T0180599

Lecture Notes in Computer Science 14266

Founding Editors

Gerhard Goos
Juris Hartmanis

The series Lecture Notes in Computer Science (LNCS), including its subseries Lecture Notes in Artificial Intelligence (LNAI) and Lecture Notes in Bioinformatics (LNBI), has established itself as a medium for the publication of new developments in computer science and information technology research, teaching, and education.

LNCS enjoys close cooperation with the computer science R & D community, the series counts many renowned academics among its volume editors and paper authors, and collaborates with prestigious societies. Its mission is to serve this international community by providing an invaluable service, mainly focused on the publication of conference and workshop proceedings and postproceedings. LNCS commenced publication in 1973.

Terry R. Payne · Valentina Presutti · Guilin Qi ·
María Poveda-Villalón · Giorgos Stoilos ·
Laura Hollink · Zoi Kaoudi · Gong Cheng ·
Juanzi Li
Editors

The Semantic Web –
ISWC 2023

22nd International Semantic Web Conference
Athens, Greece, November 6–10, 2023
Proceedings, Part II

 Springer

Editors
Terry R. Payne 🆔
University of Liverpool
Liverpool, UK

Guilin Qi 🆔
Southeast University
Nanjing, China

Giorgos Stoilos 🆔
Huawei Technologies R&D UK
Edinburgh, UK

Zoi Kaoudi 🆔
IT University of Copenhagen
Copenhagen, Denmark

Juanzi Li 🆔
Tsinghua University
Beijing, China

Valentina Presutti 🆔
University of Bologna
Bologna, Italy

María Poveda-Villalón 🆔
Universidad Politécnica de Madrid
Madrid, Spain

Laura Hollink 🆔
Centrum Wiskunde and Informatica
Amsterdam, The Netherlands

Gong Cheng 🆔
Nanjing University
Nanjing, China

ISSN 0302-9743   ISSN 1611-3349 (electronic)
Lecture Notes in Computer Science
ISBN 978-3-031-47242-8   ISBN 978-3-031-47243-5 (eBook)
https://doi.org/10.1007/978-3-031-47243-5

This Springer imprint is published by the registered company Springer Nature Switzerland AG
The registered company address is: Gewerbestrasse 11, 6330 Cham, Switzerland

Paper in this product is recyclable.

Preface

The International Semantic Web Conference (ISWC), started in 2002, aims to provide a platform for Semantic Web researchers and practitioners from around the world to share and exchange advanced techniques, and experiences in Semantic Web and related areas. Now in its 22nd edition, the ISWC has become the flagship conference for the Semantic Web and Knowledge Graph community to discuss and present the latest advances in machine-understandable semantics, large-scale knowledge resource construction, logical reasoning, and semantic interoperability and multi-agent applications.

ISWC continues its tradition of being the premier international forum, having been hosted in 9 countries and 20 cities worldwide since its inception. This year, ISWC 2023 convened in Athens, Greece, bringing together researchers, practitioners, and enthusiasts in the Semantic Web and Knowledge Graph community for valuable face-to-face interactions and discussions. ISWC 2023 received 411 submissions, authored by 1,457 distinct authors from 46 different countries, reflecting the ever-growing interest and participation in the field. Building on the rigorous reviewing processes of previous editions, our review processes this year were equally comprehensive and constructive. Each submitted paper underwent meticulous evaluation, considering criteria such as originality, novelty, empiricism, and reproducibility. We extend our heartfelt gratitude to all the authors, reviewers, and organizers who have contributed to making this conference possible.

The recent upsurge in Artificial Intelligence (AI) driven by Large Language Models (LLMs) brings new challenges and opportunities to the Semantic Web and Knowledge Graph community. LLMs have massive parameterized knowledge, can generate fluent content, engage in natural language interactions with humans, and have the ability to accomplish multi-scenario tasks. At the same time, we notice that LLMs still have some limitations in terms of knowledge hallucination and interpretability, as well as the planning ability of knowledge reasoning and complex problem-solving. Currently, we need to re-examine the relationship between LLMs and Semantic Web and Knowledge Graphs. This conference also hopes to fully communicate and discuss these problems, and together promote the research and application of combining knowledge-driven and data-driven AI.

In-depth exploration of these various aspects was addressed in invited keynotes given by three distinguished professors, and a panel with invited panelists from industry and academia. The keynote of Gerhard Weikum was entitled "Knowledge Graphs in the Age of Large Language Models" and outlined research opportunities that could leverage synergies between LLMs and Knowledge Graphs. Deborah L. McGuinness's keynote was entitled "Semantic Web Research in the Age of Generative Artificial Intelligence" and rethinks how generative AI holds great potential for Semantic Web research and applications in general and ontology-related work. The keynote entitled "ChatGLM: An Alternative to ChatGPT", presented by Jie Tang, introduced and discussed technical details on how to build a ChatGPT-style intelligent system and shared lessons learned during the development of ChatGLM. A panel led by Vassilis Christophides and Heng Ji delved into the topic of neuro-symbolic AI, which aims to enhance statistical AI (machine learning) with the complementary capabilities of symbolic AI (knowledge and reasoning).

The research track was chaired by Terry Payne and Valentina Presutti, and in keeping with previous conferences, solicited novel and significant research contributions addressing theoretical, analytical, and empirical aspects of the Semantic Web. A total of 170 full paper submissions were received across a broad set of topics. As with previous years, the most popular topics included knowledge representation and reasoning, and the construction and use of Knowledge Graphs. Many submissions focused on the use of reasoning and query answering, with a number addressing engineering, maintenance, and alignment tasks for ontologies. Likewise, there was a healthy batch of submissions on search, query, integration, and the analysis of knowledge. Finally, following the growing interest in neuro-symbolic approaches, there was a rise in the number of studies that focus on the use of Large Language Models and Deep Learning techniques such as Graph Neural Networks.

As ever, the Program Committee (PC) was fundamental in reviewing and providing guidance to the papers, both in determining what should be accepted in terms of maturity and quality, and in shaping the final version of each paper through detailed comments and recommendations. For this, we had the help of 264 PC members from 34 countries, and a further 39 Senior Program Committee (SPC) members who helped oversee the reviewing process and were responsible for drafting the meta-reviews for all of the papers. Finally, an additional 56 external reviewers, solicited by PC members, assisted by contributing valuable additional reviews to the process. Continuing the trend of previous editions of ISWC, the Research Track was double-blind, with each paper receiving at least three reviews, and the majority getting four. Reproducibility and novelty continued to be a fundamental component of every submission, with the requirement to provide supplementary material wherever possible. In the end, 33 papers were accepted, resulting in an acceptance rate of 19.4%, which was consistent with that of previous research tracks at ISWC.

The Resources Track, chaired by Guilin Qi and María Poveda-Villalón, focused on the promotion and sharing of resources that support, enable, or utilize Semantic Web research, and in particular datasets, ontologies, software, and benchmarks, among others. This track received 70 papers for review. Each paper was subject to a rigorous single-blind review process involving at least three PC and SPC members, and program chairs considered both the papers and the author responses. The main review criteria focused on impact (novelty of the resource), reusability, design and technical quality, and availability. Eventually, 17 papers were accepted. The Resources Track was aided by 7 SPC and 54 PC members, and 12 additional reviewers.

The In-Use Track this year was chaired by Giorgos Stoilos and Laura Hollink. This track provides a forum to explore the benefits and challenges of applying Semantic Web and Knowledge Graph technologies in concrete, practical use cases, in contexts ranging from industry to government and society. In total, eight full papers were accepted out of 25 full paper submissions (32% acceptance rate). All submissions were thoroughly reviewed in a single-blind process by at least three and in some cases even four PC members. Submissions were assessed in terms of novelty (of the proposed use case or solution), uptake by the target user group, demonstrated or potential impact, as well as overall soundness and quality. An Objection and Response phase was also implemented this year in line with the other tracks of the conference. Overall, 32 PC members and three additional reviewers participated in a rigorous review process.

The Industry Track, this year chaired by Daniel Garijo and Jose Manuel Gomez-Perez, covers all aspects of innovative commercial or industrial-strength Semantic Technologies and Knowledge Graphs to showcase the state of adoption. This track received 19 papers for review, of which 12 were accepted (63% acceptance rate) following a single-blind review process. The 17 members of the PC assessed each submission in terms of qualitative and quantitative business value, as well as the innovative aspects, impact, and lessons learned of applying Knowledge Graph and semantic technologies in the application domain.

The Workshop and Tutorial Track, chaired by Heiko Paulheim and Bo Fu, presented a total of 10 selected workshops covering established and emerging topics as part of the conference program, including knowledge engineering and management (e.g., ontology design and patterns, knowledge base construction, evolution, and preservation), acquisition, integration, and manipulation of knowledge (e.g., ontology matching, as well as the storing, querying, and benchmarking of knowledge graphs), visualization and representation of knowledge for human users (e.g., interactive visual support for ontologies, linked data, and knowledge graphs), applied emerging areas that assist the advancement of Semantic Web research (e.g., deep learning for knowledge graphs), as well as semantic technologies in use (e.g., industrial information modeling, ontology design for cultural heritage, and open knowledge bases such as Wikidata). In addition, two tutorials were offered as part of the conference program to foster discussions and information exchange for researchers and practitioners working to overcome challenges surrounding knowledge discovery in spatial data and neuro-symbolic artificial intelligence for smart manufacturing.

The Semantic Web Challenges Track was jointly chaired by Valentina Ivanova and Wen Zhang. Four challenges were selected for the track, all of them held before in some of the previous editions of either the ISWC or ESWC conference series. Each of the challenges provides a common environment and datasets to evaluate and compare the systems in various settings and tasks. The challenges covered various topics ranging from reasoners evaluation to creating knowledge graphs from tabular data as well as from pretrained language models and query answering. Two of the challenges were collocated with workshops focusing on similar topics, which provided a ground for extended discussion around emerging research and demonstrating it in proof-of-concept solutions. The accepted challenges were: 2nd edition of LM-KBC: Knowledge Base Construction from Pretrained Language Models (collocated with the 1st Workshop on Knowledge Base Construction from Pre-Trained Language Models (KBC-LM)), 2nd edition of The Scholarly QALD Challenge, 5th edition of SemTab: Semantic Web Challenge on Tabular Data to Knowledge Graph Matching (collocated with the 18th International Workshop on Ontology Matching) and the 3rd edition of Semantic Reasoning Evaluation Challenge (SemREC 2023).

The Posters and Demos Track was chaired by Irini Fundulaki and Kouji Kozaki. This track complements the paper tracks of the conference by offering an opportunity to present late-breaking research results, on-going projects, and speculative as well as innovative work in progress. The Posters and Demos Track encourages presenters and participants to submit papers that have the potential to create discussions about their work that provide valuable input for the future work of the presenters. At the same time, it offers participants an effective way to broaden their knowledge on a variety of research topics and to network with other researchers. This track received 101 papers for review, of which 57 were accepted (56% acceptance rate). Among the accepted papers, 29 were poster papers and 28 were demo papers. The 55 members of the PC were involved in a double-blind review process and assessed each submission based on a variety of criteria such as novelty, relevance to the Semantic Web, impact, technical contribution, and readability.

The Doctoral Consortium (DC) was chaired by Claudia d'Amato and Jeff Pan. The DC is another fundamental event of ISWC. It gives PhD students the opportunity to present their research ideas and initial results and to receive constructive feedback from senior members of the community. This year's DC received 24 submissions. Each submission was reviewed by three members of a PC that consisted of 35 members in total. Based on the reviews, which were managed in agreement with a single-blind review process, 17 submissions were accepted to be published in the DC proceedings edited by CEUR, and the students of these submissions were invited to present their ideas and work during the DC sessions of the conference, where they received further feedback from senior conference attendees. The DC also hosted a career-advice session, consisting of senior researchers providing career advice with an open Q&A session.

Our thanks go to our local organization team, led by local chair Manolis Koubarakis, Dimitris Plexousakis, and George Vouros, who worked tirelessly to ensure a seamless conference experience. Their meticulous management of all conference activities was truly commendable.

We would like to thank the diligent work of Zoi Kaoudi and Gong Cheng, who have been instrumental in the preparation of the ISWC 2023 proceedings. Their efforts have not only ensured the quality of the conference materials but have also facilitated the sharing of conference data in a reusable and open format.

The success of ISWC 2023 has been widely disseminated within the Semantic Web and Knowledge Graph community, thanks to the tireless efforts of Ioannis Chrysakis, Ioannis Karatzanis, and Lei Hou. Their unwavering commitment to spreading news and updates has greatly contributed to the conference's visibility and reach.

Sponsorship plays a pivotal role in bringing the conference to fruition. We would like to express our gratitude to sponsorship chairs Haofen Wang, Andrea Nuzzolese, and Evgeny Kharlamov, who worked tirelessly to secure support and promote the conference to our sponsors, making ISWC 2023 possible in its current form. We also extend our sincerest thanks to all our sponsors for their invaluable contributions. Also, we are especially thankful to our Student Grants Chairs, Cogan Shimizu and Eleni Tsalapati, whose hard work enabled students to actively participate in this conference.

Finally, our heartfelt gratitude extends to the entire organizing committee, a dedicated family of chairs who have embarked on this complex yet remarkable journey to deliver ISWC 2023. We would also like to express our appreciation to the Semantic Web Science Association (SWSA) for their invaluable support and constant presence throughout ISWC's 22 year history.

Juanzi Li, ISWC 2023 General Chair, on behalf of all the editors.

September 2023

Terry R. Payne
Valentina Presutti
Guilin Qi
María Poveda-Villalón
Giorgos Stoilos
Laura Hollink
Zoi Kaoudi
Gong Cheng
Juanzi Li

Organization

General Chair

Juanzi Li   Tsinghua University, China

Local Chairs

Manolis Koubarakis	National and Kapodistrian University of Athens, Greece
Dimitris Plexousakis	Foundation for Research and Technology Hellas and University of Crete, Greece
George Vouros	University of Piraeus, Greece

Research Track Chairs

Terry R. Payne	University of Liverpool, UK
Valentina Presutti	University of Bologna, Italy

Resources Track Chairs

Guilin Qi	Southeast University, China
María Poveda-Villalón	Universidad Politécnica de Madrid, Spain

In-Use Track Chairs

Giorgos Stoilos	Huawei Technologies R&D, UK
Laura Hollink	Centrum Wiskunde & Informatica, The Netherlands

Workshops and Tutorials Chairs

Heiko Paulheim	University of Mannheim, Germany
Bo Fu	California State University Long Beach, USA

Industry Track Chairs

Jose Manuel Gomez-Perez   Expert AI, Spain
Daniel Garijo   Universidad Politécnica de Madrid, Spain

Doctoral Consortium Chairs

Claudia d'Amato   University of Bari, Italy
Jeff Z. Pan   University of Edinburgh, UK

Posters, Demos, and Lightning Talks Chairs

Irini Fundulaki   Foundation for Research and Technology Hellas,
                                   Greece
Kozaki Kouji   Osaka Electro-Communication University, Japan

Semantic Web Challenge Chairs

Valentina Ivanova   RISE Research Institutes of Sweden, Sweden
Wen Zhang   Zhejiang University, China

Panel Chairs

Vassilis Christophides   ENSEA, ETIS, France
Heng Ji   University of Illinois at Urbana-Champaign, USA

Sponsor Chairs

Haofen Wang   Tongji University, China
Andrea Nuzzolese   National Research Council, Italy
Evgeny Kharlamov   Bosch Center for AI, Germany and University of
                                   Oslo, Norway

Proceedings and Metadata Chairs

Zoi Kaoudi   IT University of Copenhagen, Denmark
Gong Cheng   Nanjing University, China

Student Grants Chairs

Cogan Shimizu   Wright State University, USA
Eleni Tsalapati   National and Kapodistrian University of Athens,
                                 Greece

Web Presence and Publicity Chairs

Ioannis Chrysakis   Foundation for Research and Technology Hellas,
                                 Greece and Ghent University and KU Leuven,
                                 Belgium
Ioannis Karatzanis   Foundation for Research and Technology Hellas,
                                 Greece
Lei Hou   Tsinghua University, China

Research Track Senior Program Committee

Maribel Acosta   Ruhr University Bochum, Germany
Irene Celino   Cefriel, Italy
Gong Cheng   Nanjing University, China
Michael Cochez   Vrije Universiteit Amsterdam, The Netherlands
Oscar Corcho   Universidad Politécnica de Madrid, Spain
Julien Corman   Free University of Bozen-Bolzano, Italy
Mauro Dragoni   Fondazione Bruno Kessler - FBK-IRST, Italy
Jérôme Euzenat   Inria and Univ. Grenoble Alpes, France
Aldo Gangemi   University of Bologna - CNR-ISTC, Italy
Chiara Ghidini   Fondazione Bruno Kessler, Italy
Peter Haase   metaphacts, Germany
Olaf Hartig   Linköping University, Sweden
Aidan Hogan   Universidad de Chile, Chile
Wei Hu   Nanjing University, China
Ernesto Jimenez-Ruiz   City, University of London, UK
Sabrina Kirrane   Vienna University of Economics and Business,
                                 Austria

Markus Luczak-Roesch	Victoria University of Wellington, New Zealand
Maria Vanina Martinez	Artificial Intelligence Research Institute (IIIA-CSIC), Spain
Gabriela Montoya	Aalborg University, Denmark
Boris Motik	University of Oxford, UK
Magdalena Ortiz	Vienna University of Technology, Austria
Francesco Osborne	Open University, UK
Matteo Palmonari	University of Milano-Bicocca, Italy
Marta Sabou	Vienna University of Economics and Business, Austria
Elena Simperl	King's College London, UK
Hala Skaf-Molli	University of Nantes - LS2N, France
Kavitha Srinivas	IBM, USA
Valentina Tamma	University of Liverpool, UK
Serena Villata	CNRS - Laboratoire d'Informatique, Signaux et Systèmes de Sophia-Antipolis, France
Domagoj Vrgoc	Pontificia Universidad Católica de Chile, Chile
Kewen Wang	Griffith University, Australia
Yizheng Zhao	Nanjing University, China

Research Track Program Committee

Ibrahim Abdelaziz	IBM Research, USA
Shqiponja Ahmetaj	TU Vienna, Austria
Mirza Mohtashim Alam	Institut für Angewandte Informatik, Germany
Harith Alani	Open University, UK
Panos Alexopoulos	Textkernel B.V., Netherlands
Samah Alkhuzaey	University of Liverpool, UK
João Paulo Almeida	Federal University of Espírito Santo, Brazil
Julián Arenas-Guerrero	Universidad Politécnica de Madrid, Spain
Hiba Arnaout	Max Planck Institute for Informatics, Germany
Luigi Asprino	University of Bologna, Italy
Amr Azzam	WU Vienna, Austria
Carlos Badenes-Olmedo	Universidad Politécnica de Madrid, Spain
Ratan Bahadur Thapa	University of Oslo, Norway
Payam Barnaghi	Imperial College London, UK
Pierpaolo Basile	University of Bari, Italy
Russa Biswas	Karlsruhe Institute of Technology & FIZ Karlsruhe, Germany
Christian Bizer	University of Mannheim, Germany
Eva Blomqvist	Linköping University, Sweden

Carlos Bobed	University of Zaragoza, Spain
Alexander Borgida	Rutgers University, USA
Paolo Bouquet	University of Trento, Italy
Zied Bouraoui	CRIL - CNRS & Univ. Artois, France
Janez Brank	Jožef Stefan Institute, Slovenia
Carlos Buil Aranda	Universidad Técnica Federico Santa María, Chile
Davide Buscaldi	LIPN, Université Sorbonne Paris Nord, France
Jean-Paul Calbimonte	University of Applied Sciences and Arts Western Switzerland HES-SO, Switzerland
Pablo Calleja	Universidad Politécnica de Madrid, Spain
Antonella Carbonaro	University of Bologna, Italy
Valentina Anita Carriero	University of Bologna, Italy
Pierre-Antoine Champin	Inria/W3C, France
Victor Charpenay	Mines Saint-Etienne, Univ Clermont Auvergne, INP Clermont Auvergne, France
Vinay Chaudhri	JPMorgan Chase & Co., USA
David Chaves-Fraga	Universidad Politécnica de Madrid, Spain
Jiaoyan Chen	University of Manchester, UK
Sijin Cheng	Linköping University, Sweden
Philipp Cimiano	Bielefeld University, Germany
Andrei Ciortea	University of St. Gallen, Switzerland
Pieter Colpaert	Ghent University – imec, Belgium
Philippe Cudre-Mauroux	U. of Fribourg, Switzerland
Victor de Boer	Vrije Universiteit Amsterdam, The Netherlands
Daniele Dell'Aglio	Aalborg University, Denmark
Danilo Dessì	University of Cagliari, Italy
Stefan Dietze	GESIS - Leibniz Institute for the Social Sciences, Germany
Anastasia Dimou	KU Leuven, Belgium
Shusaku Egami	National Institute of Advanced Industrial Science and Technology, Japan
Fajar J. Ekaputra	Vienna University of Economics and Business, Austria
Paola Espinoza-Arias	BASF, Spain
David Eyers	University of Otago, New Zealand
Alessandro Faraotti	IBM, Italy
Michael Färber	Karlsruhe Institute of Technology, Germany
Daniel Faria	INESC-ID, Instituto Superior Técnico, Universidade de Lisboa, Portugal
Catherine Faron	Université Côte d'Azur, France
Javier D. Fernández	F. Hoffmann-La Roche AG, Switzerland
Sebastián Ferrada	Linköping University, Sweden

Jan-Christoph Kalo   Vrije Universiteit Amsterdam, The Netherlands
Maulik R. Kamdar   Elsevier Inc., The Netherlands
Takahiro Kawamura   National Agriculture and Food Research
                                    Organization, Japan
Maria Keet   University of Cape Town, South Africa
Mayank Kejriwal   University of Southern California, USA
Ilkcan Keles   Aalborg University/TomTom, Denmark
Neha Keshan   Rensselaer Polytechnic Institute, USA
Ankesh Khandelwal   Amazon, USA
Evgeny Kharlamov   University of Oslo, Norway
Elmar Kiesling   Vienna University of Economics and Business,
                                    Austria
Craig Knoblock   USC Information Sciences Institute, USA
Haridimos Kondylakis   Foundation of Research & Technology-Hellas,
                                    Greece
Stasinos Konstantopoulos   NCSR Demokritos, Greece
Roman Kontchakov   Birkbeck, University of London, UK
Manolis Koubarakis   National and Kapodistrian University of Athens,
                                    Greece
Adila A. Krisnadhi   Universitas Indonesia, Indonesia
Markus Krötzsch   TU Dresden, Germany
Benno Kruit   Vrije Universiteit Amsterdam, The Netherlands
Jose Emilio Labra Gayo   Universidad de Oviedo, Spain
André Lamurias   Aalborg University, Denmark
Agnieszka Lawrynowicz   Poznan University of Technology, Poland
Danh Le Phuoc   TU Berlin, Germany
Maxime Lefrançois   Mines Saint-Étienne, France
Huanyu Li   Linköping University, Sweden
Tianyi Li   University of Edinburgh, UK
Wenqiang Liu   Tencent Inc., China
Carsten Lutz   Universität Bremen, Germany
Maria Maleshkova   Helmut-Schmidt-Universität, Germany
Thomas Meyer   University of Cape Town and CAIR, South Africa
Pascal Molli   University of Nantes - LS2N, France
Pierre Monnin   Orange, France
Deshendran Moodley   University of Cape Town, South Africa
Varish Mulwad   GE Research, India
Summaya Mumtaz   University of Oslo, Norway
Raghava Mutharaju   IIIT-Delhi, India
Hubert Naacke   Sorbonne Université, LIP6, France
Shinichi Nagano   Toshiba Corporation, Japan
Axel-Cyrille Ngonga Ngomo   Paderborn University, Germany

Vinh Nguyen	National Library of Medicine, NIH, USA
Andriy Nikolov	AstraZeneca, UK
Inna Novalija	Jožef Stefan Institute, Slovenia
Werner Nutt	Free University of Bozen-Bolzano, Italy
Andrea Giovanni Nuzzolese	Consiglio Nazionale delle Ricerche, Italy
Julian Padget	University of Bath, UK
Ankur Padia	Philips Research North America, USA
Peter Patel-Schneider	Independent Researcher, USA
Evan Patton	Massachusetts Institute of Technology, USA
Rafael Peñaloza	University of Milano-Bicocca, Italy
Bernardo Pereira Nunes	Australian National University, Australia
Romana Pernisch	Vrije Universiteit Amsterdam, The Netherlands
Alina Petrova	University of Oxford, UK
Francesco Piccialli	University of Naples Federico II, Italy
Sofia Pinto	Universidade de Lisboa, Portugal
Giuseppe Pirrò	University of Calabria, Italy
Alessandro Piscopo	BBC, UK
Dimitris Plexousakis	University of Crete, Greece
Axel Polleres	Vienna University of Economics and Business, Austria
Ehsan Qasemi	University of Southern California, USA
Yuzhong Qu	Nanjing University, China
Alexandre Rademaker	IBM Research and EMAp/FGV, Brazil
David Ratcliffe	Microsoft, Australia
Achim Rettinger	Trier University, Germany
Martin Rezk	Google, USA
Mariano Rico	Universidad Politécnica de Madrid, Spain
Giuseppe Rizzo	LINKS Foundation, Italy
Edelweis Rohrer	Universidad de la República, Uruguay
Dumitru Roman	SINTEF AS/University of Oslo, Norway
Oscar Romero	Universitat Politècnica de Catalunya, Spain
Miguel Romero Orth	Universidad de Adolfo Ibañez, Chile
Henry Rosales-Méndez	University of Chile, Chile
Marco Rospocher	Università degli Studi di Verona, Italy
Jose Rozanec	Jožef Stefan Institute, Slovenia
Anisa Rula	University of Brescia, Italy
Harald Sack	FIZ Karlsruhe, Leibniz Institute for Information Infrastructure & KIT Karlsruhe, Germany
Tomer Sagi	Aalborg University, Denmark
Satya Sahoo	Case Western Reserve University, USA
Angelo Antonio Salatino	Open University, UK
Muhammad Saleem	University of Leipzig, Germany

Marco Luca Sbodio	IBM Research, Ireland
Francois Scharffe	University of Montpellier, France
Konstantin Schekotihin	Alpen-Adria Universität Klagenfurt, Austria
Ralf Schenkel	Trier University, Germany
Juan F. Sequeda	data.world, USA
Cogan Shimizu	Wright State University, USA
Kuldeep Singh	Cerence GmbH and Zerotha Research, Germany
Nadine Steinmetz	TU Ilmenau, Germany
Armando Stellato	University of Rome Tor Vergata, Italy
Gerd Stumme	University of Kassel, Germany
Mari Carmen Suárez-Figueroa	Universidad Politécnica de Madrid, Spain
Zequn Sun	Nanjing University, China
Vojtěch Svátek	University of Economics, Czech Republic
Ruben Taelman	Ghent University – imec, Belgium
Hideaki Takeda	National Institute of Informatics, Japan
Kerry Taylor	Australian National University, Australia
Andreas Thalhammer	F. Hoffmann-La Roche AG, Switzerland
Krishnaprasad Thirunarayan	Wright State University, USA
Steffen Thoma	FZI Research Center for Information Technology, Germany
Ilaria Tiddi	Vrije Universiteit Amsterdam, The Netherlands
David Toman	University of Waterloo, Canada
Riccardo Tommasini	INSA de Lyon - LIRIS Lab, France
Raphael Troncy	Eurecom, France
Takanori Ugai	Fujitsu Ltd., Japan
Guillermo Vega-Gorgojo	Universidad de Valladolid, Spain
Ruben Verborgh	Ghent University – imec, Belgium
Haofen Wang	Tongji University, China
Zhe Wang	Griffith University, Australia
Yisong Wang	Guizhou University, China
Xiaxia Wang	Nanjing University, China
Meng Wang	Southeast University, China
Peng Wang	Southeast University, China
Xin Wang	Tianjin University, China
Ruijie Wang	University of Zurich, Switzerland
Simon Werner	Trier University, Germany
Xander Wilcke	Vrije Universiteit Amsterdam, The Netherlands
Honghan Wu	University College London, UK
Josiane Xavier Parreira	Siemens AG Österreich, Austria
Ikuya Yamada	Studio Ousia Inc., Japan
Qiang Yang	King Abdullah University of Science and Technology, Saudi Arabia

Fouad Zablith   American University of Beirut, Lebanon
Fadi Zaraket   American University of Beirut, Lebanon
Xiaowang Zhang   Tianjin University, China
Lu Zhou   Flatfeecorp, Inc., USA
Antoine Zimmermann   École des Mines de Saint-Étienne, France

Research Track Additional Reviewers

Mehdi Azarafza   Andrea Mauri
Moritz Blum   Sebastian Monka
Alexander Brinkmann   Simon Münker
Luana Bulla   Sergi Nadal
Yanping Chen   Janna Omeliyanenko
Panfeng Chen   Wolfgang Otto
Sulogna Chowdhury   Trupti Padiya
Fiorela Ciroku   Despina-Athanasia Pantazi
Yuanning Cui   George Papadakis
Hang Dong   Ralph Peeters
Daniel Fernández-Álvarez   Zhan Qu
Giacomo Frisoni   Youssra Rebboud
Carlos Golvano   Qasid Saleem
Abul Hasan   Muhammad Salman
Johannes Hirth   Alyssa Sha
Viet-Phi Huynh   Chen Shao
Monika Jain   Basel Shbita
Varvara Kalokyri   Sarah Binta Alam Shoilee
Keti Korini   Lucia Siciliani
Kyriakos Kritikos   Gunjan Singh
Kai Kugler   Eleni Tsalapati
Kabul Kurniawan   Roderick van der Weerdt
Anh Le-Tuan   Binh Vu
Fandel Lin   Xinni Wang
Anna Sofia Lippolis   Jinge Wu
Pasquale Lisena   Ziwei Xu
Yun Liu   Jicheng Yuan
Tiroshan Madhushanka   Albin Zehe

Resources Track Senior Program Committee

Enrico Daga   Open University, UK
Antoine Isaac   Europeana & VU Amsterdam, The Netherlands
Tong Ruan   ECUST, China

Ruben Taelman   Ghent University, Belgium
Maria-Esther Vidal   TIB, Germany
Xiaowang Zhang   Tianjin University, China
Antoine Zimmermann   École des Mines de Saint-Étienne, France

Resources Track Program Committee

Vito Walter Anelli   Politecnico di Bari, Italy
Ghislain Atemezing   ERA - European Union Agency for Railways, France
Debanjali Biswas   GESIS Leibniz Institute for the Social Sciences, Germany
Oleksandra Bruns   FIZ Karlsruhe, Leibniz Institute for Information Infrastructure & KIT Karlsruhe, Germany
Pierre-Antoine Champin   Inria/W3C, France
David Chaves-Fraga   Universidade de Santiago de Compostela, Spain
Andrea Cimmino Arriaga   Universidad Politécnica de Madrid, Spain
Jérôme David   Université Grenoble Alpes, France
Anastasia Dimou   KU Leuven, Belgium
Elvira Amador-Domínguez   Universidad Politécnica de Madrid, Spain
Pablo Fillottrani   Universidad Nacional del Sur, Argentina
Florian Grensing   University of Siegen, Germany
Tudor Groza   Perth Children's Hospital, Australia
Peter Haase   metaphacts, Germany
Fatma-Zohra Hannou   École des Mines de Saint-Étienne, France
Ana Iglesias-Molina   Universidad Politécnica de Madrid, Spain
Clement Jonquet   MISTEA (INRAE) and LIRMM (U. Montpellier), France
Yavuz Selim Kartal   GESIS Leibniz Institute for Social Sciences, Germany
Zubeida Khan   Council for Scientific and Industrial Research, South Africa
Christian Kindermann   Stanford University, UK
Tomas Kliegr   Prague University of Economics and Business, Czechia
Jakub Klímek   Charles University, Czechia
Agnieszka Lawrynowicz   Poznan University of Technology, Poland
Maxime Lefrançois   École des Mines de Saint-Étienne, France
Allyson Lister   University of Oxford, UK
Zola Mahlaza   University of Cape Town, South Africa
Maria Maleshkova   Helmut-Schmidt-Universität Hamburg, Germany

Milan Markovic	University of Aberdeen, UK
Patricia Martín-Chozas	Ontology Engineering Group, Spain
Hande McGinty	Ohio University, USA
Lionel Medini	University of Lyon1 - LIRIS/CNRS, France
Nandana Mihindukulasooriya	IBM Research AI, USA
Pascal Molli	University of Nantes - LS2N, France
Alessandro Mosca	Free University of Bozen-Bolzano, Italy
Ebrahim Norouzi	FIZ Karlsruhe, Leibniz Institute for Information Infrastructure & KIT Karlsruhe, Germany
Rafael Peñaloza	University of Milano-Bicocca, Italy
María del Mar Roldán-García	Universidad de Málaga, Spain
Catherine Roussey	INRAE, France
Harald Sack	FIZ Karlsruhe, Leibniz Institute for Information Infrastructure & KIT Karlsruhe, Germany
Umutcan Serles	University of Innsbruck, Austria
Patricia Serrano Alvarado	University of Nantes - LS2N, France
Cogan Shimizu	Wright State University, USA
Blerina Spahiu	Università degli Studi di Milano-Bicocca, Italy
Valentina Tamma	University of Southampton, UK
Walter Terkaj	CNR-STIIMA, Italy
Tabea Tietz	FIZ Karlsruhe, Leibniz Institute for Information Infrastructure & KIT Karlsruhe, Germany
Jörg Waitelonis	FIZ Karlsruhe – Leibniz Institute for Information Infrastructure, Germany
Meng Wang	Tongji University, China
Zhichun Wang	Beijing Normal University, China
Tianxing Wu	Southeast University, China
Lan Yang	University of Galway, Ireland
Ondřej Zamazal	Prague University of Economics and Business, Czechia
Ningyu Zhang	Zhejiang University, China
Ziqi Zhang	Accessible Intelligence, UK

Resources Track Additional Reviewers

Cristobal Barba-Gonzalez	Aljosha Köcher
Antonio Benítez-Hidalgo	Edna Ruckhaus
Giovanni Maria Biancofiore Biancofiore	Mayra Russo
Jean-Paul Calbimonte	Andre Valdestilhas
Dario Di Palma	Miel Vander Sande
Florian Grensing	Lei Zhang

In-Use Track Program Committee

Nathalie Aussenac-Gilles	IRIT CNRS, France
Martin Bauer	NEC Laboratories Europe, Germany
Maria Bermudez-Edo	University of Granada, Spain
Stefan Bischof	Siemens AG Österreich, Austria
Carlos Buil Aranda	Universidad Técnica Federico Santa María, Chile
Oscar Corcho	Universidad Politécnica de Madrid, Spain
Philippe Cudre-Mauroux	University of Fribourg, Switzerland
Christophe Debruyne	Université de Liège, Belgium
Jose Manuel Gomez-Perez	expert.ai, Spain
Damien Graux	Huawei Technologies, UK
Daniel Gruhl	IBM Almaden Research Center, USA
Peter Haase	Metaphacts, Germany
Nicolas Heist	University of Mannheim, Germany
Aidan Hogan	Universidad de Chile, Chile
Tomi Kauppinen	Aalto University, Finland
Mayank Kejriwal	University of Southern California, USA
Craig Knoblock	University of Southern California, USA
Maxime Lefrançois	École des Mines de Saint-Étienne, France
Vanessa Lopez	IBM Research Europe, Ireland
Michael Luggen	University of Fribourg, Switzerland
Ioanna Lytra	Semantic Web Company, Austria
Beatrice Markhoff	Université de Tours, France
Andriy Nikolov	AstraZeneca, UK
Declan O'Sullivan	Trinity College Dublin, Ireland
Matteo Palmonari	University of Milano-Bicocca, Italy
Artem Revenko	Semantic Web Company, Austria
Mariano Rico	Universidad Politécnica de Madrid, Spain
Dezhao Song	Thomson Reuters, USA
Danai Symeonidou	INRAE, France
Josiane Xavier Parreira	Siemens AG Österreich, Austria
Matthäus Zloch	GESIS - Leibniz Institute for the Social Sciences, Germany

In-Use Track Additional Reviewers

Basel Shbita
Fandel Lin
Binh Vu

Sponsors

Below we report the list of sponsors that joined before the completion of the proceedings, *i.e.*, September 18th, 2023.

For the final list of sponsors in every category, please visit https://iswc2023.semant icweb.org/sponsors/.

Diamond Sponsor

https://www.createlink.com/

Platinum Sponsor

https://www.zhipuai.cn/

Gold Plus Sponsors

https://www.bosch.com/

IBM **Research**

http://www.research.ibm.com/

Gold Sponsors

metaphacts

https://metaphacts.com/

Google

https://www.google.com/

Leibniz Institute
for the Social Sciences

https://www.gesis.org/

ontotext

https://www.ontotext.com/

ebay

https://www.ebay.com/

https://www.huawei.com/

Silver Plus Sponsor

https://www.journals.elsevier.com/artificial-intelligence

Silver Sponsor

QUALCO
Group

https://qualco.group/

Sponsor

https://www.bupsolutions.com/

Best Paper Award Sponsor

https://www.springer.com/series/558

Invited Speaker Support

https://www.eurai.org/

Keynote Speeches and Panels

Knowledge Graphs in the Age of Large Language Models

Gerhard Weikum

Max Planck Institute for Informatics, Saarbruecken, Germany
weikum@mpi-inf.mpg.de

Abstract. Large knowledge graphs (KG's) have become a key asset for search engines and other use cases (see, e.g., [1–5]). They are partly based on automatically extracting structured information from web contents and other texts, using a variety of pattern-matching and machine-learning methods. The semantically organized machine knowledge can be harnessed to better interpret text in news, social media and web tables, contributing to question answering, natural language processing (NLP) and data analytics.

A recent trend that has revolutionized NLP is to capture knowledge latently by billions of parameters of language models (LM's), learned at scale from huge text collections in a largely self-supervised manner (see, e.g., [6, 7]). These pre-trained models form the basis of fine-tuning machine-learning solutions for tasks that involve both input texts and broad world knowledge, such as question answering, commonsense reasoning and human-computer conversations (see, e.g., [8–10]).

This talk identifies major gaps in the coverage of today's KG's, and discusses potential roles of large language models towards narrowing thee gaps and constructing the next KG generation. The talk outlines research opportunities that could leverage synergies between LM's and KG's.

References

1. Hogan, A., et al.: Knowledge graphs. ACM Comput. Surv. **54**(4), 71:1–71:37 (2021)
2. Weikum, G., Dong, X.L., Razniewski, S., Suchanek, F.M.: Machine knowledge: creation and curation of comprehensive knowledge bases. Found. Trends Databases **10**(2–4), 108–490 (2021)
3. Weikum, G.: Knowledge graphs 2021: a data odyssey. Proc. VLDB Endow. **14**(12), 3233–3238 (2021)
4. Noy, N.F., et al.: Industry-scale knowledge graphs: lessons and challenges. Commun. ACM **62**(8), 36–43 (2019)
5. Dong, X.L.: Generations of knowledge graphs: the crazy ideas and the business impact. Proc. VLDB Endow. **16** (2023)

6. Liu, P.: et al.: Pre-train, prompt, and predict: a systematic survey of prompting methods in natural language processing. ACM Comput. Surv. **55**(9), 195:1–195:35 (2023)
7. Zhaom, W.X., et al.: A Survey of Large Language Models. CoRR abs/2303.18223 (2023)
8. Hu, L.: A Survey of Knowledge-Enhanced Pre-trained Language Models. CoRR abs/2211.05994 (2022)
9. Pan, S., et al.: Unifying Large Language Models and Knowledge Graphs: A Roadmap. CoRR abs/2306.08302 (2023)
10. Pan, J.Z., et al.: Large Language Models and Knowledge Graphs: Opportunities and Challenges. CoRR abs/2308.06374 (2023)

Semantic Web Research in the Age of Generative Artificial Intelligence

Deborah L. McGuinness

Rensselaer Polytechnic Institute, Troy, NY, USA
dlm@cs.rpi.edu

We are living in an age of rapidly advancing technology. History may view this period as one in which generative artificial intelligence is seen as reshaping the landscape and narrative of many technology-based fields of research and application. Times of disruptions often present both opportunities and challenges. We will briefly discuss some areas that may be ripe for consideration in the field of Semantic Web research and semantically-enabled applications.

Semantic Web research has historically focused on representation and reasoning and enabling interoperability of data and vocabularies. At the core are ontologies along with ontology-enabled (or ontology-compatible) knowledge stores such as knowledge graphs. Ontologies are often manually constructed using a process that (1) identifies existing best practice ontologies (and vocabularies) and (2) generates a plan for how to leverage these ontologies by aligning and augmenting them as needed to address requirements. While semi-automated techniques may help, there is typically a significant manual portion of the work that is often best done by humans with domain and ontology expertise.

This is an opportune time to rethink how the field generates, evolves, maintains, and evaluates ontologies. It is time to consider how hybrid approaches, i.e., those that leverage generative AI components along with more traditional knowledge representation and reasoning approaches to create improved processes.

The effort to build a robust ontology that meets a use case can be large. Ontologies are not static however and they need to evolve along with knowledge evolution and expanded usage. There is potential for hybrid approaches to help identify gaps in ontologies and/or refine content. Further, ontologies need to be documented with term definitions and their provenance. Opportunities exist to consider semi-automated techniques for some types of documentation, provenance, and decision rationale capture for annotating ontologies.

The area of human-AI collaboration for population and verification presents a wide range of areas of research collaboration and impact. Ontologies need to be populated with class and relationship content. Knowledge graphs and other knowledge stores need to be populated with instance data in order to be used for question answering and reasoning. Population of large knowledge graphs can be time consuming. Generative AI holds the promise to create candidate knowledge graphs that are compatible with the ontology schema. The knowledge graph should contain provenance information at least identifying how the content was populated and where the content came from. Efforts also need to be made to verify that the populated content is correct and current. This is an area of opportunity since language models predict likely completions for prompts and most do not have built in capabilities to check their answers.

While generative AI is evolving, at least one theme is emerging. Many are proposing a human-AI collaborative assistant approach (e.g., Microsoft's Copilot [1], Google's Assistant [2], Zoom's AI Companion [3], etc.). This is not new, expert system assistants and semantic technology assistants have been proposed, implemented, and deployed for decades. However, the interactive nature of the current language models along with the constant coverage in the press have drastically expanded awareness and usage of large language model services and tools. Gartner's latest AI hype cycle [4], for example, has helped increase attention to many areas of AI that are subfields of the Semantic Web or Generative AI or a combination of both. Further, the diversity of users has expanded. People who do not have computer science experience are now experimenting with these tools and the use cases seem to be expanding almost daily.

Opportunities and challenges increase with the wider range of users and usage types. When some content is automatically generated potentially from models that have been trained on data that is either inaccurate, out of date, or that contains assumptions and biases, the need for rigorous validation grows. Further, as these hybrid approaches proliferate, transparency and explainability become even more critical. Transparency should not just include content related to what a model was trained on but also how it was evaluated. While the field of validation and verification has existed for decades, it becomes more essential now as hybrid systems become more pervasive. We expect not only that benchmark research will grow, but also services that provide experimentation and testing will grow. We have experimented with a kind of "sandbox" for checking answers [5] from some of the large language models, connecting the entities to known structured data sources, such as Wikidata, and then exploring services that attempt to support or refute answers. While this is just one kind of exploratory harness, we believe many more will and should arise.

The generative AI conversation and explosion has the potential to accelerate research and applications and may initiate a kind of Semantic Web Renaissance as more people call for transparency and understanding of technology. At the same time, as communities are raising issues related to bias, fairness, and potential regulation, ethical considerations and responsible use must be at the forefront of our efforts. Ultimately, the opportunities may be more boundless than they have ever been in the history of Semantic Web research and technology.

References

1. Copilot. https://news.microsoft.com/reinventing-productivity/
2. Google Assistant. https://assistant.google.com/
3. Zoom Blog. https://blog.zoom.us/zoom-ai-companion/
4. Gartner Hype Cycle. https://www.gartner.com/en/articles/what-s-new-in-artificial-intelligence-from-the-2023-gartner-hype-cycle
5. RPI's Tetherless World Constellation Large Language Model/Knowledge Graph Fact Checker Demo. https://inciteprojects.idea.rpi.edu/chatbs/app/chatbs/

ChatGLM: An Alternative to ChatGPT

Jie Tang

KEG, Tsinghua University, China
jietang@tsinghua.edu.cn

Large Language Models (LLMs), such as ChatGPT, GPT-4, Claude, PaLM, ChatGLM, Llama, Gemini, and Falcon, have revolutionized the field of artificial intelligence (AI) and substantially advanced the state of the art in various AI tasks, such as language understanding, text generation, image processing, and multimodal modeling. However, these powerful models also pose significant challenges to their safe and ethical deployment. The problem has become more serious since Open AI stopped sharing its techniques behind the GPT series. We present ChatGLM, an alternative to ChatGPT. We discuss technical details on how to build a ChatGPT-style system and share lessons we learned during the development of ChatGLM. Models and codes introduced in this paper are publicly available[1].

Base Model. To build ChatGLM, a powerful base model was necessary. We have developed GLM-130B [5], a bilingual (English and Chinese) language model with 130 billion parameters pre-trained using 1 trillion text tokens. Different from GPT-3, its model architecture is based on teh General Language Model (GLM) [2], a new pre-training method based on autoregressive blank-filling. In GLM, we randomly blank out continuous spans of tokens from the input text and train the model to reconstruct the spans using autoregressive pre-training. In this way, both bidirectional and unidirectional attention can be learned in a single framework. With only with three-fourths of the parameters of GPT-3, GLM-130B can achieve comparable, or even better performance on a wide range of benchmarks (112 tasks) and also outperforms PaLM 540B in many cases.

CodeGeex. We augmented the GLM base model with more code data—it is believed that the code data can help enhance the reasoning ability of the base model. Similar to Open AI's Codex, we first developed a separate model called CodeGeeX [6] using 850 billion tokens of 23 programming languages. CodeGeeX can achieve the best performance on HumanEval among all open code generation models. Based on CodeGeeX, we developed extensions on Visual Studio Code, JetBrains, and Cloud Studio with over 200,000 users.

WebGLM. The lack of dynamic information is a challenge for LLMs. One can fool the base model with simple questions such as "What is the weather now?" We present WebGLM [4], to augment the base model with web search and retrieval capabilities. In WebGLM, we have developed an LLM-augmented retriever, a bootstrapped generator,

---

[1] https://github.com/THUDM.

and a human preference-aware scorer, which successfully offers an efficient and cost-effective solution to address the limitation of the lack of dynamic information, with comparable quality to WebGPT.

ChatGLM. The base model cannot perfectly understand human intentions, follow complicated instructions, and communicate in multi-turn dialogues. Hence, the alignment training is critical for developing ChatGLM in practice. We take the following three steps to align the base model to human preference. First, *Supervised Fine-tuning (SFT)*: We collect initial queries by our existing web demonstrations (after data desensitization) and annotators' creation, including both single-round and multi-round. Second, *Feedback Bootstrapping (FB)*: We iteratively improve the quality of ChatGLM using feedback from annotators. We guide annotators to score model responses from different dimensions, including safety, factuality, relevance, helpfulness, and human preferences. Only top-scored responses are finally added to the next iteration of training. Third, *Reinforcement Learning From Human Feedback (RLHF)*: RLHF can help address flaws in specific situations, such as rejecting responses, safety issues, generating mixtures of bilingual tokens, multi-turn coherence, and some typical tasks.

VisualGLM. We further develop VisualGLM to enable ChatGLM with the ability to understand images, an important function in GPT-4. It has a visual encoder EVA-CLIP that produces image feature sequences. A Qformer model has been trained to bridge the vision model and ChatGLM. After pre-training on 330M Chinese and English image-text pairs and fine-tuning with extensive visual question answering (VQA) data, VisualGLM can effectively align visual information with the semantic nuances of natural language.

In future work, we are still trying to combine multi-modality and multi-task learning into a unified pre-training framework [1, 3], and investigate super alignment to help computers *understand* and solve real-world complicated problems.

References

1. Ding, M., et al.: CogView: mastering text-to-image generation via transformers. In: NeurIPS 2021, pp. 19822–19835 (2021)
2. Du, Z., et al.: GLM: general language model pretraining with autoregressive blank infilling. In: ACL 2022, pp. 320–335 (2022)
3. Lin, J., et al.: M6: multi-modality-to-multi-modality multitask mega-transformer for unified pretraining. In: KDD 2021, pp. 3251–3261 (2021)
4. Liu, X., et al.: WebGLM: towards an efficient web-enhanced question answering system with human preferences. In: KDD 2023, pp. 4549–4560 (2023)
5. Zeng, A., et al.: GLM-130B: an open bilingual pre-trained model. In: ICLR 2023 (2023)
6. Zheng, Q., et al.: CodeGeeX: a pre-trained model for code generation with multilingual benchmarking on HumanEval-X. In: KDD 2023, pp. 5673–5684 (2023)

Panel on Neuro-Symbolic AI

Efi Tsamoura[1], Vassilis Christophides[2], Antoine Bosselut[3], James Hendler[4],
Ian Horrocks[5], and Ioannis Tsamardinos[6]

[1]Samsung AI, Cambridge, UK
efi.tsamoura@samsung.com
[2]ETIS, ENSEA, France
vassilis.christophides@ensea.fr
[3]EPFL, Switzerland
[4]Rensselaer Polytechnic Institute, USA
[5]University of Oxford, UK
[6]University of Crete, Greece

The emerging paradigm of *neuro-symbolic Artificial Intelligence* (AI) stems from the recent efforts to enhance statistical AI (machine learning) with the complementary capabilities of symbolic AI (knowledge and reasoning). In neuro-symbolic AI, symbolic knowledge is used to guide deep models, while offering a path toward grounding symbols and inducing knowledge from low-level sensory data. Neuro-symbolic AI aims to demonstrate the capability to (i) solve hard problems requiring cognitive capabilities (ii) learn with significantly fewer data, ultimately for a large number of tasks rather than one narrow task (iii) provide inherently understandable and controllable decisions and actions.

The success stories and the research challenges of neuro-symbolic AI are the main topics of a panel that will take place in Athens, in November 2023 as part of the 22nd International Semantic Web Conference (ISWC).

A few indicative questions for the panel are:

– What have been the main reasons for developing neuro-symbolic techniques, e.g., explainability, accuracy, or scalability?
– Are there any success stories of blending logic with neural models? Are there any killer application scenarios in the semantic Web, NLP, computer vision, or other areas?
– Is logic the right formalism to address the limitations of the neural models and vice versa?
– What are the main (foundational) problems involved in integrating deep learning with logic? Are uncertain logics the "glue" between these two paradigms?
– How important is understanding the human brain to develop effective neuro-symbolic techniques and vice versa?
– Do neuro-symbolic techniques relate to other AI paradigms like causal AI, hybrid AI and artificial general intelligence (AGI)?
– How logic can help to explain neural models?

Contents – Part II

In-Use Track

Contents – Part I

Resources Track

HOLY: An Ontology Covering the Hydrogen Market

Kiara M. Ascencion Arevalo(✉) ⓘ, Christoph Neunsinger ⓘ, Roland Zimmermann ⓘ,
Ralph Blum, and Kendra Weakly ⓘ

Technische Hochschule Georg Simon Ohm, Bahnhofstraße 87, 90402 Nürnberg, Germany
kiaramarnitt.ascencionarevalo@th-nuernberg.de

Abstract. This paper presents the *Hydrogen Ontology* (*HOLY*), a domain ontology modeling the complex and dynamic structures of hydrogen-based markets.
The hydrogen economy has become a politically and economically crucial sector for the transition to renewable energy, accelerating technological and socioeconomic innovations. However, the attainment of market insights requires a large
variety of informational concepts which are predominantly found in unstructured
text data. *HOLY* provides the necessary structure for the representation of these
concepts. Through a top-down approach, *HOLY* defines taxonomies based on a
hierarchical structure of products and applications. In addition, to ensure reusability, the ontology incorporates components from established ontologies in its structure. As a result, *HOLY* consists of over 100 classes defining information about
organizations, projects, components, products, applications, markets, and indicators. Hence, our work contributes to the systemic modeling of the hydrogen domain
with a focus on its value chain. Formally, we represent and validate the ontology
with Semantic Web Technologies. *HOLY* includes lexical-semantic information
(e.g., synonyms, hyponyms, definitions, and examples) to simplify data integration into knowledge acquisition systems. Therefore, we provide a foundation for
the retrieval, storage, and delivery of market insights. A first application based on
HOLY at the Fraunhofer IIS offers an up-to-date market overview of developments
in the fuel cell environment.

Keywords: Hydrogen Ontology · Market Modeling · Ontology Engineering ·
Ontology-based Information Extraction · Value Chain Representation · PEM
Fuel Cell

1 Introduction

The hydrogen market is currently undergoing rapid changes. It is predicted to nearly
double in size from 170 billion USD in 2021 to about 300 billion USD by 2027 [1],
and - being a possible source for the green energy transition - it obtains strategic importance for nations. The most significant contributor is the European Union (EU) with its
EU Hydrogen Strategy[1]. However, other countries such as China, India, and the United

---

[1] Cf., https://energy.ec.europa.eu/topics/energy-systems-integration/hydrogen_en.

© The Author(s) 2023
T. R. Payne et al. (Eds.): ISWC 2023, LNCS 14266, pp. 3–17, 2023.
https://doi.org/10.1007/978-3-031-47243-5_1

States are also working to push this sector forward [2]. Consequently, the hydrogen sector is becoming attractive to companies investing in hydrogen projects. It also raises challenges concerning competition, development, and identification of key technologies to overcome current infrastructure limitations and political obstacles [3]. Hence, industrial, governmental, and research institutions require continuous monitoring of market developments to assess and tune their strategies.

In order to monitor developments in such a dynamic market, several aspects have to be addressed. Firstly, dynamically-changing market structures (e.g., the emergence of new stakeholders or new relations between existing stakeholders) as well as technological developments (e.g., improvements of specific fuel cell [FC] types) must be modeled in relation to each other. Secondly, these types of insights come from varying sources (e.g., publications [4], magazines [2], public institutions[2], company websites[3], and newspapers[4]). In other words, it is required to structure the necessary information (i.e., which data entities and data relationships are of interest) and enable a continuous process of retrieval (R), storage (S), and delivery (D) for the above-mentioned institutions.

To represent heterogeneous information (e.g., about markets and technology), domain ontologies capturing the conceptual patterns of a domain have been proposed in literature (e.g., in business [5], for infrastructure [6], or in the technology domain [7]). Ontologies provide a common representation of the structure of information in a particular domain by defining a shared vocabulary to enable people and software agents to share information [8].

Existing proposals are, to the authors' knowledge, sparse and insufficient in capturing the relevant information in the hydrogen domain. Therefore, the research question, *'How can knowledge about hydrogen-related microeconomic systems (domains) be modeled to enable extraction of market insights?'* guided our research.

We propose the domain-specific *Hydrogen Ontology* (*HOLY*) as a structural backbone for the hydrogen sector's R, S, and D processes, serving as a continuously-growing knowledge base for strategic foresight purposes. The development of *HOLY* is based on the *Linked Open Terms* (*LOT*) approach [9], an established methodology in the semantic literature used in different domains (e.g., in agriculture [10], information and communication technology [11], environmental management and sustainability [12], and in industrial context [13]). *HOLY* is already being used by the Fraunhofer Institute for Integrated Systems (IIS) for R, S, and D of market insights in the Atlant-H[5] project. The project aims to create a tool for automatically analyzing international market activities in the hydrogen environment. Hence, it employs natural language processing (NLP) for retrieval R and a graph database for storage S. Delivery D is based on SPARQL, a query language for the Resource Description Framework (RDF). Query results are presented in a user-friendly business intelligence front-end[6]. The ontology advances the

---

[2] Cf., https://energy.ec.europa.eu/topics/energy-systems-integration/hydrogen_en.

[3] Cf., https://www.ballard.com/fuel-cell-solutions/fuel-cell-power-products.

[4] Cf., https://www.theguardian.com/environment/2018/sep/17/germany-launches-worlds-first-hydrogen-powered-train.

[5] Atlant-H: https://www.scs.fraunhofer.de/de/referenzen/atlant-H.html.

[6] Atlant-H Front-end Demo: https://tinyurl.com/yr964ycu.

understanding of information conceptualization in a large, dynamically-changing market while considering an automated process (R, S, D). At the same time, *HOLY* provides a structured, yet dynamically-adaptable market model for the business community in the hydrogen sector.

Section 2 introduces related work, focusing on the usage of ontologies to model technical and market-related subjects and as enablers for the extraction of knowledge. Our approach for *HOLY* is detailed in Sect. 3, where we follow *LOT*'s set of structured development steps. We conclude with a summary and an outlook on future work in Sect. 4.

2 Related Work

Using domain ontologies to satisfy the analytical needs of market participants is a widespread practice among institutions. The EU used ontologies in the early 2000s within the Environmental Data Exchange Network for Inland Water (EDEN-IW) project to model information on water quality by integrating heterogeneous databases from governments [14]. The Market Blended Insight (MBI) project offered an approach to model a Business-to-Business (B2B) market in a closed domain setting with seven key partners. It includes market models in its ontology engineering process [5]. Domain ontologies position themselves as a recurring solution for areas requiring conceptual modeling and integrating information from different data sources [15].

In the hydrogen domain, knowledge graphs have been used to facilitate knowledge representation and discovery in the field of scientific research [16–18]. Additionally, interest in monitoring information pertaining to the hydrogen market can be seen in the creation of databases for hydrogen projects[7,8], and hydrogen companies[9]. To monitor the hydrogen market, the European Union realizes a rather broad approach based on the Tools for Innovation Monitoring (TIM) toolset [19, 20]. The interactive tool uses graph-based visualizations; however, these are not based on knowledge graphs or ontologies, but on the co-occurrence of keywords in the same texts [19, 20]. Nevertheless, interesting insights (e.g., into weak signals) are presented in curated reports (for 2021, see [21]).

For ontology development, reusing and building on existing, established ontologies is essential. *The Organization Ontology* was created in 2010 as a core ontology for company information, providing a logical structure for linked company data across numerous domains which includes roles and memberships [22]. The *Registered Organization Vocabulary* expanded upon *The Organization Ontology* in 2013 by extending the formal organization section with unique properties for displaying legal status and economic activities [23]. These activities can be classified using internationally accepted standards such as the Nomenclature of Economic Activities (NACE) [24], the Standard Industrial Classification [25], or the International Standard Industrial Classification [26]. In 2020, the *euBusinessGraph* added depth on registered businesses in the European Union by focusing on information concerning the harmonization of a company's legal type, its registered economic activity, geographic location, founding date, classification

---

[7] Cf., https://www.iea.org/data-and-statistics/data-product/hydrogen-projects-database.

[8] Cf., https://commodityinside.com/reports/global-green-hydrogen-projects-database/

[9] Cf., https://www.enerdata.net/research/h2-database.html.

as a start-up, and classifications for being state-owned or independent using concepts from the *Registered Organization Vocabulary* [27].

Ontologies are also utilized for Ontology Based Information Extraction (OBIE). OBIE is the conceptual structuring of information coming from Information Extraction (IE) technologies [28]. Hence, OBIE systems utilize ontological structures to filter for relevant terms or enrich them by setting extracted information into context with other information. For example, Raza Rizvi et al. [29] use ontologies to enable generalization of their OBIE system and extraction of tabular information from documents irrespective of the domain. Furthermore, the MUSING IE architecture relies on an ontology to consolidate information from its different sources (e.g., company profiles from Yahoo! Finance, company websites, newspaper articles, and company reports) concerning knowledge about companies, region-specific insights, and economic indicators [28].

3 The Hydrogen Ontology (HOLY)

3.1 Methodology

This paper's methodology for ontology development is based on the *LOT* framework [9], as shown in Fig. 1. In the requirements specification stage, the ontology's requirements (i.e., the goal, scope, use cases, and functional requirements) are identified. The implementation stage is an iterative process where a conceptual model describing the problem and its solution is created; this model is formalized in an ontological language, such as RDF, to generate machine-readable models and including metadata. Additionally, existing ontologies are identified and integrated into the developed structure. In the publication stage, the ontology is made available online via its URI, in both human-readable documentation and machine-readable file formats. The maintenance stage aims to keep the ontology updated throughout its lifecycle. Hence, activities can be triggered during the development process or later on. As a supporting activity, knowledge acquisition is constantly present in the ontology development process. Knowledge acquisition[10] relies on a range of sources including interviews, publicly-available resources from websites, magazines, books, non-ontological and ontological types as well as best practices.

The results of each stage are described in the following chapters. In addition to the *LOT* framework, guidance from *Ontology Development 101* by Noy & McGuinness [30] is applied to develop class definitions, hierarchies, properties, and class instantiations. Methods for knowledge acquisition follow the NeOn Methodology [31].

3.2 Ontology Requirements Specification

HOLY was developed within the Atlant-H hydrogen project to structure information from the hydrogen economy and serve as the backbone of an OBIE and NLP-powered text processing system for automatic market activity analysis. Hereby, *HOLY*'s objective is the representation of domain knowledge of the hydrogen sector to track developments in the market. Consequently, *HOLY* is intended to be used for decision-making, market monitoring, and to facilitate research planning for industry players, governmental

---

[10] HOLY Knowledge Acquisition Process: https://purl.org/holy/knowledge_acquisition.

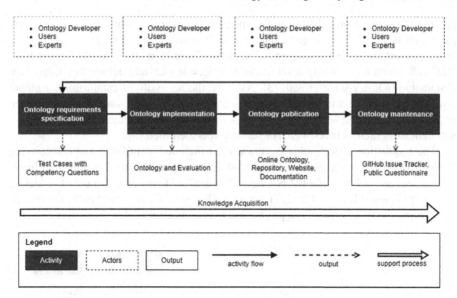

Fig. 1. The *Linked Open Terms* (*LOT*) Framework used to develop the *Hydrogen Ontology*.

institutions, and research institutions. In addition, *HOLY*'s lexical-semantic information and structure facilitate performing Natural Language tasks such as Named Entity Recognition and Question Answering, which are employed to extract information from natural language sources automatically. Aside from the requirements of the Atlant-H project, other potential use cases[11] have been identified. These applications extend to various additional stakeholders, such as technology providers, investors, product users, and educational institutions.

The specification of ontology requirements was carried out by utilizing different inputs and models gathered from the knowledge acquisition process. In order to cover domain knowledge of the hydrogen sector, the ontology incorporates both market structures and technological knowledge of the hydrogen domain. The former requires concepts and relationships of market actors, their roles, and interactions, while the latter requires concepts and relationships of hydrogen technologies and their components.

Michael E. Porter's 'Five Forces' framework structure has been identified as an appropriate source for market structure conceptualization. Porter's 'Five Forces' is an established, domain-independent framework used to evaluate the competitiveness of industries. The framework is based on five forces in a market [32]. These forces are used to identify required structures and corresponding knowledge (e.g., economic activities coming from NACE and definitions coming from the Cambridge Dictionary).

Market insights are derived from the report 'Geopolitics of the Energy Transformation: The Hydrogen Factor' of the International Renewable Energy Agency (IRENA)

---

[11] HOLY Use Case Specifiation: https://purl.org/holy/use_case_specification.

[2], the Hydrogen Council [3], the European Commission[12], news articles, and company websites[13]. The Hydrogen Council is an initiative comprising 150 organizations that represent the global hydrogen value chain. Their Hydrogen Insight Report from 2022 reflects on the maturity level of the hydrogen market and defines key factors for sustainable industry-wide growth [3]. As such, the necessity of establishing a global coverage perspective with details on geolocations was revealed since major hydrogen players are distributed worldwide [2]. Furthermore, the importance of tracking projects and indicators such as investments or funding was identified [3].

The acquisition of technological knowledge included identifying and categorizing the hydrogen market and its underlying products, components, and composition. Information was derived from the IRENA report [2], leading to the requirement of modeling the structure as displayed in Fig. 2. The structure follows the energetical path of hydrogen by showing the value chain from production to the end-user.

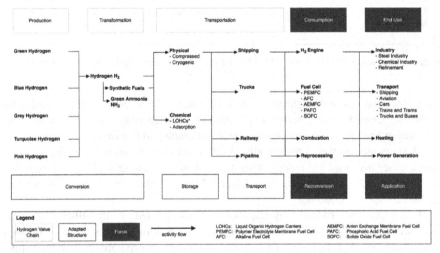

Fig. 2. Hydrogen Market Value Chain adapted and simplified from the IRENA report [2] and Information from TÜV Süd[14].

Concepts and definitions were extracted from the analysis of descriptions of governmental institutions[15], websites from active market participants[16], and scientific journals [32]. In order to properly represent said concepts for NLP tasks, it is required to include lexical-semantic data in the ontology. Therefore, synonyms, definitions, and examples for each class are included.

---

[12] Cf., https://energy.ec.europa.eu/topics/energy-systems-integration/hydrogen_en.

[13] Cf., https://www.ballard.com/fuel-cell-solutions/fuel-cell-power-products.

[14] Cf., https://www.tuvsud.com/en/themes/hydrogen/explore-the-hydrogen-value-chain.

[15] Cf., https://www.energy.gov/eere/fuelcells/hydrogen-storage.

[16] Cf., https://www.ballard.com/fuel-cell-solutions/fuel-cell-power-products.

Every value chain stage of the hydrogen market can be detailed to a high granularity level. To exemplify detailed modeling of the different stages through *HOLY*, we extensively modeled the reconversion stage (i.e., reconversion of hydrogen into electrical power). More specifically, we focused on the established Proton-exchange Membrane Fuel Cell (PEMFC) technology, a sub-technology of fuel cells that is forecasted to receive the fastest commercial growth among fuel cell technologies in the next few years. At the same time, it is prognosed to stay in competition with other maturing and potentially upcoming fuel cell technologies [2].

We used test cases to formalize the functional ontology requirements identified. Test cases are formal descriptions of input, action, and outcomes used to ensure that a Linked Data resource conforms to a given set of requirements [33] - in this case, our ontology requirements specification document (ORSD)[17]. As such, they enable the evaluation of the quality and interoperability of *HOLY* by verifying that the terms are clearly and unambiguously defined [34]. Test cases were collected from industry participants as a set of competency questions as part of the Atlant-H project. We then defined our test cases based on the competency question in collaboration with Fraunhofer IIS internal market experts and H2Ohm[18] hydrogen experts. Ontology requirements and corresponding test cases as either 'Technological' or 'Market' depending on the type of information to which they are related. A comprehensive list of our test cases can be found in our repository[19].

3.3 Ontology Implementation

In order to address the ORSD, two orthogonal dimensions - market and hydrogen technology - have to be conceptualized in the ontology.

The **market dimension** requires terms which enable the development of reusable abstract microeconomic structures. As a result, *HOLY* consists of the six main classes listed below and conceptualizes market relationships such as production, cooperation, geographic placement, and provision of goods or services.

- **Product:** delineates relevant and substitute technologies, products, and their components along the hydrogen value chain to cover the need for segmentation outlined by the market.
- **Application:** covers use cases for products and technologies under the categories of stationary and mobile applications.
- **Organization:** contains structural information about market participants and organization types following NACE.
- **GeographicMarket:** focuses on geographic units at the level of countries and continents. Smaller units (e.g., states or provinces) are mapped to these two classes.
- **Project:** provides a structure to classify project types by purpose and state and display their market role using object properties connected to the other five classes.

---

[17] HOLY Requirements Specification: https://purl.org/holy/requirements.

[18] Institut für Angewandte Wasserstoffforschung, Elektro- und Thermochemische Energiesysteme (H2Ohm): https://www.th-nuernberg.de/einrichtungen-gesamt/in-institute/institut-fuer-angewandte-wasserstoffforschung-elektro-und-thermochemische-energiesysteme/.

[19] HOLY Test Cases: https://purl.org/holy/test_cases.

- **Indicator:** has connections to all other classes, allowing it to store performance information.

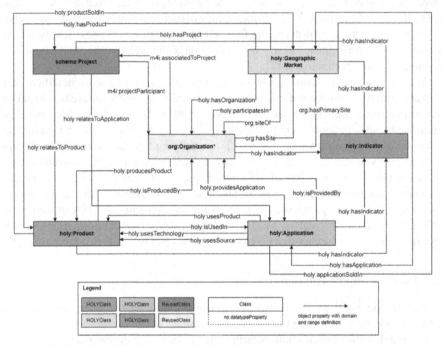

Fig. 3. Overview of the *Hydrogen Ontology*'s six main classes and related properties.

Figure 3 provides an overview of the ontology schema including main classes and relationships. Organization and Project classes are defined by existing ontologies - *The Organization Ontology (org)* and *Schema.org (schema)* respectively - while the other classes belong to *HOLY*'s vocabulary. The subclasses of *org:Organization* and *holy:GeographicMarket* structure information to identify rivalry within the market based on segmentation by a player's economic activity and geographic location. The alignment with terms from official economic nomenclatures under *org:Organization* enables identification of buyers and suppliers. A threat of substitutes is addressed using the classes *holy:Product* and *holy:Application* by providing a structure to cluster PEMFCs and their substitutes according to their related applications. The class *schema:Project* provides a set of terms to model market players' efforts to develop the industry and classify them by objective (e.g., research-oriented, product-oriented, infrastructure-oriented or oriented to projects concerning circular economy) and state (finished, ongoing, or planned). The class *holy:Indicator* categorizes strategic information influencing the strength of a market participant and barriers faced by parties interested in competing in the hydrogen industry. Indicators are, for example, market share, investment, market size, and patents. Hence, the model covers the 'Market' requirements from the ORSD.

The **hydrogen dimension** specifies products and component classes related to the hydrogen domain and splits the market into segments along the stages of the hydrogen value chain (conversion, storage, transport, and reconversion). The separation between products and their components enables detailed insights into product composition. The modeling example of PEMFC technology embeds a more detailed level of granularity into the product taxonomy. A part of the hydrogen schema is shown in the following Fig. 4, illustrating different types of products on multiple levels of abstraction.

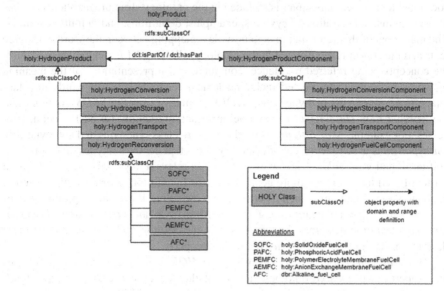

Fig. 4. A fragment from *HOLY*'s taxonomy focused on the *holy:HydrogenProduct* and *holy:HydrogenProductComponent* classes. A complete representation is available in the *HOLY* documentation[20].

With the purpose of ensuring the reusability and extensibility of the ontology, existing ontological concepts are integrated into *HOLY*'s structure. Following best practices, *HOLY* applies a multi-tiered approach to enable semantic interoperability using a range of ontologies - from top-level to low-level abstractions - across different domain sections [35]. The frameworks of *RDF Schema* (*RDFS*) and *Simple Knowledge Organisation System* (*SKOS*) act as top-level ontologies in *HOLY* and provide extended structures of hierarchical knowledge representation, establishing a common vocabulary. *RDFS* is used to define concepts and relationships while *SKOS* enables lexical-semantic information integration.

Mid-level ontologies cover areas of representation such as organizations, locations, and projects. *The Organization Ontology* provides a widely used and accepted framework for classifying organizations. *Schema.org*'s vocabulary delivers extensions to classify a project while providing structures for geographic segmentation. Lower-level ontologies extend these mid-level ontologies by building upon their class structures [35]. The *Registered Organization Vocabulary* (*rov*) extends *The Organization Ontology* regarding organizations' classifications and economic activities. At the same time, the *euBusinessGraph* (*ebg*) expands the *Registered Organization Vocabulary* even further towards

---

[20] HOLY Documentation: https://purl.org/holy/doc.

additional company classification criteria such as defining whether an organization is state-owned, publicly traded, or a start-up [27]. *Schema.org* is enriched with the *Metadata4Ing* (*m4i*) ontology, which provides an extended information structure for identifying project participants and the status of projects. The *DBpedia Ontology* (*dbo*) offers geographic mapping through entity linking against its knowledge graph [36].

To facilitate OBIE, which utilizes NLP methods to extract information, natural language descriptors for the classes on both dimensions are necessary. To this end, an additional lexical-semantic layer is included in the ontology structure, explicitly declaring synonyms, abbreviations, keywords, examples, definitions, and definition sources. The main goal of this information is to provide a mapping between the words in source texts and the concepts represented in the ontology, allowing NLP techniques to identify the concepts being referred to. Hence, computational representations of the meaning of words in context are created including lexical relations between words in a language (e.g., synonyms or hyponyms). *HOLY* primarily uses the *SKOS* ontology and the *Wordnet RDF Ontology* (wn) to model information required for NLP pipeline processes. For example, *skos:altLabel* is used to capture class synonyms and abbreviations, *wn:hyponym* is used to represent relevant keywords that denote subtypes of a more general term, and *skos:hiddenLabel* is used for class-relevant keywords that can be used for text-based indexing in a more general context. In addition, *skos:example* is used to annotate specific examples such as companies (e.g., Plug Power Inc.), product names (e.g., FCwave™), or applications (e.g., Toyota Mirai) available on the market. The property *skos:definition* describes the terms used in the ontology, and the sources of these descriptions are given using the *dct:references* property.

The *Hydrogen Ontology* is built using OWL 2. *HOLY* combines newly created classes and properties with existing ontologies and vocabularies such as *The Organization Ontology*, *Schema.org*, and the *euBusinessGraph*. *HOLY* consists of 109 classes (6 main classes and 103 sub-classes), 35 object properties, 8 data properties, 544 instances, and actively uses 5 annotation properties. The distribution between native and foreign classes and properties implemented in *HOLY* is listed in Table 1.

Table 1. Distribution of native and foreign classes and properties in *HOLY.*

Class and Property Type	Main Classes	Sub-classes	Object Properties	Data Properties	Annotation Properties
Native	4	97	18	0	0
Foreign	2	6	17	8	5
Total	6	103	35	8	5

3.4 Evaluation

An evaluation was performed following various criteria. In order to evaluate the RDF implementation of the *Hydrogen Ontology*, it was cross-checked for ontology pitfalls. These ontology pitfalls cover human understanding, logical consistency, elimination of modeling issues and errors in the representation of the real world, and compliance with the ontology language [36]. The validation was realized with the *OntOlogy Pitfall Scanner* (*OOPS!*). *OOPS!* is a web-based ontology checker which helps to validate ontologies by identifying previously-defined ontology pitfalls. Evaluation results of *OOPS!* contain a list of pitfalls and their severity alongside the categories 'minor', 'important', and 'critical' [37].

When cross-checking the *Hydrogen Ontology*, 12 minor issues and one important issue were detected. Two minor issues referred to classes merging different concepts and ten referred to inverse relations not being explicitly declared. Six out of the ten inverse relations labeled as not declared are object properties directly taken from *The Organization Ontology* and the *Registered Organization Vocabulary*. Creating inverse relationships for the remaining four inverse relationships would be redundant and leads to an increase of important pitfalls of recursive definitions. The two minor issues related to classes merging different concepts come from organization types created by following NACE. Modifying the structure would hinder adherence to the NACE standard. The important issue (recursive definition) is derived from using a class and its definition from *Schema.org*. Nevertheless, the ontology's consistency and reasoning are not affected by these pitfalls, as they are caused by the generality of *OOPS!* which is necessary to cover different knowledge models.

Additionally, following the *LOT* framework, test cases were used to verify the fit to functional requirements. Throughout the evaluation, four approaches using SPARQL were followed, similar to those followed by Lisena et al. [38].

1. **Explicit Relations:** query for relations that directly connect classes
   Example: 'Which applications are there for a given product?'
2. **Inference/Aggregation:** query using aggregation or inference (e.g., group by, count, property chains, etc.)
   Example: 'In which vehicles are PEM fuel cells more often used?'
3. **Linked Open Data:** query required information outside the scope of the model, but accessible through Linked Open Data (e.g., DBpedia)
   Example: 'In which countries is a given company present?'
4. **OBIE:** query requiring an extension of the model or information extraction through NLP, as is present in an OBIE system.
   Example: 'Do product components change over time?'

Some test cases required additional information obtainable through an OBIE system. As an example, assume that we are interested in the change of PEMFC components over time. In that case, we require a temporal structure and data gathered across a time span. Hence, in the fourth approach, information from the Atlant-H use case was used to evaluate whether requirements could be answered; we consider all other cases to be satisfied by the ontology. Table 2 shows a summary of our results classified by test case type.

3.5 Publishing

The *Hydrogen Ontology* is implemented in RDF format and published[21] under a Creative Commons 4.0 CC-BY-SA license. The ontology requirements specification process as well as validation and evaluation results are available in the resource repository[22].

---

[21] HOLY URL: https://purl.org/holy/ns.
[22] HOLY repository: https://purl.org/holy/repository.

Table 2. Type of SPARQL Queries by Test Case type for *HOLY* listing.

Type	Explicit Relation	Inference/Aggregation	LOD	OBIE	Total
Technological	5	2	0	1	8
Market	3	1	6	0	10
Total	8	3	6	1	18

Ontology documentation is accessible online[23]. Other related resources developed and published in the context of this work are attainable through the Future Engineering homepage[24].

3.6 Maintenance

In order to support the continued use of the ontology, a maintenance plan has been developed which aims to continually evaluate the structure and accuracy of the ontology and provide feedback regarding areas of high potential for future growth endeavors. For bug detection, we employ the GitHub issue tracker which keeps control of the list of issues. For the identification of new requirements, a questionnaire[25] consisting of fixed, mostly open-ended questions has been made publicly available to allow for external input about the current state of the hydrogen market. Submissions will be regularly reviewed and considered regarding changes for further versions of *HOLY*.

4 Contribution and Future Work

In this paper, we introduced the *Hydrogen Ontology*, a domain ontology modeling the hydrogen economy. We followed the *LOT* framework and developed an ontology which combines established business models with technological domain knowledge. As such, *HOLY*'s structure is composed of two orthogonal dimensions. The first comprises six main classes representing market structures while the second organizes technological knowledge in hierarchical structures to enable the classification of products along the hydrogen value chain and the identification of components and substitutes. We included existing ontologies and vocabularies to address reusability challenges and allow expansion within other segments. To handle heterogeneous and fast-growing data sources, the model includes a lexical-semantic layer, which provides the necessary information to aid NLP of texts in the hydrogen domain, thus facilitating the construction of an OBIE system around the ontology. Additionally, the ontology was validated through a pitfall scanner and evaluated to ensure the satisfaction of its functional requirements.

At the time of writing, the published version of the ontology is being used in the Atlant-H project and is planned to be applied in the follow-up project from Atlant-H, also in cooperation with the Fraunhofer IIS. As part of this project, we intend to expand and improve the *HOLY* model. Thus, future research may extend the conceptual model to other hydrogen technologies or value chain stages. Similarly, classes like *Projects* and *Indicators* can be further detailed (e.g., via subclasses) to provide a more comprehensive

---

[23] HOLY Documentation: https://purl.org/holy/doc.

[24] HOLY Website: https://purl.org/holy.

[25] Maintenance feedback questionnaire: https://purl.org/holy/feedback.

market representation. Moreover, to ensure support of OBIE systems, integrated lexical-semantic information for NLP should be further evaluated to ensure proper coverage concerning available natural text in the domain (e.g., hydrogen market-related press releases, news, and publications). Furthermore, *HOLY's* applicability is not limited to the Atlant-H project alone, as it is intended to be employed in other third-party hydrogen projects such as the DuraFuelCell project, a German national research project led by the H2Ohm.

Resource Availability Statement: Source code for *HOLY*, test cases, ontology requirements specification, use case specification, maintenance feedback questionnaire, and Atlant-H use case are available from Github[26]. The *Hydrogen Ontology* and its documentation are available from Zenodo[27]. The *HOLY* website is available from the Technische Hochschule Nürnberg Georg Simon Ohm[28]. The *Hydrogen Ontology* is published under the Creative Commons 4.0 CC-BY-SA license.

Acknowledgements. This work has been supported by the Future Engineering Research Group, a research collaboration between the Technische Hochschule Nürnberg Georg Simon Ohm and the Fraunhofer IIS. In addition, we would like to thank Rene Dorsch from the Fraunhofer IIS for the useful discussion and comments on the manuscript.

Author Contribution. Conceptualization, K.A.; Methodology, K.A., C.N.; Software, K.A., C.N.; Validation, K.A.; Formal Analysis, C.N.; Investigation, K.A., C.N.; Data Curation, K.A., C.N., K.W.; Writing-original draft, K.A., C.N.; Writing-review and editing, K.A., C.N., K.W., R.Z., R.B.; Visualization, C.N., K.W.; Supervision, K.A., R.Z., R.B.; Project Administration, K.A. All authors have read and approved the final version of the manuscript.

References

1. Global Market Insights: Hydrogen Market Size, Forecast Report 2021–2027. https://www.gminsights.com/industry-analysis/hydrogen-market. Accessed 03 Aug 2022
2. IRENA: Geopolitics of the Energy Transformation: The Hydrogen Factor. International Renewable Energy Agency, Abu Dhabi (2022)
3. McKinsey & Company, Hydrogen Council: Hydrogen Insights 2022. Hydrogen Council (2022)
4. Fan, L., Tu, Z., Chan, S.H.: Recent development of hydrogen and fuel cell technologies: a review. Energy Rep. **7**, 8421–8446 (2021). https://doi.org/10.1016/j.egyr.2021.08.003
5. Zuo, L., et al.: Supporting multi-view user ontology to understand company value chains. In: Bernstein, A., et al. (eds.) ISWC 2009. LNCS, vol. 5823. Springer, Heidelberg (2009). https://doi.org/10.1007/978-3-642-04930-9_58
6. El-Gohary, N.M., El-Diraby, T.E.: Domain ontology for processes in infrastructure and construction. J. Constr. Eng. Manag. **136**, 730–744 (2010). https://doi.org/10.1061/(ASCE)CO.1943-7862.0000178
7. Haghgoo, M., Sychev, I., Monti, A., Fitzek, F.: SARGON – smart energy domain ontology. Smart Cities (2020). https://doi.org/10.1049/iet-smc.2020.0049

---

[26] GitHub: https://purl.org/holy/repository.
[27] Zenodo: https://doi.org/10.5281/zenodo.7447958.
[28] HOLY Website: https://purl.org/holy.

8. Leontis, N.B., et al.: The RNA ontology consortium: an open invitation to the RNA community. RNA **12**, 533–541 (2006). https://doi.org/10.1261/rna.2343206
9. Poveda-Villalón, M., Fernández-Izquierdo, A., Fernández-López, M., García-Castro, R.: LOT: an industrial oriented ontology engineering framework. Eng. Appl. Artif. Intell. **111**, 104755 (2022). https://doi.org/10.1016/j.engappai.2022.104755
10. Nguyen, Q.-D., Roussey, C., Poveda-Villalón, M., de Vaulx, C., Chanet, J.-P.: Development experience of a context-aware system for smart irrigation using CASO and IRRIG ontologies. Appl. Sci. **10**, 1803 (2020). https://doi.org/10.3390/app10051803
11. Tailhardat, L., Chabot, Y., Troncy, R.: NORIA-O: an ontology for anomaly detection and incident management in ICT systems, **13**. IOS Press (2022). https://doi.org/10.3390/app100 51803
12. Espinoza-Arias, P., Poveda-Villalón, M., Corcho, O.: Using LOT methodology to develop a noise pollution ontology: a Spanish use case. J. Ambient. Intell. Humaniz. Comput. **11**, 4557–4568 (2020). https://doi.org/10.1007/s12652-019-01561-2
13. de Roode, M., Fernández-Izquierdo, A., Daniele, L., Poveda-Villalón, M., García-Castro, R.: SAREF4INMA: a SAREF extension for the industry and manufacturing domain, **17**. IOS Press (2020)
14. Stjernholm, M., Poslad, S., Zuo, L., Sortkj, O., Huang, X.: The EDEN-IW ontology model for sharing knowledge and water quality data between heterogeneous databases. In: EnviroInfo 2004 (2004)
15. Munir, K., Sheraz Anjum, M.: The use of ontologies for effective knowledge modelling and information retrieval. Appl. Comput. Inform. **14**, 116–126 (2018). https://doi.org/10.1016/j. aci.2017.07.003
16. Seurin, P., et al.: H2-golden-retriever: methodology and tool for an evidence-based hydrogen research grantsmanship. http://arxiv.org/abs/2211.08614 (2022). https://doi.org/10.48550/ arXiv.2211.08614
17. Lin, R., Fang, Q., Wu, B.: Hydro-graph: a knowledge graph for hydrogen research trends and relations. Int. J. Hydrog. Energy **45**, 20408–20418 (2020). https://doi.org/10.1016/j.ijhydene. 2019.12.036
18. Zhang, M., Yang, R., Xu, J.: Construction and analysis of scientific research knowledge graph in the field of hydrogen energy technology. In: Liang, Q., Wang, W., Mu, J., Liu, X., Na, Z. (eds.) AIC 2022. LNEE, vol. 871, pp. 392–402. Springer, Singapore (2023). https://doi.org/ 10.1007/978-981-99-1256-8_46
19. European Commission. Joint Research Centre: Text mining for horizon scanning: an insight into agricultural research and innovation in Africa. Publications Office, LU (2020)
20. Moro, A., Joanny, G., Moretti, C.: Emerging technologies in the renewable energy sector: a comparison of expert review with a text mining software. Futures **117**, 102511 (2020). https:// doi.org/10.1016/j.futures.2020.102511
21. European Commission. Joint Research Centre: Weak signals in science and technologies in 2021: technologies at a very early stage of development that could impact the future. Publications Office, LU (2022)
22. World Wide Web Consortium: The Organization Ontology (2014). http://www.w3.org/TR/ 2014/REC-vocab-org-20140116/
23. World Wide Web Consortium: Registered Organization Vocabulary (2013). http://www.w3. org/TR/2013/NOTE-vocab-regorg-20130801/
24. EUROSTAT: NACE rev. 2. Office for Official Publications of the European Communities, Luxembourg (2008)
25. Prosser, L. (ed.): UK Standard Industrial Classification of Economic Activities 2007 (SIC 2007): Structure and Explanatory Notes. Palgrave Macmillan, Basingstoke (2008)
26. United Nations ed: International Standard Industrial Classification of All Economic Activities (ISIC). United Nations, New York (2008)

27. Roman, D., et al.: The euBusinessGraph ontology: a lightweight ontology for harmonizing basic company information. Semant. Web **13**, 41–68 (2021). https://doi.org/10.3233/SW-210424

28. Saggion, H., Funk, A., Maynard, D., Bontcheva, K.: Ontology-based information extraction for business intelligence. In: Aberer, K., et al. (eds.) ISWC ASWC 2007 2007. LNCS, vol. 4825, pp. 843–856. Springer, Heidelberg (2007). https://doi.org/10.1007/978-3-540-76298-0_61

29. Rizvi, S.T.R., Mercier, D., Agne, S., Erkel, S., Dengel, A., Ahmed, S.: Ontology-based information extraction from technical documents: In: Proceedings of the 10th International Conference on Agents and Artificial Intelligence, pp. 493–500. SCITEPRESS - Science and Technology Publications, Funchal, Madeira, Portugal (2018). https://doi.org/10.5220/0006596604930500

30. Noy, N.F., McGuinness, D.L.: Ontology development 101: a guide to creating your first ontology

31. Suárez-Figueroa, M.C., Gómez-Pérez, A., Motta, E., Gangemi, A. (eds.): Ontology Engineering in a Networked World. Springer, Heidelberg (2012). https://doi.org/10.1007/978-3-642-24794-1

32. Porter, M.E.: Towards a dynamic theory of strategy. Strateg. Manag. J. **12**, 95–117 (1991). https://doi.org/10.1002/smj.4250121008

33. Peroni, S.: A simplified agile methodology for ontology development. In: Dragoni, M., Poveda-Villalón, M., Jimenez-Ruiz, E. (eds.) OWLED ORE 2016 2016. LNCS, vol. 10161, pp. 55–69. Springer, Cham (2017). https://doi.org/10.1007/978-3-319-54627-8_5

34. Schekotihin, K., Rodler, P., Schmid, W., Horridge, M., Tudorache, T.: Test-driven ontology development in Protégé. In: Proceedings of the 9th International Conference on Biological Ontology, ICBO 2018 (2018)

35. Rudnicki, R., Smith, B., Malyuta, T., Mandrick, W.: Best practices of ontology development, p. 16 (2016)

36. Lehmann, J., et al.: DBpedia – a large-scale, multilingual knowledge base extracted from Wikipedia. Semant. Web **6**, 167–195 (2015). https://doi.org/10.3233/SW-140134

37. Poveda-Villalón, M., Suárez-Figueroa, M.C., Gómez-Pérez, A.: Validating ontologies with OOPS!. In: ten Teije, A., et al. (eds.) EKAW 2012. LNCS, vol. 7603, pp. 267–281. Springer, Heidelberg (2012). https://doi.org/10.1007/978-3-642-33876-2_24

38. Lisena, P., et al.: Capturing the semantics of smell: the odeuropa data model for olfactory heritage information. In: Groth, P., et al. (eds.) ESWC 2022. LNCS, vol. 13261, pp. 387–405. Springer, Cham (2022). https://doi.org/10.1007/978-3-031-06981-9_23

MMpedia: A Large-Scale Multi-modal Knowledge Graph

Yinan Wu[1], Xiaowei Wu[1], Junwen Li[1], Yue Zhang[1], Haofen Wang[2], Wen Du[3], Zhidong He[3], Jingping Liu[1], and Tong Ruan[1(✉)]

[1] School of Information Science and Engineering, East China University of Science and Technology, Shanghai, China
y21220035@mail.ecust.edu.cn, {jingpingliu,ruantong}@ecust.edu.cn
[2] College of Design and Innovation, Tongji University, Shanghai, China
[3] DS Information Technology, Shanghai, China

Abstract. Knowledge graphs serve as crucial resources for various applications. However, most existing knowledge graphs present symbolic knowledge in the form of natural language, lacking other modal information, e.g., images. Previous multi-modal knowledge graphs have encountered challenges with scaling and image quality. Therefore, this paper proposes a highly-scalable and high-quality multi-modal knowledge graph using a novel pipeline method. Summarily, we first retrieve images from a search engine and build a new Recurrent Gate Multi-modal model to filter out the non-visual entities. Then, we utilize entities' textual and type information to remove noisy images of the remaining entities. Through this method, we construct a large-scale multi-modal knowledge graph named MMpedia, containing 2,661,941 entity nodes and 19,489,074 images. As we know, MMpedia has the largest collection of images among existing multi-modal knowledge graphs. Furthermore, we employ human evaluation and downstream tasks to verify the usefulness of images in MMpedia. The experimental result shows that both the state-of-the-art method and multi-modal large language model (e.g., VisualChatGPT) achieve about a 4% improvement on Hit@1 in the entity prediction task by incorporating our collected images. We also find that the multi-modal large language model is hard to ground entities to images. The dataset (https://zenodo.org/record/7816711) and source code of this paper are available at https://github.com/Delicate2000/MMpedia.

Keywords: Multi-modal · Knowledge graph · Entity grounding

1 Introduction

Knowledge Graph (KG) is an important resource and has been applied to various applications such as text classification [6], recommendation [52] and question answering [1]. KGs (e.g., DBpedia [21] and Wikidata [44]) contain a large volume of symbol knowledge. The symbol knowledge is usually represented in the form of RDF triples $< h, r, t >$, where h and t are the head and tail entity respectively, and r is the relation between h and t.

© The Author(s), under exclusive license to Springer Nature Switzerland AG 2023
T. R. Payne et al. (Eds.): ISWC 2023, LNCS 14266, pp. 18–37, 2023.
https://doi.org/10.1007/978-3-031-47243-5_2

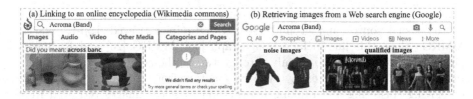

Fig. 1. Traditional MMKG construction methods

Problem Statement. However, most existing KGs illustrate the entity in the form of natural language without other modal information such as visual or audio [57]. This results in two problems. **(1)** In the cognitive domain, this situation limits machines' ability to know the physical world. For example, for human beings, we form the concept of *cat* based on the experience of living with a cat. However, for machines, it is challenging to understand what *cat* is as humans do, since symbols or text alone can not bridge the entity *cat* with the experience of cats. Hence, it is necessary to ground entities in KGs to corresponding images, which provides visual experiences for machines. **(2)** In the application domain, grounding entities in KGs to images can enhance machines' performance on various NLP tasks, including relation extraction (RE) [18], named entity recognition [5] and recommendation [38]. In most cases, the integration of visual features has the potential to resolve issues that are difficult to be comprehended from symbolic and textual representations. For example, in RE, given the sentence *JustinBieber (JB) and HaileyBaldwin (HB) arriving at LIV club* from the MNRE dataset [56], it is challenging to determine the social relation between "JB" and "HB" because the text does not provide any semantics of their relation. Fortunately, with the additional information (e.g., age and gender) from images of "JB" and "HB", the relation (Couple) is easier to be inferred.

Hence, in this paper, we aim to help machines understand *what the entity is* by providing high-quality images for KGs.

Limits of Previous MMKGs. Several multi-modal KGs (MMKGs) with entities grounded to images have been proposed. These MMKGs are constructed by collecting images from *online encyclopedias* (OEs) or *web search engines* (WSEs) while either of them still has limitations in providing sufficient and high-quality images for entities.

The first category considers *OEs* (e.g., Wikipedia) as the visual source since they provide images (e.g., Wikimedia commons[1]) as auxiliary information to depict entities. MMKGs built through this category include IMGpedia [13] and Visualsem [2] with data-linking and image-text matching methods. The images in them are relatively reliable and come with textual annotations. However, these MMKGs are hard to scale **due to the limited number of entities in OEs**. For example, given an entity *Acroma_ (band)* in DBpedia, we can not find its images because it is absent from Wikimedia commons as shown in Fig. 1(a).

---

[1] http://commons.wikimedia.org.

To improve scalability, the second category considers *WSEs* (e.g., Google) as the visual source and ground the entity to its retrieved Top-K images. MMKGs alone this line include Imagegraph [30], MMKG [26] and Richpedia [46], which are constructed mainly through two methods: (1) generating unambiguous queries with the entity type information from triples [26,30] and (2) employing clustering and ranking information to select images retrieved from WSEs [46]. Nevertheless, these MMKGs suffer from relatively low image quality due to two reasons. Firstly, **both (1) and (2) overlook the removal of non-visual entities, which leads to mismatched images.** Non-visual entities lack a clear visual representation and can not be described in images. For example, given the entity *Idealism*, it is difficult to find an image that accurately reflects it. In contrast, entities with specific visual representations are known as visual entities (e.g., Cat). Secondly, **both (1) and (2) are limited to filtering noisy images retrieved from WSEs.** For example, even with the unambiguous query Acroma (band) generated by (1), some high-ranked images that do not match the corresponding entity still remain as shown in Fig. 1(b). Furthermore, there are many noisy images and they may belong to the same class (e.g., shirt in Fig. 1(b)), making it challenging to remove them via (2).

Our Idea and Contribution. In this paper, we construct a large-scale MMKG named MMpedia, which is both highly-scalable and high-quality. This MMKG is built by a novel pipeline method that retrieves images from WSEs (the second category) to ensure the scalability. To ensure image quality, we address the above two issues: (1) non-visual entities in KG and (2) noisy images in WSEs. Specifically, to solve (1), we model the non-visual entity filtering task as a binary classification problem to judge whether the entity is visualizable. In this task, we build a new Recurrent Gate Multi-modal model (RGMM) where the classifier receives the multi-modal features extracted from multiple images and text. To solve (2), we implement a double-filtering process. Firstly, we filter images not depicting the given entity with the text information. To this end, we employ a pre-trained image-text model (e.g., CLIP [32]) to compute the matching score between the textual description and retrieved images. Secondly, we introduce CV models to compare the types of objects in images with the pre-defined entity type. Note that the type information is not leveraged in the query to match with the context of images for two reasons. First, many noisy images with the context containing type-based query are retrieved from WSEs. For example, the context of *shirt.img* in Fig. 1(b) is *Acroma Band T-Shirt*, which includes the entity *Acroma* and type *Band*. Second, even with the type-based query, WSEs would return images whose context does not include the type, making the type information useless. For example, for the query *Johnny G (Cyclist)*, the contexts of most retrieved images do not have the type *Cyclist*. In contrast, our approach removes noisy images directly using visual information, rather than relying on the context. Our contributions are summarized as follows:

- We propose a novel pipeline method to construct MMKGs, which consists of the following steps: entity information collection, non-visual entity filtering, entity-image matching and entity type detection.

- We construct a MMKG named MMpedia containing 2,661,941 entities and 19,489,074 images. As we know, MMpedia has the biggest image dataset among existing MMKGs. The accuracy of our images reaches 84.91% after human evaluation.
- Experimental results verify the effectiveness of our proposed method and collected images. In the entity prediction task, both the state-of-the-art method and multi-modal large language model (e.g., VisualChatGPT [50]) achieve about a 4% improvement on Hit@1 by incorporating our collected images.

2 Related Work

We first introduce existing two opposite MMKG construction methods. One is to label images with symbols and another is to grounding entities to images. Then we introduce a closely related task cross-modal retrieval.

Labeling images with symbols can be mainly classified into two categories. The first way is to directly extract visual entities and relations from an image. Chen et al. [8] propose NEIL to automatically extract generic relations from online images. Krishna et al. [20] construct Visual Genome with the images from YFCC100M [40] and MS-COCO [24]. However, they can only obtain limited relation categories. To address this problem, the second way is to extract knowledge from multi-modal information [22,49]. GAIA [22] and Resin [49] first extract event knowledge from multimedia news and then link them to KGs. Although they enrich relation categories, this way requires multi-modal data and a pre-defined schema for different event types, which restricts the scale of MMKGs.

Grounding entities to images mainly includes two groups. One way is to collect images from OEs. Ferrada et al. construct IMGpedia [13] by linking the entity to Wikimedia Commons. Alberts et al. build VisualSem [2] that regards Babelnet [29] as the visual source and addresses the known issue of noisy images [4,10] via image-text matching. Images in OEs are commonly more qualified than those retrieved from WSEs. However, this way is hard to provide images for all entities due to entity differences between OEs and KGs. Another way is to collect images from WSEs. Onoro et al. [30] collect images for FB15K [3] and construct ImageGraph for answering visual-relational queries. Based on DBpedia, Yago [37] and FB15K, Liu et al. [26] retrieve Top-20 images from WSEs and build MMKG. Wang et al. [46] construct Richpedia via employing K-means on images and remaining Top-20 images of each cluster. Although these works provide rich visual resources for KGs, they have limitations on image quality.

Cross-modal retrieval (CMR) is mainly classified into two groups according to the textual query: (1) object-centric and (2) scene-centric [17]. The former compares the objects in the given text with the object in images for CMR. For example, Corbiere et al. [11] retrieve images for fashion-related objects by training two independent uni-modal models with weakly annotated data. Wang et al. [45] propose SCAN to retrieve images based on the given food objects. The latter considers the relation between multiple objects to retrieve the images.

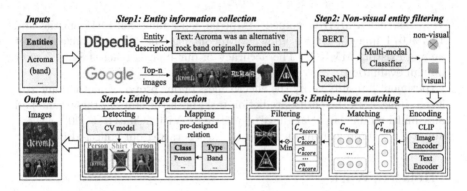

Fig. 2. The frame of our proposed pipeline method. We first collect entity information and remove non-visual entities with a multi-modal classifier. Then, we take entities' textual and type information to remove noisy images.

Liu et al. [25] explicitly model objects and relations with GSMN. Mafla et al. [28] propose StacMR, which utilizes GCN to obtain context representation of images and scene text. Cheng et al. [9] present ViSTA to encode image patches and scene text with mid-level fusion. However, both of them focus on abstract concepts (e.g., man) and are limited to grounding a specific entity to images.

3   MMpedia Construction

In this paper, we aim to construct a MMKG via providing high-quality images for entities in KGs. For example, given the entity *Acroma_ (band)*, we expect to collect images about its members or live performances. To this end, we propose a novel four-step pipeline method, as shown in Fig. 2.

3.1   Entity Information Collection

In this step, we aim to collect entities' textual and visual information for the subsequent non-visual entity filtering and removal of noisy images. To acquire textual information, we retrieve it from KGs as they provide high-quality abstracts for entities. To obtain sufficient candidate images, we build a crawler and retrieve images from a WSE. Specifically, given an entity, we first replace its special characters with space as the query. Then we input the query into a WSE and collect Top-n returned images. For example, the query for the entity "Juan_Pablo_Plada" is "Juan Pablo Plada" because WSEs (e.g., Google) are confused by the character "_".

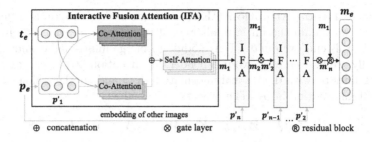

Fig. 3. The multi-modal fusion process of our Recurrent Gate Multi-modal model.

3.2 Non-visual Entity Filtering

Based on the collected entity information, we expect to remove the non-visual entities which can not be characterized visually. To this end, we regard the task of non-visual entity filtering as a binary classification problem $f(m_e) = 0/1$. Given an entity e, the input is its retrieved Top-n images and textual description and the output is 0 (*non-visual*) or 1 (*visual*). f is denoted as a multi-modal classifier and m_e represents the embedding of multi-modal information.

Since WSEs easily introduce noisy images for entities and existing multi-modal fusion methods have limitations in processing multiple images mixed with noise data, we propose a Recurrent Gate based Multi-modal Model (RGMM) as shown in Fig. 3. The core idea of the model is a recurrent structure which employs the Interactive Fusion Attention (IFA) module and gate mechanism to select useful information for multi-modal fusion at each iteration.

Uni-Modal Feature Extraction. Given the Top-n images and text of an entity e, we utilize pre-trained uni-modal models to extract n image features $\boldsymbol{p}_e$ and text feature $\boldsymbol{t}_e$. Specifically, to achieve $\boldsymbol{p}_e$, we first obtain the embedding $\boldsymbol{p}'_i$ of each image P_i by a visual feature extractor (e.g., ResNet [16]). Then we feed $\boldsymbol{p}'_i$ into a fully connected layer and return the transformed image representation $\boldsymbol{p}_i$. Finally, we treat the list $[\boldsymbol{p}_1, ..., \boldsymbol{p}_n]$ as $\boldsymbol{p}_e$. This process can be formalized as

$$\boldsymbol{p}_i = ResNet(P_i) \in \mathbb{R}^{d_p}, \boldsymbol{p}'_i = \boldsymbol{W}_p \boldsymbol{p}_i + \boldsymbol{b}_p \in \mathbb{R}^{d_t}, \boldsymbol{p}_e = [\boldsymbol{p}_1, ..., \boldsymbol{p}_n], \quad (1)$$

where $\boldsymbol{W}_p \in \mathbb{R}^{d_p * d_t}, \boldsymbol{b}_p \in \mathbb{R}^{d_t}$ are learnable parameters .

To achieve $\boldsymbol{t}_e$, we first concatenate the text of e with the special tokens $\langle CLS \rangle$, $\langle SEP \rangle$ and feed it into a pre-trained language model (e.g., BERT [12]) to obtain the text representation $\boldsymbol{T}'$. Then, we employ average pooling on $\boldsymbol{T}'$ to obtain $\boldsymbol{t}_e$ [34]. The process is computed as

$$\boldsymbol{T}' = BERT([\langle CLS \rangle, w_1, ..., w_k, \langle SEP \rangle]), \boldsymbol{t}_e = \frac{\sum_{i=0}^{k+1} \boldsymbol{t}_i}{k+2} \in \mathbb{R}^{d_t}, \quad (2)$$

where $[w_1, ..., w_k]$ is a sequence of tokens from e's text and $\boldsymbol{t}_i \in \boldsymbol{T}'$ is the embedding of the corresponding token.

Interactive Fusion Attention (IFA). After achieving two kinds of features p_e and t_e, we obtain the initial multi-modal representation m_1 with $p_1 \in p_e$ and t_e. To this end, we build a IFA module to merge multi-modal information. Specifically, we first employ two independent co-attention [27] layers for p_1 and t_e. One refines p_1 with the textual information in t_e and another refines t_e with the visual information in p_1. The process is defined as

$$p'_1 = MHAtt(Q = W_{Q_p}p_1, K = W_{K_p}t_e, V = W_{V_p}t_e)_h \in \mathbb{R}^{d_t}, \qquad (3)$$

$$t'_e = MHAtt(Q = W_{Q_t}t_e, K = W_{K_t}p'_1, V = W_{V_t}p'_1)_h \in \mathbb{R}^{d_t}, \qquad (4)$$

where $MHAtt(\cdot)_h$ is h heads' attention mechanism and W_Q, W_K, W_V are learnable parameters. Then we concatenate the co-attention outputs p'_1 and t'_e and fuse them with a self-attention layer, which is formalized as

$$m_1 = SAtt(p'_1 \oplus t'_e) = MHAtt(Q, K, V = p'_1 \oplus t'_e)_h \in \mathbb{R}^{d_t}, \qquad (5)$$

where $\oplus$ represents concatenation. We denote Eq. (3) to (5) as IFA.

Recurrent Structure. After achieving m_1, we obtain the final multi-modal representation m_e by iteratively fusing $p_i, 2 \leq i \leq n$ into m_1 with IFA and a gate mechanism. To begin with, we reverse the list of image features $[p_2, ..., p_n]$ to $S = [p_n, p_{n-1}, ..., p_2]$ as the input of IFA. The reason is that the recurrent structure tends to forget previously input information [54] and we expect RGMM to lay emphasis on the features of high-ranked images sorted by WSEs. Next, at the i-th step, we first feed the i-th image feature $S[i]$ and the multi-modal fusion result at $(i-1)$-th step m'_{i-1} into IFA to obtain the multi-modal representation m_i, which is formalized as

$$m_i = IFA(m'_{i-1}, S[i]). \qquad (6)$$

We then input m'_{i-1} and m_i into the gate layer and outputs m'_i, which is also the input of $(i+1)$-th step. The gate layer is defined as

$$Z = Sigmoid(W_m m_i + b_m) \in \mathbb{R}^{d_t}, m'_i = Z \odot m_i + (1 - Z) \odot m'_{i-1} \in \mathbb{R}^{d_t}, \quad (7)$$

where $W_m \in \mathbb{R}^{d_t * d_t}$, $b_m \in \mathbb{R}^{d_t}$ are learnable parameters, $1 \in \mathbb{R}^{d_t}$ donates as an all-ones vector and $\odot$ represents element-wise production. Finally, we feed m_1 and the final multi-modal fusion result m'_n into a residual block to obtain m_e, which reinforces the visual information in the Top-1 image.

After obtaining m_e, we feed it into a binary classifier. The classifier consists of two fully connected layers and a softmax function. If the classifier outputs 0, we judge the entity as non-visualizable.

3.3   Entity-Image Matching

In most cases, some images retrieved from WSEs (e.g., Google) do not depict the corresponding entity. For example, given the query "Acroma (band)", WSE returns some images of Acroma's previous Facebook logo. Hence, we introduce entity-image matching and employ a pre-trained image-text model named CLIP [32] to remove these images. For each entity, we treat its textual description and retrieved images as input and CLIP outputs their matching score.

Specifically, given an entity e, we first feed its textual description T_e into the text encoding part of CLIP and return the embedding $c_{e_{text}} \in \mathbb{R}^{d_c}$. Then we encode e's retrieved images $[P_1, ..., P_n]$ with the visual encoding part of CLIP. After obtaining the embedding of text $c_{e_{text}} \in \mathbb{R}^{d_c}$ and images $c_{e_{img}} \in \mathbb{R}^{n*d_c}$, we employ outer product on them to compute the image-text matching degree. The process can be formulated as

$$c_{e_{text}} = Enc_{text}(T_e), c_{e_{img}} = [c_{img}^1, ..., c_{img}^n] = Enc_{image}([P_1, ..., P_n]), \quad (8)$$

$$c_{e_{score}} = [c_{score}^1, ..., c_{score}^n] = c_{e_{text}} c_{e_{img}}^T \in \mathbb{R}^{d_n}, \quad (9)$$

where $c_{score}^i \in \mathbb{R}$ represents the matching score between the text T_e and image P_i. If c_{score}^i is lower than the pre-defined threshold, we remove P_i.

3.4   Entity Type Detection

Although we have removed noisy images not depicting the corresponding entity with model CLIP and the text information, some remaining images may still not be the appropriate visual representation. For example, for the entity *Acroma*, images such as a shirt with "*Acroma*" and a WordArt "*Acroma*" are considered valid by CLIP. These images illustrate the given entity but do not allow us to associate *Acroma* with "band". Hence, in this paper, we take the type information of entities to conduct further filtering. The core idea is to employ CV models to detect the entity class from a candidate image and assess whether the result aligns with the type information.

Specifically, given an entity e and one of its candidate images P_i, we first retrieve e's type information A_e from KGs (e.g., DBpedia). Then we map A_e to the expected entity classes $C_e' = [C_1', C_2', ..., C_n']$ using a manually constructed type-to-class list $L_{A \to C}$ (e.g., Band → [Person]), where *class* is from COCO [24] and imagenet dataset [35]. After obtaining C_e', we employ pre-trained CV models YOLO [33] and VGG [36] to identify entity classes $C_e = [C_1, C_2, ..., C_m]$ from P_i. Finally, we calculate the intersection of C_e' and C_e to determine whether P_i should be removed. This process is formalized as

$$Y = \Omega(L_{A \to C}(A_e), CV(P_i)) \quad (10)$$

where $\Omega(\cdot)$ denotes the Boolean function judging whether the intersection is an empty set. If the output is true, we remove the P_i.

4   MMpedia Analysis

In this section, we first report the dataset statistics of MMpedia and typical MMKGs. Then we give a detailed analysis of the image quality and diversity.

Table 1. Comparison between MMpedia and typical MMKGs. (We report triples of relations between entities in KG. The triples in IMGpedia and Richpedia are relations between entities and images)

KG	Nodes	Images	Triples(KG)
IMGpedia [13]	14,765,300	14,765,300	-
Imagegraph [30]	14,870	829,931	564,010
MMKG [26]	45,011	37,479	814,127
Richpedia [46]	29,985	2,915,770	-
VisualSem [2]	89,896	938,100	1,481,007
MMpedia (Ours)	2,661,941	**19,489,074**	**5,960,965**

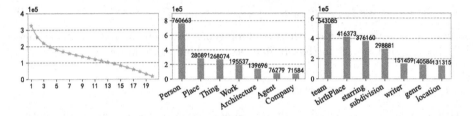

Fig. 4. The distribution of images per node (left) and most common numerical categories of entities (middle) and relations (right) in MMpedia.

MMpedia Statistics. We perform our proposed method on the KG DBpedia, which has a well-defined ontology and contains 7,195,709 entity nodes, 633 relation categories, and 21,687,345 triples. Based on this KG, we construct a MMKG named MMpedia, including 598 relation categories, 5,960,965 triples and 19,489,074 images for 2,661,941 entity nodes. Table 1 reports the statistic of our MMpedia and other typical MMKGs. MMpedia has the biggest image dataset among existing MMKGs. Note that IMGpedia has the most entities while it is built by data linking without powerful means to supervise the image quality. To better understand MMpedia, we report the distribution of images per node and high-frequency entity and relation categories in Fig. 4. Around 45% of entities have one to five images and each entity has 7.3 images on average. For entities, we note that *Person* is the most numerous entity type of all 362 categories, accounting for 28.57%. The number of *Place, Thing, Work,* and *ArchitecturalStructure* also exceeds 10^5. For relations, we observe that *team, birthPlace, starring, subdivision, writer, genre* and *location* take a high proportion in total of 598 categories, all exceeding 10^5.

Image Quality. Since there is no ground truth, we employ manual and automatic evaluation to verify the image quality in MMpedia. For manual evaluation, we invite three CV research students. The criteria is that if an image reflects what the corresponding entity is, it is labeled as 1. Otherwise, it is labeled as 0. Before manual evaluation begins, we conduct a test for all participants. To this end, we crawl 1,000 image-text pairs from Wikipedia and randomly select 100 correct and 100 incorrect pairs for each participant to evaluate. We start the manual evaluation when every participant achieves a test accuracy of 95%. During the manual evaluation process, we randomly select 500 entities with 3,415 images. We also add 200 noisy images to assess the quality of the evaluation, which provides a basis for final accuracy calculations. The three participants recall 0.98, 0.96 and 0.99 of these noisy images, respectively. The current MMpedia achieves 84.91% accuracy on the weighted average and 81.14% on T@3, where T@k means an image is labeled as 1 by k people. The Fleiss' kappa [14] is 0.836, showing the consistency of human evaluation. Additionally, to evaluate the quality of images associated with "nodes pairs", we randomly select 500 pairs of Top-1 images corresponding to the head-tail entities, which are sorted by the proposed pipeline method. The average accuracy is 88.20% and the Fleiss' kappa is 0.859. For automatic evaluation, we introduce two downstream tasks to verify the image quality in Sect. 5.2.

Image Diversity. Similarly, we employ human evaluation on 3,415 images of 500 entities to verify the image diversity of MMpedia. We first evaluate each entity's diversity by calculating the percentage of similar image pairs. For example, given an entity e with n_e images, we will build $n_p = 0.5 * n_e * (n_e - 1)$ image pairs. If there are s_e similar image pairs, the diversity score d of e will be $d = \frac{n_p - s_e}{n_p}$. Then, we compute the average diversity of each entity as the diversity score of the whole dataset. Finally, our current MMpedia reaches the average diversity score of 90.07% and the Fleiss' kappa is 0.807.

5 Experiment

Through the experiment, we expect to demonstrate the effectiveness of our proposed pipeline method and collected images. We first report implementation details of the pipeline method. Then we introduce *entity prediction* and *relation prediction* to verify that our collected images are helpful for downstream tasks. Finally, we give a detailed analysis on MMpedia construction.

5.1 Implementation Details

We give detailed information about each step in the proposed method, including the input-output, data analysis and hyperparameter settings.

Entity information collection collects 3,494,367 entities with the information of type, textual description and candidate images. First, for 7,195,709 entity nodes in DBpedia, we remove 2,600,603 entity nodes that are similar to others (e.g., *Herbowo* and *Herbowo__Tenure__1*). Second, for the remaining 4,595,106 entities, we take SPARQL API[2] to retrieve the corresponding 3,668,041 textual descriptions and 4,264,106 type information from DBpedia and Wikidata. We remove entities missing the abstract or type. Finally, we crawl Top-20

---

[2] https://dbpedia.org/sparql.

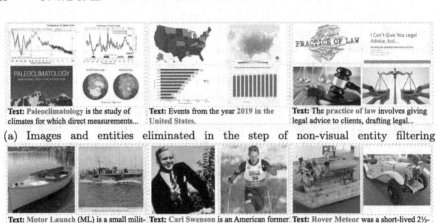

Text: Paleoclimatology is the study of climates for which direct measurements...   **Text:** Events from the year 2019 in the United States.   **Text:** The practice of law involves giving legal advice to clients, drafting legal...

(a) Images and entities eliminated in the step of non-visual entity filtering

Text: Motor Launch (ML) is a small military vessel in Royal Navy service. It was... **Filterd:** An image of 1910 Mathis launch   **Text:** Carl Swenson is an American former cyclist and cross-country skier. He... **Filterd:** An image of Karl Swenson   **Text:** Rover Meteor was a short-lived 2½-litre or 2-litre medium-sized car made... **Filterd:** An image of Rolls-Royce Meteor

(b) Images eliminated (left) and remained (right) in the step of entity-image matching

Text: Weedflower is a 2006 American children's historical novel by Cynthia... **Type:** Book   **Text:** Novembre is an Italian heavy metal band, formed in Rome in 1990. **Type:** Band   **Text:** Pratibhasthali is a girls school started by Acharya Vidyasagar. Schools are... **Type:** School

(c) Images eliminated (left) and remained (right) in the step of entity type detection

Fig. 5. Case studies of each step in proposed pipeline methods. The entities in KG are marked in red, while entities depicted by noisy images are marked in blue. (Color figure online)

images from Google for each entity. Since some entities have less than 20 images in Google, there are 66,399,460 images for remained 3,494,367 entities.

Non-visual entity filtering judges 3,136,997 entities into visualizable and 357,370 entities into non-visualizable. We employ ResNet50 and BERT$_{BASE}$ to embed the Top-5 images and the text respectively, where $d_p = 2048$ and $d_t = 768$. During the training process, we run for 50 epochs with a batch size of 32. We choose AdamW as the optimizer and the learning rate is 1e-4.

Since the model is supervised and there is no public labeled data for non-visual entity filtering, we construct a dataset based on Wordnet. We first sample 200 entities from Wordnet and research the path between the root node r and them in the 'hyponymy' hierarchy. Given an entity e and its path, we observe two regularities: (1) If $pathLength|(e, r)| \leq 5$ and the node "Abstraction" appears in the path, e is commonly to be 0 (non-visualizable) and (2) If e is a leaf node and the node "Abstraction" not appears in the path, e is commonly to be 1 (visualizable). Based on (1) and (2), we crawled 2,142 entities and give them unsupervised labels. Then we collect their textual information and images from DBpedia and Google, respectively. Finally, we invite three volunteers to revise the unsupervised label based on the criteria that if the Top-5 images of an entity reflect it, its label should be 1, and vice versa. The Fleiss' kappa is 0.798 and we revise the unsupervised label of an entity if it is corrected by three volunteers at the same time. Note that these volunteers are different with those in Sect. 4. Finally, we collect 1,182 visual entities and 960 non-visual entities and randomly split them as 1328/406/408 for training, validation and testing respectively. Our classifier reaches the F1 score of 92.88% on the test dataset.

To intuitively understand non-visualizable and visualizable, we give some cases. As shown in Fig. 5(a), it is hard to find an image reflecting *Paleoclimatology*, which is a scientific discipline, not a data table or a globe. By contrast, images (right) reflect the corresponding entity, as shown in Fig. 5(b) and 5(c).

Entity-image matching remains 2,785,592 entity nodes and 22,274,190 images. We introduce the pre-trained CLIP to perform *Entity-image matching*. We sample the images of 500 entities and conduct a statistical analysis on the CLIP results. Finally, we define $Min_{CLIP} = 29$ as the threshold since we observe that most noisy images have a CLIP score of lower than 29. Figure 5(b) gives the cases to intuitively demonstrate the effectiveness of this step.

Entity type detection remains 2,661,941 entity nodes and 19,489,074 images. We first manually construct a type-to-class list containing 1,179 mappings, where *type* is from DBpedia containing 141 entity type information and *class* is from COCO and ImageNet containing 1080 image recognition classes (e.g., Ship → [Boat, Fireboat, Ocean liner]). Then we introduce YOLOv5 and VGG19 to perform image recognition. The input is 10,293,162 candidate images and 1,306,957 entity type information. For each image, the recognized entity class consists of all results from YOLOv5 and Top-3 ones from VGG19. Figure 5(c) gives the cases to intuitively demonstrate the effectiveness of this step.

5.2 Downstream Tasks

To verify the usefulness of MMpedia, we employ its images in two real-world tasks: (1) *entity prediction* and (2) *relation prediction* [53]. We conduct the experiment on DB15K [26] which is a sub-graph of DBpedia. Since there are non-visual entities in DB15K, we need to filter the triples. Specifically, we first remove the triples if the head-tail entity can not find corresponding images in MMpedia. Then we further filter the triples containing one-shot relation or head-tail entity. Finally, we remain 23,055 triples and split them as 16,384/ 3,389/ 3,282 for training, validation and testing. The splitting principle is that entities and relations in validation and test sets need to appear in the training set. The vocabulary size is 5,239 and the number of relation categories is 158.

Entity Prediction. Given a triple fact $< h, r, t >$, entity prediction requires models to complete the missing head or tail information. Taking the tail entity prediction as an example, the input is the image of h and the textual information of $< h, r >$. For each test example, we first replace t with all candidate entities and then record the ranking of them in descending order based on the predicted scores. We report four metrics: MRR, MR, Hit@1, and Hit@10, where MR and

Table 2. The performance of BERT-based models on the entity prediction task. We highlight the data using our collected images in gray. ↑ means that higher values provide better performance while ↓ means that lower values provide better performance.

Method	Head Entity prediction				Tail Entity prediction			
	MRR↑	MR↓	Hit@1↑	Hit@10↑	MRR↑	MR↓	Hit@1↑	Hit@10↑
BERT	10.94	439.43	5.00	22.73	23.67	157.37	14.78	40.77
+ResNet50+Noise	10.91	441.36	5.09	22.09	23.61	152.84	14.20	42.23
+ResNet50+Our	**12.27**	**423.43**	**5.94**	24.95	**25.44**	**147.27**	**16.33**	**43.93**
ViLT+Noise	10.70	639.71	4.88	22.58	22.90	249.83	14.47	40.74
ViLT+Our	12.08	596.34	5.45	**26.02**	24.60	226.54	16.30	42.47

Table 3. The result of SOTA MKGC and KGC models on the entity prediction task.

Method	Head Entity prediction				Tail Entity prediction			
	MRR↑	MR↓	Hit@1↑	Hit@10↑	MRR↑	MR↓	Hit@1↑	Hit@10↑
Translational Distance Models								
ComplEX	22.98	1476.31	17.40	33.18	20.23	2125.34	15.39	29.77
RotatE	26.14	784.91	20.69	36.53	39.16	579.77	31.23	53.84
LineaRE	26.34	418.47	21.43	36.02	34.38	309.99	27.57	47.54
RSME+Google	25.90	622.46	20.78	35.01	40.78	308.95	33.00	55.48
RSME+Our	26.93	547.08	21.57	36.41	42.10	274.74	34.34	57.10
MoSE+Google	29.04	338.24	21.25	42.60	43.84	123.16	33.79	62.87
MoSE+Our	29.99	**329.28**	22.73	**43.27**	45.62	**122.13**	35.89	63.92
Pre-trained Language Models								
KG-BERT	3.68	543.54	0.91	7.46	7.53	493.58	2.43	17.06
MKGformer+Google	29.01	379.07	22.82	40.13	44.62	135.50	35.83	61.61
MKGformer+Our	**30.05**	371.30	**23.85**	42.02	**48.17**	128.20	**39.49**	**65.14**

MRR are the mean rank and reciprocal rank of all correct entities, respectively and Hit@k represents the proportion of correct entities existing in Top-k.

First, to verify whether our collected images reflect the corresponding entity, we design an A/B testing. The input of experiment A_1 is h and r while experiment B_1 has two kinds of input: (1) h, r and h's image in MMpedia (+Our) and (2) h, r and an image of another entity (+Noise). For the input "The r of h is [MASK]" of experiment A_1, we employ $BERT_{base}$ as the backbone, where a classifier is connected to the [MASK] representation. For the experiment B_1, we introduce BERT+ResNet50 [43] and ViLT [19] to predict t. As shown in Table 2, BERT+ResNet50 and ViLT with (+Our) outperform BERT, indicating that image features are helpful for *entity prediction*. Moreover, both methods with (+Noise) achieve no significant improvement than BERT, demonstrating that the improvement is mainly due to the input image rather than the added visual encoder. Hence, our collected images provide effective visual information.

Second, to evaluate whether our collected images improve the performance of state-of-the-art (SOTA) multi-modal knowledge graph completion (MKGC) models, we design an A/B testing. For each MKGC

Table 4. The results of relation prediction.

Methods	MRR↑	MR↓	Hit@1↑	Hit@3↑	Hit@10↑
ComplEX	41.48	26.11	24.38	55.30	69.35
RotatE	65.51	5.29	50.79	76.93	91.99
KG-BERT	73.36	2.95	57.86	88.48	96.92
RSME+Google	68.34	4.03	51.86	83.21	93.60
RSME+Our	69.51	3.76	53.05	84.89	94.64
MoSE+Google	72.24	6.20	59.08	83.58	93.48
MoSE+Our	74.54	6.07	63.01	85.10	93.69
MKGformer+Google	78.96	2.20	65.90	91.62	98.35
MKGformer+Our	**80.34**	**2.12**	**68.31**	**91.74**	**98.57**

model, the input of experiment A_2 is h, r and h's image crawled from Google (+Google) while B_2 is h, r and h's image from MMpedia (+Our). We introduce two SOTA MKGC models MoSE [55] and MKGformer [7]. Following them, we also introduce four uni-modal KGC models ComplEX [42], RotatE [39], LineaRE [31], KG-BERT [53] and one MKGC model RSME [47]. As shown in Table 3, MKGC models +Our outperform other methods. Compared with MKGC models +Google, MKGC models +Our achieve at most 3.5% improvement on Hit@1, indicating that our collected images enhance MKGC models' performance.

Relation Prediction. Given a triple $< h, ?, t >$, models are required to complete the missing r. The input is h, t and two images of h and t respectively. The evaluation metrics are the same as those in *entity prediction*.

To evaluate whether our collected images are useful to improve MKGC models' performance on relation prediction, we design an A/B testing. For each MKGC model, the input of experiment A_3 is h, t and images (+ Google) while B_3 is h, t and images (+Our). As shown in Table 4, MKGC models outperform uni-modal KGC models, indicating that the visual information is beneficial for *relation prediction*. Compared with MKGC models +Google, MKGC models +Our achieve at most 4.0% improvement on Hit@1. Hence, our collected images enhance the model's performance on *relation prediction*.

5.3 Detailed Analysis

In this section, we make a detailed analysis on *non-visual entity filtering*, *entity type detection* and the multi-modal large language model (M-LLM).

To verify whether images reflect non-visual entities, we still design an A/B testing. For experiment A_4, the input is h and r. For experiment B_4, the input is h, r and two kinds of h's image: (1) +Google and (2) filtered by steps 3 and 4 (+Our w/o 2). We first select 6,657 triples from DB15K where h is non-visualizable. Then we split the triples into 4,644/970/1043 for training, validation and testing. We denote this dataset as D_{nv}. Finally, we also employ BERT-based

Table 5. Tail entity prediction on D_{nv}. We denote w/o k as removing the step k.

Methods	Input	MRR↑	MR↓	Hit@1↑	Hit@3↑	Hit@10↑
BERT	(h, r)	**42.21**	53.77	**30.29**	46.40	**68.55**
BERT+ResNet50	+Google	41.49	**52.04**	29.62	45.83	67.31
	+Our w/o 2	41.89	59.47	29.91	**46.60**	68.36
ViLT	+Google	39.99	104.76	29.15	46.02	60.88
	+Our w/o 2	40.26	94.64	29.82	45.35	60.79

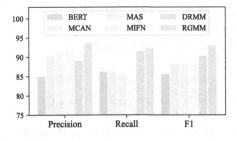 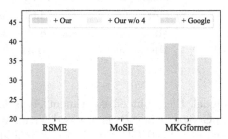

Fig. 6. Non-visual entity filtering.   **Fig. 7.** Entity type detection.

models to perform tail entity prediction. As shown in Table 5, either (+Google) or (+Our w/o 2) do not enhance BERT's performance, showing the necessity of filtering non-visual entities. To evaluate our proposed RGMM, we compare it with some typical SOTA multi-modal interaction methods. The baselines contain BERT, MAS [48], MCAN [51], MIFN [23] and DRMM [41]. Among them, MIFN and DRMM can process multiple images. We train all models on the dataset depicted in the Sect. 5.1 with the same hyperparameters. As shown in Fig. 6, RGMM can filter non-visual entities more effectively.

To evaluate whether entity type detection improves the image quality, we compare MKGC models' performance on three kinds of images: (1) +Our, (2) filtered without *entity type detection* (+Our w/o 4) and (3) +Google. For the dataset depicted in Sect. 5.2, we first replace the images of 844 entities with those filtered via *entity type detection*. Then we also employ MKGC models to conduct tail entity prediction. As shown in Fig. 7, the performance of MKGC models decreases on Hit@1, showing the effectiveness of *entity type detection*.

To evaluate whether M-LLMs generate high-quality images for the given entity, we introduce VisualChatGPT (VCG). The input is the prompt *"Please generate an image of [entity]. [entity's abstract]"* and the output is a generated image. We sample 200 entities from DBpedia and invite the participants in Sect. 4 to evaluate the images generated by VCG. VCG achieves an average accuracy of 0.29 and the Flessi's Kappa is 0.870. The reasons for error cases are mainly classified into two groups. The first group is an image depicting another entity of the same type as the given entity, accounting for 59%. For example, given the entity *Masuisuimatamaalii Tauaua-Pauaraisa*, VCG gener-

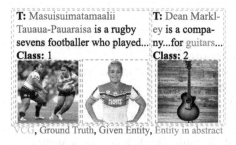
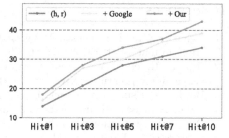

Fig. 8. Case study of VCG.   **Fig. 9.** The result of VCG.

ates a *another_person.jpg* as shown in Fig. 8. The second group is an image of another entity appeared in the given abstract, accounting for 28%. For example, as shown in Fig. 8, given the company *Dean Markley*, VCG generates a *guitar.jpg*, where *guitar* appears in the given abstract. Hence, grounding entities to images remains a challenge for M-LLMs. **To evaluate whether our collected images are helpful for M-LLMs**, we randomly select 200 triples and compare the performance of VCG on three kinds of input: (1) h and r, (2) h, r +Our and (3) h, r +Google. VCG is asked to reorder the list of candidate t based on the given h, r. The prompt consists of task definition, one positive example and two negative examples [15]. As shown in Fig. 9, our collected images improve VCG's performance on *tail entity prediction*.

6 Conclusion

In this paper, we present a large-scale MMKG named MMpedia. To this end, we propose a novel pipeline method, which first collects images from a WSE and filters non-visual entities with a multi-modal classifier, and then leverage entities' textual and type information to remove noisy images. Through the pipeline method, MMpedia is constructed, containing 2,661,941 entities and 19,489,074 images. As we know, MMpedia boasts the largest number of images among existing MMKGs. Extensive experiments are conducted to demonstrate the effectiveness of our proposed method. Furthermore, the images in MMpedia are helpful for different downstream tasks.

Acknowledgements. This work was supported by the Shanghai Municipal Special Fund for Promoting High-quality Development of Industries (2021-GZL-RGZN-01018) and the Shanghai Sailing Program (23YF1409400).

References

1. Aghaei, S., Raad, E., Fensel, A.: Question answering over knowledge graphs: a case study in tourism. IEEE Access **10**, 69788–69801 (2022)
2. Alberts, H., et al.: VisualSem: a high-quality knowledge graph for vision and language. arXiv preprint arXiv:2008.09150 (2020)
3. Bordes, A., Usunier, N., Garcia-Duran, A., Weston, J., Yakhnenko, O.: Translating embeddings for modeling multi-relational data. In: Advances in Neural Information Processing Systems, vol. 26 (2013)
4. Calabrese, A., Bevilacqua, M., Navigli, R.: Fatality killed the cat or: BabelPic, a multimodal dataset for non-concrete concepts. In: Proceedings of the 58th Annual Meeting of the Association for Computational Linguistics, pp. 4680–4686 (2020)
5. Chen, D., Li, Z., Gu, B., Chen, Z.: Multimodal named entity recognition with image attributes and image knowledge. In: Jensen, C.S., et al. (eds.) DASFAA 2021. LNCS, vol. 12682, pp. 186–201. Springer, Cham (2021). https://doi.org/10.1007/978-3-030-73197-7_12
6. Chen, Q., Wang, W., Huang, K., Coenen, F.: Zero-shot text classification via knowledge graph embedding for social media data. IEEE Internet Things J. **9**(12), 9205–9213 (2021)
7. Chen, X., et al.: Hybrid transformer with multi-level fusion for multimodal knowledge graph completion. arXiv preprint arXiv:2205.02357 (2022)
8. Chen, X., Shrivastava, A., Gupta, A.: NEIL: extracting visual knowledge from web data. In: Proceedings of the IEEE International Conference on Computer Vision, pp. 1409–1416 (2013)
9. Cheng, M., et al.: ViSTA: vision and scene text aggregation for cross-modal retrieval. In: Proceedings of the IEEE/CVF Conference on Computer Vision and Pattern Recognition, pp. 5184–5193 (2022)
10. Colla, D., Mensa, E., Radicioni, D.P., Lieto, A.: Tell me why: computational explanation of conceptual similarity judgments. In: Medina, J., et al. (eds.) IPMU 2018. CCIS, vol. 853, pp. 74–85. Springer, Cham (2018). https://doi.org/10.1007/978-3-319-91473-2_7
11. Corbiere, C., Ben-Younes, H., Ramé, A., Ollion, C.: Leveraging weakly annotated data for fashion image retrieval and label prediction. In: Proceedings of the IEEE International Conference on Computer Vision Workshops, pp. 2268–2274 (2017)
12. Devlin, J., Chang, M.W., Lee, K., Toutanova, K.: BERT: pre-training of deep bidirectional transformers for language understanding. arXiv preprint arXiv:1810.04805 (2018)
13. Ferrada, S., Bustos, B., Hogan, A.: IMGpedia: a linked dataset with content-based analysis of Wikimedia images. In: d'Amato, C., et al. (eds.) ISWC 2017. LNCS, vol. 10588, pp. 84–93. Springer, Cham (2017). https://doi.org/10.1007/978-3-319-68204-4_8
14. Fleiss, J.L.: Measuring nominal scale agreement among many raters. Psychol. Bull. **76**(5), 378 (1971)
15. Gao, J., Zhao, H., Yu, C., Xu, R.: Exploring the feasibility of ChatGPT for event extraction. arXiv preprint arXiv:2303.03836 (2023)
16. He, K., Zhang, X., Ren, S., Sun, J.: Deep residual learning for image recognition. In: Proceedings of the IEEE Conference on Computer Vision and Pattern Recognition, pp. 770–778 (2016)
17. Hendriksen, M., Vakulenko, S., Kuiper, E., de Rijke, M.: Scene-centric vs. object-centric image-text cross-modal retrieval: a reproducibility study. arXiv preprint arXiv:2301.05174 (2023)

18. Kang, H., et al.: TSPNet: translation supervised prototype network via residual learning for multimodal social relation extraction. Neurocomputing **507**, 166–179 (2022)
19. Kim, W., Son, B., Kim, I.: ViLT: vision-and-language transformer without convolution or region supervision. In: International Conference on Machine Learning, pp. 5583–5594. PMLR (2021)
20. Krishna, R., et al.: Visual genome: connecting language and vision using crowdsourced dense image annotations. Int. J. Comput. Vision **123**(1), 32–73 (2017)
21. Lehmann, J., et al.: DBpedia-a large-scale, multilingual knowledge base extracted from Wikipedia. Semant. Web **6**(2), 167–195 (2015)
22. Li, M., et al.: Gaia: a fine-grained multimedia knowledge extraction system. In: Proceedings of the 58th Annual Meeting of the Association for Computational Linguistics: System Demonstrations, pp. 77–86 (2020)
23. Li, Y., Li, J., Jin, H., Peng, L.: Focusing attention across multiple images for multimodal event detection. In: ACM Multimedia Asia, pp. 1–6. Association for Computing Machinery (2021)
24. Lin, T.-Y., et al.: Microsoft COCO: common objects in context. In: Fleet, D., Pajdla, T., Schiele, B., Tuytelaars, T. (eds.) ECCV 2014. LNCS, vol. 8693, pp. 740–755. Springer, Cham (2014). https://doi.org/10.1007/978-3-319-10602-1_48
25. Liu, C., Mao, Z., Zhang, T., Xie, H., Wang, B., Zhang, Y.: Graph structured network for image-text matching. In: Proceedings of the IEEE/CVF Conference on Computer Vision and Pattern Recognition, pp. 10921–10930 (2020)
26. Liu, Y., Li, H., Garcia-Duran, A., Niepert, M., Onoro-Rubio, D., Rosenblum, D.S.: MMKG: multi-modal knowledge graphs. In: Hitzler, P., et al. (eds.) ESWC 2019. LNCS, vol. 11503, pp. 459–474. Springer, Cham (2019). https://doi.org/10.1007/978-3-030-21348-0_30
27. Lu, J., Batra, D., Parikh, D., Lee, S.: ViLBERT: pretraining task-agnostic visiolinguistic representations for vision-and-language tasks. In: Advances in Neural Information Processing Systems, vol. 32 (2019)
28. Mafla, A., Rezende, R.S., Gomez, L., Larlus, D., Karatzas, D.: StacMR: scene-text aware cross-modal retrieval. In: Proceedings of the IEEE/CVF Winter Conference on Applications of Computer Vision, pp. 2220–2230 (2021)
29. Navigli, R., Ponzetto, S.P.: BabelNet: the automatic construction, evaluation and application of a wide-coverage multilingual semantic network. Artif. Intell. **193**, 217–250 (2012)
30. Oñoro-Rubio, D., Niepert, M., García-Durán, A., González, R., López-Sastre, R.J.: Answering visual-relational queries in web-extracted knowledge graphs. arXiv preprint arXiv:1709.02314 (2017)
31. Peng, Y., Zhang, J.: LineaRE: simple but powerful knowledge graph embedding for link prediction. In: 2020 IEEE International Conference on Data Mining (ICDM), pp. 422–431. IEEE (2020)
32. Radford, A., et al.: Learning transferable visual models from natural language supervision. In: International Conference on Machine Learning, pp. 8748–8763. PMLR (2021)
33. Redmon, J., Divvala, S., Girshick, R., Farhadi, A.: You only look once: unified, real-time object detection. In: Proceedings of the IEEE Conference on Computer Vision and Pattern Recognition, pp. 779–788 (2016)
34. Reimers, N., Gurevych, I.: Sentence-BERT: sentence embeddings using Siamese BERT-networks. arXiv preprint arXiv:1908.10084 (2019)
35. Russakovsky, O., et al.: Imagenet large scale visual recognition challenge. Int. J. Comput. Vision **115**(3), 211–252 (2015)

36. Simonyan, K., Zisserman, A.: Very deep convolutional networks for large-scale image recognition. arXiv preprint arXiv:1409.1556 (2014)
37. Suchanek, F.M., Kasneci, G., Weikum, G.: Yago: a core of semantic knowledge. In: Proceedings of the 16th International Conference on World Wide Web, pp. 697–706 (2007)
38. Sun, R., et al.: Multi-modal knowledge graphs for recommender systems. In: Proceedings of the 29th ACM International Conference on Information & Knowledge Management, pp. 1405–1414 (2020)
39. Sun, Z., Deng, Z.H., Nie, J.Y., Tang, J.: Rotate: knowledge graph embedding by relational rotation in complex space. arXiv preprint arXiv:1902.10197 (2019)
40. Thomee, B., et al.: YFCC100M: the new data in multimedia research. Commun. ACM **59**(2), 64–73 (2016)
41. Tong, M., Wang, S., Cao, Y., Xu, B., Li, J., Hou, L., Chua, T.S.: Image enhanced event detection in news articles. In: Proceedings of the AAAI Conference on Artificial Intelligence, pp. 9040–9047 (2020)
42. Trouillon, T., Welbl, J., Riedel, S., Gaussier, É., Bouchard, G.: Complex embeddings for simple link prediction. In: International Conference on Machine Learning, pp. 2071–2080. PMLR (2016)
43. Tsimpoukelli, M., Menick, J.L., Cabi, S., Eslami, S., Vinyals, O., Hill, F.: Multimodal few-shot learning with frozen language models. Adv. Neural. Inf. Process. Syst. **34**, 200–212 (2021)
44. Vrandečić, D., Krötzsch, M.: Wikidata: a free collaborative knowledgebase. Commun. ACM **57**(10), 78–85 (2014)
45. Wang, H., et al.: Cross-modal food retrieval: learning a joint embedding of food images and recipes with semantic consistency and attention mechanism. IEEE Trans. Multimedia **24**, 2515–2525 (2021)
46. Wang, M., Wang, H., Qi, G., Zheng, Q.: Richpedia: a large-scale, comprehensive multi-modal knowledge graph. Big Data Res. **22**, 100159 (2020)
47. Wang, M., Wang, S., Yang, H., Zhang, Z., Chen, X., Qi, G.: Is visual context really helpful for knowledge graph? A representation learning perspective. In: Proceedings of the 29th ACM International Conference on Multimedia, pp. 2735–2743 (2021)
48. Wang, X., et al.: PromptMNER: prompt-based entity-related visual clue extraction and integration for multimodal named entity recognition. In: Bhattacharya, A., et al. (eds.) DASFAA 2022. LNCS, vol. 13247, pp. 297–305. Springer, Cham (2022). https://doi.org/10.1007/978-3-031-00129-1_24
49. Wen, H., et al.: Resin: a dockerized schema-guided cross-document cross-lingual cross-media information extraction and event tracking system. In: Proceedings of the 2021 Conference of the North American Chapter of the Association for Computational Linguistics: Human Language Technologies: Demonstrations, pp. 133–143 (2021)
50. Wu, C., Yin, S., Qi, W., Wang, X., Tang, Z., Duan, N.: Visual ChatGPT: talking, drawing and editing with visual foundation models. arXiv preprint arXiv:2303.04671 (2023)
51. Wu, Y., Zhan, P., Zhang, Y., Wang, L., Xu, Z.: Multimodal fusion with co-attention networks for fake news detection. In: Findings of the Association for Computational Linguistics: ACL-IJCNLP 2021, pp. 2560–2569 (2021)
52. Yang, Y., Zhu, Y., Li, Y.: Personalized recommendation with knowledge graph via dual-autoencoder. Appl. Intell. **52**(6), 6196–6207 (2022)
53. Yao, L., Mao, C., Luo, Y.: KG-BERT: BERT for knowledge graph completion. arXiv preprint arXiv:1909.03193 (2019)

54. Zhao, J., Huang, F., Lv, J., Duan, Y., Qin, Z., Li, G., Tian, G.: Do RNN and LSTM have long memory? In: International Conference on Machine Learning, pp. 11365–11375. PMLR (2020)

55. Zhao, Y., et al.: MoSE: modality split and ensemble for multimodal knowledge graph completion. arXiv preprint arXiv:2210.08821 (2022)

56. Zheng, C., Wu, Z., Feng, J., Fu, Z., Cai, Y.: MNRE: a challenge multimodal dataset for neural relation extraction with visual evidence in social media posts. In: 2021 IEEE International Conference on Multimedia and Expo (ICME), pp. 1–6. IEEE (2021)

57. Zhu, X., et al.: Multi-modal knowledge graph construction and application: a survey. arXiv preprint arXiv:2202.05786 (2022)

Ontology Repositories and Semantic Artefact Catalogues with the OntoPortal Technology

Clement Jonquet[1,2(✉)] , John Graybeal[3] , Syphax Bouazzouni[1] ,
Michael Dorf[3] , Nicola Fiore[4] , Xeni Kechagioglou[4] , Timothy Redmond[3] ,
Ilaria Rosati[5,6] , Alex Skrenchuk[3] , Jennifer L. Vendetti[3] , Mark Musen[3] ,
and members of the OntoPortal Alliance

[1] LIRMM, University of Montpellier & CNRS, Montpellier, France
jonquet@lirmm.fr
[2] MISTEA, University of Montpellier, INRAE & Institut Agro, Montpellier, France
[3] BMIR, School of Medicine, Stanford University, Stanford, USA
jgraybeal@stanford.edu
[4] LifeWatch ERIC, Service Centre, Lecce, Italy
[5] CNR-IRET, National Research Council, Institute of Research on Terrestrial, Ecosystems,
Lecce, Italy
[6] LifeWatch Italy, University of Salento, Lecce, Italy

Abstract. There is an explosion in the number of ontologies and semantic artefacts being produced in science. This paper discusses the need for common platforms to receive, host, serve, align, and enable their reuse. Ontology repositories
and semantic artefact catalogues are necessary to address this need and to make
ontologies FAIR (Findable, Accessible, Interoperable, and Reusable). The Onto-
Portal Alliance (https://ontoportal.org) is a consortium of research and infrastructure teams dedicated to promoting the development of such repositories based on
the open, collaboratively developed OntoPortal software. We present the OntoPortal technology as a generic resource to build ontology repositories and semantic
artefact catalogues that can support resources ranging from SKOS thesauri to
OBO, RDF-S, and OWL ontologies. The paper reviews the features of OntoPortal
and presents the current and forthcoming public and open repositories built with
the technology maintained by the Alliance.

Keywords: ontologies · semantic artefacts · ontology repository · ontology
services · vocabulary server · terminology service · ontology registry · semantic
artefact catalogue

© The Author(s) 2023
T. R. Payne et al. (Eds.): ISWC 2023, LNCS 14266, pp. 38–58, 2023.
https://doi.org/10.1007/978-3-031-47243-5_3

1 Introduction

In all areas of science, many ontologies (or more broadly semantic artefacts[1]) are used to represent and annotate data in a standardized manner. Semantic artefacts have become a master element to achieve the FAIR Data Principles [1] and have been discussed as research objects that themselves need to be FAIR [2–4]. However, those semantic artefacts are spread out, in different formats, of different size, with different structures and from overlapping domains. Therefore, there is a need for common platforms to receive and host them, to serve them, to align them, and to enable their reuse in miscellaneous communities and use cases. In other words, with the explosion in the number of ontologies and semantic artefacts available, *ontology repositories* or more broadly, *semantic artefact catalogues* are now mandatory.

Ontology repositories are usually developed to address the needs of certain communities. Their functionalities span from simple listings with metadata description (i.e., libraries) to rich platforms offering various advanced ontology-based services (i.e., repositories), including browsing, searching, visualizing, computing metrics, annotating, recommending, accessing data, assessing FAIRness, sometimes even editing. More generally, ontology repositories help ontology users to deal with ontologies without asking the users to manage them or to engage in the complex and long process of developing them. Plus, as with any other data, repositories help make ontologies FAIR (Findable, Accessible, Interoperable, and Re-usable) [5, 6].

The OntoPortal Alliance (https://ontoportal.org) is a consortium of several research and infrastructure teams and a company dedicated to promoting the development of ontology repositories—in science and other disciplines—based on the open, collaboratively developed OntoPortal open-source software. Teams in the Alliance develop and maintain several openly accessible ontology repositories and semantic artefact catalogues. These ontology repositories include BioPortal, the primary and historical source of OntoPortal code, but also AgroPortal, EcoPortal, MatPortal and more, as illustrated in Fig. 1. The OntoPortal Alliance's original motivation and vision [7] was to reuse outcomes and experiences obtained in the biomedical domain—an area where the use of ontologies has always been important—to serve and advance other scientific disciplines.

In this paper, we present the OntoPortal technology as a generic resource to build ontology repositories or, more broadly, semantic artefact catalogues that can simultaneously co-host and fully support resources that span from SKOS thesauri to OBO, RDF-S, and OWL ontologies. We briefly review the span of OntoPortal-generic features, from the ones originally developed and provided by BioPortal [8, 9], to the new ones developed in the context of other projects such as AgroPortal or EcoPortal [10]. Then, we present the OntoPortal Alliance, the consortium maintaining the software as an open-source collaborative project. As an "evaluation" of our technology, we list the

---

[1] "Semantic artefact" is a broader term that has recently emerged in Europe used to include ontologies, terminologies, taxonomies, thesauri, vocabularies, metadata schemas, and other standards. "Semantic Artefact Catalogues" is also a broader term to include "ontology repositories/libraries/registries" or "terminology/vocabulary services/servers". Despite the use of American spelling thru out the article, we use the British spelling for these expressions. In the context of this paper, we will also often simply use only the words 'ontology' and 'repository'.

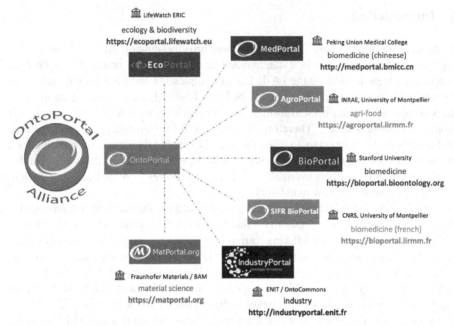

Fig. 1. Current public installations of OntoPortal. Missing installation(s) done by Cogni.zone (private) and many private deployments, as well as new portals in 2023.

current uses of the OntoPortal technology, focusing mainly on the current and coming public and open repositories built with the technology maintained by the Alliance.

2   Related Work on Semantic Artefact Catalogues[2]

2.1   From Ontology Libraries and Repositories to Semantic Artefact Catalogues

With the growing number of developed ontologies, ontology libraries and repositories have been a long-time interest in the semantic web community. Ding & Fensel [11] presented in 2001 a review of *ontology libraries*: *"A system that offers various functions for managing, adapting and standardizing groups of ontologies. It should fulfill the needs for re-use of ontologies."* Ontology libraries usually register ontologies and provide metadata description. The terms *collection, listing* or *registry* were also later used to describe similar concepts to ontology libraries. All correspond to systems that help reuse or find ontologies by simply listing them (e.g., DAML, Protégé or DERI listings) or by offering structured metadata to describe them (e.g., FAIRSharing, BARTOC, Agrisemantics Map). But those systems do not support any services beyond description, including services based on the content of the ontologies. In the biomedical domain, the OBO Foundry [12] is a reference library effort to help the biomedical and biological communities build their ontologies with an enforcement of design and reuse principles. A number of services and tools are built to work with this library of semantic artefacts.

---

[2] This section reuses and updates elements in the introduction chapter of [45].

Hartman et al. [13] introduced in 2009 the concept of *ontology repository*: "*A structured collection of ontologies (...) by using an Ontology Metadata Vocabulary. References and relations between ontologies and their modules build the semantic model of an ontology repository. Access to resources is realized through semantically-enabled interfaces applicable for humans and machines.*". Multiple ontologies repositories have been developed since then, with advanced features such as search, metadata management, visualization, personalization, mappings, annotation and recommendation services, as well as application programming interfaces to query their content/services. Here again the biomedical domain has seen a lot of resources (not necessarily synchronized), such as the NCBO BioPortal [8], OntoBee [14], the EBI Ontology Lookup Service [15] and AberOWL [16]. We have seen also repository initiatives such as the Linked Open Vocabularies [17], OntoHub [18], and the Marine Metadata Initiative's Ontology Registry and Repository [19] and its earth science counterpart, the ESIP Federation's Community Ontology Repository. By the end of the 2000's, the topic was of high interest as illustrated by the 2010 ORES workshop [20] and the 2008 Ontology Summit.[3] More recently, the SIFR BioPortal [21] prototype was built to develop a French Annotator and experiment with multilingual issues in BioPortal [22]. The first reuse of the OntoPortal technology to develop a free and open, community-driven ontology repository in the spirit of BioPortal, but for agri-food, was AgroPortal, started at the end of 2015 [23]. D'Aquin & Noy [24] and Naskar and Dutta [25] provided the latest reviews of ontology repositories.

In parallel, there have been efforts to index any semantic web data online (including ontologies) and offer search engines such as Swoogle and Watson [26, 27]. We cannot consider these "semantic web indexes" as ontology libraries, even if they support some features of ontology repositories (e.g., search). Other similar products are *terminology services* or *vocabulary servers* which are usually developed to host one or a few terminologies for a specific community (e.g., SNOMED-CT terminology server, UMLS-KS, CLARIN vocabulary services, OpenTheso, etc.); they are usually not semantic web compliant and did not handle the complexity of ontologies, although an increasing number of terminology services are getting compliant with SKOS (Simple Knowledge Organization System) [28]. We can also cite the ARDC Research Vocabularies Australia (https://vocabs.ardc.edu.au) using multiple technologies such as PoolParty and SSISVoc.

In the following, we will focus on ontology repositories considering they offer both ontology-focused services (i.e., services for ontologies) and ontology-based services (i.e., services using ontologies). We will also name them now *semantic artefact catalogues*, a term which emerged in the forum and discussions around building the European Open Science Cloud (e.g., [29]) and which translates the idea that such catalogues are not only for ontologies but must offer common services for a wide range of semantic artefacts.

2.2 Generic Ontology Repository and Semantic Artefact Catalogue Technology

In the end of the 2000's, the Open Ontology Repository Initiative (OORI) [30] was a collaborative effort to develop a federated infrastructure of ontology repositories. At that time, the effort already reused the NCBO BioPortal technology [31] that was the

---

[3] http://ontolog.cim3.net/wiki/OntologySummit2008.html.

most advanced open-source technology for managing ontologies at that time. Later, the initiative studied OntoHub [18] technology for generalization but the Initiative is now discontinued.

In the context of our projects, to avoid building new ontology repositories from scratch, most of the authors have considered which of the technologies cited above were reusable. While there is a strong difference between "open source" (most of them are) and "made to be reused" we think only the NCBO BioPortal and OLS were really generic ontology repository candidates for both their construction and documentation. OLS technology has always been open source but some significant changes (e.g., the parsing of OWL) facilitating the reuse of the technology for other portals were done with OLS 3.0 released in December 2015. Until very recently (2022), in the context of the NFDI projects (https://terminology.tib.eu), we had not seen another public repository built with OLS. On the other hand, the NCBO BioPortal was developed from scratch as a domain-independent and open-source software. Although it has been very early reused by ad-hoc projects (e.g., at OORI, NCI, and MMI), it is only in 2012, with the release of BioPortal 4.0 that the technology, made of multiple various components was packaged as a virtual appliance, a virtual server machine embedding the complete code and deployment environment, allowing anyone to set up a local ontology repository and customize it. The technology is denoted as OntoPortal since 2018.

Skosmos [32] is another alternative originally built in for reuse, but it only supports browsing and search for SKOS vocabularies. For instances Finto (https://finto.fi) or Loterre (www.loterre.fr) have adopted Skosmos as backend technology. Another example is VocPrez, an open-source technology developed by a company adopted for examples by the Geoscience Australia Vocabularies system (https://vocabs.ga.gov.au) or by the NERC Vocabulary Server (http://vocab.nerc.ac.uk). Another technology is ShowVoc, based on the same technological core as VocBench but it appears to have drawn inspiration from OntoPortal in terms of its design and services.

A full comparison of the different semantic artefact catalogue technologies is not the subject of this paper, but we strongly believe the OntoPortal technology implements the highest number of features and requirements in our projects. Indeed, there are two other major motivations for reusing this technology: (i) to avoid re-developing tools that have already been designed and extensively used and instead contribute to long term support of a shared technology; and (ii) to offer the same tools, services and formats to multiple user communities, to facilitate the interface and interaction between domains and interoperability.

3   OntoPortal Technology

The OntoPortal virtual appliance is mainly made available as an OVF file (Open Virtualization Format) to deploy on a server. Amazon Machine Instances are also available. Once installed, an OntoPortal instance provides an out-of-the-box semantic artefact catalogue web application with a wide range of features. A demo server can be visited at https://demo.ontoportal.org. Administrators of the platform can then include the desired semantic artefacts directly, reach out to their users to let them upload resources, or both. In the following, we review the OntoPortal architecture and default OntoPortal services—many of these have been presented and published already in the context of referenced publications of BioPortal or subsequent projects. Then, we describe the latest services and functionalities developed by members of the Alliance that are being discussed and step-by-step included in the main code branch when relevant.

3.1 OntoPortal Standard/Default Technical Architecture

OntoPortal is a complex system composed of multiple –coherently connected– stacks depending on the services implemented. Most of the components (listed in Table 1) are developed in Ruby (www.ruby-lang.org). Sometimes, they rely or reuse third party technologies, especially in the storage layer.

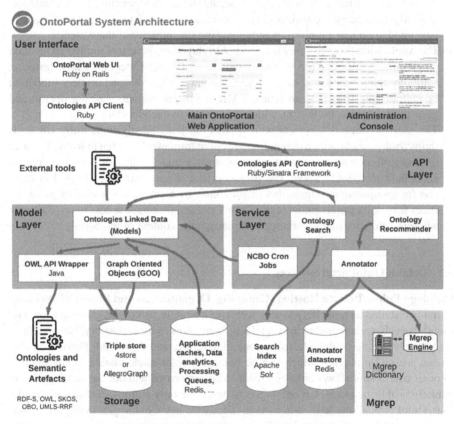

Fig. 2. OntoPortal system architecture.

The OntoPortal system architecture is presented in Fig. 2. It is structured in several layers briefly described here:

- The storage layer is mainly made of a triple-store which saves each semantic artefact RDF content in a distinct graph, as well as other data (metadata records, mappings, projects, users, etc.). We have always used 4store (https://github.com/4store), a very efficient and scalable RDF database. The technology being outdated, we are transitioning to other triple-stores. This layer also uses: (i) Redis-based key-value storage for application caches and the Annotator dictionary datastore; (ii) Solr search engine (https://solr.apache.org) to index and retrieve ontologies content data with the Search service.

- The model layer implements all the models (objects) of the business logic and the mechanisms to parse the semantic artefact source files using the OWL-API (https://github.com/owlcs/owlapi) and persist/retrieve them from the triple-store using our built-in Object-Relational-Mapping-like library, called GOO.
- The service layer, with Ruby/Sinatra (https://sinatrarb.com), implements the core OntoPortal services working with the models: Search, Annotator and Recommender. When necessary, these services rely on specific storage components and external tools (e.g., Mgrep concept recognizer [33]). A command line administration tool was also integrated to do jobs monitoring and managing the integrity of the system.
- The Application Programming Interface (API) layer implements a unified application programming interface for all the models (e.g., Group, Category, Class, Instance, Ontology, Submission, Mapping, Project, Review, Note, User) and services supported by OntoPortal. The API can return XML or custom formats, but the default and most-used output is JSON-LD, which uses JSON to encode RDF.
- The user interface is a typical web application built mostly with Ruby On Rails (https://rubyonrails.org), a popular open-source framework written in Ruby. The user interface offers a set of various views to display and use the services and components built in the API layer. The user interface is customized for logged-in users and for groups/organizations that display their own sub-set of resources using the slices feature. Administrators of the OntoPortal instance have access to an additional administration console to monitor, and manage the content of the portal.

3.2 Default OntoPortal Services

Ontology Public/Private Hosting, Grouping, Organization and Slices: When OntoPortal is installed as a publicly visible web application in its default configuration, end users[4] can self-register and upload artefacts themselves to the repository. New artefacts are publicly visible by default, for anyone to find, use, and download. OntoPortal also allows private ontologies, which can be managed by or made visible to any number of other users. This allows ontology work to be performed without the ontology being publicly visible, or a subset of ontologies to be visible only within a certain community. Plus, OntoPortal allows logged-in users to specify the list of ontologies to display in their own user interface. Within an installation, semantic resources are organized in groups and/or categories that are specialized by each portal. Typically, groups associate ontologies from the same project or organization whereas categories are about the ontology

---

[4] We call "end users" the final users of an OntoPortal instance i.e., stakeholders interested in hosting or using an ontology on that deployed OntoPortal installation. We distinguish the end user role from the role performed by administrators of the installation, who in some sense also "use" the technology.

Table 1. OntoPortal components code repositories (https://github.com/ontoportal).

Name	Description	Technology
ontoportal_web_ui	Frontend Rails-based web application for OntoPortal	RubyOnRails
ontologies_api_ruby_client	A Ruby client for accessing the OntoPortal hypermedia API	Ruby
ontologies_api	Hypermedia and data API for OntoPortal services	Sinatra (Ruby)
ontologies_linked_data	Models and serializers for OntoPortal objects and services backed by triple-store	Ruby
goo	Graph Oriented Objects (GOO) for Ruby. An RDF/SPARQL-based "ORM"	Ruby
ncbo_annotator	OntoPortal Annotator which annotates text with semantic terms	Ruby
ncbo_ontology_recommender	OntoPortal Recommender which recommends relevant ontologies for text or keywords	Ruby
ncbo_cron	Cron jobs that run on a regular basis in the infrastructure	Ruby
owlapi_wrapper	A command line utility that wraps the Java OWL API for parsing RDF-S, OWL, and OBO ontologies	Java

subjects/topics. OntoPortal also offers a "slice" mechanism to allow users to interact (both via API and UI) only with a subset of ontologies in an installation. If browsing the slice, all the portal features will be restricted to the chosen subset, enabling users to focus on their specific use cases.

Library, Versioning and Search: The primary mission of an OntoPortal installation is to host and serve ontologies and semantic artefacts. The portals accept resources in multiple knowledge representation languages: OWL, RDF-S, SKOS, OBO and UMLS-RRF.[5] Ontologies are semantically described with rich metadata (partially extracted from the source files), and a browsing user interface allows to quickly identify, with faceted search, the ontologies of interest based on their metadata. The portal can also consider some resources as "views" of main ones. The technology is not a version control system like GitHub—which provides complementary services—but will store all ontology versions (called "submissions"), whether manually submitted or automatically

---

[5] Actually, OntoPortal uses the OWLAPI (https://github.com/owlcs/owlapi) to parse source files. It will therefore accept every knowledge representation language and format supported by this third-party tool.

pulled.[6] Each version's metadata record is saved[7] and differences from one version to the other are computed, which enables a historical overview of the ontology as it evolves. Only the latest versions of ontologies are indexed and loaded in the backend but all source files and diffs are available. Beyond the metadata record, OntoPortal loads each ontology's content in a triple-store and indexes the content (classes, properties and values) with Solr to allow searching across the ontologies by keyword or identifier.

Ontology Browsing and Content Visualization: OntoPortal lets users visualize a class/concept or property within its hierarchy, as well as see related information for this entity (as relations included in the source file).[8] Some key properties (e.g., preferred labels, synonyms, definitions), even if encoded by custom properties in a given source file, are explicitly "mapped" (by the portal or the submitter) to a common model that offers a baseline for OntoPortal services. For each ontology, several web widgets (e.g., "Autocomplete jump-to term" or "Hierarchy tree") are automatically provided and can be embedded in external web applications to facilitate the reuse/visualization of ontology entities.

Mappings: Another key service of OntoPortal is a mapping repository that stores 1-to-1 mappings between classes or concepts. The mappings in OntoPortal are first-class citizens that can be identified, stored, described, retrieved and deleted. Mappings can be explicitly uploaded from external sources and reified as a resource described with simple provenance information and an explicit relation (e.g., owl:sameAs, skos:exactMatch). The portal automatically creates some mappings when two classes share the same URI (indicating reuse of that URI) or the same UMLS CUI and generates simple "lexical mappings" with the LOOM algorithm [34]. Although the LOOM mappings are not semantic (based only on syntactic matching), they quickly indicate the overlap of an ontology with all the other ones in a portal, and suggest possible terms to investigate in other ontologies. OntoPortal does not yet support the new Simple Semantic Standard for Ontology Mapping (SSSOM) format [35], although steps toward this have started in the AgroPortal project.

Community Feedback, Change Requests and Projects: OntoPortal includes some community-oriented features [36] such as: (i) *Ontology reviews*: for each ontology, a review can be written by a logged-in user; this feature is currently rebuild and thus deactivated by default. (ii) *Notes* can be attached in a forum-like mode to a specific artefact or class/concept, in order to discuss the ontology (its design, use, or evolution) or allow users to propose changes. (iii) *Change requests* can be submitted, and in some cases directly transferred to external systems such as a GitHub issue tracker. (iv) *Projects*

---

[6] An ontology submission can be performed as a single submission of a provided file, or as an ongoing service to monitor a particular public location (a 'pull URL'). When the ontology is configured with a pull URL, the file at that source is immediately downloaded and parsed. Each subsequent night the submission service checks the pull URL, and if the source file there has changed, it will automatically create a new submission.

[7] This is important to support the FAIR Principle A2.

[8] An OntoPortal content page always has a direct URL, that could be used to dereference an ontology URI.

can be defined, and their use of specific ontologies recorded, to materialize the ontology-project relation and demonstrate concrete uses of an ontology. Ontology developers (or any registered users) can subscribe to email notifications to be informed each time a user note or mapping is added to their ontologies of interest.

Ontology-Based Annotation with the Annotator: OntoPortal features the Annotator, a domain-agnostic text annotation service that will identify semantic artefact classes or concepts inside any raw text [37]. The user can control which ontologies are used to perform the text annotation. The Annotator workflow is based on a highly efficient syntactic concept recognition tool (using concept names and synonyms) [33], and on a set of semantic expansion algorithms that leverage the semantics in ontologies (e.g., subclass relations and mappings). It is also used as a component of the system to recommend ontologies for given text input, as described hereafter.

Ontology Recommendation with the Recommender: OntoPortal includes the Recommender an ontology recommendation service [38] which suggests relevant semantic artefacts for a provided text or keyword list. The Recommender evaluates the relevance of an ontology according to four different criteria: (1) the extent to which the ontology covers the input data; (2) the acceptance of the ontology in the community (number of views in the portal); (3) the level of detail of the ontology classes that cover the input data; and (4) the specialization of the ontology to the domain of the input data. The user can configure the weights of the four criteria, and can choose to rank the most relevant individual ontologies, or sets of ontologies. The OntoPortal Recommender is arguably the most powerful ontology discovery and recommendation tool available in public semantic repositories.

Automated Access: REST API and SPARQL Endpoint: OntoPortal provides two different endpoints for accessing its content: (i) a REST web service API that returns JSON-LD; (ii) a SPARQL endpoint [39]. These endpoints are consistent across all the OntoPortal deployments, so software written originally to query a specific portal (most commonly BioPortal) can be used equally well to query any other OntoPortal deployment, assuming that deployment makes its endpoints accessible. The REST web service API provides access to all the resources (read/write) and services described above, and queries are highly customizable using various request parameters. To efficiently handle large result sets, pagination is available for the majority of the endpoints. The SPARQL web service provides direct read-only access to the OntoPortal triple store. Since OntoPortal is developed to work with semantic web technologies and artefacts, all of its content (ontologies, mappings, metadata, notes, and projects) is stored in an RDF triple store. For security, some OntoPortal installations (like BioPortal itself) choose not to make the primary triple store queryable. In these cases, a copy of the triple store can be made accessible [39].

Many external applications developed by the biomedical semantics community to use BioPortal can be adapted to work with any other portal; examples include OntoMaton, OntoCAT, Zooma, Galaxy, REDCap, and FAIRsharing. More recently, we have seen tools developed directly considering multiple OntoPortal endpoints e.g., https://github.com/cthoyt/ontoportal-client, and we are discussing federating search and other queries/services across all public OntoPortal systems.

3.3 Additional Features and Services Developed by the Alliance

The features described above were originally developed for BioPortal and after adopted and sometime improved by members of the Alliance, which now is established as the baseline for OntoPortal technology. However, with new adopters and use cases, the Alliance has proposed new ideas and developed new functionalities. The additional features presented in this section have been developed in the context of the SIFR BioPortal [21], AgroPortal [23], and EcoPortal [10] projects. The Alliance is now incorporating some of these contributions into the core OntoPortal code.

Enhanced Mapping Features: AgroPortal enhanced its mappings repository with several more advanced features. Originally any mapping's source and target object could only be in the local repository, but AgroPortal added the ability for the target entity to be in another instance of the OntoPortal technology ('inter-portal') or in any external semantic resource. AgroPortal can also import mappings in bulk from a JSON file[9] (submitting multiple mappings previously required multiple calls to the API). AgroPortal can also recognize SKOS mappings explicitly defined in semantic artefact source files, and can serve those mappings (both in UI and API) alongside all of the other ones in the mapping repository.

Enhanced Semantic Annotation Workflow: The SIFR BioPortal offers natural language-based enhancements of the Annotator making it first available for French text, but also adding three scoring methods to rank semantic annotations by order of importance [40]. It also introduced significant improvements that support clinical context detection (i.e., in the context of clinical text, the Annotator can detect negation, experiencer—the person experiencing the symptom or event—and temporality) [22] that were eventually made available for English in OntoPortal.

Extended Ontology Metadata Model and Instances: To facilitate the ontology identification and selection process and promote FAIRness, AgroPortal implemented an extended metadata model based on MOD1.4 [41] to better support descriptions of ontologies and their relations. Such a model enabled multiple features in the portal [5] such as: additional filtering options when selecting ontologies, a *Landscape* page which shows synthetized metadata-based analytics for all the ontologies in the portal, and FAIRness assessment. AgroPortal also now supports OWL instances—in addition to the classes and properties in the standard OntoPortal—and displays the instances in the user interface.

Ontology FAIRness Assessment with O'FAIRe: AgroPortal implemented the Ontology FAIRness Evaluation (O'FAIRe) methodology [6, 42] in a tool that automatically assesses the level of FAIRness –i.e., to which degree a digital object adheres to the FAIR principles–of semantic artefacts within the portal. The assessment relies on 61 questions answered using the extended ontology metadata or the portal's own services. When working on O'FAIRe, we demonstrated the importance of relying on ontology repositories to harmonize and harness unified metadata and thus allow FAIRness assessment.

---

[9] This bulk load will accept a file generated by an extension of the SSSOM python tool (https://github.com/mapping-commons/sssom-py) which transforms SSSOM mappings to OntoPortal format. (Some information is lost, as the OntoPortal mapping format is still currently less expressive than SSSOM.).

Extended SKOS Support: AgroPortal added new functions to support SKOS resources as the standard OntoPortal code is still limited [43]. The new functions handle and represent SKOS concept schemes, collections and SKOS-XL elements if used in the displayed thesaurus. AgroPortal offers state-of-the-art innovative browsing approaches to discover and navigate concepts in SKOS thesauri that make extensive use of scheme and collections.

Assigning DOIs and Connecting with VocBench: EcoPortal development focused on improving the provenance aspects of OntoPortal and supporting the collaborative creation and maintenance of the semantic artefacts, in particular of SKOS thesauri. EcoPortal added the ability to: (i) graphically administrate groups and categories of semantic artefacts and (ii) request a Digital Object Identifier (DOI) for resources hosted in the portal using Datacite services (https://datacite.org/dois.html). The DOI assignment depends on an editorial workflow that evaluates the ontology's maturity and pertinence to the ecological domain. To support collaborative work on the portal's semantic artefacts, EcoPortal integrated a connector to the VocBench 3 system (https://vocbench.unirom a2.it), which provides a web-based, multilingual, collaborative development capability.

4 OntoPortal Open-Source Project Organization

The OntoPortal Alliance has a main goal of synchronizing and sharing research and development efforts. The group's motivations are: (i) to represent OntoPortal adopters and end users; (ii) to maximize the OntoPortal state-of-the-art service portfolio; (iii) to improve OntoPortal software while managing several parallel and different installations; (iv) to increase semantic uptake in science communities; and (v) to increase the ecosystem's long-term support.

The Alliance is committed to be an open community and is working to ease participation by providing installation and deployment procedures, detailed documentation, and in the future training and tutorials for all stakeholders. We are spending a considerable amount of time to create a resource for the community and support it (e.g., average of 4 support emails per day for BioPortal, 3 per week for AgroPortal) and document it. In 2022, we launched an annual 3-day-workshop [44] that we see as key to fostering our growing community. The Alliance is setting-up three documents (https://ont oportal.github.io/documentation) to reach multiple stakeholders: (i) A *user guide* documents domain- and portal-specific capabilities. This targets OntoPortal end users—either ontology developers who want to host an ontology on one of the portals, or users who want to access and reuse ontologies. The user guide can be specialized by each project in the Alliance to adjust to specific needs of a community or to document a portal specific feature. (ii) An *admin guide* documents how to set up the system and manage the content. This is typically addressed to the technical person involved in deploying, running and monitoring the server but also to the content administrator who will supervise the semantic artefacts loaded, perform artefact curation, and provide outreach to the end users. (iii) A *developer guide* documents how to develop new features and make contributions to the core technology, thereby sharing work back with the rest of the Alliance.

The code packaged and running within the appliance is available on the OntoPortal GitHub (https://github.com/ontoportal) and licensed BSD-2, so every administrator or developer can easily get the relevant branches or forks and redeploy the code in the appliance. We strongly encourage Alliance partners (and other open-source contributors) to fork the OntoPortal GitHub repositories to enable traceability and collaborative contributions via their pull requests. Besides code sharing, we use GitHub for issues, discussions, decision-making and overall project management. Wherever feasible the OntoPortal project follows best practices for developing and supporting open-source projects. The documentation and the OntoPortal website materials are being enhanced and made more community-maintainable. Both have been ported to GitHub too and can be maintained by the community as any other technical projects (Table 2). These mechanisms allow all community members to improve the public presence of both the software and the organization.

The key idea behind the deployment of community- or domain-specific semantic repositories is to provide closer and better connections to the end users in those communities. To address its user communities, the Alliance relies on the support provided by each project deploying an installation. We have implemented a free licensing system that we use to trace the many applications of the technology, identify potential collaborators and Alliance members, and maintain an ongoing connection to the adopters, so that we can notify them of timely improvements and get feedback. In some cases, if the Alliance collaborates with industry or the private sector, we discuss the appropriate terms and conditions and possible financial participation.

Table 2. OntoPortal project description repositories (https://github.com/ontoportal).

Name	Description	Technology
ontoportal-project	OntoPortal Alliance centralized repository for the management of the OntoPortal project	none
website	Source code for OntoPortal product and Alliance website at http://ontoportal.org	Jekyll (Ruby)
documentation	Source code for user, admin and developer guides at https://ontoportal.github.io/documentation	Jekyll (Ruby)
literature	Different research articles related to OntoPortal software	PDF

5   Usage of the OntoPortal Technology

In place of an evaluation section, we hereafter briefly present the uses of our technology: either by public and open repositories but also local, private and temporal uses. We believe the choices to reuse our technology made by such a large variety of projects and use cases, in multiple scientific domains, is the best assessment of its value.

5.1 Current Open Domain or Project Specific OntoPortal Installation

In September 2022, we conducted a survey among the 10 main Alliance participants to date (Table 3). We obtained a sense of a typical OntoPortal installation: a public (open and free) community repository where anyone can contribute ontologies, with on average 50/60 ontologies, of which more than 50% are exclusive to that repository (that is, unavailable in any other OntoPortal repository). The content is generally multilingual (77%)—despite a lack of support for this in the core software—and mostly in OWL or SKOS format. Ontologies are mostly added by content administrators performing significant or moderate content curation, even when end users can also add ontologies. This tends to change with broader adoption of the portals. Indeed, a typical OntoPortal installation is concretely used by a few groups (dozens to hundreds of users) and animated by a 1-to-3-person team. If a developer is in this team, the portal tends to develop new functionalities.

In the survey, we requested and received detailed information about several facets of the projects. The most important reason people wanted to run an OntoPortal instance was the value of running a community-specific ontology repository, while the least important reason was BioPortal's reliability. Most installations have not determined any policy for adding ontologies to the collection, and had relatively little outreach (it is likely too soon for many projects). There is a lot of interest in adding diverse features, and several responses alluded to improving the ability to re-use ontologies in various ways. Many groups expressed interest in leading a shared development activity.

5.2 Other Running Installations of the OntoPortal Technology

Beyond the domain-specific portal reuses in the Alliance, the OntoPortal technology is deployed by many external parties with other objectives. For instance, hospitals reuse the technology in-house to use services such as the Annotator on sensitive data.

In the past, those uses of the OntoPortal technology were hard to track since users provide no feedback or report to the OntoPortal providers unless they need explicit support. Through 2015, the virtual appliance file was downloaded or deployed from Amazon Machine Images more than 140 times. Since version 3.0 of the OntoPortal software in 2020, the appliance incorporates a "call home" feature and a free registration solution that together help track the number and status of other OntoPortal installations. In the past 3 years, 98 unique accounts have registered 135 OntoPortal appliances. In 2022, 60 unique appliance IDs called home including 19 running in Amazon Machine Instances. These numbers demonstrate the large adoption of the OntoPortal technology beyond the Alliance and public repositories.

Table 3. Current members of the OntoPortal Alliance as of early 2023.

Name	URL	Domain	Supporting organization	Release
BioPortal	https://bioportal.bio ontology.org	Biomedicine, life sciences, general	Stanford University	2005

Foundational and most complex project of all OntoPortal deployments. Has over 1 million API accesses per day, a complex infrastructure and many users whose activities are cumbersome to track. Software has always been open and the baseline for the OntoPortal appliance since 2012. For scalability and robustness reasons, the BioPortal infrastructure is much more complex than the default OntoPortal. BioPortal has experimented with some features (e.g., visualization, notes, data annotation) that were discontinued

SIFR BioPortal	https://bioportal.lir mm.fr	Medicine (focus on French)	LIRMM (CNRS & Univ. of Montpellier)	2014

Dedicated biomedical instance for French use cases especially built to develop the SIFR Annotator semantic annotation web service. Mutualize developments with the AgroPortal to keep them generic, domain-agnostic, activated and parameterized in different OntoPortal installations

AgroPortal	https://agroportal.lir mm.fr	Agri-food and environment	INRAE (originally LIRMM)	2015

Generic tool for any kind of semantic artefacts related to agri-food while keeping an "ontology research" dimension. Offers heavy curation and harmonization of the metadata as well as new services (landscape and O'FAIRe) based on these metadata. Implemented many upgrades (mappings, annotation, and metadata) while remaining backward-compatible with OntoPortal default codebase. The AgroPortal project was the first to show that different ontology repositories could be used to reach out to other and new communities (technically and scientifically)

EcoPortal	https://ecoportal.lif ewatch.eu	Ecology, biodiversity	LifeWatch ERIC and Italian national node	2019

Based on a study started in 2017, recent funding support—and endorsement by LifeWatch ERIC—gives the platform visibility and sustainability. Developed a new service that permits creators/authors to request and obtain a DOI for hosted semantic artefacts. Incorporated mandatory metadata fields from the DataCite specification. Offers ability to use an internal instance of VocBench, accessing it from the portal and signing in with the same credentials thus providing a quite complete solution for managing semantic artefacts over full lifecycle

MedPortal	http://medportal.bmi cc.cn	Medicine (focus on Chinese)	Peking Union Medical College	2020

National Population Health Data Center (BMICC) instance collecting and integrating ontologies in the biomedical domain in order to support related research in China. Providing ontology service for ontologies in Chinese including annotation

Cogni.zone	N/A	Total Energies	Cogni.zone (SME)	2020

(continued)

Table 3. (*continued*)

Name	URL	Domain	Supporting organization	Release
As a company that installs OntoPortal for clients Congi.zone has a different perspective on use cases, challenges, and clients. Installed the appliance using the Microsoft Azure cloud and coordinated an extensive security evaluation of the product (security was identified as a challenging issue to address). Extensive semantic knowledge and installations provide many technical and marketing opportunities				
MatPortal	https://matportal.org	Material sciences	Fraunhofer Materials, BAM, NFDI Matwerk	2021
Aims to accelerate the development and reuse of ontologies in materials sciences. Appreciates crucial functionalities for ontology development such as visualization, search, mappings, and annotations. Further developments include specific features to support the development of standards-specific ontologies in alignment with the Smart Standards initiatives				
IndustryPortal	http://industryportal.enit.fr	Industry and manufacturing	ENIT	2022
Managing the proliferation of semantic artefacts in the industrial domain, and evaluating the level of FAIRness of artefacts. Supported by H2020 OntoCommons, an EU project to standardize industrial data documentation through harmonized ontologies. Strong motivation on making things interoperable, aligning the semantic artefacts and ensuring their FAIRness				
VODANA	(to come)	Health/COVID	VODAN Africa	2021
Advancing tracking and management of COVID-19 in Africa. VODAN Africa teams have adapted OntoPortal for redistribution to health centers and clinics throughout Africa, serving country-specific vocabularies from locally managed repositories. The VODANA project researched and demonstrated the best ways to package OntoPortal as part of an application set installed on pre-configured laptops				
BiodivPortal	(to come)	Biodiversity	NFDI4Biodiversity	2023
NDFI4biodiv is a node of the NFDI infrastructure projects in Germany. Adopting OntoPortal for developing the next generation of the GFBio terminology service. Convergence and partnership with EcoPortal being discussed. Extensive experience with mappings of semantic artefacts and ontology evolution to bring in the technology features in the future				
EarthPortal	(to come)	Earth/Env.	CNRS/Data Terra	2023
Developed during the FAIR-IMPACT project by Data Terra (French research infrastructure on solid earth, ocean, continental surfaces and atmosphere). Aims to be a reference repository for any kind of semantic artefacts related to earth and environmental sciences, and amplify the development and reuse of ontologies in these communities. To address specific communities' needs and propose new features				

6 Perspectives and Discussion

The Alliance members are working on multiple technical improvements of the OntoPortal technology. These improvements include: (i) Multilingual support for artefact content; (ii) internationalization of the user interface; (iii) Fully SSSOM-compliant mapping repository with enhanced mapping features e.g., connect to third party tools for ontology alignment; (iv) Docker container-based setup/installation of OntoPortal; (v) SPARQL query editor and viewer; (vi) Consolidated and harmonized metadata model; (vii) Historical view of the evolution of a semantic artefact (metrics, differencing); (viii) Decoupling dependencies on current triple-store backend to support alternative triple-stores; (ix) Refactoring the feedback and notes mechanism and connect modification requests to codebase repositories such as GitHub; (x) Accelerated, simplified, and more transparent ontology submissions; (xi) Federated search capabilities across multiple repositories; (xii) New and improved user interfaces; and (xiii) improve the overall system performance.

With the proliferation of semantic artefact catalogues—either using the OntoPortal technology or not—the semantic ecosystem for scientific research becomes more complex for many end users. Because scientific domains and projects overlap, some ontologies might be hosted in multiple portals, or conversely a set of ontologies may be split across multiple portals, and different versions of the same ontology may be presented in different catalogues. Our philosophy is that ontology developers should decide how their ontology should be deployed, whether in one or many portals. On our side, we will work to provide the best possible federation of our portals. Our challenge is to better coordinate to be sure semantic artefact metadata and versions are synchronized, ontology developers are aware where their resources are deployed (without having to explicitly deal with multiple portals), and our services federate results of services like search, annotation and recommendations.

In the context of FAIR-IMPACT, a Horizon Europe project within the *European Open Science Cloud*, some members of the Alliance and other parties are investigating the life cycle of FAIR semantic artefacts. We are reviewing governance models for semantic artefacts and discussing the role the catalogues have to play in this governance. Within this project, we are also building on the *Metadata for Ontology Description and Publication* initiative (https://github.com/FAIR-IMPACT/MOD) to provide a DCAT-based vocabulary to describe semantic artefacts and their catalogues. We expect to make these descriptions available via a standard application programming interface that ontology repositories and semantic artefact catalogues, including the OntoPortal technology and also extending beyond it, can implement to improve their interoperability and ease the reuse of their resources.

The OntoPortal Alliance has many other development opportunities beyond the ongoing tasks described above. Each member of the Alliance brings unique vision and potential for improvements to the software. These improvements will make the OntoPortal systems steadily more interoperable, more interconnected, more powerful, and easier to install, operate, and update. However, these development opportunities are not without challenges. Creating a common open-source project, and an emerging organization and governance model to coordinate changes and evolutions, only begin the work needed for a robust collaborative software capability. Achieving successful results require a combination of factors: community commitment to a common, yet improvable, technical solution; technical approaches for accepting modifications that allow each participating organization autonomy to select its own system configuration; funding commitments that allow both the OntoPortal Alliance and its contributing members to thrive; and continuing buy-in to the common mission of the Alliance.

7 Conclusion

In the semantic web and linked open data world, the impact of BioPortal is easily illustrated by the famous Linked Open Data cloud diagram that since 2017 includes ontologies imported from the NCBO BioPortal (most of the Life Sciences section): We like to duplicate this impact in multiple scientific domains. In [5, 6], we argued about the importance of ontology repositories to make semantic artefacts FAIR. In this paper, we have presented a domain-agnostic, open and collaboratively developed technology for building such repositories.

The demand for semantic services can be seen not just in the growing deployment of OntoPortal systems, but the increasing presence and capabilities of other semantic artefact catalogues, often developed on their own with ad-hoc technology and brand-new code. We believe the timing—and community maturity—is right to invest some energy in a common, shared yet customizable and adaptable technology for semantic artefact catalogues. The OntoPortal Alliance, with its OntoPortal technology and world-wide base of members and system users, is uniquely positioned to move semantic artefact catalogues and ontology repositories to the next level of adoption and value to the research community. We anticipate accelerated progress and engagement from researchers, Alliance members, funders, and sponsors as we pursue the Alliance mission.

Resource Availability Statement

- Source code for OntoPortal is available here: https://github.com/ontoportal and documentation is centralized here: https://ontoportal.github.io/documentation.
- The product and the Alliance are publicly and generally presented in the OntoPortal website here: https://ontoportal.org.
- License terms are described here: https://ontoportal.github.io/documentation/administration/general/licensing.
- OntoPortal support can be reach at support@ontoportal.org.
- Each specific OntoPortal instance project can be contacted via their specific portal listed in Table 3. Those are generally public, open source and provide free support as well as the code on GitHub e.g., https://github.com/ontoportal/ontoportal_web_ui/forks.
- Release notes are usually available in forked GitHub repositories. BioPortal historical release notes are here: https://www.bioontology.org/wiki/BioPortal_Release_Notes; AgroPortal's ones are here: https://github.com/agroportal/project-management.
- In a near future, we will use a software PID provider (e.g., Software Heritage) to long term identify our software and the related releases and the Codemeta standard to define our product metadata.

Acknowledgement. This work has been supported by the D2KAB project (ANR-18-CE23-0017), the French NUMEV-IRT OntoPortal Alliance (ANR-10-LABX-20), the Horizon Europe FAIR-IMPACT project (grant #101057344) and the U.S. National Institutes of Health BioPortal U24 grant (1U24GM143402). The Alliance is also supported by the research bodies and organizations of its members. We thank and acknowledge here the discussions, engagement and participation of the Alliance members and any external parties that provide contributions or feedback on our technology or our running OntoPortal installations.

References

1. Wilkinson, M.D., et al.: The FAIR guiding principles for scientific data management and stewardship. Sci. Data **3** (2016). https://doi.org/10.1038/sdata.2016.18
2. Poveda-Villalón, M., Espinoza-Arias, P., Garijo, D., Corcho, O.: Coming to terms with FAIR ontologies. In: Keet, C.M., Dumontier, M. (eds.) EKAW 2020. LNCS, vol. 12387, pp. 255–270. Springer, Cham (2020). https://doi.org/10.1007/978-3-030-61244-3_18
3. Amdouni, E., Jonquet, C.: FAIR or FAIRer? An integrated quantitative FAIRness assessment grid for semantic resources and ontologies. In: Garoufallou, E., Ovalle-Perandones, MA., Vlachidis, A. (eds.) MTSR 2021. CCIS, vol. 1537, pp. 67–80. Springer, Cham (2022). https://doi.org/10.1007/978-3-030-98876-0_6
4. Coxid, S.J.D., Gonzalez-Beltranid, A.N., Magagna, B., Marinescu, M.-C.: Ten simple rules for making a vocabulary FAIR (2021). https://doi.org/10.1371/journal.pcbi.1009041
5. Jonquet, C., Toulet, A., Dutta, B., Emonet, V.: Harnessing the power of unified metadata in an ontology repository: the case of AgroPortal. Data Semant. **7**, 191–221 (2018). https://doi.org/10.1007/s13740-018-0091-5
6. Amdouni, E., Bouazzouni, S., Jonquet, C., O'faire, C.J.: O'FAIRe makes you an offer: metadata-based automatic FAIRness assessment for ontologies and semantic resources. Int. J. Metadata Semant. Ontol. **16**, 16–46 (2022). https://doi.org/10.13039/501100001665
7. Graybeal, J., Jonquet, C., Fiore, N., Musen, M.A.: Adoption of BioPortal's ontology registry software: the emerging OntoPortal community. In: 13th Plenary Meeting of the Research Data Alliance, Poster session, Philadelphia, PA, USA (2019)
8. Noy, N.F., et al.: BioPortal: ontologies and integrated data resources at the click of a mouse. Nucleic Acids Res. **37**, 170–173 (2009). https://doi.org/10.1093/nar/gkp440
9. Whetzel, P.L., et al.: BioPortal: enhanced functionality via new Web services from the national center for biomedical ontology to access and use ontologies in software applications. Nucleic Acids Res. **39**, 541–545 (2011). https://doi.org/10.1093/nar/gkr469
10. Kechagioglou, X., Vaira, L., Tomassino, P., Fiore, N., Basset, A., Rosati, I.: EcoPortal: an environment for FAIR semantic resources in the ecological domain. In: 3rd International Workshop on Semantics for Biodiversity (S4BioDiv 2021). CEUR, Bolzano, Italy (2021)
11. Ding, Y., Fensel, D.: Ontology library systems: the key to successful ontology re-use. In: 1st Semantic Web Working Symposium, SWWS 2001, pp. 93–112. CEUR-WS.org, Stanford, CA, USA (2001)
12. Smith, B., et al.: The OBO Foundry: coordinated evolution of ontologies to support biomedical data integration. Nat. Biotechnol. **25**, 1251–1255 (2007). https://doi.org/10.1038/nbt1346
13. Hartmann, J., Palma, R., Gómez-Pérez, A.: Ontology repositories. In : Handbook on Ontologies, pp. 551–571 (2009). https://doi.org/10.1007/978-3-540-92673-3
14. Ong, E., et al.: Ontobee: a linked ontology data server to support ontology term dereferencing, linkage, query and integration. Nucleic Acids Res. **45**, D347–D352 (2016). https://doi.org/10.1093/nar/gkw918
15. Côté, R.G., Jones, P., Apweiler, R., Hermjakob, H.: The ontology lookup service, a lightweight cross-platform tool for controlled vocabulary queries. BMC Bioinform. **7**, 97 (2006). https://doi.org/10.1186/1471-2105-7-97

16. Hoehndorf, R., Slater, L., Schofield, P.N., Gkoutos, G.: V: Aber-OWL: a framework for ontology-based data access in biology. BMC Bioinform. **16**, 1–9 (2015). https://doi.org/10.1186/s12859-015-0456-9

17. Vandenbussche, P.-Y., Atemezing, G.A., Poveda-Villalon, M., Vatant, B.: Linked open vocabularies (LOV): a gateway to reusable semantic vocabularies on the Web. Semant. Web **1**, 1–5 (2014). https://doi.org/10.3233/SW-160213

18. Till, M., Kutz, O., Codescu, M.: Ontohub: a semantic repository for heterogeneous ontologies. In: Theory Day in Computer Science, DACS 204, Bucharest, Romania, p. 2 (2014)

19. Rueda, C., Bermudez, L., Fredericks, J.: The MMI ontology registry and repository: a portal for marine metadata interoperability. In: MTS/IEEE Biloxi - Marine Technology for Our Future: Global and Local Challenges, OCEANS 2009, Biloxi, MS, USA, p. 6. (2009)

20. D'Aquin, M., Castro, A.G., Lange, C., Viljanen, K. (eds.): 1st Workshop on Ontology Repositories and Editors for the Semantic Web, ORES 2010. CEUR-WS.org, Hersonissos, Greece (2010)

21. Jonquet, C., Annane, A., Bouarech, K., Emonet, V., Melzi, S.: SIFR BioPortal: un portail ouvert et générique d'ontologies et de terminologies biomédicales françaises au service de l'annotation sémantique. In: 16th Journées Francophones d'Informatique Médicale, JFIM 2016, Genève, Suisse, p. 16 (2016)

22. Tchechmedjiev, A., Abdaoui, A., Emonet, V., Zevio, S., Jonquet, C.: SIFR annotator: ontology-based semantic annotation of French biomedical text and clinical notes. BMC Bioinform. **19**, 405–431 (2018). https://doi.org/10.1186/s12859-018-2429-2

23. Jonquet, C., et al.: AgroPortal: a vocabulary and ontology repository for agronomy. Comput. Electron. Agric. **144**, 126–143 (2018). https://doi.org/10.1016/j.compag.2017.10.012

24. D'Aquin, M., Noy, N.F.: Where to publish and find ontologies? A survey of ontology libraries. Web Semant. **11**, 96–111 (2012). https://doi.org/10.1016/j.websem.2011.08.005

25. Naskar, D., Dutta, B.: Ontology libraries : a study from an ontofier and an ontologist perspectives. In: 19th International Symposium on Electronic Theses and Dissertations, ETD 2016, Lille, France, pp. 1–12 (2016)

26. Ding, L., et al.: Swoogle: a semantic web search and metadata engine. In: Grossman, D.A., Gravano, L., Zhai, C., Herzog, O., Evans, D. (eds.) 13th ACM Conference on Information and Knowledge Management, CIKM 2004. ACM, Washington DC (2004)

27. D'Aquin, M., Baldassarre, C., Gridinoc, L., Angeletou, S., Sabou, M., Motta, E.: Watson: a gateway for next generation semantic web applications. In: Poster & Demonstration Session at the 6th International Semantic Web Conference, ISWC 2007, Busan, Korea, p. 3 (2007)

28. Miles, A., Bechhofer, S.: SKOS simple knowledge organization system reference. W3C recommendation 18, W3C (2009)

29. Corcho, O., Eriksson, M., Kurowski, K., et al.: EOSC interoperability framework (2021). https://data.europa.eu/doi/10.2777/620649

30. Obrst, L., Baclawski, K.: The OOR initiative – an update announcing the new OOR logo designed by: Ali Hashemi, pp. 1–23 (2011)

31. Whetzel, P.L., Team, N.: NCBO technology: powering semantically aware applications. Biomed. Semant. **4S1**, 49 (2013). https://doi.org/10.1186/2041-1480-4-S1-S8

32. Suominen, O., et al.: Publishing SKOS vocabularies with Skosmos. Manuscript submitted for review (2015)

33. Dai, M., et al.: An efficient solution for mapping free text to ontology terms. In: American Medical Informatics Association Symposium on Translational BioInformatics, AMIA-TBI 2008, San Francisco, CA, USA (2008)

34. Ghazvinian, A., Noy, N.F., Musen, M.A.: Creating mappings for ontologies in biomedicine: simple methods work. In: American Medical Informatics Association Annual Symposium, AMIA 2009, Washington DC, USA, pp. 198–202 (2009)

35. Matentzoglu, N., et al.: A simple standard for sharing ontological mappings (SSSOM). Database 2022 (2022). https://doi.org/10.1093/database/baac035
36. Noy, N.F., Dorf, M., Griffith, N.B., Nyulas, C., Musen, M.A.: Harnessing the power of the community in a library of biomedical ontologies. In: Clark, T., Luciano, J.S., Marshall, M.S., Prud'hommeaux, E., Stephens, S. (eds.) Workshop on Semantic Web Applications in Scientific Discourse, SWASD 2009, Washington DC, USA, p. 11 (2009)
37. Jonquet, C., Shah, N.H., Musen, M.A.: The open biomedical annotator. In: American Medical Informatics Association Symposium on Translational BioInformatics, AMIA-TBI 2009, San Francisco, CA, USA, pp. 56–60 (2009)
38. Martinez-Romero, M., Jonquet, C., O'Connor, M.J., Graybeal, J., Pazos, A., Musen, M.A.: NCBO ontology recommender 2.0: an enhanced approach for biomedical ontology recommendation. Biomed. Semant. **8** (2017). https://doi.org/10.1186/s13326-017-0128-y
39. Salvadores, M., Horridge, M., Alexander, P.R., Fergerson, R.W., Musen, M.A., Noy, N.F.: Using SPARQL to query BioPortal ontologies and metadata. In: Cudré-Mauroux, P., et al. (eds.) ISWC 2012. LNCS, vol. 7650, pp. 180–195. Springer, Heidelberg (2012). https://doi.org/10.1007/978-3-642-35173-0_12
40. Melzi, S., Jonquet, C.: Scoring semantic annotations returned by the NCBO annotator. In: Paschke, A., Burger, A., Romano, P., Marshall, M.S., Splendiani, A. (eds.) 7th International Semantic Web Applications and Tools for Life Sciences, SWAT4LS 2014, p. 15. CEUR-WS.org, Berlin, Germany (2014)
41. Dutta, B., Toulet, A., Emonet, V., Jonquet, C.: New generation metadata vocabulary for ontology description and publication. In: Garoufallou, E., Virkus, S., and Alemu, G. (eds.) 11th Metadata and Semantics Research Conference, MTSR 2017, Tallinn, Estonia (2017). https://doi.org/10.1007/978-3-319-70863-8_17
42. Amdouni, E., Bouazzouni, S., Jonquet, C.: O'FAIRe: ontology FAIRness evaluator in the AgroPortal semantic resource repository. In: Groth, P., et al. (eds.) SWC 2022. LNCS, vol. 13384. Springer, Cham (2022). https://doi.org/10.1007/978-3-031-11609-4_17
43. Jonquet, C., Bouazzouni, S.: State-of-the-art browsing of SKOS resources in AgroPortal. In: NKOS Consolidated Workshop, Daegu, South Korea (2023)
44. Jonquet, C., Graybeal, J., OntoPortal Alliance, M. of the: OntoPortal Workshop 2022 Report, Montpellier, France (2022)
45. Jonquet, C.: Ontology Repository and Ontology-Based Services – Challenges, contributions and applications to biomedicine & agronomy (2019). https://tel.archives-ouvertes.fr/

AsdKB: A Chinese Knowledge Base for the Early Screening and Diagnosis of Autism Spectrum Disorder

Tianxing Wu[1,2(✉)], Xudong Cao[1], Yipeng Zhu[1], Feiyue Wu[1], Tianling Gong[1], Yuxiang Wang[3], and Shenqi Jing[4,5]

[1] Southeast University, Nanjing, China
{tianxingwu,xudongcao,yipengzhu,wufeiyue,gtl2019}@seu.edu.cn
[2] Key Laboratory of New Generation Artificial Intelligence Technology and Its Interdisciplinary Applications (Southeast University), Ministry of Education, Nanjing, China
[3] Hangzhou Dianzi University, Hangzhou, China
lsswyx@hdu.edu.cn
[4] The First Affiliated Hospital of Nanjing Medical University, Nanjing, China
[5] Nanjing Medical University, Nanjing, China
jingshenqi@jsph.org.cn

Abstract. To easily obtain the knowledge about autism spectrum disorder and help its early screening and diagnosis, we create AsdKB, a Chinese knowledge base on autism spectrum disorder. The knowledge base is built on top of various sources, including 1) the disease knowledge from SNOMED CT and ICD-10 clinical descriptions on mental and behavioural disorders, 2) the diagnostic knowledge from DSM-5 and different screening tools recommended by social organizations and medical institutes, and 3) the expert knowledge on professional physicians and hospitals from the Web. AsdKB contains both ontological and factual knowledge, and is accessible as Linked Data at https://w3id.org/asdkb/. The potential applications of AsdKB are question answering, auxiliary diagnosis, and expert recommendation, and we illustrate them with a prototype which can be accessed at http://asdkb.org.cn/.

Keywords: Autism Spectrum Disorder · Knowledge Base · Ontology

1 Introduction

Autism spectrum disorder (ASD) is a kind of neurodevelopmental disability which begins before the age of 3 years and can last throughout a person's whole life. People with ASD have problems in social communication and interaction, and may have stereotypic or repetitive behaviors (or interests). According to the most recent statistics [17] published by the Centers for Disease Control and Prevention (CDC), about 1 in 36 children aged 8 years has been identified with ASD, and this proportion is quite high. However, there is no quantitative

T. R. Payne et al. (Eds.): ISWC 2023, LNCS 14266, pp. 59–75, 2023.
https://doi.org/10.1007/978-3-031-47243-5_4

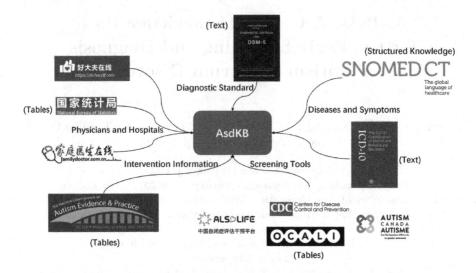

Fig. 1. The data sources for building AsdKB.

medical test to diagnose such a disorder, and professional physicians only use screening tools and look at the behaviors for some time to make a diagnosis. In this way, many children cannot receive a final diagnosis until much older, which causes the children with ASD might not get the early help they need. In China, the situation on screening and diagnosing the children with ASD maybe much worse compared with western developed countries. The 2020 China rehabilitation report of children developmental disorder[1] points out that the ASD incidence in China is around 1% and the number of ASD children is more than three million, but the number of professional physicians who can diagnose ASD is only about 500, let alone the number of board certified behavior analysts. This does hinder the timely diagnosis on ASD, which inspires us to think about if we can apply artificial intelligence techniques to solve the early screening and diagnosis of ASD. The key problem is how to extract and integrate ASD relevant knowledge from heterogeneous sources to support upper-level intelligent applications.

To solve this problem, we build AsdKB, a Chinese knowledge base for the early screening and diagnosis of ASD, from various sources (see Fig. 1), such as SNOMED CT [5] (a large collection of medical terms), ICD-10[2] (the 10th revision of the classification system of diseases published by WHO) clinical descriptions on mental and behavioural disorders [21], DSM-5 [1] (the 5th edition of diagnostic and statistical manual of mental disorders), the screening tools recommended by CDC and so on. Specifically, we first build an ontology covering important concepts about the screening and diagnosis of ASD from DSM-5, ICD-10 clinical descriptions on mental and behavioural disorders, SNOMED CT, CDC materials, and other Web sources. Using this ontology as the schema, we

---

[1] http://pkucarenjk.com/news-family/2303.html.

[2] https://en.wikipedia.org/wiki/ICD-10.

then extract and integrate factual knowledge on diseases, diagnosis, experts, and others. Besides, we use and develop Web crawler and natural language processing (NLP) tools for data extraction, keyword extraction, knowledge extraction, machine translation, and etc., over various formats of data, including text, tables, and structured knowledge. All classes, properties, and instances in AsdKB are identified by permanent dereferenceable URIs in w3id[3]. All data are available as RDF dump files on Zenodo[4], and the basic information of the AsdKB project can be accessed at Github[5]. All the resources are published under CC BY-SA 4.0. The main contributions of this paper are summarized as follows:

- We first build a Chinese knowledge base for the early screening and diagnosis of ASD, i.e., AsdKB, which contains both ontological and factual knowledge, and publish it following Linked Data best practices.
- We present a prototype system on question answering, auxiliary diagnosis, and expert recommendation with AsdKB, and discuss how to support the early screening and diagnosis of ASD with this system.

The rest of this paper is organized as follows. Section 2 introduces the process of ontology building. Section 3 describes the extraction of factual knowledge. Section 4 presents the potential applications of AsdKB. Section 5 outlines related work, and we conclude in the last section.

2   Ontology Building

This section introduces the process of building the AsdKB ontology as the schema which is used to guide extracting and integrating factual knowledge from various sources. We follow Ontology Development 101 [20] to build the ontology (Fig. 2 shows a part of it) as follows.

Step 1: Determine the domain and scope of the ontology. AsdKB is expected to cover the ASD relevant knowledge on the early screening and diagnosis, so the ontology needs to cover important concepts in widely recognized materials about the screening and diagnosis of ASD. Here, we select relevant materials from CDC, DSM-5, ICD-10, SNOMED-CT, and other Web sources.

Step 2: Consider reusing existing ontologies. In this part, we reuse the standard RDF, RDFS, and OWL vocabularies, including `rdf:type` linking from instances to classes, `rdfs:label` recording the Chinese (or English) labels of classes and properties, `rdfs:comment` providing textual descriptions to clarify meanings of classes, `rdfs:subClassOf` describing the class hierarchy, equivalent classes are linked by `owl:equivalentClass` from the AsdKB ontology to other ontologies, and `rdfs:domain` and `rdfs:range` specifying the resources and values of a property are instances of one or more classes, respectively.

---

[3] https://w3id.org/asdkb/.
[4] https://zenodo.org/record/8199698.
[5] https://github.com/SilenceSnake/ASDKB.

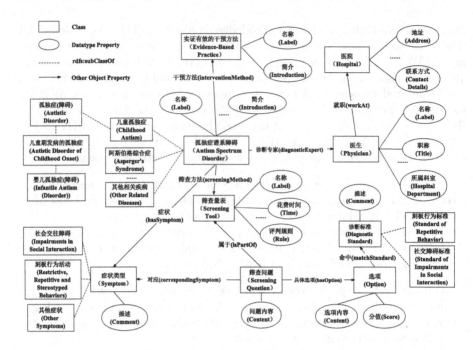

Fig. 2. A part of the AsdKB ontology.

Step 3: Enumerate important terms in the ontology. We read the ASD materials from CDC, DSM-5, ICD-10, SNOMED CT and other Web sources mentioned in the first step, to manually identify a list of important concept-level terms. For example, important symptom concepts in disease knowledge include "Impairments in Social Interaction" and " Restrictive, Repetitive and Stereotyped Behaviors". Important concepts in expert knowledge include "Physician" and "Hospital". Besides, "Screening Tool" and "Diagnostic Standard" are related to screening and diagnosis.

Step 4: Define the classes and the class hierarchy. Based on the previous identified important terms, we start to create disease classes (e.g., "Autism Spectrum Disorder" and "Asperger's Syndrome"), diagnosis classes (e.g., "Screening Tool" and "Screening Question"), expert classes (e.g., "Physician" and "Hospital"), and others. For the class hierarchy, we consider the hierarchies within disease classes, symptom classes, and diagnosis classes, respectively. For example, as shown in Fig. 2, we have "Asperger's Syndrome rdfs:subClassOf Autism Spectrum Disorder" and "Standard of Social Interaction rdfs:subClassOf Diagnostic Standard". Specifically, we have created a class "Screening Question" in the diagnosis classes to facilitate the exploration of the association between instances of "Screening Question" and "Diagnostic Standard".

Step 5: Define the properties of classes. After selecting classes from the list of terms, we start to attach properties to classes using rdfs:domain. We distinguish datatype properties and object properties. For example, for the class "Physician", we have the object property workAt and datatype properties Name, Title, Specialty, Hospital Department, and etc.

Step 6: Define the facets of the properties. We specify the value type of each property by defining rdfs:range. The range of a datatype property is an XML Schema datatype. For example, the ranges of properties Address (attached to the class "Hospital") and Score (attached to the class "Option") are xsd:string and xsd:float, respectively. Besides, the range of an object property is a class. For example, the range of hasSymptom is the "Symptom".

Step 7: Create instances. We do not define instances in the ontology but only use it as the schema of AsdKB. The creation of instances belongs to factual knowledge extraction, and it will be described in Sect. 3.

Statistics About the AsdKB Ontology. The built ontology is currently online: https://w3id.org/asdkb/ontology/. It contains 32 classes, 25 datatype properties, and 16 object properties. The maximum depth of a class in the class hierarchy is 4. Note that we apply google translate[6] to translate the English labels of all elements in the ontology into Chinese ones, and also perform careful manual proofreading and correction.

Mapping to Other Ontologies. To facilitate schema knowledge sharing across different ontologies, We map our AsdKB ontology to the Unified Medical Language System [2] (UMLS) and the Autism DSM-ADI-R (ADAR) ontology [19]. UMLS is the largest integrated biomedical ontology covering the vocabularies from around 200 sources including SNOMED CT, DSM-5, FMA [23], and etc. ADAR is built from Autism Diagnostic Interview-Revised [16] (ADI-R), which is a structured interview used for autism diagnosis. ADAR focuses on autism symptom classification, and it constructs many fine-grained symptom classes, e.g., "First walked unaided" and "Daily spontaneous and meaningful speech", which are taken as instances in AsdKB. This is why we do not directly re-use ADAR in AsdKB.

Since the disease classes in the AsdKB ontology are extracted from SNOMED CT, which is also a part of UMLS, such classes are naturally linked to UMLS (see the Example 1 in Fig. 3). For the rest eighteen classes in AsdKB, we submit each of their labels to UMLS Metathesaurus Browser[7] and manually make comparisons between the returned classes and submitted ones to decide whether there exist owl:equivalentClass or rdfs:subClassOf relations (the Example 2 in Fig. 3 gives a mapping result). Besides, we apply AgreementMakerLight [6] to mapping the AsdKB ontology to ADAR, and the Example 3 in Fig. 3 also shows a mapping result.

---

[6] https://translate.google.com/.
[7] https://uts.nlm.nih.gov/uts/umls/home.

```
Example 1:
<https://w3id.org/asdkb/ontology/class/autism_spectrum_disorder>  owl:equivalentClass
<https://uts.nlm.nih.gov/uts/umls/concept/C1510586> .

Example 2:
<https://w3id.org/asdkb/ontology/class/physician>  rdfs:subClassOf
<https://uts.nlm.nih.gov/uts/umls/concept/C0031831> .

Example 3:
<https://w3id.org/asdkb/ontology/class/restrictive_repetitive_and_stereotyped_behaviors>
owl:equivalentClass
<http://purl.org/autism-ontology/class/1.0/autism-rules.owl#Restricted_and_Repetitive_Behavior> .
```

Fig. 3. Examples of mapping the AsdKB ontology to UMLS and ADAR.

3   Factual Knowledge Extraction

This section presents the extraction of factual knowledge of ASD. Due to limited spaces, we do not explain every detail but focus on the main content.

3.1   Disease Knowledge

For disease knowledge, we need to extract the factual knowledge about disease and symptom instances according to the AsdKB ontology. Disease instances (e.g., "Atypical Rett syndrome") are derived from SNOMED CT, and they are actually the leaf nodes in the disease taxonomy in SNOMED CT. For each disease instance, we extract the values of the properties: Label (instance name), SCTID (the term ID in SNOMED CT), ICD-10 code (the corresponding ICD-10 category), and Synonym from SNOMED CT, respectively. We also manually design templates (i.e., regular expressions) to extract the values of properties Introduction (a brief description of the given disease instance), Patient Groups (e.g., "children" or "female children"), and Pathogeny (e.g., "genetic and environmental factors") from ICD-10 clinical descriptions on mental and behavioural disorders [21], respectively. Besides, for the values of properties Label, Synonym, Introduction, Patient Groups, and Pathogeny, we obtain the corresponding Chinese versions by Google Translate and manual proofreading. We collect 49 disease instances relevant to ASD in total, and their corresponding property information.

Symptom instances are also extracted from ICD-10 clinical descriptions on mental and behavioural disorders. We model the symptom instance extraction as the task of sequence labeling. We first take each paragraph as a document, and apply Term Frequency-Inverse Document Frequency [15] (TF-IDF) to identify keywords. Based on this, we then label a small amount of symptom instances in the corpus to train an extraction model. Here, we use BioBERT [14], a pretrained biomedical language representation model for biomedical text mining, to encode each word as an embedding. Afterwards, we utilize BiLSTM [7] to capture textual context features for each word. Finally, we apply conditional random fields [13] to finishing sequence labeling, which naturally classifies symptom instances to the pre-defined symptom classes, i.e., "Impairments in Social Interaction", " Restrictive, Repetitive and Stereotyped Behaviors", and "Other Symptoms". High-quality results of sequence labeling obtained by the trained model will be added to the labeled data to train a new model. We repeat this process until the maximum number of iterations is reached. Google Translate is also used to get the Chinese description of each symptom instance. Figure 4 shows the triples of the symptom <https://w3id.org/asdkb/instance/symptom64>. Finally, We collect 65 symptom instances in total.

```
<https://w3id.org/asdkb/instance/symptom64>   rdfs:comment
"a resistance to changes in routine or in details of the personal environment (such as the movement
of ornaments or furniture in the family home)."@en .

<https://w3id.org/asdkb/instance/symptom64 >   rdfs:comment
"对日常生活或个人环境细节变化的抵制（如家庭中装饰品或家具的移动）"@zh .

<https://w3id.org/asdkb/instance/symptom64 >   rdf:type
<https://w3id.org/asdkb/ontology/class/restrictive_repetitive_and_stereotyped_behaviors> .
```

Fig. 4. An example of the triples containing a symptom instance.

3.2 Diagnostic Knowledge

For diagnostic knowledge, we extract the factual knowledge on the instances of diagnostic standards, screening tools, screening questions, and the corresponding options. Instances of diagnostic standards are acquired from the Chinese edition[8] of DSM-5 [1], so we only have Chinese descriptions for the instances of diagnostic standards. We follow a similar process used for extracting symptom instances, and only replace the pre-trained model BioBERT with a more general model BERT [11] because BioBERT does not support Chinese but BERT does. Different from symptom instances, instances of diagnostic standards do not refer to specific behaviors or activities of the people with ASD, they actually present textual summarizations for specific classes of diagnostic standards (i.e., "Standard of Repetitive Behavior" and "Standard of Impairments in Social Interaction"). For example, an instance of diagnostic standards in AsdKB is expressed as " 眼神接触、手势、面部表情、身体定位或言语语调等方面的缺乏、减少或不合规的使用 (abnormalities in eye contact and body language or deficits in understanding and use of gestures)", which corresponds to multiple symptom instances, e.g., " 不会进行对视 (without eye contact)" and "很少微笑 (rarely smile)". We collect 43 instances of diagnostic standards in total.

Regarding instances of screening tools, screening questions, and options, we extract them and the corresponding property values from the websites of social

---

[8] https://www.worldcat.org/zh-cn/title/1052824369.

organizations and medical institutes, including CDC[9], ALSOLIFE[10] (China ASD Evaluation and Intervention Platform), Autism Canada[11], and OCALI[12] (The Ohio Center for Autism and Low Incidence). Instances of screening tools in AsdKB are actually screening scales, which have the properties Introduction (basic information and instructions), Author, User (the one filling in the scale, e.g., parents or teacher), Age (applicable ages of screening targets), Time (the time it takes to fill in the scale), Rule (screening principles and details), and Screening Boundary (the score of screening boundary after finishing the scale). After careful selection, we extract twenty instances of screening tools, containing fifteen English screening scales and five Chinese ones, such as ABC [12], CARS2 [24], and M-CHAT [27]. Google Translate is used here to translate English scales into Chinese ones, and manual proofreading is also conducted.

For instances of screening questions and options, they can be directly obtained from screening scales through table extraction. Besides keeping their textual content as the property, we also establish correspondingSymptom relationships between instances of screening questions and symptom instances, and matchStandard relationships between option instances and instances of diagnostic standards. These two kinds of relationships (i.e., object properties) benefit to the interpretability of screening results. For example, as shown in Fig. 5, AsdKB can tell users that the current question investigates what specific symptoms are and whether the current option matches some diagnostic standard or not, in order to help users better understand screening questions and provide explanations to screening results. To identify correspondingSymptom relationships, we first use FNLP [22] to perform Chinese word segmentation on the instances of screening questions and symptom instances. After removing stopwords, we then compare string similarities between two word sequences to decide whether the correspondingSymptom relationship exists. The method of extracting matchStandard relationships is similar to that of correspondingSymptom relationships, and the only difference is to additionally consider the property Score of each option. If an option has the highest score or lowest score, it means the result of the current screening question is abnormal or normal (it ups to the design of screening scales), and abnormal results could help identify matchStandard relationships.

3.3   Expert Knowledge

For expert knowledge, we extract factual knowledge of the instances of professional physicians, and the hospitals they work at, from the Web. We select two famous Chinese healthcare websites The Good Doctor[13] and Family Doctor[14]

---

[9] https://www.cdc.gov/ncbddd/autism/hcp-screening.html#Tools.

[10] https://www.alsolife.com/autism/screen/.

[11] https://autismcanada.org/autism-explained/screening-tools/.

[12] https://www.ocali.org/project/assessment_measures.

[13] https://www.haodf.com/.

[14] https://www.familydoctor.com.cn/.

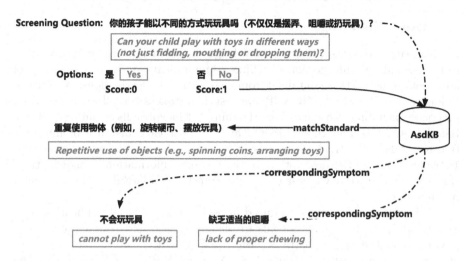

Fig. 5. An example to show the benefits of `correspondingSymptom` and `matchStandard` relationships.

as the data sources to extraction, so the string values of some datatype properties are only presented in Chinese. We first submit the following keywords "孤独症, 自闭症, 孤独症谱系障碍 (ASD)", "广泛性发育障碍 (pervasive developmental disorders)", "儿童孤独症 (childhood autism)", and "阿斯伯格综合症 (Asperger's syndrome)", to the search engines of the selected websites, which locates the Web pages of professional physicians on ASD. Faced with the structures like infobox tables in Wikipedia, we then extract physician instances and the values of properties `Name`, `Title` (e.g., "主任医师 (chief physician)" and "主治医师 (attending physician)"), `Specialty` (e.g., "各类儿童精神障碍 (various types of mental disorders in childhood)"), `Hospital Department` (e.g., "儿童保健科 (child healthcare department)" and "精神科 (psychiatry department)"), and `workAt` (i.e., hospital instances). We collect 499 physician instances in total.

According to the values of the property `workAt`, we locate the Web pages of hospital instances. Similar to the extraction on physician instances and the corresponding property information, we extract the hospital instances and the values of properties `Name`, `Address`, `Contact Details`, and `Hospital Level` (e.g., "三甲医院 (Grade-A tertiary hospital)"). We collect 270 hospital instances in total.

Since physician and hospital instances are extracted from different sources, we perform instance matching using heuristics. Given two hospital instances, if their values for at least one of the properties `Address` and `Contact Details` are the same, they are treated as equivalent. Given two physician instances, if their values for the property `workAt` are equivalent, and the values for the properties `Name` and `Title` are the same respectively, these two instances are determined as equivalent. Equivalent instances are fused as one instance in AsdKB.

3.4 Other Knowledge

In this part, we extract factual knowledge on the instances of intervention methods, and the information of China administrative divisions. Instances of intervention methods are obtained from The National Clearinghouse on Autism Evidence and Practice[15] (NCAEP), and such instances are all evidence-based practices, including "Discrete Trial Training", "Social Skills Training", "Peer-Based Instruction and Intervention", and etc. For each instance of intervention methods, we extract the values of properties Label (instance name) and Introduction (a brief description on the instance information). English string values are translated to Chinese by Google Translate, and we also conduct careful proofreading.

With expert knowledge introduced in Sect. 3.3, a potential application is to seek expertise help from physicians to diagnosis. In order to find professional physicians in the target districts, cities, and provinces, we extract instances of China administrative divisions from National Bureau of Statistics[16]. The extracted instances are specific districts, cities, and provinces, and we also build locateAt relationships among them. To link each hospital to the corresponding administrative divisions, we first use Amap (a leading provider of digital map in China) API[17] to get the latitude and longitude of each hospital by inputting the value of property address. With the information of latitudes and longitudes, Amap API can return the corresponding districts, cities, and provinces of hospitals. Besides, we record the Population of each instance of China administrative divisions, which could help regional analysis on ASD.

3.5 Quality of AsdKB

AsdKB contains 6,166 entities (including conceptual entities, i.e., classes, and individual entities, i.e., instances) and 69,290 triples in total. All class URIs in the namespace http://w3id.org/asdkb/ontology/class/ and instance URIs in the namespace http://w3id.org/asdkb/instance/ are dereferenceable. To evaluate the quality of AsdKB, we design two evaluation methods: accuracy evaluation, and task evaluation.

Accuracy Evaluation. There is no ground truth available, and it is impossible to evaluate all triples manually. Therefore, we apply a random evaluation strategy. We first randomly select 100 entities distributed across classes and instances, and obtain 732 triples. These samples can reflect the distribution of triples in the entire knowledge base. We then conduct manual labeling to evaluate the accuracy of the samples. The accuracy of the entire AsdKB is estimated by evaluating the accuracy of the samples.

Five graduate students participate in the labeling process. We provide three choices, which are *correct*, *incorrect*, and *unknown* to label each sample. After

---

[15] https://ncaep.fpg.unc.edu/.

[16] http://www.stats.gov.cn/.

[17] https://github.com/amapapi.

each student label all the samples, we calculate the average accuracy. Finally, similar to YAGO [10], Zhishi.me [28], and Linked Open Schema [29], we use the Wilson interval [3] when $\alpha = 5\%$ to extend our findings on the subset to the entire knowledge base. The Wilson interval is a binomial proportion confidence interval calculated from the results of a series of Bernoulli trials, and α is the significance level. For the randomly selected 732 triples, the average *correct* votes is 712, so the accuracy is $97.02\% \pm 1.21\%$, and it demonstrates the high quality of AsdKB.

Task Evaluation. Besides the accuracy of the triples in AsdKB, we try to evaluate the effectiveness of AsdKB in answering real-world ASD relevant questions. Thus, we collect 100 frequently asked questions (e.g., "孤独症都有哪些临床表现？ (What are the clinical symptoms of autism?)" and "哪些干预方法是有效的？ (Which interventions are effective?)") on ASD from Chinese healthcare websites The Good Doctor and Family Doctor (introduced in Sect. 3.3), which are also the data sources of the expert knowledge in AsdKB. We store AsdKB in a graph database Neo4j [26], and also invite five graduate students to manually write Cypher (Neo4's graph query language) queries for the collected questions so as to check whether the returned query results can answer the questions. According to the above evaluation, AsdKB can answer 81 questions, i.e., the coverage reaches to 81%, which reflects the practicality of AsdKB.

4   Application of AsdKB

To illustrate the potential application of AsdKB, this section describes the implementation of a prototype system[18] for the early screening and diagnosis of ASD based on AsdKB. This system has three main applications, including question answering, auxiliary diagnosis, and expert recommendation. Users of this system are parents, teachers, and caregivers.

4.1   Question Answering

We implement a natural language question answering (QA) system based on AsdKB, and expect that the QA system can answer various common-sense and factual questions on ASD. As mentioned in Sect. 3.5, AsdKB is stored in Neo4j, so we aim to translate each natural language question to a Cypher query, in order to query the graph database to return the answer. We use two strategies to design the QA system. The first one is to manually write common ASD relevant natural language query patterns (i.e., regular expressions) according to AsdKB ontology and the corresponding Cypher query templates. If a user query matches one of our patterns, then we construct and execute the corresponding Cypher query based on the pre-defined Cypher query template to get the answer. If the user query does not match our patterns, we use the second strategy, which applies the idea of the method for translating natural language questions to formal queries with semantic query graph modeling [31] to generating the Cypher query.

---

[18] http://asdkb.org.cn/.

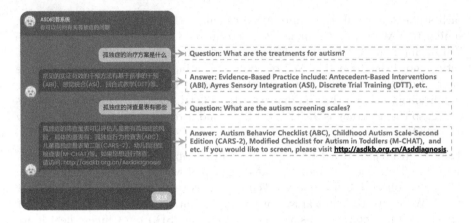

Fig. 6. The interface of the QA system.

Figure 6 shows the interface of our QA system. We also detect the intention of each question to check whether the user would like to further fill in screening scales. If so, the system will directly give the link of auxiliary diagnosis to help choose screening scales (see Fig. 6). The intention identification is modeled as a task of binary classification, where we use BERT to encode questions in the labeled data, and then train a SVM [9] classifier to predict whether users are willing to conduct screening or not.

4.2 Auxiliary Diagnosis

We have developed an auxiliary diagnosis system based on AsdKB. This system provides users with screening scales to assess the risk of being ASD. As long as the screening result of a screening scale shows a risk, the system will prompt the user to seek professional medical evaluation and recommend experts using our expert recommendation system (will be introduced in Sect. 4.3).

As shown in Fig. 7(a), before filling the screening scales, users can select appropriate screening conditions based on their situations, such as the child's age and existing symptoms, and the system will return the corresponding screening scales with a brief introduction (see Fig. 7(b)). Figure 7(c) shows the questions and options when filling in the ABC screening scale. After completing a screening scale, the system will give the screening result (i.e., risky or not) based on the total score of all options and the screening boundary.

When users are filling in screening scales, they can check what specific symptoms the current question investigates to better understand the question, so as to help make a choice more precisely. Besides, after completing screening scales, this system can also analyze which option matches some diagnostic standard, to provide explanations of the screening results. More details have already been introduced in Sect. 3.2 and Fig. 5.

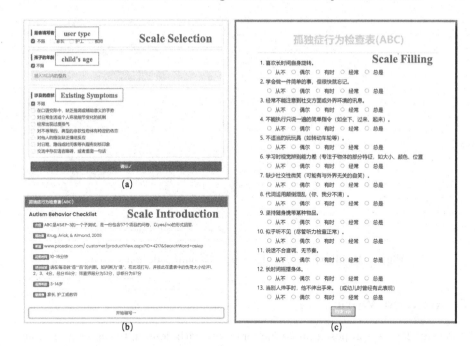

Fig. 7. An illustration of the auxiliary diagnosis system.

4.3   Expert Recommendation

If our auxiliary diagnosis system reports the risk of being ASD, users may have requirements to find experts on diagnosing ASD in the target administrative divisions. Thus, we design an expert recommendation system with facet search on AsdKB. Users can choose the target province, city and district by selecting a checkbox or directly clicking their locations on the map (see Fig. 8). The recommendation result is a list of professional physicians with their names, titles, hospital departments, hospitals, hospital addresses, and specialties.

The recommendation has two steps: candidate physician generation and candidate physician ranking. In candidate physician generation, we use the location information of hospitals in AsdKB to match user selected administrative divisions, and the physicians in AsdKB working at such hospitals are candidates. Note that if no candidate physician returns, we will consider more hospitals in surrounding administrative divisions by distance calculation with latitudes and longitudes. In the candidate physician ranking, three aspects are taken into consideration. Firstly, the higher the title, the higher the ranking. Secondly, the higher the hospital level, the higher the ranking. Finally, the higher the number of thumbs up minus the number of thumbs down (Fig. 8 gives an example), the higher the ranking.

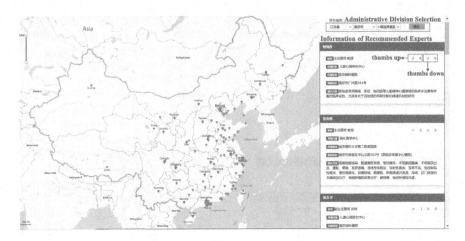

Fig. 8. An illustration of the expert recommendation system.

5   Related Work

Tu et al. [25] first proposed an autism ontology with domain terms and relationships relevant to autism phenotypes. The main target is to enable user queries and inferences about such phenotypes using data in the NDAR repository, but it does not include DSM criteria, so it does not support diagnosis of ASD. McCray et al. [18] also developed an ASD-phenotype ontology assessing and comparing different ASD diagnostic instruments, but it also does not include DSM-IV or DSM-5 criteria phenotypes. ADAR [19] extends an ontology proposed by Tu et al [25]. with additional SWRL rules to infer phenotypes from ADI-R [16] items, and it covers various symptoms and features of DSM IV and DSM-5 diagnostic criteria, such as difficulties with social interaction, language and communication issues, and stereotyped and repetitive behaviors. However, many fine-grained classes are actually instances in the generic sense.

The most recent work is AutismOnt [8], an ontology for autism diagnosis and treatment, which covers various covers autism research directions. AutismOnt includes the classes: Diagnosis, Risk Factors, Treatments, Strength and Weakness, Services, Lifespan Issues, Profile, and Family Relationships. However, although the authors claim that AutismOnt is available in the NCBO BioPortal, it cannot be found in the repository.

Some large-scale medical knowledge bases also contain ASD knowledge. For example, SNOMED CT [5] contains a large-scale number of medical terms, and the disease classes in AsdKB also comes from SNOMED CT, but it does not cover other kinds of knowledge, such as diagnostic knowledge and expert knowledge. Yuan et al. [30] proposed a method for constructing knowledge graphs with minimal supervision based on unstructured biomedical domain-specific contexts. They collected 24,687 abstracts of articles related to ASD from PubMed[19], and

---

[19] https://pubmed.ncbi.nlm.nih.gov/.

constructed a knowledge graph on ASD. However, they did not design the ontology and the knowledge graph is not publicly available. CMeKG [4] is a Chinese medical knowledge graph developed using natural language processing and text mining techniques from a large amount of medical text data. CMeKG mistakenly uses drugs as the treatment for ASD, but drugs are only used to alleviate the complications of ASD in fact.

Compared with all existing works, AsdKB is the first publicly available Chinese knowledge base on ASD, and it contains both ontological and factual knowledge about diseases, diagnosis, experts, and others. AsdKB has been applied in developing applications of the early screening and diagnosis of ASD.

6   Conclusions and Future Work

We develop and publish a Chinese knowledge base on ASD called AsdKB by extracting and integrating knowledge from various data sources with different formats. To the best of our knowledge, AsdKB is the most comprehensive ASD knowledge base on the Web, and it supports the different applications on the early screening and diagnosis of ASD, such as question answering, auxiliary diagnosis, and expert recommendation. However, there are still some limitations to our work that we plan to address in the future.

Quality of AsdKB. During our preliminary evaluations of AsdKB, we discovered that the entities contained within the knowledge base are of high quality. However, errors do exist during the automatic extraction process. These errors stem from a variety of factors such as the quality of the original data sources, differences in data formats, and our integration methods. To address this issue, we plan to introduce crowd-sourcing techniques to fix the existing errors in AsdKB and study automatic error detection methods to ensure the accuracy of knowledge in the process of knowledge update.

Applications of AsdKB. We have explored various applications for AsdKB, including QA, auxiliary diagnosis, and expert recommendation. The integrated prototype system has demonstrated the potential for AsdKB to play a critical role in early ASD screening and diagnosis. To further improve the accuracy of QA and auxiliary diagnosis, we will incorporate data-driven machine learning models on more user log data in our prototype system. In addition to this, we plan to analyze electronic medical records if possible using AsdKB to assist physicians in ASD diagnosis. By analyzing medical histories, symptoms, and other relevant information using AsdKB, physicians can make more accurate diagnosis and give appropriate and personalised treatment suggestions to the people with ASD.

Acknowledgements. This work is supported by the NSFC (Grant No. 62006040, 62072149), the Project for the Doctor of Entrepreneurship and Innovation in Jiangsu Province (Grant No. JSSCBS20210126), the Fundamental Research Funds for the Central Universities, and ZhiShan Young Scholar Program of Southeast University.

References

1. American Psychiatric Association: Diagnostic and Statistical Manual of Mental Disorders: DSM-5, vol. 5 (2013)
2. Bodenreider, O.: The unified medical language system (UMLS): integrating biomedical terminology. Nucleic Acids Res. **32**(Suppl. 1), D267–D270 (2004)
3. Brown, L.D., Cai, T.T., DasGupta, A.: Interval estimation for a binomial proportion. Stat. Sci. **16**(2), 101–133 (2001)
4. Byambasuren, O., et al.: Preliminary study on the construction of Chinese medical knowledge graph. J. Chin. Inf. Process. **33**(10), 1–9 (2019)
5. Donnelly, K.: SNOMED-CT: the advanced terminology and coding system for eHealth. Stud. Health Technol. Inform. **121**, 279 (2006)
6. Faria, D., Pesquita, C., Santos, E., Palmonari, M., Cruz, I.F., Couto, F.M.: The AgreementMakerLight ontology matching system. In: Meersman, R., et al. (eds.) OTM 2013. LNCS, vol. 8185, pp. 527–541. Springer, Heidelberg (2013). https://doi.org/10.1007/978-3-642-41030-7_38
7. Graves, A., Schmidhuber, J.: Bidirectional LSTM networks for improved phoneme classification and recognition. Neural Netw. **18**(5–6), 602–610 (2005)
8. Hassan, M.M., Mokhtar, H.M.: AutismOnt: an ontology-driven decision support for autism diagnosis and treatment. Egypt. Inform. J. **23**(1), 95–103 (2022)
9. Hearst, M.A., Dumais, S.T., Osuna, E., Platt, J., Scholkopf, B.: Support vector machines. IEEE Intell. Syst. Appl. **13**(4), 18–28 (1998)
10. Hoffart, J., Suchanek, F.M., Berberich, K., Weikum, G.: YAGO2: a spatially and temporally enhanced knowledge base from Wikipedia. Artif. Intell. **194**, 28–61 (2013)
11. Kenton, J.D.M.W.C., Toutanova, L.K.: BERT: pre-training of deep bidirectional transformers for language understanding. In: Proceedings of NAACL, pp. 4171–4186 (2019)
12. Krug, D.A., Arick, J., Almond, P.: Behavior checklist for identifying severely handicapped individuals with high levels of autistic behavior. Child Psychol. Psychiatry Allied Disciplines (1980)
13. Lafferty, J.D., McCallum, A., Pereira, F.C.: Conditional random fields: probabilistic models for segmenting and labeling sequence data. In: Proceedings of ICML, pp. 282–289 (2001)
14. Lee, J., et al.: BioBERT: a pre-trained biomedical language representation model for biomedical text mining. Bioinformatics **36**(4), 1234–1240 (2020)
15. Leskovec, J., Rajaraman, A., Ullman, J.D.: Mining of Massive Data Sets. Cambridge University Press, Cambridge (2020)
16. Lord, C., Rutter, M., Le Couteur, A.: Autism diagnostic interview-revised: a revised version of a diagnostic interview for caregivers of individuals with possible pervasive developmental disorders. J. Autism Dev. Disord. **24**(5), 659–685 (1994)
17. Maenner, M.J., et al.: Prevalence and characteristics of autism spectrum disorder among children aged 8 years - autism and developmental disabilities monitoring network, 11 sites, United States, 2020. MMWR Surveill. Summ. **72**(2), 1 (2023)
18. McCray, A.T., Trevvett, P., Frost, H.R.: Modeling the autism spectrum disorder phenotype. Neuroinformatics **12**, 291–305 (2014)
19. Mugzach, O., Peleg, M., Bagley, S.C., Guter, S.J., Cook, E.H., Altman, R.B.: An ontology for autism spectrum disorder (ASD) to infer ASD phenotypes from autism diagnostic interview-revised data. J. Biomed. Inform. **56**, 333–347 (2015)

20. Noy, N.F., McGuinness, D.L.: Ontology development 101: a guide to creating your first ontology. Technical report, Standford University (2001)
21. World Health Organization: The ICD-10 Classification of Mental and Behavioural Disorders: clinical descriptions and diagnostic guidelines. World Health Organization (1992)
22. Qiu, X., Zhang, Q., Huang, X.J.: FudanNLP: a toolkit for Chinese natural language processing. In: Proceedings of ACL, pp. 49–54 (2013)
23. Rosse, C., Mejino Jr, J.L.: The foundational model of anatomy ontology. In: Anatomy Ontologies for Bioinformatics: Principles and Practice, pp. 59–117 (2008)
24. Schopler, E., Van Bourgondien, M., Wellman, G., Love, S.: Childhood Autism Rating Scale-Second Edition (CARS-2). Western Psychological Services, Los Angeles (2010)
25. Tu, S.W., Tennakoon, L., O'Connor, M., Shankar, R., Das, A.: Using an integrated ontology and information model for querying and reasoning about phenotypes: the case of autism. In: AMIA Annual Symposium Proceedings, vol. 2008, p. 727 (2008)
26. Webber, J.: A programmatic introduction to Neo4j. In: Proceedings of SPLASH, pp. 217–218 (2012)
27. Wright, K., Poulin-Dubois, D.: Modified checklist for autism in toddlers (M-CHAT): validation and correlates in infancy. Compr. Guide Autism 80, 2813–2833 (2014)
28. Wu, T., et al.: Knowledge graph construction from multiple online encyclopedias. World Wide Web 23, 2671–2698 (2020)
29. Wu, T., Wang, H., Qi, G., Zhu, J., Ruan, T.: On building and publishing linked open schema from social web sites. J. Web Semant. 51, 39–50 (2018)
30. Yuan, J., et al.: Constructing biomedical domain-specific knowledge graph with minimum supervision. Knowl. Inf. Syst. 62, 317–336 (2020)
31. Zou, L., Huang, R., Wang, H., Yu, J.X., He, W., Zhao, D.: Natural language question answering over RDF: a graph data driven approach. In: Proceedings of SIGMOD, pp. 313–324 (2014)

TEC: Transparent Emissions Calculation Toolkit

Milan Markovic[1($\boxtimes$)] , Daniel Garijo[2] , Stefano Germano[3] ,
and Iman Naja[4]

[1] Interdisciplinary Centre for Data and AI, School of Natural and Computing
Sciences, University of Aberdeen, Aberdeen, UK
milan.markovic@abdn.ac.uk
[2] Ontology Engineering Group, Universidad Politécnica de Madrid, Madrid, Spain
daniel.garijo@upm.es
[3] Department of Computer Science, University of Oxford, Oxford, UK
stefano.germano@cs.ox.ac.uk
[4] Knowledge Media Institute, The Open University, Milton Keynes, UK
iman.naja@open.ac.uk

Abstract. Greenhouse gas emissions have become a common means for
determining the carbon footprint of any commercial activity, ranging
from booking a trip or manufacturing a product to training a machine
learning model. However, calculating the amount of emissions associated with these activities can be a difficult task, involving estimations of
energy used and considerations of location and time period. In this paper,
we introduce the Transparent Emissions Calculation (TEC) toolkit, an
open source effort aimed at addressing this challenge. Our contributions
include two ontologies (ECFO and PECO) that represent emissions conversion factors and the provenance traces of carbon emissions calculations (respectively), a public knowledge graph with thousands of conversion factors (with their corresponding YARRRML and RML mappings)
and a prototype carbon emissions calculator which uses our knowledge
graph to produce a transparent emissions report.
Resource permanent URL: https://w3id.org/tec-toolkit.

Keywords: Ontology · GHG Emissions · Carbon Accounting ·
Transparency

1 Introduction

The Net Zero agenda has gained significant traction across the world, with over
40 countries worldwide requiring organisations to periodically calculate and
report their greenhouse gas (GHG) emissions [29]. Calculating them requires
real-world data observations quantifying various aspects of business activities
(e.g., amount of fuel consumed by a fleet of vehicles) and additional resources
such as methodologies for transforming activity data into GHG estimates (also
referred to as emissions scores). Reported emissions scores may differ depending on various factors including the calculation methodology and software used,

T. R. Payne et al. (Eds.): ISWC 2023, LNCS 14266, pp. 76–93, 2023.
https://doi.org/10.1007/978-3-031-47243-5_5

geopolitical location, government requirements for reporting methods, applicable emissions conversion factors (ECFs), and the type of reported GHG emissions. Emissions calculations may also include unintentional errors, such as the use of ECFs which might be out of date, from unreliable publishers, or incorrectly applied to a specific activity, thus causing erroneous results. In addition, organisations may have a vested interest in deliberately under-reporting on certain aspects of carbon footprint if they deem it could have negative impact on the company image [20].

While reporting requirements may differ from one country to another, organisations are expected to be transparent about their submitted results. Achieving such transparency may be challenging as it requires a clear history of which ECFs were used and how the emissions scores were calculated including details about the origin and accuracy of the input data. These details are typically communicated in the form of free text reports which are not suitable for automated processing. However, such transparency is necessary to support assessments evaluating the trustworthiness and meaningful comparison of emissions scores reported by organisations across different sectors over time. We argue that provenance traces of such calculations described in the form of Knowledge Graphs (KGs) potentially provide a machine-understandable solution to this challenge by making the calculations more transparent and providing the means for automated processing and analysis. This is a core motivation for our Transparent Emissions Calculation (TEC) toolkit which aims to address this issue by providing ontologies and software tools for enhancing the transparency of emissions calculations using KGs. Our contributions include:

- Two ontologies for representing carbon emissions calculations: the Emission Conversion Factor Ontology (ECFO) and the Provenance of Emission Calculations Ontology (PECO)
- Machine-actionable mappings for transforming open ECFs data to a KG described using ECFO
- A public KG comprising of open data containing ECFs published by two different sources [10, 24]
- A logic-based data validation module for the information included in the KG
- A prototype software implementation of a Semantic Machine Learning Impact calculator using various components of the TEC toolkit

The remainder of the paper is structured as follows: Sect. 2 describes related work including existing software solutions for supporting emissions calculations and semantic models considering the concept of GHG emissions; Sect. 3 describes the design of the TEC toolkit; Sect. 4 introduces ECFO and PECO ontologies, their design methodology and evaluation; Sect. 5 describes the validation of ECFO through building a public KG of ECFs; Sect. 6 describes the Semantic MLI calculator built to evaluate PECO's and ECFO's utility in the context of a software application; and Sect. 7 concludes the paper with final remarks and discussion of future work.

2 Related Work

Several ontologies have been proposed to model different aspects or sources of energy emissions, applied to different domains: in the manufacturing domain, Zhu *et al.* [42] present a carbon footprint labeling ontology to support calculation and inference of the carbon footprints of products and services (unfortunately no longer available). In [41], Zhou *et al.* present an ontology for cutting tool configuration with the goal to reduce the time, cost, and carbon footprint, while in [40] Zhang *et al.* present an ontology for modelling the carbon footprint of manufacturing mechanical products. In the logistics domain, Torres [35] describes an ontology which models performance metrics for freight transportation including safety, mobility, traffic congestion, and environment sustainability. In the built environment domain, Petri *et. al.* [31] presents an ontology that supports a digital twin model aimed at performance measurement and optimisation which include energy consumption and savings. Finally, the Open Energy Ontology[1] (OEO) [4] is a large community-led open source ontology designed for use in energy systems analysis and modelling across energy domains and to date has grown to contain over 1430 classes. The scope of these ontologies goes beyond representing conversion factor metadata, focusing on specific domains. These approaches propose mechanisms to capture emission activities (e.g., burning fuel) and consider emission factors as process attributes which qualify them. However, none of these efforts represent metadata of the corresponding ECFs used to quantify emissions or the calculations they take part in, which is the focus of our work. In fact, to the best of our knowledge, no other vocabulary focuses on capturing the provenance of emission calculations e.g., by aligning it with W3C standards (such as PROV [25] for provenance, Time [7] for applicable periods or SOSA for observations [19]) to facilitate data consumption and interoperability. A first step in this direction was presented in [17], but it was based on a more generic model and did not provide specific concepts and relations for ECFs.

From a data perspective, most countries that mandate emissions reporting require organisations to use resources provided by their governments to estimate, calculate and report emissions, with some of them providing tools to support these activities. For example, the UK government publishes an updated list of ECFs yearly as open data [10], and provides a toolkit where users can manually estimate their emissions [11]. In the US, the United States Environmental Protection Agency also publishes emission conversion factors on a yearly basis [36], along with a corresponding online platform[2] where users may enter data manually via web-forms. The GHG Protocol publishes spreadsheets to assist in the reporting of emissions by country, city, or sector [18] and the Intergovernmental Panel on Climate Change (IPCC) provides an emission factor database and application [23]. While accessing these data sources is free, working with the integrated data is challenging, as it is often made available in heterogeneous spreadsheets.

---

[1] https://openenergy-platform.org/ontology.

[2] https://ghgreporting.epa.gov.

Companies aim to address this data integration gap with generic (e.g., IBM [22] and Oracle [30]) and domain specific emissions calcualtors (e.g., in the logistics domain [5] and in the agriculture domain [2]). However, the opaque nature of these tools prevents their results to be easily validated or explained which becomes especially problematic in case of varying results for the same activity generated by different solutions [8,34].

Recent efforts such as Climatiq [6] have also appeared to provide API access to multi-agency ECF data in a developer-friendly format. However, these databases are not free and the APIs use application-specific request parameters (e.g., names of the units, activity identifiers) which are not defined in a formal reusable vocabulary.

3   TEC Toolkit Design

We identified the key design requirements of the TEC toolkit by assessing current UK government [10] practices for reporting ECFs and through discussions with carbon accounting experts who contributed to the development of the competency questions for our ontologies. Our requirements were also influenced by a literature review of the state of the art, in particular by current practices for measuring the impact of training AI models based on the hardware, duration and location used for training [24]. Below we summarise the main aspects of the TEC toolkit design:

Purpose: To provide the means for representing, generating, sharing, querying, and validating semantic provenance descriptions of GHG emissions calculation processes including their inputs (e.g., ECFs for different emission sources) and resulting emissions scores.

Scope: The toolkit aims to represent and map the ECFs published by different authoritative data sources with open licenses, along with their usage in emissions calculations. To narrow the scope, we targeted the UK Department for Business, Energy & Industrial Strategy (BEIS) as a data source, and calculated the provenance of ML emissions as the main activity track.

Target Users: (*1*) Organisations which report on their emissions; (*2*) Researchers in the carbon accounting domain who would like to use the toolkit or expand on its components; (*3*) Software engineers who build software to support emissions calculation processes; (*4*) Auditors and compliance officers who may use the ECF KG and other TEC toolkit software to evaluate the GHG emissions reports submitted by organisations; and (*5*) Policy-makers aiming to standardise machine-understandable GHG emissions reporting and automated carbon footprint analysis across industry sectors.

Intended Uses: (*1*) Supporting transparency by providing tools to record provenance of reported emissions scores; (*2*) Supporting the automated validations of emissions calculations to reduce errors; (*3*) Integrating data resources (e.g., ECFs) required to perform and analyse the results of emissions calculations from heterogeneous sources, and support their comparison.

Competency Questions: Based on our requirements, we created competency questions for our vocabularies, which are available online[3],[4] together with example SPARQL queries and test datasets.

Governance: The TEC Toolkit is open for contributions from the community. All our repositories include contribution guidelines specifying how to propose new terms to our ontologies, new mappings for existing open datasets, or suggest new open datasets to integrate. New suggestions are addressed through GitHub issues.

4   TEC Toolkit Ontologies

The TEC toolkit contains two ontologies: the Emission Conversion Factor Ontology (ECFO)[5] and Provenance of Emission Calculations Ontology (PECO)[6]. Both ontologies are open source (CC-BY 4.0 license) and are maintained in public GitHub repositories.[7]

4.1   Methodology

We followed the Linked Open Terms methodology (LOT) [32], which proposes designing ontologies in four phases. For the first phase, the ontology requirements specification, we collected competency questions as outlined in Sect. 3. We decided to separate our ontologies in two separate vocabularies (Emission Conversion Factor Ontology (ECFO) and Provenance of Emission Calculations Ontology (PECO)), in order to ease their reusability in an independent manner. Each ontology has its corresponding requirement specification document (ORSD). ORSDs are organised as a CSV with one question per line in one column and the terms in the ontology used to address it in another column (new or reused from other vocabularies).

For the second phase (ontology implementation) we used Protégé [28] with the OWL syntax, and used LOV [37] to look for existing terms. For ECFO (see Sect. 4.2), we reused concepts from W3C PROV [25], Quantities, Units, Dimensions, and Types (QUDT) [12], Simple Knowledge Organization System (SKOS) [27], and W3C OWL-Time [7] to represent different metadata associated with an emission conversion factor. For PECO (see Sect. 4.2), we reused concepts from PROV, QUDT, and Semantic Sensor Network Ontology (SOSA) [19] ontologies to describe the provenance of emissions calculations. Ontologies were evaluated against their competency questions, as outlined in Sect. 4.4.

For the third phase (ontology publication) we generated the ontology documentations using WIDOCO [13], manually improving the results to add illustrative examples. Both ontologies have been made available using permanent URLs

---

[3] CQs for ECFO: https://github.com/TEC-Toolkit/ECFO/tree/main/cqs.

[4] CQs for PECO: https://github.com/TEC-Toolkit/PECO/tree/main/cqs.

[5] https://w3id.org/ecfo.

[6] https://w3id.org/peco.

[7] https://github.com/TEC-Toolkit/ECFO, https://github.com/TEC-Toolkit/PECO.

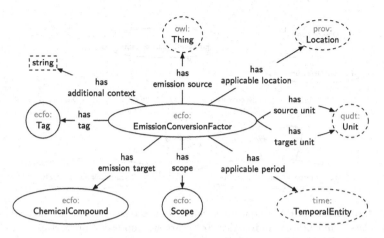

Fig. 1. Main entities of ECFO ontology. Solid ellipses represent classes, dashed ellipses refer to classes in external ontologies, dashed rectangles are RDFS datatypes and arrows represent properties.

through the w3id platform,[8] enabling content negotiation in multiple serialisations (RDF/XML, TTL, NT, JSON-LD). Each ontology has its own version IRI and a change log with the terms that differ between versions.

Finally, for the fourth phase (ontology maintenance) we tracked new issues, bugs and new requirements through GitHub issue trackers in the corresponding ontology repositories.

4.2   Emission Conversion Factors Ontology (ECFO)

ECFO aims to provide a generic model for describing the values of ECFs and their associated metadata. We represent ECFs as first class citizens, as shown in Fig. 1. Our terms have the *ecfo* prefix, while terms from imported ontologies such as W3C Time and W3C PROV use their corresponding prefixes (*time, prov*). *Ecfo:EmissionConversionFactor* represents the coefficient value used in GHG emissions calculations (i.e., activity data x emission conversion factor = GHG emissions). Each ECF instance uses *rdf:value* property to link the conversion factor value as *xsd:float*. An ECF instance is also linked (using *ecfo:hasSourceUnit*) to information about the unit of measurement (*qudt:Unit*) that corresponds to the calculation input (i.e., activity data) for which the conversion factor was designed. For example, an ECF for calculating emissions from petrol may expect the quantity of the burnt fuel to be expressed in litres. The type of the emissions source (e.g., petrol) is linked to the ECF instance via property *ecfo:hasEmissionSource*. The range of this property is *owl:Thing* as the emissions source may be conceptualised in different ways, for example, as a tangible object (e.g., fuels) but also as an event (e.g., hotel stay). An

---

[8] https://github.com/perma-id/w3id.org/#permanent-identifiers-for-the-web.

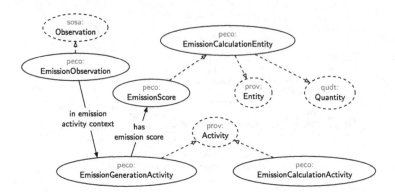

Fig. 2. Main entities of PECO ontology. Solid ellipses represent classes, dashed ellipses refer to classes in external ontologies, solid arrows represent properties and dashed arrows indicate RDFS subClassOf.

ECF may be further described using the *ecfo:Tag* concept and data property *ecfo:hasAdditionalContext* (e.g., to explain whether the ECF is considering a gross or net calorific value, or associations with specific types of machinery). Furthermore, GHG emissions are globally classified under one of three scopes [39]: direct emissions generated by activities owned or controlled by an organisation are considered Scope 1; indirect energy emissions resulting from the activities of an organisation at sources not owned or controlled by it are considered Scope 2 (e.g., purchased electricity or heat, steam and cooling) and all other indirect emissions generated by an organisation's activities at sources not owned or controlled by it are considered Scope 3 (e.g., purchased materials). ECFs may refer to the same emission source (e.g., fuel) but their values will differ significantly depending on the scope they fall under. Therefore, the term *ecfo:Scope* is used to associate each ECF instance with its relevant scope. The property *ecfo:hasTargetUnit* specifies the unit of the resulting emission factor calculated using the specific ECF (this is typically Kilograms). The kind of the emission factor (e.g., CO_2) is defined trough the *ecfo:hasEmissionTarget* property. ECFs also vary over time and the location for which they were calculated. For example, electricity generation in UK will have multiple ECFs for different years as the decarbonisation efforts of the grid progress over time. For this purpose, ECFs may use *ecfo:hasApplicablePeriod* and *ecfo:hasApplicableLocation* to further contextualise their application. Lastly, we reuse the *dc:publisher* property to link ECFs to the agent responsible for publishing the ECF values and the *prov:wasDerivedFrom* one to link an ECF to the dataset it was obtained from.

4.3   Provenance of Emission Calculation Ontology (PECO)

Figure 2 shows an overview of the PECO vocabulary, which describes provenance traces of carbon emissions calculations by capturing the quantifiable measurements of energy estimates (i.e., activity data) and ECFs used to estimate the carbon emissions. For example, PECO helps to capture the emissions produced when electricity is consumed by machinery to manufacture a product, the petrol used to make a car journey, etc. In addition, the ontology captures data transformations that may occur before energy estimates are used with relevant ECFs.

Calculation steps are described using *peco:EmissionCalculationEntity* and *peco:EmissionCalculationActivity* which are modelled as subclasses of PROV's *prov:Entity* and *prov:Activity* respectively. A *peco:EmissionCalculationEntity* can represent any quantifiable value that was used during the calculation and the different calculation steps are linked into causal chains of events when emission calculation entities are used and generated by emission calculation activities. The *peco:EmissionCalculationEntity* is a subclass of *qudt:Quantity* to integrate mechanisms for expressing quantity values, quantity kinds and units from the QUDT ontology. The standard SOSA vocabulary is used to describe the real-world observation context (*peco:EmissionObservation*) which produces some *sosa:Result* described as *peco:EmissionCalculationEntity*. This can be observed either by a human (e.g., person reporting how long the machine was used for) or machine sensor (e.g., smart meter recording the electricity usage) and can be linked to a specific *sosa:FeatureOfInterest* (e.g., type of machine) as well as properties describing the duration of the observation period. PECO defines *peco:inEmissionActivityContext* that links the real world observations which influence emissions calculations to *peco:EmissionGenerationActivity* representing the specific activities the emissions relate to (e.g., production of goods). For convenience, the object property *peco:hasEmissionScore* may be used to link the calculated *peco:EmissionScore* to the *peco:EmissionGenerationActivity* to simplify queries that do not require to traverse the entity/activity chains documenting the full calculation process. For a more detailed example of a domain-specific emissions calculation trace annotated using PECO see Sect. 6.2.

4.4   ECFO and PECO Validation

Following our methodology, we validated both ontologies by converting their corresponding competency questions into SPARQL queries and assessing their results against real world data produced by our use cases. The CQs from ECFO have been tested against the Emission Conversion Factors KG (see Sect. 5), while the CQs from PECO have been tested against provenance traces of the Semantic Machine Learning Impact calculator (see Sect. 6). Competency questions in SPARQL and their corresponding results are available online.[9,10]

We also used the OntOlogy Pitfall Scanner (OOPS!) [33] to detect potential modeling errors, and its sister tool FOOPS! [14] to assure compliance with the Findable, Accessible, Interoperable and Reusable principles [38]. Following the feedback from these analyses, we improved our ontologies with missing metadata

---

[9] https://github.com/TEC-Toolkit/ECFO/blob/main/cqs/README.md.
[10] https://github.com/TEC-Toolkit/PECO/blob/main/cqs/README.md.

Table 1. Conversion factors imported in our knowledge graph, along with their applicable period and publisher.

Source	BEIS	BEIS	BEIS	BEIS	BEIS	BEIS	BEIS	MLI
Year	2022	2021	2020	2019	2018	2107	2016	2002–19
Number of ECFs	6464	6284	6140	6163	6192	6178	4977	81

and registered them in the Linked Open Vocabularies registry [37]. The reports and corresponding discussion are available online.[11,12]

5   Emission Conversion Factors Knowledge Graph

We populated ECFO with open data from two different sources. The first one is the BEIS, an open authoritative data source issuing GHG ECFs in the UK. The second source is the Machine Learning CO2 Impact Calculator [24], an open source initiative which aims to estimate the emissions of training Machine Learning models. We detail the steps followed for integrating these sources into a KG below. The resultant KG and mappings are publicly available online[13] (mappings are available under an Apache 2.0 license) [15].

5.1   Data Sources

Table 1 provides an overview of the number of ECFs in our KG, together with their publisher and publication year. In total, we include more than 42400 ECFs from diverse activities, ranging from burning fuels to driving cars of different sizes, or spending a night in a hotel.

BEIS Data: BEIS publishes annual reports of GHG emission conversion factors, together with the methodology used to estimate them. Since 2016, these data are published in a flat file CSV format, indicating the scope of the emission (Scope 1, 2, or 3), the source and target units, the type of the emission being converted to (e.g., CO_2, CH_4, etc.) as well as an up to four-level categorisation of the emission source. For example, delivery vehicles (level 1) may be vans (level 2) of certain dimensions or weight (level 3). Each combination of levels has a unique ECF value during a year, hence the high number of ECFs shown in Table 1.

In order to convert these data into a KG, we separated columns mixing units and pollutants (e.g., "kg of CO_2") and we added a column recording the valid period of time for each ECF. We then aligned units, chemical compounds and locations to Wikidata terms using Open Refine [9] and curated each result manually. Finally, we removed rows with no value for an ECF, and rows where the value was not a number. For example, we discovered that a low number of ECFs had an estimated value of "< 1". After discussing with experts, we decided not to impute a value and exclude them from our KG.

---

[11] ECFO reports: https://github.com/TEC-Toolkit/ECFO/issues/15.

[12] PECO reports: https://github.com/TEC-Toolkit/PECO/issues/7.

[13] https://github.com/TEC-Toolkit/cfkg.

MLI Calculator Data: The MLI calculator includes a manually curated CSV file detailing 81 different ECFs used by the tool to calculate emissions for different cloud providers around the world, separated by different compute regions (i.e., locations of data centres)[14]. We expanded this CSV file with additional information such as Wikidata IRIs corresponding to the countries associated with the compute regions, converted the ECF values for source units in kWh (i.e., to match the format in BEIS data), and where possible we also followed the referenced sources of conversion factors and extracted the applicable period range. Some source references (e.g., eGRID) were insufficiently described with missing links to the source data/tool hence we did not include these in our KG. We also fixed discrepancies between the reported conversion factors and the corresponding source references. For example, a reference used to support conversion factor value for Tokyo (Japan) only contained information about Hong Kong (China). Another reference supporting conversion factors used for Japan mentioned an ECF of 0.37kg- CO_2/kWh, however, the tool used factor 0.516. Where such discrepancies were found, we did not include applicable period range in our Knowledge Graph since the source of the ECF is unknown. We also removed the reference supporting the reported conversion factor. All reported conversion factors have been assigned a Scope 2, as they are related to electricity usage.

5.2   Transforming Data Sources to RDF

We transformed all sources using RML mappings[15] for each source file. Mappings have been developed and tested using YARRRML and Matey [21] and executed with the Morph-KGC engine [3] in RML format. All mappings include the source of the original data source in order to preserve the provenance of each ECF. For BEIS data, mapping files for each year are similar, but required small changes due to column renames in the source files. We believe that providing the mappings will help in integrating additional data sources from future years.

In total, our KG contains 662992 triples, which we expect to grow as new data sources become integrated. To help executing SPARQL queries, we have set up a public SPARQL endpoint[16] using the Fuseki Triplestore.[17]

All URIs in our KG have a permanent URL, and follow the structure:

https://w3id.org/ecfkg/i/{Region}/{Publisher}/{Year}/{cfid}

Where {*Region*}, {*Publisher*} and {*Year*} correspond to the applicable location, the responsible organisation and the year of publication of the conversion factor (respectively) and {*cfid*} corresponds to the identifier of the ECF within the source dataset.

---

[14] https://github.com/TEC-Toolkit/Semantic_Machine_Learning_Impact_Calculator/blob/main/src/main/resources/static/data/impact.csv.

[15] https://rml.io/specs/rml.

[16] See instructions at https://github.com/TEC-Toolkit/cfkg#sparql-endpoint.

[17] https://jena.apache.org/documentation/fuseki2.

5.3   Data Validation with Semantic Rules

We built a data validation module based on Datalog [1] rules and SPARQL queries. This allows a very high flexibility and expressivity while keeping the reasoning tractable. In addition to these advantages, Datalog has been chosen due to the wide availability of various high-performance solvers that support advanced features such as stratified negation as failure and aggregation. This way it is possible to express complex behaviours in the form of simple rules and benefit from the efficient solvers available for evaluating Datalog programs.

After loading the data and the ontology, Datalog rules are processed to infer new relations, and then ASK queries are used to check whether *unwanted* relations (i.e., those that represent violations of the conditions we want to validate) have any instances.[18]

By interacting with domain experts, we identified the following initial *checks* to validate:

Net/Gross CV

The *Net CV* value must be greater than or equal to the *Gross CV* value.

Kg of CO_2e

The sum of the values of all gas emissions (i.e., CO_2, CH_4 and NO_2) must be less than or equal to the *kg of* CO_2e value for the ECF referring to the same "activity".

Non-negative ECF

ECFs must be non-negative.

All these checks can be easily and naturally expressed by simple Datalog rules. For instance, the rule below identifies conversion factors (conflictingCF) where the *Net CV* value is less than the *Gross CV* value:

```
eov:conflictingCF(?CF_Net, ?CF_Gross) :-
    eov:sameCF(?CF_Net, ?CF_Gross) ,
    [?CF_Net, ecfo:hasAdditionalContext, "Energy - Net CV" ] ,
    [?CF_Gross, ecfo:hasAdditionalContext, "Energy - Gross CV" ] ,
    [?CF_Net, ecfo:hasEmissionTarget, ?EmissionTarget] ,
    [?CF_Gross, ecfo:hasEmissionTarget, ?EmissionTarget] ,
    ecfo:hasTargetUnit(?CF_Net, ?TargetUnit) ,
    ecfo:hasTargetUnit(?CF_Gross, ?TargetUnit) ,
    rdf:value(?CF_Net, ?Value_Net) ,
    rdf:value(?CF_Gross, ?Value_Gross) ,
    ?Value_Net < ?Value_Gross .
```

where sameCF is an additional relation based on properties in our ontologies to identify two ECFs that refer to the same "activity", and the prefix eov is used to generate unique IRIs for the data validation module.

All the details and the full set of rules used can be found in the online repository on GitHub[19] [16]. Note that the proposed approach allows to add new checks

---

[18] The entire process for hundreds of thousands of triples is completed in seconds on a standard laptop and uses only a few MB of RAM.

[19] https://github.com/TEC-Toolkit/Data-Validation.

just in a couple of steps[20] and effortlessly include new data to validate (all that is required is to import the relevant RDF files, and they will be automatically included in all checks).

6   Semantic Machine Learning Impact Calculator

We adapted an existing MLI calculator [24] to assess PECO when describing provenance traces of emissions calculations. We modified its code to (1) make use of our public ECF KG; (2) generate a provenance trace of the emissions calculation process, thus supporting the generation of a transparency report; and (3) include validation rules which assess whether the selected ECF is outdated, and if so to provide alternatives. This level of transparency is currently not available in other carbon footprint calculators. We named our extension the Semantic Machine Learning Impact (SMLI) calculator, and made it available online[21] [26] under MIT license.

6.1   Calculator Overview

The SMLI calculator[22] was built using a SpringBoot framework[23] with HTML and JavaScript client interface. The client extends the functionality of the original MLI calculator with the ability to document the emissions calculation trace in a JSON-LD object, fetch information about relevant ECFs from the remote KG, and evaluate the provenance trace using the application's REST services. Java-based backend services utilise Apache Jena library[24] to query a remote SPARQL endpoint and also to execute validation queries on the local in-memory model containing the provenance trace uploaded by the client.

The emissions calculation process employed by the calculator depends on user input including the location of the computation (e.g., Google Cloud Platform in asia-east1 region), hardware used (e.g., A100 PCIe 40/80 GB), and the number of hours it was used for. The subsequent emissions calculation contains two steps:

- Estimate electricity use in kWh by multiplying the hardware consumption (based on its associated thermal design power specification) and the duration of the ML model training.
- Calculate the final emission score by multiplying the estimated energy use in kWh by the relevant ECF that is applicable to the region where the ML model training took place.

Note that SMLI is suitable for some use cases more than others. While it is useful for calculating general estimates of carbon footprint for ML training, the embedded assumptions (e.g., use of thermal design power property of GPU as a proxy measurement) should be assessed by the end users before the calculator is applied in specific use cases.

---

[20] https://github.com/TEC-Toolkit/Data-Validation#add-another-validation-check.
[21] https://github.com/TEC-Toolkit/Semantic_Machine_Learning_Impact_Calculator.
[22] Demo: https://calculator.linkeddata.es.
[23] https://spring.io.
[24] https://jena.apache.org.

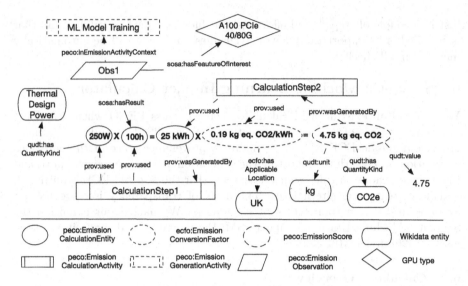

Fig. 3. An overview of the estimation (4.75 kg of CO₂e) produced by SMLI calculator (center) and its corresponding machine-readable trace aligned to PECO and ECFO. Some quantities have been simplified for clarity.

6.2   Emissions Calculation Provenance Trace

Figure 3 illustrates a portion of the provenance trace generated by the SMLI calculator. The centre of the figure depicts the aforementioned two-step emissions calculation process for training a ML model on a specific GPU hardware for 100 h. The emissions calculation process begins the with user input detailing the duration of the ML model training (*Obs1*) that links the observed value (*peco:EmissionCalculationEntity*) and the observed hardware (*sosa:FeatureOfInterest*) to the specific ML model training activity (*peco:EmissionGenerationActivity*). This is then multiplied by the thermal design power property corresponding to the specific GPU (*peco:EmissionCalculationEntity*) to produce an estimation of electricity usage in kWh which is captured as an output of the first calculation step (*peco:EmissionCalculationActivity*). The second calculation step multiplies this value with the value of the relevant conversion factor (*ecfo:EmissionConversionFactor*) to produce an estimate of the emissions released (*peco:EmissionScore*) during the ML model training. The generated provenance trace can be downloaded in a JSON-LD format.

Activity	Input	Output
Emission Score Calculation	Emission Conversion Factor - 0.19338kg [carbon dioxide equivalent]	Emission Score - 4.75E0kg [carbon dioxide equivalent]
	Energy Used - 25kWh [electricity]	
Estimate Electricity Use in kW/h	Duration of Use - 100h [time]	Energy Used - 25kWh [electricity]
	Watt Consumption - 250W [thermal design power]	

Fig. 4. Part of the transparency report detailing inputs and outputs of emission calculation activities generated from the provenance trace.

Source Unit	Target Unit	Applicable Period Start	Applicable Period End	Applicable Location	CF Value	Source	Emission Score
kWh	kg	2022-01-01T00:00:00	2022-12-31T23:59:59	United Kingdom	0.19338	link	4.75kg [carbon dioxide equivalent]
kWh	kg	2021-01-01T00:00:00	2021-12-31T23:59:59	United Kingdom	0.21233	link	5.25kg [carbon dioxide equivalent]

Fig. 5. Details of the Scope 2 electricity ECFs contained in the ECF KG and linked to the selected region of compute ordered by the applicable period. The highlighted ECF corresponds to the most recent year and is used to calculate the final emission score and included in the provenance trace.

6.3 Explaining Emissions Calculation Provenance Traces

To enhance the transparency of the calculation process, the SMLI calculator queries the provenance trace to retrieve the individual steps, inputs and outputs involved in the process (Fig. 4) including the intermediate step of estimating energy consumption based on the thermal design power property of the hardware used to perform the ML training). For each input/output the calculator shows their recorded labels, corresponding quantities with units, and the type (i.e., *qudt:QuantityKind*) of the quantity they represent.

Additionally, users are presented with a detailed overview of the ECF used to perform the calculations. The calculator is designed to query for ECF where the linked *ecfo:hasEmissionSource* value corresponds to electricity usage reported under Scope 2. For example, the information illustrated in Fig. 5 describes an ECF that converts energy expressed in kWh into kg of CO_2e and that its value is applicable to year 2022. The resulting emission score in this particular case (4.75 kg of CO_2e) is calculated based on the user input reporting a usage of hardware with 250 W thermal design power for the period of 100 h (see Fig. 4). Where ECFs for multiple years exist in the ECF KG that correspond to the location of the compute (e.g., UK-based Google Cloud Platform europe-west2), multiple rows with corresponding information (including alternative emission scores for other years) are shown.

6.4   Assessing Provenance Traces

Semantic descriptions of emissions calculations may be further processed by validation services that help users to detect discrepancies in the calculation process, assess the quality of results, etc. To demonstrate this benefit, the software also executes SPARQL queries aimed at testing whether the ECFs used to calculate the emission score are up to date and reference the source from which they were derived. For example, to retrieve any outdated ECF recorded in the provenance trace the following SPARQL query is executed:

```
SELECT DISTINCT ?cf ?cf_value ?time
WHERE {
    ?entity a peco:EmissionScore;
        prov:wasGeneratedBy/prov:used ?cf.
    ?cf ecfo:hasApplicablePeriod/time:hasEnd/time:inXSDDate ?time;
        rdf:value ?cf_value.
    FILTER (?time < now())
}
```

If an outdated CF is selected, a warning will appear at the bottom of the page to alert users.

7   Conclusions and Future Work

In this paper we have presented the TEC toolkit, a novel ontological approach for modelling information about GHG ECFs and the provenance of GHG emissions calculations. Our toolkit includes mappings to describe two public data sources in RDF (which we have used to generate a public KG containing thousands of ECFs) and an application for estimating transparent emissions of training machine learning models built on top of our KG.

Our approach presents an open-source alternative to commercial non-semantic platforms for ECF aggregation, and demonstrates our vision of future-generation software tools producing transparent and machine-understandable records of emissions calculations that can be easily integrated and holistically analysed trough automated means. Our framework also aids in validating data consistency values, and tracking the provenance of sources the data was derived from in case corrections are needed.

In future work, we will explore how semantic descriptions of domain specific business activities (e.g., farming operations, product manufacturing, business travel, etc.) can be automatically associated with estimates of emissions source quantities (e.g., amounts of electricity/fuel used) to enable automated emission scores calculations. Our planned use cases for the resource will initially focus on the AgriFood domain (helping UK farmers specify their farm carbon emissions accurately) and attaching provenance metadata to the emission estimates of machine learning models in Spanish Knowledge Spaces, e.g., to compare ML models by taking their emissions into account. We will also explore aligning emissions sources with existing ontologies in the energy domain (such as the Open Energy Ontology and Wikidata) in order to help intereoperability.

In addition to integrating additional open source datasets of ECFs (EPA, IPCC), we also aim to expand on the evaluations of ECFO and PECO by consulting with expert users which may lead to further extensions of these models. Finally, we would also like to explore how search and comparison of ECFs from multiple sources could be streamlined by leveraging the semantic nature of data.

Acknowledgements. This work was supported by eBay, Samsung Research UK, Siemens AG, the EPSRC projects ConCur (EP/V050869/1), UK FIRES (EP/S019111/1) and EATS (EP/V042270/1), the EU Horizon 2020 project GATEKEEPER (No 857223) and by the Comunidad de Madrid under the Multiannual Agreement with Universidad Politécnica de Madrid (UPM) in the line Support for R&D projects for Beatriz Galindo researchers, in the context of the V PRICIT (Regional Programme of Research and Technological Innovation) and through the call Research Grants for Young Investigators from UPM. For the purpose of open access, the author has applied a Creative Commons Attribution (CC BY) [or other appropriate open licence] licence to any Author Accepted Manuscript version arising from this submission.

References

1. Abiteboul, S., Hull, R., Vianu, V.: Foundations of Databases. Addison-Wesley, Boston (1995). http://webdam.inria.fr/Alice/
2. agrecalc: Agrecalc the farm carbon calculator. https://www.agrecalc.com/. Accessed 05 May 2023
3. Arenas-Guerrero, J., Chaves-Fraga, D., Toledo, J., Pérez, M.S., Corcho, O.: Morph-KGC: scalable knowledge graph materialization with mapping partitions. Semant. Web (2022). https://doi.org/10.3233/SW-223135
4. Booshehri, M., et al.: Introducing the open energy ontology: enhancing data interpretation and interfacing in energy systems analysis. Energy AI **5**, 100074 (2021). https://doi.org/10.1016/j.egyai.2021.100074
5. Carbon Care: CO_2 emissions calculator. https://www.carboncare.org/en/co2-emissions-calculator.html. Accessed 05 May 2023
6. Climatiq: API reference. https://www.climatiq.io/docs. Accessed 08 May 2023
7. Cox, S., Little, C.: Time Ontology in OWL. W3C candidate recommendation draft, W3C, November 2022. https://www.w3.org/TR/2022/CRD-owl-time-20221115/
8. Čuček, L., Klemeš, J.J., Kravanja, Z.: A review of footprint analysis tools for monitoring impacts on sustainability. J. Clean. Prod. **34**, 9–20 (2012)
9. Delpeuch, A., et al.: Openrefine/openrefine: Openrefine v3.7.2, April 2023. https://doi.org/10.5281/zenodo.7803000

10. Department for Energy Security and Net Zero and Department for Business, Energy & Industrial Strategy: Government conversion factors for company reporting of greenhouse gas emissions. Online at GOV.UK, June 2022. https://www.gov.uk/government/collections/government-conversion-factors-for-company-reporting

11. Department of Environment, Food & Rural Affairs: Emissions factors toolkit. Online at GOV.UK, November 2021. https://laqm.defra.gov.uk/air-quality/air-quality-assessment/emissions-factors-toolkit/

12. FAIRsharing.org: QUDT; Quantities, Units, Dimensions and Types, May 2022. https://doi.org/10.25504/FAIRsharing.d3pqw7

13. Garijo, D.: WIDOCO: a wizard for documenting ontologies. In: d'Amato, C., et al. (eds.) ISWC 2017. LNCS, vol. 10588, pp. 94–102. Springer, Cham (2017). https://doi.org/10.1007/978-3-319-68204-4_9

14. Garijo, D., Corcho, O., Poveda-Villalón, M.: Foops!: an ontology pitfall scanner for the fair principles. In: International Semantic Web Conference (ISWC) 2021: Posters, Demos, and Industry Tracks. CEUR Workshop Proceedings, vol. 2980. CEUR-WS.org (2021). http://ceur-ws.org/Vol-2980/paper321.pdf

15. Garijo, D., Markovic, M.: TEC-Toolkit/cfkg: CFKG 1.0.0: first release of the ECF KG, May 2023. https://doi.org/10.5281/zenodo.7916096

16. Germano, S.: TEC-Toolkit/Data-Validation: Data Validation v1.0.0, May 2023. https://doi.org/10.5281/zenodo.7916359

17. Germano, S., Saunders, C., Horrocks, I., Lupton, R.: Use of semantic technologies to inform progress toward zero-carbon economy. In: Hotho, A., et al. (eds.) ISWC 2021. LNCS, vol. 12922, pp. 665–681. Springer, Cham (2021). https://doi.org/10.1007/978-3-030-88361-4_39

18. Green House Gas Protocol: Calculation tools. Online at ghgprotocol.org. https://ghgprotocol.org/calculation-tools. Accessed 02 May 2023

19. Haller, A., Janowicz, K., Cox, S., Phuoc, D.L., Taylor, K., Lefrancois, M.: Semantic Sensor Network Ontology. W3C recommendation, W3C, October 2017. https://www.w3.org/TR/2017/REC-vocab-ssn-20171019/

20. He, R., Luo, L., Shamsuddin, A., Tang, Q.: Corporate carbon accounting: a literature review of carbon accounting research from the Kyoto Protocol to the Paris Agreement. Account. Finance 62(1), 261–298 (2022). https://doi.org/10.1111/acfi.12789

21. Heyvaert, P., De Meester, B., Dimou, A., Verborgh, R.: Declarative rules for linked data generation at your fingertips! In: Proceedings of the 15th ESWC: Posters and Demos (2018)

22. IBM: IBM Envizi ESG Suite. https://www.ibm.com/products/envizi. Accessed 05 May 2023

23. Intergovernmental Panel on Climate Change: Efdb emission factor database, November 2020. https://www.ipcc-nggip.iges.or.jp/EFDB/main.php. Accessed 28 Apr 2023

24. Lacoste, A., Luccioni, A., Schmidt, V., Dandres, T.: Quantifying the carbon emissions of machine learning. arXiv preprint arXiv:1910.09700 (2019)

25. Lebo, T., Sahoo, S., McGuinness, D.: PROV-O: the PROV ontology. W3C recommendation, W3C, April 2013. http://www.w3.org/TR/2013/REC-prov-o-20130430/

26. Markovic, M., Garijo, D.: TEC-Toolkit/Semantic_Machine_Learning_Impact_Calculator: SMLI Calculator 1.0.0: Stable release, May 2023. https://doi.org/10.5281/zenodo.7916120

27. Miles, A., Bechhofer, S.: SKOS Simple Knowledge Organization System Reference. W3C recommendation, W3C, August 2009. http://www.w3.org/TR/2009/REC-skos-reference-20090818/
28. Musen, M.A.: The protégé project: a look back and a look forward. AI Matters **1**(4), 4–12 (2015). https://doi.org/10.1145/2757001.2757003
29. Singh, N., Longendyke, L.: A global look at mandatory greenhouse gas reporting programs. Online at wri.org. https://www.wri.org/insights/global-look-mandatory-greenhouse-gas-reporting-programs. Accessed 14 Apr 2023
30. Oracle: Automate environmental data collection. https://www.oracle.com/applications/ebusiness/products/environmental-accounting-and-reporting/. Accessed 05 May 2023
31. Petri, I., Rezgui, Y., Ghoroghi, A., Alzahrani, A.: Digital twins for performance management in the built environment. J. Ind. Inf. Integr. **33**, 100445 (2023)
32. Poveda-Villalón, M., Fernández-Izquierdo, A., Fernández-López, M., García-Castro, R.: Lot: an industrial oriented ontology engineering framework. Eng. Appl. Artif. Intell. **111**, 104755 (2022). https://doi.org/10.1016/j.engappai.2022.104755
33. Poveda-Villalón, M., Gómez-Pérez, A., Suárez-Figueroa, M.C.: Digital twins for performance management in the built environment. Int. J. Semant. Web Inf. Syst. (IJSWIS) **10**(2), 7–34 (2014)
34. Sukhoveeva, O.: Carbon calculators as a tool for assessing greenhouse gas emissions from livestock. Dokl. Earth Sci. **497**, 266–271 (2021). Springer
35. Torres, E.J.: Ontology-driven integration of data for freight performance measures. The University of Texas at El Paso (2016)
36. United States Environmental Protection Agency: GHG emission factors hub. Online at epa.gov, April 2023. https://www.epa.gov/climateleadership/ghg-emission-factors-hub
37. Vandenbussche, P.Y., Atemezing, G.A., Poveda-Villalón, M., Vatant, B.: Linked open vocabularies (LOV): a gateway to reusable semantic vocabularies on the web. Semant. Web **8**(3), 437–452 (2017)
38. Wilkinson, M.D., et al.: The fair guiding principles for scientific data management and stewardship. Sci. Data **3**(1), 1–9 (2016)
39. World Business Council for Sustainable Development and World Resource Institute: The greenhouse gas protocol - a corporate accounting and reporting standard, revised edition. Online at ghgprotocol.org. https://ghgprotocol.org/sites/default/files/standards/ghg-protocol-revised.pdf. Accessed 07 Apr 2023
40. Zhang, Y., Yi, J., Wang, Z., He, L.: A customization-oriented carbon footprint service for mechanical products. In: IOP Conference Series: Earth and Environmental Science, vol. 291, p. 012024. IOP Publishing (2019)
41. Zhou, G., Lu, Q., Xiao, Z., Zhou, C., Yuan, S., Zhang, C.: Ontology-based cutting tool configuration considering carbon emissions. Int. J. Precis. Eng. Manuf. **18**(11), 1641–1657 (2017). https://doi.org/10.1007/s12541-017-0193-2
42. Zhu, W., Zhou, G., Yen, I.L., Hwang, S.Y.: A CFL-ontology model for carbon footprint reasoning. In: Proceedings of the 2015 IEEE 9th International Conference on Semantic Computing (IEEE ICSC 2015), pp. 224–231 (2015). https://doi.org/10.1109/ICOSC.2015.7050810

SemOpenAlex: The Scientific Landscape in 26 Billion RDF Triples

Michael Färber[1]([✉])(iD), David Lamprecht[1](iD), Johan Krause[1](iD), Linn Aung[2](iD), and Peter Haase[2](iD)

[1] Institute AIFB, Karlsruhe Institute of Technology (KIT), Karlsruhe, Germany
michael.faerber@kit.edu, {david.lamprecht,johan.krause}@student.kit.edu
[2] metaphacts GmbH, Walldorf, Germany
{la,ph}@metaphacts.com

Abstract. We present *SemOpenAlex*, an extensive RDF knowledge graph that contains over 26 billion triples about scientific publications and their associated entities, such as authors, institutions, journals, and concepts. SemOpenAlex is licensed under CC0, providing free and open access to the data. We offer the data through multiple channels, including RDF dump files, a SPARQL endpoint, and as a data source in the Linked Open Data cloud, complete with resolvable URIs and links to other data sources. Moreover, we provide embeddings for knowledge graph entities using high-performance computing. SemOpenAlex enables a broad range of use-case scenarios, such as exploratory semantic search via our website, large-scale scientific impact quantification, and other forms of scholarly big data analytics within and across scientific disciplines. Additionally, it enables academic recommender systems, such as recommending collaborators, publications, and venues, including explainability capabilities. Finally, SemOpenAlex can serve for RDF query optimization benchmarks, creating scholarly knowledge-guided language models, and as a hub for semantic scientific publishing.

Data and Services: https://semopenalex.org
https://w3id.org/SemOpenAlex
Code: https://github.com/metaphacts/semopenalex/
Data License: Creative Commons Zero (CC0)
Code License: MIT License

Keywords: Scholarly Data · Open Science · Digital Libraries

1 Introduction

With the increasing number of scientific publications, staying up-to-date with current research presents a significant challenge. For instance, in 2022 alone, more than 8 million scientific publications were registered [1]. To explore related scholarly entities such as authors and institutions, researchers rely on a range of methods from search interfaces to recommendation systems [2,3]. One effective way to model the underlying scholarly data is to represent it as an RDF

© The Author(s) 2023
T. R. Payne et al. (Eds.): ISWC 2023, LNCS 14266, pp. 94–112, 2023.
https://doi.org/10.1007/978-3-031-47243-5_6

knowledge graph (KG). Doing so facilitates standardization, visualization, and interlinking with Linked Data resources [4]. Consequently, scholarly KGs play a pivotal role in transforming document-centric scholarly data into interconnected and machine-actionable knowledge structures [2].

However, available scholarly KGs have one or several of the following limitations. Firstly, they rarely contain an exhaustive catalog of publications across all disciplines [5]. Secondly, they often cover only certain disciplines, such as computer science [6]. Thirdly, they are not regularly updated, rendering many analyses and business models obsolete [7]. Fourthly, they often contain usage restrictions [8]. Lastly, even if they fulfill these requirements, they are not available according to W3C standards such as RDF [1,9]. These issues hinder the application of scientific KGs on a broad scale, such as in comprehensive search and recommender systems, or for scientific impact quantification. For instance, the Microsoft Academic Graph was discontinued in 2021 [10], which hinders further updates to its derivative in RDF, the Microsoft Academic Knowledge Graph (MAKG) [7]. This leaves a gap that the novel OpenAlex dataset aims to fill [1]. However, the data in OpenAlex is not available in RDF and does not comply with Linked Data Principles [11]. Consequently, OpenAlex cannot be considered a KG, which makes semantic queries, integration into existing applications, or linking to additional resources non-trivial. At first glance, integrating scholarly data about scientific papers into Wikidata and thus contributing to the WikiCite initiative may seem like an obvious solution. However, apart from the dedicated schema, the volume of the data is already so large that the Blazegraph triplestore which is used in the Wikidata Query Service reaches its capacity limit, preventing any integration [12] (see Sect. 2).

In this paper, we introduce *SemOpenAlex*, an extremely large RDF dataset of the academic landscape with its publications, authors, sources, institutions, concepts, and publishers. SemOpenAlex consists of more than 26 billion semantic triples and includes over 249 million publications from all academic disciplines. It is based on our rich ontology (see Sect. 3.1) and includes links to other LOD sources such as Wikidata, Wikipedia, and the MAKG. To ensure easy and efficient use of SemOpenAlex's integration with the LOD cloud, we provide a public SPARQL endpoint. In addition, we provide a sophisticated semantic search interface that allows users to retrieve real-time information about contained entities and their semantic relationships (e.g., displaying co-authors or an author's top concepts – information, which is not directly contained in the database but obtained through semantic reasoning). We also provide the full RDF data snapshots to enable big data analysis. Due to the large size of SemOpenAlex and the ever-increasing number of scientific publications being integrated into SemOpenAlex, we have established a pipeline using AWS for regularly updating SemOpenAlex entirely without any service interruptions. Additionally, to use SemOpenAlex in downstream applications, we trained state-of-the-art knowledge graph entity embeddings. By reusing existing ontologies whenever possible, we ensure system interoperability in accordance with FAIR principles [13] and pave the way for the integration of SemOpenAlex into the Linked Open

Data Cloud. We fill the gap left by the discontinuation of MAKG by providing monthly updates that facilitate ongoing monitoring of an author's scientific impact, tracking of award-winning research, and other use cases using our data [14,15]. By making SemOpenAlex free and unrestricted, we empower research communities across all disciplines to use the data it contains and integrate it into their projects. Initial use cases and production systems that use SemOpenAlex already exist (see Sect. 5).

Overall, we make the following contributions:

1. We create an *ontology* for SemOpenAlex reusing common vocabularies.
2. We create the SemOpenAlex *knowledge graph* in RDF, covering 26 billion triples, and provide all *SemOpenAlex* data, code, and services for public access at https://semopenalex.org/:
   (a) We provide monthly updated RDF data snapshots free of charge on AWS S3 at `s3://semopenalex` (via browser: https://semopenalex.s3.amazonaws.com/browse.html), accepted as AWS Open Data project.[1]
   (b) We make all URIs of SemOpenAlex resolvable, allowing SemOpenAlex to be part of the Linked Open Data cloud.[2]
   (c) We index all data in a triple store and make it publicly available via a SPARQL endpoint (https://semopenalex.org/sparql).
   (d) We provide a semantic search interface including entity disambiguation to access, search, and visualize the knowledge graph and its statistical key figures in real time.
3. We provide state-of-the-art knowledge graph embeddings for the entities represented in SemOpenAlex using high-performance computing.

In the following, we first discuss related work (see Sect. 2) and describe the SemOpenAlex ontology and RDF data (see Sect. 3), before presenting the SemOpenAlex entity embeddings (see Sect. 4). Subsequently, we outline existing and potential use cases (see Sect. 5), before we conclude the paper (see Sect. 6).

2   Related Work

A comparison of scholarly RDF datasets is presented in Table 1. It is obvious from the table that SemOpenAlex (1) is the only RDF KG that follows the Linked Data Principles, (2) is fully open, (3) contains a vast amount of bibliographic information from all scientific disciplines, and (4) is regularly updated, making it a valuable resource in various contexts (see Sect. 5).

The OpenAIRE Research Graph provides open and free access to metadata of 145 million publications, datasets, and software via an API, a SPARQL endpoint,

---

[1] The AWS Open Data Sponsorship program covers the cost of storing and retrieving all SemOpenAlex data, ensuring the long-term sustainability of our project. Upon request, it was confirmed that Zenodo does not support the provision of SemOpenAlex data due to its size.

[2] See, e.g. `curl -H "Accept:text/n3"` https://semopenalex.org/work/W4239696231.

Table 1. Statistical comparison of scholarly RDF datasets.

	OpenAIRE	AceKG	Wikidata	COCI	MAKG	SemOpenAlex
# Works	145M	62M	42M	76M	239M	249M
# Triples	1.4B	3.13B	–	1.4B	8B	26.4B
# References	0	480M	288M	1.4B	1.4B	1.7B
Snapshot size	100 GB	113 GB	120 GB	1.5 TB	1.4 TB	1.7 TB
Regular updates			(✓)	✓		✓
SPARQL endpoint			✓	✓	✓	✓
Entity embeddings					✓	✓

OpenAIRE as of March 2021, AceKG as of 2018, Wikidata as of Dec. 2022, the OpenCitations Index of Crossref open DOI-to-DOI citations (COCI) as of Oct. 2022, the MAKG as of March 2021, and SemOpenAlex as of March 2023

and database dumps [16]. However, not only is the number of publications significantly lower than in SemOpenAlex but on May 8, 2023, OpenAIRE stopped its LOD services and closed the SPARQL endpoint.[3]

WikiCite[4] has incorporated bibliographic metadata into Wikidata, but SemOpenAlex covers considerably more metadata (e.g., 249M papers vs. 42M), including additional properties such as papers' abstracts. While using Wikidata as a central KG and regularly importing SemOpenAlex information seems logical, the scalability of the Blazegraph triplestore backend which hosts the Wikidata Query Service is limited, and Wikimedia has announced a plan to delete scholarly articles in case of bulk imports.[5]

AceKG [17] is a database containing 62 million publications, along with academic details related to authors, fields of study, venues, and institutes. AceKG data is modeled in RDF. However, unlike our approach, it does not use existing vocabularies, lacks a publicly available triple store, and does not offer continuous updates. All data is sourced from a company's database.

OpenCitations focuses on publications and their citation relationships [18]. Specifically, it covers metadata about publications and their citations, but not descriptions of affiliated organizations (institutions) or hosting conferences and journals (venues). OpenCitations includes several datasets, including the OpenCitations Index of Crossref Open DOI-to-DOI Citations (COCI) with 76 million items to date, and smaller datasets such as the OpenCitations Corpus (OCC) and OpenCitations in Context Corpus (CCC) [5].

The Microsoft Academic Knowledge Graph (MAKG) is based on the Microsoft Academic Graph (MAG), containing information on publications, authors, institutions, venues, and concepts [7,19]. The MAKG has high coverage

---

[3] See https://www.openaire.eu/pausing-our-lod-services.
[4] See http://wikicite.org/.
[5] See https://m.wikidata.org/wiki/Wikidata:SPARQL_query_service/WDQS_back end_update/Blazegraph_failure_playbook.

Table 2. SemOpenAlex entity types and number of instances (as of March 2023).

Entity Type	# Instances
Work	249,450,604
Author	135,360,159
Source	226,413
Institution	108,618
Concept	65,073
Publisher	7,017

across scientific domains and has enabled novel use cases. However, it will no longer be updated due to lack of source data [10]. Several analyses have assessed the MAG and MAKG, revealing the need for improvements in areas such as citation accuracy, concept assignment, and disambiguation [20–23]. Compared to MAKG, SemOpenAlex provides a similar schema, but provides fresh data that is in addition cleaned by an author name disambiguation provided by OpenAlex and a neater mapping of concepts to papers using the Simple Knowledge Organization System (SKOS) ontology [24,25].

Further notable scholarly KGs are the DBLP KG[6] and the Open Research Knowledge Graph (ORKG) [26]. DBLP provides only high-quality metadata about computer science publications, resulting in a coverage of roughly 6 million publications [6]. ORKG is a project that aims to provide a KG infrastructure for semantically capturing and representing the content of research papers [2, 27]. ORKG contains a relatively small set of more than 25,000 publications, however, with many RDF statements, indicating considerable semantic richness. Due to their different focuses, SemOpenAlex can complement ORKG as an LOD data source: while SemOpenAlex provides a broad basis of metadata about a massive amount of publications and related entities in RDF (with a focus on high coverage, see Table 2), ORKG focuses on modeling scientific contributions as well as methodology aspects, which are manually curated (with a focus on high data quality and key insights of papers).

3   SemOpenAlex

In the following, we describe the design of the SemOpenAlex ontology (Sect. 3.1) and the process of generating SemOpenAlex data (Sect. 3.2). We also explain how we publish and enable user interaction with the data (Sect. 3.3), and present key statistics of the KG (Sect. 3.4). Furthermore, we evaluate to what extent SemOpenAlex meets linked data set descriptions and rankings (Sect. 3.5).

---

[6] See https://www.dagstuhl.de/en/institute/news/2022/dblp-in-rdf.

3.1   Ontology of SemOpenAlex

We developed an ontology following the best practices of ontology engineering reusing as much existing vocabulary as possible. An overview of the entity types, the object properties, and the data type properties is provided in Fig. 1. Overall, the ontology of SemOpenAlex covers *13 entity types*, including the main entity types *works, authors, institutions, sources, publishers and concepts*, as well as *87 relation types*.

Table 3. Used ontologies, their corresponding prefixes and namespace.

Ontology	Prefix	Associated URI
SemOpenAlex	:	https://semopenalex.org/class/
SemOpenAlex	soa:	https://semopenalex.org/property/
OpenAlex	oa:	http://openalex.org/
XML Schema	xsd:	http://www.w3.org/2001/XMLSchema#
OWL	owl:	http://www.w3.org/2002/07/owl#
RDF	rdf:	http://www.w3.org/1999/02/22-rdf-syntax-ns#
RDF Schema	rdfs:	http://www.w3.org/2000/01/rdf-schema#
Dubin Core	dcterms:	http://purl.org/dc/terms/
CiTO	cito:	http://purl.org/spar/cito/
FaBiO	fabio:	http://purl.org/spar/fabio/
BiDO	bido:	http://purl.org/spar/bido/
DataCite	datacite:	http://purl.org/spar/datacite
PRISM	prism:	http://prismstandard.org/namespaces/basic/2.0/
DBpedia	dbo:	https://dbpedia.org/ontology/
DBpedia	dbp:	https://dbpedia.org/property/
FOAF	foaf:	http://xmlns.com/foaf/0.1/
W3 ORG	org:	http://www.w3.org/ns/org#
GeoNames	gn:	https://www.geonames.org/ontology#
SKOS	skos:	http://www.w3.org/2004/02/skos/core#

We reused the vocabularies listed in Table 3. To describe publications, researchers, and institutions, we leveraged established Semantic Publishing and Referencing (SPAR) ontologies [28], such as FaBiO and CiTO. FaBiO is used to describe specific identifiers such as a work's PubMedID, while CiTO represents citing relationships between works. For bibliographic metadata, such as a work's publication date and abstract, we used the Dublin Core ontology (DCterms). To represent more generic features and relations, we relied on cross-domain

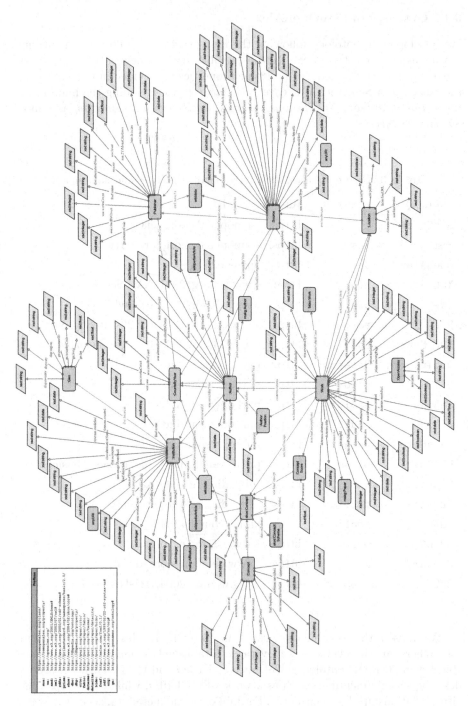

Fig. 1. Ontology of SemOpenAlex.

ontologies such as DBpedia and the W3 Organization Ontology (W3 ORG). The works are classified using a concept hierarchy, which we represented in a SKOS vocabulary of 65k SKOS concepts and semantic relations (`skos:broader` and `skos:related`). The concepts are further linked with Wikidata entities, allowing for additional interoperability and providing multi-lingual labels.

3.2 Knowledge Graph Creation Process

The raw OpenAlex data was presumably designed for data processing (e.g., abstracts are provided as inverted index and not provided as one string). To create an RDF KG based on the OpenAlex dump files, major changes in the data formatting and the data modeling are necessary. In the following, we outline the essential steps of this transformation process.

Transformation. We carry out a number of distinct steps for the transformation that can be reproduced via the code in our GitHub repository.[7]

1. *Data Preprocessing:* We download the OpenAlex snapshot in compressed `.jsonl` format from its AWS S3 bucket and use the Python multiprocessing package for efficient parallel processing of the large amount of data. To ensure valid triple generation according to the *W3C RDF 1.1 Concepts and Abstract Syntax*[8] later, we remove problematic characters from literal values, such as non-escaped backslashes in URLs or newlines in publication titles. Additionally, we convert the abstracts, which are included in OpenAlex as an inverted index, to plain text to improve accessibility.
2. *RDF Generation:* We transform the preprocessed data from JSON into RDF according to the ontology shown in Fig. 1. For the generation of the triples, we draw on the rdflib Python package,[9] which offers functionality to handle, process and validate RDF data. During triple serialization, we create a buffer subgraph that is written once a fixed number of statements is reached to reduce the number of I/O operations. In total, we generate 26,401,183,867 RDF triples given the data snapshot as of 2023-03-28.
3. *Compression and Deployment:* The RDF data generated for SemOpenAlex takes up 1.7 TB in the TriG format[10] when uncompressed. To make the data more manageable, we compress it into .gz archives, resulting in a reduction of over 80% in file size to 232 GB. These compressed files are then imported into the GraphDB triple store and made available for download as an open snapshot. Additionally, we provide a data sample on GitHub.

---

[7] See https://github.com/metaphacts/semopenalex.
[8] See https://www.w3.org/TR/rdf11-concepts/#section-Graph-Literal.
[9] See https://github.com/RDFLib/rdflib/.
[10] TriG is an extension of Turtle, extended to support representing a complete RDF dataset (see https://www.w3.org/TR/trig/).

Update Mechanism. To ensure that SemOpenAlex remains up-to-date, we perform the transformation process described earlier on a monthly basis, which involves downloading the latest OpenAlex snapshot. This enables us to observe temporal dynamics in the data, and ensures that SemOpenAlex provides the most recent information available. The updated version of the data is available through all three access points (RDF dump, SPARQL endpoint, and visual interface). The update process is semi-automated and takes approximately five days to complete on an external server instance. We use one AWS instance to provide SemOpenAlex services and one instance to process the next SemOpenAlex release. Changes to SemOpenAlex data resulting from changes in the raw OpenAlex files are tracked using announcements via the OpenAlex mailing list. Several adaptations have been performed in this way in the past.

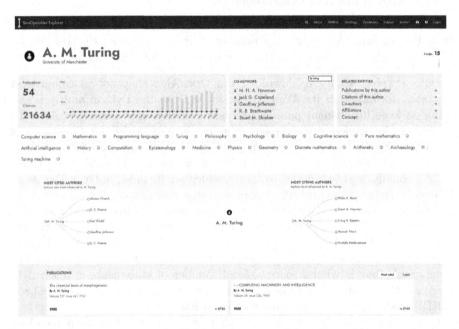

Fig. 2. Author overview page for A.M. Turing, accessible at https://semopenalex.org/author/A2430569270.

3.3   Data Publishing and User Interaction

Our KG is publicly accessible at https://semopenalex.org/. We utilize the metaphactory knowledge graph platform [29] on top of a GraphDB triple store to deploy the KG. metaphactory serves as a Linked Data publication platform and ensures that the URIs of SemOpenAlex are fully resolvable. The data is published in machine-readable RDF formats as well as human-readable HTML-based templates using content negotiation. Figure 2 displays the page for the URI https://semopenalex.org/author/A2430569270.

Among other features, the interface provided for SemOpenAlex enables users to: (1) access SemOpenAlex through a search interface with filtering options; (2) visualize arbitrarily large sub-graphs for objects and relations of interest; (3) formulate and execute SPARQL queries to retrieve objects from the graph using a provided SPARQL endpoint; (4) examine the ontology of SemOpenAlex; (5) obtain key statistics for each object in SemOpenAlex in a dashboard, as shown in the screenshot in Fig. 2; (6) assess the underlying multi-level concept hierarchy; and (7) interact with further linked entities such as co-authors or concepts and access external resources such as links to Wikidata.

3.4   Key Statistics of SemOpenAlex and Example SPARQL Queries

In this subsection, we present several statistics that we generated based on queries using our SPARQL endpoint. We provide the queries on GitHub.

Figure 3 shows the number of papers published in the field of machine learning and natural language processing by researchers from Karlsruhe Institute of Technology from 2000 to 2021. While the number of machine learning papers

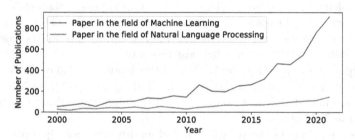

Fig. 3. Number of publications published in machine learning and natural language processing by researchers from Karlsruhe Institute of Technology.

Table 4. Number of institution for the countries with the most institutions.

Country	# Institutions
US	32,814
GB	7,743
DE	5,096
CN	4,856
JP	4,031
FR	3,965
IN	3,731
CA	3,498

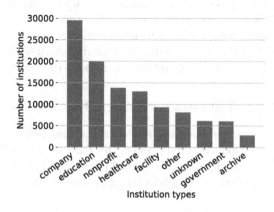

Fig. 4. Distribution of institution types.

```
PREFIX foaf: <http://xmlns.com/foaf/0.1/>
PREFIX xsd: <http://www.w3.org/2001/XMLSchema#>
PREFIX dcterms: <http://purl.org/dc/terms/>
PREFIX soa: <https://semopenalex.org/property/>
PREFIX skos: <http://www.w3.org/2004/02/skos/core#>

SELECT DISTINCT ?paperTitle ?citedByCount ?firstAuthorName
WHERE {
   ?paper dcterms:title ?paperTitle .
   ?paper soa:hasConcept ?Concept .
   ?Concept skos:prefLabel "Semantic Web"^^xsd:string .
   ?paper soa:citedByCount ?citedByCount .
   ?paper soa:hasAuthorPosition ?authorPosition .
   ?authorPosition soa:position "first"^^xsd:string .
   ?authorPosition soa:hasAuthor ?firstAuthor .
   ?firstAuthor foaf:name ?firstAuthorName .
}
ORDER BY DESC(?citedByCount)
LIMIT 100
```

List. 1. Querying the top 100 most cited papers with the concept "Semantic Web" as well as their citation count and first author.

received a sharp increase from 2015, the number of papers in the field of natural language processing increased at a rather constant rate. SemOpenAlex enables institutions to create such relevant key figures and trends in the context of strategic controlling in a simple and cost-free way.

SemOpenAlex covers the worldwide scientific landscape and contains publications from institutions around the globe. In total, institutions from 225 different countries are included. The 8 countries with the highest number of institutions are shown in Table 4.

By distinguishing between eight types of institutions, SemOpenAlex enables differentiated data analyses. In Fig. 4, we can see the distribution of the 108,618 unique institutions across the different types. We can see that the majority of the organizations are companies, followed by educational and nonprofit institutions.

Listing 1 shows an example of how SemOpenAlex can be queried with SPARQL. This query retrieves the top 100 most cited papers in the field of semantic web, along with their citation counts and first authors. It is worth noting that this query cannot be executed on other scholarly KGs like the MAKG, as they do not cover information about the author's position for a given paper.

3.5   Linked Data Set Descriptions and Ratings

Following the licensing model of the underlying OpenAlex data,[11] we provide all SemOpenAlex data under the *CC0 license*, which grants users the right to freely build upon, enhance, and reuse the works for any purpose without restriction, paving the way for other researchers and software engineers to build upon

---

[11] See https://openalex.org/about.

SemOpenAlex in any context. The RDF data files are available for unrestricted and free download as they are hosted with the AWS Open Data program.[12]

We can categorize SemOpenAlex according to the two kinds of 5-star rating schemes in the Linked Data context:

- *Tim Berners-Lee's 5-star deployment scheme for Open Data*[13]: Our SemOpenAlex RDF dataset is a 5-star data set according to this scheme, because we provide our data in RDF (leading to 4 stars) and the (1) entity URIs are linked to Wikidata, Wikipedia and the MAKG and (2) our vocabulary URIs to other vocabularies (leading to 5 stars).
- *Linked Data vocabulary star rating* [30]: This rating is intended to rate the use of vocabulary within Linked (Open) Data. By providing a turtle file, by linking our vocabulary to other vocabularies (see the SPAR ontologies), we are able to provide the vocabulary with 4 stars.

Aside from the SemOpenAlex RDF documents, we provide the following linked data set descriptions (all available at https://semopenalex.org/):

- *Turtle:* We provide our ontology as a Turtle file describing the used classes, object properties, and data type properties.
- *VoID:* We provide a VoID file to describe our linked data set with an RDF schema vocabulary.

4   Graph Embeddings for SemOpenAlex

Apart from creating and providing the SemOpenAlex data set and services (e.g., the SPARQL endpoint), we computed embeddings for all SemOpenAlex entities. Entity embeddings have proven to be useful as implicit knowledge representations in a variety of scenarios, as we describe in Sect. 5. Based on the SemOpenAlex data in RDF, we trained entity embeddings based on several state-of-the-art embedding techniques and compared the performance of the respective results with regard to link prediction tasks. Specifically, we applied the following approaches: TransE [31], DistMult [32], ComplEx [33], a GraphSAGE neural network [34], and a graph attention network [35]. To address the nontrivial challenges associated with training on SemOpenAlex as a very large knowledge graph, we employed the Marius framework [36]. Marius[14] is designed to optimize resource utilization by pipelining hard disk, CPU, and GPU memory during training, thereby reducing idle times. In our evaluation, we opted for a configuration of 100 embedding dimensions, a batch size of 16,000, and trained for 3 epochs on a high-performance computing system (bwUniCluster 2.0) using Python 3.7, Marius 0.0.2, PyTorch 1.9.1, and CUDA 11.2.2. These parameters are in line with previous research on large-scale entity embeddings [24].

---

[12] See https://aws.amazon.com/opendata/open-data-sponsorship-program/.

[13] See http://5stardata.info/.

[14] See https://marius-project.org.

The computational effort required for the different embedding techniques varied, with the GraphSAGE and the graph attention network approaches requiring the most memory. These methods used up to 716 GB of CPU RAM and took the longest time to train, with each epoch taking roughly 24 h. Despite the resource-intensive nature of the GraphSAGE and graph attention network approaches, DistMult yielded the highest mean reciprocal rank (MRR) score in our link prediction evaluation (see all evaluation results on GitHub). Therefore, we provide the DistMult-based embedding vectors for all entities online.[15]

5   Use Cases of SemOpenAlex

Scholarly KGs have proven to be a valuable data basis for various use cases and scenarios, such as analyzing research dynamics between academia and industry [37], scientific impact quantification [14,38], and linking research data sets to publications [39]. This is also reflected in the high number of citations of the reference publications of the MAG [40] and MAKG [7].[16] In the following, we focus on existing and potential use cases of SemOpenAlex.

Scholarly Big Data Analytics and Large-Scale Scientific Impact Quantification. SemOpenAlex can serve for scientific impact quantification and innovation management. For instance, OpenAlex has been utilized as a comprehensive and reliable data source to rank researchers and institutions worldwide on `research.com`.[17] InnoGraph is a new project that leverages OpenAlex to represent innovation ecosystems as a KG for innovation management and forecasting [41]. By using SemOpenAlex as underlying database for such projects and efforts, the need to deal with cumbersome data integration issues can be reduced. Currently, universities such as KIT rely on paid scholarly services like those from Springer Nature for measuring their performance and ranking as a university [42]. However, in the future, these institutions can use SemOpenAlex as a free database to run analytics and evaluations on all relevant publications and associated entities.

Scholarly Search and Recommender Systems. Recommendation systems – both content-based and collaborative filtering-based – have become increasingly important in academia to help scientists navigate the overwhelming amount of available information resulting from the exponential increase in the number of publications. In this paper, we provide entity embeddings for nearly all existing entities in the scientific landscape, which can be used directly to build state-of-the-art recommender systems. These systems can recommend items such as papers to read and cite, as well as venues and collaborators [43]. SemOpenAlex

---

[15] See https://doi.org/10.5281/zenodo.7912776.

[16] Sinha et al. [40] have obtained 1,041 citations and Färber [7] has obtained 115 citations as of April 28, 2023, according to Google Scholar.

[17] See   https://research.com/university/materials-science/humboldt-university-of-berlin.

can be utilized to make these recommendations explainable, as symbolic information from the KG can be shown to the user. Due to SemOpenAlex's rich ontology, including various entity types, SemOpenAlex can serve as a realistic dataset for training and evaluating state-of-the-art graph neural networks designed for heterogeneous information networks and with a specific focus on scalability and semantics. Moreover, our rich KG can be utilized to provide recommendations in complex scenarios, such as finding the optimal consortium for large, possibly interdisciplinary research projects. In the context of semantic search, SemOpenAlex can be used for entity linking, annotating scientific texts [44] or tables [45] for enhanced search capabilities.

Semantic Scientific Publishing. SemOpenAlex is a part of the Linked Open Data Cloud and contains links to other data sources such as Wikidata, Wikipedia, and MAKG. As a result, it significantly contributes to the use of linked data in areas such as digital libraries and information retrieval [46]. SemOpenAlex has a unique selling point among available scientific knowledge graphs, with its coverage of publications worldwide and across all scientific disciplines, totaling around 250 million publications (see Table 2), and its regular updates. SemOpenAlex can serve as a central catalog for publications, researchers, and research artifacts, to which other data repositories and KGs can link. This creates an opportunity to use SemOpenAlex as a basis for modeling scientific artifacts, such as datasets, scientific methods, and AI models, and thus beyond SemOpenAlex' current scope. This information may be modeled in separate, interlinked KGs or as part of SemOpenAlex in the future. For instance, the Data Set Knowledge Graph [39], which currently links 600,000 publications in which datasets are mentioned to the MAKG, can now link datasets to papers in SemOpenAlex. Similarly, semantic representations of datasets and scientific methods [47], as well as representations of scientific facts and claims mentioned in full-text articles [48], can be linked to publications and authors in SemOpenAlex to provide rich context information as explanations of academic recommender systems. Furthermore, links between SemOpenAlex and KGs modeling AI models and their energy consumption, such as the Green AI Knowledge Graph [49], can be used to combine previously isolated data for performing complex analytics. In this way, questions of strategic controlling, such as "How green are the AI models developed at my institution?" [49], can be automatically answered. Finally, it makes sense to link full-text paper collections to SemOpenAlex, for instance, to leverage its concept schema, since SemOpenAlex applies concept tags to all its papers published globally and across all scientific fields. An excellent example of an existing paper collection linked to SemOpenAlex is unarXive 2022 [50], sourced from two million arXiv papers.

Research Project Management and Modeling. KGs have become increasingly important in supporting research projects by providing a structured representation of various research entities and their relationships [51]. These project-specific KGs encapsulate a diverse range of research entities, such as topics, methods, tasks, materials, organizations, researchers, their skills, interests, and activities, as well as research outputs and project outcomes. To facilitate the

development and support of KGs for research projects, SemOpenAlex serves
as a knowledge hub by providing existing data on project participants and
relevant research. Researchers can use tools and vocabularies provided by the
Competency Management Ontology [52] to seamlessly describe their skills, current research interests, and activities in terms of the entities already contained
in SemOpenAlex. Moreover, SemOpenAlex's concept hierarchy allows for the
construction of ontologies for specific research domains, streamlining research
tasks such as performing a state-of-the-art analysis for a research area. Existing
resources from SemOpenAlex can be integrated into KG-based project bibliographies, enhancing collaboration between researchers through resource sharing.

SemOpenAlex has already been used to provide a comprehensive and structured overview of research projects. In particular, personalized dashboards have
been created by metaphacts that display recently added publications from
SemOpenAlex that are relevant to the current research context. Newly created
resources within a project, such as research papers and datasets, can also be
described and linked to SemOpenAlex. Ultimately, published results become a
valuable part of SemOpenAlex.

Groundwork for Scientific Publishing in the Future. One can envision
that the working style of researchers will considerably change in the next few
decades [53, 54]. For instance, publications might not be published in PDF format
any more, but in either an annotated version of it (with information about the
claims, the used methods, the data sets, the evaluation results, and so on) or in
the form of a flexible publication form, in which authors can change the content
and, in particular, citations, over time. SemOpenAlex can be easily combined
with new such data sets due to its structure in RDF. Furthermore, ORKG is
an ongoing effort that targets the semantic representation of papers and their
scientific contributions. We argue that SemOpenAlex can be used as data basis
for ORKG in the sense that with SemOpenAlex, users do not need to take care
of first creating papers and authors in the ORKG, but to directly import or link
the corresponding information from SemOpenAlex, which has its focus on being
a comprehensive KG covering all scientific publications worldwide.

Knowledge-Guided Language Models. Large language models, including
ChatGPT and GPT-4, have been criticized for their lack of explainability and
their failure to provide reliable in-text citations to reference literature. Often,
when citations are provided, they are incorrect and reflect "hallucinations". In
this context, SemOpenAlex represents a valuable repository for guiding language
models in providing reliable references to scientific literature and as a basis for
text-editing generative models. With metadata of 250 million scientific works,
SemOpenAlex can serve as a valuable resource for source attribution and improving the accuracy and quality of scientific writing generated by these models.

Benchmarking. SemOpenAlex is a prime example of big data, fulfilling the
"4 V's" criteria: it is very large, with a wide variety of information types (including papers, authors, institutions, venues, and various data formats), contains
uncertainties, and is updated periodically. This makes it suitable for bench-

marking systems and approaches, particularly in the context of querying large, realistic KGs [55]. In fact, the MAKG has already been used for this purpose [56] and we expect SemOpenAlex to follow suit.

6   Conclusions

In this paper, we presented a comprehensive RDF dataset with over 26 billion triples covering scholarly data across all scientific disciplines. We outlined the creation process of this dataset and discussed its characteristics. Our dataset supports complex analyses through SPARQL querying. By making the SPARQL endpoint publicly available and the URIs resolvable, we enriched the Linked Open Data cloud with a valuable source of information in the field of academic publishing. We offer RDF dumps, linked dataset descriptions, a SPARQL endpoint, and trained entity embeddings online at https://semopenalex.org/. In the future, we plan to incorporate metadata about funding programs to enable in-depth and comprehensive evaluations of funding lines of governments and institutions [51,57,58].

Acknowledgments. This work was partially supported by the German Federal Ministry of Education and Research (BMBF) as part of the project IIDI (01IS21026D). The authors acknowledge support by the state of Baden-Württemberg through bwHPC.

References

1. Priem, J., Piwowar, H., Orr, R.: OpenAlex: a fully-open index of scholarly works, authors, venues, institutions, and concepts. arXiv preprint arXiv:2205.01833 (2022)
2. Auer, S., Kovtun, V., Prinz, M., Kasprzik, A., Stocker, M., Vidal, M.E.: Towards a knowledge graph for science. In: Proceedings of the 8th International Conference on Web Intelligence, Mining and Semantics. WIMS'18, June 2018, pp. 1–6 (2018)
3. Christensen, A.: Wissenschaftliche Literatur entdecken: Was bibliothekarische Discovery-Systeme von der Konkurrenz lernen und was sie ihr zeigen können. LIBREAS, Library Ideas (2022)
4. Hogan, A., Blomqvist, E., Cochez, M., d'Amato, C., et al.: Knowledge graphs. Synth. Lect. Data Semant. Knowl. **12**(2), 1–257 (2021)
5. Peroni, S., Shotton, D.: OpenCitations, an infrastructure organization for open scholarship. Quant. Sci. Stud. **1**(1), 428–444 (2020)
6. Aleman-Meza, B., Hakimpour, F., Budak Arpinar, I., Sheth, A.P.: SwetoDblp ontology of Computer Science publications. J. Web Semant. **5**(3), 151–155 (2007)
7. Färber, M.: The Microsoft academic knowledge graph: a linked data source with 8 billion triples of scholarly data. In: Proceedings of the 18th International Semantic Web Conference. ISWC'19, pp. 113–129 (2019)
8. Waltman, L., Larivière, V.: Special issue on bibliographic data sources. Quant. Sci. Stud. **1**(1), 360–362 (2020)
9. Manghi, P., Mannocci, A., Osborne, F., Sacharidis, D., Salatino, A., Vergoulis, T.: New trends in scientific knowledge graphs and research impact assessment. Quant. Sci. Stud. **2**(4), 1296–1300 (2021)

10. Microsoft Research: Next Steps for Microsoft Academic - Expanding into New Horizons, May 2021. https://www.microsoft.com/en-us/research/project/academic/articles/microsoft-academic-to-expand-horizons-with-community-driven-approach/
11. Berners-Lee, T.: Linked Data - Design Issues, July 2006. https://www.w3.org/DesignIssues/LinkedData.html
12. WDQS Search Team: WDQS Backend Alternatives Working Paper (2022). Version 1.1, 29 March 2022. Wikimedia Foundation, San Franciscio, CA, USA. https://www.wikidata.org/wiki/File:WDQS_Backend_Alternatives_working_paper.pdf
13. Wilkinson, M.D., Dumontier, M., Aalbersberg, I.J., et al.: The FAIR guiding principles for scientific data management and stewardship. Sci. Data **3**(1) (2016)
14. Huang, Y., Lu, W., Liu, J., Cheng, Q., Bu, Y.: Towards transdisciplinary impact of scientific publications: a longitudinal, comprehensive, and large-scale analysis on Microsoft Academic Graph. Inf. Process. Manag. **59**(2) (2022)
15. Wagner, C.S., Horlings, E., Whetsell, T.A., Mattsson, P., Nordqvist, K.: Do nobel laureates create prize-winning networks? An analysis of collaborative research in physiology or medicine. PLOS ONE **10**(7) (2015)
16. Manghi, P., et al.: OpenAIRE Research Graph Dump (June 2022) Version Number: 4.1 https://doi.org/10.5281/zenodo.6616871
17. Wang, R., et al.: AceKG: a large-scale knowledge graph for academic data mining. In: Proceedings of the 27th ACM International Conference on Information and Knowledge Management. CIKM'18, pp. 1487–1490 (2018)
18. Peroni, S., Dutton, A., Gray, T., Shotton, D.: Setting our bibliographic references free: towards open citation data. J. Doc. **71**(2), 253–277 (2015)
19. Sinha, A., et al.: An overview of microsoft academic service (MAS) and applications. In: Proceedings of the 24th International Conference on World Wide Web, Florence Italy, ACM, pp. 243–246, May 2015
20. Herrmannova, D., Knoth, P.: An analysis of the Microsoft Academic graph. D-Lib Mag. **22**(9/10) (2016)
21. Visser, M., van Eck, N.J., Waltman, L.: Large-scale comparison of bibliographic data sources: Scopus, Web of Science, Dimensions, Crossref, and Microsoft Academic. Quant. Sci. Stud. **2**(1), 20–41 (2021)
22. Chen, C.: A glimpse of the first eight months of the COVID-19 literature on Microsoft Academic graph: themes, citation contexts, and uncertainties. Front. Res. Metrics Anal. **5** (2020)
23. Wang, K., Shen, Z., Huang, C., Wu, C.H., Dong, Y., Kanakia, A.: Microsoft Academic Graph: when experts are not enough. Quant. Sci. Stud. **1**(1), 396–413 (2020)
24. Färber, M., Ao, L.: The Microsoft Academic knowledge graph enhanced: author name disambiguation, publication classification, and embeddings. Quant. Sci. Stud. **3**(1), 51–98 (2022)
25. Tay, A., Martín-Martín, A., Hug, S.E.: Goodbye, Microsoft Academic - hello, open research infrastructure? May 2021. https://blogs.lse.ac.uk/impactofsocialsciences/2021/05/27/goodbye-microsoft-academic-hello-open-research-infrastructure/
26. Auer, S., et al.: Improving access to scientific literature with knowledge graphs. Bibliothek Forschung und Praxis **44**(3), 516–529 (2020)
27. Jaradeh, M.Y., et al.: Open research knowledge graph: next generation infrastructure for semantic scholarly knowledge. In: Proceedings of the 10th International Conference on Knowledge Capture. K-CAP'19, Marina Del Rey, CA, USA, pp. 243–246 (2019)
28. Peroni, S., Shotton, D.: The SPAR ontologies. In: Proceedings of the 17th International Semantic Web Conference. ISWC'18, pp. 119–136 (2018)

29. Haase, P., Herzig, D.M., Kozlov, A., Nikolov, A., Trame, J.: Metaphactory: a platform for knowledge graph management. Semant. Web **10**(6), 1109–1125 (2019)
30. Janowicz, K., Hitzler, P., Adams, B., Kolas, D., Vardeman, C.: Five stars of linked data vocabulary use. Semant. Web **5**(3), 173–176 (2014)
31. Bordes, A., Usunier, N., Garcia-Durán, A., Weston, J., Yakhnenko, O.: Translating embeddings for modeling multi-relational data. In: Proceedings of the 26th International Conference on Neural Information Processing Systems - Volume 2. NIPS'13, Red Hook, NY, USA, pp. 2787–2795. Curran Associates Inc. (2013)
32. Yang, B., Yih, W.t., He, X., Gao, J., Deng, L.: Embedding entities and relations for learning and inference in knowledge bases. arXiv preprint arXiv:1412.6575 (2014)
33. Trouillon, T., Welbl, J., Riedel, S., Gaussier, E., Bouchard, G.: Complex Embeddings for Simple Link Prediction, June 2016
34. Hamilton, W.L., Ying, R., Leskovec, J.: Inductive representation learning on large graphs, September 2018. arXiv:1706.02216
35. Veličković, P., Cucurull, G., Casanova, A., Romero, A., Liò, P., Bengio, Y.: Graph attention networks. arXiv preprint arXiv:1710.10903 (2017)
36. Waleffe, R., Mohoney, J., Rekatsinas, T., Venkataraman, S.: MariusGNN: resource-efficient out-of-core training of graph neural networks (2022)
37. Angioni, S., Salatino, A., Osborne, F., Recupero, D.R., Motta, E.: AIDA: a knowledge graph about research dynamics in academia and industry. Quant. Sci. Stud. **2**(4), 1356–1398 (2021)
38. Schindler, D., Zapilko, B., Krüger, F.: Investigating software usage in the social sciences: a knowledge graph approach. In: Proceedings of the Extended Semantic Web Conference. ESWC'20, pp. 271–286 (2020)
39. Färber, M., Lamprecht, D.: The data set knowledge graph: creating a linked open data source for data sets. Quant. Sci. Stud. **2**(4), 1324–1355 (2021)
40. Sinha, A., et al.: An overview of Microsoft Academic Service (MAS) and applications. In: Proceedings of the 24th International Conference on World Wide Web Companion. WWW'15, pp. 243–246 (2015)
41. Massri, M.B., Spahiu, B., Grobelnik, M., Alexiev, V., Palmonari, M., Roman, D.: Towards innograph: a knowledge graph for AI innovation. In: Companion Proceedings of the ACM Web Conference, pp. 843–849 (2023)
42. Marginson, S.: University rankings and social science. Eur. J. Educ. **49**(1), 45–59 (2014)
43. Hu, Z., Dong, Y., Wang, K., Sun, Y.: Heterogeneous graph transformer. In: Proceedings of the Web Conference, pp. 2704–2710 (2020)
44. Färber, M., Nishioka, C., Jatowt, A.: ScholarSight: visualizing temporal trends of scientific concepts. In: Proceedings of the 19th ACM/IEEE on Joint Conference on Digital Libraries. JCDL'19, pp. 436–437 (2019)
45. Lou, Y., Kuehl, B., Bransom, E., Feldman, S., Naik, A., Downey, D.: S2abEL: a dataset for entity linking from scientific tables. arXiv preprint arXiv:2305.00366 (2023)
46. Carrasco, M.H., Luján-Mora, S., Maté, A., Trujillo, J.: Current state of linked data in digital libraries. J. Inf. Sci. **42**(2), 117–127 (2016)
47. Färber, M., Albers, A., Schüber, F.: Identifying used methods and datasets in scientific publications. In: Proceedings of the Workshop on Scientific Document Understanding Co-located with 35th AAAI Conference on Artificial Intelligence. SDU@AAAI'21 (2021)
48. Fathalla, S., Vahdati, S., Auer, S., Lange, C.: Towards a knowledge graph representing research findings by semantifying survey articles. In: Proceedings of the 21st

International Conference on Theory and Practice of Digital Libraries. TPDL'17, pp. 315–327 (2017)

49. Färber, M., Lamprecht, D.: The green AI ontology: an ontology for modeling the energy consumption of AI models. In: Proceedings of the 21st International Semantic Web Conference. ISWC'22 (2022)

50. Saier, T., Krause, J., Färber, M.: unarxive 2022: All arXiv publications preprocessed for NLP, including structured full-text and citation network. In: Proceedings of the 2023 Joint Conference on Digital Libraries. JCDL'23 (2023)

51. Diefenbach, D., Wilde, M.D., Alipio, S.: Wikibase as an infrastructure for knowledge graphs: the EU knowledge graph. In: Hotho, A., et al. (eds.) ISWC 2021. LNCS, vol. 12922, pp. 631–647. Springer, Cham (2021). https://doi.org/10.1007/978-3-030-88361-4_37

52. Heist, N., Haase, P.: Flexible and extensible competency management with knowledge graphs. In: Proceedings of the 20th International Semantic Web Conference. ISWC'21 (2021)

53. Hoffman, M.R., Ibáñez, L.D., Fryer, H., Simperl, E.: Smart papers: dynamic publications on the blockchain. In: Proceedings of the 15th Extended Semantic Web Conference. ESWC'18, pp. 304–318 (2018)

54. Jaradeh, M.Y., Auer, S., Prinz, M., Kovtun, V., Kismihók, G., Stocker, M.: Open research knowledge graph: towards machine actionability in scholarly communication. CoRR abs/1901.10816 (2019)

55. Cossu, M., Färber, M., Lausen, G.: Prost: distributed execution of SPARQL queries using mixed partitioning strategies. In: Proceedings of the 21st International Conference on Extending Database Technology, EDBT 2018, Vienna, Austria, 26–29 March 2018, OpenProceedings.org, pp. 469–472 (2018)

56. Bassani, E., Kasela, P., Raganato, A., Pasi, G.: A multi-domain benchmark for personalized search evaluation. In: Proceedings of the 31st ACM International Conference on Information and Knowledge Management, pp. 3822–3827 (2022)

57. Dzieżyc, M., Kazienko, P.: Effectiveness of research grants funded by European Research Council and Polish National Science Centre. J. Informetrics **16**(1) (2022)

58. Jonkers, K., Zacharewicz, T., et al.: Research Performance Based Funding Systems: A Comparative Assessment. Publications Office of the European Union, Luxembourg (2016)

Comprehensive Analysis of Freebase and Dataset Creation for Robust Evaluation of Knowledge Graph Link Prediction Models

Nasim Shirvani-Mahdavi⬤, Farahnaz Akrami, Mohammed Samiul Saeef,
Xiao Shi, and Chengkai Li⁽✉⁾⬤

University of Texas at Arlington, Arlington, TX 76019, USA
{nasim.shirvanimahdavi2,farahnaz.akrami,mohammedsamiul.saeef,
xiao.shi}@mavs.uta.edu, cli@uta.edu

Abstract. Freebase is amongst the largest public cross-domain knowledge graphs. It possesses three main data modeling idiosyncrasies. It has a strong type system; its properties are purposefully represented in reverse pairs; and it uses mediator objects to represent multiary relationships. These design choices are important in modeling the real-world. But they also pose nontrivial challenges in research of embedding models for knowledge graph completion, especially when models are developed and evaluated agnostically of these idiosyncrasies. This paper lays out a comprehensive analysis of the challenges associated with the idiosyncrasies of Freebase and measures their impact on knowledge graph link prediction. The results fill an important gap in our understanding of embedding models for link prediction as such models were never evaluated using a proper full-scale Freebase dataset. The paper also makes available several variants of the Freebase dataset by inclusion and exclusion of the data modeling idiosyncrasies. It fills an important gap in dataset availability too as this is the first-ever publicly available full-scale Freebase dataset that has gone through proper preparation.

Keywords: Knowledge graph completion · Link prediction · Knowledge graph embedding · Benchmark dataset

1 Introduction

Knowledge graphs (KGs) encode semantic, factual information as triples of the form (subject s, predicate p, object o). They can link together heterogeneous data across different domains for purposes greater than what they support separately. KGs have become an essential asset to a wide variety of tasks and applications in the fields of artificial intelligence and machine learning [13,24], including natural language processing [47], search [46], question answering [22], and recommender systems [49]. Thus, KGs are of great importance to many technology companies [17,30] and governments [3,29].

T. R. Payne et al. (Eds.): ISWC 2023, LNCS 14266, pp. 113–133, 2023.
https://doi.org/10.1007/978-3-031-47243-5_7

To develop and robustly evaluate models and algorithms for tasks on KGs, access to large-scale KGs is crucial. But publicly available KG datasets are often much smaller than what real-world scenarios render and require [23]. For example, FB15k and FB15k-237 [10,39], two staple datasets for knowledge graph completion, only have less than 15,000 entities in each. As of now, only a few cross-domain common fact KGs are both large and publicly available, including DBpedia [7], Freebase [8], Wikidata [41], YAGO [37], and NELL [12].

With more than 80 million nodes, Freebase is amongst the largest public KGs. It comprises factual information in a broad range of domains. The dataset possesses several data modeling idiosyncrasies which serve important practical purposes in modeling the real-world. *Firstly*, Freebase properties are purposefully represented in reverse pairs, making it convenient to traverse and query the graph in both directions [31]. *Secondly*, Freebase uses mediator objects to facilitate representation of n-ary relationships [31]. *Lastly*, Freebase's strong de facto type system categorizes each entity into one or more types, the type of an entity determines the properties it may possess [9], and the label of a property *almost* functionally determines the types of the entities at its two ends.

Albeit highly useful, the aforementioned idiosyncrasies also pose nontrivial challenges in the advancement of KG-oriented technologies. Specifically, when algorithms and models for intelligent tasks are developed and evaluated agnostically of these data modeling idiosyncrasies, one could either miss the opportunity to leverage such features or fall into pitfalls without knowing. One example is that for knowledge graph link prediction—the task of predicting missing s in triple (?, p, o) or missing o in (s, p, ?)—many models [33,42] proposed in the past decade were evaluated using FB15k, a small subset of Freebase full of reverse triple pairs. The reverse triples lead to data leakage in model evaluation. The consequence is substantial over-estimation of the models' accuracy and thus faulty and even reversed comparison of their relative strengths [5].

This paper provides four variants of the Freebase dataset by inclusion/exclusion of mediator objects and reverse triples. It also provides a Freebase type system which is extracted to supplement the variants. It lays out a comprehensive analysis of the challenges associated with the aforementioned idiosyncrasies of Freebase. Using the datasets and the type system, it further measures these challenges' impact on embedding models (e.g., TransE [10] and ComplEx [40]) which are most extensively employed for knowledge graph link prediction. Furthermore, the datasets underwent thorough cleaning in order to improve their utility and to remove irrelevant triples from the original Freebase data dump [18]. The methodology, code, datasets, and experiment results produced from this work, available at https://github.com/idirlab/freebases, are significant contributions to the research community, as follows.

The paper fills an important gap in dataset availability. To the best of our knowledge, ours is the first-ever publicly available full-scale Freebase dataset that has gone through proper preparation. Specifically, our Freebase variants were prepared in recognition of the aforementioned data modeling idiosyncrasies, as well as via thorough data cleaning. On the contrary, the Freebase data dump has all types of triples tangled together, including even data about the operation of Freebase itself which are not common knowledge facts; Freebase86m [51], the only other public full-scale Freebase dataset, also mixes together metadata (such as data related to Freebase type system), administrative data, reverse triples, and mediator objects.

The paper also fills an important gap in our understanding of embedding models for knowledge graph link prediction. Such models were seldom evaluated using the full-scale Freebase. When they were, the datasets used (e.g., the aforementioned Freebase86m) were problematic, leading to unreliable results. The experiments on our datasets inform the research community several important results that were never known before, including 1) the true performance of link prediction embedding models on the complete Freebase, 2) how data idiosyncrasies such as mediator objects and reverse triples impact model performance on the complete Freebase data, and 3) similarly, how the mixture of knowledge facts, metadata and administrative data impact model performance.

The datasets and results are highly relevant to researchers and practitioners, as Freebase remains the single most commonly used dataset for link prediction, by far. Upon examining all full-length publications appeared in 12 top conferences in 2022, we found 53 publications used datasets commonly utilized for link prediction. The conferences, the papers, and the datasets used in them are listed in a file "papers.xlsx" in GitHub repository https://github.com/idirlab/freebases. Amongst these publications, 48 utilized datasets derived from Freebase, only 3 publications used a Freebase dataset at its full scale, specifically Freebase86m, while 8 made use of datasets from Wikidata. The properly processed full-scale Freebase datasets from this work can facilitate researchers and practitioners in carrying out large-scale studies on knowledge graph completion and beyond.

The dataset creation was nontrivial. It required extensive inspection and complex processing of the massive Freebase data dump, for which documents are scarce. None of the idiosyncrasies, as articulated in Sects. 3 and 4, was defined or detailed in the data dump itself. Figuring out the details required iterative trial-and-error in examining the data. To the best of our knowledge, more detailed description of these idiosyncrasies is not available anywhere else. If one must learn to examine Freebase and prepare datasets from scratch, the process has a steep learning curve and can easily require many months. Our datasets can thus accelerate the work of many researchers and practitioners.

The datasets and experimentation design can enable comparison with non-conventional models and on other datasets. Our methodology of processing and analyzing data is extensible to other datasets with similar data modeling idiosyncrasies, such as YAGO3-10 and WN18 which have redundant and reverse relations [5] and Wikidata which represents multiary relationships using *statements*. The experiment design could be extended to studying the impact of multiary relationships in Wikidata on various kinds of link prediction models. Further, given the datasets and experiment results made available in this paper, it becomes possible to compare the real performance of conventional embedding models and hyper-relational fact models [20,34,44,50] on a full-scale Freebase dataset that includes multiary relationships (i.e., mediator objects).

2   Freebase Basic Concepts

This section provides a summary of basic terminology and concepts related to Freebase. We aim to adhere to [9,19,25,31] in nomenclature and notation.

RDF: Freebase is available from its data dumps [18] in N-Triples RDF (Resource Description Format) [25]. An RDF graph is a collection of triples (s, p, o), each comprising a *subject* s, an *object* o, and a *predicate p*. An example triple is (James Ivory, */film/director/film*, A Room with a View).

Topic (entity, node): In viewing Freebase as a graph, its nodes can be divided into *topics* and *non-topics*. Topics are distinct entities, e.g., James Ivory in Fig. 1. An example of non-topic nodes is CVT (Compound Value Type) nodes which are used to represent n-ary relations (details in Sect. 3). Other non-topic nodes are related to property, domain and type (see below). Each topic and non-topic node has a unique *machine identifier* (MID), which consists of a prefix (either /m/ for Freebase Identifiers or /g/ for Google Knowledge Graph Identifiers) followed by a base-32 identifier. For example, the MID of James Ivory is /m/041d94. For better readability, we use the names (i.e., labels) of topics and non-topics in presenting triples in this paper. Inside the dataset, though, they are represented by MIDs.

Type and **domain:** Freebase topics are grouped into *types* semantically. A topic may have multiple types, e.g., James Ivory's types include */people/person* and */film/director*. Types are further grouped into *domains*. For instance, domain *film* includes types such as */film/actor*, */film/director*, and */film/editor*.

Property (predicate, relation, edge): *Properties* are used in Freebase to provide facts about topics. A property of a topic defines a relationship between the topic and its property value. The property value could be a literal or another topic. Property labels are structured as /[domain]/[type]/[label]. The /[domain]/[type] prefix identifies the topic's type that a property belongs to, while [label] provides an intuitive meaning of the property. For example, topic James Ivory has the property */people/person/date_of_birth* with value 1928-06-07. This property is pertinent to the topic's type */people/person*. The topic also has another property */film/director/film*, on which the value is another topic A Room with a View, as shown in Fig. 1. This property is pertinent to another type of the topic—*/film/director*. A relationship is represented as a triple, where the triple's predicate is a property of the topic in the triple's subject. In viewing Freebase as a graph, a property is a directed edge from the subject node to the object node. The type of an edge (i.e., *edge type*) can be distinctly identified by the label of the edge (i.e., the property label). The occurrences of an edge type in the graph are *edge instances*.

Schema: The term schema refers to the way Freebase is structured. It is expressed through types and properties. The schema of a type is the collection of its properties. Given a topic belonging to a type, the properties in that type's schema are applicable to the topic. For example, the schema of type */people/person* includes property */people/person/date_of_birth.* Hence, each topic of this type (e.g., James Ivory) may have the property.

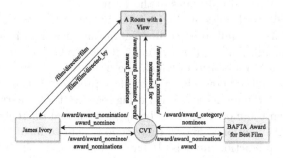

Fig. 1. A small fragment of Freebase, with a mediator node

3   Idiosyncrasies of Freebase and Challenges They Pose

Freebase is the single most commonly used dataset for the task of link prediction, as mentioned in Sect. 1. The Freebase raw data dump contains more than 80 million nodes, more than 14,000 distinct relations, and 1.9 billion triples. It has a total of 105 domains, 89 of which are diverse *subject matter domains*—domains describing real-world facts [13]. This section explains several idiosyncrasies of Freebase's data modeling design choices, and their impacts on link prediction.

3.1   Reverse Triples

When a new fact was included into Freebase, it would be added as a pair of reverse triples (s, *p*, o) and (s, p^{-1}, o) where p^{-1} is the reverse of *p*. Freebase denotes reverse relations explicitly using a special relation */type/property/reverse_property* [16,31]. For instance, */film/film/directed_by* and */film/director/film* are reverse relations, as denoted by a triple (**/film/film/directed_by**, */type/property/reverse_property*, **/film/director/film**). Thus, (James Ivory, */film/director/film*, A Room With A View) and (A Room With A View, */film/film/directed_by*, James Ivory) form reverse triples, shown as two edges in reverse directions in Fig. 1.

Several previous studies discussed the pitfalls in including reverse relations in datasets used for knowledge graph link prediction task [4,5,15,39]. The popular benchmark dataset FB15k (a relatively small subset of Freebase), created by Bordes et al. [10], was almost always used for this task. Toutanova and

Chen [39] noted that FB15k contains many reverse triples. They constructed another dataset, FB15k-237, by only keeping one relation out of any pair of reverse relations. The pitfalls associated with reverse triples in datasets such as FB15k can be summarized as follows. 1) Link prediction becomes much easier on a triple if its reverse triple is available. Hence, the reverse triples led to substantial over-estimation of model accuracy, which is verified by experiments in [5]. 2) Instead of complex models, one may achieve similar results by using statistics of the triples to derive simple rules of the form $(s, p_1, o) \Rightarrow (o, p_2, s)$ where p_1 and p_2 are reverse. Such rules are highly effective given the prevalence of reverse relations [5,15]. 3) The link prediction scenario for such data is non-existent in the real-world at all. For such intrinsically reverse relations that always come in pair, there is not a scenario in which one needs to predict a triple while its reverse is already in the knowledge graph. More precisely, this is a case of excessive *data leakage*—the model is trained using features that otherwise would not be available when the model needs to be applied for real inference.

For all reasons mentioned above, there is no benefit to include reverse triples in building link prediction models. If one still chooses to include them, care must be taken to avoid the aforementioned pitfalls. Particularly, a pair of reverse triples should always be placed together in either training or test set.

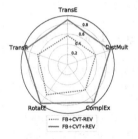 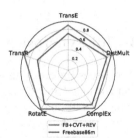

Fig. 2. Impact of reverse triples on MRR† of embedding models

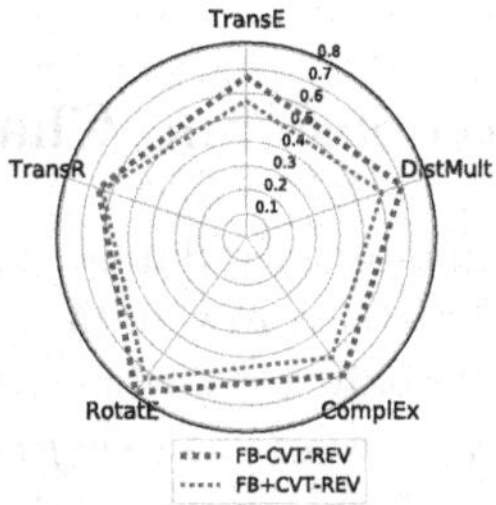

Fig. 3. Impact of mediator nodes on MRR† of embedding models

Fig. 4. Impact of non-subject matter triples on MRR† of embedding models

The impact of reverse triples was previously only examined on small-scale datasets FB15k and FB15k-237 [4,5,15,39]. Our corresponding experiment results on full-scale Freebase thus answer an important question for the first time. While the full results and experiment setup are detailed in Sect. 7 (specifically Table 7 and Fig. 5), here we summarize the most important observations. Figure 2 compares the performance of several representative link predication models on a commonly used performance measure MRR†, using two new full-scale Freebase datasets created by us (details of dataset creation in Sect. 6). FB+CVT+REV is obtained after cleaning the Freebase data dump and removing irrelevant data, and in FB+CVT-REV reverse relations are further removed by only keeping one relation out of each reverse pair. Similar to the comparison

Table 1. Link prediction performance (MRR$^\top$) on FB+CVT-REV vs. FB+CVT+REV

	FB+CVT-REV			FB+CVT+REV		
Model	unidir	bidir	all	unidir	bidir	all
TransE	0.72	0.56	0.57	0.75	0.89	0.88
DistMult	0.65	0.60	0.61	0.70	0.94	0.92
ComplEx	0.67	0.61	0.62	0.69	0.94	0.92
TransR	0.66	0.63	0.64	0.75	0.94	0.93
RotatE	0.67	0.74	0.73	0.73	0.96	0.94

Table 2. Link prediction performance (MRR$^\top$) on FB-CVT-REV vs. FB+CVT-REV

	FB-CVT-REV			FB+CVT-REV		
Model	binary	concatenated	all	binary	multiary	all
TransE	0.60	0.90	0.67	0.57	0.96	0.57
DistMult	0.64	0.89	0.70	0.61	0.77	0.61
ComplEx	0.66	0.90	0.71	0.62	0.80	0.62
TransR	0.58	0.92	0.66	0.63	0.87	0.64
RotatE	0.76	0.92	0.80	0.73	0.88	0.73

results on small-scale FB15k vs. FB15k-237, the results on the full-scale datasets also show drastic decrease of model accuracy after removal of reverse triples and thus overestimation of model performance due to reverse triples.

We further break down the results by categorizing all relations into two groups—*unidirectional relations* (denoted as "unidir" in Table 1 and Table 3) which do not have reverse relations and *bidirectional relations* (denoted "bidir") which have reverse relations in the original Freebase data dump. In Table 1, the columns labeled "all" correspond to Fig. 2 and are for both categories of relations together. As the table shows, while the performance degradation is universal, the drop is significantly more severe for bidirectional relations due to removing reserve triples.

Table 3. Link prediction results on FB15k-237 vs. FB15k

	FB15k-237						
Model	MRR$^\top$ (unidir)	MRR$^\top$ (bidir)	MRR$^\top$ (all)	MR$^\downarrow$	Hits@1$^\top$	Hits@3$^\top$	Hits@10$^\top$
TransE	0.35	0.22	0.24	257.75	0.14	0.28	0.44
DistMult	0.31	0.23	0.24	385.12	0.14	0.27	0.43
ComplEx	0.30	0.22	0.23	425.38	0.14	0.25	0.42
TransR	0.54	0.58	0.57	196.99	0.52	0.59	0.67
RotatE	0.39	0.22	0.24	288.43	0.16	0.26	0.42
	FB15k						
Model	MRR$^\top$ (unidir)	MRR$^\top$ (bidir)	MRR$^\top$ (all)	MR$^\downarrow$	Hits@1$^\top$	Hits@3$^\top$	Hits@10$^\top$
TransE	0.56	0.63	0.63	46.55	0.49	0.73	0.83
DistMult	0.60	0.69	0.68	59.92	0.57	0.76	0.86
ComplEx	0.59	0.76	0.74	66.37	0.66	0.81	0.88
TransR	0.63	0.66	0.66	66.09	0.57	0.72	0.80
RotatE	0.63	0.68	0.68	50.28	0.57	0.75	0.85

To put the discussion in context, we reproduced the results on FB15k and FB15k-237 using DGL-KE [51], which is the framework we used in this study for experiments on large-scale datasets. The results (Table 3) are mostly consistent with previously reported results using frameworks for small-scale datasets (e.g., LibKGE [11]), barring differences that can be attributed to implementations of different frameworks. Comparing Table 1 and Table 3, we can observe that models' performance on full-scale datasets is significantly higher than the small-scale counterpart, unsurprisingly given the much larger datasets. What are common for both small-scale and large-scale datasets are the performance degradation due to removal of reverse triple as well as the observations regarding unidirectional vs. bidirectional relations.

3.2   Mediator Nodes

Mediator nodes, also called CVT nodes, are used in Freebase to represent n-ary relationships [31]. For example, Fig. 1 shows a CVT node connected to an award, a nominee, and a work. This or similar approach is necessary for accurate modeling of the real-world. Note that, one may convert an n-ary relationship centered at a CVT node into $\binom{n}{2}$ binary relationships between every pair of entities, by concatenating the edges that connect the entities through the CVT node. While such a transformation may help reduce the complexity of algorithmic solutions, it results in loss of information [44] and is irreversible [33], and thus it may not always be an acceptable approach as far as data semantics is concerned. Nevertheless, most prior studies of knowledge graph link prediction use Freebase datasets without CVT nodes, e.g., FB15k and FB15k-237, which applied the aforementioned transformation. Though lossful for Freebase-like KGs, the insights gained using such datasets could be more applicable toward graphs with only binary relationships.

When multiary relationships (i.e., CVT nodes) are present, link prediction could become more challenging as CVT nodes are long-tail nodes with limited connectivity. Nonetheless, impact of CVT nodes on the effectiveness of current link prediction approaches is unknown. This paper for the first time presents experiment results in this regard, on full-scale Freebase datasets. While Sect. 7 presents the full results, here we highlight the most important observations.

Figure 3 shows the performance ($\mathtt{MRR}^\uparrow$) of various models on two of our new datasets, FB-CVT-REV and FB+CVT-REV (dataset details in Sect. 6). In both datasets, reverse relations are removed by keeping only one relation out of every reverse pair so that we can solely focus on the impact of CVT nodes. CVT nodes are kept in FB+CVT-REV but removed from FB-CVT-REV by the concatenation approach discussed in Sect. 6. All models performed worse when CVT nodes are present, verifying our earlier analysis.

We further broke down the results by categorizing all relations into two groups—binary relations and multiary (or concatenated) relations. Binary relations are between two regular entities. While multiary relations in FB+CVT-REV connect regular entities with CVT nodes, concatenated relations in FB-CVT-REV are the binary relations converted from multiary relations. In Table 2, the columns labeled "all" correspond to Fig. 3 and are for both categories of relations together. These results show that most models perform better on concatenated relations than multiary relations, further verifying the aforementioned challenges posed by CVT nodes. Furthermore, for all models and datasets, the models' accuracy on concatenated/multiary relations are substantially higher than that on binary relations. This could be due to different natures of binary and multiary relations in the datasets and is worth further examination.

3.3   Metadata and Administrative Data

As stated in [13], Freebase domains can be divided into 3 groups: implementation domains, Web Ontology Language (OWL) domains, and subject matter domains. Freebase implementation domains such as */dataworld/* and */freebase/* include triples that convey schema and technical information used in creation of Freebase. According to [18], */dataworld/* is "a domain for schema that deals with operational or infrastructural information" and */freebase/* is "a domain to administer the Freebase application." For example, */freebase/mass_data_operation* in the */freebase/* domain is a type for tracking large-scale data tasks carried out by Freebase data team. OWL domains contain properties such as *rdfs:domain* and *rdfs:range* for some predicates p. *rdfs:domain* denotes to which type the subject of any triple of predicate p belongs, and *rdfs:range* denotes the type of the object of any such triple [6]. For example, the domain and range of the predicate *film/director/film* are *director* and *film*, respectively.

Different from implementation domains and OWL domains, subject matter domains contain triples about knowledge facts. We call (s, p, o) a subject matter triple if s, p and o belong to subject matter domains. Computational tasks and applications thus need to be applied on this category of domains instead of the other two categories. However, about 31% of the Freebase86m [51] triples fall under non-subject matter domains, more specifically implementation domains since OWL domains were removed from Freebase86m. These domains are listed in Table 4, to show concretely what they are about. The purposes of some of these domains were explained earlier in this section. We have created 4 datasets in which only the triples belonging to subject matter domains are retained. We also provide the information related to type system as discussed in Sect. 3. The details of this process are discussed in Sect. 6.

Table 4. Statistics of implementation domains in Freebase86m

Domain	#Triples	%Total
/common/	48,610,556	14.4
/type/	26,541,747	7.8
/base/	14,253,028	4.2
/freebase/	7,705,605	2.3
/dataworld/	6,956,819	2.1
/user/	322,215	0.1
/pipeline/	455,377	0.1
/kp_lw/	1,034	0.0003

Table 5. Link prediction performance (MRR[†]) on Freebase86m and FB+CVT+REV

Model	Freebase86m			FB+CVT+REV
	subj matter	non-subj matter	all	all
TransE	0.74	0.68	0.72	0.88
DistMult	0.91	0.64	0.83	0.92
ComplEx	0.91	0.64	0.83	0.92
TransR	0.76	0.39	0.65	0.93
RotatE	0.92	0.56	0.82	0.94

Figure 4 shows the impact of non-subject matter triples by comparing the performance ($MRR^{\uparrow}$) of link prediction models on Freebase86m and our new dataset FB+CVT+REV, which includes only subject matter triples. The figure shows the adverse effect of non-subject matter triples. Table 5 further breaks down the results separately on subject matter and non-subject matter triples. The results clearly show that the models struggled on non-subject matter triples.

4   Freebase Type System

Freebase categorizes each topic into one or more types and each type into one domain. Furthermore, the triple instances satisfy *pseudo* constraints as if they are governed by a rigorous type system. Specifically, 1) given a node, its types set up constraints on the labels of its properties; the /[domain]/[type] segment in the label of an edge in most cases is one of the subject node's types. To be more precise, this is a constraint satisfied by 98.98% of the nodes—we found 610,007 out of 59,896,902 nodes in Freebase (after cleaning the data dump; more to be explained later in Sect. 6) having at least one property belonging to a type that is not among the node's types. 2) Given an edge type and its edge instances, there is *almost* a function that maps from the edge type to a type that all subjects in the edge instances belong to, and similarly *almost* such a function for objects. For instance, all subjects of edge *comedy/comedian/genres* belong to type */comedy/comedian* and all their objects belong to */comedy/comedy_genre*. Particularly, regarding objects, the Freebase designers explained that every property has an "expected type" [9]. For each edge type, we identified the most common entity type among all subjects and all objects in its instances, respectively. To this end, we filtered out the relations without edge labels in Freebase data dump, since the type of a property is known by its label. Given 2,891 such edge types with labels out of 3,055 relations in our dataset FB-CVT-REV (explained in Sect. 6), for 2,011, 2,510, 2,685, and 2,723 edge types, the most common entity type among subjects covers 100%, 99%, 95%, and 90% of the edge instances, respectively. With regard to objects, the numbers are 2,164, 2,559, 2,763, and 2,821, for 100%, 99%, 95%, and 90%, respectively.

Given the *almost* true constraints reflected by the aforementioned statistics, we created an explicit type system, which can become useful when enforced in various tasks such as link prediction. Note that Freebase itself does not explicitly specify such a type system, even though its data appear to follow guidelines that approximately form the type system, e.g., the "expected type" mentioned earlier. Our goal in creating the type system is to, given an edge type, designate a *required type* for its subjects (and objects, respectively) from a pool of candidates formed by all types that the subjects (objects, respectively) belong to. As an example, consider edge type */film/film/performance* and the entities *o* at the object end of its instances. These entities belong to types {*/film/actor*, */tv/tv_actor*, */music/artist*, */award/award_winner*, */people/person*}, which thus form the candidate pool. We select the required type for its object end in two steps, and the same procedure is applied for the subject/object ends of all edge types.

In *step 1*, we exclude a candidate type t if $P(o \in t) < \alpha$, i.e., the probability of the object end of */film/film/performance* belonging to t is less than a threshold α. The rationale is to keep only those candidates with sufficient coverage. In the dataset, $P(o \in$ */film/actor$) = 0.9969$, $P(o \in$ */tv/tv_actor$) = 0.1052$, $P(o \in$ */music/artist$) = 0.0477$, $P(o \in$ */award/award_winner$) = 0.0373$, and $P(o \in$ */people/person$) = 0.998$. Using threshold $\alpha = 0.95$, */tv/tv_actor*, */music/artist* and */award/award_winner* were excluded. In *step 2*, we choose the most *specific* type among the remaining candidates. The most specific type is given by $\arg\min_t \sum_{t' \neq t} P(o \in t | o \in t')$, where t and t' are from remaining candidates. $P(o \in t | o \in t')$ is the conditional probability of a Freebase entity o belonging to type t given that it also belongs to type t'. In the dataset, $P(o \in$ */people/person* $| o \in$ */film/actor$) = 0.9984$ and $P(o \in$ */film/actor* $| o \in$ */people/person$) = 0.1394$. Thus, we assigned */film/actor* as the required entity type for objects of edge type */film/film/performance* because it is more specific than */people/person*, even though */people/person* had slightly higher coverage.

The type system we created can be useful in improving link prediction. A few studies in fact employed type information for such a goal [21,45]. Particularly, embedding models can aim to keep entities of the same type close to each other in the embedding space [21]. Further, type information could be a simple, effective model feature. For instance, given the task of predicting the objects in (James Ivory, */film/director/film*, ?), knowing the object end type of */film/director/film* is */film/film* can help exclude many candidates. Finally, type information can be used as a constraint for generating more useful negative training or test examples. For instance, a negative example (James Ivory, */film/director/film*, BAFTA Award for Best Film) has less value in gauging a model's accuracy since it is a trivial case, as BAFTA Award for Best Film is not of type */film/film*.

5   Defects of Existing Freebase Datasets

Over the past decade, several datasets were created from Freebase. This section reviews some of these datasets and briefly discusses flaws associated with them.

FB15k [10] includes entities with at least 100 appearances in Freebase that were also available in Wikipedia based on the *wiki-links* database [14]. Each included relation has at least 100 instances. 14,951 entities and 1,345 relations satisfy these criteria, which account for 592,213 triples included into FB15k. These triples were randomly split into training, validation and test sets. This dataset suffers from data redundancy in the forms of reverse triples, duplicate and reverse-duplicate relations. Refer to [5] for a detailed discussion of such.

FB15k-237 [39], with 14,541 entities, 237 relations and 309,696 triples, was created from FB15k in order to mitigate the aforementioned data redundancy. Only the most frequent 401 relations from FB15k are kept. Near-duplicate and reverse-duplicate relations were detected, and only one relation from each pair of such redundant relations is kept. This process further decreased the number of relations to 237. This step could incorrectly remove useful information, in two scenarios. 1) False positives. For example, hypothetically *place_of_birth* and *place_of_death* may have many overlapping subject-object pairs, but they are not semantically redundant. 2) False negatives. The creation of FB15k-237 did not resort to the accurate reverse relation information encoded by *reverse_property* in Freebase. For example, */education/educational_institution/campuses* and */education/educational_institution_campus/educational_institution* are both in FB15k-237 but they are reverse relations according to *reverse_property*.

Freebase86m is created from the last Freebase data dump and is employed in evaluating large-scale knowledge graph embedding frameworks [28,51]. It includes 86,054,151 entities, 14,824 relations and 338,586,276 triples. No information is available on how this dataset was created. We carried out an extensive investigation to assess its quality. We found that 1) 31% of the triples in this dataset are non-subject matter triples from Freebase implementation domains such as */common/* and */type/*, 2) 23% of the dataset's nodes are mediator nodes, and 3) it also has abundant data redundancy since 38% of its triples form reverse triples. As discussed in Sect. 3, non-subject matter triples should be removed; reverse triples, when not properly handled, lead to substantial over-estimation of link predication models' accuracy; and the existence of mediator nodes presents extra challenges to models. Mixing these different types of triples together, without clear annotation and separation, leads to foreseeably unreliable models and results. Section 7 discusses in detail the impact of these defects in Freebase86m.

6   Data Preparation

Variants of the Freebase Dataset. We created four variants of the Freebase dataset by inclusion/exclusion of reverse triples and CVT nodes. Table 6 presents the statistics of these variants, including number of entities, number of relations, and number of triples. The column "CVT" indicates whether each dataset includes or excludes CVT nodes, and the column "reverse" indicates whether the dataset includes or excludes reverse triples. Correspondingly, the dataset names use +/− of CVT/REV to denote these characteristics. The type system we created is also provided as auxiliary information. Metadata and administrative triples are removed, and thus the variants only include subject matter triples. The rest of this section provides details about how the variants were created from the original Freebase data dump, which is nontrivial largely due to the scarcity of available documentation.

Table 6. Statistics of the four variants of Freebase

Variant	CVT	reverse	#Entities	#Relations	#Triples
FB-CVT-REV	×	×	46,069,321	3,055	125,124,274
FB-CVT+REV	×	✓	46,077,533	5,028	238,981,274
FB+CVT-REV	✓	×	59,894,890	2,641	134,213,735
FB+CVT+REV	✓	✓	59,896,902	4,425	244,112,599

URI Simplification. In a Freebase triple (subject, *predicate*, object), each component that is not a literal value is identified by a URI (uniform resource identifier) [25]. For simplification and usability, we removed URI prefixes such as "<*http://rdf.freebase.com/>*", "<*http://rdf.freebase.com/ns/>*" and "<*http://www.w3.org/[0-9]*/[0-9]*/[0-9]*-*>*". We only retained URI segments corresponding to domains, types, properties' labels, and MIDs. These segments are dot-delimited in the URI. For better readability, we replaced the dots by "/". For example, URI <*http://rdf.freebase.com/ns/film.director.film>* is simplified to */film/director/film*. Likewise, <*http://rdf.freebase.com/ns/award.award_winner>* and <*http://rdf.freebase.com/ns/m.0zbqpbf>*, which are the URIs of a Freebase type and an MID, are simplified to */award/award_winner* and /m/0zbqpbf. The mapping between original URIs and simplified labels are also included in our datasets as auxiliary information.

Extracting Metadata. The non-subject matter triples are used to extract metadata about the subject matter triples. We created a mapping between Freebase entities and their types using predicate */type/object/types*. Using predicate */type/object/name*, we created a lookup table mapping the MIDs of entities to their labels. Similarly, using predicate */type/object/id*, we created lookup tables mapping MIDs of Freebase domains, types and properties to their labels.

Detecting Reverse Triples. As discussed in Sect. 3, Freebase has a property */type/property/reverse_property* for denoting reverse relations. A triple (r1, */type/property/reverse_property*, r2) indicates that relations *r1* and *r2* are reverse of each other. When we remove reverse triples to produce FB-CVT-REV and FB+CVT-REV, i.e., triples belonging to reverse relations, we discard all triples in relation *r2*.

Detecting Mediator Nodes. Our goal is to identify and separate all mediator (CVT) nodes. It is nontrivial as Freebase does not directly denote CVT nodes although it does specify 2,868 types as *mediator types*. According to our empirical analysis, a mediator node can be defined as a Freebase object that belongs to at least one mediator type but was given no label. One example is object /m/011tzbfr which belongs to the mediator type */comedy/comedy_group_membership* but has no label. Once we found all CVTs, we created Freebase variants with and without such nodes. The variants without CVTs were produced by creating concatenated edges that collapse CVTs and merge intermediate edges (edges with at least one CVT endpoint). For instance, the triples (BAFTA Award for Best Film, */award/award_category/nominees*, CVT) and (CVT, */award/award_nomination/award_nominee*, James Ivory) in Fig. 1 would be concatenated to form a new triple (BAFTA Award for Best Film, */award/award_category/nominees–/award/award_nomination/award_nominee*, James Ivory). Note that, in converting n-ary relationships to binary relationships, the concatenation does not need to be carried out along edges in the same direction. For each pair of reverse triples only one is kept, and the choice of which one to keep is random. Two edges connected to the same CVT node thus can have various combinations of directions, depending how their reverse edges were randomly removed. Moreover, the performance of the models cannot be affected by these random selection of reverse triple removal.

7   Experiments

Task. The *link prediction* task as described in [10] is particularly widely used for evaluating different embedding methods. Its goal is to predict the missing h or t in a triple (h, r, t). For each test triple (h, r, t), the head entity h is replaced with every other entity h' in the dataset, to form *corrupted* triples. The original test triple and its corresponding corrupted triples are ranked by their scores according to a scoring function. The scoring function takes learned entity and relation representations as input. The rank of the original test triple is denoted $rank_h$. The same procedure is used to calculate $rank_t$ for the tail entity t. A method with the ideal performance should rank the test triple at top.

Evaluation Measures. We gauge the accuracy of embedding models by several commonly used measures in [10] and follow-up studies, including $Hits@1^{\uparrow}$, $Hits@3^{\uparrow}$, $Hits@10^{\uparrow}$, $MR^{\downarrow}$ (Mean Rank), and $MRR^{\uparrow}$ (Mean Reciprocal Rank). An upward/downward arrow beside a measure indicates that methods with greater/ smaller values by that measure possess higher accuracy. Instead of directly using the above-mentioned raw metrics', we use their corresponding *filtered* metrics [10], denoted $FHits@1^{\uparrow}$, $FHits@3^{\uparrow}$, $FHits@10^{\uparrow}$, $FMR^{\downarrow}$, and $FMRR^{\uparrow}$. In calculating these measures, corrupted triples that are already in training, test or validation sets do not participate in ranking. In this way, a model is not penalized for ranking other correct triples higher than a test triple.

Models. We trained and evaluated five well-known link prediction embedding models—TransE [10], TransR [27], DistMult [48], ComplEx [40], and RotatE [38]—on the four variant datasets of Freebase discussed in Sect. 6. TransE, RotatE and TransR are three representative translational distance models. DistMult and ComplEx are semantic matching models that exploit similarity-based scoring functions [51].

Experiment Setup. Multi-processing, multi-GPU distributed training frameworks have recently become available to scale up embedding models [26,51,52]. Our experiments were conducted using one such framework, DGL-KE [51], with the settings and hyperparameters suggested in [51]. The experiments used an Intel-based machine with a Xeon E5-2695 processor running at 2.1 GHz, Nvidia Geforce GTX1080Ti GPU, and 256 GB RAM. The datasets were randomly divided into training, validation and test sets with the split ratio of 90/5/5, as in [51]. In our two datasets with CVT nodes, we made sure that a CVT node present in the test or validation set is also present in the training set. More details on experiment setup as well as training and inference time logs are available from our GitHub repository.

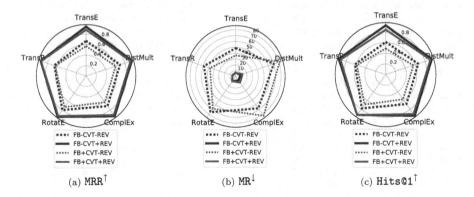

Fig. 5. Link prediction performance on our four new variants of Freebase

Results on Full-Scale vs. Small-Scale Freebase Datasets. The experiment results are reported in Table 7 and Fig. 5. Link prediction results on full-scale Freebase datasets have never been reported before, barring results on problematic datasets such as Freebase86m which we explained in Sect. 3.3. Our datasets FB-CVT-REV and FB-CVT+REV can be viewed as the full-scale counterparts of FB15k-237k and FB15k (of which the results are in Table 3), respectively. Comparing the results on the full-scale and small-scale datasets shows that models have much stronger performance on the full-scale datasets. Our goal is not to compare different models or optimize the performance of any particular model. Rather, the significant performance gap between the full-scale and small-scale Freebase datasets is worth observing and not reported before. This accuracy difference could be attributed to the dataset size difference, as is the case in machine learning in general. Results like these suggest that our datasets can provide opportunities to evaluate embedding models more realistically.

Impact of Reverse Relations. The impact of reverse relations at the scale of the full Freebase dataset was never studied before. This paper thus fills the gap. As Fig. 5 and Table 7 show, results on the two variants without CVT nodes—FB-CVT-REV (reverse relations excluded) and FB-CVT+REV (reverse relations included)—present substantial over-estimation of link prediction models' accuracy when reverse triples are included. So do the results on the two variants with CVT nodes—FB+CVT-REV and FB+CVT+REV.

Impact of Mediator Nodes. As articulated in Sect. 3.2, no prior work has studied the impact of mediator nodes on link prediction, regardless of dataset

Table 7. Link prediction performance on four new Freebase variants and Freebase86m

Table 8. Triple classification results on FB15k-237

	FB-CVT-REV				
Model	MRR$^\uparrow$	MR$^\downarrow$	Hits@1$^\uparrow$	Hits@3$^\uparrow$	Hits@10$^\uparrow$
TransE	0.67	48.49	0.61	0.70	0.78
DistMult	0.70	70.49	0.66	0.72	0.77
ComplEx	0.71	67.74	0.68	0.73	0.78
TransR	0.66	58.55	0.62	0.68	0.74
RotatE	0.80	75.72	0.78	0.81	0.84

	FB-CVT+REV				
Model	MRR$^\uparrow$	MR$^\downarrow$	Hits@1$^\uparrow$	Hits@3$^\uparrow$	Hits@10$^\uparrow$
TransE	0.94	6.07	0.92	0.95	0.97
DistMult	0.95	9.23	0.94	0.96	0.97
ComplEx	0.95	8.43	0.95	0.96	0.97
TransR	0.94	5.98	0.93	0.95	0.96
RotatE	0.96	10.43	0.95	0.96	0.97

	FB+CVT-REV				
Model	MRR$^\uparrow$	MR$^\downarrow$	Hits@1$^\uparrow$	Hits@3$^\uparrow$	Hits@10$^\uparrow$
TransE	0.57	36.12	0.49	0.61	0.75
DistMult	0.61	81.84	0.56	0.63	0.70
ComplEx	0.62	83.20	0.57	0.64	0.70
TransR	0.64	47.52	0.58	0.66	0.75
RotatE	0.73	68.43	0.69	0.75	0.80

	FB+CVT+REV				
Model	MRR$^\uparrow$	MR$^\downarrow$	Hits@1$^\uparrow$	Hits@3$^\uparrow$	Hits@10$^\uparrow$
TransE	0.88	5.60	0.84	0.92	0.96
DistMult	0.92	12.92	0.91	0.93	0.95
ComplEx	0.92	13.27	0.91	0.93	0.95
TransR	0.93	6.07	0.91	0.94	0.96
RotatE	0.94	10.26	0.93	0.95	0.96

	Freebase86m				
Model	MRR$^\uparrow$	MR$^\downarrow$	Hits@1$^\uparrow$	Hits@3$^\uparrow$	Hits@10$^\uparrow$
TransE	0.72	23.27	0.65	0.77	0.87
DistMult	0.83	45.54	0.81	0.84	0.87
ComplEx	0.83	46.55	0.81	0.84	0.86
TransR	0.65	71.91	0.61	0.68	0.74
RotatE	0.82	65.46	0.81	0.82	0.84

	consistent h			
Model	Precision	Recall	Acc	F1
TransE	0.52	0.59	0.52	0.55
DistMult	0.53	0.51	0.53	0.52
ComplEx	0.54	0.48	0.53	0.51
RotatE	0.52	0.53	0.52	0.52

	inconsistent h			
Model	Precision	Recall	Acc	F1
TransE	0.81	0.69	0.76	0.74
DistMult	0.94	0.87	0.91	0.90
ComplEx	0.94	0.88	0.91	0.91
RotatE	0.89	0.83	0.87	0.86

	consistent t			
Model	Precision	Recall	Acc	F1
TransE	0.58	0.54	0.57	0.56
DistMult	0.59	0.55	0.58	0.57
ComplEx	0.60	0.56	0.59	0.58
RotatE	0.60	0.47	0.58	0.53

	inconsistent t			
Model	Precision	Recall	Acc	F1
TransE	0.90	0.82	0.86	0.86
DistMult	0.95	0.89	0.92	0.92
ComplEx	0.95	0.90	0.93	0.92
RotatE	0.87	0.78	0.83	0.82

scale. Comparing the results on the two variants without reverse triples—FB-CVT-REV (mediator nodes excluded) and FB+CVT-REV (mediator nodes included), as illustrated in Fig. 5 and Table 7, shows that the existence of CVT nodes led to weaker model accuracy. Although the results on FB-CVT+REV and FB+CVT+REV are over-estimations since they both retained reverse triples, similar observation regarding mediator nodes is still made—the models are slightly less accurate on FB+CVT+REV (mediator nodes included) than FB-CVT+REV (mediator nodes excluded). More detailed analyses remain to be done, in order to break down different impacts of individual factors that contribute to the performance degeneration, such as the factors analyzed in Sect. 3.2. Our newly created datasets will facilitate research in this direction.

Freebse86m vs. FB+CVT+REV. Comparing the results on these two datasets, as shown in Table 7 and Fig. 4, reveals that the existence of non-subject matter triples degenerates model performance. In general, non-subject matter triples and subject-matter triples should be examined separately given their fundamental difference. Mixing them together hinders robust understanding of embedding models' effectiveness in predicting knowledge facts.

Usefulness of the Type System. To demonstrate the usefulness of the Freebase type system we created (Sect. 4), we evaluated embedding models' performance on the task of triple classification [43] using the LibKGE library [11]. This task is the binary classification of triples regarding whether they are true or false facts. We needed to generate a set of negative triples in order to conduct this task. The type system proves useful in generating type-consistent negative samples. When triple classification was initially used for evaluating models [36,43], negative triples were generated by randomly corrupting head or tail entities of test and validation triples. The randomly generated negative test cases are not challenging as they mostly violate type constraints which were discussed in Sect. 4, leading to overestimated classification accuracy. Pezeshkpour et al. [32] and Safavi et al. [35] noted this problem and created harder negative samples. Inspired by their work, we created two sets of negative samples for test and validation sets of FB15k-237. One set complies with type constraints and the other violates such constraints. To generate a type consistent negative triple for a test triple (h, r, t), we scan the ranked list generated for tail entity prediction to find the first entity t' in the list that has the expected type for the objects of relation r. We then add the corrupted triple (h, r, t') to the set of type consistent negative triples for tail entities if it does not exists in FB15k-237. We repeat the same procedure to corrupt head entities and to create negative samples for validation data. To generate type-violating negative triples we just make sure the type of the entity used to corrupt a positive triple is different from the original entity's type. The results of triple classification on these new test sets are presented in Table 8. Note that Table 8 does not include TransR since it is not implemented in LibKGE. The results in the table show that the models' performance on type-consistent negative samples are much lower than their performance on type-violating negative samples.

8   Conclusion

We laid out a comprehensive analysis of the challenges associated with Freebase data modeling idiosyncrasies, including CVT nodes, reverse properties, and type system. To tackle these challenges, we provide four variants of the Freebase dataset by inclusion and exclusion of these idiosyncrasies. We further conducted experiments to evaluate various link prediction models on these datasets. The results fill an important gap in our understanding of embedding models for knowledge graph link prediction as such models were never evaluated using a proper full-scale Freebase dataset. The paper also fills an important gap in dataset availability as this is the first-ever publicly available full-scale Freebase dataset that has gone through proper preparation.

Acknowledgments. This material is based upon work supported by the National Science Foundation under Grants IIS-1719054 and IIS-1937143.

Resource Availability Statement. The code and experiment results produced from this work are available from GitHub [1] and the datasets are made available at Zenodo [2].

References

1. The GitHub repository of Freebases (2022). https://github.com/idirlab/freebases
2. Freebase datasets for robust evaluation of knowledge graph link prediction models (2023). https://doi.org/10.5281/zenodo.7909511
3. Open knowledge network roadmap: powering the next data revolution (2023). https://new.nsf.gov/tip/updates/nsf-releases-open-knowledge-network-roadmap-report
4. Akrami, F., Guo, L., Hu, W., Li, C.: Re-evaluating embedding-based knowledge graph completion methods. In: Proceedings of the 27th ACM International Conference on Information and Knowledge Management, pp. 1779–1782. Association for Computing Machinery, Turin, Italy (2018)
5. Akrami, F., Saeef, M.S., Zhang, Q., Hu, W., Li, C.: Realistic re-evaluation of knowledge graph completion methods: an experimental study. In: Proceedings of the 2020 ACM Special Interest Group on Management of Data International Conference on Management of Data, pp. 1995–2010. Association for Computing Machinery, Portland, Oregon, USA (2020)
6. Allemang, D., Hendler, J.: Semantic Web for the Working Ontologist: Effective Modeling in RDFS and OWL. Elsevier, Online (2011)
7. Auer, S., Bizer, C., Kobilarov, G., Lehmann, J., Cyganiak, R., Ives, Z.: DBpedia: a nucleus for a web of open data. In: Aberer, K., et al. (eds.) Proceedings of the 6th International Semantic Web Conference and 2nd Asian Semantic Web Conference. LNCS, vol. 4825, pp. 722–735. Springer, Cham (2007). https://doi.org/10.1007/978-3-540-76298-0_52
8. Bollacker, K., Evans, C., Paritosh, P., Sturge, T., Taylor, J.: Freebase: a collaboratively created graph database for structuring human knowledge. In: Proceedings of the 2008 ACM Special Interest Group on Management of Data International Conference on Management of Data, pp. 1247–1250. Association for Computing Machinery, Vancouver, Canada (2008)
9. Bollacker, K., Tufts, P., Pierce, T., Cook, R.: A platform for scalable, collaborative, structured information integration. In: International Workshop on Information Integration on the Web, pp. 22–27. AAAI Press, Vancouver, British Columbia (2007)
10. Bordes, A., Usunier, N., Garcia-Durán, A., Weston, J., Yakhnenko, O.: Translating embeddings for modeling multi-relational data. In: Proceedings of the 26th International Conference on Neural Information Processing Systems, pp. 2787–2795. Curran Associates, Lake Tahoe, Nevada, United States (2013)

11. Broscheit, S., Ruffinelli, D., Kochsiek, A., Betz, P., Gemulla, R.: LibKGE - a knowledge graph embedding library for reproducible research. In: Proceedings of the 2020 Conference on Empirical Methods in Natural Language Processing: System Demonstrations, pp. 165–174. Association for Computational Linguistics, Online (2020)

12. Carlson, A., Betteridge, J., Kisiel, B., Settles, B., Hruschka, E.R., Mitchell, T.M.: Toward an architecture for never-ending language learning. In: Twenty-Fourth AAAI Conference on Artificial Intelligence, pp. 1306–1313. AAAI Press, New York, USA (2010)

13. Chah, N.: Freebase-triples: a methodology for processing the Freebase data dumps. arXiv preprint arXiv:1712.08707 (2017)

14. Code, G.: Wikipedia links data (2012). https://code.google.com/archive/p/wiki-links/. Accessed 9 June 2022

15. Dettmers, T., Pasquale, M., Pontus, S., Riedel, S.: Convolutional 2D knowledge graph embeddings. In: Proceedings of the 32nd AAAI Conference on Artificial Intelligence, pp. 1811–1818. AAAI Press, New Orleans, Louisiana, USA (2018)

16. Färber, M.: Semantic Search for Novel Information. IOS Press, Amsterdam (2017)

17. Ferrucci, D., et al.: Building Watson: an overview of the DeepQA project. AI Mag. **31**(3), 59–79 (2010)

18. Google: Freebase data dumps (2013). https://developers.google.com/freebase. Accessed 11 Nov 2022

19. Grant, J., Beckett, D.: RDF test cases (2004). https://www.w3.org/TR/rdf-testcases/

20. Guan, S., Jin, X., Wang, Y., Cheng, X.: Link prediction on N-ary relational data. In: The World Wide Web Conference, pp. 583–593. Association for Computing Machinery, San Francisco, CA, USA (2019)

21. Guo, S., Wang, Q., Wang, B., Wang, L., Guo, L.: Semantically smooth knowledge graph embedding. In: Proceedings of the 53rd Annual Meeting of the Association for Computational Linguistics and the 7th International Joint Conference on Natural Language Processing, pp. 84–94. Association for Computational Linguistics, Beijing, China (2015)

22. Hao, Y., et al.: An end-to-end model for question answering over knowledge base with cross-attention combining global knowledge. In: Proceedings of the 55th Annual Meeting of the Association for Computational Linguistics, pp. 221–231. Association for Computational Linguistics, Vancouver, Canada (2017)

23. Hu, W., et al.: Open graph benchmark: datasets for machine learning on graphs. Adv. Neural Inf. Process. Syst. **33**, 22118–22133 (2020)

24. Ji, S., Pan, S., Cambria, E., Marttinen, P., Philip, S.Y.: A survey on knowledge graphs: representation, acquisition, and applications. IEEE Trans. Neural Networks Learn. Syst. **33**(2), 494–514 (2021)

25. Klyne, G.: Resource description framework (RDF): Concepts and abstract syntax (2004). http://www.w3.org/TR/2004/REC-rdf-concepts-20040210/

26. Lerer, A., et al.: PyTorch-BigGraph: a large scale graph embedding system. Proc. Mach. Learn. Syst. **1**, 120–131 (2019)

27. Lin, Y., Liu, Z., Sun, M., Liu, Y., Zhu, X.: Learning entity and relation embeddings for knowledge graph completion. In: Proceedings of the 29th AAAI Conference on Artificial Intelligence, pp. 2181–2187. AAAI Press, Austin, Texas, USA (2015)

28. Mohoney, J., Waleffe, R., Xu, H., Rekatsinas, T., Venkataraman, S.: Marius: learning massive graph embeddings on a single machine. In: 15th USENIX Symposium on Operating Systems Design and Implementation, pp. 533–549. The Advanced Computing Systems Association, Online (2021)

29. Networking, information technology research, development: Open knowledge network: Summary of the big data IWG workshop (2018). https://www.nitrd.gov/open-knowledge-network-summary-of-the-big-data-iwg-workshop/
30. Noy, N., Gao, Y., Jain, A., Narayanan, A., Patterson, A., Taylor, J.: Industry-scale knowledge graphs: lessons and challenges. Commun. ACM **62**(8), 36–43 (2019)
31. Pellissier Tanon, T., Vrandečić, D., Schaffert, S., Steiner, T., Pintscher, L.: From Freebase to Wikidata: the great migration. In: Proceedings of the 25th International Conference on World Wide Web, pp. 1419–1428. Association for Computing Machinery, Montreal, Canada (2016)
32. Pezeshkpour, P., Tian, Y., Singh, S.: Revisiting evaluation of knowledge base completion models. In: Automated Knowledge Base Construction, p. 10. OpenReview, Online (2020)
33. Rossi, A., Barbosa, D., Firmani, D., Matinata, A., Merialdo, P.: Knowledge graph embedding for link prediction: a comparative analysis. ACM Trans. Knowl. Discov. Data (TKDD) **15**(2), 1–49 (2021)
34. Rosso, P., Yang, D., Cudré-Mauroux, P.: Beyond triplets: hyper-relational knowledge graph embedding for link prediction. In: Proceedings of The Web Conference 2020, pp. 1885–1896. Association for Computing Machinery, Online (2020)
35. Safavi, T., Koutra, D.: CoDEx: a comprehensive knowledge graph completion benchmark. In: Proceedings of the 2020 Conference on Empirical Methods in Natural Language Processing, pp. 8328–8350. Association for Computational Linguistics, Online (2020)
36. Socher, R., Chen, D., Manning, C.D., Ng, A.: Reasoning with neural tensor networks for knowledge base completion. In: Proceedings of the 26th International Conference on Neural Information Processing Systems, pp. 926–934. Curran Associates, Lake Tahoe, United States (2013)
37. Suchanek, F.M., Kasneci, G., Weikum, G.: YAGO: a large ontology from Wikipedia and WordNet. J. Web Semant. **6**(3), 203–217 (2008)
38. Sun, Z., Deng, Z.H., Nie, J.Y., Tang, J.: RotatE: knowledge graph embedding by relational rotation in complex space. In: Proceedings of the International Conference on Learning Representations, pp. 926–934. OpenReview.net, New Orleans, LA, USA (2019)
39. Toutanova, K., Chen, D.: Observed versus latent features for knowledge base and text inference. In: Proceedings of the 3rd Workshop on Continuous Vector Space Models and their Compositionality, pp. 57–66. Association for Computational Linguistics, Beijing, China (2015)
40. Trouillon, T., Welbl, J., Riedel, S., Gaussier, É., Bouchard, G.: Complex embeddings for simple link prediction. In: Proceedings of the 33rd International Conference on Machine Learning, pp. 2071–2080. JMLR.org, New York City, NY, USA (2016)
41. Vrandečić, D., Krötzsch, M.: Wikidata: a free collaborative knowledge base. Commun. ACM **57**(10), 78–85 (2014)
42. Wang, Q., Mao, Z., Wang, B., Guo, L.: Knowledge graph embedding: a survey of approaches and applications. IEEE Trans. Knowl. Data Eng. **29**(12), 2724–2743 (2017)
43. Wang, Z., Zhang, J., Feng, J., Chen, Z.: Knowledge graph embedding by translating on hyperplanes. In: Proceedings of the 28th AAAI Conference on Artificial Intelligence, pp. 1112–1119. AAAI Press, Québec City, Québec, Canada (2014)
44. Wen, J., Li, J., Mao, Y., Chen, S., Zhang, R.: On the representation and embedding of knowledge bases beyond binary relations. In: Proceedings of the International

Joint Conference on Artificial Intelligence, pp. 1300–1307. IJCAI, New York City, USA (2016)

45. Xie, R., Liu, Z., Sun, M., et al.: Representation learning of knowledge graphs with hierarchical types. In: Proceedings of International Joint Conference on Artificial Intelligence, vol. 2016, pp. 2965–2971. IJCAI, New York City, USA (2016)

46. Xiong, C., Power, R., Callan, J.: Explicit semantic ranking for academic search via knowledge graph embedding. In: Proceedings of the 26th International Conference on World Wide Web, pp. 1271–1279. Association for Computing Machinery, Perth, Australia (2017)

47. Yang, B., Mitchell, T.: Leveraging knowledge bases in LSTMs for improving machine reading. In: Proceedings of the 55th Annual Meeting of the Association for Computational Linguistics (vol. 1: Long Papers), pp. 1436–1446. Association for Computational Linguistics, Vancouver, Canada (2017)

48. Yang, B., Yih, W.T., He, X., Gao, J., Deng, L.: Embedding entities and relations for learning and inference in knowledge bases. In: Proceedings of the International Conference on Learning Representations, p. 12. OpenReview.net, San Diego, CA, USA (2015)

49. Zhang, F., Yuan, N.J., Lian, D., Xie, X., Ma, W.Y.: Collaborative knowledge base embedding for recommender systems. In: Proceedings of the 22nd ACM SIGKDD International Conference on Knowledge Discovery and Data Mining, pp. 353–362. Association for Computing Machinery, San Francisco, CA, USA (2016)

50. Zhang, R., Li, J., Mei, J., Mao, Y.: Scalable instance reconstruction in knowledge bases via relatedness affiliated embedding. In: Proceedings of the 2018 World Wide Web Conference, pp. 1185–1194. Association for Computing Machinery, Lyon, France (2018)

51. Zheng, D., et al.: DGL-KE: training knowledge graph embeddings at scale. In: Proceedings of the 43rd International ACM SIGIR Conference on Research and Development in Information Retrieval, pp. 739–748. Association for Computing Machinery, Xi'an, China (2020)

52. Zhu, Z., Xu, S., Qu, M., Tang, J.: GraphVite: a high-performance CPU-GPU hybrid system for node embedding. In: The World Wide Web Conference, pp. 2494–2504. Association for Computing Machinery, San Francisco, CA, USA (2019)

The SAREF Pipeline and Portal—An Ontology Verification Framework

Maxime Lefrançois$^{(\boxtimes)}$ and David Gnabasik

Mines Saint-Étienne, Univ Clermont Auvergne, INP Clermont Auvergne, CNRS,
UMR 6158 LIMOS, 42023 Saint-Étienne, France
{maxime.lefrancois,david.gnabasik}@emse.fr

Abstract. The Smart Applications REFerence Ontology (SAREF)
defines a modular set of versioned ontologies that enable semantic interoperability between different Internet of Things (IoT) vendor solutions
across various IoT industries. The European Telecommunications Standards Institute Specialist Task Force (ETSI STF) 578 recently completed the "Specification of the SAREF Development Framework and
Workflow and Development of the SAREF Community Portal for User
Engagement". This project specifies the development pipeline and workflow needed to accelerate the development of SAREF and its extensions
along with the development of software that automates the generation of
ontology portal content from SAREF sources on the public ETSI Forge.
This paper describes the SAREF Pipeline that provides an efficient and
robust support infrastructure for the Continuous Integration and Delivery of semantic ontology development.

Keywords: SAREF · ETSI · SmartM2M · Ontology · Semantic ·
IoT · Continuous Delivery · Quality control · Pipeline

1 Introduction

The Smart Applications REFerence Ontology (SAREF) defines a modular set
of versioned ontologies that enable semantic interoperability between different
Internet of Things (IoT) vendor solutions across various IoT industries [5,17].
SAREF was promoted by the European Commission in collaboration with the
European Telecommunications Standards Institute (ETSI) *SmartM2M* technical committee to design a common data model to limit the fragmentation of
the Internet of Things (IoT) by enabling interoperability between solutions from
different vendors across various IoT industries, thus contributing to the development of the global digital marketplace and the European data spaces.

The value of SAREF is strongly correlated with the size of its community of
users, and also to the agility of the SAREF developers to improve the SAREF
ontologies and react to raised issues. As such, SAREF users' community and the
industry actors need be attracted to SAREF with clear web documentation and
a clear indication about how to provide their input and the kind of input that

T. R. Payne et al. (Eds.): ISWC 2023, LNCS 14266, pp. 134–151, 2023.
https://doi.org/10.1007/978-3-031-47243-5_8

they can provide. ETSI Specialist Task Force (STF) 578 recently completed the "Specification of the SAREF Development Framework and Workflow and Development of the SAREF Community Portal for User Engagement". The ultimate project goal is to enable SAREF users in various industries to contribute to and maintain SAREF without requiring specialized or advanced ontology engineering skills, so as to lower the level of support needed by ETSI members, and in particular SmartM2M members. Experts participating in STF 578 specified the general development framework for the SAREF ontology and its extensions, generally referred to as *SAREF projects*, in the ETSI TS 103 673 technical specification [13], and the sources of SAREF were migrated to the public ETSI Forge portal https://saref.etsi.org/sources/.

This paper provides an overview of this ETSI TS 103 673 technical specification, with an emphasis on the specification of requirements for *SAREF project repositories*: git repositories that contain the sources of a SAREF project. It then provides a functional and technical overview of the *SAREF Pipeline* software, that automates checking the compliance of SAREF project repositories against this specification, and automates the generation of the static documentation website. The SAREF pipeline is openly available under an open BSD-3-Clause license at https://saref.etsi.org/sources/saref-pipeline/. It has already been used to accelerate the development of version 3 of SAREF and the 12 published SAREF extensions, and to generate the contents of the public SAREF community portal available at https://saref.etsi.org/

The rest of this paper is organized as follows. Section 2 describes related work. Section 3 describes the modular architecture of the SAREF ontology core and its extensions. Section 4 provides an overview of ETSI TS 103 673, especially who and how SAREF ontology development proceeds, and which rules SAREF project repositories must comply to. Section 5 describes the SAREF Pipeline software and how it is configured for continuous integration and delivery. Section 6 qualifies the impact, reusability and availability of the SAREF Pipeline and discusses current work. Section 7 offers our conclusions.

2   Related Work

Automation in ontology engineering aims to accelerate the production of high quality ontology artifacts by automating manual or redundant tasks and preventing bad releases. For example linting tools[1] supporting the ontology editing process limit the difficulty of editing ontologies of good quality. Examples include Jena Eyeball,[2] and RDFLint[3]. The latter is integrated in the extension *RDF language support via rdflint*[4] of Visual Studio Code, and allows to execute

---

[1] Linting, named after a UNIX pre-processor command for the C language, is an approach that consists of statically analyzing software source code to detect errors, bugs, or style mistakes.

[2] https://jena.apache.org/documentation/archive/eyeball/eyeball-manual.html.

[3] https://github.com/imas/rdflint.

[4] https://marketplace.visualstudio.com/items?itemName=takemikami.vscode-rdflint.

SPARQL queries, to validate SHACL constraints, or to validate that literals are well formed. Command line interfaces available in software such as Apache Jena[5] also help automating common tasks in ontology development.

The ROBOT tool [22] developed by the Open Biological and Biomedical Ontologies (OBO)[6] community provides ontology processing commands for a variety of bio-medical/disease research tasks such as commands for converting formats, filtering axioms, invoking a reasoner for logical validation and automatic classification (where all direct inferred *subClassOf* axioms are added to the ontology), creating and extracting import modules, verifying the correct execution of SPARQL unit test queries, and running reports. Although ROBOT itself is not a workflow manager, the various ROBOT commands are often combined into automated workflows using a separate task execution system such as GNU Make. The main release artifacts are an OWL file and an OBO file. Since ROBOT was designed to enforce many of the OBO Foundry conventions, ROBOT helps guarantee that released ontologies are free of certain types of logical errors and conform to standard quality control checks, thereby increasing the overall robustness and efficiency of the ontology development life cycle. ROBOT also employs the OWL API library. Whereas ROBOT facilitates the ontology engineering in the bio-medical research community, SAREF's engineering mandate is the unified interoperability of IoT sensor networks from multiple industries and use-cases.

Authors in [4] identified data standards and reporting formats that use version control and summarize common practices in earth and environmental sciences. Just as Agile methods aim to improve collaborations between software project customers and developers, DevOps methods improve collaborations between developers and IT operations professionals. Jenkins, Travis CI, Circle CI, Gitlab CI/CD, Github Actions, are all frameworks that allow to specify task pipelines that will be executed automatically when, for example, a commit is pushed to the server. Before the democratization of these frameworks, a few preliminary approaches were proposed in the ontology engineering community using Github applications[7]. For example VoCol [20] or OnToology [2]. *Ontology Development Kit* (ODK) [27] uses Travis CI to run workflows with ROBOT. CI/CD pipelines are reported for the publication of different ontologies, such as the Financial Industry Business Ontology (FIBO) in [1], the International Data Spaces Information Model (IDSA) in [3], and the CASE Cyber Ontology[8]. Specific GitHub actions are available on the GitHub marketplace for running RDFLint[9], validating RDF syntaxes[10,11], or validating RDF files against SHACL shapes[12] or ShEx [31].

---

[5] https://jena.apache.org/documentation/tools/index.html.
[6] https://obofoundry.org/.
[7] https://docs.github.com/en/developers/apps.
[8] https://github.com/marketplace/actions/case-ontology-validator.
[9] https://github.com/marketplace/actions/setup-rdflint.
[10] https://github.com/marketplace/actions/rdf-syntax-check.
[11] https://github.com/marketplace/actions/validate-rdf-with-jena.
[12] https://github.com/marketplace/actions/validate-shacl.

3   SAREF - A Modular and Versioned Suite of Ontologies

As illustrated in Fig. 1, the SAREF suite of ontologies is composed of ontologies that define generic patterns such as SAREF4SYST [12], a core ontology SAREF Core [14] illustrated in Fig. 2, and different extensions developed for distinct vertical domains: SAREF4ENER for energy [6], SAREF4ENVI for environment [8], SAREF4BLDG for smart buildings [8], SAREF4CITY for smart cities, SAREF4INMA for industry and manufacturing, SAREF4AGRI for agriculture and food, SAREF4AUTO for automotive [9], SAREF4EHAW for e-health and ageing well [10], SAREF4WEAR for wearables [11], SAREF4WATR for water management [7], and SAREF4LIFT for smart lifts [15].

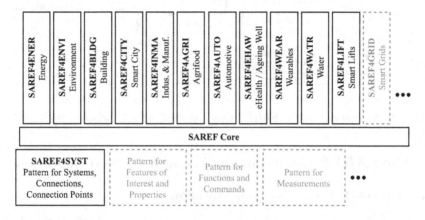

Fig. 1. The SAREF suite of ontologies with its different modules. Dashed blocks are under development in ongoing projects.

SAREF Projects are formally endorsed by ETSI as Technical Specification documents, and therefore adopt the *semantic versioning* approach as specified by the ETSI version numbering system for documents.[13] Each SAREF project version is tagged with three numbers: a *major*, a *technical*, and a *non-technical*. A major increment indicates a break in backward compatibility. A technical increment indicates technical changes. A non-technical increment indicates an editorial change.

---

[13] https://portal.etsi.org/Services/editHelp/How-to-start/Document-procedures-and-types/Version-numbering-system.

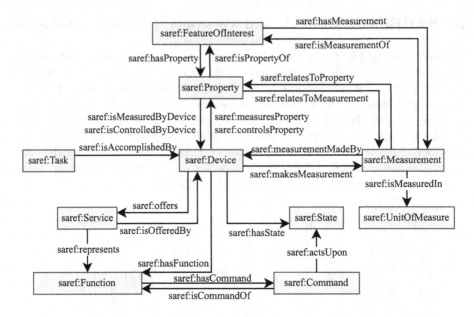

Fig. 2. An overview of the SAREF Core ontology V3.1.1 (adapted from [14])

4   The SAREF Development Framework and Workflow

4.1   The SAREF Development Workflow

In general, the development of SAREF ontologies follows the Linked Open Terms (LOT) methodology [29], which adopts a V-model approach with conditional jumps to previous development stages. The following roles are defined in [13, Clause 5]:

Steering Board member: steers the development of SAREF extensions, community participation, and underlying infrastructure.

Technical Board member: maintains the SAREF public forge and portal.

Project Leader: performs SAREF project management tasks.

Ontology Developer: uses their in-depth understanding of ontology development to interactively modify the ontology during the development cycle. Ontology developers create and modify the different development artefacts, provide new requirements to the ontology, validate whether they are satisfied or not when implemented, and make decisions regarding what contributions are included in the ontology.

Contributor: proposes contributions to the ontology given their domain-specific knowledge.

Ontology User: is interested in any of the SAREF projects or in proposing a new project.

Different workflows are established:

Workflow 1: new SAREF project versions [13, Clause 6.1].
Workflow 2: project version development [13, Clause 7.1].
Workflow 3: project release (publication) [13, Clause 8.1].

Workflow 1 applies to new versions of the SAREF Core, new versions of existing SAREF extensions, or initial versions (V1.1.1) of new SAREF extensions. For example, Fig. 3 illustrates the workflow for the development of different project versions from the SAREF community of users. The project version development workflow is founded upon the issues recorded in the corresponding SAREF project issue tracker on the public ETSI Forge portal. The issue tracker not only presents a single point of development interaction, but also tracks development activity and discussions. Any update to a SAREF project version is made through a change request that is posted as an issue in the corresponding git repository of the public forge, where it is assigned an issue number. Issues include change requests related to new ontology requirements, defects, or improvements in the ontology specification, in the ontology tests and examples, or in the ontology documentation. Any contributor can create a new change request or review and discuss existing change requests. Steering Board members then review these change requests. Ontology developers also review change requests, propose, and review implementations of accepted change requests. The project leader ensures that the change requests are approved by SmartM2M and that the implementations of the change requests satisfy the requested change.

4.2   SAREF Project Repositories on the ETSI Forge

SAREF Projects may correspond to SAREF Core or a SAREF Extension. Each SAREF Extension is assigned an identifier that is based on a four letter code. SAREF Projects are hosted in a git repository on the public ETSI Forge https://saref.etsi.org/sources/. *Release branches* are used instead of tags to identify releases, thus allowing continuous evolution of the documentation or examples after the ontology version is published. SAREF project repositories therefore have four different types of branches:

- `issue-x` branches to work on an issue,
- `develop-vx.y.z` branches to work on a version,
- `prerelease-vx.y.z` branches to work on the final validation of the ontology,
- `release-vx.y.z` branches for published versions.

Protection rules are defined to prevent ontology developers from directly pushing their changes to `development-vx.y.z` branches or from directly accepting merge requests in `prerelease-vx.y.z` branches. In addition, the `saref-portal` repository[14] contains the static resources of the SAREF public documentation portal, and a file `.saref-repositories.yml` that references each of the SAREF projects whose documentation needs to be generated on the portal.

---

[14] https://saref.etsi.org/sources/saref-portal.

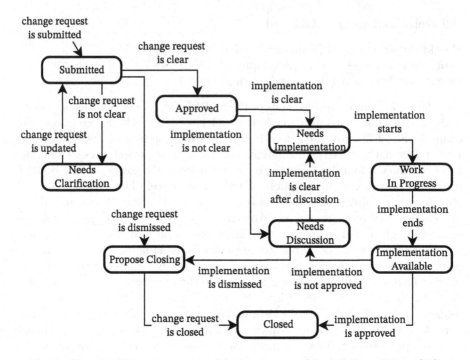

Fig. 3. The SAREF project version development workflow (adapted from [13])

4.3 SAREF Project Version Specification and Documentation

Clause 9 in the ETSI TS 103 673 technical specification [13, Clause 9] outlines the rules to which each SAREF project repository must comply. All these rules, summarized below, are automatically checked by the SAREF Pipeline.

Clause 9.2. The SAREF project version directory shall[15] contain a README.md, a LICENSE file, and folders requirements, ontology, tests, examples, documentation.

Clauses 9.3.1. and 9.3.2. The requirements directory should contain a file requirements.csv. If present, this file shall be a UTF-8 encoded CSV file with specific delimiter, quote character, and specific header row.

Clause 9.4.1. The ontology directory shall contain the ontology document of the project version saref.ttl for SAREF Core, saref4abcd.ttl for SAREF extension SAREF4ABCD. This file shall contain the sources of a consistent OWL2 DL ontology in the Turtle 1.1 format.

Clause 9.4.2. If the document contains a base or prefix declarations, they shall conform to the ones given in this clause.

---

[15] ETSI draft editing rules disallow the use of the MUST keyword. The highest level of specification enforcement is SHALL.

Clause 9.4.3.1. specifies which ontology series IRI and which ontology version IRI shall be used, along with version-related metadata such as owl:versionInfo, vann:preferredNamespacePrefix, vann:preferredNamespaceUri, and owl:prior Version if applicable.

Clause 9.4.3.2. specifies which ontology metadata shall, should, or may be defined, and which value and/or datatype they shall have if they are defined. In general the use of Dublin Core terms is enforced. Ontology imports are often a source of versioning problems. This clause stipulates that supporting ontologies are imported by their version IRI and not by the ontology series identifier. For example, SAREF4LIFT V1.1.1 imports SAREF Core V3.1.1, SAREF4SYST V1.1.2, and SAREF4BLDG V1.1.2. This rule effectively avoids imported ontology versioning issues.

Clause 9.4.3.3. defines who can be considered a creator or a contributor to the SAREF project version, and how they may be described in the ontology. In general persons are described using IRIs or blank nodes, which then shall be instances of schema:Person and further described using a schema:givenName and schema:familyName. Affiliations shall be described as instances of schema:Organization.

Clause 9.4.4.1. defines which namespace shall be used for terms defined in the ontology document, and which naming convention shall be used for classes and properties.

Clause 9.4.4.2. enforces the use of rdfs:label and rdfs:comment metadata on terms, which should at least have one rdf:langString datatype with the en language tag.

Clause 9.4.5. specifies that the ontology shall satisfy the OWL2 DL profile, with the exception that unknown datatypes may be used. It shall be consistent, it should not present ontology development pitfalls as per the OntOlogy Pitfall Scanner! (OOPS!) [30], and every declared class should be satisfiable.

Clause 9.5.1. and 9.5.2. The `tests` directory should contain a file `tests.csv`. If present, this file shall be a UTF-8 encoded CSV file with specific delimiter, quote character, and given header row.

Clause 9.6.1. The `examples` directory should contain example documents that illustrate how the ontology can be used in practice. Every example document shall be a consistent OWL2 DL ontology in the Turtle 1.1 format. Main classes and properties should be illustrated with at least one example.

Clause 9.6.2. Specifies allowed prefixes and base declarations in examples.

Clause 9.6.3. The example document shall be declared as a dctype:Dataset. It shall be asserted to conform to (dct:conformsTo) the SAREF project version IRI. It additionally may conform to other SAREF project specific versions, or some ontology published by international Standard Development Organizations. Additional metadata elements shall be used.

Clause 9.6.4. The RDF graph in the example document, when augmented with an ontology declaration that imports all the ontologies the example conforms to, shall satisfy the OWL2 DL profile, with the exception that unknown datatypes may be used, and shall be consistent.

Clause 9.7.1. The `documentation` directory should contain documentation sources to provide human-readable documentation for the ontology and how it can be used in practice. These documentation sources are for `creators`, `contributors`, `abstract`, `description`, `examples`, `references`, `acknowledgements`. They shall be a HTML snippet and have the extension .html or be a markdown snippet and have extension .md.

Clause 9.7.2. Diagrams should be included in a directory `documentation/diagrams`, and adopt graphical notations from [18].

5   Quality Control and Requirements Verification with the SAREF Pipeline

The SAREF Pipeline software verifies the conformance to the specification summarized in Sect. 4.3, and generates the HTML documentation of SAREF. It can be run on a SAREF project repository, or on the `saref-portal` repository for verifying all the SAREF projects and generating the complete documentation of SAREF to be deployed on the public SAREF community portal. This section provides technical details about this software, how the checks are performed, and how it is used.

5.1   User Interface, Execution Modes, Error Reporting

The SAREF Pipeline operates in either a graphical mode (Fig. 4) or a command line interface (Fig. 5) depending upon the ontology developer's preference. Choosing an *execution mode* determines the thoroughness and coverage of the pipeline tests and usually depends on the development stage:

develop some metadata such as version numbers are not checked;

release thorough check of the repository which must be clean (contain no tracked and modified files);

portal pre-release run on the `saref-portal` repository to operate a strict check and generate the documentation for all pre-release and release branches of the source repositories;

portal release same as above, but only considers release branches.

The ontology engineer may also choose to skip some tasks such as the analysis of examples, the generation of the HTML documentation for terms, or the generation of the HTML documentation altogether.

The SAREF Pipeline provides a detailed but easy-to-read global view of all the identified warnings and errors. Violation of *shall* clauses trigger errors, while violation of *should* clauses trigger warnings. The logs are formatted in HTML in the GUI and markdown in the CLI, which is convenient to create nicely-formatted issues rapidly to collaboratively deal with problems.[16] In addition, a log file in the JUnit report format is generated, which can be used by GitLab to provide an overview of the issues in Merge Requests.[17]

---

[16] example: https://labs.etsi.org/rep/saref/saref4agri/-/issues/1.

[17] Test reports in Merge Request on GitLab: https://docs.gitlab.com/ee/ci/testing/unit_test_reports.html.

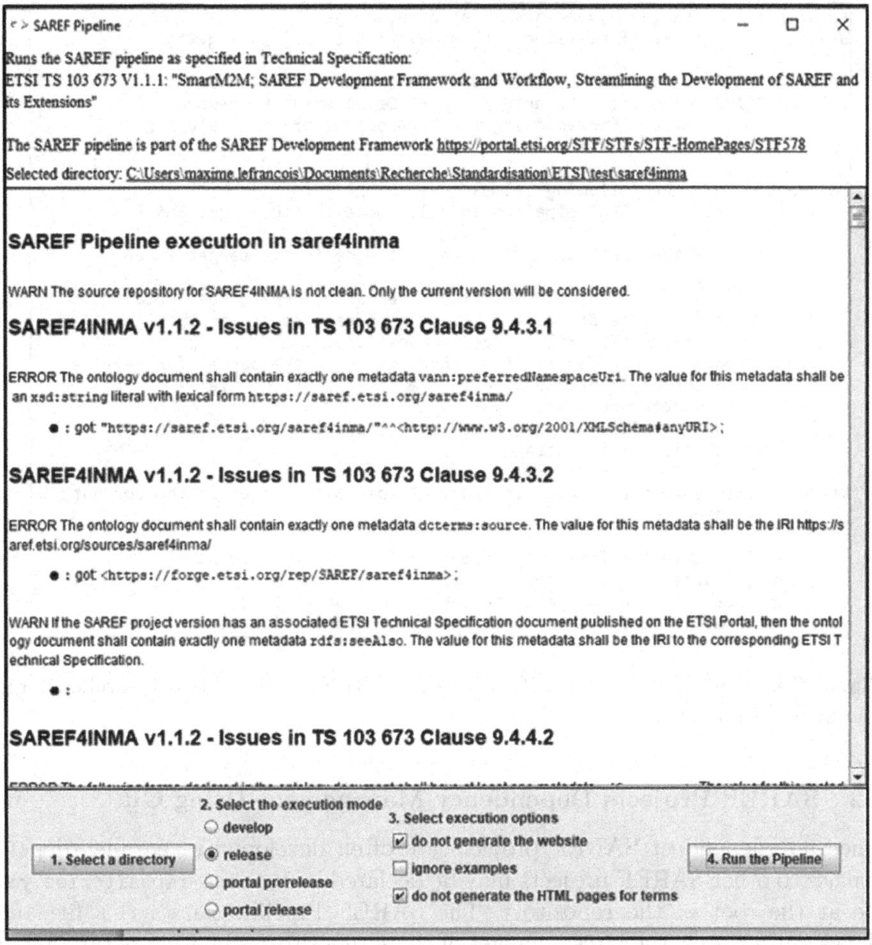

Fig. 4. Graphical User Interface (GUI) of the SAREF Pipeline https://saref.etsi.org/
sources/saref-pipeline/

```
saref-pipeline/target$ java -jar saref-pipeline.jar
usage: java -jar saref-pipeline.jar <mode> [<options>] [<target>]

Runs the SAREF pipeline as specified in Technical Specification:
  ETSI TS 103 673 V1.1.1: "SmartM2M; SAREF Development Framework and
            Workflow, Streamlining the Development of SAREF and its
            Extensions"

<mode> can take the following values:
  develop    Run the SAREF pipeline in relax mode in the target SAREF
             project
  release    Run the SAREF pipeline in strict mode in the target SAREF
             project
  prerelease-portal   Operate a strict check and generate the portal for
             pre-release or release branches of each source in the
             configuration file `.saref-repositories.yml`
  release-portal   Operate a strict check generate the portal for release
             branches of each source in the configuration file
             `.saref-repositories.yml`
  clean      Remove all files generated by the previous executions
  help       Displays this message

<target> points to the target directory. By default, target is the current
             directory.

<options> can take the following values:
  -e,--no-examples   Do not check examples
  -s,--no-site       Do not generate the static portal
  -t,--no-terms      Do not generate the static portal for terms
```

Fig. 5. Command Line Interface (CLI) of the SAREF Pipeline https://saref.etsi.org/sources/saref-pipeline/

5.2   SAREF Projects Dependency Management Using Git

Since interdependent SAREF projects are often developed in parallel, dependencies to other SAREF projects may be declared in a .saref-repositories.yml file at the root of the repository. The SAREF Pipeline parses this file and clones and/or pulls the latest changes of those repositories in a temporary folder sources. It prompts the user for credentials for non-public repositories.

If the ontology document or if an example imports one of these SAREF ontologies in a specific version, then this folder is checked out at the corresponding branch (release, prerelease, or develop branch) before the ontology file is loaded.

Other checks use git operations. For example in Clause 9.4.3.1 the SAREF Pipeline computes the ontology version IRI from the version number in the branch name (not possible if on a issue-x branch), and the desired value for owl:priorVersion based on the list of release-x.y.z branches.

5.3   Testing Requirement Satisfaction with Themis

Requirements (requirements.csv file) and tests (tests.csv file) are sent to the Themis service [16] which automatically generates OWL Axioms based on Lexico-Syntactic patterns analysis of the tests, and checks that the ontology contains the generated axioms.

5.4   Checks Based on SHACL

SHACL shapes [23] are used for verifying clauses 9.4.3.1 (ontology IRI and ontology version IRI), 9.4.3.2 (ontology metadata), 9.4.3.3 (creators and contributors), 9.4.4.2 (ontology terms metadata), and 9.6.3. (example declaration). The general process is as follows:

Step 1: The SAREF Pipeline loads the RDF graph containing SHACL shape stubs[18] for the clause being verified;

Step 2: The RDF graph containing the SHACL shapes is updated with information that is computed on-the-fly;

Step 3: The RDF graph of the ontology or the example being tested is evaluated against the SHACL shapes;

Step 4: The conformance result (a RDF Graph) is queried for warnings and errors, which are logged.

Updates in Step 2 include:

- adding localized violation messages (all clauses);
- computing the expected ontology series IRI, objects for the owl:versionIRI, owl:versionInfo and owl:priorVersion annotations, and preferred prefix and namespace metadata (Clause 9.4.3.1);
- removing some metadata checks when running in **develop** (relaxed) mode (Clause 9.4.3.2);
- expliciting the target nodes for shapes that verify metadata for terms: only those terms that have the namespace of the ontology are required to have a label and a comment in that ontology (Clause 9.4.4.2);
- computing to which ontology the example shall conform to (Clause 9.6.3).

5.5   Checks Using OWL API and Hermit

Checking Clauses 9.4.5 and 9.6.4 involves the use of the OWL API library [21]. Violations to the OWL2 DL profile are logged, except those related to undefined datatypes[19]. Then the consistency of the ontology or example is verified using Hermit [19], and optionally a maximum of 10 inconsistency explanations are logged. Finally, the coherence of each class in the signature except owl:Nothing is checked, and optionally a maximum of 10 incoherence explanations are logged.

As the SAREF Pipeline generally relies on Apache Jena and Git for dependency management, a specific `OntologyParser` realization class was developed such that OWL API can consume Jena RDF Models, and potentially checkout repositories in specific branches while resolving imports.

Before checking examples, the dctype:Dataset and dct:conformsTo declarations are replaced by owl:Ontology and owl:imports, respectively. This way,

---

[18] Stubs for SHACL shapes are available at https://saref.etsi.org/sources/saref-pipeline/-/tree/master/src/main/resources/shapes.

[19] Violations of type `UseOfDefinedDatatypeInDatatypeRestriction`, `UseOfDefinedDatatypeInLiteral`, `UseOfUndeclaredDatatype`, and `UseOfUnknownDatatype`.

OWL API can resolve imports and check the consistency of the example plus the ontologies it conforms to. In addition, all the classes in the signature of the example and the ontologies it conforms to are checked for coherence.

5.6 Documentation Generation

The last phase in the SAREF Pipeline execution is the generation of the documentation in a folder `site`, that is ultimately served on the SAREF Portal https://saref.etsi.org/ using an Apache 2 web server. Documentation is generated for ontology versions, examples, and terms, and an `.htaccess` document is generated to implement content negotiation and redirection from every ontology IRI to its most recent version IRI.

For ontology versions and examples, the source Turtle file is first copied to an appropriate directory. Then different other RDF serializations are generated in RDF/XML, N-triples, N3, and JSON-LD. Finally, an HTML documentation is generated. See for example https://saref.etsi.org/core/v3.1.1/. For each SAREF term t, an RDF Graph is created with the result of a SPARQL DESCRIBE t query evaluated on the last version of the ontology that defines this term. This graph is augmented with rdfs:isDefinedBy metadata that point to each ontology version IRI that defines this term, and custom ex:usedBy metadata that point to each ontology version IRI that uses this term. For terms also different RDF serializations are generated and an HTML documentation is generated. See for example https://saref.etsi.org/core/Command.

The HTML documentation generation process is inspired by LODE [28], but developed as a set of 61 named TEMPLATE, SELECT and FUNCTION SPARQL-Generate queries,[20] which are executed using version 2.0 of the SPARQL-Generate engine [24,26].[21] This transformation is executed on the RDF Graph of the ontology augmented with the RDF Graph of imported ontology versions, explicit entity declarations, and annotations with literal values (especially labels and comments) for all the entities that are used but not declared in this ontology. This allow the SPARQL-Generate transformations to generate class and property hierarchies, and add tooltips for all terms with the appropriate label and comment. It also incorporates the documentation snippets from the `documentation` folder, optionally converting markdown snippets to HTML if required.

The documentation generation tool does not yet generate multilingual documentation, although initial efforts towards internationalization has been done.[22]

---

[20] Available in the `main/resources/documentation` folder of the `saref-pipeline`.

[21] SPARQL-Generate 2.0 with GENERATE, TEMPLATE, SELECT, and FUNCTION queries has no dedicated publication yet. More information can be obtained from the website and presentation at https://ci.mines-stetienne.fr/sparql-generate/, and https://www.slideshare.net/maximelefrancois86/overview-of-the-sparqlgenerate-language-and-latest-developments.

[22] See https://labs.etsi.org/rep/saref/saref-pipeline/-/blob/master/src/main/resources/documentation/en.properties.

5.7   Continuous Integration and Delivery

The SAREF Pipeline is configured to run using the *Continuous Integration and Continuous Delivery* (CI/CD) features of the ETSI Forge, which is an instance of GitLab. Each SAREF project repository is configured such that the SAREF Pipeline is run in different modes and with different options depending on the type of branch where a commit is pushed:

issue and develop branches run `java -jar saref-pipeline.jar develop -s` (relaxed mode without generating the static portal), then publish an HTML report file to the snapshot area of the SAREF portal (deleted after one day) at `https://saref.etsi.org/snapshot/$CI_PIPELINE_ID/report.html`, even if the pipeline identified errors;

pre-release branches run `java -jar saref-pipeline.jar release -t` (do not generate the static portal for terms) then publish the generated report and partial static portal to the snapshot area of the SAREF portal at `https://saref.etsi.org/snapshot/$CI_PIPELINE_ID/report.html`, even if the pipeline identified errors;

release branches run `java -jar saref-pipeline.jar release -t` and, if successful, trigger the CI/CD pipeline on the `master` branch of `saref-portal`

The CI/CD process on the `master` branch of the `saref-portal` project is a three stage process:

Step 1: run `java -jar saref-pipeline.jar release-portal`,

Step 2: publish the generated report and static portal to the staging area of the SAREF portal (deleted after one week) at `https://saref.etsi.org/staging/$CI_PIPELINE_ID/`,

Step 3: if the portal in the staging area seems fine, this step can be manually triggered to publish the generated static portal to https://saref.etsi.org/.

6   Discussion and Current Work

Compared to the existing approaches listed in Sect. 2, the SAREF Pipeline is developed for a modular and versioned suite of ontologies, each having its sources in a separate git repository. It is usable both as GUI, CLI, and in CI/CD pipelines, and integrates many different semantic web technologies such as Apache Jena, OWL API, the Hermit reasoner, OOPS!, SHACL, Themis, SPARQL-Generate. It produces detailed error reporting, and generates a public documentation portal for the whole suite of SAREF ontologies and the terms they define. The SAREF Pipeline is publicly available under the open-source ETSI Forge license (BSD-3-Clause LICENSE) at the stable URL https://saref.etsi.org/sources/saref-pipeline. It is further registered on Zenodo with DOI 10.5281/zenodo.7913535 and has therefore an associated canonical citation. Its documentation, in terms of the list of checks it operates, is part of the

ETSI TS 103 673 technical specification which benefits from the ETSI standardization principles in terms of openness, maintenance, availability, and stability.[23] The SAREF Pipeline already had an impact in raising the quality level of all the SAREF ontologies, and publishing the public SAREF community portal https://saref.etsi.org/. Although originally tailored for the SAREF ontology development framework, it is currently used by projects outside ETSI to prepare new candidate extensions to SAREF. For example the newly created ETSI work item for SAREF4ENER V1.2.1, is based on contributions from the H2020 InterConnect project.[24]

Extensions to ETSI TS 103 673 and the SAREF Pipeline are planned in the context of the ongoing ETSI STF 653[25], which aims at consolidating the suite of SAREF ontologies into a more homogeneous and predictable structure, using operationalized ontology patterns. The initial observation that motivated STF 653 is that, even within the SAREF developer community, modeling and naming choices are sometimes varied and conflicting. The primary technique to resolve modeling discrepancies was to use *namespaces* to label the concepts and terms in each module. Choosing a distinct namespace for each module makes it easy to identify from which module a term originates. However, this approach poses several problems. First, it is sometimes difficult as a user of these ontologies to remember what the namespace is for each term. We have, for example, a variety of subclasses of saref:Property spread across the namespaces of the different extensions, depending on when they were first defined: saref:Temperature, saref:Humidity, saref:Power, s4ener:PowerMax, s4ener:PowerStandardDeviation, s4inma:Size, saref:Light, s4envi:LightProperty. Second, experience shows that it is sometimes necessary to move a term from one module to another. For example SAREF4CITY V1.1.1 introduced the concept of s4city:FeatureOfInterest, and it was decided during the development of SAREF Core V3.1.1 that this concept would be moved into the core ontology. So it is now identified by saref:FeatureOfInterest, and the SAREF4CITY implementations had to be modified. This problem would not have arisen if an approach based on a unique namespace had been adopted. Also, some SAREF developers decided to extend saref:Property not using classes, but using instances. Example include s4envi:Frequency, s4wear:SoundLevel, s4wear:BatteryRemainingTime, s4watr:Conductivity, s4wear:Temperature. Ongoing work in STF 653 therefore aims at defining ontology patterns to guide the development of SAREF extensions, and operationalizing them in the SAREF Pipeline.

7 Conclusion

The SAREF Pipeline integrates the SAREF development and documentation generation pipeline, as part of the SAREF Development Framework. It automatically checks the conformance of SAREF project repositories to the technical

---

[23] https://www.etsi.org/standards/standards-making.
[24] https://portal.etsi.org/webapp/WorkProgram/Report_WorkItem.asp? WKI_ID=68491.
[25] https://portal.etsi.org/xtfs/#/xTF/653.

specification ETSI TS 103 673. It has been applied on all the SAREF ontologies, and was used to generate the public SAREF community portal https://saref.etsi. org/. It is made available as open source under an open license to the semantic web community for the development of new SAREF extension, and could be adapted for other ontology development projects. ETSI TS 103 673 and the SAREF pipeline speed up the evolution of the current and future extensions of SAREF, and help reducing the costs of developing these extensions.

To summarize its main benefits, the SAREF Pipeline provides an efficient and robust support infrastructure for the continuous integration and continuous delivery of the modular and versioned suite of SAREF ontologies, which cover multiple application domains of the IoT. In particular, the SAREF Pipeline:

- Operates on a modular and versioned suite of ontologies;
- Operationalizes conformance checking against ETSI TS 103 673;
- Combines several semantic web technologies to automate checks;
- Is used by ontology developers as a GUI, and by CI/CD pipelines as CLI;
- Produces detailed error reporting, and generates documentation;
- Has been used to verify all SAREF ontologies, and is used to shape new SAREF extensions.

Acknowledgements. The development of the SAREF Pipeline has been funded by ETSI STF 578. The authors thank the other experts involved in this project, who contributed to the definition of the SAREF development workflow detailed in Sect. 4.1, and to online web services OOPS! and Themis that are called by the SAREF Pipeline. Ongoing development is funded by ETSI STF 653.

Resource Availability Statement. Source code of the SAREF Pipeline is available from the ETSI Forge (https://saref.etsi.org/sources/saref-pipeline). It is also registered on Zenodo with DOI 10.5281/zenodo.7913534 (https://doi.org/10.5281/zenodo. 7913534). The canonical citation is [25].

References

1. Allemang, D., Garbacz, P., Gradzki, P., Kendall, E., Trypuz, R.: An infrastructure for collaborative ontology development, lessons learned from developing the financial industry business ontology (FIBO). In: Formal Ontology in Information Systems. IOS Press (2022)
2. Alobaid, A., Garijo, D., Poveda-Villalón, M., Santana-Perez, I., Fernández-Izquierdo, A., Corcho, O.: Automating ontology engineering support activities with ontoology. J. Web Semant. **57**, 100472 (2019)
3. Bader, S., et al.: The international data spaces information model – an ontology for sovereign exchange of digital content. In: Pan, J.Z., et al. (eds.) ISWC 2020. LNCS, vol. 12507, pp. 176–192. Springer, Cham (2020). https://doi.org/10.1007/ 978-3-030-62466-8_12
4. Crystal-Ornelas, R., et al.: A guide to using GitHub for developing and versioning data standards and reporting formats. Earth Space Sci. **8**(8), e2021EA001797 (2021)

5. Daniele, L., den Hartog, F., Roes, J.: Created in close interaction with the industry: the Smart Appliances REFerence (SAREF) ontology. In: Cuel, R., Young, R. (eds.) FOMI 2015. LNBIP, vol. 225, pp. 100–112. Springer, Cham (2015). https://doi.org/10.1007/978-3-319-21545-7_9
6. ETSI: SmartM2M; Extension to SAREF; Part 1: Energy Domain. ETSI Technical Specification 103 410-1 V1.1.2, May 2020
7. ETSI: SmartM2M; Extension to SAREF; Part 10: Water Domain. ETSI Technical Specification 103 410-10 V1.1.1, July 2020
8. ETSI: SmartM2M; Extension to SAREF; Part 2: Environment Domain. ETSI Technical Specification 103 410-2 V1.1.2, May 2020
9. ETSI: SmartM2M; Extension to SAREF; Part 7: Automotive Domain. ETSI Technical Specification 103 410-7 V1.1.1, July 2020
10. ETSI: SmartM2M; Extension to SAREF; Part 8: eHealth/Ageing-well Domain. ETSI Technical Specification 103 410-8 V1.1.1, July 2020
11. ETSI: SmartM2M; Extension to SAREF; Part 9: Wearables Domain. ETSI Technical Specification 103 410-9 V1.1.1, July 2020
12. ETSI: SmartM2M; SAREF consolidation with new reference ontology patterns, based on the experience from the SEAS project. ETSI Technical Specification 103 548 V1.1.2, June 2020
13. ETSI: SmartM2M; SAREF Development Framework and Workflow, Streamlining the Development of SAREF and its Extensions. ETSI Technical Specification 103 673 V1.1.1 (2020). https://www.etsi.org/deliver/etsi_ts/103600_103699/103673/01.01.01_60/ts_103673v010101p.pdf
14. ETSI: SmartM2M; Smart Applications; Reference Ontology and oneM2M Mapping. ETSI Technical Specification 103 264 V3.1.1, February 2020
15. ETSI: SmartM2M; Extension to SAREF; Part 11: Lift Domain. ETSI Technical Specification 103 410-11 V1.1.1, July 2021
16. Fernández-Izquierdo, A., García-Castro, R.: Themis: a tool for validating ontologies through requirements. In: Software Engineering and Knowledge Engineering, pp. 573–753 (2019)
17. García-Castro, R., Lefrançois, M., Poveda-Villalón, M., Daniele, L.: The ETSI SAREF ontology for smart applications: a long path of development and evolution, pp. 183–215. Wiley-IEEE Press (2023). https://doi.org/10.1002/9781119899457.ch7
18. Garijo, D., Poveda-Villalón, M.: Best practices for implementing fair vocabularies and ontologies on the web. In: Applications and Practices in Ontology Design, Extraction, and Reasoning, vol. 49, pp. 39–54 (2020)
19. Glimm, B., Horrocks, I., Motik, B., Stoilos, G., Wang, Z.: HermiT: an OWL 2 reasoner. J. Autom. Reason. **53**(3), 245–269 (2014). https://doi.org/10.1007/s10817-014-9305-1
20. Halilaj, L., et al.: VoCol: an integrated environment to support version-controlled vocabulary development. In: Blomqvist, E., Ciancarini, P., Poggi, F., Vitali, F. (eds.) EKAW 2016. LNCS (LNAI), vol. 10024, pp. 303–319. Springer, Cham (2016). https://doi.org/10.1007/978-3-319-49004-5_20
21. Horridge, M., Bechhofer, S.: The OWL API: a Java API for OWL ontologies. Semant. Web **2**(1), 11–21 (2011)
22. Jackson, R.C., Balhoff, J.P., Douglass, E., Harris, N.L., Mungall, C.J., Overton, J.A.: Robot: a tool for automating ontology workflows. BMC Bioinf. **20**(1), 1–10 (2019)
23. Knublauch, H., Kontokostas, D.: Shapes Constraint Language (SHACL). W3C Recommendation, W3C, 20 July 2017

24. Lefrançois, M., Zimmermann, A., Bakerally, N.: A SPARQL extension for generating RDF from heterogeneous formats. In: Blomqvist, E., Maynard, D., Gangemi, A., Hoekstra, R., Hitzler, P., Hartig, O. (eds.) ESWC 2017. LNCS, vol. 10249, pp. 35–50. Springer, Cham (2017). https://doi.org/10.1007/978-3-319-58068-5_3
25. Lefrançois, M.: SAREF pipeline, May 2023. https://doi.org/10.5281/zenodo.7913535
26. Lefrançois, M., et al.: SPARQL-generate/SPARQL-generate: 2.0.12, October 2022. https://doi.org/10.5281/zenodo.7141122
27. Matentzoglu, N., Mungall, C., Goutte-Gattat, D.: Ontology development kit, July 2021. https://doi.org/10.5281/zenodo.6257507
28. Peroni, S., Shotton, D., Vitali, F.: The live OWL documentation environment: a tool for the automatic generation of ontology documentation. In: ten Teije, A., et al. (eds.) EKAW 2012. LNCS (LNAI), vol. 7603, pp. 398–412. Springer, Heidelberg (2012). https://doi.org/10.1007/978-3-642-33876-2_35
29. Poveda-Villalón, M., Fernández-Izquierdo, A., Fernández-López, M., García-Castro, R.: LOT: an industrial oriented ontology engineering framework. Eng. Appl. Artif. Intell. **111**, 104755 (2022)
30. Poveda-Villalón, M., Gómez-Pérez, A., Suárez-Figueroa, M.C.: OOPS! (ontology pitfall scanner!): an on-line tool for ontology evaluation. Int. J. Semant. Web Inf. Syst. (IJSWIS) **10**(2), 7–34 (2014)
31. Publio, G.C., Gayo, J.E.L., Colunga, G.F., Menendéz, P.: Ontolo-CI: continuous data validation with shex. In: Proceedings of Poster and Demo Track and Workshop Track of the 18th International Conference on Semantic Systems co-located with 18th International Conference on Semantic Systems, SEMANTiCS 2022 (2022)

The RML Ontology: A Community-Driven Modular Redesign After a Decade of Experience in Mapping Heterogeneous Data to RDF

Ana Iglesias-Molina[1]([✉])(iD), Dylan Van Assche[2](iD), Julián Arenas-Guerrero[1](iD),
Ben De Meester[2](iD), Christophe Debruyne[3](iD), Samaneh Jozashoori[4,5](iD),
Pano Maria[6], Franck Michel[7](iD), David Chaves-Fraga[1,8,9](iD),
and Anastasia Dimou[9](iD)

[1] Ontology Engineering Group, Universidad Politécnica de Madrid, Madrid, Spain
ana.iglesiasm@upm.es
[2] IDLab, Department of Electronics and Information Systems, Ghent University - imec, Ghent, Belgium
[3] Montefiore Institute, University of Liège, Liège, Belgium
[4] metaphacts GmbH, Walldorf, Germany
[5] TIB - Leibniz Information Center for Science and Technology, Hanover, Germany

[6] Skemu, Schiedam, Netherlands
[7] University Cote d'Azur, CNRS, Inria, I3S, Nice, France
[8] Universidade de Santiago de Compostela, Santiago de Compostela, Spain
[9] KU Leuven – Flanders Make@KULeuven – Leuven.AI, Leuven, Belgium

Abstract. The Relational to RDF Mapping Language (R2RML) became a W3C Recommendation a decade ago. Despite its wide adoption, its potential applicability beyond relational databases was swiftly explored. As a result, several extensions and new mapping languages were proposed to tackle the limitations that surfaced as R2RML was applied in real-world use cases. Over the years, one of these languages, the RDF Mapping Language (RML), has gathered a large community of contributors, users, and compliant tools. So far, there has been no well-defined set of features for the mapping language, nor was there a consensus-marking ontology. Consequently, it has become challenging for non-experts to fully comprehend and utilize the full range of the language's capabilities. After three years of work, the W3C Community Group on Knowledge Graph Construction proposes a new specification for RML. This paper presents the new modular RML ontology and the accompanying SHACL shapes that complement the specification. We discuss the motivations and challenges that emerged when extending R2RML, the methodology we followed to design the new ontology while ensuring its backward compatibility with R2RML, and the novel features which increase its expressiveness. The new ontology consolidates the potential of RML, empowers practitioners to define mapping rules for constructing RDF graphs that were previously unattainable, and allows developers to implement systems in adherence with [R2]RML.

© The Author(s) 2023
T. R. Payne et al. (Eds.): ISWC 2023, LNCS 14266, pp. 152–175, 2023.
https://doi.org/10.1007/978-3-031-47243-5_9

Resource type: Ontology/**License**: CC BY 4.0 International
DOI: 10.5281/zenodo.7918478/**URL**: http://w3id.org/rml/portal/

Keywords: Declarative Language · R2RML · RML · Knowledge
Graph

1   Introduction

In 2012, the Relational to RDF Mapping Language (R2RML) [37] was released
as a W3C Recommendation. The R2RML ontology [8] provides a vocabulary
to describe how an RDF graph should be generated from data in a relational
database (RDB). Although R2RML gained wide adoption, its potential applicability beyond RDBs quickly appeared as a salient need [49,63,76,87].

Targeting the generation of RDF from heterogeneous data sources other than
RDBs, several extensions [49,76,87] preserving R2RML's core structure were
proposed. As R2RML and the growing number of extensions were applied in a
wider range of use cases, more limitations became evident [76]. Consequently,
these languages were further extended with different features, e.g., the description of input data sources or output RDF (sub)graphs [76,96], data transformations [40,47,66,69], support for RDF-star [48,91], etc. Over the years, the RDF
Mapping Language (RML) has gathered a large community of contributors and
users, and a plethora of systems [26,95] and benchmarks [31,33,59].

Until recently, there was no well-defined, agreed-upon set of features for the
RML mapping language, nor was there a consensus-marking ontology covering
the whole set of features. Consequently, it has become challenging for non-experts
to fully comprehend this landscape and utilize all capabilities without investing
a substantial research effort. Therefore, the W3C Community Group on Knowledge Graph Construction [3], with more than 160 members, has convened every
two weeks to review the RML specification over the past three years.

In this paper, we present the new modular RML ontology and the accompanying SHACL shapes [61] that complement the specification. We discuss the
motivations and challenges that emerged by extending R2RML, the methodology
we followed to design the new ontology while ensuring its backward compatibility
with R2RML, and the novel features which increase its expressiveness. The new
RML ontology and specification is the result of an attempt to (i) address multiple
use cases from the community [30] (ii) streamline and integrate various features
proposed to support these use cases, and (iii) adopt agreed-upon design practices
that make it possible to come up with a coherent, integrated whole consisting
of a core ontology [97] and multiple feature-specific modules [41,46,64,98]. The
presented ontology consolidates the potential of RML enabling the definition of
mapping rules for constructing RDF graphs that were previously unattainable,
and the development of systems in adherence with both R2RML and RML.

This paper is organized as follows: In Sect. 2, we present the relevant concepts
of R2RML and RML. In Sect. 3, we outline the motivations that drive this work
and the challenges we tackle. In Sect. 4, we describe the methodology employed

to redesign the RML ontology while maintaining backward compatibility, and in Sect. 5 the modules introduced with the various features. In Sect. 6, we present the early adoption and potential impact, followed by related work in Sect. 7. We conclude the paper with a summary of the presented contributions and future steps in Sect. 8.

2   Background: R2RML

R2RML mapping rules (Listing 2) are grouped within `rr:TriplesMap` (line 1), which contain one `rr:LogicalTable`, one `rr:SubjectMap` and zero to multiple `rr:PredicateObjectMap`. The `rr:LogicalTable` (lines 2–3) describes the input RDB, while `rr:SubjectMap` (lines 4–5) specifies how the subjects of the triples are created. A `rr:PredicateObjectMap` (lines 6–9) generates the predicate-object pairs with one or more `rr:PredicateMap` (line 7) and one or more `rr:ObjectMap` (lines 8–9). Zero or more `rr:GraphMap`, which indicate how to generate named graphs, can be assigned to both `rr:SubjectMap` and `rr:PredicateObjectMap`. It is also possible to join `rr:LogicalTables` replacing `rr:ObjectMap` by `rr:RefObjectMap`, which uses the subject of another *Triples Map* indicated in `rr:parentTriplesMap` as the object of the triple. This join may have a condition to be performed, which is indicated using `rr:joinCondition`, `rr:child`, and `rr:parent`. *Subject Map*, *Predicate Map*, *Object Map*, and *Graph Map* are subclasses of `rr:TermMap`, which define how to generate RDF terms. *Term Maps* can be (i) *constant-valued*, i.e., always generating the same RDF term (line 7); (ii) *column-valued*, i.e., the RDF terms are directly obtained from cells of a column in the RDB (line 9); or (iii) *template-valued*, i.e., the RDF terms are composed from the data in columns and constant strings (line 5).

```
1  PERSON      , MARK, DATE
2  Duplantis  , 6.22, 02-25-2023
3  Guttormsen , 6.00, 03-10-2023
4  Vloon      , 5.91, 02-25-2023
```

Listing 1: *ATHLETES* table.

```
1  <#MarksTM> a rr:TriplesMap;
2    rr:logicalTable [
3      rr:tableName "ATHLETES" ];
4    rr:subjectMap [
5      rr:template ":{NAME}" ];
6    rr:predicateObjectMap [
7      rr:predicate :mark;
8      rr:objectMap [
9        rr:column "MARK" ] ]  .
```

Listing 2: R2RML mapping rules.

According to the R2RML specification, an R2RML processor is a system that, given a set of R2RML mapping rules and an input RDB, can construct RDF graphs. Therefore, an R2RML processor should have an SQL connection to the input RDB where the tables reside and a base IRI used to resolve the relative IRIs produced by the R2RML mapping rules.

3   Motivation and Challenges

In this section, we discuss the limitations of generalizing R2RML to construct RDF graphs from heterogeneous data sources and their impact on the ontology. We also consider the required extensions for the ontology to construct RDF graphs that were not possible before, e.g., RDF collections and containers or RDF-star [56]. Based on these limitations, we group the challenges in the following high-level categories: data input and RDF output, schema and data transformations, collections and containers, and RDF-star.

Data Input and RDF Output. In R2RML, the desired RDF graph is constructed from tables residing in only one RDB. R2RML recommends to hard-code the connection to the RDB in the R2RML processor, hence, rules in a mapping document cannot refer to multiple input RDBs.

To date, a wide range of data formats and structures is considered beyond RDBs, such as CSV, XML, or JSON. These sources may be available locally or via web APIs, statically, or streaming. Thus, a flexible approach for constructing RDF graphs from a combination of these diverse inputs is desired [95]. The R2RML ontology needs to be extended to also describe what the data source is for each set of mapping rules, e.g., a NoSQL DB or a Web API, and what the data format is, e.g., CSV, JSON or XML. In addition, a per row iteration pattern is assumed for RDBs, but this may vary for other data formats.

RML [49] proposed how to describe heterogeneous data assuming originally that these data appear in local files and a literal value specifies the path to the local file. In parallel, xR2RML [76] proposed how to extend R2RML for the document-oriented MongoDB. A more concrete description of the data sources and their access, e.g., RDBs, files, Web APIs, etc. was later proposed [50], relying on well-known vocabularies to describe the data sources, e.g., DCAT [74], VOID [23], or SPARQL-SD [101] and further extended [96] to also describe the output RDF (sub)graphs. The description of NULL values [94], predetermined in RDBs but not in other data sources, has not been addressed yet.

Schema and Data Transformations. Integrating heterogeneous data goes beyond schema-level transformations, as it usually involves additional data-level transformations [67]. The R2RML ontology describes the schema transformations, i.e., the correspondences between the ontology and the data schema. It delegates data transformations and joins to the storage layer, by using operators in SQL queries. However, not all data formats can leverage similar operators, e.g., JSON does not have a formal specification to describe its data transformation, nor do all formats' operators cover the same data transformations, e.g., XPath offers a different set of operators compared to SQL. Moreover, there are cases in which such pre-processing is not possible, e.g., for streaming data. Thus, the R2RML ontology needs to be extended to describe such data transformations.

RML+FnO [39], R2RML-F [47], its successor FunUL [66] or D-REPR [100] are examples of the proposals providing support to data operations. However, only RML+FnO describes the transformation functions declaratively. RML+FnO has been well adopted in the community by being included in a number of RML-compliant engines [25,58,59,86] and RML+FnO-specific translation engines [65,85]. Nevertheless, a more precise definition to address ambiguities and a simplification of introduced (complex) constructs is needed.

Collections and Containers. RDF containers represent open sets of RDF terms, ordered (`rdf:Sequence`) or unordered (`rdf:Bag`, `rdf:Alt`). Their member terms are denoted with the `rdf:_n` properties[1]. RDF collections refer solely to type `rdf:List` that represents a closed-ordered list of RDF terms. An RDF list is built using cons-pairs; the first cons-pair of a list refers to an element of that list with the `rdf:first` property, and the `rdf:rest` to the remainder list. All list elements should be traversed via `rdf:rest` until the empty list `rdf:nil`. Generating RDF collections and containers in R2RML, while possible, results in a cumbersome and limited task. A container's properties `rdf:_n` are typically generated only when a key in the form of a positive integer is yielded from the data source. By contrast, there is no elegant way to model a list's cons-pairs with R2RML if the list is of arbitrary length.

Due to the need for RDF containers and collections in several projects [75], e.g., both the Metadata Authority Description Schema [15] and W3C's XHTML Vocabulary [7] use RDF containers, and both OWL [102] and SHACL [68] use RDF collections. The xR2RML [76] vocabulary supported the generation of nested collections and containers within the same data source iteration (e.g., within one result among the results returned by the MongoDB database). Its vocabulary also allowed to change the iterator within a term map and yield nested collections and containers. By contrast, [45] provided terms for creating (nested) collections and containers from within an iteration (same row) and across iterations (across rows) and provided a property for retaining empty collections and containers. The ontology presented in [45] also provided directive for generating collections or containers whose members may have different term types, whereas [76]'s vocabulary provided support for one term type. The vocabulary of both approaches did not provide support for named collections and containers, nor the generation of these as subjects.

RDF-star. RDF-star [55] introduces the *quoted triple* term, which can be embedded in the subject or object of another triple. Quoted triples may be asserted (i.e., included in the graph) or not. RDF-star quickly gained popularity, leading to its adoption by a wide range of systems [4] (e.g., Apache Jena [24], Oxigraph [78]) and the formation of the RDF-star Working Group [5].

The inception of RDF-star came after R2RML. Therefore, R2RML only considered the generation of RDF. The principal challenge is the generation of quoted and asserted triples, which requires a dedicated extension. RML-star [48] and R2RML-star [91] are extensions of R2RML to construct RDF-star graphs,

---

[1] n is a strictly positive natural number denoting the nth element in that container.

however, the latter comes with limitations and it is not backward compatible with R2RML. Our ontology includes the RML-star extension to enable the generation of RDF-star graphs, remaining backward compatible with R2RML.

4 Methodology

We followed the Linked Open Terms (LOT) methodology [80] to redesign the R2RML ontology, as well as to generalize and modularize it. The methodology includes four major stages: *Requirements Specification, Implementation, Publication*, and *Maintenance*. We describe below how we follow these steps to develop the RML ontology and the accompanying SHACL shapes.

Requirements. The requirements to build the RML ontology are mainly derived from three sources: (i) the legacy of the R2RML ontology, (ii) the scientific publications which proposed different extensions [63,95], and (iii) the experience of the community of R2RML and RML to build upon their limitations. The latter has been gathered from GitHub issues [20] and summarized as *mapping challenges* [13]. The complete set of requirements for each module can be accessed from the ontology portal [21]. These requirements cover both the base needs and fine-grained features for generating triples with mapping rules. On the one hand, how to generate subjects, predicate, objects, datatypes, language tags, and named graphs in both a static (constant) and dynamic (from data sources) manner (RML-Core). On the other hand, the description and access of input data sources and target output data (RML-IO); RDF Collections and Containers to create lists from diverse terms (RML-CC); data transformation functions with their desired output and input parameters (RML-FNML); and quoting *Triples Maps* to create asserted and non-asserted RDF-star triples (RML-star).

Implementation. We build the RML ontology based on the requirements in a modular manner maintaining its backward compatibility with R2RML. We use a GitHub organization [2] to summarize issues and coordinate asynchronously.

Modularity. The ontology is composed of 5 modules: RML-Core, RML-IO, RML-CC, RML-FNML, and RML-star. We opt for a modular design to facilitate its development and maintenance, as each module can be adjusted independently without affecting the rest. This choice facilitates also its reuse and adoption, as RML processors can implement specific modules instead of the entire ontology.

Modeling. The modeling of each module is carried out independently. A version is drafted from the requirements and presented to the community. For this iteration step, we draft the proposal using ontology diagrams that follow the Chowlk notation [34], and some use cases with examples. Once it is agreed that the model is accurate and meets the requirements, the ontology is encoded.

Encoding. We encode the ontology using OWL [28] and its application profile using SHACL [68]. We deliberately use both to distinguish between the model, which is described in OWL, and the constraints described as SHACL shapes. The latter specifies how the different ontology constructs should be used within a mapping document, e.g. a *Triples Map* can only contain exactly one *Subject Map*. Hence, they allow to validate the mapping rules' correctness, depending on which modules are used. This way, RML processors can indicate which module they support and verify the mapping rules' compliance before executing them.

Backward Compatibility. The new RML ontology is backward compatible with the previous [R2]RML ontologies [17]. We first gather all terms affected from the RML-Core and RML-IO modules (the other modules only introduce new features), and define correspondences between the past and new resources. We identify two kinds of correspondences: (i) *equivalences* if a resource is used in the same manner and its semantics is not significantly changed (e.g., `rr:SubjectMap` is equivalent to `rml:SubjectMap`); and (ii) *replacements* if a resource is superseded by another one (e.g., `rr:logicalTable` is replaced by `rml:logicalSource`). A summary of these correspondences is available online [18] as well as a semantic version to enable automatic translation of mapping rules [17].

Evaluation. We evaluate the ontology with OOPS! [81] and check for inconsistencies using the HermiT reasoner. If all issues are solved, a module is deployed.

Table 1. List of modules of the RML ontology.

Module	Description	Ontology
RML-Core [97]	Schema Transformations	http://w3id.org/rml/core
RML-IO [98]	Source and Target	http://w3id.org/rml/io
RML-CC [46]	Collections and Containers	http://w3id.org/rml/cc
RML-FNML [41]	Data Transformations	http://w3id.org/rml/fnml
RML-star [64]	RDF-star	http://w3id.org/rml/star

Publication. All modules of the RML ontology are managed and deployed independently from a separate GitHub repository, and published using a W3ID URL under the CC-BY 4.0 license. Each repository contains the ontology file, its documentation (created using Widoco [52]), requirements, associated SHACL shapes, and the module's specification. We follow a unified strategy for the resources' IRIs. The RML ontology resources use a single prefix IRI to make it convenient for users to convert their RML mappings to the new RML ontology, while clearly stating which module each resource belongs to. We publish the complete ontology at http://w3id.org/rml/, and a summary of all modules with links to all their related resources (i.e. SHACL shapes, issues, specifications, etc.) is available at the ontology portal [21] and in Table 1.

Maintenance. To ensure that the ontology is updated with error corrections and new updates during its life cycle, the GitHub issue tracker of each module will be used to gather suggestions for additions, modifications, and deletions. We discuss every major modification asynchronously and in the W3C KG Construction Community Group meetings until they are agreed upon, which triggers another round of implementation and publication, leading to new releases.

5 Artifacts: Ontologies and Shapes

The RML ontology consists of 5 modules: (i) **RML-Core** (Sect. 5.1) describes the schema transformations, generalizes and refines the R2RML ontology, and becomes the basis for all other modules; (ii) **RML-IO** (Sect. 5.2) describes the input data and output RDF (sub)graphs; (iii) **RML-CC** (Sect. 5.3) describes how to construct RDF collections and containers; (iv) **RML-FNML** (Sect. 5.4) describes data transformations; and (v) **RML-star** (Sect. 5.5) describes how RDF-star can be generated. Figure 1 shows an overview of all modules of the RML ontology and how they are connected. The modules build upon the RML-Core, which, in turn, builds upon R2RML, but are independent among one another. We illustrate each module by continuing the example in Sect. 2.

5.1 RML-Core: Schema Transformations

The RML-Core is the main module of the RML ontology, which generalizes and refines the R2RML ontology; all the other modules build on top of it. The RML-Core ontology consists of the same concepts as the R2RML ontology (rml:TriplesMap, rml:TermMap, rml:SubjectMap, rml:PredicateMap, rml:ObjectMap, rml:PredicateObjectMap, and rml:ReferencingObjectMap), but redefines them to distinguish them from the R2RML counterparts.

RML-Core refines the R2RML ontology by introducing the concept of *Expression Map* rml:ExpressionMap (Listing 4, lines 6 & 9). An *Expression Map* is a mapping construct that can be evaluated on a data source to generate values during the mapping process, the so-called *expression values*. The R2RML specification allowed such mapping constructs (template-based, column-based or constant-based) which can only be applied to subject, predicate, object and named graph terms. In RML, the *Expression Map* can be a *template expression* specified with the property rml:template, a *reference expression* specified with the property rml:reference, or a *constant expression*, specified with the property rml:constant. A *Term Map* becomes a subclass of *Expression Map*.

With the introduction of the *Expression Map*, the language, term type, parent and child properties can be specified using any *Expression Map*, and not only a predefined type of expression. To achieve this, the following concepts are introduced as subclasses of the *Expression Map*: (i) rml:LanguageMap, whose shortcut rml:language can be used if it is a constant-valued *Expression Map*; (ii)

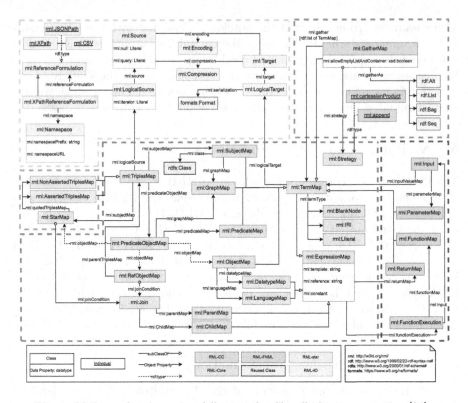

Fig. 1. RML ontology overview following the Chowlk diagram notation [34].

`rml:DatatypeMap`, whose shortcut `rml:datatype` can be used if it is a constant-valued *Expression Map*; (iii) `rml:ParentMap`, whose shortcut `rml:parent` can be used if it is a reference-valued *Expression Map*; and (iv) `rml:ChildMap`, whose shortcut `rml:child` can be used if it is a reference-valued *Expression Map*.

Listing 4 shows an example of a basic mapping to create RDF triples from the JSON file in Listing 3, and whose *Logical Source* is defined in Listing 5.

```
1  [ { "NAME": "Duplantis",        7       "MARK": "6.00",
2      "RANK": "1",                8       "DATE": 03-10-2023},
3      "MARK": "6.22",             9  { "NAME": "Vloon",
4      "DATE": 02-25-2023},        10      "RANK": "3",
5    { "NAME": "Guttormsen",       11      "MARK": "5.91",
6      "RANK": "2",                12      "DATE": 02-25-2023} ]
```

Listing 3: Input JSON file with ranks and their specific date for athletes.

```
1  <#RankTriplesMap> a rml:TriplesMap;
2    rml:logicalSource <#JSONSource>;
3    rml:subjectMap <#RankSubjectMap>;
4    rml:predicateObjectMap [ a rml:PredicateObjectMap;
5      rml:predicate ex:rank;
6      rml:objectMap [ a rml:ObjectMap, rml:ExpressionMap;
7      rml:reference "$.RANK"; ] ] .
8
9  <#RankSubjectMap> a rml:SubjectMap, rml:ExpressionMap;
10   rml:template "{$.NAME}" .
```

Listing 4: RML-Core example to generate a subject from a template, a predicate from a constant, and an object from a reference expression.

5.2 RML-IO: Source and Target

RML-IO complements RML-Core describing the input data sources and how they can be retrieved. To achieve this, RML-IO defines the *Logical Source* (with rml:LogicalSource) for describing the input data, and the *Source* (rml:Source) for accessing the data. The *Logical Source* specifies the grammar to refer to the input data via the *Reference Formulation* (rml:ReferenceFormulation). For instance, in Listing 5, the *Reference Formulation* is JSONPath (Line 4). RML-IO refers to a set of predefined *Reference Formulations* (JSONPath, XPath, etc.) but others can be considered as well. Besides the *Reference Formulation*, the *Logical Source* also defines how to iterate over the data source through the iteration pattern with the property rml:iteration (Line 5). In a *Triples Map*, the property rml:logicalSource specifies the *Logical Source* to use and should be specified once. The *Source* specifies how a data source is accessed by leveraging existing specifications; and indicates when values should be considered NULL (rml:null) and a query if needed (rml:query) e.g., SQL or SPARQL query. In a *Logical Source*, the property rml:source refers to exactly one *Source*.

Similarly, RML-IO includes the *Logical Target* (rml:LogicalTarget) and the *Target* (rml:Target) to define how the output RDF is exported. A *Logical Target* includes the properties rml:serialization to indicate in which RDF serialisation the output should be encoded, and rml:target to refer to exactly one *Target*. The *Logical Target* can be optionally specified in any *Term Map* e.g., *Subject* or *Graph Map*. The *Target* is similar to the *Source*, indicating how the output target can be accessed, and has 2 properties: (i) rml:compression to specify if the RDF output will be compressed and, if so, how e.g., GZip, and (ii) rml:encoding to define the encoding e.g., UTF-8.

Both *Source* and *Target* consider the re-use of existing vocabularies to incorporate additional features to access data, such as DCAT [74], SPARQL-SD [101], VoID [23], D2RQ [36], and CSVW [93]. Listing 5 shows an example of an RML mapping that describes a JSON file (Listing 3) with a *Logical Source* (lines 1–5).

A *Logical Target* is also used to export the resulting triples to a Turtle file with GZip compression (lines 7–12). Since the *Logical Target* is specified within the subject (line 18), all triples with that subject are exported to this target.

```
1   <#JSONSource> a rml:LogicalSource;
2     rml:source [ a rml:Source, dcat:Distribution;
3       dcat:accessURL <file://ranks.json> ];
4     rml:referenceFormulation rml:JSONPath;
5     rml:iterator "$.[*]"; .
6
7   <#FileTarget> a rml:LogicalTarget;
8     rml:target [ a rml:Target, void:Dataset;
9       void:dataDump <file:///data/dump.ttl.gz>;
10      rml:compression rml:gzip;
11      rml:encoding rml:UTF-8 ];
12    rml:serialization rml:Turtle; .
13
14  <#RankTriplesMap> a rml:TriplesMap;
15    rml:logicalSource <#JSONSource>;
16    rml:subjectMap <#RankSubjectMap> .
17
18  <#RankSubjectMap> rml:logicalTarget <#FileTarget> .
```

Listing 5: Input data from the *ranked.json* file is described with DCAT. An output file in Turtle serialization with GZip compression is described with VoID.

5.3   RML-CC: Collections and Containers

As the RML Collections and Containers module is fundamentally new, the Community Group formulated a set of functional requirements that the RML Containers and Collections specification should meet: One should be able to: (i) collect values from one or more *Term Maps*, including multi-valued *Term Maps*; (ii) have control over the generation of empty collections and containers; (iii) generate nested collections and containers; (iv) group different term types; (v) use a generated collection or container as a subject; and (vi) assign an IRI or blank node identifer to a collection or container. Based on these requirements, the RML-CC module was introduced which consists of a new concept, the *Gather Map* rml:GatherMap, two mandatory properties (rml:gather and rml:gatherAs) and two optional properties. Even though the module is limited with respect to its ontology terms, significant effort is expected for the RML processors to support it. Thus, we decided on keeping it as a separate module.

We specified the *Gather Map* (rml:GatherMap) as a *Term Map* with 2 mandatory properties: (i) rml:gather to specify the list of *Term Maps* used for the generation of a collection or container, and (ii) rml:gatherAs to indicate what is generated (one of the rdf:List, rdf:Bag, rdf:Seq, and rdf:Alt). The rml:gather contains any type of *Term Map* including *Referencing Term Maps* (to use the subjects generated by another *Triples Map*) which are treated as multi-valued *Term Maps*. Other properties were defined with default values to facilitate the use of this extension: `rml:allowEmptyListAndContainer` and `rml:strategy`. By default, a *Gather Map* shall not yield empty containers and collections; the predicate `rml:allowEmptyListAndContainer` must be set to true to preserve them[2]. Also, by default, the values of multiple multi-valued *Term Maps* will be appended from left to right; `rml:append` is the default `rml:strategy`. Alternatively, the `rml:cartesianProduct` strategy that instructs to carry out a Cartesian product between the terms generated by each *Term Map*. The `rml:strategy` renders the vocabulary *extensible*; RML implementations may propose their own strategies for generating collections and containers from a list of multi-valued term maps.

Listing 6 demonstrates the support for 4 of the aforementioned requirements: the collection of values from a multi-valued *Term Map*, the generation of a named collection, and the collection as a subject. It generates a subject that will be related to a list via `ex:contains`. The values of that list are collected from a multi-valued *Term Map* generating IRIs from the names and generates the following RDF: `:Ranking23 ex:contains (:Duplantis :Guttormsen :Vloon)`.

```
1   <#RankingListTM> a rml:TriplesMap;
2     rml:logicalSource <#JSONSource>;
3     rml:subjectMap [ rml:constant :Ranking23 ];
4     rml:predicateObjectMap [
5       rml:predicate ex:contains;
6       rml:objectMap [
7         rml:gather (
8           [ rml:template "{$.*.NAME}"; rml:termType rml:IRI ] );
9         rml:gatherAs rdf:List; ] ] .
```

Listing 6: The use of a *Gather Map* to generate a list of terms. The RDF collection `:Ranking23` will be generated using the name data reference.

If a *Gather Map* is an empty *Expression Map*, a new blank node is created for the head node of each generated collection or container (the first cons-pair in the case of a collection). Conversely, when providing a template, constant or reference, the head node is assigned the generated IRI or blank node identifier. If unchecked, this may lead to the generation of collections or containers that share the same head node, which we refer to as ill-formed. Therefore, the specification details the behavior that a processor must adopt: when a gather map creates a named collection or container, it must first check whether a named collection or container with the same head node IRI or blank node identifier already exists, and if so, it must append the terms to the existing one.

5.4   RML-FNML: Data Transformations

The RML-FNML module enables the declarative evaluation of data transformation functions defined using the Function Ontology (FnO) [40] in RML. Thus,

---

[2] E.g., an empty list could explicitly represent that the number 1 has no prime factors.

the data transformation functions in RML are independent of specific processors. Functions and Executions are described with FnO, while FNML declares the evaluation of FnO functions in terms of specific data sources. The *evaluation* of a function is defined through a *Function Execution* (rml:FunctionExecution), where a *Function Map* (rml:FunctionMap) defines the function. The input values' definitions are provided through *Term Maps* using *Inputs* (rml:Input), which in turn include *Parameter Maps* (rml:ParameterMap) referring to *Function Parameters* defined by FnO. The *Function Execution*'s output is declared using a *Return Map* (rml:ReturnMap) and referred to by the rml:return property, enabling the reference to a specific output of a function's multiple outputs.

```
1    <#RankTriplesMap> a rml:TriplesMap;
2      rml:logicalSource <#JSONSource>;
3      rml:subjectMap    <#RankSubjectMap>;
4      rml:predicateObjectMap [
5        rml:predicate ex:date;
6        rml:objectMap [
7          rml:functionExecution <#Execution>;
8          rml:return ex:dateOut ] ] .
9
10   <#Execution> a rml:FunctionExecution;
11     rml:function ex:parseDate;
12     rml:input [ a rml:Input;
13       rml:parameter ex:valueParam;
14       rml:inputValueMap [ rml:reference "$.DATE" ] ] ,
15     [ a rml:Input;
16       rml:parameter ex:dateFormatParam;
17       rml:inputValueMap [ rml:constant "MM-DD-YYYY" ] ] .
```

Listing 7: The function ex:parseDate parses the referenced DATE value using the "MM-DD-YYYY" pattern, and returns a parsed date.

Listing 7 shows the use date formatting function. Within an *Object Map*, the *Function Execution* (Line 7) and type of *Return* (Line 8) are defined. The *Function Execution* describes which *Function* is used (Line 11) and its two *Inputs*: the data reference (Lines 12–14) and the output date format (Lines 15–17).

5.5   RML-star: RDF-star Generation

The building block of RML-star [48] is the *Star Map* (rml:StarMap). A *Star Map* can be defined in a *Subject* or an *Object Map*, generating quoted triples in the homonymous positions of the output triples. The *Triples Map* generating quoted triples is connected to a *Star Map* via the object property rml:quotedTriplesMap. Quoted *Triple Maps* specify whether they are asserted (rml:AssertedTriplesMap) or non-asserted (rml:NonAssertedTriplesMap). Listing 8 uses an *Asserted Triples Map* (lines 1–5) to generate triples of the mark of some athletes, annotated using a *Star Map* with the date on which the marks were accomplished (lines 7–11).

```
1   <#QuotedRankTM> a rml:AssertedTriplesMap;
2     rml:logicalSource <#JSONSource>;
3     rml:subjectMap <#RankSubjectMap>;
4     rml:predicateObjectMap [ rml:predicate :mark;
5       rml:objectMap [ rml:reference "$.MARK"; ] ] .
6
7   <#DateTM> a rml:TriplesMap;
8     rml:logicalSource <#JSONSource> ;
9     rml:subjectMap [ rml:quotedTriplesMap <#QuotedRankTM> ] ;
10    rml:predicateObjectMap [ rml:predicate :date;
11      rml:objectMap [ rml:reference "$.DATE"; ] ] .
```

Listing 8: The <#QuotedRankTM> generates asserted triples that are also quoted by rml:quotedTriplesMap property from <#DateTM> .

6   Early Adoption and Potential Impact

Over the years, the RML mapping language has gathered a large community of contributors and users, a plethora of systems were developed [26,95], benchmarks were proposed [31,33,59], and tutorials were performed [9–12,16,99].

During the last decade, many initiatives have used the different extensions of R2RML which contributed to the modular RML ontology to construct RDF graphs from heterogeneous data for e.g., COVID-19-related data [77,84,90], bio-diversity [22,62,79], streaming data analysis and visualisation [38,44], social networks' data portability [43], social media archiving [73], supply chain data integration [42], public procurement [88], agriculture [29], federated advertisement profiles [72]. These extensions were also incorporated in services, e.g., Chimera [53], Data2Services [14], InterpretME [35], and even the Google Enterprise Knowledge Graph to construct and reconcile RDF [6].

As the modules of the RML ontology take shape, an increasing number of systems embrace its latest version. The RMLMapper [58], which was so far the RML reference implementation, currently supports the RML-Core and RML-IO modules. The SDM-RDFizer [59,60] and Morph-KGC [25], two broadly-used RML processors, already integrate the generation of RDF-star with the RML-star module in their systems. Additionally, Morph-KGC also supports transformation functions using the RML-FNML module. The adoption of RML was facilitated by YARRRML [57], a human-friendly serialization of RML. Yatter [32] is a YARRRML translator that already translates this serialization to the RML-Core, RML-star, RML-IO and RML-FNML modules. The increasing number of systems that support different modules illustrate the benefits of the modular approach of the RML ontology: each system implements a set of modules, without the necessity of offering support for the complete ontology, while different use cases can choose a system based on their modules' support.

As an increasing number of systems support the RML ontology proposed in this paper, several real-world use cases already adopted the ontology as well.

NORIA [92] extends RMLMapper in their MASSIF-RML [82] system, implemented at Orange, to construct RDF graphs for anomaly detection and incident management. InteGraph [70] uses RML to construct RDF graphs in the soil ecology domain and CLARA [19] to construct RDF-star for educational modules, both using Morph-KGC. At the European level, two governmental projects use RML to integrate their data into RDF graphs. In the transport domain, the European Railway Agency constructs RDF from the Register of Infrastructure data, distributed in XML, using RML mapping rules [83] and taking advantage of the RML-IO module. The Public Procurement Data Space [54] is an ongoing project that integrates procurement data, distributed in various formats, from all EU member states using the e-Procurement Ontology [1], and mapping rules in RML with the RML-Core and RML-star modules on the roadmap.

The RML ontology and SHACL shapes are maintained by the W3C Knowledge Graph Construction Community Group, and part of the larger International Knowledge Graph Construction community. This community will continue to maintain these resources and a call for systems to incorporate the new specification and ontology will be launched. The aim is to have at least two reference implementations for each module in RML systems by the end of 2023.

7   Related Work

A large amount of mapping languages have been proposed to enable the construction of RDF graphs from different data sources [63,95]. Apart from the RDF-based languages that considerably influence the RML ontology (see Sect. 3), we highlight here the popular alternatives that rely on the syntax of query (SPARQL-Generate [71], SPARQL-Anything [27], NORSE [89]), constraint (e.g., ShExML [51]) or data-serialisation (e.g., D-REPR [100]) languages.

SPARQL-Generate [71] leverages the expressive power of the SPARQL query language and extends it with additional clauses to describe the input data. It offers a relatable way to RML for handling the input data: it supports a wide range of data sources, describes their access and defines an iterator and reference formulations to describe input data. While SPARQL-Generate describes input data and its access, it does not consider the specification of target formats as the new RML ontology does. SPARQL-Generate supports collection and containers, but they can only be placed as objects; embedded collections and containers are not allowed. Last, despite developed over Apache Jena, which already supports RDF-star and SPARQL-star, the GENERATE clause proposed by SPARQL-Generate, does not support RDF-star graph construction at the moment.

SPARQL-Anything [27] introduces *Facade-X* to override the SERVICE clause as its input data description. It implements all SPARQL and SPARQL-star features, including the generation of RDF-star graphs. However, the construction of well-formed collections and containers with the CONSTRUCT clause is limited. To overcome this, SPARQL-Anything proposes a bespoke function fx:bnode that ensures that the same blank node identifiers are returned for the same input. Hence, while blank nodes are addressed, the generation of lists remains complex.

Both SPARQL-Generate and SPARQL-Anything, offer limited support for data transformations, as they are bounded to the ones already provided by their corresponding implementations. While SPARQL allows custom functions, these are implementation-dependent. The addition of declarative data transformations, as the new RML ontology proposes, is not possible.

More recently, Stadler et al. [89] present an approach that processes SPARQL CONSTRUCT queries translated from RML mappings. This approach also includes an extended implementation of the SERVICE operator to process non-RDF data sources. These sources are described with NORSE, a tailored vocabulary for this implementation that allows including RML source descriptions inside queries. Hence, this approach completely relies on the expressiveness of RML features while leveraging SPARQL implementations.

Despite the expressive power of these languages, the systems implementing them need to provide a complete support for SPARQL and extend the language with new clauses or modify the semantics of existing ones to support the construction of RDF graphs. The modular approach presented for the RML ontology allows having a set of basic features to be implemented by the systems, without forcing support for the entire language, and ensures the long-term sustainability, as new modules of the ontology can be proposed without affecting current ones.

8   Conclusions and Future Steps

We present the RML ontology as a community-driven modular redesign of R2RML and its extensions to generate RDF graphs from heterogeneous data sources. Our work is driven by the limitations of R2RML and the extensions proposed over the years. We present our motivation for following a modular design, backward compatible with R2RML. We discussed how each module was designed accompanied by its SHACL shapes, addressing the identified challenges.

The quick adoption of the RML ontology by some of its most used systems, and the number of initiatives and companies that have already incorporated RML, creates a favorable ecosystem for the adoption of RML as the standard for generating RDF graphs from heterogeneous data. The modular design allows us to easily adjust the adequate module with future requirements following an agile methodology. A thorough versioning system will be enabled to keep track of the new versions and badges will be provided for systems to indicate which modules and versions of these modules they support.

As future steps, the community is willing to initiate the process of turning this resource into a W3C Recommendation. Hence, a *Final Community Group Report* will be published with all the resources presented in this paper, so the SW community can start providing feedback on the specifications to finally, draft a W3C Working Group charter. From a technical perspective, we want to develop further use cases to ensure a thorough validation of the new implementations. Finally, test-cases for each module and validation with SHACL shapes will also be further refined to provide an exhaustive validation resource.

Acknowledgements. We would like to thank María Poveda-Villalón and Maxime Lefrançois for their insights and help with the publication of this ontology.

Ana Iglesias-Molina is supported by the project *Knowledge Spaces* (Grant PID2020-118274RB-I00 funded by MCIN/AEI/10.13039/501100011033). Dylan Van Assche is supported by the Special Research Fund of Ghent University under grant BOF20/DOC/132. Ben de Meester is supported by SolidLab Vlaanderen (Flemish Government, EWI and RRF project VV023/10). Julián Arenas-Guerrero is partially supported by the Euratom Research and Training Programme 2019–2020 under grant agreement No 900018 (ENTENTE project). David Chaves-Fraga is partially supported by the Galician Ministry of Culture, Education, Professional Training, and University, by the European Regional Development Fund (ERDF/FEDER program) through grant ED431C2022/19 and by the Madrid Government (Comunidad de Madrid-Spain) under the Multiannual Agreement with Universidad Politécnica de Madrid in the line Support for R&D projects for Beatriz Galindo researchers, in the context of the V PRICIT (Regional Programme of Research and Technological Innovation). Anastasia Dimou is partially supported by Flanders Make, the strategic research centre for the manufacturing industry and the Flanders innovation and entrepreneurship (VLAIO) via the KG3D project. The collaboration of Dylan Van Assche, Ben De Meester, Christophe Debruyne, David Chaves-Fraga and Anastasia Dimou is stimulated by the KG4DI FWO scientific research network (W001222N).

References

1. eProcurement Ontology (ePO). https://github.com/OP-TED/ePO. Accessed 9 May 2023
2. GitHub Organization of the Knowledge Graph Construction W3C Community Group. https://www.github.com/kg-construct/. Accessed 9 May 2023
3. Knowledge Graph Construction Community Group. https://www.w3.org/community/kg-construct/. Accessed 9 May 2023
4. RDF-star Implementations. https://w3c.github.io/rdf-star/implementations.html. Accessed 9 May 2023
5. RDF-star Working Group. https://www.w3.org/groups/wg/rdf-star. Accessed 9 May 2023
6. Run an entity reconciliation job from the Google Cloud console. https://cloud.google.com/enterprise-knowledge-graph/docs/entity-reconciliation-console. Accessed 9 May 2023
7. XHTML Vocabulary (2010). https://www.w3.org/1999/xhtml/vocab. Accessed 9 May 2023
8. R2RML: RDB to RDF Mapping Language Schema (2012). https://www.w3.org/ns/r2rml#. Accessed 9 May 2023
9. Tutorial: Generating and Querying (Virtual) Knowledge Graphs from Heterogeneous Data Sources (2019). https://oeg-dataintegration.github.io/kgc-tutorial-2019. Accessed 9 May 2023
10. Tutorial: How to build a knowledge graph (2019). https://2019.semantics.cc/satellite-events/how-build-knowledge-graph. Accessed 9 May 2023
11. Tutorial: How to build large knowledge graphs efficiently (LKGT) (2020). https://stiinnsbruck.github.io/lkgt/. Accessed 9 May 2023
12. Tutorial: Knowledge Graph Construction using Declarative Mapping Rules (2020). https://oeg-dataintegration.github.io/kgc-tutorial-2020. Accessed 9 May 2023

13. Knowledge Graph Construction Open Challenges (2021). https://w3id.org/kg-construct/workshop/2021/challenges.html. Accessed 9 May 2023
14. Data2Services: RML Transformations (2022). https://d2s.semanticscience.org/docs/d2s-rml. Accessed 9 May 2023
15. Metadata Authority Description Schema (2022). https://www.loc.gov/standards/mads/. Accessed 9 May 2023
16. Tutorial: Knowledge Graph Construction (2022). https://w3id.org/kg-construct/costdkg-eswc-tutorial. Accessed 9 May 2023
17. Backwards Compatibility (2023). http://w3id.org/rml/bc. Accessed 9 May 2023
18. Backwards Compatibility Portal (2023). https://w3id.org/rml/portal/backwards-compatibility.html. Accessed 9 May 2023
19. Clara Project (2023). https://gitlab.univ-nantes.fr/clara/pipeline. Accessed 9 May 2023
20. RML Core issues (2023). https://github.com/kg-construct/rml-core/issues. Accessed 9 May 2023
21. RML Ontology Portal (2023). http://w3id.org/rml/portal/. Accessed 9 May 2023
22. Aisopos, F., et al.: Knowledge graphs for enhancing transparency in health data ecosystems. Semant. Web (2023). https://doi.org/10.3233/SW-223294
23. Alexander, K., Cyganiak, R., Hausenblas, M., Zhao, J.: Describing Linked Datasets with the VoID Vocabulary. Interest Group Note, World Wide Web Consortium (2011). https://www.w3.org/TR/void/
24. Apache Software Foundation: Apache Jena (2021). https://jena.apache.org
25. Arenas-Guerrero, J., Chaves-Fraga, D., Toledo, J., Pérez, M.S., Corcho, O.: Morph-KGC: scalable knowledge graph materialization with mapping partitions. Semant. Web (2022). https://doi.org/10.3233/SW-223135
26. Arenas-Guerrero, J., et al.: Knowledge graph construction with R2RML and RML: an ETL system-based overview. In: Proceedings of the 2nd International Workshop on Knowledge Graph Construction, vol. 2873. CEUR Workshop Proceedings (2021). http://ceur-ws.org/Vol-2873/paper11.pdf
27. Asprino, L., Daga, E., Gangemi, A., Mulholland, P.: Knowledge graph construction with a FaçAde: a unified method to access heterogeneous data sources on the web. ACM Trans. Internet Technol. **23**(1) (2023). https://doi.org/10.1145/3555312
28. Bechhofer, S., et al.: OWL Web Ontology Language. W3C Recommendation, World Wide Web Consortium (2004). https://www.w3.org/TR/owl-ref/
29. Bilbao-Arechabala, S., Martinez-Rodriguez, B.: A practical approach to cross-agri-domain interoperability and integration. In: 2022 IEEE International Conference on Omni-Layer Intelligent Systems (COINS), pp. 1–6. IEEE (2022)
30. Chaves, D., et al.: kg-construct/use-cases: v1.0 (2023). https://doi.org/10.5281/zenodo.7907172
31. Chaves-Fraga, D., Endris, K.M., Iglesias, E., Corcho, O., Vidal, M.E.: What are the parameters that affect the construction of a knowledge graph? In: Panetto, H., Debruyne, C., Hepp, M., Lewis, D., Ardagna, C., Meersman, R. (eds.) Proceedings of the Confederated International Conferences, pp. 695–713. Springer, Cham (2019). https://doi.org/10.1007/978-3-030-33246-4_43
32. Chaves-Fraga, D., et al.: oeg-upm/yatter: v1.1.0 (2023). https://doi.org/10.5281/zenodo.7898764
33. Chaves-Fraga, D., Priyatna, F., Cimmino, A., Toledo, J., Ruckhaus, E., Corcho, O.: GTFS-Madrid-Bench: a benchmark for virtual knowledge graph access in the transport domain. J. Web Semant. **65**, 100596 (2020)

34. Chávez-Feria, S., García-Castro, R., Poveda-Villalón, M.: Chowlk: from UML-based ontology conceptualizations to OWL. In: Groth, P., et al. (eds.) The Semantic Web: 19th International Conference, ESWC 2022, Hersonissos, Crete, Greece, 29 May–2 June 2022, Proceedings. LNCS, vol. 13261, pp. 338–352. Springer, Cham (2022). https://doi.org/10.1007/978-3-031-06981-9_20

35. Chudasama, Y., Purohit, D., Rohde, P.D., Gercke, J., Vidal, M.E.: InterpretME: a tool for interpretations of machine learning models over knowledge graphs. Submitted to Semant. Web J. (2023). https://www.semantic-web-journal.net/system/files/swj3404.pdf

36. Cyganiak, R., Bizer, C., Garbers, J., Maresch, O., Becker, C.: The D2RQ mapping language. Technical report, FU Berlin, DERI, UCB, JP Morgan Chase, AGFA Healthcare, HP Labs, Johannes Kepler Universität Linz (2012). http://d2rq.org/d2rq-language

37. Das, S., Sundara, S., Cyganiak, R.: R2RML: RDB to RDF Mapping Language. W3C Recommendation, World Wide Web Consortium (2012). http://www.w3.org/TR/r2rml/

38. De Brouwer, M., et al.: Distributed continuous home care provisioning through personalized monitoring & treatment planning. In: Companion Proceedings of the Web Conference 2020. ACM (2020). https://doi.org/10.1145/3366424.3383528

39. De Meester, B., Dimou, A., Verborgh, R., Mannens, E.: An ontology to semantically declare and describe functions. In: Sack, H., Rizzo, G., Steinmetz, N., Mladenić, D., Auer, S., Lange, C. (eds.) ESWC 2016, P&D. LNCS, vol. 9989, pp. 46–49. Springer, Cham (2016). https://doi.org/10.1007/978-3-319-47602-5_10

40. De Meester, B., Seymoens, T., Dimou, A., Verborgh, R.: Implementation-independent function reuse. Futur. Gener. Comput. Syst. **110**, 946–959 (2020). https://doi.org/10.1016/j.future.2019.10.006

41. De Meester, B., Van Assche, D., Iglesias-Molina, A., Jozashoori, S., Chaves-Fraga, D.: RML-FNML Ontology: Functions (2023). https://doi.org/10.5281/zenodo.7919856

42. De Mulder, G., De Meester, B.: Implementation-independent knowledge graph construction workflows using FnO composition. In: Third International Workshop on Knowledge Graph Construction (2022). https://ceur-ws.org/Vol-3141/paper4.pdf

43. De Mulder, G., De Meester, B., Heyvaert, P., Taelman, R., Verborgh, R., Dimou, A.: PROV4ITDaTa: transparent and direct transfer of personal data to personal stores. In: Proceedings of The Web Conference (2021). https://doi.org/10.1145/3442442.3458608

44. De Paepe, D., et al.: A complete software stack for IoT time-series analysis that combines semantics and machine learning—lessons learned from the Dyversify project. Appl. Sci. **11**(24), 11932 (2021). https://doi.org/10.3390/app112411932

45. Debruyne, C., McKenna, L., O'Sullivan, D.: Extending R2RML with support for RDF collections and containers to generate MADS-RDF datasets. In: Kamps, J., Tsakonas, G., Manolopoulos, Y., Iliadis, L.S., Karydis, I. (eds.) Research and Advanced Technology for Digital Libraries - 21st International Conference on Theory and Practice of Digital Libraries, TPDL 2017, Thessaloniki, Greece, 18–21 September 2017, Proceedings. LNCS, vol. 10450, pp. 531–536. Springer, Cham (2017). https://doi.org/10.1007/978-3-319-67008-9_42

46. Debruyne, C., Michel, F., Iglesias-Molina, A., Van Assche, D., Chaves-Fraga, D., Dimou, A.: RML-CC Ontology: Collections and Containers (2023). https://doi.org/10.5281/zenodo.7919852

47. Debruyne, C., O'Sullivan, D.: R2RML-F: towards sharing and executing domain logic in R2RML mappings. In: Proceedings of the 9th Workshop on Linked Data on the Web, vol. 1593. CEUR Workshop Proceedings (2016). http://ceur-ws.org/Vol-1593/article-13.pdf

48. Delva, T., Arenas-Guerrero, J., Iglesias-Molina, A., Corcho, O., Chaves-Fraga, D., Dimou, A.: RML-Star: a declarative mapping language for RDF-Star generation. In: International Semantic Web Conference, ISWC, P&D, vol. 2980. CEUR Workshop Proceedings (2021). http://ceur-ws.org/Vol-2980/paper374.pdf

49. Dimou, A., Vander Sande, M., Colpaert, P., Verborgh, R., Mannens, E., Van de Walle, R.: RML: a generic language for integrated RDF mappings of heterogeneous data. In: Proceedings of the 7th Workshop on Linked Data on the Web, vol. 1184. CEUR Workshop Proceedings (2014). http://ceur-ws.org/Vol-1184/ldow2014_paper_01.pdf

50. Dimou, A., Verborgh, R., Vander Sande, M., Mannens, E., Van de Walle, R.: Machine-interpretable dataset and service descriptions for heterogeneous data access and retrieval. In: Proceedings of the 11th International Conference on Semantic Systems - SEMANTICS 2015. ACM Press (2015). https://doi.org/10.1145/2814864.2814873

51. García-González, H., Boneva, I., Staworko, S., Labra-Gayo, J.E., Lovelle, J.M.C.: ShExML: improving the usability of heterogeneous data mapping languages for first-time users. PeerJ Comput. Sci. **6**, e318 (2020)

52. Garijo, D.: WIDOCO: a wizard for documenting ontologies. In: d'Amato, C., et al. (eds.) 6th International Semantic Web Conference, Vienna, Austria, vol. 10588, pp. 94–102. Springer, Cham (2017). https://doi.org/10.1007/978-3-319-68204-4_9

53. Grassi, M., Scrocca, M., Carenini, A., Comerio, M., Celino, I.: Composable semantic data transformation pipelines with Chimera. In: Proceedings of the 4th International Workshop on Knowledge Graph Construction. CEUR Workshop Proceedings (2023)

54. Guasch, C., Lodi, G., Van Dooren, S.: Semantic knowledge graphs for distributed data spaces: the public procurement pilot experience. In: Sattler, U., et al. (eds.) The Semantic Web-ISWC 2022: 21st International Semantic Web Conference, Virtual Event, 23–27 October 2022, Proceedings, vol. 13489, pp. 753–769. Springer, Cham (2022). https://doi.org/10.1007/978-3-031-19433-7_43

55. Hartig, O.: Foundations of RDF* and SPARQL* (an alternative approach to statement-level metadata in RDF). In: Proceedings of the 11th Alberto Mendelzon International Workshop on Foundations of Data Management and the Web. CEUR Workshop Proceedings, vol. 1912 (2017)

56. Hartig, O., Champin, P.A., Kellogg, G., Seaborne, A.: RDF-star and SPARQL-star. W3C Final Community Group Report (2021). https://w3c.github.io/rdf-star/cg-spec/2021-12-17.html

57. Heyvaert, P., De Meester, B., Dimou, A., Verborgh, R.: Declarative rules for linked data generation at your fingertips! In: Gangemi, A., et al. (eds.) ESWC 2018. LNCS, vol. 11155, pp. 213–217. Springer, Cham (2018). https://doi.org/10.1007/978-3-319-98192-5_40

58. Heyvaert, P., De Meester, B., et al.: RMLMapper (2022). https://github.com/RMLio/rmlmapper-java

59. Iglesias, E., Jozashoori, S., Chaves-Fraga, D., Collarana, D., Vidal, M.E.: SDM-RDFizer: an RML interpreter for the efficient creation of RDF knowledge graphs. In: Proceedings of the 29th ACM International Conference on Information and Knowledge Management, CIKM, pp. 3039–3046. Association for Computing Machinery (2020). https://doi.org/10.1145/3340531.3412881
60. Iglesias, E., Vidal, M.E.: SDM-RDFizer-Star (2022). https://github.com/SDM-TIB/SDM-RDFizer-Star
61. Iglesias-Molina, A., et al.: RML Ontology and Shapes (2023). https://doi.org/10.5281/zenodo.7918478
62. Iglesias-Molina, A., Chaves-Fraga, D., Priyatna, F., Corcho, O.: Enhancing the maintainability of the Bio2RDF project using declarative mappings. In: Proceedings of the 12th International Conference on Semantic Web Applications and Tools for Health Care and Life Sciences, vol. 2849, pp. 1–10. CEUR Workshop Proceedings (2019). https://ceur-ws.org/Vol-2849/paper-01.pdf
63. Iglesias-Molina, A., Cimmino, A., Ruckhaus, E., Chaves-Fraga, D., García-Castro, R., Corcho, O.: An ontological approach for representing declarative mapping languages. Semant. Web 1–31 (2022). https://doi.org/10.3233/sw-223224
64. Iglesias-Molina, A., Van Assche, D., Arenas-Guerrero, J., Chaves-Fraga, D., Dimou, A.: RML-star Ontology (2023). https://doi.org/10.5281/zenodo.7919845
65. Jozashoori, S., Chaves-Fraga, D., Iglesias, E., Vidal, M.E., Corcho, O.: FunMap: efficient execution of functional mappings for knowledge graph creation. In: Pan, J.Z., et al. (eds.) Proceedings of the 19th International Semantic Web Conference, ISWC. LNCS, vol. 12506, pp. 276–293. Springer, Cham (2020). https://doi.org/10.1007/978-3-030-62419-4_16
66. Junior, A.C., Debruyne, C., Brennan, R., O'Sullivan, D.: FunUL: a method to incorporate functions into uplift mapping languages. In: Proceedings of the 18th International Conference on Information Integration and Web-Based Applications and Services, pp. 267–275. Association for Computing Machinery (2016). https://doi.org/10.1145/3011141.3011152
67. Knoblock, C.A., Szekely, P.: Exploiting semantics for big data integration. AI Mag. **36**(1), 25–38 (2015). https://doi.org/10.1609/aimag.v36i1.2565
68. Knublauch, H., Kontokostas, D.: Shapes Constraint Language (SHACL) (2017). https://www.w3.org/TR/shacl/
69. Kyzirakos, K., et al.: GeoTriples: transforming geospatial data into RDF graphs using R2RML and RML mappings. J. Web Semant. **52–53**, 16–32 (2018). https://doi.org/10.1016/j.websem.2018.08.003
70. Le Guillarme, N., Thuiller, W.: A practical approach to constructing a knowledge graph for soil ecological research. Eur. J. Soil Biol. **117**, 103497 (2023). https://doi.org/10.1016/j.ejsobi.2023.103497
71. Lefrançois, M., Zimmermann, A., Bakerally, N.: A SPARQL extension for generating RDF from heterogeneous formats. In: Blomqvist, E., Maynard, D., Gangemi, A., Hoekstra, R., Hitzler, P., Hartig, O. (eds.) Proceedings of the 14th Extended Semantic Web Conference. LNCS, vol. 10249, pp. 35–50. Springer, Cham (2017). https://doi.org/10.1007/978-3-319-58068-5_3
72. Lieber, S., De Meester, B., Verborgh, R., Dimou, A.: EcoDaLo: federating advertisement targeting with linked data. In: Blomqvist, E., et al. (eds.) SEMANTICS 2020. LNCS, vol. 12378, pp. 87–103. Springer, Cham (2020). https://doi.org/10.1007/978-3-030-59833-4_6
73. Lieber, S., et al.: BESOCIAL: a sustainable knowledge graph-based workflow for social media archiving. In: Further with Knowledge Graphs, pp. 198–212. IOS Press (2021). https://doi.org/10.3233/SSW210045

74. Maali, F., Erickson, J.: Data Catalog Vocabulary (DCAT). W3C Recommendation, World Wide Web Consortium (2014). https://www.w3.org/TR/vocab-dcat/
75. McKenna, L., Bustillo, M., Keefe, T., Debruyne, C., O'Sullivan, D.: Development of an RDF-enabled cataloguing tool. In: Kamps, J., Tsakonas, G., Manolopoulos, Y., Iliadis, L., Karydis, I. (eds.) Research and Advanced Technology for Digital Libraries - 21st International Conference on Theory and Practice of Digital Libraries, TPDL 2017, Thessaloniki, Greece, 18–21 September 2017, Proceedings. LNCS, vol. 10450, pp. 612–615. Springer, Cham (2017). https://doi.org/10.1007/978-3-319-67008-9_55
76. Michel, F., Djimenou, L., Faron-Zucker, C., Montagnat, J.: Translation of relational and non-relational databases into RDF with xR2RML. In: Monfort, V., Krempels, K., Majchrzak, T.A., Turk, Z. (eds.) WEBIST 2015 - Proceedings of the 11th International Conference on Web Information Systems and Technologies, Lisbon, Portugal, 20–22 May 2015, pp. 443–454. SciTePress (2015). https://doi.org/10.5220/0005448304430454
77. Michel, F., et al.: Covid-on-the-Web: knowledge graph and services to advance COVID-19 research. In: Pan, J.Z., et al. (eds.) ISWC 2020. LNCS, vol. 12507, pp. 294–310. Springer, Cham (2020). https://doi.org/10.1007/978-3-030-62466-8_19
78. Pellissier Tanon, T.: Oxigraph (2023). https://doi.org/10.5281/zenodo.7749949
79. Pérez, A.Á., Iglesias-Molina, A., Santamaría, L.P., Poveda-Villalón, M., Badenes-Olmedo, C., Rodríguez-González, A.: EBOCA: evidences for biomedical concepts association ontology. In: Corcho, O., Hollink, L., Kutz, O., Troquard, N., Ekaputra, F.J. (eds.) Knowledge Engineering and Knowledge Management: 23rd International Conference, EKAW 2022, Bolzano, Italy, 26–29 September 2022, Proceedings, vol. 13514, pp. 152–166. Springer, Cham (2022). https://doi.org/10.1007/978-3-031-17105-5_11
80. Poveda-Villalón, M., Fernández-Izquierdo, A., Fernández-López, M., García-Castro, R.: LOT: an industrial oriented ontology engineering framework. Eng. Appl. Artif. Intell. 111, 104755 (2022). https://doi.org/10.1016/j.engappai.2022.104755
81. Poveda-Villalón, M., Gómez-Pérez, A., Suárez-Figueroa, M.C.: OOPS! (OntOlogy Pitfall Scanner!): an on-line tool for ontology evaluation. Int. J. Semant. Web Inf. Syst. 10(2), 7–34 (2014). https://doi.org/10.4018/ijswis.2014040102
82. Ranaivoson, M., Tailhardat, L., Chabot, Y., Troncy, R.: SMASSIF-RML: a Semantic Web stream processing solution with declarative data mapping capability based on a modified version of the RMLMapper-java tool and extensions to the StreamingMASSIF framework (2023). https://github.com/Orange-OpenSource/SMASSIF-RML
83. Rojas, J.A., et al.: Leveraging semantic technologies for digital interoperability in the European railway domain. In: Hotho, A., et al. (eds.) The Semantic Web-ISWC 2021: 20th International Semantic Web Conference, ISWC 2021, Virtual Event, 24–28 October 2021, Proceedings 20, vol. 12922, pp. 648–664. Springer, Cham (2021). https://doi.org/10.1007/978-3-030-88361-4_38
84. Sakor, A., et al.: Knowledge4COVID-19: a semantic-based approach for constructing a COVID-19 related knowledge graph from various sources and analyzing treatments' toxicities. J. Web Semant. 75, 100760 (2023)
85. Samaneh Jozashoori, E.I., Vidal, M.E.: Dragoman (2022). https://github.com/SDM-TIB/Dragoman

86. Şimşek, U., Kärle, E., Fensel, D.: RocketRML - a NodeJS implementation of a use-case specific RML mapper. In: Proceedings of the 1st International Workshop on Knowledge Graph Building, vol. 2489, pp. 46–53. CEUR Workshop Proceedings (2019). http://ceur-ws.org/Vol-2489/paper5.pdf

87. Slepicka, J., Yin, C., Szekely, P., Knoblock, C.A.: KR2RML: an alternative interpretation of R2RML for heterogeneous sources. In: Proceedings of the 6th International Workshop on Consuming Linked Data, vol. 1426. CEUR Workshop Proceedings (2015). http://ceur-ws.org/Vol-1426/paper-08.pdf

88. Soylu, A., et al.: TheyBuyForYou platform and knowledge graph: expanding horizons in public procurement with open linked data. Semant. Web **13**(2), 265–291 (2022)

89. Stadler, C., Bühmann, L., Meyer, L.P., Martin, M.: Scaling RML and SPARQL-based knowledge graph construction with apache spark. In: Proceedings of the 4th International Workshop on Knowledge Graph Construction. CEUR Workshop Proceedings (2023)

90. Steenwinckel, B., et al.: Facilitating COVID-19 meta-analysis through a literature knowledge graph. In: Proceedings of 19th International Semantic Web Conference (2020)

91. Sundqvist, L.: Extending VKG Systems with RDF-star Support (2022). https://ontop-vkg.org/publications/2022-sundqvist-rdf-star-ontop-msc-thesis.pdf

92. Tailhardat, L., Chabot, Y., Troncy, R.: Designing NORIA: a knowledge graph-based platform for anomaly detection and incident management in ICT systems. In: Proceedings of the 4th International Workshop on Knowledge Graph Construction. CEUR Workshop Proceedings (2023)

93. Tennison, J., Kellogg, G., Herman, I.: Generating RDF from Tabular Data on the Web. W3C Recommendation, World Wide Web Consortium (2015). https://www.w3.org/TR/csv2rdf/

94. Toussaint, E., Guagliardo, P., Libkin, L., Sequeda, J.: Troubles with nulls, views from the users. Proc. VLDB Endow. **15**(11), 2613–2625 (2022). https://doi.org/10.14778/3551793.3551818

95. Van Assche, D., Delva, T., Haesendonck, G., Heyvaert, P., De Meester, B., Dimou, A.: Declarative RDF graph generation from heterogeneous (semi-)structured data: a systematic literature review. J. Web Semant. **75**, 100753 (2023). https://doi.org/10.1016/j.websem.2022.100753

96. Van Assche, D., et al.: Leveraging web of things W3C recommendations for knowledge graphs generation. In: Brambilla, M., Chbeir, R., Frasincar, F., Manolescu, I. (eds.) Web Engineering. LNCS, vol. 12706, pp. 337–352. Springer, Cham (2021). https://doi.org/10.1007/978-3-030-74296-6_26

97. Van Assche, D., Iglesias-Molina, A., Dimou, A., De Meester, B., Chaves-Fraga, D., Maria, P.: RML-Core Ontology: Generic Mapping Language for RDF (2023). https://doi.org/10.5281/zenodo.7919848

98. Van Assche, D., Iglesias-Molina, A., Haesendonck, G.: RML-IO Ontology: Source and Target (2023). https://doi.org/10.5281/zenodo.7919850

99. Van Herwegen, J., Heyvaert, P., Taelman, R., De Meester, B., Dimou, A.: Tutorial: knowledge representation as linked data: tutorial. In: Proceedings of the 27th ACM International Conference on Information and Knowledge Management, pp. 2299–2300 (2018)

100. Vu, B., Pujara, J., Knoblock, C.A.: D-REPR: a language for describing and mapping diversely-structured data sources to RDF. In: Proceedings of the 10th International Conference on Knowledge Capture, pp. 189–196. Association for Computing Machinery (2019). https://doi.org/10.1145/3360901.3364449

101. Williams, G.: SPARQL 1.1 Service Description. W3C Recommendation, World Wide Web Consortium (2013). https://www.w3.org/TR/sparql11-service-description/
102. Williams, G.T.: OWL 2 Web Ontology Language: Document Overview. W3C Recommendation, World Wide Web Consortium (2012). https://www.w3.org/TR/owl2-overview/

SPARQL_edit: Editing RDF Literals in Knowledge Graphs via View-Update Translations

Sascha Meckler[1(✉)] and Andreas Harth[1,2]

[1] Fraunhofer IIS, Fraunhofer Institute for Integrated Circuits IIS, Erlangen, Germany
{sascha.meckler,andreas.harth}@iis.fraunhofer.de
[2] University of Erlangen-Nuremberg, Erlangen, Germany

Abstract. In order to improve the adoption of knowledge graphs (KG) in everyday work, non-technical users must be empowered to not only view but to write data in a KG. Whereas most available software tools focus on displaying information, the presented solution helps business users to execute write operations for correcting wrong values or inserting missing values. SPARQL_edit is a Web application that enables users without any knowledge of SPARQL or RDF to view query results and instantly edit RDF literal values of the knowledge graph. The main concept can be summarized as 'editable SPARQL result table'. If a user modifies the value of an RDF literal in the view, a generic view-update algorithm translates the change into a SPARQL/Update query that updates the correct RDF triple in the KG. Similar to the view update problem in databases, there are restrictions of the SPARQL language features that can be used for creating a view with unambiguous updates to the graph.

1 Introduction

The application of Semantic Web technologies in enterprises has received increasing attention from both the research and industrial side. Information is often stored in a knowledge graph (KG), "a graph of data intended to accumulate and convey knowledge of the real world, whose nodes represent entities of interest and whose edges represent relations between these entities" [19]. There are openly available knowledge graphs such as DBpedia, Wikidata or Freebase and commercial enterprise-related KGs. Enterprise knowledge graphs (EKG) are designed for the use inside a company with applications from search and recommendations, commerce and finance to social networks [19]. The adoption of KGs for connecting data and knowledge inside an organisation was popularised by the big tech corporations, namely Google, Facebook, Microsoft, eBay and IBM [22]. EKG can be seen as an implementation of linked enterprise data by means of a "semantic network of concepts, properties, individuals and links representing and referencing foundational and domain knowledge relevant for an enterprise" [15]. Despite their different application domains, EKGs have common features: EKGs integrate data from different internal and external heterogeneous data

T. R. Payne et al. (Eds.): ISWC 2023, LNCS 14266, pp. 176–193, 2023.
https://doi.org/10.1007/978-3-031-47243-5_10

sources resulting in millions or billions of nodes and edges. Ontologies are typically used to define relationships between concepts and serve as a data schema. Artificial intelligence is used for knowledge extraction from unstructured data or for reasoning, the inference of new facts from existing ones. Every EKG requires an initial refinement and techniques to keep the graph up-to-date with corporate operations to guarantee a high quality knowledge base.

KGs can be built with different graph-structured data models but EKG are typically labelled property graphs or directed edge-labelled graphs built upon the Resource Description Framework (RDF) [9], the standard data model for the Web of Data. This paper focuses on RDF KGs that are queried with SPARQL [17], the query language of the Semantic Web.

The life-cycle of a KG can be divided into the creation, hosting, curation and the deployment phase [28]. In the creation and hosting process the KG is built from semantically annotated data which was generated by mapping data from heterogeneous sources into the graph format. The curation process includes tasks for cleaning and enriching in order to improve the correctness and completeness of the newly created KG. If errors are detected, the mapping rules are modified to correct the graph output. Even after the KG cleaning, there are still faulty values in the graph data that cannot be found by cleaning algorithms or the data engineers. There is still the need for manual changes after the deployment, e.g. for updating values or the correction of wrong values.

To simplify the work with KGs, the effort for maintaining and updating single values in a KG must be reduced. Instead of contacting a data engineer or re-executing the whole creation process, non-expert users should be able to update wrong values immediately by themselves. However, non-technical users are usually not familiar with RDF graph structures and the SPARQL query language. This leads to the overarching research question of how to enable lay users to update single values in an EKG. This question can be divided into more specific sub-questions:

- Is it possible to create an editable view of KG data where changes made by the user are automatically handed back to the original graph?
- Can we automatically translate a change to a SPARQL query result (view) into a SPARQL/Update query? Under what circumstances can an algorithm create unambiguous database updates?
- Which requirements and features are necessary for an end-user application?

This paper presents SPARQL_edit, a demo implementation of a generic solution that allows users to display arbitrary SPARQL query results in a table with editable input fields for RDF literal results. We explain an algorithm that translates the user's changes into a SPARQL/Update query that alters the correct RDF triples in the KG. The view-update algorithm constructs a SPARQL/Update query from the initial SPARQL/Select query, the query results and the changed RDF literal value. Similar to the view update problem in databases, there are restrictions to the SPARQL language features that can be used inside the initial query. This paper evaluates the benefits and shortcomings of this generic approach and discusses restrictions to the SPARQL grammar. Our main contribution is the practical study of a SPARQL-based view-update application for the use with RDF knowledge graphs.

The following section introduces a practical application example that showcases the functioning of SPARQL_edit. Section 3 describes related read-write Linked Data systems and the relation to the view update problem which is known from relational databases. The view-update algorithm and its restrictions are discussed in Sect. 4. It is followed by the description of the implementation in Sect. 5 and a study of the applicability of the presented solution in terms of performance and collaborative work in Sect. 6.

2   Practical Example

The concept of SPARQL_edit is based on the assumption that users are familiar with working on tabular data in spreadsheets. Graph data from a KG is presented in a table where cells of RDF literal solutions can be edited. A user story for the application in an enterprise environment is the correction of a product catalog in the EKG: While preparing the delivery bill for a customer, Bob notices that the billing software fetched an incorrect weight attribute for a product from the EKG. Bob wants to update the product weight in the EKG but he is not familiar with SPARQL. Bob opens SPARQL_edit in his browser and loads the 'Product Catalog View' configuration that Alice from the IT department shared with him. SPARQL_edit then displays a table with the product data. After filtering the table rows, Bob changes the cell with the wrong weight value and submits the change which is immediately applied to the company's EKG.

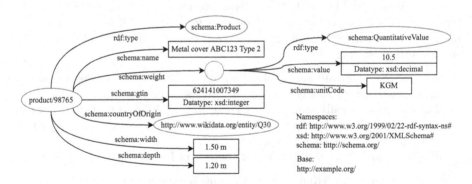

Fig. 1. Product graph from a fictional graph G of a dataset D

Figure 1 shows a graph of the exemplary product whose weight property shall be changed. After loading the 'Product Catalog View' in the SPARQL_edit Web application, Bob filters the displayed table for the desired product with a certain GTIN number. He uses the form controls to change the weight value as shown in Fig. 2. The 'Product Catalog View' has been created with the SPARQL/Select query from Listing 1.1. When Bob changes the weight value, the algorithm generates the SPARQL/Update query shown in Listing 1.2. If Bob submits his change, the application will send this update query to the graph store and refresh the values in the table by re-executing the original SPARQL/Select query. After the initial loading of the view, the literal update process consists of four steps:

1. Algorithm generates a SPARQL/Update query
2. SPARQL/Update query from step 1 is sent to the SPARQL server
3. Original SPARQL/Select query of the view is rerun
4. User interface is updated with values from step 3.

3   Related Work

Different software tools have been developed to support users who do not know the concepts of RDF and Semantic Web and also expert users in their work with Linked Data and KG. Most tools and techniques focus on the exploration and visualisation of semantically connected data which is either distributed across the Web or stored in a central location. However, there are only few software tools that allow users to execute write operations in a generic and reusable way. Generic read-write systems without explicit mapping rules between the presentation of data and the database struggle with the view update problem. This section presents related read-write Linked Data systems and gives an introduction to the database view update problem. After this, solutions for creating database-to-RDF mappings with write capabilities are listed.

3.1   Read-Write Linked Data Systems

Tabulator. Following Tim Berners-Lee's concept of a read-write Linked Data Web, "it is essential that the Data Web should not be read-only" [2]. Tim Berners-Lee and his colleagues developed Tabulator [3], a Web of Data browser with write capabilities that allows users to modify and extend information within the browser interface. In Tabulator, changes to a resource are submitted back to the Web server using an HTTP and SPARQL-based protocol. Berners-Lee et al. [3] discuss the difficulties that arise with write functionality. These difficulties are related to the view update problem which is described in Sect. 3.2.

RDF-to-Form Mapping. Software tools such as RDFauthor [32] facilitate RDF editing by creating a bidirectional mapping between RDF data and Web HTML forms by making use of semantic markup annotations like RDFa. Rdf Edit eXtension (REX) [30] uses RDFa-like HTML attributes to create a mapping between an RDF graph and the model of the HTML form controls. When a user changes a value in the form controls, REX generates and executes a SPAR-QL/Update query based on the semantic annotations. Moreover, RDForms [11] is a library for creating form-based RDF editors by using a templating mechanism which uses bidirectional mapping rules to translate between the Web form and the RDF graph. In contrast to RDFauthor, REX and RDForms, SPARQL_edit

Fig. 2. Editing of an RDF literal value in the user interface of SPARQL_edit

```
PREFIX rdf: <http://www.w3.org/1999/02/22-rdf-syntax-ns#>
PREFIX schema: <http://schema.org/>
SELECT ?product ?name ?gtin ?weight
FROM <http://example.org/dataset/graph>
WHERE {
  ?product rdf:type schema:Product ;
    schema:name ?name ;
    schema:gtin ?gtin ;
    schema:weight [
      schema:value ?weight
    ]
  FILTER (lang(?name) = 'en')
}
```

Listing 1.1. SPARQL/Select query for the product catalog view in Fig. 2

```
PREFIX rdf: <http://www.w3.org/1999/02/22-rdf-syntax-ns#>
PREFIX xsd: <http://www.w3.org/2001/XMLSchema#>
PREFIX schema: <http://schema.org/>
WITH <http://example.org/dataset/graph>
DELETE { ?g_0 schema:value "10.5"^^xsd:decimal. }
INSERT { ?g_0 schema:value "8.8"^^xsd:decimal. }
WHERE {
  <http://example.org/product/98765> rdf:type schema:Product;
    schema:name "Metal cover ABC123 Type 2"@en;
    schema:gtin 624141007349;
    schema:weight ?g_0.
  ?g_0 schema:value "10.5"^^xsd:decimal.
}
```

Listing 1.2. SPARQL/Update query generated for changing the weight RDF triple

does not require the upfront definition of mapping rules or form annotations. In SPARQL_edit, an algorithm automatically translates a change to a form control into an appropriate SPARQL/Update query that will manipulate the underlying RDF graph. Instead of embedding information in the HTML form, SPARQL_edit gathers the necessary inputs for the algorithm from the view defined by a SPARQL/Select query and the current database state.

Solid Pod Managers. Today, the read-write Linked Data Web is extended with Social Linked Data (Solid)[1], a new set of technical concepts and standards for building a decentralized social Web. The key concept is the storage of personal data in a user-managed personal online data store (Pod) whose resource management is based on the Linked Data Platform (LDP) [29]. With Solid, a new category of read-write Linked Data tools emerged: Pod managers or browsers. Pod managers can be seen as successors of LDP clients [34] that use Solid authentication and authorization. Pod managers like SolidOS (Databrowser)[2] or Pod-Browser[3] provide a GUI for resource management and triple editing of RDF documents in a Solid Pod. The Solid protocol [8] allows document updates via HTTP PUT requests and via PATCH requests that include Notation 3 (N3) [1] rules defining the update operation. Although the document-based update is different to our query-based approach, the N3 update rules have similarities with the queries in SPARQL_edit. A Solid `InsertDeletePatch` typically includes an insertion, a deletion and a condition formula that is evaluated against the target RDF document similar to a `DELETE-INSERT-WHERE` SPARQL/Update query.

PoolParty GraphEditor. Besides the open-source tools, there are proprietary solutions that are often incorporated into commercial Semantic Web or KG platforms. PoolParty's GraphEditor[4] provides a graphical user interface that guides users in the creation of views for graph editing. The proprietary tool helps users to visually build queries, filter the results and perform inline editing to single or multiple triples of the KG. GraphEditor automatically generates a SPARQL query based on the selected graphs, the chosen properties from the selected vocabulary as well as the user-defined filters and is able to "refine triples, create or change relations among their properties or their names and labels and even create new resources" [27]. Since SPARQL_edit has a similar motivation as PoolParty's GraphEditor – to build an easily usable application for directly editing data in a KG – it shares the same design principle of having customizable views on a KG and follows the same concept of in-line editing by means of editable fields in query results. Whereas GraphEditor is strongly integrated in the proprietary platform of PoolParty, SPARQL_edit is a lightweight stand-alone application that can be used with any SPARQL 1.1 query/update endpoint.

---

[1] cf., https://solidproject.org/.
[2] cf., https://github.com/SolidOS/solidos.
[3] cf., https://github.com/inrupt/pod-browser.
[4] cf., https://www.poolparty.biz/poolparty-grapheditor.

3.2   Database View Update Problem

The (database) view update problem with its origin in the field of relational databases describes the problem of translating updates on a view into equivalent updates on the database. There are cases in which the translation of a view update is not unique, ill-defined or even impossible. Calculated update queries may create inconsistencies in the database or have side-effects on the derived view [14]. In general, there are two opposed approaches for solving the view update problem [14]: In the first approach, the view includes all permissible view updates together with their translations. This approach requires the explicit definition of translation rules on how to update the database for each possible update operation in the view. The second solution are general view update translators which are based on the analysis of the conceptual schema dependencies or on the concept of a view complement in order to create unique view update translations. The database update is calculated from the view definition, the view update, additional information and the current database state. This automatic translation is comfortable because the database engineer must not define the translation rules like in the first approach. However, the general approach only allows a limited range of view updates that can be translated correctly and the database engineer has to check if the calculated translations are right [14]. For answering the question whether a view is updatable, it is necessary to check if the mapping from the database relations to the view is invertible and if a view update has a translation [13].

The research for relational databases and the SQL query language can be transferred to graph databases, RDF and SPARQL. Berners-Lee et al. [3] discuss the problem of mapping changes in a Web page (presentation) to the underlying Web data that may originate from different Web servers in the context of their tool Tabulator. Whereas Tabulator is focused on linked documents on the Web, SPARQL_edit is working on views defined by SPARQL queries. SPARQL_edit belongs to the group of general view update translators that trade expressivity for generality. We accepted the restrictions for the set of possible view updates to create a lightweight tool which does not require much upfront configuration and is therefore more efficient than developing a domain-specific application.

3.3   Database-to-RDF Mappings

Several techniques and software tools have been developed to create a (virtual) RDF graph from a relational database (RDB) by applying specific mapping rules. The use of an ontology-based mediation layer for accessing data from relational databases is often labeled as Ontology-Based Data Access (OBDA). RDB-to-RDF solutions like D2RQ [5], R2RML [31] and OBDA implementations such as Ontop [7] or Mastro [6] provide RDF views on relational databases or expose a virtual SPARQL endpoint for querying. Although most RDB-to-RDF and OBDA systems are limited to read operations, there have been efforts to create a bidirectional read-write access by reversing the RDB-to-RDF mappings. OntoAccess [18] explicitly supports write access by means of translating

SPARQL/Update operations to SQL. Information and integrity constraints for the database schema are included in the mapping rules in order to identify update requests that cannot be executed by the database engine. D2RQ++ and D2RQ/Update are similar extensions to the D2RQ mapping platform which allow the execution of SPARQL/Update statements on the virtual RDF graph. D2RQ++ and D2RQ/Update differ in the way they handle the translation of SPARQL to a number of SQL statements [12]. Unbehauen and Martin [33] presented a solution for read-write access to graphs that are mapped with the R2RML language. Ontology- and source-level updates have also been examined for OBDA systems [10]. Writing RDF/SPARQL updates back into the RDB naturally leads to the view update problem explained in Sect. 3.2. The translation of a SPARQL/Update query into one or more SQL statements is especially complicated because SPARQL/Update can potentially modify the data and schema triples at the same time [33]. Most solutions with write capabilities are limited to basic relation-to-class and attribute-to-property mappings [20].

4   View-Update Algorithm

The result of a SPARQL/Select query Q is a solution sequence Ω, an unordered list of zero or more solutions from graph pattern matching and operations on the initial matching solutions. Each solution (mapping) $\mu \in \Omega$ has a set of bindings of variables to RDF terms $\mu : V \to T$ [17]. In the JSON serialization of SPARQL results [26], Ω is represented in an array which is the value of the `bindings` key inside the `results` key. Each member ("result binding") representing a solution mapping μ is a JSON object that encodes the bound values, i.e. RDF terms, for each variable v from Q. In the result table, each column represents a variable and each solution produces a row.

4.1   Translation of a Literal Update into a SPARQL/Update Query

The SPARQL_edit algorithm illustrated in Fig. 3 translates the change of a literal value l in the solution μ_{ed} into a DELETE-INSERT-WHERE SPARQL/Update query Q^-. The basic idea behind the algorithm is to rebuild the original SPARQL/Select query Q so that it only affects the single RDF triple whose object literal value shall be changed. This is done by replacing every variable $v \in V$ in Q with the URIs or literal values from the solution $\mu_{ed} \in \Omega$ that is represented in the row with the edited value. In order to have solution mappings for every variable, Q is altered to select all variables (SELECT *). The triple patterns with replaced variables are then used for building the update query Q^-. In order to output Q^-, the algorithm requires the input of

- the original SPARQL/Select query (Q),
- the solution mapping/result binding (μ_{ed}) for the edited table row
- and the previous and new literal values (l_{old}, l_{new}).

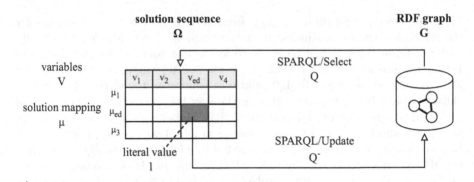

Fig. 3. Principle of the SPARQL_edit algorithm

Algorithm Steps. The algorithm follows four sequential steps for building Q^-:

1. In a first step, information about the edited literal value is collected. This includes the name, datatype, language, old and new values of l.
2. Then, the graph patterns in the WHERE clause of Q are analysed. The algorithm filters and stores Basic Graph Patterns (BGP) and Optional Graph Patterns (OGP). The algorithm finds the triple pattern that includes the particular variable v_{ed} in object position whose solution mapping μ_{ed} was edited. If the triple pattern is part of an OGP, the OGP must be treated like a BGP.
3. In the third step, the WHERE clause for Q^- is built. For each BGP that was collected in the second step, all named variables are replaced with named nodes (URIs) or concrete literal values from μ_{ed}. A variable in subject position is either set to a named node or, in case of an unnamed variable (blank node), set to a named variable. Blank nodes are replaced with named variables so that the subject can be referenced later in the DELETE and INSERT templates. Blank nodes are prohibited in a SPARQL/Update DELETE template, because a new blank node never matches anything in the graph and therefore never results in any deletion [24]. A predicate variable is always replaced with a named node whereas a variable in object position is bound to either a named node, a literal value or a blank node.
4. Next, the DELETE and INSERT templates for Q^- are defined and the update query is assembled. Both templates are built from the same triple pattern which included v_{ed}. In case of the DELETE template, the triple's object holds the old value l_{old} from μ_{ed}. The triple in the INSERT template has the new user-defined literal value l_{new} in the object position. Finally, Q^- is completed by replicating the prefixes of Q. If Q uses a FROM statement to specify the default graph for the query, a matching WITH clause is added to Q^-.

Insert Mode. The algorithm is capable of generating SPARQL/Update queries for updating existing literal values, but also for inserting missing RDF literals. However, the insert mode has two prerequisites: First, the variable v_{ed} must be defined inside an optional graph pattern (OGP) in the WHERE clause of Q.

Otherwise, there would be no table row representing a solution mapping which is missing a literal value for v_{ed}. The second requirement is that Ω includes at least one solution mapping that binds v_{ed} to an RDF literal term $\mu : v_{ed} \rightarrow lit$. This literal result is used as a template for new literals the user wants to insert. The insert mode introduces a new edge case for the algorithm. If the OGP is composed of an n-ary relation [25], the INSERT template has to include all successive triples needed for the construction of a new blank node with the user-defined literal. In practice, the insert mode is useful to fill in gaps in the KG data which may originate from mapping incomplete data sources to RDF.

4.2   Query Restrictions

According to the two classes of solutions for the view update problem [14], the SPARQL_edit algorithm belongs to the general view update translators where the database update is automatically calculated from the view definition (Q), the view update (l_{new}) and the current database state (μ_{ed}). However, this comfortable update generation only allows a limited range of view updates that can be translated correctly. The database engineer who creates the views has to check if the calculated translations are right.

The presented algorithm supports simple SPARQL/Select queries on the default graph specified with or without a single FROM clause. If the original query Q defines a certain graph as the default graph with a FROM clause, a corresponding WITH clause is attached to Q^-. There can only be one WITH clause as it "defines the graph that will be modified or matched against for any of the subsequent elements (in DELETE, INSERT, or WHERE clauses) if they do not specify a graph explicitly" [24]. In the case of multiple FROM clauses, the default graph is the RDF merge of the graphs which is ambiguous for any update translations. Despite that, the algorithm might be extended to support SPARQL/Select queries with named graphs using the FROM NAMED clause. With explicitly named graphs, the changed graph could be tracked and included in a SPARQL/Update query of the form:

DELETE { GRAPH <g1>{ s p o } } INSERT { GRAPH <g1>{ s p o2 } }
    USING NAMED <g1> WHERE { ... }

The algorithm supports SPARQL/Select queries with a graph pattern that is composed of one or more BGPs and OGPs that may contain triple patterns with variables, blank nodes and filters (FILTER). The query can include filter statements and solution sequence modifier (ORDER, LIMIT or OFFSET). When creating Q^-, the algorithm removes any filters because the replacement of the variables with explicit values makes filters obsolete. Any other query constructs are currently not supported by the algorithm. For example, the algorithm cannot support SPARQL/Select queries with irreversible functions like aggregation (GROUP BY) or bindings (BIND). Table 1 specifies the restrictions to the original SPARQL 1.1 grammar. The restrictions have been studied empirically and must be further examined based on the formal models for the SPARQL language. To help expert users with the creation of "updatable" views, the query editor in

Table 1. Restricted SPARQL grammar for SPARQL_edit in EBNF notation. The table lists rules that differ from the original SPARQL 1.1 grammar [17]. Unsupported language features are crossed out.

[2]   Query   ::=

    Prologue
    (SelectQuery ~~| ConstructQuery | DescribeQuery |~~
       ~~AskQuery~~)
    ValuesClause

[7]   SelectQuery   ::=

    SelectClause DatasetClause?~~*~~ WhereClause
    SolutionModifier

[9]   SelectClause   ::=

    'SELECT' ('DISTINCT' | 'REDUCED')? (
    (Var ~~| ('(' Expression 'AS' Var ')')~~)+ | '*')

[13]   DatasetClause   ::=

    'FROM' (DefaultGraphClause
    ~~| NamedGraphClause~~)

[18]   SolutionModifier   ::=

    ~~GroupClause?~~
       ~~HavingClause?~~ OrderClause? LimitOffsetClauses?

[53]   GroupGraphPattern   ::=

    '{' (~~SubSelect |~~ GroupGraphPatternSub) '}'

[56]   GraphPatternNotTriples   ::=

    ~~GroupOrUnionGraphPattern |~~
    OptionalGraphPattern | ~~MinusGraphPattern~~
    ~~| GraphGraphPattern | ServiceGraphPattern |~~
    Filter ~~| Bind | InlineData~~

[83]   PropertyListPathNotEmpty ::=

    (~~VerbPath |~~ VerbSimple) ObjectListPath
      (';' ((~~VerbPath |~~ VerbSimple)
      ObjectList)?)*

[98]   TriplesNode   ::=

    ~~Collection |~~ BlankNodePropertyList

[100]   TriplesNodePath   ::=

    ~~CollectionPath |~~ BlankNodePropertyListPath

[109]   GraphTerm   ::=

    iri | RDFLiteral | NumericLiteral |
    BooleanLiteral | BlankNode ~~| NIL~~

SPARQL_edit marks queries which are not compliant with this subset of the SPARQL grammar.

Unambiguous Update Guaranty. Due to the structural freedom of RDF and the ambiguous nature of RDF blank nodes, it is possible to construct graphs where Q^- has unwanted side-effects on other RDF triples. In these edge cases with RDF blank nodes, the graph pattern of Q^- matches more than one RDF triple in the graph. An example in the context of the product graph from Fig. 1 would be a product node which has two identical weight properties connected to two different blank nodes which have again the same predicate (`schema:value`) and equal literals (e.g. `"10.5"^^xsd:decimal`). The two blank nodes might have different triples apart from the value triple. In this special case, Q^- from Listing 1.2 would change the weight literal value of the first and the second blank node. To guarantee safe RDF literal updates for cases with RDF blank nodes, an additional SPARQL/Select query Q_{check} is used to verify that Q^- updates exactly one RDF triple. Q_{check} is a simple SPARQL/Select query that uses the `WHERE` clause from Q^-. Depending on the size of its solution sequence $|\Omega|$, we can distinguish three cases:

- $|\Omega| = 0$: The graph pattern matching has no result because the relevant triples in the graph have been changed in the meantime.
- $|\Omega| = 1$: The ideal case in which Q^- will affect exactly one RDF triple.
- $|\Omega| \geq 2$: Q^- is ambiguous and would alter more than one RDF triple.

URI Editing. In principle, the algorithm could be generalized for editing not only literal objects but also object URIs. However, changes to the URI of an RDF triple's object can have drastic effects on the whole graph. Any URI alteration could disconnect or connect parts of the graph. The consequences of a URI modification for the graph structure cannot be foreseen from the tabular representation. From a user perspective, a lay user should not be able to change the graph structure by accident.

5   Implementation

SPARQL_edit is designed as a standalone Web application which is usable on different devices without installation. SPARQL_edit is implemented in JavaScript and TypeScript as a React single-page-application that can be served from any Web server or content delivery network. The application acts as a SPARQL client and renders the query results as an HTML table with HTML5 input controls for literal results. In order to simulate in-place editing of cells, a change submission immediately triggers an update query and refreshes the table to give feedback to the user. SPARQL_edit requires that the SPARQL server provides an endpoint for SPARQL 1.1 updates [24] and that it allows Cross-Origin Resource Sharing, a browser security feature for cross-domain HTTP requests.

Similar to the approach of rdfedit [23], SPARQL_edit uses configuration objects that are created by experts to simplify the work for non-technical users. Lay users can simply load predefined "SPARQL views" that include all information that is necessary for SPARQL_edit to create a certain table of data from a KG. A "SPARQL view" configuration is an RDF graph including information about:

– the SPARQL endpoint (query and update URL of an RDF dataset),
– the SPARQL/Select query for the view,
– metadata (description, originator, modification date, etc.) and
– the security mechanism for requests to the SPARQL server.

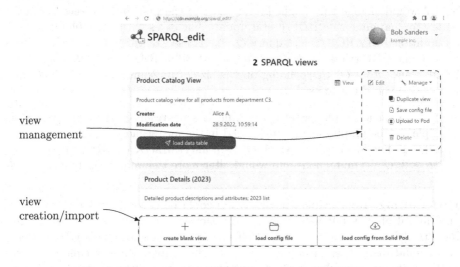

Fig. 4. Management of "SPARQL views" in SPARQL_edit

Instead of a back-end (database), the client-side application uses the HTML5 Web Storage to save view configurations in the browser. To allow for easy sharing of view configurations, views can be exported to or imported from text-based files in the JSON-LD RDF format. A KG expert is able to create and test a specific view configuration, upload it to a Web server or a Solid Pod and share it with one or more colleagues. In this way, non-technical users can work with predefined views on the KG without knowledge about SPARQL and RDF. Figure 4 shows the UI controls for the management of views in SPARQL_edit.

6   Applicability

The applicability of the presented solution in an enterprise scenario concerns the cooperation of several people and the performance in case of large data sets.

6.1   Performance

Many Linked Data exploration and visualisation solutions pay too little attention to performance and scalability because they load a complete KG or dataset into memory [4]. SPARQL_edit only loads the SPARQL query results for a specific view which is usually only a subset of the whole graph. Due to the SPARQL/Update mechanism, single changes are applied directly via the SPARQL endpoint of the KG without re-writing the graph and without writing any RDF files.

The execution times of RDF literal update cycles for different sizes of solutions sequences are shown in Fig. 5. The comparison of the running times for the four steps from Sect. 2 reveal that the transmission and processing of the SPARQL results are the key drivers for the execution time of a complete literal update cycle for growing numbers of query solutions. The algorithm and the SPARQL/Update query are independent of the number of SPARQL results. The algorithm is responsible for less than one percent of the total execution time because it only uses the solution $\mu_{ed} \in \Omega$ which was modified. The running time of the algorithm merely depends on the number of triple patterns in the SPARQL/Select query. Experiments revealed a linear rise from 0.10 to 0.18 ms on average when continuously increasing the number of triple patterns with variables from two to thirty. The reason for the increase are several loops over the triple patterns of Q in the algorithm.

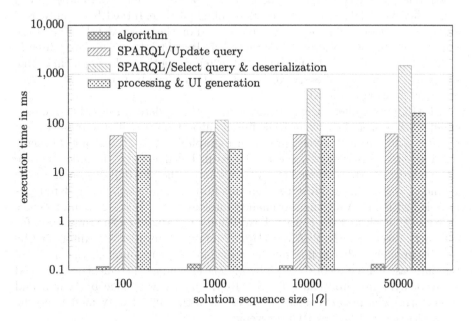

Fig. 5. Average execution times of the steps of a SPARQL_edit literal update cycle

6.2   Concurrent Literal Editing

If two SPARQL_edit users are concurrently editing the same triples of the same graph, inconsistencies may occur because the algorithm uses a slightly outdated state of the database for generating the update query Q^-. When the user loads a "SPARQL view", the application sends the specified SPARQL/Select query Q to the specified SPARQL endpoint of a dataset D and receives the solution sequence Ω. This Ω represents the solution for Q on a graph $G \in D$ at the time of the query evaluation. If relevant triples in G are modified by another user before Q^- is executed, Q^- is ineffective because its triple patterns do not match with the new triples in G. Although the ineffectiveness of Q^- can be considered as fail-safe, this behavior is very irritating to the user. This race condition can by prevented by means of the ambiguity check from Sect. 4.2. Prior to Q^-, SPARQL_edit executes the SPARQL/Select query Q_{check} to verify that Q^- will update exactly one RDF triple. If Q_{check} has no query results ($|\Omega| = 0$), the application notifies the user that the values of the selected table row have been changed in the meantime. The user can reload the view to see the current state of the KG.

6.3   Update Logging

Until today, an EKG is typically built with data from different databases which is translated to RDF as part of the KG building pipeline. If the EKG is only used for query answering, data changes are executed on the source databases and the building pipeline is rerun to update the graph. But if triples are updated directly in the KG, these changes would be lost after repeating the building pipeline. One solution is the logging of every KG update so that it can be reapplied after every new instantiation of the KG.

SPARQL_edit offers a feature for logging the update queries that are executed when a user changes an RDF literal value. On every literal update, a log is inserted into a user-defined provenance graph $G_{prov} \in D$. Instead of executing a separate insert query, the logging is included into Q^- in order to take advantage of the transactional query execution at the SPARQL endpoint. Q^- is extended with additional insert statements for the update log. The update log is modeled with PROV-O, the provenance ontology of the W3C [21], and includes at least Q^- itself and the captured execution time. Based on the timestamp for the query execution, the SPARQL/Update queries from multiple editors can be sorted chronologically. Following the principle of event sourcing, the states of the database can be reconstructed by adding up update increments. A detailed study of dynamic provenance for SPARQL updates was done by Halpin and Cheney [16] who researched the combination of the W3C PROV model and the semantics of SPARQL for RDF provenance.

If SPARQL_edit demanded users to login, e.g. using Solid authentication, the update logging could be used to track user activities – which user has made which change at which time.

7 Conclusion

To improve the adoption of enterprise knowledge graphs, non-expert users must be able to easily maintain and update single values in the graph. We present SPARQL_edit, a Web application that enables users without any knowledge about SPARQL or RDF to view query results and instantly edit or insert missing RDF literal values. The browser application connects to a SPARQL endpoint and presents query results in an interactive table that helps users to make changes to literal contents of the underlying RDF data. Expert users can create configurations for loading specific views on the KG data and share them with business users. The functionality, performance and applicability of our solution was studied by means of a demo implementation. In addition to the update algorithm, the open-source application implements features for view management and collaborative work.

The algorithm behind the SPARQL_edit application translates a change in a view into a SPARQL/Update query for updating the original KG. The generic view update translation approach reduces the upfront work for data engineers. In contrast to most existing read-write Linked Data tools, it is not necessary to explicitly define RDF translation rules. However, the automatic update query generation comes with restrictions which limit the possible views on the KG data. Therefore, we defined restrictions to the SPARQL query language that are necessary for the creation of "updatable" views. Although the restrictions have been studied empirically, they must be further examined based on the formal models for the SPARQL query language. Furthermore, the generic approach could be extended so that data engineers can define translations for problematic cases that exceed the capabilities of the algorithm.

Acknowledgments. This work was funded by the Bavarian State Ministry of Economic Affairs and Media, Energy and Technology within the research program "Information and Communication Technology" (grant no. DIK0134/01).

Resource Availability Statement. Source code for the view-update algorithm and the Web application described in Sect. 5 are available from Github (cf., https://github.com/wintechis/sparqledit).

References

1. Berners-Lee, T., Connolly, D.: Notation3 (N3): a readable RDF syntax. W3C team submission. W3C (2011). http://www.w3.org/TeamSubmission/2011/SUBM-n3-20110328/
2. Berners-Lee, T., O'Hara, K.: The read-write linked data web. Phil. Trans. R. Soc. A **371**, 20120513 (2013). https://doi.org/10.1098/rsta.2012.0513
3. Berners-Lee, T., et al.: Tabulator redux: browsing and writing linked data. In: Bizer, C., et al. (eds.) Proceedings of the WWW2008 Workshop on Linked Data on the Web, LDOW. CEUR-WS (2008)

4. Bikakis, N., Sellis, T.: Exploration and visualization in the web of big linked data: a survey of the state of the art. In: Proceedings of the Workshops of the EDBT/ICDT 2016 Joint Conference (2016)

5. Bizer, C., Seaborne, A.: D2RQ - treating non-RDF databases as virtual RDF graphs. In: Proceedings of the 3rd International Conference on Semantic Web Conference, ISWC 2004. LNCS. Springer, Heidelberg (2004)

6. Calvanese, D., et al.: The MASTRO system for ontology-based data access. Semant. Web **2**, 43–53 (2011). https://doi.org/10.3233/SW-2011-0029

7. Calvanese, D., et al.: OBDA with the Ontop framework. In: Lembo, D., Torlone, R., Marrella, A. (eds.) 23rd Italian Symposium on Advanced Database Systems, SEBD (2015)

8. Capadisli, S., Berners-Lee, T., Verborgh, R., Kjernsmo, K.: Solid protocol. Technical report. solidproject.org (2021). https://solidproject.org/TR/2021/protocol-20211217

9. Cyganiak, R., Wood, D., Lanthaler, M.: RDF 1.1 concepts and abstract syntax. W3C recommendation. W3C (2014). https://www.w3.org/TR/2014/REC-rdf11-concepts-20140225/

10. De Giacomo, G., Lembo, D., Oriol, X., Savo, D.F., Teniente, E.: Practical update management in ontology-based data access. In: d'Amato, C., et al. (eds.) ISWC 2017. LNCS, vol. 10587, pp. 225–242. Springer, Cham (2017). https://doi.org/10.1007/978-3-319-68288-4_14

11. Dörr, T.: RDF in HTML-forms. https://rdforms.org/. Accessed 18 Jul 2023

12. Eisenberg, V., Kanza, Y.: D2RQ/Update: updating relational data via virtual RDF. In: Proceedings of the 21st International Conference on World Wide Web, WWW 2012, Companion, pp. 497–498. ACM, New York (2012). https://doi.org/10.1145/2187980.2188095

13. Franconi, E., Guagliardo, P.: The view update problem revisited (2012). https://doi.org/10.48550/ARXIV.1211.3016

14. Furtado, A.L., Casanova, M.A.: Updating relational views. In: Kim, W., Reiner, D.S., Batory, D.S. (eds.) Query Processing in Database Systems. Topics in Information Systems, pp. 127–142. Springer, Heidelberg (1985). https://doi.org/10.1007/978-3-642-82375-6_7

15. Galkin, M., Auer, S., Scerri, S.: Enterprise knowledge graphs: a backbone of linked enterprise data. In: 2016 IEEE/WIC/ACM International Conference on Web Intelligence (WI), Omaha, USA, pp. 497–502. IEEE Computer Society (2016). https://doi.org/10.1109/WI.2016.0083

16. Halpin, H., Cheney, J.: Dynamic provenance for SPARQL updates. In: Mika, P., et al. (eds.) ISWC 2014. LNCS, vol. 8796, pp. 425–440. Springer, Cham (2014). https://doi.org/10.1007/978-3-319-11964-9_27

17. Harris, S., Seaborne, A.: SPARQL 1.1 query language. W3C recommendation. W3C (2013). https://www.w3.org/TR/2013/REC-sparql11-query-20130321/

18. Hert, M., Reif, G., Gall, H.C.: Updating relational data via SPARQL/update. In: Proceedings of the 2010 EDBT/ICDT Workshops, EDBT 2010. ACM, New York (2010). https://doi.org/10.1145/1754239.1754266

19. Hogan, A., et al.: Knowledge Graphs. Synthesis Lectures on Data, Semantics, and Knowledge, Springer, Cham (2022). https://doi.org/10.1007/978-3-031-01918-0

20. Konstantinou, N., Spanos, D.: Materializing the Web of Linked Data. Springer, Cham (2015). https://doi.org/10.1007/978-3-319-16074-0

21. McGuinness, D., Lebo, T., Sahoo, S.: PROV-O: The PROV Ontology. W3C recommendation. W3C (2013). https://www.w3.org/TR/2013/REC-prov-o-20130430/

22. Noy, N., et al.: Industry-scale knowledge graphs: lessons and challenges. Commun. ACM **62**(8), 36–43 (2019). https://doi.org/10.1145/3331166
23. Pohl, O.: rdfedit: user supporting web application for creating and manipulating RDF instance data. In: Closs, S., Studer, R., Garoufallou, E., Sicilia, M.-A. (eds.) MTSR 2014. CCIS, vol. 478, pp. 54–59. Springer, Cham (2014). https://doi.org/10.1007/978-3-319-13674-5_6
24. Polleres, A., Gearon, P., Passant, A.: SPARQL 1.1 update. W3C recommendation. W3C (2013). https://www.w3.org/TR/2013/REC-sparql11-update-20130321/
25. Rector, A., Noy, N.: Defining n-ary relations on the semantic web. W3C note. W3C (2006). https://www.w3.org/TR/2006/NOTE-swbp-n-aryRelations-20060412/
26. Seaborne, A.: SPARQL 1.1 query results JSON format. W3C recommendation. W3C (2013). https://www.w3.org/TR/2013/REC-sparql11-results-json-20130321/
27. Semantic Web Company: PoolParty GraphEditor - overview (2022). https://help.poolparty.biz/en/user-guide-for-knowledge-engineers/enterprise-features/poolparty-grapheditor---overview.html. Accessed 18 Jul 2023
28. Simsek, U., et al.: Knowledge Graph lifecycle: building and maintaining knowledge graphs. In: Proceedings of the 2nd International Workshop on Knowledge Graph Construction, KGC 2021, vol. 2873. CEUR-WS (2021)
29. Speicher, S., Malhotra, A., Arwe, J.: Linked data platform 1.0. W3C recommendation. W3C (2015). https://www.w3.org/TR/2015/REC-ldp-20150226/
30. Stadler, C., Arndt, N., Martin, M., Lehmann, J.: RDF editing on the web with REX. In: SEMANTICS 2015, SEM 2015. ACM (2015)
31. Sundara, S., Das, S., Cyganiak, R.: R2RML: RDB to RDF mapping language. W3C recommendation. W3C (2012). https://www.w3.org/TR/2012/REC-r2rml-20120927/
32. Tramp, S., Heino, N., Auer, S., Frischmuth, P.: RDFauthor: employing RDFa for collaborative knowledge engineering. In: Cimiano, P., Pinto, H.S. (eds.) EKAW 2010. LNCS (LNAI), vol. 6317, pp. 90–104. Springer, Heidelberg (2010). https://doi.org/10.1007/978-3-642-16438-5_7
33. Unbehauen, J., Martin, M.: SPARQL update queries over R2RML mapped data sources. In: Eibl, M., Gaedke, M. (eds.) INFORMATIK 2017, pp. 1891–1901. Gesellschaft für Informatik, Chemnitz, Germany (2017). https://doi.org/10.18420/in2017_189
34. W3C: LDP implementations. https://www.w3.org/wiki/LDP_Implementations. Accessed 18 Jul 2023

LDkit: Linked Data Object Graph Mapping Toolkit for Web Applications

Karel Klíma[1(✉)], Ruben Taelman[2], and Martin Nečaský[1]

[1] Department of Software Engineering, Faculty of Mathematics and Physics, Charles
University, Prague, Czechia
{karel.klima,martin.necasky}@matfyz.cuni.cz
[2] IDLab, Department of Electronics and Information Systems, Ghent University –
IMEC, Ghent, Belgium
ruben.taelman@ugent.be

Abstract. The adoption of Semantic Web and Linked Data technologies in web application development has been hindered by the complexity of numerous standards, such as RDF and SPARQL, as well as the challenges associated with querying data from distributed sources and a variety of interfaces. Understandably, web developers often prefer traditional solutions based on relational or document databases due to the higher level of data predictability and superior developer experience. To address these issues, we present LDkit, a novel Object Graph Mapping (OGM) framework for TypeScript designed to provide a model-based abstraction for RDF. LDkit facilitates the direct utilization of Linked Data in web applications, effectively working as the data access layer. It accomplishes this by querying and retrieving data, and transforming it into TypeScript primitives according to user defined data schemas, while ensuring end-to-end data type safety. This paper describes the design and implementation of LDkit, highlighting its ability to simplify the integration of Semantic Web technologies into web applications, while adhering to both general web standards and Linked Data specific standards. Furthermore, we discuss how LDkit framework has been designed to integrate seamlessly with popular web application technologies that developers are already familiar with. This approach promotes ease of adoption, allowing developers to harness the power of Linked Data without disrupting their current workflows. Through the provision of an efficient and intuitive toolkit, LDkit aims to enhance the web ecosystem by promoting the widespread adoption of Linked Data and Semantic Web technologies.

Keywords: Linked Data · Developer experience · Data abstraction

1 Introduction

The Semantic Web and Linked Data have emerged as powerful technologies to enrich the World Wide Web with structured and interlinked information [3]. Despite their potential, the adoption of these technologies by web application

T. R. Payne et al. (Eds.): ISWC 2023, LNCS 14266, pp. 194–210, 2023.
https://doi.org/10.1007/978-3-031-47243-5_11

developers has been hindered the challenging nature of querying distributed Linked Data in web applications [4], referred to as the expressivity/complexity trade-off.

Expressivity in Linked Data typically pertains to the ability to represent rich semantics and relationships between resources, often using ontologies and vocabularies [11]. The more expressive the data model, the more accurately and precisely it can represent the intended meaning and relationships between entities.

On the other hand, complexity refers to the difficulty in querying, processing, and managing the data. As the expressiveness of the Linked Data model increases, so does the complexity of the underlying query language, such as SPARQL [9], and the processing algorithms required to handle the data. This can lead to increased development effort, computational resources, and time needed to work with the data.

In order to leverage Linked Data in web applications, developers need to overcome these challenges. In recent years, several projects have been developed that address these needs, most prominently the Comunica [19] query engine, and LDflex [23], a domain-specific language for querying and manipulating RDF. These tools abstract away some of the complexity of Linked Data by simplifying querying mechanisms, without sacrificing expressiveness. Nevertheless, the Linked Data tooling ecosystem for web application development remains limited, as the tools and libraries available today may not be as mature or feature-rich as those for more established web development technologies.

In the past decade, the landscape of web development has undergone significant changes, with web technologies maturing considerably. The emergence of powerful web application frameworks, such as React[1] and Angular[2], has led to a rapid increase in the development and deployment of front-end web applications. The rise of TypeScript[3], a strongly typed programming language that builds on JavaScript, has brought a variety of benefits to the whole web ecosystem. The addition of a static typing system allows for strict type checking at compile-time, leading to improved code quality, enhanced developer productivity, and better tooling support. These technologies have provided developers with robust tools, enabling them to create sophisticated and feature-rich web applications more efficiently than ever before.

The growing complexity of web applications has highlighted the need for new types of data abstractions. Traditional data access patterns may no longer be sufficient to address the unique challenges posed by modern web development, such as the architecture split between back-end and front-end systems, or integrating with diverse APIs.

To address the needs of modern web developers, we introduce LDkit, a novel Linked Data abstraction designed to provide a type-safe and developer-friendly way for interacting with Linked Data from within web applications.

---

[1] https://react.dev/.

[2] https://angular.io/.

[3] https://www.typescriptlang.org/.

LDkit enables developers to directly utilize Linked Data in their web applications by providing mapping from Linked Data to simple, well-defined data objects; it shields the developer from the challenges of querying, fetching and processing RDF data.

In this paper, we present the design and implementation of LDkit, highlighting its ability to simplify the integration of Semantic Web technologies into web applications and improve the overall developer experience. By providing an efficient and intuitive toolkit, LDkit aims to promote the widespread adoption of Linked Data and Semantic Web technologies in web applications.

The rest of the paper is organized as follows. Section 2 introduces the related work, and Sect. 3 discusses requirements for LDkit as a viable Linked Data abstraction. Section 4 provides overview of design, implementation and embedding of LDkit in web applications, followed by Sect. 5 that evaluates LDkit from three distinct perspectives, including a real-world usage of the framework. We conclude in Sect. 6 and identify directions for future research.

2   Related Work

2.1   Web Application Data Abstractions

There are various styles of abstractions over data sources to facilitate access to databases in web development. These abstractions often cater to different preferences and use cases.

Object-Relational Mapping (ORM) and Object-Document Mapping (ODM) abstractions map relational or document database entities to objects in the programming language, using a data schema. They provide a convenient way to interact with the database using familiar object-oriented paradigms, and generally include built-in type casting, validation and query building out of the box. Examples of ORM and ODM libraries for JavaScript/TypeScript include *Prisma*[4], *TypeORM*[5] or *Mongoose*[6]. Corresponding tools for graph databases are typically referred to as Object-Graph Mapping (OGM) or Object-Triple Mapping (OTM) [14] libraries, and include *Neo4j OGM*[7] for Java and *GQLAlchemy*[8] for Python.

Query Builders provide a fluent interface for constructing queries in the programming language, with support for various database types. They often focus on providing a more flexible and composable way to build queries compared to ORM/ODM abstractions, but lack convenient development features like automated type casting. A prominent query builder for SQL databases in web application domain is *Knex.js*[9].

---

[4] https://www.prisma.io/.
[5] https://typeorm.io/.
[6] https://mongoosejs.com/.
[7] https://github.com/neo4j/neo4j-ogm.
[8] https://github.com/memgraph/gqlalchemy.
[9] https://knexjs.org/.

Driver-based abstractions provide a thin layer over the database-specific drivers, offering a simplified and more convenient interface for interacting with the database. An examples of a driver-based abstraction heavily utilized in web applications is the *MongoDB Node.js Driver*[10].

Finally, *API-based Data Access* abstractions facilitate access to databases indirectly through APIs, such as RESTful or GraphQL APIs. They provide client-side libraries that make it easy to fetch and manipulate data exposed by the APIs. Examples of API-based data access libraries include *tRPC*[11] and *Apollo Client*[12].

Each style of abstraction caters to different needs and preferences, ultimately the choice of abstraction style depends on the project's specific requirements and architecture, as well as the database technology being used. There are however several shared qualities among these libraries that contribute to a good developer experience. All of these libraries have *static type support*, which is especially beneficial for large or complex projects, where maintaining consistent types can significantly improve developer efficiency. Another aspect is *good tooling support*: these libraries often provide integrations with popular development tools and environments. This support can include autocompletion, syntax highlighting, and inline error checking, which further enhances the developer experience and productivity. Furthermore, most of these libraries offer a consistent API across different database systems, which simplifies the process of switching between databases or working with multiple databases in a single application. Finally, abstracting away low-level details allows developers to focus on their application's logic rather than dealing with the intricacies of the underlying database technology.

2.2   JavaScript/TypeScript RDF Libraries

JavaScript is a versatile programming language that can be utilized for both front-end development in browsers and back-end development on servers. As Linked Data and RDF have gained traction in web development, several JavaScript libraries have emerged to work with RDF data. These libraries offer varying levels of RDF abstraction and cater to different use cases.

Most of the existing libraries conform to the RDF/JS Data model specification [2], sharing the same RDF data representation in JavaScript for great compatibility benefits. Often, RDF libraries make use of the JSON-LD (JavaScript Object Notation for Linked Data) [17], a lightweight syntax that enables JSON objects to be enhanced with RDF semantics. JSON-LD achieves this by introducing the concept of JSON-LD *context*, which serves as a dictionary that maps JSON keys to RDF property and type IRIs. This mapping allows for JSON objects to be interpreted as RDF graphs, and can also be used independently of JSON-LD documents.

---

[10] https://github.com/mongodb/node-mongodb-native.
[11] https://github.com/trpc/trpc.
[12] https://github.com/apollographql/apollo-client.

One of the most comprehensive projects is *Comunica* [19], a highly modular and flexible query engine for Linked Data, enabling developers to execute SPARQL queries over multiple heterogeneous data sources with extensive customizability.

LDflex [23] is a domain-specific language that provides a developer-friendly API for querying and manipulating RDF data with an expressive, JavaScript-like syntax. It makes use of JSON-LD contexts to interpret JavaScript expressions as SPARQL queries. While it does not provide end-to-end type safety, LDflex is one of the most versatile Linked Data abstractions that are available. Since it does not utilize a fixed data schema, it is especially useful for use cases where the underlying Linked Data is not well defined or known.

There are also several object-oriented abstractions that provide access to RDF data through JavaScript objects. *RDF Object*[13] and *SimpleRDF*[14] enable per-property access to RDF data through JSON-LD context mapping. *LDO (Linked Data Objects)*[15] leverage ShEx [15] data shapes to generate RDF to JavaScript interface, and static typings for the JavaScript objects. *Soukai-solid*[16] provides OGM-like access to Solid Pods[17] based on a proprietary data model format.

Except for LDflex, the major drawback of all the aforementioned Linked Data abstractions is that they require pre-loading the source RDF data to memory. For large decentralized environments like Solid, this pre-loading is often impossible, and we instead require discovery of data during query execution [22]. While these libraries offer valuable tools for working with RDF, when it comes to web application development, none of them provides the same level of type safety, tooling support and overall developer experience as their counterparts that target relational or document databases.

In recent years, the GraphQL[18] interface has gained popularity as an alternative to REST interfaces, due to its flexible data retrieval, strongly typed schema, and the ability to group multiple REST requests into one. A notable element of this interface is the GraphQL query language, which is popular among developers due to its ease of use and wide tooling support. However, GraphQL uses custom interface-specific schemas, which are difficult to federate over, and have no relation to the RDF data model.

That is why, in the recent years, we have seen several initiatives [1,20,21] attempting to bridge the worlds of GraphQL and RDF, by translating GraphQL queries into SPARQL, with the goal of lowering the entry-barrier for writing queries over RDF. While these initiatives addressed the problems to some extent, there are still several drawbacks to this approach. Most notably, it requires the deployment of a GraphQL server, which is not always possible or desirable,

---

[13] https://github.com/rubensworks/rdf-object.js.
[14] https://github.com/simplerdf/simplerdf.
[15] https://github.com/o-development/ldo.
[16] https://github.com/NoelDeMartin/soukai-solid.
[17] https://solidproject.org/.
[18] https://graphql.org/.

depending on the use case. Furthermore, this extra architectural layer may add significant performance overhead.

3   Requirements Analysis

The goal of LDkit is to provide a type-safe and developer-friendly abstraction layer for interacting with Linked Data from within web applications. Based on our research of common web data abstractions and Linked Data libraries, we have identified a set of primary requirements for LDkit that are necessary to achieve this goal.

R1 Embraces Linked Data heterogenity
   The inherent heterogeneity of Linked Data ecosystem arises due to the decentralized nature of Linked Data, where various data sources, formats, and ontologies are independently created and maintained by different parties [4]. As a result, data from multiple sources can exhibit discrepancies in naming conventions, data models, and relationships among entities, making it difficult to combine and interpret the information seamlessly [12]. LDkit should embrace this heterogeneity by supporting the querying of Linked Data from multiple data sources and various formats.

R2 Provides a simple way of Linked Data model specification
   The core of any ORM, ODM or OGM framework is a specification of a data model. This model is utilized for shielding the developer from the complexities of the underlying data representation. It is a developer-friendly programming interface for data querying and validation that encapsulates the complexity of the translation between the simplified application model and the underlying data representation. In LDkit, the data model should be *easy to create and maintain*, and separable from the rest of the application so that it can be *shared* as a standalone artifact. LDkit should aim to offer a comprehensive RDF data abstraction while simplifying the data structure by default, ensuring efficient use in web applications. Simultaneously, it must allow users to override the default behavior to fine-tune the processes of RDF data querying, retrieval, and processing.

R3 Has a flexible architecture
   A Linked Data abstraction for web applications needs to encompass several inter-related processes, such as generating SPARQL queries based on the data model, executing queries across one or more data sources, and transforming RDF data to JavaScript primitives and vice-versa. In LDkit, each of these processes should be implemented as a standalone component for maximum *flexibility*. A flexible architecture allows LDkit to *adapt* to varying use cases and requirements, making it suitable for a wide range of web applications that leverage Linked Data. Developers can *customize* the framework to their specific needs, modify individual components, or extend the functionality to accommodate unique requirements. Finally, as Linked Data and web technologies evolve, a flexible architecture ensures that LDkit remains relevant

and can accommodate new standards, formats, or methodologies that may emerge in the *future*.

R4 Provides solid developer experience

LDkit can achieve a good developer experience by focusing on several key aspects. First, LDkit should provide a clear and intuitive API to make the learning curve more manageable for developers new to the framework. Second, the toolkit should leverage TypeScript's type safety features, enabling better tooling support and error prevention. This provides developers with instantaneous feedback in the form of autocomplete or error highlighting within their development environment. Third, LDkit must ensure compatibility with popular web application libraries and frameworks, allowing developers to incorporate LDkit into their existing workflows more easily. By focusing on these aspects, LDkit can create a positive developer experience that fosters rapid adoption and encourages the effective use of the framework for reading and writing Linked Data in web applications.

R5 Adheres to existing Web standards and best practices

LDkit should adhere to both general web standards and web development best practices, and Linked Data specific standards for several reasons. First, compliance with established standards ensures interoperability and seamless integration with existing web technologies, tools, and services, thereby enabling developers to build on the current web ecosystem's strengths. Second, adhering to Linked Data specific standards fosters best practices and encourages broader adoption of Linked Data technologies, contributing to a more robust and interconnected Semantic Web. Finally, compliance with existing web standards allows for the long-term sustainability and evolution of the LDkit framework, as it can adapt and grow with the ever-changing landscape of web technologies and standards.

4   LDkit

We have designed LDkit OGM library according to the aforementioned requirements. In this section, we provide a high level perspective of LDkit capabilities and discuss some of its most important components.

Let us illustrate how to display simple Linked Data in a web application, using the following objective:

Query DBpedia for Persons. A person should have a name property and a birth date property of type date. Find me a person by a specific IRI.

The example in Listing 1.1 demonstrates how to query, retrieve and display Linked Data in TypeScript using LDkit in only 20 lines of code.

On lines 4–11, the user creates a data *Schema*, which describes the shape of data to be retrieved, including mapping to RDF properties and optionally their data type. On line 13, they create a *Lens* object, which acts as an intermediary between Linked Data and TypeScript paradigms. Finally, on line 18, the user requests a data artifact using its resource IRI and receives a plain JavaScript object that can then be printed in a type-safe way.

```
1  import { createLens } from "ldkit";
2  import { dbo, xsd } from "ldkit/namespaces";
3
4  const PersonSchema = {
5    "@type": dbo.Person,
6    "name": dbo.birthName,
7    "birthDate": {
8      "@id": dbo.birthDate,
9      "@type": xsd.date,
10   },
11 } as const;
12
13 const Persons = createLens(PersonSchema, {
14   sources: ["https://dbpedia.org/sparql"]
15 });
16
17 const adaIri = "http://dbpedia.org/resource/Ada_Lovelace";
18 const ada = await Persons.findByIri(adaIri);
19
20 console.log(ada.name); // "The Hon. Augusta Ada Byron"
21 console.log(ada.birthDate); // Date object of 1815-12-10
22
```

Listing 1.1. LDkit usage example

Under the hood, LDkit performs the following:

- Generates a SPARQL query based on the data schema.
- Queries remote data sources and fetches RDF data.
- Converts RDF data to JavaScript plain objects and primitives.
- Infers TypeScript types for the provided data.

4.1 Data Schema

On the conceptual level, a data schema is a definition of a data shape through which one can query RDF data, similar to a data model for standard ORM libraries. Specifically, the schema describes a class of entities defined by RDF type(s) and properties.

We have designed the LDkit *schema* based on the following criteria:

- LDkit can generate SPARQL queries based on the schema.
- LDkit can use the schema as a mapping definition between RDF and JavaScript primitives (both ways).
- LDkit can infer a correct TypeScript type from the schema.
- Developer can adjust the resulting data shape; specifically, they can require some properties to be optional or arrays.
- Developer can nest schemas within other schemas.

– Developer can reuse and share schemas independently of LDkit.
– Schemas must be easy to create and should be self-explanatory.

A *schema* is a plain TypeScript object that follows the formal specification defined in Listing 1.2. LDkit schemas are based on JSON-LD context format, and simple JSON-LD contexts can be easily transformed to LDkit schemas. Having the schema defined in TypeScript allows for end-to-end data type safety. In addition, developers may benefit from autocomplete features and syntax checks within their development environment, to aid schema reuse and composition.

```
1  type Schema = {
2    "@type": Iri | Iri[];
3    [key: string]: Iri | Property;
4  }
5  type Property = {
6    "@id": Iri;
7    "@type"?: DatatypeIri;
8    "@context"?: Schema;
9    "@optional"?: true;
10   "@array"?: true;
11   "@multilang"?: true;
12 }
13 type Iri = string
14 type DatatypeIri = /* supported data type, e.g. xsd:date */
```

Listing 1.2. Formal specification of LDkit schema in TypeScript

4.2 Reading and Writing Data

In LDkit, reading and writing data is realized through *Lens*.

A data *Lens* turns a particular data *Schema* to an interactive entity repository. Conceptually, a Lens represents a collection of data *entities* that conform to the specified Schema. The interface of Lens follows the data mapper architectural pattern, facilitating bidirectional transfer of data between an RDF data store and in-memory data representation of *entities*, which are plain JavaScript objects. In background, Lens handle building and executing SPARQL queries, data retrieval and transformation according to the data Schema.

A Lens instance provides the following data access interface:

– **find([where], [limit]): entity[]** retrieves all entities that correspond to the data schema, optionally applies additional conditions and limit
– **findByIri(iri): entity** retrieves an entity with a particular resource IRI
– **count([where]): number** counts all entities that correspond to the data schema, optionally applies additional conditions
– **insert(...entities)** creates new entities in the data source

- **update(...entities)** updates entity properties in the data source
- **delete(...iris)** removes entities from data source based on their IRI.

When any of these methods are invoked, LDkit creates an appropriate SPARQL or SPARQL UPDATE [7] query and execute it against the underlying data source. Consequently, in order to modify data, the data source must permit update operations. The algorithm that generates the queries is complex, as it takes into account payload of the interface methods, as well as data schema, therefore its description is out of scope of this article.

The presented interface is similar to other data mapper-based TypeScript frameworks and covers all basic data reading and manipulation. Listing 1.3 demonstrates how this interface may be used to retrieve and update a data entity.

```
1  const Persons = createLens(PersonSchema);
2
3  const alanIri = "http://dbpedia.org/resource/Alan_Turing";
4  const alan = await Persons.findByIri(alanIri);
5
6  alan.name = "Not Alan Turing"; // fictitious name
7  alan.birthDate = new Date("1900-01-01"); // fictitious birth date
8  await Persons.update(alan);
```

Listing 1.3. Example of reading and writing data in LDkit

While the Lens interface is expressive enough to cover common cases of working with data that are structured in a relational fashion, it may be insufficient or inconvenient for some advanced use cases, such as working with large arrays possibly containing thousands of items. While LDkit supports reading such arrays, modifying them with operations like *insert a value to array* or *remove a value from array* may be cumbersome to perform through the standard interface. For these cases, the Lens exposes advanced methods for the developer to interact directly with RDF, either in the form of SPARQL query or RDF quads:

- **query(sparqlQuery)** retrieves entities based on a custom SPARQL query
- **updateQuery(sparqlQuery)** performs a SPARQL UPDATE query on the data source
- **insertData(quads[])** inserts RDF quads array to data source
- **deleteData(quads[])** removes RDF quads array from data source.

4.3 Data Sources and Query Engine

In LDkit, a *Query engine* is a component that handles execution of SPARQL queries over data sources. The query engine must follow the RDF/JS Query specification [18] and implement the `StringSparqlQueryable` interface.

LDkit ships with a simple default query engine that lets developers execute queries over a single SPARQL endpoint. It is lightweight and optimized for browser environment, and it can be used as a standalone component, independently of the rest of LDkit. The engine supports all SPARQL endpoints that conform to the SPARQL 1.1 specification [9].

LDkit is fully compatible with Comunica-based query engines. Comunica [19] provides access to RDF data from multiple sources and various source types, including Solid pods, RDF files, Triple/Quad Pattern Fragments, and HDT files.

4.4　Current Limitations

While the presented data model of LDkit reduces complexity of SPARQL and RDF, it introduces some trade-offs, as it is not as expressive. First, reverse relations are not yet supported. That could be useful for scenarios when one needs to display incoming links. In order to achieve this, the developer needs to provide a custom SPARQL query that would produce a graph corresponding to the specified schema. Second, there is the issue of multiplicity of RDF properties: contrary to the world of relational databases, where each cell in a table usually corresponds to a single value, the world of Linked Data does not have this constraint. As a result, there may be an unknown number of triples with the same RDF property linked to a particular resource. This may either be by design, if the data is supposed to represent a set of values, or the data may be of poor quality and there may be some duplicates. Ultimately, the developer needs to choose, whether they prefer to read one, albeit random, value, or an array of values that may be redundant.

4.5　LDkit Components

Thanks to its modular architecture, components comprising the LDkit OGM framework can be further extended or used separately, accommodating advanced use cases of leveraging Linked Data in web applications. Besides *Schema*, *Lens* and *Query engine* already presented, there are other components and utilities that can be used by developers to facilitate working with Linked Data. The `Decoder` and `Encoder` components transform data from RDF to JavaScript plain objects and vice-versa based on the provided data schema. The `QueryBuilder` generates SPARQL CRUD queries based on a data schema. Furthermore, there is a universal SPARQL query builder available, allowing for type-safe SPARQL query composition, and a set of utilities for working with RDF quads. Finally, LDkit also includes *Namespaces* definitions for popular Linked Data vocabularies, such as Dublin Core [5], FOAF [6] or Schema.org [16].

This level of flexibility means that LDkit could also support other query languages, such as GraphQL.

4.6　LDkit Distribution and Sustainability

The TypeScript implementation of LDkit is available under the MIT license on GitHub at https://github.com/karelklima/ldkit, via the *DOI 10.5281/zen-*

odo.7905468, and the persistent URL https://doi.org/10.5281/zenodo.7905468, and has an associated canonical citation [13].

Following the standard practices, LDkit is published as an NPM package[19] and as a Deno module[20]. To make adoption easy for new developers, documentation and examples are available at https://ldkit.io or linked from the GitHub repository.

In order to demonstrate our commitment to the long-term maintenance and improvement of LDkit, we have developed a comprehensive sustainability plan. Our team guarantees a minimum of five years of ongoing maintenance, during which we will be dedicated to addressing any issues, optimizing performance, and ensuring compatibility with the evolving Linked Data landscape. LDkit has already been adopted by several academic and non-academic projects, with more projects set to incorporate it in the future. This growing user base helps to guarantee ongoing interest and support for the framework. As LDkit continues to be used in new research projects, our team will work closely with the academic community to gather feedback and identify areas for further improvement. Finally, we have identified several features that are not yet included in LDkit but will enhance its capabilities and usefulness in the future. Our team will actively work on incorporating these features into LDkit, ensuring its continued relevance and applicability to a wide range of use cases. By implementing this sustainability plan, we aim to ensure that LDkit remains a valuable and dependable resource for web developers and researchers working with Linked Data, both now and in the years to come.

5   Evaluation

In this section, we present the evaluation of LDkit from three distinct perspectives to provide a comprehensive assessment of the framework's capabilities. First, we discuss the primary requirements that LDkit aims to address and how it satisfies these needs. Second, we demonstrate a real-world use case of LDkit to showcase its practical applicability in web applications. Finally, we examine the framework's performance.

5.1   Requirements Reflection

Earlier in this paper, we presented a list of five primary requirements that LDkit must meet in order to provide a developer-friendly abstraction layer for interacting with Linked Data from within web applications.

LDkit provides a simple way of Linked Data model specification (**R2**) through *schema*, which is a flexible mechanism for developers to define their own custom data models and RDF mappings that are best suited for their application's requirements. The schema syntax is based on JSON-LD context, and as such it

---

[19] https://www.npmjs.com/package/ldkit.
[20] https://deno.land/x/ldkit.

assumes its qualities: it is self-explanatory and easy to create, and can be reused, nested, and shared independently of LDkit.

Thanks to the flexible data model definition and interoperability with the Comunica query engine, LDkit effectively embraces Linked Data heterogenity (**R1**) by providing means to query Linked Data from various data sources, formats, and vocabularies. Furthermore, its modular architecture (**R3**) allows for a high level of customization. LDkit components can be adapted and extended to accommodate unique requirements, or used standalone for advanced use cases.

LDkit offers good developer experience (**R4**) in several ways. Its API for reading and writing Linked Data is simple and intuitive, and should feel familiar even to the developers new to RDF, as it is inspired by interfaces of analogous model-based abstractions of relational databases. By incorporating end-to-end data type safety, which is the biggest differentiator from LDflex, LDkit provides unmatched tooling support, giving developers instantaneous feedback in the form of autocomplete or error highlighting within their development environment. The official website of LDkit[21] contains comprehensive documentation, along with a step-by-step "getting started" guide for new developers, and includes examples of how to use LDkit with popular web application frameworks, such as React. These aspects contribute to a positive developer experience and encourage effective use of LDkit in web applications.

Finally, LDkit adheres to and employs existing Web and Linked Data standards (**R5**), such as JSON-LD or SPARQL, to ensure interoperability and seamless integration with existing Web technologies. LDkit follows RDF/JS data model [2] and query [18] standards, making it compatible with other existing Linked Data tools, such as Comunica, and contributing to a more robust Linked Data ecosystem for web developers.

5.2   Real World Usage

LDkit is used in a project for the Czech government[22] that aims to build a set of web applications for distributed modeling and maintenance of government ontologies[23]. The ensemble is called *Assembly Line (AL)*. It allows business glossary experts and conceptual modeling engineers from different public bodies to model their domains in the form of domain vocabularies consisting of a business glossary further extended to a formal UFO-based ontology [8]. The individual domain vocabularies are managed in a distributed fashion by the different parties through AL. AL also enables interlinking related domain vocabularies and also linking them to the common upper public government ontology defined centrally. Domain vocabularies are natively represented and published[24] in SKOS (business glossary) and OWL (ontology). The AL tools have to process this native

---

[21] https://ldkit.io/.

[22] https://slovnik.gov.cz.

[23] https://github.com/datagov-cz/sgov-assembly-line is the umbrella repository that refers to the repositories of individual tools (in Czech).

[24] https://github.com/datagov-cz/ssp (in Czech).

representation of the domain vocabularies in their front-end parts. Dealing with native representation would be, however, unnecessarily complex for the front-end developers of these tools. Therefore, they use LDkit to simplify their codebase. This allows them to focus on the UX of their domain-modeling front-end features while keeping the complexity of SKOS and OWL behind the LDkit schemas and lenses. On the other hand, the native SKOS and OWL representations of the domain models make their publishing, sharing, and reuse much easier. LDkit removes the necessity to transform this native representation with additional transformation steps in the back-end components of the AL tools.

5.3   Performance

To evaluate the performance of LDkit, we considered a typical use case of working with data in web applications: displaying a list of data resources. Specifically, we envisioned a scenario of building a Web book catalog. For this catalog, our objective was to obtain a list of books from the DBpedia[25] SPARQL endpoint so that we can display it to end users. We have designed three experiments, and in each case, we query DBpedia for a list of 1000 books, using the LDkit built-in query engine. The experiments are identical except for the data schema; its complexity increases with each test case. For reproducibility purposes, we have shared the experiments on GitHub[26].

Our initial assumption was that LDkit should not add significant performance overhead, and that the majority of the execution time would be spent on querying the SPARQL endpoint, since this is often the primary bottleneck when dealing with remote data sources.

To assess LDkit performance, we measured total execution time and subtracted the time it took to query DBpedia.[27] Table 1 displays the resulting aver-

Table 1. LDkit performance evaluation results

Scenario schema	Book – title	Book – title – author(Person) – name	Book – title – author(Person) – name – country – language – genre
Query time	255 ms	359 ms	2751 ms
LDkit time	23 ms	38 ms	45 ms
Total time	278 ms	397 ms	2796 ms
Number of quads	217	3955	7123

---

[25] https://dbpedia.org/sparql.

[26] https://github.com/karelklima/ldkit/tree/main/tests/performance.

[27] Each scenario was run 10 times, and was executed using Deno JavaScript runtime. The experiment was performed on a PC with 2.40 GHz Intel i7 CPU and 8 GB RAM.

age times for each scenario and, for illustration purposes, includes a number of RDF quads that were returned by the data source.

Our findings indicate that, even with the increasing complexity of the scenarios, LDkit maintained its performance without any substantial degradation. Since LDkit uses data schema to generate SPARQL queries that are eventually passed to a pre-configured query engine, the overall performance will be therefore determined mostly by the query engine itself, which may employ advanced strategies for query processing, such as query optimization or caching [10], leading to improved query execution times.

6 Conclusion

Web application development is a rather specific software engineering discipline. When designing a website, or any other user-facing application for that matter, the developers need to think about the product side and user interface first. In short, they need to figure out what to display to users and how. Building a great user interface and experience is the primary objective. Hence, the ever-evolving web application tooling provide sophisticated abstractions and enable developers to focus on what matters the most – the end user. Popular web application frameworks, such as React, employ declarative programming paradigm, and the use of visual components as the application building blocks. Modern data access solutions are seamlessly integrated to application frameworks, to allow for easy access to data, simplified to the application domain model, in a declarative way. In that regard, from the point of view of a front-end developer, the web application architecture, and even more so data architecture, are almost an afterthought.

In this paper, we presented LDkit, a developer-friendly tool that enables using Linked Data within web applications in an easy and intuitive way.

LDkit is the result of a decade-long effort and experience of building front-end web applications that leverage Linked Data, and as such it is a successor to many different RDF abstractions that we have built along the way. It is designed to cater to the mindset of a web developer and help them focus on data itself and how to best present them to the users, abstracting away the complexity of querying, processing and adapting Linked Data.

In our future work, we aim to further extend the capabilities of LDkit, and we plan to build more sophisticated solutions for assisted generating of LDkit schemas and entire front-end applications from RDF vocabularies or data sources, allowing for rapid prototyping of Linked Data-based applications.

In conclusion, we believe that LDkit is a valuable contribution to the Linked Data community, providing a powerful and accessible tool to seamlessly integrate Linked Data into web applications. Throughout this paper, we have presented evidence to support this claim, demonstrating how LDkit addresses specific web development needs and how it can be utilized in real-world scenarios. We are confident that LDkit will contribute to further adoption of Linked Data in web applications.

References

1. Angele, K., Meitinger, M., Bußjäger, M., Föhl, S., Fensel, A.: GraphSPARQL: a GraphiQL interface for linked data. In: Proceedings of the 37th ACM/SIGAPP Symposium on Applied Computing, pp. 778–785 (2022)
2. Bergwinkl, T., Luggen, M., elf Pavlik, Regalia, B., Savastano, P., Verborgh, R.: RDF/JS: data model specification, May 2022. https://rdf.js.org/data-model-spec/
3. Berners-Lee, T., Hendler, J., Lassila, O.: The semantic web. Sci. Am. **284**(5), 34–43 (2001)
4. Bizer, C., Heath, T., Berners-Lee, T.: Linked data - the story so far. Int. J. Semant. Web Inf. Syst. **5**(3), 1–22 (2009)
5. DCMI Usage Board: DCMI metadata terms (2020). https://www.dublincore.org/specifications/dublin-core/dcmi-terms/
6. Brickley, D., Miller, L.: FOAF vocabulary specification (2014). http://xmlns.com/foaf/spec/
7. Gearon, P., Passant, A., Polleres, A.: SPARQL 1.1 update, March 2013. https://www.w3.org/TR/sparql11-update/
8. Guizzardi, G., Botti Benevides, A., Fonseca, C.M., Porello, D., Almeida, J.P.A., Prince Sales, T.: UFO: unified foundational ontology. Appl. Ontol. **17**(1), 167–210 (2022)
9. Harris, S., Seaborne, A.: SPARQL 1.1 query language, March 2013. https://www.w3.org/TR/sparql11-query/
10. Hartig, O.: An overview on execution strategies for linked data queries. Datenbank-Spektrum **13**, 89–99 (2013)
11. Heath, T., Bizer, C.: Linked Data: Evolving the Web into a Global Data Space. Synthesis Lectures on the Semantic Web: Theory and Technology, vol. 1. Morgan & Claypool Publishers (2011)
12. Hogan, A., Umbrich, J., Harth, A., Cyganiak, R., Polleres, A., Decker, S.: An empirical survey of linked data conformance. J. Web Semant. **14**, 14–44 (2012)
13. Klíma, K., Beeke, D.: karelklima/ldkit: 1.0.0, May 2023. https://doi.org/10.5281/zenodo.7905469
14. Ledvinka, M., Křemen, P.: A comparison of object-triple mapping libraries. Semant. Web **11**(3), 483–524 (2020)
15. Prud'hommeaux, E., Boneva, I., Labra Gayo, J.E., Kellog, G.: Shape Expressions Language (ShEx) 2.1, October 2019. https://shex.io/shex-semantics/
16. Schema.org: Vocabulary (2011). https://schema.org/
17. Sporny, M., Longley, D., Kellogg, G., Lanthaler, M., Lindström, N.: JSON-LD 1.1. W3C Recommendation, July 2020
18. Taelman, R., Scazzosi, J.: RDF/JS: query specification (2023). https://rdf.js.org/query-spec/
19. Taelman, R., Van Herwegen, J., Vander Sande, M., Verborgh, R.: Comunica: a modular SPARQL query engine for the web. In: Vrandečić, D., et al. (eds.) ISWC 2018. LNCS, vol. 11137, pp. 239–255. Springer, Cham (2018). https://doi.org/10.1007/978-3-030-00668-6_15
20. Taelman, R., Vander Sande, M., Verborgh, R.: GraphQL-LD: linked data querying with GraphQL. In: The 17th International Semantic Web Conference, ISW C2018, pp. 1–4 (2018)
21. Taelman, R., Vander Sande, M., Verborgh, R.: Bridges between GraphQL and RDF. In: W3C Workshop on Web Standardization for Graph Data. W3C (2019)

22. Taelman, R., Verborgh, R.: Evaluation of link traversal query execution over decentralized environments with structural assumptions. arXiv preprint arXiv:2302.06933 (2023)
23. Verborgh, R., Taelman, R.: LDflex: a read/write linked data abstraction for front-end web developers. In: Pan, J.Z., et al. (eds.) ISWC 2020. LNCS, vol. 12507, pp. 193–211. Springer, Cham (2020). https://doi.org/10.1007/978-3-030-62466-8_13

VOYAGE: A Large Collection of Vocabulary Usage in Open RDF Datasets

Qing Shi[1], Junrui Wang[1], Jeff Z. Pan[2], and Gong Cheng[1(✉)] ⓘ

[1] State Key Laboratory for Novel Software Technology, Nanjing University,
Nanjing, China
{qingshi,181840223}@smail.nju.edu.cn, gcheng@nju.edu.cn
[2] School of Informatics, University of Edinburgh, Edinburgh, UK
http://knowledge-representation.org/j.z.pan/

Abstract. Shared vocabularies facilitate data integration and application interoperability on the Semantic Web. An investigation of how vocabularies are practically used in open RDF data, particularly with the increasing number of RDF datasets registered in open data portals, is expected to provide a measurement for the adoption of shared vocabularies and an indicator of the state of the Semantic Web. To support this investigation, we constructed and published VOYAGE, a large collection of vocabulary usage in open RDF datasets. We built it by collecting 68,312 RDF datasets from 517 pay-level domains via 577 open data portals, and we extracted 50,976 vocabularies used in the data. We analyzed the extracted usage data and revealed the distributions of frequency and diversity in vocabulary usage. We particularly characterized the patterns of term co-occurrence, and leveraged them to cluster vocabularies and RDF datasets as a potential application of VOYAGE. Our data is available from Zenodo at https://zenodo.org/record/7902675. Our code is available from GitHub at https://github.com/nju-websoft/VOYAGE.

Keywords: Open RDF data · Vocabulary usage · Term co-occurrence

1 Introduction

The Semantic Web has entered its third decade. Driven by the ambitious vision of creating a Web where applications reach agreement on common vocabularies (i.e., sets of terms including classes and properties) to facilitate data integration and establish interoperability, we have witnessed the global adoption of vocabularies like schema.org [12] for annotating webpages to enhance Web search. Analyzing the practical usage of vocabularies could provide metrics and insights that are useful for measuring and understanding the adoption of vocabularies, as well as the state of the Semantic Web from the perspective of vocabulary usage.
Motivations. While the usage of a few exceptional vocabularies, such as schema.org, has been extensively analyzed, e.g., [21], such analyses are yet to

© The Author(s), under exclusive license to Springer Nature Switzerland AG 2023
T. R. Payne et al. (Eds.): ISWC 2023, LNCS 14266, pp. 211–229, 2023.
https://doi.org/10.1007/978-3-031-47243-5_12

be generalized to the majority of vocabularies used in open RDF data, mainly due to the lack of a large, representative, and timely data collection for this purpose. Note that our notion of open RDF data [25] goes beyond the conventional and relatively small RDF documents, which are the main sources of previous data collections such as Billion Triple Challenge [14] and WebDataCommons [22]. Indeed, the increasing number of large *RDF datasets registered in open data portals* (ODPs), including but not limited to the Linked Open Data (LOD) Cloud, deserve more attention. It motivates us to particularly collect such RDF datasets for analyzing their vocabulary usage.

Furthermore, existing analyses of vocabulary usage are predominantly limited to simple metrics such as the frequency of occurrence of each individual vocabulary [7,13,14,17,23,24,29,31]. While this kind of elementary analysis is useful as it provides a basis, it has been desirable to further look into more advanced and useful indicators. In particular, investigating how terms are jointly used to describe an entity may exhibit notable *patterns of term co-occurrence*, and understanding such patterns is important to a wide range of Semantic Web research tasks and applications. For example, they have already played a vital role in RDF store optimization [28] and RDF data sampling [34], which rely on the "emergent schema" these patterns represent. It motivates us to extend our mining and analysis of vocabulary usage along this direction. We believe such analysis is valuable for vocabulary reuse when constructing knowledge graphs [27].

Resource. With the above motivations, we construct VOYAGE, short for VOcabularY usAGE, a large collection for analyzing vocabulary usage in open RDF datasets. Our data sources are 68,312 RDF datasets registered in 577 ODPs we collected. From the crawled and deduplicated RDF datasets, we extracted 50,976 vocabularies containing 62,864 classes and 842,745 properties that are actually used in the data, and we extracted their 767,976 patterns of co-occurrence in entity descriptions. We published the extracted usage data with provenance information. VOYAGE meets the following quality and availability criteria.

- It is publicly available and findable as a Zenodo dataset[1] with documentation explaining the structure of each JSON file, which is also summarized in the Resource Availability Statement at the end of the paper.
- It has metadata description available in multiple formats (e.g., DCAT).
- It is published at a persistent DOI URI.[2]
- It is associated with a canonical citation [30].
- It is open under the CC BY 4.0 license.

Applications. We ate our own dog food by analyzing the usage data provided by VOYAGE from multiple angles. Specifically, for both individual vocabularies and their patterns of co-occurrence, we characterized their usage by analyzing their frequencies across RDF datasets and their diversity in each RDF dataset, and obtained a set of new findings. Besides, as another potential application

---

[1] https://zenodo.org/record/7902675.
[2] https://doi.org/10.5281/zenodo.7902675.

of our resource, we employed the patterns of co-occurrence to simultaneously cluster vocabularies and RDF datasets, and we found that the resulting clusters provided a reasonable complement to the conventional topic-based clustering, thus showing their value for downstream applications such as vocabulary recommender systems [6] and exploratory dataset search engines [5, 26].

Table 1. Statistics about Data Collection (Notes: ODP catalogues may overlap. Inaccessible ODPs/datasets and non-RDF datasets are not counted.)

ODP catalogue	#ODP	(%)	#dataset	(%)	#triple	(%)
CKAN	109	(18.89%)	15,858	(22.00%)	397,404,207	(40.96%)
DataPortals.org	110	(19.06%)	25,341	(35.15%)	555,050,054	(57.21%)
DKAN	36	(6.24%)	3,007	(4.17%)	14,345,698	(1.48%)
Open Data Portal Watch	135	(37.40%)	37,407	(51.89%)	689,106,507	(71.02%)
Socrata	398	(68.98%)	55,653	(77.20%)	427,739,164	(44.09%)
LOD Cloud	1	(0.17%)	308	(0.43%)	128,902,453	(13.29%)
Total	577	(100.00%)	72,088	(100.00%)	970,258,378	(100.00%)
After deduplication			68,312		920,501,102	

Outline. We describe data collection in Sect. 2, analyze the usage of vocabularies in Sect. 3, extract and analyze their patterns of co-occurrence in Sect. 4, based on which we co-cluster vocabularies and RDF datasets in Sect. 5. Related work is discussed in Sect. 6 before we conclude in Sect. 7.

2 Data Collection

To construct VOYAGE, we collected RDF datasets from ODPs, deduplicated the crawled datasets, and extracted vocabularies used in the crawled RDF data.

2.1 RDF Dataset Crawling

To find as many ODPs as possible, we used five large catalogues of ODPs: CKAN,[3] DataPortals.org,[4] DKAN,[5] Open Data Portal Watch,[6] and Socrata.[7] They collectively listed 1,207 distinct ODPs where 576 ODPs were accessible at the time of crawling (i.e., Q1 2022). We manually submitted the LOD Cloud as an ODP to our crawler, resulting in a total of 577 ODPs to be accessed.

For each ODP, we invoked its API to retrieve the metadata of all the *datasets* registered in this ODP. Datasets providing at least one dump file in an RDF

---

[3] https://ckan.org/.
[4] http://dataportals.org/.
[5] https://getdkan.org/.
[6] https://data.wu.ac.at/portalwatch/.
[7] https://dev.socrata.com/.

format (e.g., RDF/XML, Turtle, N-Triples) were identified as *RDF datasets*. We successfully downloaded and parsed the dump files of 72,088 RDF datasets using Apache Jena,[8] and extracted a total of 970,258,378 RDF triples.

Table 1 summarizes the data sources of VOYAGE.

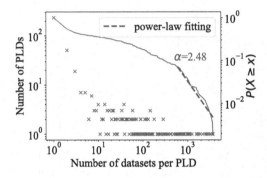

Fig. 1. Distribution (crosses) and cumulative probability distribution (curve) of the number of RDF datasets crawled from a PLD.

Table 2. Top-Ranked PLDs

PLD	#dataset	(%)
datos.gov.co	3,703	(5.42%)
cityofnewyork.us	3,575	(5.23%)
socrata.com	3,209	(4.70%)
smcgov.org	2,926	(4.28%)
dati.lombardia.it	2,683	(3.93%)
utah.gov	2,497	(3.66%)
wa.gov	2,199	(3.22%)
edmonton.ca	1,894	(2.77%)
ny.gov	1,721	(2.52%)
seattle.gov	1,711	(2.50%)

2.2   RDF Dataset Deduplication

We observed that the same RDF dataset might have been registered in multiple ODPs. However, we found it difficult to accurately identify duplicate datasets only based on their metadata, e.g., a certain dataset had different titles, different descriptions, and different download URLs in its metadata registered in different ODPs. Therefore, we employed the actual RDF data to detect duplicates.

Specifically, we regarded two crawled RDF datasets as duplicates if they were crawled from the same pay-level domain (PLD) and their dump files were parsed into two isomorphic RDF graphs. We used the BLabel algorithm [15] to test RDF graph isomorphism, and we followed [32] to decompose each RDF graph which may have a large size into a unique set of practically very small subgraphs to accelerate isomorphism testing.

After deduplication, among the 72,088 RDF datasets we kept 68,312 distinct ones, containing a total of 920,501,102 RDF triples. They were crawled from 517 PLDs. Figure 1 plots the distribution of the number of RDF datasets crawled from a PLD. The distribution appears uneven: while 285 PLDs (55.13%) contribute at most 2 RDF datasets, some PLDs contribute several thousand RDF datasets. Motivated by its highly skewed shape, we tried to fit a power law using powerlaw.[9] According to the Kolmogorov-Smirnov test, the null hypothesis that

---

[8] https://jena.apache.org/.
[9] https://github.com/jeffalstott/powerlaw.

the tail of the distribution ($X \geq 593$) fits a power law with $\alpha = 2.48$ is accepted ($p = 0.89$). However, no single PLD can dominate: as shown in Table 2, a single PLD contributes at most 5.42% of all the RDF datasets we crawled, which is important as it shows the diversity of our data sources.

2.3 Vocabulary Extraction

We extracted vocabularies that are actually used (i.e., instantiated) in the crawled RDF data. For example, a class is used in an RDF dataset if its IRI appears as the object of an RDF triple in this dataset where the predicate is rdf:type, and a property is used if its IRI appears as the predicate of an RDF triple in this dataset. Classes and properties are collectively called *terms*. A *vocabulary* is a set of terms denoted by IRIs starting with a common namespace IRI. A vocabulary is used in an RDF dataset if any of its terms is used in this dataset.

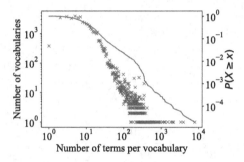

Fig. 2. Distribution (crosses) and cumulative probability distribution (curve) of the number of used terms in a vocabulary.

From the 68,312 RDF datasets we crawled, we extracted 62,864 distinct classes and 842,745 distinct properties, belonging to 50,976 distinct vocabularies. Figure 2 plots the distribution of the number of used terms in a vocabulary, with a median of 9 and a rejected power-law fitting ($p = 1.98\mathrm{E}{-}13$). While most vocabularies are small, the largest vocabulary contains 7,930 terms.

3 Frequency and Diversity in Vocabulary Usage

To characterize the usage of vocabularies provided by VOYAGE, we firstly analyzed their frequencies across all the crawled RDF datasets and their diversity in each dataset, providing a basis for the subsequent experiments. In this analysis, we excluded five language-level vocabularies since they were found to be trivially used in many RDF datasets, i.e., xsd,[10] rdf,[11] rdfs,[12] owl,[13] and skos.[14]

3.1 Frequency Analysis

We analyzed to what extent vocabularies have been shared among open RDF datasets by calculating their dataset frequencies. Figure 3 plots the distribution of the number of RDF datasets using a vocabulary. Fitting the tail of the distribution ($X \geq 837$) to a power law with $\alpha = 2.58$ is accepted ($p = 0.99$). Most vocabularies (87.41%) are only used in a single RDF dataset, but there are also 317 vocabularies used in at least ten RDF datasets. As shown in Table 3, four vocabularies are very popular and are used in RDF datasets from more than one hundred PLDs, i.e., foaf,[15] dcterms,[16] socrata,[17] and dc.[18] These observations suggest that *vocabulary sharing is common among open RDF datasets, although only a small proportion of vocabularies are widely shared.*

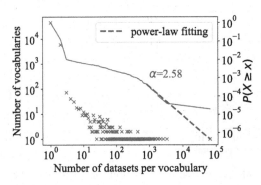

Fig. 3. Distribution (crosses) and cumulative probability distribution (curve) of the number of RDF datasets using a vocabulary.

Table 3. Top-Ranked Vocabularies

Vocabulary	#PLD	(%)
foaf	329	(63.64%)
dcterms	183	(35.40%)
socrata	162	(31.33%)
dc	117	(22.63%)
geo	58	(11.22%)
void	58	(11.22%)
admin	39	(7.54%)
schema	35	(6.77%)
dcat	34	(6.58%)
cc	27	(5.22%)

The Semantic Web community may not be very familiar with socrata. Although this vocabulary is not dereferenceable, it is used in RDF datasets from 162 PLDs, which represent an important part of RDF data in the real world.

---

[10] http://www.w3.org/2001/XMLSchema#.
[11] http://www.w3.org/1999/02/22-rdf-syntax-ns#.
[12] http://www.w3.org/2000/01/rdf-schema#.
[13] http://www.w3.org/2002/07/owl#.
[14] http://www.w3.org/2004/02/skos/core#.
[15] http://xmlns.com/foaf/0.1/.
[16] http://purl.org/dc/terms/.
[17] http://www.socrata.com/rdf/terms#.
[18] http://purl.org/dc/elements/1.1/.

3.2 Diversity Analysis

We analyzed to what extent a multiplicity of terms and vocabularies have been used in an open RDF dataset by calculating their diversity in each dataset. Figure 4 plots the distribution of the number of terms used in an RDF dataset, with a median of 11 and a rejected power-law fitting ($p = 1.60\text{E}{-}10$). In particular, four RDF datasets exhibit a complex constitution of schema where more than one thousand terms are used. Figure 5 plots the distribution of the number of vocabularies used in an RDF dataset, with a median of 3. Fitting the tail of the distribution ($X \geq 10$) to a power law with $\alpha = 3.04$ is accepted ($p = 0.43$). One RDF dataset entitled "TaxonConcept Knowledge Base" notably uses 458 vocabularies, being the largest number among all the crawled RDF datasets. These observations suggest that *it is common for an open RDF dataset to use multiple vocabularies and diverse terms*, which motivated the following analysis.

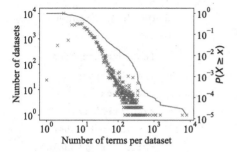

Fig. 4. Distribution (crosses) and cumulative probability distribution (curve) of the number of terms used in an RDF dataset.

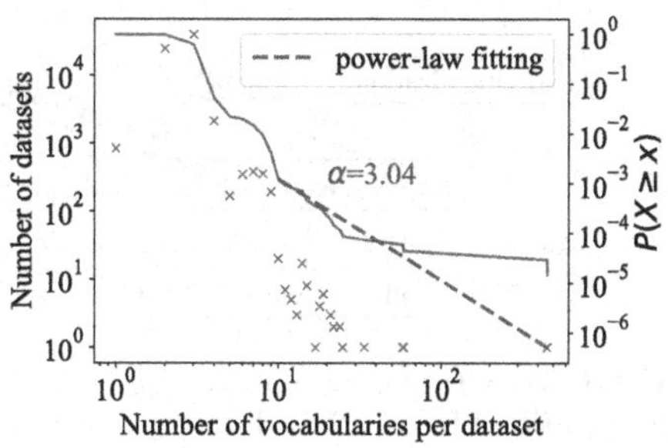

Fig. 5. Distribution (crosses) and cumulative probability distribution (curve) of the number of vocabularies used in an RDF dataset.

4 Patterns of Term Co-occurrence

The observations obtained in Sect. 3 indicate the possibility that some terms and vocabularies have been *jointly used* in many RDF datasets. In particular, terms may have been jointly used to describe many entities and hence exhibit a notable *pattern of term co-occurrence* in entity descriptions. Such patterns represent an "emergent schema" and are of particular interest. Indeed, they have been exploited in a variety of research tasks including RDF store optimization [28] and RDF data sampling [34]. Therefore, we extracted them from the crawled RDF data as part of VOYAGE, and characterized their usage by analyzing their frequencies across all the crawled RDF datasets and their diversity in each dataset.

4.1   Term Co-occurrence Extraction

Following [34], we refer to a pattern of term co-occurrence as an *entity description pattern*, or *EDP* for short. Specifically, in an RDF dataset T which contains a set of RDF triples, the EDP of an entity e consists of the sets of all the classes (C), forward properties (FP), and backward properties (BP) used in T to describe e:

$$
\begin{aligned}
\text{EDP}(e) &= \langle \text{C}(e),\ \text{FP}(e),\ \text{BP}(e)\rangle, \\
\text{C}(e) &= \{c : \exists\langle e,\ \texttt{rdf:type},\ c\rangle \in T\}, \\
\text{FP}(e) &= \{p : \exists\langle e,\ p,\ o\rangle \in T,\ p \neq \texttt{rdf:type}\}, \\
\text{BP}(e) &= \{p : \exists\langle s,\ p,\ e\rangle \in T\}.
\end{aligned}
\tag{1}
$$

For example, Fig. 6 illustrates the description of an entity in an RDF dataset, and Table 4 shows the EDP of this entity.

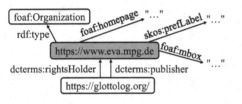

Fig. 6. An entity denoted by https://www.eva.mpg. de described in an RDF dataset.

Table 4. An Example of EDP

C	foaf:Organization
FP	foaf:homepage
	foaf:mbox
	skos:prefLabel
BP	dcterms:publisher
	dcterms:rightsHolder

From the descriptions of 58,777,001 entities in the 68,312 RDF datasets we crawled, we extracted 767,976 distinct EDPs. On average, an EDP consists of 1.14 classes, 63.31 forward properties, and 0.15 backward property, i.e., most properties used in open RDF datasets are literal-valued. For example, from one RDF dataset entitled "Higher Education Cost Data From IPEDS Utah 2000–2010", we extracted an EDP consisting of 890 terms, most of which are literal-valued properties for describing various statistic data for a year, being the largest number among all the extracted EDPs.

We particularly examined the EDPs extracted from the RDF datasets in the LOD Cloud as they might be of special interest to the Semantic Web community. These EDPs consist of relatively more classes (2.45 > 1.14) and more backward properties (0.55 > 0.15) but fewer forward properties (20.80 < 63.31), i.e., the entities in the LOD Cloud are better typed and better interlinked with each other. Since the presence of types and the completeness of interlinks are important metrics for assessing the syntactic validity and completeness of RDF data, respectively [36], these observations suggest that *the RDF datasets in the LOD Cloud exhibit relatively high data quality in terms of typing and interlinking.*

4.2   Frequency Analysis

We analyzed to what extent EDPs have been shared among open RDF datasets by calculating their dataset frequencies. Figure 7 plots the distribution of the number of RDF datasets using an EDP. Fitting the tail of the distribution ($X \geq$ 17) to a power law with $\alpha = 2.01$ is accepted ($p = 0.95$). Most EDPs (87.14%) are only used in a single RDF dataset, but there are also 464 EDPs used in more than ten RDF datasets, and 53 EDPs used in more than one hundred RDF datasets. These observations suggest that despite the decentralized nature of the Semantic Web, *a few patterns of term co-occurrence for describing entities have emerged and are shared among open RDF datasets.* Table 5 illustrates the

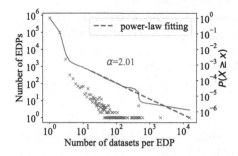

Fig. 7.   Distribution (crosses) and cumulative probability distribution (curve) of the number of RDF datasets using an EDP.

Fig. 8.   Distribution (crosses) and cumulative probability distribution (curve) of the number of RDF datasets in the LOD Cloud using an EDP.

Table 5. Top-Ranked Singleton (Top) and Non-Singleton (Bottom) EDPs

EDP	#PLD
C = ∅, FP = ∅, BP = {foaf:homepage}	128
C = ∅, FP = ∅, BP = {foaf:document}	89
C = ∅, FP = ∅, BP = {foaf:depiction}	65
C = ∅, FP = ∅, BP = {dcterms:license}	62
C = ∅, FP = ∅, BP = {foaf:workplaceHomepage}	57
C = ∅, FP = {socrata:rowID, rdfs:member}, BP = ∅	65
C = {foaf:PersonalProfileDocument}, FP = {admin:errorReportsTo, admin:generatorAgent, foaf:maker, foaf:primaryTopic}, BP = ∅	27
C = {foaf:PersonalProfileDocument}, FP = {foaf:maker, foaf:primaryTopic}, BP = ∅	17
C = {foaf:Document}, FP = {dcterms:hasFormat, foaf:primaryTopic, foaf:topic}, BP = ∅	11
C = {foaf:Document}, FP = {dc:format, rdfs:label}, BP = {dcterms:hasFormat}	11

Table 6. Top-Ranked Singleton (Top) and Non-Singleton (Bottom) EDPs in the LOD Cloud

EDP	#PLD
C = ∅, FP = ∅, BP = {dcterms:license}	42
C = ∅, FP = ∅, BP = {dcterms:subject}	32
C = ∅, FP = ∅, BP = {foaf:homepage}	31
C = ∅, FP = ∅, BP = {dcterms:creator}	31
C = ∅, FP = ∅, BP = {void:feature}	23
C = {foaf:Organization}, FP = {foaf:mbox, foaf:homepage, skos:prefLabel}, BP = {dcterms:rightsHolder, dcterms:publisher}	7
C = {dcmit:Software}, FP = {dcterms:identifier}, BP = ∅	7
C = {void:Dataset}, FP = {skos:example, skos:hiddenLabel, void:rootResource, skos:prefLabel}, BP = {void:subset, void:rootResource}	6
C = ∅, FP = ∅, BP = {dcterms:creator, dcterms:publisher}	5
C = {owl:Thing}, FP = ∅, BP = {dcterms:conformsTo}	5

most popular singleton (i.e., consisting of a single term) and non-singleton EDPs used in RDF datasets from tens to hundreds of PLDs.[19]

We particularly restricted the above distribution to the RDF datasets in the LOD Cloud. As shown in Fig. 8, fitting the tail of the distribution ($X \geq 4$) to a power law with $\alpha = 2.56$ is also accepted ($p = 0.95$). There are 55 EDPs used in more than ten RDF datasets in the LOD Cloud. These observations suggest that *the RDF datasets in the LOD Cloud also share a few patterns of co-occurrence for describing entities.* However, the most popular EDPs used in

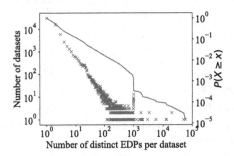
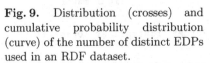
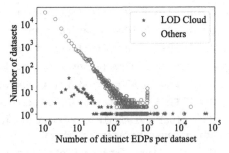

Fig. 9. Distribution (crosses) and cumulative probability distribution (curve) of the number of distinct EDPs used in an RDF dataset.

Fig. 10. Distribution of the number of distinct EDPs used in an RDF dataset in or outside the LOD Cloud.

---

[19] EDPs that solely consist of terms in the five language-level vocabularies (i.e., xsd, rdf, rdfs, owl, and skos) are excluded from Table 5 and Table 6.

the LOD Cloud illustrated in Table 6 differ from those in Table 5. There are descriptions of organizations and software in Table 6, not limited to descriptions of documents in Table 5.

4.3 Diversity Analysis

We analyzed to what extent a multiplicity of distinct EDPs have been used in an open RDF dataset by calculating their diversity in each dataset. Figure 9 plots the distribution of the number of distinct EDPs used in an RDF dataset, with a median number of 2 and a rejected power-law fitting ($p = 7.92E{-}4$). Nearly half of the RDF datasets (44.70%) use only a single EDP that describes all the entities, i.e., each of these RDF datasets describes all the entities in a homogeneous manner. There are also 24 RDF datasets using more than ten thousand distinct EDPs. For example, one RDF dataset entitled "Open Food Facts" describes entities in a highly heterogeneous manner, using 19,693 distinct EDPs which represent different combinations of nutrition facts about food products.

We particularly divided the distribution in Fig. 9 into two distributions in Fig. 10: one over all the RDF datasets in the LOD Cloud, and the other over those outside. The two distributions are noticeably different. The RDF datasets in the LOD Cloud use relatively more distinct EDPs in terms of median (14 > 2). The distribution over the LOD Cloud peaks at 5 EDPs, while most RDF datasets outside the LOD Cloud (67.68%) use at most 2 distinct EDPs. These observations suggest that *most RDF datasets outside the LOD Cloud contain nearly homogeneous entity descriptions, and the RDF datasets in the LOD Cloud describe entities in a relatively heterogeneous manner.*

One potential application of this kind of analysis is for choosing a suitable RDF store. For example, among RDF store solutions [1], a property table stores the description of each entity in a row, and each column stores the values of a distinct property, thereby allowing to retrieve entities having multiple specified property values without join operations. Property table is suitable for storing an RDF dataset using one or a few distinct EDPs, since otherwise there will be many null values which waste space. By contrast, vertical partitioning separately stores the values of different properties in different tables. A triple table stores all the RDF triples in a single table. Vertical partitioning and triple table are more suitable for storing an RDF dataset using a large number of distinct EDPs, since there will be no null values despite more joins at query time.

5   Clusters of Vocabularies Based on Co-occurrence

In this section, we exemplify another potential application of the extracted EDPs. We leveraged them to cluster vocabularies and RDF datasets. The generated clusters can be used in recommendation to support serendipitous discovery of vocabularies and RDF datasets. As we will see in this section, such EDP-based clusters are complementary to the conventional topic-based clusters.

5.1   Clustering Method

Graph Construction. Our clustering method relies on the following tripartite relation between RDF datasets, EDPs, and vocabularies: RDF datasets use EDPs which consist of terms belonging to vocabularies. To represent this relation, we constructed a tripartite *dataset-EDP-vocabulary graph*, where nodes represent RDF datasets, EDPs, and vocabularies; edges connect each EDP with all the RDF datasets using it, and with all the vocabularies its constituent terms belong to. For example, the dataset illustrated in Fig. 6 and the EDP illustrated in Table 4 are represented by two adjacent nodes; the EDP node is also adjacent with three vocabulary nodes representing foaf, skos, and dcterms.

Graph Clustering. Our idea is to exploit vocabulary co-occurrence in RDF data to simultaneously cluster RDF datasets and vocabularies via their connections with EDPs. We converted it into the problem of finding two co-clusterings on the dataset-EDP-vocabulary graph: one between EDPs and RDF datasets, and the other between EDPs and vocabularies, subject to that the consensus between the clusters of EDPs in the two co-clusterings should be maximized.

We solved this problem by using MV-ITCC [35], which is a multi-view co-clustering algorithm. Specifically, we treated EDPs as the main items to be clustered by the algorithm, and treated RDF datasets and vocabularies as items' features in two different views. We used MV-ITCC to compute a two-sided two-view clustering, where the items (i.e., EDPs) were clustered by exploiting the agreement and disagreement between different views, and the features in each view (i.e., RDF datasets or vocabularies) were simultaneously clustered.

5.2   Implementation Details

Preprocessing. We constructed a dataset-EDP-vocabulary graph from VOYAGE. Subject to the scalability of the MV-ITCC algorithm, we performed the following preprocessing to reduce the size of the graph and extract its core structure. First, we removed all the infrequent vocabularies used in RDF datasets from less than five PLDs, and we removed five language-level vocabularies as described in Sect. 3 as well as the socrata vocabulary since they have been trivially used in many RDF datasets. We also removed the RDF datasets that only use these vocabularies, and removed the EDPs whose constituent terms only belong to these vocabularies. Second, we merged the nodes representing EDPs whose constituent terms belong to exactly the same set of vocabularies, i.e., adjacent with the same set of vocabulary nodes in the graph. It actually generalized EDPs from the term level to the more coarse-grained vocabulary level. Finally, we removed all the isolated nodes from the graph.

Parameter Selection. Applying the MV-ITCC algorithm to the constructed dataset-EDP-vocabulary graph required specifying the expected numbers of clusters of RDF datasets, EDPs, and vocabularies, denoted by k_d, k_e, and k_v, respectively. To find their optimal setting, we heuristically searched each parameter from $\lceil 0.5\sqrt{\frac{n}{2}} \rceil$ to $\lceil 1.5\sqrt{\frac{n}{2}} \rceil$ in $\lceil 0.1\sqrt{\frac{n}{2}} \rceil$ increments, where n denotes the number of items to be clustered. Specifically, for each k_e, we found an optimal setting

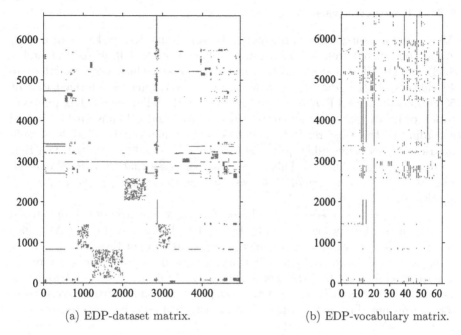

(a) EDP-dataset matrix.   (b) EDP-vocabulary matrix.

Fig. 11. Adjacency matrix representation of the dataset-EDP-vocabulary graph.

of k_d and k_v as follows. For each k_d-k_v combination, we employed the ITCC algorithm to compute a co-clustering of the bipartite EDP-dataset subgraph, and a co-clustering of the bipartite EDP-vocabulary subgraph. We measured the similarity between the clusters of EDPs in the two co-clusterings by calculating their adjusted rand index (ARI), and chose the k_d-k_v combination featuring the best ARI to form a k_e-k_d-k_v combination. Finally, we chose the k_e-k_d-k_v combination featuring the highest quality of co-clustering measured by Silhouette Coefficient.

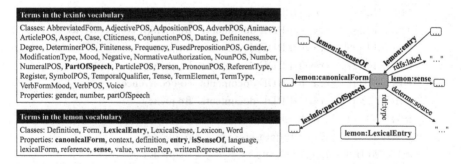

Fig. 12. Left: two vocabularies with few overlaps in the names of their constituent terms. Right: the description of an entity using terms in both vocabularies.

5.3   Cluster Analysis

After preprocessing and parameter selection, our dataset-EDP-vocabulary graph constructed from VOYAGE was reduced to 4,958 RDF dataset nodes, 6,584 merged EDP nodes, and 64 vocabulary nodes, which were grouped into 45 clusters of RDF datasets and 6 clusters of vocabularies intermediated by 52 clusters of merged EDPs. Figure 11 visualizes the adjacency matrix representation of its two bipartite subgraphs, where rows and columns are rearranged according to the clusters. Both matrices contain many noticeable dense submatrices representing subgraphs where nodes are densely connected, i.e., they represent cohesive clusters. This observation suggests that *open RDF datasets and vocabularies both exhibit distinguishable clusters based on the patterns of vocabulary co-occurrence.*

We compared our co-occurrence-based clusters with conventional topic-based clusters of vocabularies generated by Latent Dirichlet Allocation (LDA), which was fed with a set of pseudo documents each consisting of the names of all the terms in a vocabulary. We found 678 pairs of vocabularies that were clustered by our approach but not by LDA. For example, Fig. 12 illustrates two vocabularies, lexinfo[20] and lemon,[21] having few overlaps in the names of their constituent terms, thus not clustered by LDA. By contrast, their constituent terms co-occur

Table 7. Existing Analyses of Vocabulary Usage

	Data collection	Vocabulary usage analysis
LDOW'12 [23]	crawled RDF documents	frequency
JoWS'12 [16]	crawled RDF documents	frequency, co-occurrence
CSWS'12 [7]	crawled RDF documents	frequency
CSWS'12 [31]	crawled RDF documents	frequency
WI'12 [2]	crawled RDF documents	frequency, co-occurrence
ESWC'13 [10]	crawled RDF documents	co-occurrence
COLD'13 [9]	crawled RDF documents	co-occurrence, dynamics
ISWC'13 [4]	crawled RDF documents	frequency, co-occurrence
JoWS'13 [8]	crawled RDF documents	frequency, co-occurrence
ISWC'14 [29]	crawled RDF documents	frequency
ISWC'14 [22]	crawled RDF documents	frequency, co-occurrence
DPD'15 [11]	crawled RDF documents	co-occurrence
OIR'17 [24]	crawled RDF documents	frequency
ISWC'19 [14]	crawled RDF documents	frequency
ISWC'19 [17]	EuroDP datasets	frequency
JDIQ'20 [13]	LOD datasets	frequency

---

[20] http://www.lexinfo.net/ontology/2.0/lexinfo#.
[21] http://lemon-model.net/lemon#.

in 4 EDPs, thus clustered by our approach. This result is reasonable because lexinfo is exactly a vocabulary created to be used with lemon. These observations suggest that *our co-occurrence-based clusters of vocabularies provide a useful complement to the conventional topic-based clusters.*

6   Related Work

We are among the first to construct and publish a large collection that is specifically for analyzing vocabulary usage in open RDF datasets. Our analysis offers new measures that differ from previous analyses of vocabulary usage in Table 7.

Our analysis is focused on the patterns of term co-occurrence represented by EDPs, which have also been considered in previous analyses. For example, Dividino et al. [9] investigated the dynamics of EDPs. Gottron et al. [10,11] compared the informativeness of class sets and property sets. However, their analyses treated all the crawled RDF documents as a whole, whereas we separately analyzed each RDF dataset and obtained new findings, e.g., we characterized the diversity of vocabularies and EDPs used in each RDF dataset. In [2,4,8,16,22], RDF datasets were also separately analyzed, but these analyses were relatively coarse-grained—characterizing vocabulary co-occurrence in RDF datasets, whereas our more fine-grained analysis characterizes term co-occurrence in entity descriptions to provide a more accurate measurement.

Many analyses of vocabulary usage did not address co-occurrence as ours but they only reported frequencies [7,13,14,17,23,24,29,31]. A few researches were focused on the usage of a particular vocabulary such as GoodRelations [18] or schema.org [21]. Instead of vocabulary usage, some works analyzed vocabulary definitions [19,20] and inter-vocabulary links derived from their definitions [3,33]. All these analyses are considered orthogonal to our analysis of co-occurrence.

Another distinguishing feature of our VOYAGE is that we collected RDF datasets from ODPs. By contrast, previous analyses mostly crawled RDF documents from the Web and then heuristically grouped RDF documents into RDF datasets by PLD [16,29]. Such heuristic construction of pseudo RDF datasets may suffer from inaccuracy. A recent study gave attention to the RDF datasets in the LOD Cloud [13]. We further extended the scope by also crawling RDF datasets registered in many other ODPs. Our comparative analysis of the RDF datasets in and outside the LOD Cloud revealed their large differences.

7   Conclusion

We have constructed and published VOYAGE, a large collection of vocabulary usage from a diverse set of open RDF datasets, with a particular focus on the patterns of term co-occurrence in entity descriptions. We conclude the paper with a discussion of its impact, reusability, and future plans.

Impact. Different from previous data collections, our VOYAGE is sourced from RDF datasets registered in ODPs, and provides the usage of vocabularies, terms, and their patterns of co-occurrence extracted from each RDF dataset. It facilitates measuring the adoption of vocabularies and reviewing the state of the Semantic Web from a new angle. Indeed, our analysis of frequency and diversity in vocabulary usage has revealed some new findings of interest to the Semantic Web community and the open data community. Our observations collectively reflect that the Semantic Web is not too far away from establishing interoperability via shared vocabularies. This result is expected to encourage the continued adoption of Semantic Web technologies.

Reusability. Our presented analysis of VOYAGE is not exhaustive, and VOYAGE has the potential to be used in further analyses. For example, in some experiments we ablated the LOD Cloud to be specifically analyzed, and one may partition the RDF datasets and/or vocabularies in VOYAGE in a different way to perform comparative analysis. VOYAGE can also be applied in other scenarios. For example, we have showed its usefulness in vocabulary clustering, and one may explore its value for other tasks. Reusing and extending VOYAGE is easy since we have documented the structure of its JSON files.

Plans for the Future. VOYAGE is sourced from RDF datasets registered in ODPs, which is complementary to the sources of other existing data collections such as WebDataCommons. Therefore, we plan to extend VOYAGE with vocabulary usage extracted from the latest version of WebDataCommons[22] and from a re-crawl of the Billion Triple Challenge dataset.[23] As for long-term maintenance, we plan to periodically (i.e., yearly or more frequently) recollect all the data sources and publish updated vocabulary usage.

Acknowledgements. This work was supported by the NSFC (62072224) and the Chang Jiang Scholars Program (J2019032).

Resource Availability Statement:. VOYAGE is available from Zenodo at https://zenodo.org/record/7902675. For each of the accessed 577 ODPs, its name, URL, API type, API URL, and the IDs of RDF datasets collected from it are given in `odps.json`. For each of the crawled 72,088 RDF datasets, its ID, title, description, author, license, dump file URLs, and PLDs are given in `datasets.json`. The IDs of the deduplicated 68,312 RDF datasets and whether they are in the LOD Cloud are given in `deduplicated_datasets.json`. The extracted 62,864 classes, 842,745 properties, and the IDs of RDF datasets using each term are given in `terms.json`. The extracted 50,976 vocabularies, the classes and properties in each vocabulary, and the IDs of RDF datasets using each vocabulary are given in `vocabularies.json`. The extracted 767,976 distinct EDPs and the IDs of RDF datasets using each EDP are given in `edps.json`. The clusters of vocabularies generated by MV-ITCC and LDA are given in `clusters.json`. All the experiments presented in the paper can be reproduced from the above files, for which some helpful scripts are available from GitHub at https://github.com/nju-websoft/VOYAGE.

---

[22] http://webdatacommons.org/structureddata/#results-2022-1.
[23] https://zenodo.org/record/2634588.

References

1. Ali, W., Saleem, M., Yao, B., Hogan, A., Ngomo, A.N.: A survey of RDF stores & SPARQL engines for querying knowledge graphs. VLDB J. **31**(3), 1–26 (2022). https://doi.org/10.1007/s00778-021-00711-3
2. Ashraf, J., Hussain, O.K.: Analysing the use of ontologies based on usage network. In: WI 2012, pp. 540–544 (2012). https://doi.org/10.1109/WI-IAT.2012.203
3. Asprino, L., Beek, W., Ciancarini, P., van Harmelen, F., Presutti, V.: Observing LOD using equivalent set graphs: it is mostly flat and sparsely linked. In: Ghidini, C., et al. (eds.) ISWC 2019, Part I. LNCS, vol. 11778, pp. 57–74. Springer, Cham (2019). https://doi.org/10.1007/978-3-030-30793-6_4
4. Bizer, C., Eckert, K., Meusel, R., Mühleisen, H., Schuhmacher, M., Völker, J.: Deployment of RDFa, Microdata, and Microformats on the web – a quantitative analysis. In: Alani, H., et al. (eds.) ISWC 2013, Part II. LNCS, vol. 8219, pp. 17–32. Springer, Heidelberg (2013). https://doi.org/10.1007/978-3-642-41338-4_2
5. Brickley, D., Burgess, M., Noy, N.F.: Google dataset search: building a search engine for datasets in an open Web ecosystem. In: WWW 2019, pp. 1365–1375 (2019). https://doi.org/10.1145/3308558.3313685
6. Cheng, G., Gong, S., Qu, Y.: An empirical study of vocabulary relatedness and its application to recommender systems. In: Aroyo, L., et al. (eds.) ISWC 2011, Part I. LNCS, vol. 7031, pp. 98–113. Springer, Heidelberg (2011). https://doi.org/10.1007/978-3-642-25073-6_7
7. Cheng, G., Liu, M., Qu, Y.: NJVR: The NanJing vocabulary repository. In: Li, J., Qi, G., Zhao, D., Nejdl, W., Zheng, H.T. (eds.) Semantic Web and Web Science. Springer Proceedings in Complexity, pp. 265–272. Springer, New York (2013). https://doi.org/10.1007/978-1-4614-6880-6_23
8. Cheng, G., Qu, Y.: Relatedness between vocabularies on the Web of data: a taxonomy and an empirical study. J. Web Semant. **20**, 1–17 (2013). https://doi.org/10.1016/j.websem.2013.02.001
9. Dividino, R.Q., Scherp, A., Gröner, G., Grotton, T.: Change-a-LOD: does the schema on the Linked Data Cloud change or not? In: COLD 2013 (2013)
10. Gottron, T., Knauf, M., Scheglmann, S., Scherp, A.: A systematic investigation of explicit and implicit schema information on the linked open data cloud. In: Cimiano, P., Corcho, O., Presutti, V., Hollink, L., Rudolph, S. (eds.) ESWC 2013. LNCS, vol. 7882, pp. 228–242. Springer, Heidelberg (2013). https://doi.org/10.1007/978-3-642-38288-8_16
11. Gottron, T., Knauf, M., Scherp, A.: Analysis of schema structures in the Linked Open Data graph based on unique subject URIs, pay-level domains, and vocabulary usage. Distrib. Parallel Databases **33**(4), 515–553 (2014). https://doi.org/10.1007/s10619-014-7143-0
12. Guha, R.V., Brickley, D., Macbeth, S.: Schema.org: evolution of structured data on the Web. Commun. ACM **59**(2), 44–51 (2016). https://doi.org/10.1145/2844544
13. Haller, A., Fernández, J.D., Kamdar, M.R., Polleres, A.: What are links in Linked Open Data? A characterization and evaluation of links between knowledge graphs on the Web. ACM J. Data Inf. Qual. **12**(2), 9:1–9:34 (2020). https://doi.org/10.1145/3369875
14. Herrera, J.-M., Hogan, A., Käfer, T.: BTC-2019: the 2019 billion triple challenge dataset. In: Ghidini, C., et al. (eds.) ISWC 2019, Part II. LNCS, vol. 11779, pp. 163–180. Springer, Cham (2019). https://doi.org/10.1007/978-3-030-30796-7_11

15. Hogan, A.: Canonical forms for isomorphic and equivalent RDF graphs: algorithms for leaning and labelling blank nodes. ACM Trans. Web **11**(4), 22:1–22:62 (2017). https://doi.org/10.1145/3068333

16. Hogan, A., Umbrich, J., Harth, A., Cyganiak, R., Polleres, A., Decker, S.: An empirical survey of Linked Data conformance. J. Web Semant. **14**, 14–44 (2012). https://doi.org/10.1016/j.websem.2012.02.001

17. Ibáñez, L.-D., Millard, I., Glaser, H., Simperl, E.: An assessment of adoption and quality of linked data in European Open government data. In: Ghidini, C., et al. (eds.) ISWC 2019, Part II. LNCS, vol. 11779, pp. 436–453. Springer, Cham (2019). https://doi.org/10.1007/978-3-030-30796-7_27

18. Kowalczuk, E., Potoniec, J., Lawrynowicz, A.: Extracting usage patterns of ontologies on the Web: a case study on GoodRelations vocabulary in RDFa. In: OWLED 2014, pp. 139–144 (2014)

19. Abdul Manaf, N.A., Bechhofer, S., Stevens, R.: The current state of SKOS vocabularies on the web. In: Simperl, E., Cimiano, P., Polleres, A., Corcho, O., Presutti, V. (eds.) ESWC 2012. LNCS, vol. 7295, pp. 270–284. Springer, Heidelberg (2012). https://doi.org/10.1007/978-3-642-30284-8_25

20. Matentzoglu, N., Bail, S., Parsia, B.: A corpus of OWL DL ontologies. In: DL 2013, pp. 829–841 (2013)

21. Meusel, R., Bizer, C., Paulheim, H.: A web-scale study of the adoption and evolution of the schema.org vocabulary over time. In: WIMS 2015, p. 15 (2015). https://doi.org/10.1145/2797115.2797124

22. Meusel, R., Petrovski, P., Bizer, C.: The WebDataCommons Microdata, RDFa and Microformat dataset series. In: Mika, P., et al. (eds.) ISWC 2014, Part I. LNCS, vol. 8796, pp. 277–292. Springer, Cham (2014). https://doi.org/10.1007/978-3-319-11964-9_18

23. Mika, P., Potter, T.: Metadata statistics for a large Web corpus. In: LDOW 2012 (2012)

24. Nogales, A., Urbán, M.Á.S., Barriocanal, E.G.: Measuring vocabulary use in the Linked Data Cloud. Online Inf. Rev. **41**(2), 252–271 (2017). https://doi.org/10.1108/OIR-06-2015-0183

25. Pan, J.Z.: Resource description framework. In: Staab, S., Studer, R. (eds.) Handbook on Ontologies. IHIS, pp. 71–90. Springer, Heidelberg (2009). https://doi.org/10.1007/978-3-540-92673-3_3

26. Pan, J.Z., Thomas, E., Sleeman, D.: ONTOSEARCH2: searching and querying Web ontologies. In: WWW/Internet 2006, pp. 211–218 (2006)

27. Pan, J.Z., Vetere, G., Gómez-Pérez, J.M., Wu, H. (eds.): Exploiting Linked Data and Knowledge Graphs in Large Organisations. Springer, Cham (2017). https://doi.org/10.1007/978-3-319-45654-6

28. Pham, M.-D., Boncz, P.: Exploiting emergent schemas to make RDF systems more efficient. In: Groth, P., et al. (eds.) ISWC 2016, Part I. LNCS, vol. 9981, pp. 463–479. Springer, Cham (2016). https://doi.org/10.1007/978-3-319-46523-4_28

29. Schmachtenberg, M., Bizer, C., Paulheim, H.: Adoption of the linked data best practices in different topical domains. In: Mika, P., et al. (eds.) ISWC 2014, Part I. LNCS, vol. 8796, pp. 245–260. Springer, Cham (2014). https://doi.org/10.1007/978-3-319-11964-9_16

30. Shi, Q., Wang, J., Pan, J.Z., Cheng, G.: VOYAGE: a large collection of vocabulary usage in open RDF datasets (2023). https://doi.org/10.5281/zenodo.7902675

31. Stadtmüller, S., Harth, A., Grobelnik, M.: Accessing information about Linked Data vocabularies with vocab.cc. In: Li, J., Qi, G., Zhao, D., Nejdl, W., Zheng,

HT. (eds.) Semantic Web and Web Science. Springer Proceedings in Complexity, pp. 391–396. Springer, New York (2012). https://doi.org/10.1007/978-1-4614-6880-6_34

32. Tummarello, G., Morbidoni, C., Bachmann-Gmür, R., Erling, O.: RDFSync: efficient remote synchronization of RDF models. In: Aberer, K., et al. (eds.) ASWC/ISWC -2007. LNCS, vol. 4825, pp. 537–551. Springer, Heidelberg (2007). https://doi.org/10.1007/978-3-540-76298-0_39

33. Vandenbussche, P., Atemezing, G., Poveda-Villalón, M., Vatant, B.: Linked Open Vocabularies (LOV): a gateway to reusable semantic vocabularies on the Web. Semant. Web **8**(3), 437–452 (2017). https://doi.org/10.3233/SW-160213

34. Wang, X., et al.: PCSG: pattern-coverage snippet generation for RDF datasets. In: Hotho, A., et al. (eds.) ISWC 2021. LNCS, vol. 12922, pp. 3–20. Springer, Cham (2021). https://doi.org/10.1007/978-3-030-88361-4_1

35. Xu, P., Deng, Z., Choi, K., Cao, L., Wang, S.: Multi-view information-theoretic co-clustering for co-occurrence data. In: AAAI 2019, pp. 379–386 (2019). https://doi.org/10.1609/aaai.v33i01.3301379

36. Zaveri, A., Rula, A., Maurino, A., Pietrobon, R., Lehmann, J., Auer, S.: Quality assessment for Linked Data: a survey. Semant. Web **7**(1), 63–93 (2016). https://doi.org/10.3233/SW-150175

Linked Data Objects (LDO):
A TypeScript-Enabled RDF Devtool

Jackson Morgan[✉] [iD]

O.team, Washington DC 20001, USA
`jackson@o.team`

Abstract. Many RDF devtools exist for JavaScript that let developers read and modify RDF data, but they often opt to use proprietary interfaces and don't fully leverage the methods of reading and writing data with which JavaScript developers are familiar. This paper introduces Linked Data Objects (LDO), a JavaScript-based devtool designed to make reading and writing RDF as similar to programming traditional TypeScript applications as possible. LDO generates TypeScript typings and a JSON-LD context from an RDF Shape like ShEx. A JavaScript Proxy uses the generated code to serve as an abstracted interface for an underlying RDF/JS dataset, allowing the developer to manipulate RDF as a TypeScript object literal. LDO is currently in use in a small number of RDF-based projects and our user studies indicate that LDO's interface-parity with TypeScript object literals is preferable to proprietary interfaces in other JavaScript RDF devtools. Finally, this paper proposes future work to make LDO even more approachable for JavaScript developers.

Keywords: RDF · Devtool · JavaScript · TypeScript

Resource Type: Software Framework
License: MIT License
Permanent URL: https://purl.archive.org/o.team/ldo
Canonical Citation: https://doi.org/10.5281/zenodo.7909200

1 Introduction

Ease of use is paramount for JavaScript developers when they are evaluating which devtool to use in their project, and members of the semantic web community are rightfully striving to make RDF as approachable for novice developers as possible [20]. There have been many approaches to making RDF accessible in JavaScript, the web's native language.

Some libraries like RDF/JS [1], clownface [2], Tripledoc [3], and rdflib [4] implement unique interfaces for accessing and modifying data. For example, RDF/JS employs its own methods like `quad`, `namedNode`, and `dataset` to manipulate data. A developer can create a new quad by writing (Fig. 1):

© The Author(s), under exclusive license to Springer Nature Switzerland AG 2023
T. R. Payne et al. (Eds.): ISWC 2023, LNCS 14266, pp. 230–246, 2023.
https://doi.org/10.1007/978-3-031-47243-5_13

```
dataset.add(quad(namedNode("a"), namedNode("b"), namedNode("c")))
```

Fig. 1. Creating a new quad in RDF/JS

While this might be a straightforward technique for anyone versed in the semantic web, it is daunting for new developers who need to read API documentation and the basic concepts of linked data to use it properly.

We hypothesize that the closer the developer experience is to the native environment they're used to, the easier it will be for a developer to use a tool, even if advanced use-cases require those developers to leave the comfort zone of their native environment. Many RDF devtools have employed techniques that work towards that goal. In this paper, we will explore those techniques and present Linked Data Objects (LDO), a library designed to allow developers to easily use RDF in a TypeScript setting specifically.

2 Related Work

A plethora of JavaScript libraries exist to help JavaScript developers use RDF data. In this section, we discuss these libraries, the design choices they made, and their strengths and weaknesses.

Matching JSON's Interface. JSON is the primary data structure for JavaScript, and therefore is an interface that feels natural for JavaScript developers. A few libraries acknowledge this in their design, most notably JSON-LD [5]. As a serialization of RDF, JSON-LD lets developers read and write data to a document using JSON's interface. Its ease of use is probably why many of the subsequently referenced libraries – including LDO – use it as a basis.

JSON-LD is not without its flaws, however. Pure JSON is a tree, not a graph. This means that with raw JSON-LD, a developer cannot traverse a full circuit of the graph without searching the graph for a certain node. It is possible to flatten a JSON-LD document so that a developer can directly look up objects by their subject ids, however, this would require extra work on the part of the developer. A true match of JSON's interface would allow a developer to use uninterrupted chaining (Fig. 2).

```
// uninterrupted chaining
person.friend.name
// chaining interrupted by a lookup on a flat JSON-LD doc
jsonldDocument[person.friend["@id"]].name
```

Fig. 2. A comparison of uninterrupted chaining and a lookup on flattened JSON-LD

Libraries that use JSON-LD as a base interface like rdf-tools [9] and shex-methods [10] are limited by JSON-LD's raw structure as a tree.

Schemas. While RDF's formal semantics follow the open world assumption [21], TypeScript naturally follows a closed world assumption. To reconcile this, many libraries have adopted a Schema system to define how data should be structured.

Schema systems fall into three categories. Firstly, some devtools like LDflex [6], RDF Object [7], and SimpleRDF [8] ask the user to provide a JSON-LD context. While this is a simple solution, JSON-LD contexts do not strongly define the "shape" of an RDF node (as languages like ShEx and SHACL do) and lacks useful features like asserting a predicate's cardinality (as languages like OWL do). For example, JSON-LD contexts only define possible fields, not where those fields should be used. A context may define the existence of fields "name", "friends", "file extension", and "dpi", but not clarify that only "name" and "friends" should be used on a "Person" node.

Secondly, some devtools translate a language with strong definitions into a JSON-LD context. For example, rdf-tools [9] generates a context from OWL, and shex-methods [10] generates a context from ShEx [15]. Unlike the libraries that depend on JSON-LD context alone, these libraries have provisions to ensure certain predicates are only used on their intended types.

Thirdly, some devtools like Semantika [11] and ts-rdf-mapper [12] ask the user to define the schema in JavaScript itself. They develop their own unique JavaScript interface to let the developer define how their actions in JavaScript translate to RDF. These libraries are similar to Java libraries in the semantic web space including So(m)mer [26] and Jenabean [27] which use Java decorators to achieve the same goal.

If the goal is to design a devtool that is as close to JavaScript as possible, the third option sounds like the obvious technique to employ, but it does have a downside. Any development work done to define a schema in a JavaScript-only environment is not transferable to other languages. Philosophically, semantic data should be equally as usable on any platform no matter what language it's using. Having a single schema that works with multiple programming languages (like OWL, ShEx, or SHACL) makes it easier for developers on many different platforms to read and write the same semantic data.

For LDO, we have decided to employ the second option, using a strongly defined language-agnostic schema (in our case ShEx). As will be discussed in the "User Studies" section, this design choice has a negative impact on approachability for JavaScript developers who are unfamiliar with RDF. However, the "Future Work" section discusses the potential for a universal schema library accessible to all developers. In that future, the relative unapproachability of RDF schemas for JavaScript developers is inconsequential.

TypeScript. Multiple studies [13, 14] have shown that strongly typed languages are more useful for developers than weakly typed languages because strongly typed languages permit useful tools like auto-suggest and type checking that inform developers how to interact with data.

While many libraries like RDF/JS [1], clownface [2], Tripledoc [3], and rdflib [4] use TypeScript, their typings apply to the interface for accessing data and not the data itself. Other libraries like rdf-tools [9], shex-methods [10], and ts-rdf-mapper [12] generate typings based on a schema. This allows developers to know, for example, that a "Person" has a "name" field that is type "string." We decided to do the same for LDO.

Similar Java Libraries. LDO is conceptually similar to Java RDF code generators like Owl2Java [28]. These take some standard (like OWL) and generatse POJOs that can be used in the project. However, providing a native-feeling environment is a bit more difficult in JavaScript than Java. In Java, developers are used to interacting with a class and methods, so a code generator only needs to generate methods that match a given schema-like input. That could be an approach in JavaScript, but JavaScript developers are more likely to interact with data through raw JSON rather than JavaScript classes. That's why LDO considers all operations that could possibly be done on a raw JSON object literal (the " =" operator, the "delete" operator, array iterators, array methods, chaining etc.).

The aforementioned libraries and their design decisions are displayed in Table 1.

Table 1. Various RDF JavaScript Devtools rated on Design Considerations

Library	Has a JSON-like interface	Not represented as a tree	Uses a Schema	Typings are generated from Schema
RDF/JS [1]		✓		
clownface [2]		✓		
Tripledoc [3]		✓		
rdflib [4]		✓		
JSON-LD [5]	✓		JSON-LD Context	
LDflex [6]		✓	JSON-LD Context	
RDF Object [7]		✓	JSON-LD Context	
SimpleRDF [8]	✓	✓	JSON-LD Context	
rdf-tools [9]	✓		Generated (OWL)	✓
shex-methods [10]			Generated (ShEx)	✓
Semantika [11]		✓	Defined in JS	
ts-rdf-mapper [12]	✓	✓	Defined in JS	✓
So(m)mer [26]	N/A	✓	Defined in Java	✓
jenabean [27]	N/A	✓	Defined in Java	✓
Owl2Java [28]	N/A	✓	Generated (OWL)	✓
LDO	✓	✓	Generated (ShEx)	✓

3 Linked Data Objects (LDO)

Linked Data Objects (LDO) is designed to satisfy the design considerations discussed above. It contains two main libraries: ldo[1] and ldo-cli[2]. We will also mention a few dependencies that were built to support LDO: shexj2typeandcontext[3], jsonld-dataset-proxy[4] and o-dataset-pack[5].

Generally, LDO's developer experience is divided into five steps (as described in Fig. 3): (1) building from the schema, (2) parsing raw RDF, (3) creating a Linked Data Object, (4) reading/modifying data, and (5) converting data back to raw RDF.

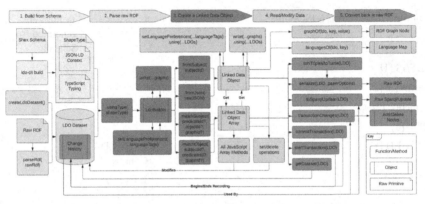

Fig. 3. A diagram showing all the developer-facing methods and their intended flow as a developer experience.

3.1 Building From the Schema

As mentioned in the "Related Work" section, we decided to orient the LDO around a language-agnostic schema. We chose ShEx [15] as our schema system for relatively arbitrary reasons: ShEx is more popular in the Solid [30] community. However, we architected the system to be able to also accommodate alternatives like SHACL [16] if a converter is built.

By itself, a ShEx schema isn't useful for LDO. It can validate raw RDF, but as LDO strives to interact with data in a JSON-like way, two pieces of data must first be derived from a ShEx schema. First, a corresponding JSON-LD context can be derived from a schema to inform LDO about the shape at runtime, and second, a TypeScript typing can also be derived from the schema to perform type checking at compile-time (or more accurately in the case of TypeScript, transpile-time) and in a developer's IDE.

---

[1] https://purl.archive.org/o.team/ldo.

[2] https://purl.archive.org/o.team/ldo-cli.

[3] https://purl.archive.org/o.team/shexj2typeandcontext.

[4] https://purl.archive.org/o.team/jsonld-dataset-proxy.

[5] https://purl.archive.org/o.team/o-dataset-pack.

As TypeScript typings are required before compile-time, the schema conversion script must be run before then. A command line interface (CLI) is a common design pattern to execute such scripts, and LDO has an accompanying cli called ldo-cli.

Ldo-cli makes it easy for developers to set up their projects. By running one command in their TypeScript project (npx ldo-cli init), ldo-cli will install all required dependencies, create a folder for developers to store their ShEx schemas, provide an example ShEx schema, and add the "build" command to their project's metadata file (package.json).

Once the developer has initialized their project, they can modify and add ShEx schemas to their "shapes" folder. Running ldo build --input {shapesPath} --output {outputPath} or simply npm run build:ldo runs the script to convert shapes into context and typings.

As an example, suppose a developer uses the ShEx Schema defined in Fig. 4.

```
PREFIX ex: <https://example.com/>
PREFIX foaf: <http://xmlns.com/foaf/0.1/>
PREFIX rdfs: <http://www.w3.org/2000/01/rdf-schema#>
PREFIX xsd: <http://www.w3.org/2001/XMLSchema#>
PREFIX ns: <http://www.w3.org/1999/02/22-rdf-syntax-ns#>
ex:FoafProfile EXTRA a {
  foaf:name xsd:string
  // rdfs:comment "A profile has 1 names" ;
  foaf:title ns:langString *
  // rdfs:comment "A profile has 0-∞ titles, and they could have translations" ;
  foaf:knows @ex:FoafProfile *
  // rdfs:comment "A profile has 0-∞ friends." ;
}
```

Fig. 4. An example ShEx shape that will be used in all future examples

The "build" command uses the shexj2typeandcontext library which iterates over ShExJ (ShEx's JSON-LD serialization). It builds a context by inferring a predicate name. If a predicate is not explicitly labeled with rdfs:label, shexj2typeandcontext will choose a field name by looking at the end of a predicate URI. For example, the predicate http://xmlns.com/foaf/0.1/name will translate to a field name of name. The library also includes contingencies for overlapping field names. Any fields that could have more than one object are marked with "@container": "@set".

This interpretation does not exactly map to the interpretation outlined in the JSON-LD specification as the absence of a "@container" field does not officially mean a cardinality of 1 in JSON-LD. Therefore, in this version of LDO, developers should only use a JSON-LD context that was generated by the "build" command and not one that was generated externally.

The example above produces this context in Fig. 5.

```
export const foafProfileContext: ContextDefinition = {
  name: {
    "@id": "http://xmlns.com/foaf/0.1/name",
    "@type": "http://www.w3.org/2001/XMLSchema#string",
  },
  title: {
    "@id": "http://xmlns.com/foaf/0.1/title",
    "@type": "http://www.w3.org/1999/02/22-rdf-syntax-ns#langString",
    "@container": "@set",
  },
  knows: {
    "@id": "http://xmlns.com/foaf/0.1/knows",
    "@type": "@id",
    "@container": "@set",
  },
};
```

Fig. 5. JSON-LD context generated by ldo-cli given the example ShEx shape.

Once a context is produced, shex2typeandcontext iterates over the ShExJ object a second time to construct the TypeScript typings. It uses the field names defined in the context to create TypeScript interfaces. The library does not account for every feature in ShEx as mentioned in the "Future Work" section; however, it does handle enough to be usable on basic schemas. The example shape above produces the following typing (Fig. 6):

```
export interface FoafProfile {
  "@id"?: string;
  "@context"?: ContextDefinition;
  name: string;
  title?: string[];
  knows?: FoafProfile[];
}
```

Fig. 6. TypeScript typings generated by ldo-cli given the example ShEx shape.

Finally, the "build" script produces a resource called a "ShapeType." ShapeTypes combine typings, context, and other metadata into one object so that it can easily be imported by the developer.

3.2 Parsing Raw RDF

A developer could receive RDF in many forms and can use LDO's `parseRdf()` function to convert it. ParseRdf uses N3.js [17] and JSON-LD Streaming Parser [18] to accept turtle, n-triples, JSON-LD, or any RDF/JS compatible dataset and converts it into an "LdoDataset." LdoDatasets implement the RDF/JS Dataset [19] interface but have an additional method that lets the developer create Linked Data Objects (Fig. 7).

```
const rawTurtle = `
@prefix example: <https://example.com/>.
@prefix foaf: <http://xmlns.com/foaf/0.1/>.
@prefix xsd: <http://www.w3.org/2001/XMLSchema#>.
@prefix ns: <http://www.w3.org/1999/02/22-rdf-syntax-ns#>.
example:Taggart
   foaf:name "Peter Quincy Taggart" ;
   foaf:knows example:Lazarus .
example:Lazarus
   foaf:name "Lazarus of Tev'Meck" ;
   foaf:title "Doctor"^^ns:langString ;
   foaf:title "Docteur"@fr ;
   foaf:knows example:Taggart .
`;
const ldoDataset = await parseRdf(rawTurtle, { format: "Turtle" });
```

Fig. 7. Use of the parsedRdf function preceded by raw RDF that will be used in upcoming examples.

3.3   Creating the Linked Data Object

A Linked Data Object represents a specific type and a specific subject inside a dataset. The developer can provide the expected type with the usingType() method by providing the "ShapeType" generated in step one. The usingType() method returns an "LdoBuilder," a class that will help build a Linked Data Object for the given type.

Some methods on the LdoBuilder, like the write() and setLanguagePreferences() methods, set preferences for the eventual Linked Data Object, but only return an LdoBuilder so that preferences can be set using the method chaining design pattern [22]. We will cover the specifics of write and setLanguagePreferences in the next section.

Finally, the developer must define the subject(s) they want their Linked Data Object to represent. The most common way of doing this is the fromSubject() method which returns a Linked Data Object representing the provided subject ID (Fig. 8).

```
import { FoafProfileShapeType } from "./ldo/foafProfile.shapeTypes";
const taggart = ldoDataset
 .usingType(FoafProfileShapeType)
 .setLanguagePreferences("en", "@none")
 .fromSubject("https://example.com/Taggart");
```

Fig. 8. Method chaining to get a Linked Data Object with the usingType and fromSubject methods.

The fromJson() method serves a similar purpose as the fromSubject() method, but instead of accepting a Subject ID, it accepts raw JSON. This JSON is then processed, added to the dataset, and turned into a Linked Data Object to return.

The matchSubject() and matchObject() methods are two more advanced ways to create a Linked Data Object. They both return arrays of Linked Data Objects corresponding to the matching predicate, object, and graph in matchSubject's case or the matching subject, predicate, and graph in matchObject's case (See Fig. 9). These two methods require knowledge of quads and the underlying data structure of RDF. Therefore, it is expected that only users with knowledge of RDF will use these methods.

```
const listOfAllPeopleWhoKnowLazarus = ldoDataset
  .usingType(FoafProfileShapeType)
  .matchSubject(
    "http://xmlns.com/foaf/0.1/knows",
    "https://example.com/Lazarus",
    null
  );
const listOfAllPeopleKnownByLazarus = ldoDataset
  .usingType(FoafProfileShapeType)
  .matchObject(
    "https://example.com/Lazarus",
    "http://xmlns.com/foaf/0.1/knows",
    null
  );
```

Fig. 9. Advanced matching methods for constructing a set of Linked Data Objects

3.4 Reading/Modifying Data

Linked Data Objects. A Linked Data Object is built with the library "jsonld-dataset-proxy." This uses JavaScript's "Proxy" object [23] to intercept and redefine fundamental operations of an object. A Linked Data Object adopts the same interface as a traditional JavaScript object, but under the hood, it is translating any fundamental operation into an operation on a dataset (See Figs. 10 and 11).

```
console.log(taggart.name);
// translates to
console.log(
  ldoDataset.match(
    namedNode("https://example.com/Taggart"),
    namedNode("http://xmlns.com/foaf/0.1/name"),
    null
  ).toArray()[0].object.value
);
```

Fig. 10. A JSON get operation translates to a "match" operation on an RDF Dataset

Notice that in Fig. 11, setting a new name is translated to both "delete" and "add" operations. If the "name" field in the generated JSON-LD context contained the metadata `"@container": "@set"`, the Linked Data Object would have only done an add operation because it interprets a "set container" as permission to allow multiple quads with the "name" predicate.

While most JSON operations perfectly map to RDF operations, some require creative interpretation. For example, in LDO, `delete taggart.knows[0]` and `tagart.knows[0]= undefined` are different operations. The first will remove all quads associated with an object (in this case, it would remove all quads associated

```
taggart.name = "Jason Nesmith";
// translates to
ldoDataset.deleteMatches(
  namedNode("https://example.com/Taggart"),
  namedNode("http://xmlns.com/foaf/0.1/name")
);
ldoDataset.add(quad(
  namedNode("https://example.com/Taggart"),
  namedNode("http://xmlns.com/foaf/0.1/name"),
  literal("Jason Nesmith")
));
```

Fig. 11. A JSON set operation translates to a delete and add operation on an RDF Dataset

with Dr. Lazarus), and the second will only delete the adjoining quad (in this case Dr. Lazarus still exists, but Taggart doesn't know him). While this is a departure from the JSON-purist approach we've taken thus-far, we believe it is necessary here because both operations are useful for a developer.

Linked Data Object Arrays. LDO will create an array for any key with a cardinality of over 1. Linked Data Object Arrays are more than just an array of Linked Data Objects, they are JavaScript proxies themselves that intercept fundamental operations. As such, reading from or writing to an index (for example `taggart.knows[0]`) and every JavaScript array method translates to operations on the underlying RDF dataset.

One point of difference is that JavaScript arrays are ordered, and RDF sets are not. This difference is especially relevant when implementing JavaScript array methods that depend on the ordered nature of arrays like `splice()` or `sort()`. In the spirit of keeping LDO as similar to JSON as possible, Linked Data Object Arrays maintain an internal state that keeps track of the order of entities. However, developers are warned not to depend on order as edge cases like modifying the dataset without a Linked Data Object can cause the ordering to change unexpectedly.

Non-JSON Concepts. RDF contains features like graph support and language tag support that don't perfectly map onto JSON paradigms. While the JSON-LD specification has solutions for these features, we found that they break the simplicity of the TypeScript typings generated in step 1. Instead, we opted to handle these features by using functions outside of the Linked Data Object.

Graph Support. Every quad has a graph, and to enable graph support, LDO needs to answer two questions for the developer: "How do I discover which graph certain specific information is on?" and "If I add new data, how do I control which graphs it is written to?".

The first question can be answered with the `graphOf()` function. This function essentially lets the developer describe a triple using a Linked Data Object (the subject), a key on that object (the predicate), and an array index in the case that the key has a cardinality of greater than 1 (the object). It returns an array of all graphs on which that triple exists. For example, `graphOf(taggart, "knows", 0)` might return "[defaultGraph]" because the triple `ex:Taggart foaf:knows ex:Lazarus` exists on the default graph.

The second question is answered with the `write()`.`using()` function. The developer can provide a list of RDF-JS compatible graph nodes to the `write` function and a list of Linked Data Objects to the `using` method, and any succeeding triple additions to the dataset will be made in the defined graphs. The write graphs can also be defined when creating the linked data object using the `write()` method on the LdoBuilder (Fig. 12).

```
console.log(graphOf(taggart, "name")); // Logs [defaultGraph]
write(namedNode("otherGraph")).using(taggart);
taggart.name = "Jason Nesmith";
console.log(graphOf(taggart, "name")); // Logs [otherGraph]
```

Fig. 12. A demonstration of graph support in LDO

Language Tag Support. Having access to all languages of a langString is nice to have, but in most cases, developers have a preference for a specific language, and can use the `setLangaugePreferences()`.`using()` function to communicate that with LDO (Fig. 13).

```
const titleLanguageMap = languagesOf(taggart, "title");
titleLanguageMap.en?.add("Commander").add("Mr.");
titleLanguageMap.es?.add("Comandante").add("Sr.");
titleLanguageMap["@none"].add("Captain").add("Mr.");
setLanguagePreferences("es", "@none").using(taggart);
console.log(taggart.title[0]); // Logs Comandante
```

Fig. 13. A demonstration of Language Tag support in LDO

3.5   Converting Data Back to Raw RDF

Once modifications have been made to the data, developers will want to convert their data back into a form that's applicable outside of LDO. This form could be an RDF JS Dataset – in which case the `getDataset()` function can be used – or an RDF serialization like turtle, n-triples, or JSON-LD – in which case the `serialize()`, `toTurtle()`, `toJsonLd()`, and `toNTriples()` functions can be used.

Tracking Changes. Some systems, like Solid [30], allow SPARQL update queries to modify data, developers interfacing with such systems may prefer update queries over raw RDF documents. To build a SPARQL update query, we first must keep track of changes made by the developer. LdoDataset extends TransactionalDataset from the "o-dataset-pack" library. A transactional dataset keeps an internal record of all changes made during a transaction. To start a transaction, the developer can use the `startTransaction()` function and to end a transaction, they can use the `commitTransaction()` function (Fig. 14).

```
startTransaction(taggart);
taggart.name = "Jason Nesmith";
// Logs:
// DELETE DATA {
//   <https://example.com/Taggart> <http://xmlns.com/foaf/0.1/name>
//   "Peter Quincy Taggart" .
// }; INSERT DATA {
//   <https://example.com/Taggart> <http://xmlns.com/foaf/0.1/name>
//   "Jason Nesmith" .
// }
console.log(await toSparqlUpdate(taggart));
commitTransaction(taggart);
startTransaction(taggart);
// Logs "" because no changes are in this transaction
console.log(await toSparqlUpdate(taggart));
```

Fig. 14. A demonstration of transactions and change tracking

4 User Studies

To validate the design consideration assumptions, we conducted interviews with nine software engineers of varying proficiency (five with no proficiency in RDF but experience in JavaScript and four with RDF proficiency). Interview subjects were recruited by a social media post on our personal Twitter and LinkedIn pages as well as invitations to friends. Each one-hour study consisted of an opening interview discussing the participant's knowledge of JavaScript and RDF followed by a hands-on study. Participants were asked to clone a starter TypeScript repo and were given a string of turtle-format RDF representing a user profile. They were then asked to use LDO to change the name listed on the profile. Afterwards, participants were questioned about their experience. Finally, they were asked to read the documentation for another new-developer focused JavaScript library, LDflex, and provide an opinion on its interface choices versus LDO's. LDflex was selected a tool for comparison as both tools focus on developer friendliness for RDF. The major takeaways from the user interviews are listed below.

Building Schemas. The process of writing and building schemas was generally understood by RDF proficient participants. Each of them navigated the build process and understood the purpose of the generated files when asked. Though one did express concern for RDF novices, noting "I think it would be hard to teach them how to write ShEx and Turtle."

Novices had a more difficult time with schemas, they were unable to construct their own schemas and relied on an auto-generated version. One participant went as far as saying that they preferred LDflex to LDO because it is "easier to use and to get something off the ground more quickly. There are fewer steps." LDflex relies on a simple JSON-LD context as its schema replacement. This participant believed that it would be easier for them to build a JSON-LD context on their own than a ShEx schema.

Converting From Raw RDF. Converting from raw RDF to a Linked Data Object was similarly difficult. Even one of the experienced RDF developers stumbled on the process saying, "I got confused around the [RDF/JS] dataset term because at that point, all I worked with is rdflib," thus showing that familiarity of RDF/JS interfaces are not universal and will require additional education even with seasoned RDF JavaScript developers.

While the RDF novices were unphased by the existence of a Dataset, the `parseRdf()` function presented a challenge. "BaseIRI was a bit difficult, but I might have gotten it given a bit of time. I'm just doing pattern matching." Indeed, every novice struggled with RDF parsing and particularly didn't understand the concept of a BaseIRI. A BaseIRI is often necessary when parsing raw RDF, but understanding it does require knowledge of RDF's quirks that novice developers don't possess.

One novice, however, did have positive feedback for the conversion stage saying, "Given that there's an example that I can copy paste, I know that I need to call these two functions to turn it into an object."

Manipulating Data. Once users had overcome the setup process, feedback was generally positive about manipulating data. The experienced RDF subjects expressed praise for the simplicity of LDO versus other libraries they've used. "In [other libraries I've used] I need to create a service from scratch… I'm writing the construct query directly. There's no update. You have to delete and insert triples. So, [LDO] simplified this," one said. "I do think having the types is helpful… it was really, really easy to read/write data and change it," said another.

Further positive feedback came from the novice participants. "There seems like there's a lot of value there if you're doing a lot of complicated operations. I do think having the types is helpful." Additionally, they affirmed the approachability of JSON-congruence, noting a preference for LDO's editing interface over LDflex's. "[LD-Flex's] syntax is really weird. Await on a foreach loop? You need to learn a new syntax which is extra work."

An unexpected recipient of praise was LDO's transaction system. One experienced RDF developer said, "That's cool that you can start the transaction and it's almost like a database. That's new. I don't remember any of these other libraries letting you do that. I really like that." Though, one of the non-RDF developers was confused that you didn't need to commit a transaction before calling `toSparqlUpdate()`.

5 Case Studies

LDO has also been used in a few projects. This section details two such projects and the experience of the developers working on them. Beyond the projects listed here, a small community of developers are using LDO, yielding 17 stars on GitHub and 1,719 total downloads from NPM as of May 8th, 2023.

Capgemini and Försäkringskassan. Försäkringskassan (the Swedish Social Insurance Agency) is a Swedish government agency responsible for financial welfare including, but not limited to, pensions, housing benefits, child allowances, and immigrant support. They approached Capgemini, a global consulting company, with the problem of digitizing welfare legislation. By representing legislation as linked data, they hope to provide automated tools to deliver social insurance as dictated by law.

Capgemini developer, Arne Hassel, decided to use LDO for the Försäkringskassan project proof of concept. "I'm very happy with LDO... I've used rdflib which is very powerful, but very verbose. Inrupt's client libraries are also powerful but don't connect with the vision of the data in my mind. LDO makes it feel more natural to work with the data," he said. "For me, the most vital part of LDO is that it has a very easy to understand representation of the graph. It works from subjects and you have properties that represent the predicates and you can follow that. For me, it's a very neat way of working with data, especially with types... That's one of the core things I like: it's as close to JSON as possible."

The proof of concept is built using React, and Arne has built his own React hooks like useResource() and useSubject() that correspond to parts of the LDO interface. For now, the project has read-only requirements, and modifying and writing data is not required, though Arne says that this will be a requirement in the future.

Arne was undaunted by LDO's setup process. "Ldo is easy once you have it set up. It's simple for me because I understand the concept of ShEx." Though he mitigated his praise saying, "There are reasons that I wouldn't use LDO. It's a one-man project, so I'm very comfortable with using it for proof of concepts, but when it comes to applying it to big production environments, I need some kind of assurance that someone will be able to fix bugs in a decent amount of time." He contrasted this with other devtools like rdflib which has existed for a long time or "inrupt/solid-client" which is supported by a well-funded company (Inrupt). "LDO feels the most natural to me, so if I could be sure there was support, that would be my choice."

Internet of Production Alliance. The Internet of Production Alliance is an organization focused on building open infrastructure in manufacturing. One of their initiatives is the Open Know-How (OKH) initiative which seeks to make designs and documentation for manufactured goods open, accessible, and discoverable. Alliance member, Max Wardeh wanted to build an application that would store designs and documentation on a Solid server and needed a tool to work with the RDF metadata for each of the manufactured goods. He chose LDO.

"I don't think we could have gotten [the OKH Solid project] done in the tight deadline without LDO," he said, "especially because we were changing things about the ontology during the project itself." He noted that the ability to update ShEx shapes as the ontology for their project changed helped decrease development time. Because LDO generated TypeScript typings, he was easily able to track where code needed to be updated with every change.

In Max's case, the use of ShEx wasn't a deterrent. In fact, he noted that LDO made it easier to work with Solid due to existing ShEx shapes. "We were able to use other established shapes like the 'Solid Profile,' and 'Solid File Structure' shapes. This was really key, especially as someone who's never done something in Solid before."

However, Max acknowledged that LDO is not useful in every use case. "In my mind, LDO is a front-end thing. If I were building out a data pipeline of some sort and the data is stored in triples, I'd probably go for RDF.ex for that kind of use case." This assessment is commensurate with the target audience for LDO.

6 Future Work

While LDO has made progress towards more usable RDF devtools, there is room for improvement as seen in the user interviews and beyond. Fortunately, the NL-Net foundation has agreed to fund part of the future work for LDO.

Novice Developer Ease-of-Use. As seen in the "User Studies" section, one of the points of contention with LDO's design was the requirement to create a ShEx schema. Developers did not want to learn a new language to define a schema. One simple solution is building support for a schema language that's more comfortable for JavaScript developers like JSON Schema [24]. JSON Schema is a well-adopted schema language structured using JSON. JSON-LD Schema [29] expands JSON Schema for use in RDF. The only feature that a JavaScript developer may find daunting is the fact that JSON-LD Schema encourages developers to define URLs in order to make the jump to its status as an RDF Schema.

Ultimately, when it comes to schemas, defining predicates with URLs is unavoidable and is therefore inherently unapproachable to novice JavaScript developers. It might be prudent to say that schemas should only be defined by experienced developers and then distributed to novice developers via known mediums like NPM. Downloading schemas is not only easier for novice developers, but it also encourages data-interoperability as projects will have the same definitions for objects. This potential future could make RDF development even easier than traditional software development as the user will no longer need to define or research their own data standards when they start a project. They can depend on data standards created by the community that are easily downloadable.

Another point of user contention was the process of fetching raw RDF and converting it into a Linked Data Object. Optimizing this process was out of scope for this paper, but user studies indicate that this should be a focus for future work. Providing a fetch library that takes as input a resource URL or query and returns a Linked Data Object would prevent a developer from needing to understand concepts like BaseIRI or various RDF content-types. Further work could even integrate with popular JavaScript libraries, like React, to make the transition to using RDF even more seamless.

Spec Compliance. As mentioned in the "Building from the Schema" section, LDO interprets the feature of a JSON-LD context in an uncompliant manner. This is because the needs for LDO do not directly map to the needs for JSON-LD. In the future, LDO should generate its own proprietary context to be used at runtime and use a JSON-LD context only for conversions between JSON-LD and other RDF serializations.

LDO's build script also only supports a subset of ShEx's features, and future work must be done to support all features in ShEx as well as all features of OWL and SHACL.

Shape Evaluation. At the moment, LDO takes for granted that a certain subject follows a given shape. This can lead to mistakes and uncompliant data. But, LDO has the potential to also be a tool to evaluate the compliance of data by running data through a shape validator.

Maintenance and Bug Fixes. Currently the NLNet foundation provides funding for continued maintenance and new features for LDO. At the time of writing, NLNet funding continues through November of 2023 at which point a proposal to renew funding will be submitted. A new funding source and maintenance plan should be found if NLNet does not renew. Given funding is not secured to maintain LDO, Jackson Morgan will maintain LDO on a volunteer basis.

7   Conclusion

Linked Data Objects (LDO) is designed to make manipulating RDF as similar to manipulating TypeScript as possible. In doing so, we've designed an experience that is more approachable for JavaScript developers. User feedback shows that LDO was successful in building an approachable developer experience for manipulating linked data, but future work can be done to make the initial setup of the devtool more approachable. Given the ongoing use of LDO in real-world projects, it has promise to be a useful tool for RDF novices and experts alike.

Acknowledgements. This project was funded through the NGI0 Entrust Fund, a fund established by NLnet with financial support from the European Commission's Next Generation Internet program, under the aegis of DG Communications Networks, Content and Technology under grant agreement No 101069594.

Resource Availability Statement: Source code for LDO and its dependencies: ldo (https://purl. archive.org/o.team/ldo), ldo-cli (https://purl.archive.org/o.team/ldo-cli), shexj2 type-andcontext (https://purl.archive.org/o.team/shexj2typeandcontext), jsonld-dataset-proxy (https:// purl.archive.org/o.team/jsonld-dataset-proxy), o-dataset-pack (https://purl.archive.org/o.team/o-dataset-pack).

References

1. RDFJS. https://rdf.js.org/. Accessed 12 July 2022
2. ClownFace Documentation. https://zazuko.github.io/clownface/#/. Accessed 12 July 2022
3. Tripledoc Documentation. https://vincenttunru.gitlab.io/tripledoc/. Accessed 12 July 2022
4. rdflib source code. https://github.com/linkeddata/rdflib.js/. Accessed 12 July 2022
5. JSON-LD. https://json-ld.org/. Accessed 12 July 2022
6. Verborgh, R., Taelman, R.: LDflex: a read/write linked data abstraction for front-end web developers. In: Pan, J.Z., et al. (eds.) ISWC 2020. LNCS, vol. 12507, pp. 193–211. Springer, Cham (2020). https://doi.org/10.1007/978-3-030-62466-8_13
7. RDF Object source code. https://github.com/rubensworks/rdf-object.js#readme. Accessed 12 July 2022
8. SimpleRDF source code. https://github.com/simplerdf/simplerdf. Accessed 12 July 2022
9. RDF Tools source ode. https://github.com/knowledge-express/rdf-tools#readme. Accessed 12 July 2022
10. Shex Methods documentation. https://ludwigschubi.github.io/shex-methods/. Accessed 12 July 2022
11. Semantika source code. https://github.com/dharmax/semantika#readme. Accessed 1 July 2022
12. ts-rdf-mapper source code. https://github.com/artonio/ts-rdf-mapper. Accessed 12 July 2022
13. Fischer, L., Hanenberg, S.: An empirical investigation of the effects of type systems and code completion on API usability using TypeScript and JavaScript in MS visual studio. In: SIGPLAN 2015, vol. 51, pp. 154–167. ACM Digital Library (2016)

14. Endrikat, S., Hanenberg, S., Robbes, R., Stefik, A.: How do API documentation and static typing affect API usability? In: Proceedings of the 36th International Conference on Software Engineering (ICSE 2014), pp. 632–642. Association for Computing Machinery (2014)
15. ShEx – Shape Expressions. http://shex.io/. Accessed 02 May 2023
16. Shape Constraint Language (SHACL). https://www.w3.org/TR/shacl/. Accessed 02 May 2023
17. Rdfjs/N3.js. https://github.com/rdfjs/N3.js/. Accessed 02 May 2023
18. JSON-LD Streaming Parser. https://github.com/rubensworks/jsonld-streaming-parser.js. Accessed 02 May 2023/
19. RDF/JS: Dataset specification 1.0. https://rdf.js.org/dataset-spec/. Accessed 02 May 2023
20. Who says using RDF is hard? https://www.rubensworks.net/blog/2019/10/06/using-rdf-in-javascript/. Accessed 02 May 2023
21. Keet, C.M.: Open world assumption. In: Dubitzky, W., Wolkenhauer, O., Cho, K.H., Yokota, H. (eds.) Encyclopedia of Systems Biology, p. 1567. Springer, New York (2013). https://doi.org/10.1007/978-1-4419-9863-7_734
22. Graversen, K.B.: Method Chaining. https://web.archive.org/web/20110222112016/http://firstclassthoughts.co.uk/java/method_chaining.html. Accessed 02 May 2023
23. EMCAScript 2024 Language Specification. https://tc39.es/ecma262/multipage/reflection.html#sec-proxy-objects. Accessed 02 May 2023
24. JSON Schema. https://json-schema.org/. Accessed 02 May 2023
25. Morgan, J.: LDO source code. Zenodo (2023). https://doi.org/10.5281/zenodo.7909200
26. So(m)mer. https://github.com/bblfish/sommer. Accessed 15 July 2023
27. jenabean. https://code.google.com/archive/p/jenabean/. Accessed 15 July 2023
28. Owl2Java. https://github.com/piscisaureus/owl2java. Accessed 15 July 2023
29. JSON-LD Schema. https://github.com/mulesoft-labs/json-ld-schema. Accessed 15 July 2023
30. Solid. https://solidproject.org/. Accessed 15 July 2023

Text2KGBench: A Benchmark
for Ontology-Driven Knowledge Graph
Generation from Text

Nandana Mihindukulasooriya[1]([✉])(iD), Sanju Tiwari[2](iD), Carlos F. Enguix[2](iD),
and Kusum Lata[3](iD)

[1] IBM Research Europe, Dublin, Ireland
nandana@ibm.com
[2] Universidad Autonoma de Tamaulipas, Victoria, Mexico
[3] Sharda University, Greater Noida, India

Abstract. The recent advances in large language models (LLM) and
foundation models with emergent capabilities have been shown to
improve the performance of many NLP tasks. LLMs and Knowledge
Graphs (KG) can complement each other such that LLMs can be used
for KG construction or completion while existing KGs can be used for
different tasks such as making LLM outputs explainable or fact-checking
in Neuro-Symbolic manner. In this paper, we present *Text2KGBench*,
a benchmark to evaluate the capabilities of language models to generate KGs from natural language text guided by an ontology. Given an
input ontology and a set of sentences, the task is to extract facts from
the text while complying with the given ontology (concepts, relations,
domain/range constraints) and being faithful to the input sentences. We
provide two datasets (i) Wikidata-TekGen with 10 ontologies and 13,474
sentences and (ii) DBpedia-WebNLG with 19 ontologies and 4,860 sentences. We define seven evaluation metrics to measure fact extraction
performance, ontology conformance, and hallucinations by LLMs. Furthermore, we provide results for two baseline models, Vicuna-13B and
Alpaca-LoRA-13B using automatic prompt generation from test cases.
The baseline results show that there is room for improvement using both
Semantic Web and Natural Language Processing techniques.

Resource Type: Evaluation Benchmark
Source Repo: https://github.com/cenguix/Text2KGBench
DOI: https://doi.org/10.5281/zenodo.7916716
License: Creative Commons Attribution (CC BY 4.0)

Keywords: Benchmark · Relation Extraction · Knowledge Graph ·
Knowledge Graph Generation · Large Language Models

1 Introduction

Knowledge Graphs (KG) are becoming popular in both industry and academia due
to their useful applications in a wide range of tasks such as question answering, recommendations, semantic search, and advanced analytics with explainability [16].

© The Author(s), under exclusive license to Springer Nature Switzerland AG 2023
T. R. Payne et al. (Eds.): ISWC 2023, LNCS 14266, pp. 247–265, 2023.
https://doi.org/10.1007/978-3-031-47243-5_14

A KG can be generated using mappings such as RDB2RDF [38] if the source is relational data or semi-structured using RML [11]. Crowdsourcing can be used to build them manually as in Wikidata [48]. However, there are cases where the data is in unstructured format in text documents and crowd-sourcing is not an option (for example, internal documents). One solution in such cases is to construct knowledge graphs using Natural Language Processing (NLP) techniques such as Named Entity Recognition (NER), Relation Extraction, Open Information Extraction, Entity Linking, and Relation Linking. There is a growing interest in the Semantic Web community to explore such approaches as seen from the workshops such as Text2KG [43,44] and NLP4KGC [46].

The recent advances in large language models (LLM) and foundation models with emergent capabilities have been shown to improve the performance in many NLP tasks [6]. KGs and LLMs can complement each other in both directions; on the one hand, LLMs can be helpful in constructing KGs and on the other hand KGs can be used to validate LLM outputs or make them explainable. Approaches such as Neuro-Symbolic AI [15] will allow using KGs and LLMs jointly. In order to foment research in this direction, the establishment of evaluation benchmarks is necessary. In this context, *Text2KGBench* is a benchmark for measuring the capabilities of LLMs for generating KGs from text conforming to a given ontology. In this version, we are not evaluating the ability to process or generate RDF/OWL representations but rather the ability of extracting facts using correct relations.

There are several manners LLMs can be adapted to this task, including fine tuning [17] (also known as model tuning), updating all model parameters, Prompt tuning [24] or Prefix-Tuning [26] by keeping the model parameters frozen and only prefixing some tunable tokens to the input text and prompt design where the model is used as it is, but the prompt or the input to the model is designed to provide a few examples of the task [6]. Each of these approaches has their pros and cons with respect to the performance, computation resources, training time, domain adaption and training data required. Our benchmark provides training data that can be used in any of those approaches.

In-context learning [31,51] with prompt design is about teaching a model to perform a new task only by providing a few demonstrations of input-output pairs at inference time. Instruction fine-tuning using approaches such as Instruct-GPT [34], Reinforcement Learning from Human Feedback (RLHF) [9,41] significantly improves the models capabilities to follow a broad range of written instructions.

A vast number of LLMs have been released in recent months [52], especially in the GPT family of models such as GPT-3 [6], ChatGPT, LLaMA [45], BLOOM [39], PaLM [8], and Bard. Such models can be easily adapted for KG generation from text with a prompt design containing instructions and contextual information.

The main contributions of this paper are:

- We propose a novel benchmark *Text2KGBench* by extending the relation extraction by guiding it with ontology and instructions. We provide two datasets, (a) Wikidata-TekGen with 10 ontologies and 13,474 sentences aligned to triples and (b) DBpedia-WebNLG with 19 ontologies and 4,860 sentences aligned to triples by reusing TekGen [1] and WebNLG [13] corpora. We define seven metrics for measuring the accuracy of fact extraction, ontology conformance and detecting hallucinations and provide evaluation scripts.

– We provide results for two baselines using open-source LLMs, including Vicuna-13B [7] and Alpaca-LoRA-13B [19,42] with in-context learning. We also provide a baseline automatic prompt generator from ontologies and approach finding best demonstration examples with sentence similarity using SBERT T5-XXL model [33,36]. We provide all generated prompts, similarities, and LLM responses for further analysis.

The rest of the paper is organized as follows. Section 2 introduces the task of the benchmark, Sect. 3 describes how the benchmark was created, Sect. 4 defines the evaluation metrics and Sect. 5 presents the baselines and evaluation results. After related work in Sect. 6, the paper concludes with some final remarks and future work in Sect. 7.

2   Task Description

This section introduces the task of *Text2KGBench*. With the recent advancements of LLMs, we envision that LLMs can be used to generate KGs guided by ontologies as illustrated in Fig. 1. Given an ontology and text corpora, the goal is to construct prompts to instruct the model to extract facts relevant to the ontology. Such extracted facts can be further validated and post-processed to create a knowledge graph.

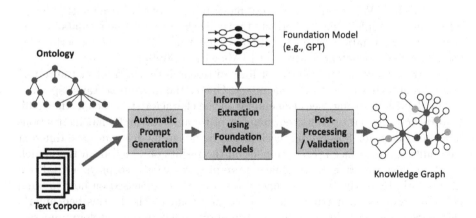

Fig. 1. Generating knowledge graphs from text guided by ontologies

In the context of the *Text2KGBench*, we define the task as a fact extraction task guided by an ontology. The proposed task is closely related to the relation extraction and relation classification tasks in literature but with an explicit ontology definition given as input. There are three main inputs to the task:

Ontology: The ontology defines the concepts of interest, a set of defined relations with their canonical names, domain and range constraints for the relations. This can be further extended with other ontological axioms to guide models.

Text Corpus: The text corpus contains the set of natural language sentences that contains facts that can be expressed using the aforementioned ontology.

Examples: Demonstrative examples or training data contains pairs of sentences and the facts extracted from them complying with the ontology.

Given these inputs, a system should be able to generate facts adhering to a set of expectations. First, the system should use the ontology and demonstrative examples as guidance on which facts to extract and which relations to be used in the output. It should follow the canonical relation names and the example output format. In the evaluation, we measure this aspect using ontology compliance metrics. Second, the system should be faithful to the input sentence. This means the system should consider only the facts mentioned in the sentence as the truth (irrespective of the knowledge it may have from pre-training). It should not include additional information that is not directly or indirectly stated or implied by the sentence. This aspect is measured by the fact extraction accuracy metrics. Finally, the system should not hallucinate i.e. it should not introduce new or fake entities/relations not mentioned in the sentence and the ontology. This aspect is measured by the hallucination metrics. Section 4 provides details of evaluation metrics.

In this version of *Text2KGBench*, we are not evaluating a system's ability to process RDF/OWL syntax or a deep understanding of OWL semantics. Thus, we are using simpler language-oriented verbalizations and triple formats for presenting the information to an LLM. Figure 2 illustrates an example of performing the task using in-context learning of LLMs with a prompt.

There are several components or lines of research that can affect the results of a system tested under this benchmark. One of the most important aspects is the model (LLM) being used. Depending on the characteristics such as the architecture, training data being used, number of parameters, and what instructions have been used for fine-tuning, each of the language models can have different capabilities, and it has a direct impact on the results obtained from the model.

Prompt engineering or automatic prompt generation also plays a vital role in this task. Recently, there is a line of research that is focused on how to build efficient prompts for getting expected outputs from LLMs. In this benchmark, the participants can design different prompts guided by an ontology and reasoning techniques can be used to develop the most efficient prompts. Related to prompt generation, another important aspect is how to find the most relevant or helpful demonstration example from training data given a test case. This can be done using sentence similarity metrics or utilizing more advanced semantic clues from the ontology.

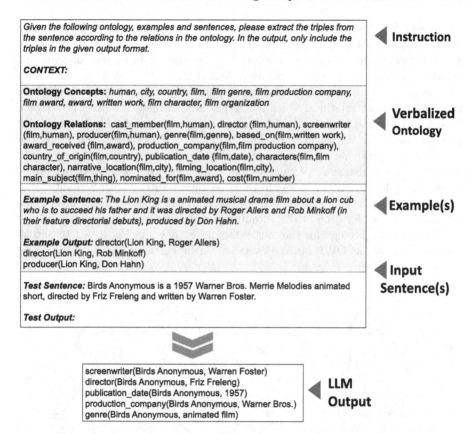

Given the following ontology, examples and sentences, please extract the triples from the sentence according to the relations in the ontology. In the output, only include the triples in the given output format. ◀ **Instruction**

CONTEXT:

Ontology Concepts: *human, city, country, film, film genre, film production company, film award, award, written work, film character, film organization*

Ontology Relations: *cast_member(film,human), director (film,human), screenwriter (film,human), producer(film,human), genre(film,genre), based_on(film,written work), award_received (film,award), production_company(film,film production company), country_of_origin(film,country), publication_date (film,date), characters(film,film character), narrative_location(film,city), filming_location(film,city), main_subject(film,thing), nominated_for(film,award), cost(film,number)* ◀ **Verbalized Ontology**

Example Sentence: *The Lion King is a animated musical drama film about a lion cub who is to succeed his father and it was directed by Roger Allers and Rob Minkoff (in their feature directorial debuts), produced by Don Hahn.* ◀ **Example(s)**

Example Output: director(Lion King, Roger Allers)
director(Lion King, Rob Minkoff)
producer(Lion King, Don Hahn)

Test Sentence: Birds Anonymous is a 1957 Warner Bros. Merrie Melodies animated short, directed by Friz Freleng and written by Warren Foster. ◀ **Input Sentence(s)**

Test Output:

screenwriter(Birds Anonymous, Warren Foster)
director(Birds Anonymous, Friz Freleng)
publication_date(Birds Anonymous, 1957)
production_company(Birds Anonymous, Warner Bros.)
genre(Birds Anonymous, animated film) ◀ **LLM Output**

Fig. 2. An example prompt for an instruction fine-tuned LLM and the generated output from the LLM model.

Post-processing and validation are also crucial for extracting the correct triples and cleaning them by removing implausible triples. Initial extraction can be done using pattern-matching techniques such as using regex. Validation of the generated triples is another open research area which can use linguistic approaches to detect hallucinations and reasoning-based approaches to validate that the generated triples are consistent with the ontology.

3 Benchmark Generation

Text2KGBench consists of two datasets: *wikidata-tekgen* and *dbpedia-webnlg*. As discussed above, each of those has a set of ontologies and corpora of text where sentences are aligned with triples according to the given ontology.

3.1 Wikidata-TekGen Dataset

This dataset is created using sentence alignments provided by TekGen corpus.

Ontology Selection. As the first step of building the dataset, we have created 10 small ontologies by reusing the concepts and relations described in Wikidata. We selected a domain, such as movies or sports and explored the concepts and relations relevant to the given domain in Wikidata. With that, a set of concepts for the domain are identified, and a sample of their instances is checked for the most frequent relations. Once a relation is identified, it's property page is used to understand the usage, and domain range constraints. For example, the property page[1] for the relation "director (P57)" describes subject and value-type constraints. Iteratively, more concepts are added to the ontology based on the domain/range constraints of the selected relations. This process is performed manually and each ontology was formulated by an author with Semantic Web expertise and reviewed by two other experts. Table 1 shows the concept and relation statistics for each of the 10 ontologies that we generated.

An example ontology for the music domain is shown in Fig. 3. All 10 ontologies are available as OWL ontologies serialized in Turtle and in a compact json format in the repo[2].

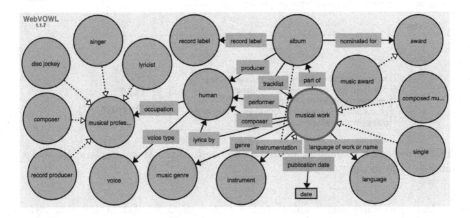

Fig. 3. An illustration of the music ontology with concepts and relations selected from Wikidata.

Triple Generation and Alignment with Sentences. Given an ontology from the previous step, a parameterized SPARQL query[3] is used to generate a set of K triples for each of the relations. The SPARQL query guaranteed that the triples confirmed the domain and range restrictions of each ontology. For example, for "director" relation, we would get triples such as director("Lion King","Roger Allers").

---

[1] https://www.wikidata.org/wiki/Property:P57.

[2] https://github.com/cenguix/Text2KGBench/tree/main/data/wikidata_tekgen/ontologies.

[3] https://github.com/cenguix/Text2KGBench/tree/main/src/benchmark.

In this dataset, we reused the TekGen corpus [1] which provides Wikidata triples aligned with corresponding sentences from Wikipedia. The TekGen corpus is generated using distant supervision and it has 16 M aligned triple-sentences covering 663 Wikidata relations. For each triple we got from the previous step, we analyzed the TekGen corpus to get an aligned sentence when available. For instance, the triple in the previous sentence will be aligned to a sentence such as "The Lion King is an animated musical drama film directed by Roger Allers and Rob Minkoff, produced by Don Hahn.". Once a sentence is found, we check all the other relations associated with the sentence in the TekGen corpus and include them also if they are part of our ontology. For example, in this sentence, director ("Lion King", "Rob Minkoff") and producer("Lion King", "Don Hahn") will also be included in the dataset.

Once we complete this process for all 10 ontologies, we generated 13,474 sentence - triple(s) alignments and they are divided into train, validation and test sets.

Manual Validations and Cleaning. Because the TekGen corpus is generated using distant supervision, it can have noise and some incorrect alignments. In order to evaluate models with a more precise set of test cases, we have manually analyzed the test sentences and selected a smaller subset of more accurately aligned sentences for each ontology. For this exercise, the annotators looked at the triple and aligned sentence in the gold standard and selected sentences that a human can easily extract the triple such that the fact is explicitly mentioned in the text. For example, "The film was also nominated for Academy Award for Best Picture." is a noisy sentence to extract the triple "nominated for(Working Girl, Academy Award for Best Picture) as it is impossible for a model to resolve coreference to understand what term "the film" is referring to, only with this sentence as input. Another example, the sentence "Welcome to Eltingville was written by Dorkin and Chuck Sheetz" is wrongly aligned with the triple director("Welcome to Eltingville", "Chuck Sheetz") because the entities co-occur in the sentence and Chuck Sheetz is both the director and the writer. For a sample of test data, the authors removed such alignments and created another test set with 939 verified sentence-triple alignments. The systems can use both the larger test set and this smaller high-quality test set for their evaluations.

Unseen Sentence Generation. One of the caveats of this benchmark is that the language models under test might have already seen these sentences or even the alignments in some form. Then it can be argued that they might have memorized some of these relations. One important aspect to evaluate is if the model performance will get affected if we test the model with unseen sentences that are not part of Wikipedia and not seen during the pre-training. For that, we invent new sentences with facts that the annotators come up with. For example, a sentence such as "John Doe starred in the movie The Fake Movie released in 2025". With this exercise, the authors generated 174 unseen sentences roughly two sentences per each relation in each ontology. Furthermore, this unseen set of sentences can be used to check how faithful the model is to the given sentence when generating the triples.

Table 1. Statistics related to the two datasets including the list of ontologies, number of types and relations in each ontology, and number of sentences aligned.

wikidata-tekgen				dbpedia-webnlg							
Ontology	Types	Rels.	Sents.	Ontology	Types	Rels	Sents.	Ontology	Types	Rels	Sents.
Movie	12	15	2800	University	15	46	156	Transport	20	68	314
Music	13	13	2243	Music	15	35	290	Monument	14	26	92
Sport	15	11	1693	Airport	14	39	306	Food	12	24	398
Book	20	12	1810	Building	14	38	275	Written Work	10	44	322
Military	13	9	750	Athlete	17	37	293	Sports Team	14	24	235
Computer	15	12	743	Politician	19	40	319	City	11	23	348
Space	15	7	666	Company	10	28	153	Artist	20	39	386
Politics	13	9	695	Celestial	8	27	194	Scientist	15	47	259
Nature	14	13	1558	Astronaut	16	38	154	Film	18	44	264
Culture	15	8	516	Comics	10	18	102				
Total			13,474	Total							4,860

3.2 DBpedia-WebNLG Dataset

The DBpedia-WebNLG dataset is created reusing the alignments in the WebNLG corpus.

Ontology Selection. Similar to the previous dataset, the first step is to create a set of ontologies. WebNLG consists of 19 categories and we created an ontology for each category. First, we analysed the triples in each category to extract the relations in each category and defined the concepts based on the domain and range constraints of those relations. The statistics for the resulting 19 ontologies are shown in Table 1.

Triple Generation and Alignment with Sentences. We have parsed the WebNLG 3.0 English dataset and collected the sentences in one of the splits (WebNLG 3triples). When creating train and test sets, we made sure that the same fact would not appear in both train and test sets. Because the alignments (verbalizations) are verified by crowdsourcing in WebNLG, there was no need for us to create a manually validated set. We generated 4,860 sentence - triple(s) alignments using WebNLG data and divided into train and test splits.

The train/val/test splits for both benchmarks were done as stratified randomized folds aiming to preserve the relation distributions as much as possible using scikit-learn. The rationale for the splits was to provide training data (examples for in-context learning or fine-tuning models) for future systems that will use the benchmark and validation data (for optimizing hyperparameters).

4   Evaluation Metrics

In this section, we present the set of evaluation metrics we use in *Text2KGBench* to measure the performance of systems for generating facts from the text. Evaluation metrics aim to validate three aspects: (i) extracted facts are accurate according to the given ontology, (ii) extracted facts conform to the given ontology, and (iii) the output doesn't include any hallucinations.

Given a prompt similar to Fig. 2, the LLM will produce a textual output that can be parsed into a set of triples, which we call LLM output triples. The expected output for each test sentence is in the ground truth files.

Fact Extraction Accuracy: This is measured using Precision (P), Recall (R), and F1 scores by comparing LLM output triples to the ground truth triples. P is calculated by dividing the number of correct LLM triples (which are part of the ground truth) by the number of LLM triples. R is calculated by dividing the number of correct LLM triples by the number of ground truth triples. F1 is calculated as the harmonic mean of the P and R. If the LLM output is empty, P, R, and F1 are set to 0. Because the set of triples are not exhaustive for a given sentence, to avoid false negatives, we follow a locally closed approach by only considering the relations that are part of the ground truth. For P, R, F1, higher numbers represent better performance.

Ontology Conformance: This is measured using the Ontology Conformance (OC) metric which is calculated as the percentage of LLM output triples conforming to the input ontology, i.e., ontology conforming LLM output triples divided by total LLM output triples. In this version, a triple is considered to be conforming to the ontology if the relation is one of the canonical relations listed in the ontology. This can be further extended to validate other restrictions such as domain, range or other ontological axioms.

Hallucinations: Hallucination is defined as the generated content that is nonsensical or unfaithful to the provided source content [21]. We calculate three hallucination metrics, subject hallucination (SH), relation hallucination (RH), and object hallucination (OH). These are calculated by comparing the generated triple to the test sentence and the ontology. For each triple, SH and OH check if the subject and object are present in either the sentence or the ontology concepts, and RH checks if the relation is present in the ontology relations. For SH and OH, we use stemming to account for inflected forms with morphological variations such as "America", "American", "Americans", etc. Each term in the subject or object and test sentence is stemmed before checking if the subject or object is present as a substring in the test sentence and/or ontology concepts. For RH, relations are matched using exact matches. In this version, RH and OC are inversely related *i.e.* 1 - OC equals to RH.

5   Baselines and Evaluation Results

In this section, we present baseline LLM models, baselines for automatic prompt generation and the evaluation results for baseline models for the two datasets of *Text2KGBench* we described in Sect. 3.

5.1   Baseline LLM Models

Vicuna-13B. Vicuna-13B [7] is an open-source LLM that fine-tunes a base LLaMA model with 70K user-shared conversations from ShareGPT. We obtained the LlaMA 13B LLM model, checkpoints, and tokenizer, through the Pyllama Github repository[4] and applied Vicuna weights from FastChat[5] as delta weights. Vicuna-13B claims 90% performance of OpenAI ChatGPT and Google Bard [56] where the authors have used a metric "Relative Response Quality" using strong LLM (GPT4) as judges to evaluate the model on open-ended questions.

Alpaca-LoRA-13B. Alpaca-LoRA[6] is a model that fine-tuned a base LLaMA model with the same 52K instructions of Alpaca model that is generated using self-instruct [50] with the OpenAI's *text-davinci-003* model. Alpaca-LoRA is fine-tuned using Low-Rank Adaptation [19] allows reducing the number of trainable parameters by a significant order by freezing the pre-trained model weights and injecting trainable rank decomposition matrices to each transformer layer.

5.2   Automatic Prompt Generation

Both our LLM models are GPT-style decoder-only models that are instruction fine-tuned. They can be used for downstream tasks by providing a prompt with an instruction. In this section, we present the steps involved in automatically creating prompts for each test sentence.

Our baseline prompt consists of our main parts: (a) Instruction, (b) Ontology description, (c) Demonstrative examples, and (d) Test sentence as illustrated in Fig. 2.

Instruction. This is a fixed instruction that we used for all test cases across the ontologies. We used the following phrase "Given the following ontology and sentences, please extract the triples from the sentence according to the relations in the ontology. In the output, only include the triples in the given output format." as the instruction. We describe the task as well as request the model to be less verbose and output only the triples in the given format.

Ontology Description. This part of the prompt provides a description of the ontology to the model as context. Each test case in our benchmark is associated with an ontology. This part of the prompts verbalizes the ontology by listing the set of concepts, and a set of relations with their domain and range constraints given by the ontology. For example, for the test case in the movie ontology, concepts will be a list such as a film, film genre, genre, film production company, film award, human etc. and the relations will be a list such as director(film, human), cast_member(film, human), award_received(film, award), genre(film, genre), production_company(film, film production company), etc. Throughout

---

[4] https://github.com/juncongmoo/pyllama.
[5] https://github.com/lm-sys/FastChat.
[6] https://github.com/tloen/alpaca-lora.

the prompt, we use the *relation(subject, object)* notation for representing relations and expect the model to follow the notation in the output.

Demonstrative Examples. This part of the prompt is used to provide the LLM with an example to show an input sentence and the expected output. LLMs are capable of In-Context Learning where they learn the task and output format from the examples provided in the prompt. The examples are taken from the training data for each of the datasets based on their similarity to the test sentence. We have used sentence similarities using Sentence Transformers (SBERT) [36] with the T5-XXL model [33]. For instance, given a test sentence such as "Super Capers, a film written by Ray Griggs, is 98 min long.", it can find the most similar sentence in training data, "English Without Tears, written by Terence Rattigan, runs 89 min." with it's aligned triples. Example output follows the same relation notation.

Test Sentence. Finally, the prompt contains the test sentence from which we want to extract the facts complying with the ontology. Similar to the example, the prompt ends with a "Test Output:"where the model is expected to generate the facts in the sentence following the same format as in the example sentence.

5.3   Evaluation Results

We run inferences for automatically generated prompts for both *Wikidata-TekGen* and *DBpedia-WebNLG* corpora and calculate the metrics discussed in Sect. 4: Precision (P), Recall (R), F1, Ontology Conformance (OC), Subject/Relation/Object Hallucinations (SH/RH/OH). Table 2 illustrates the average values across all ontologies in a given dataset. As discussed in Sect. 3, three different settings in *Wikidata-TekGen* dataset: all test cases (All), manually validated and cleaned subset (selected), and unseen sentences (Unseen) which annotated in the "Variant" column.

Each row in Table 2 is an aggregation of results from test cases across multiple ontologies (10 for Wikidata-TekGen and 19 for DBpedia-WebNLG) and Table 3 shows the results at each individual ontology level for the first row of Table 2, *i.e.*, Wikidata-TekGen - Vicuna - All. For brevity, ontology-level results for other rows are included in the project Wiki[7].

From the results, some initial observations from Table 2 on the different datasets and LLM models:

– Precision, Recall and F1 score have low intermediate values
– Ontology Conformance is pretty high in almost all entries
– Subject, Relation, Object Hallucination is relatively low

These results should be further analyzed to understand the different capbalities and limitations of LLMs in KG generation from text. An in-depth analysis of the results is out of scope of this paper due to space limitations and we expect the system papers using the benchmark to provide insights and conclusions on

---

[7] https://github.com/cenguix/Text2KGBench/wiki.

Table 2. This table summarizes average evaluation metrics for all ontologies in Wikidata-TekGen and the DBpedia-WebNLG datasets.

Dataset	Model	Variant[a]	Fact Extraction			OC	Hallucinations		
			P	R	F1		SH	RH	OH
Wikidata-TekGen	Vicuna	All	0.38	0.34	0.35	0.83	0.17	0.17	0.17
		Selected	0.42	0.39	0.38	0.84	0.11	0.16	0.14
		Unseen	0.32	0.32	0.32	0.86	0.07	0.14	0.14
	Alapaca LoRA	All	0.32	0.26	0.27	0.87	0.18	0.13	0.17
		Selected	0.33	0.27	0.28	0.87	0.12	0.13	0.17
		Unseen	0.22	0.22	0.22	0.86	0.09	0.14	0.26
DBpedia-WebNLG	Vicuna		0.34	0.27	0.30	0.93	0.12	0.07	0.28
	Alpaca-LoRA		0.32	0.23	0.25	0.91	0.16	0.09	0.38

[a]Refer to Sect. 3 for details.

Table 3. Results for Vicuna LLM All Test Cases. Numbers in bold identify the best results for each metric. Numbers underlined identify worst results.

Ontology	Fact Extraction			OC	Hallucinations		
	P	R	F1		SH	RH	OH
1. Movie Ontology	0.33	<u>0.23</u>	0.25	0.89	<u>0.26</u>	0.11	<u>0.26</u>
2. Music Ontology	0.42	0.28	0.32	0.94	0.16	**0.06**	0.22
3. Sport Ontology	0.57	0.52	0.52	0.85	0.22	0.15	0.13
4. Book Ontology	0.31	0.25	0.26	0.92	0.16	0.08	0.23
5. Military Ontology	<u>0.24</u>	0.25	<u>0.24</u>	0.8	0.19	0.2	<u>0.26</u>
6. Computer Ontology	0.38	0.35	0.35	0.85	0.15	0.15	0.11
7. Space Ontology	**0.68**	**0.67**	**0.66**	0.93	0.15	0.07	**0.08**
8. Politics Ontology	0.34	0.32	0.33	0.92	0.17	0.08	0.15
9. Nature Ontology	0.25	0.27	0.25	0.68	**0.1**	0.32	0.14
10 Culture Ontology	0.31	0.32	0.31	<u>0.59</u>	0.15	<u>0.41</u>	0.12
Ontologies Average	0.38	0.34	0.35	0.83	0.17	0.17	0.17

this aspect. As we have used LLM models as is without any fine-tuning, prompt tuning or semantic validation, we believe there is a large room for improvements.

5.4   Error Analysis

We have performed an initial error analysis to understand the errors made by the models and Table 4 shows some examples for different types of errors. In addition, we noticed that there are some false positives in hallucination due to LLMs expanding acronyms, for example, the sentence can have "NATO" where the model generates "North Atlantic Treaty Organization" as a subject. We plan to consider acronyms, aliases, etc. in hallucination calculations in the future.

Table 4. Examples of errors from the Vicuna13B model with Wikidata-TekGen

Sentence	Triple	Error Type
Aparajito won 11 international awards, including the Golden Lion and Critics Award at the Venice Film Festival, becoming the first ever film to win both.	award_received(Aparajito, Venice Film Festival)	An incorrect fact extracted. The model mistook the film festival for an award.
The Gallopin Gaucho was a second attempt at success by co-directors Walt Disney and Ub Iwerks.	directed(The Gallopin Gaucho,Walt Disney)	Ontology conformance error. The canonical relation is the director.
American Born Chinese is a graphic novel by Gene Luen Yang.	narrative_location(American Born Chinese, San Francisco)	Object hallucination. Neither the object nor the relation is mentioned in the text.
Schreck was a founding member of the Sturmabteilung.	member_of_political_party (Hermann Goring, Sturmabteilung)	Subject hallucination. Hermann Goring is not mentioned in the text.

6 Related Work

The primary aim of the knowledge graph generation task is to extract structured information from heterogeneous sources. This section will explore the Relation Extraction Benchmarks, Foundation Models for Knowledge Graph Generation and Semi-Automatic/Automatic Knowledge Graph Completion (KBC)-KG-triple generation. Relation extraction has made substantial use of the following datasets such as the New York Times (NYT)/NYT-FB dataset [32] [37] [30], TAC Relation Extraction Dataset (TACRED) [55], Large-Scale Document-Level Relation Extraction Dataset(DocRED) [53], The WEB-NLG dataset [13], FewRel dataset [14], FewRel 2.0 [12]. The relation extraction benchmarks that exist for the scientific domain are SciERC dataset [29] and SCIREX [20]. The SCIREX dataset is intended to detect both binary and n-ary relations between entities and concepts, while the SciERC dataset is intended to identify binary relations between entities in scientific papers. There are few datasets that cover multiple languages, such as Multilingual LAMA (Language Model Analysis) dataset [22], which cover 53 languages, MiLER SMiLER(Samsung Multi-Lingual Entity and Relation Extraction dataset [40] covers 14 languages, DiS-ReX [4] covers 4 languages. Through entity linking, Knowledge-Enhanced Relation Extraction Dataset (KERED) [27] gives knowledge context for entities and annotates each sentence with a relational fact. This dataset consists of NYT10m, Wikidata [48] (Wiki80 and Wiki20m).

Relation extraction benchmark datasets can be used to evaluate the performance of foundation models. A survey paper [52] has explored the history of these foundation models and summarizes different tasks. Foundation models are generally categorized into two categories: Encoder-only or Encoder-Decoder (BERT style) and Decoder-only (GPT style) [52]. BERT-style models are still challenging as they are under development and mostly available as open-source. They are considered as Mask Language Models that include RoBERTa [28], BERT [10], and T5 [35]. Decoder-only (GPT style) models (GPT-3 [6], PaLM [8], OPT [54] and BLOOM [39]) generally need finetuning on datasets of the particular downstream task. Brown et al. [6] have trained GPT-3 (an autoregressive language model) with 175 billion parameters and also tested its performance with the few-shot setting. Jeremy and Sebastian [18] have proposed an effective transfer learning method, Universal Language Model Fine-tuning (ULMFiT), for any NLP task. Brian et al. [25] explores the prompt tuning to learn soft prompts for adapting language models. Soft prompts are learned by back propagation, while GPT-3 uses discrete text prompts [49].

Vicuna [7] is an open-source chatbot and it is trained by fine-tuning LLaMA. It is shown by evaluation that Vicuna has performed more than 90% quality of Google Bard and OpenAI ChatGPT compared to other models like LLaMA and Alpaca. Alpaca [42] has been introduced as a strong, replicable instruction-following model. It is fine-tuned from the LLaMA 7B model on 52K instruction-following demonstrations.

KBC and KG-triple generation have become a hot research field with the synergy/integration with LLMs. The possibilities are limitless regarding the automatic generation of new triples via the use of LLMs and the only *"Achilles Heel"* consists of computer resources required for integrating both systems. In [5] is presented a system that generates automatically triples from natural language and code completion tasks. In this case, it is presented as input code excerpts denoting class and function definitions. They consider the use of neural networks present in pre-trained LLM's as *"black boxes"*. In [2] is presented a system that uses a GPT3 LLM with the aim of building a knowledge base semi-automatically via a multi-step process combining customized prompting techniques for predicting missing objects in triples where subjects and relations are given. In [23], the authors perform a qualitative study of large language models using ChatGPT for various tasks including KG population, KG completion, triple or fact verification and identify some challenges such as hallucination, fairness and bias, and high computational cost. And finally, we include reference [47] in this section where it is presented a benchmark dataset for assessing Knowledge Base Completion (KBC) potential for language models (LM).

7 Conclusion and Future Work

In this paper, we presented *Text2KGBench*, a benchmark for evaluating capabilities of LLMs for extracting facts from a text corpora guided by an ontology.

Limitations. In this version, we have only considered smaller-sized ontologies by design to cater for the token size limitations of LLMs. Nevertheless, in practice, there are quite larger ontologies in domains such as medicine. In future versions, we plan to include cases with much larger ontologies which will require systems to automatically select the portion of the ontology or the set of axioms that are relevant to the given input text. In addition, there is research on extending the capabilities of LLMs to handle longer contexts such as Unlimiformer [3]. Furthermore, in this version, we have separated the OWL/RDF representations of KGs by verbalizing ontologies and triples. In future versions, we will test LLMs on handing these representations directly without pre/post-processing.

Future Work. One important aspect when it comes to foundation models is bias and fairness. In future work, we would like to further extend our benchmark considering different bias variables such as gender, race/ethnicity, geographic location, etc. and create contrastive test cases to verify the fairness of LLMs when generating Knowledge Graphs from text. In other words, we would like to systematically evaluate if this process performs better for a certain subgroup based on their gender, demographics, or socioeconomic status. Furthermore, we will plan to measure more reasoning capabilities when performing fact extraction and KG generation. We plan to extend the benchmark with a dataset that requires more semantic reasoning to perform the task. In the Text2KGBench benchmark we have currently focused on available open-source LLM models. In addition, we plan to compare both LLM base-lines, Vicuna-13B and Alpaca-Lora-13B, and any emerging new open-source LLMs to the commercial OpenAI's ChatGPT[8] and GPT-4[9] LLMs.

Impact: With the popularity of GPT-like LLMs, there is a big enthusiasm for using such models jointly with KGs and for constructing KGs. Authors firmly believe that ontology-driven KG construction from text leveraging LLMs will be of interest to the Semantic Web community. To the best of our knowledge, *Text2KG* is the first benchmark for this task. We provide all the resources necessary for using and further extending the benchmark with improvements. Authors anticipate that this will inspire research in this direction by providing a way to measure and compare the performance of different approaches.

Reusability and Sustainability: There are two ongoing workshops related to KG generation from text, Text2KG[10] at ESWC and NLP4KGC[11] at the Web Conference. Furthermore, there is a proposed special issue[12] on this theme at Semantic Web journal. This will be a useful resource for evaluating approaches presented in those venues. As the authors are also co-organizers of these events, they plan

---

[8] https://openai.com/blog/chatgpt.

[9] https://openai.com/gpt-4.

[10] https://aiisc.ai/text2kg2023/.

[11] https://sites.google.com/view/nlp4kg/.

[12] https://www.semantic-web-journal.net/blog/special-issue-knowledge-graph-generation-text.

to maintain and provide improved future versions of the data in collaboration with those workshops. It's also important to note that the authors and organizations of the aforementioned workshops are not from a single organization but distributed across multiple organizations and making the proposed resource not dependent on a single organization. The code used to generate the resource is available making it possible for anyone to reproduce, improve or create derived work from it.

Resource Availability Statement: Text2KGBench dataset is available from zenodo[13], and the code that is used to generate the benchmark, evaluation scripts, baselines, LLM outputs, evaluation results are available from Github[14]. Raw datasets we used are TekGen corpus[15] and WebNLG corpus[16]. The LLM models we used are LLaMA[17] to derive Vicuna-13B[18] and Alpaca-LoRA-13B[19].For sentence similarity we used SBERT[20] with T5-XXL model[21].

References

1. Agarwal, O., Ge, H., Shakeri, S., Al-Rfou, R.: Knowledge graph based synthetic corpus generation for knowledge-enhanced language model pre-training. In: Proceedings of the 2021 Conference of the North American Chapter of the Association for Computational Linguistics: Human Language Technologies, pp. 3554–3565. Association for Computational Linguistics, Online (2021). https://doi.org/10.18653/v1/2021.naacl-main.278. https://aclanthology.org/2021.naacl-main.278
2. Alivanistos, D., Santamaría, S.B., Cochez, M., Kalo, J.C., van Krieken, E., Thanapalasingam, T.: Prompting as probing: using language models for knowledge base construction. arXiv preprint arXiv:2208.11057 (2022)
3. Bertsch, A., Alon, U., Neubig, G., Gormley, M.R.: Unlimiformer: long-range transformers with unlimited length input (2023)
4. Bhartiya, A., Badola, K., et al.: Dis-rex: a multilingual dataset for distantly supervised relation extraction. In: Proceedings of the 60th Annual Meeting of the Association for Computational Linguistics (Volume 2: Short Papers), pp. 849–863 (2022)
5. Bi, Z., et al.: Codekgc: code language model for generative knowledge graph construction. arXiv preprint arXiv:2304.09048 (2023)
6. Brown, T., et al.: Language models are few-shot learners. Adv. Neural. Inf. Process. Syst. **33**, 1877–1901 (2020)
7. Chiang, W.L., et al.: Vicuna: an open-source chatbot impressing GPT-4 with 90%* ChatGPT quality (2023). https://vicuna.lmsys.org

---

[13] https://zenodo.org/record/7916716#.ZFrX5ezML0r.
[14] https://github.com/cenguix/Text2KGBench.
[15] https://paperswithcode.com/dataset/tekgen.
[16] https://gitlab.com/shimorina/webnlg-dataset/-/tree/master/release_v3.0/en.
[17] https://github.com/juncongmoo/pyllama.
[18] https://github.com/lm-sys/FastChat.
[19] https://github.com/tloen/alpaca-lora.
[20] https://www.sbert.net/.
[21] https://huggingface.co/sentence-transformers/gtr-t5-xxl.

8. Chowdhery, A., et al.: Palm: scaling language modeling with pathways. arXiv preprint arXiv:2204.02311 (2022)

9. Christiano, P.F., Leike, J., Brown, T., Martic, M., Legg, S., Amodei, D.: Deep reinforcement learning from human preferences. In: Advances in Neural Information Processing Systems, vol. 30 (2017)

10. Devlin, J., Chang, M.W., Lee, K., Toutanova, K.: Bert: pre-training of deep bidirectional transformers for language understanding. arXiv preprint arXiv:1810.04805 (2018)

11. Dimou, A., Vander Sande, M., Colpaert, P., Verborgh, R., Mannens, E., Van de Walle, R.: RML: a generic language for integrated RDF mappings of heterogeneous data. Ldow **1184** (2014)

12. Gao, T., et al.: Fewrel 2.0: towards more challenging few-shot relation classification. In: Proceedings of the 2019 Conference on Empirical Methods in Natural Language Processing and the 9th International Joint Conference on Natural Language Processing (EMNLP-IJCNLP), pp. 6250–6255 (2019)

13. Gardent, C., Shimorina, A., Narayan, S., Perez-Beltrachini, L.: Creating training corpora for NLG micro-planners. In: Proceedings of the 55th Annual Meeting of the Association for Computational Linguistics (Volume 1: Long Papers), pp. 179–188. Association for Computational Linguistics (2017). https://doi.org/10.18653/v1/P17-1017. http://www.aclweb.org/anthology/P17-1017

14. Han, X., et al.: Fewrel: a large-scale supervised few-shot relation classification dataset with state-of-the-art evaluation. In: Proceedings of the 2018 Conference on Empirical Methods in Natural Language Processing, pp. 4803–4809 (2018)

15. Hitzler, P.: Neuro-symbolic artificial intelligence: the state of the art (2022)

16. Hogan, A., et al.: Knowledge graphs. ACM Comput. Surv. (CSUR) **54**(4), 1–37 (2021)

17. Howard, J., Ruder, S.: Universal language model fine-tuning for text classification. In: Proceedings of the 56th Annual Meeting of the Association for Computational Linguistics, pp. 328–339 (2018)

18. Howard, J., Ruder, S.: Universal language model fine-tuning for text classification. arXiv preprint arXiv:1801.06146 (2018)

19. Hu, E.J., et al.: LoRA: low-rank adaptation of large language models. In: International Conference on Learning Representations (ICLR 2022) (2022). https://openreview.net/forum?id=nZeVKeeFYf9

20. Jain, S., van Zuylen, M., Hajishirzi, H., Beltagy, I.: Scirex: a challenge dataset for document-level information extraction. In: Proceedings of the 58th Annual Meeting of the Association for Computational Linguistics, pp. 7506–7516 (2020)

21. Ji, Z., et al.: Survey of hallucination in natural language generation. ACM Comput. Surv. **55**(12) (2023). https://doi.org/10.1145/3571730

22. Kassner, N., Dufter, P., Schütze, H.: Multilingual lama: investigating knowledge in multilingual pretrained language models. In: Proceedings of the 16th Conference of the European Chapter of the Association for Computational Linguistics: Main Volume, pp. 3250–3258 (2021)

23. Khorashadizadeh, H., Mihindukulasooriya, N., Tiwari, S., Groppe, J., Groppe, S.: Exploring in-context learning capabilities of foundation models for generating knowledge graphs from text. In: Proceedings of the Second International Workshop on Knowledge Graph Generation from Text, Hersonissos, Greece, pp. 132–153. CEUR (2023)

24. Lester, B., Al-Rfou, R., Constant, N.: The power of scale for parameter-efficient prompt tuning. In: Proceedings of the 2021 Conference on Empirical Methods in

Natural Language Processing, pp. 3045–3059. Association for Computational Linguistics, Online and Punta Cana, Dominican Republic (2021). https://doi.org/10.18653/v1/2021.emnlp-main.243. https://aclanthology.org/2021.emnlp-main.243

25. Lester, B., Al-Rfou, R., Constant, N.: The power of scale for parameter-efficient prompt tuning. arXiv preprint arXiv:2104.08691 (2021)

26. Li, X.L., Liang, P.: Prefix-tuning: optimizing continuous prompts for generation. In: Proceedings of the 59th Annual Meeting of the Association for Computational Linguistics and the 11th International Joint Conference on Natural Language Processing (Volume 1: Long Papers) abs/2101.00190 (2021)

27. Lin, Y., et al.: Knowledge graph enhanced relation extraction datasets. arXiv preprint arXiv:2210.11231 (2022)

28. Liu, Y., et al.: Roberta: a robustly optimized BERT pretraining approach. arXiv preprint arXiv:1907.11692 (2019)

29. Luan, Y., He, L., Ostendorf, M., Hajishirzi, H.: Multi-task identification of entities, relations, and coreference for scientific knowledge graph construction. In: Proceedings of the 2018 Conference on Empirical Methods in Natural Language Processing, pp. 3219–3232 (2018)

30. Marcheggiani, D., Titov, I.: Discrete-state variational autoencoders for joint discovery and factorization of relations. Trans. Assoc. Comput. Linguist. **4**, 231–244 (2016)

31. Min, S., et al.: Rethinking the role of demonstrations: what makes in-context learning work? In: Proceedings of the 2022 Conference on Empirical Methods in Natural Language Processing, Abu Dhabi, United Arab Emirates, pp. 11048–11064. Association for Computational Linguistics (2022). https://aclanthology.org/2022.emnlp-main.759

32. Mintz, M., Bills, S., Snow, R., Jurafsky, D.: Distant supervision for relation extraction without labeled data. In: Proceedings of the Joint Conference of the 47th Annual Meeting of the ACL and the 4th International Joint Conference on Natural Language Processing of the AFNLP, pp. 1003–1011 (2009)

33. Ni, J., et al.: Large dual encoders are generalizable retrievers. In: Proceedings of the 2022 Conference on Empirical Methods in Natural Language Processing. Association for Computational Linguistics, Abu Dhabi, United Arab Emirates (2022)

34. Ouyang, L., et al.: Training language models to follow instructions with human feedback. arXiv preprint arXiv:2203.02155 (2022)

35. Raffel, C., et al.: Exploring the limits of transfer learning with a unified text-to-text transformer. J. Mach. Learn. Res. **21**(1), 5485–5551 (2020)

36. Reimers, N., Gurevych, I.: Sentence-BERT: sentence embeddings using Siamese BERT-networks. In: Proceedings of the 2019 Conference on Empirical Methods in Natural Language Processing. Association for Computational Linguistics (2019). http://arxiv.org/abs/1908.10084

37. Riedel, S., Yao, L., McCallum, A.: Modeling relations and their mentions without labeled text. In: Balcázar, J.L., Bonchi, F., Gionis, A., Sebag, M. (eds.) ECML PKDD 2010. LNCS (LNAI), vol. 6323, pp. 148–163. Springer, Heidelberg (2010). https://doi.org/10.1007/978-3-642-15939-8_10

38. Sahoo, S.S., et al.: A survey of current approaches for mapping of relational databases to RDF. W3C RDB2RDF Incubator Group Report, vol. 1, pp. 113–130 (2009)

39. Scao, T.L., et al.: Bloom: a 176B-parameter open-access multilingual language model. arXiv preprint arXiv:2211.05100 (2022)

40. Seganti, A., Firląg, K., Skowronska, H., Satława, M., Andruszkiewicz, P.: Multilingual entity and relation extraction dataset and model. In: Proceedings of the 16th Conference of the European Chapter of the Association for Computational Linguistics: Main Volume, pp. 1946–1955 (2021)
41. Stiennon, N., et al.: Learning to summarize with human feedback. Adv. Neural. Inf. Process. Syst. **33**, 3008–3021 (2020)
42. Taori, R., et al.: Stanford alpaca: an instruction-following llama model (2023). https://github.com/tatsu-lab/stanford_alpaca
43. Tiwari, S., et al. (eds.): Proceedings of the 1st International Workshop on Knowledge Graph Generation From Text and the 1st International Workshop on Modular Knowledge co-located with 19th Extended Semantic Conference (ESWC 2022), Hersonissos, Greece, May 30th, 2022, CEUR Workshop Proceedings, vol. 3184. CEUR-WS.org (2022). http://ceur-ws.org/Vol-3184
44. Tiwari, S., et al. (eds.): Proceedings of the 2nd International Workshop on Knowledge Graph Generation From Text and the International BiKE Challenge co-located with 20th Extended Semantic Conference (ESWC 2023), Hersonissos, Greece, May 28th, 2023, CEUR Workshop Proceedings, vol. 3447. CEUR-WS.org (2023). http://ceur-ws.org/Vol-3447
45. Touvron, H., et al.: Llama: open and efficient foundation language models. arXiv preprint arXiv:2302.13971 (2023)
46. Vakaj, E., Tiwari, S., Mihindukulasooriya, N., Ortiz-Rodríguez, F., Mcgranaghan, R.: NLP4KGC: natural language processing for knowledge graph construction. In: Companion Proceedings of the ACM Web Conference 2023, pp. 1111–1111 (2023)
47. Veseli, B., Singhania, S., Razniewski, S., Weikum, G.: Evaluating language models for knowledge base completion. arXiv preprint arXiv:2303.11082 (2023)
48. Vrandečić, D., Krötzsch, M.: Wikidata: a free collaborative knowledgebase. Commun. ACM **57**(10), 78–85 (2014)
49. Wang, A., et al.: Superglue: a stickier benchmark for general-purpose language understanding systems. In: Advances in Neural Information Processing Systems, vol. 32 (2019)
50. Wang, Y., et al.: Self-instruct: aligning language model with self generated instructions. arXiv preprint arXiv:2212.10560 (2022)
51. Xie, S.M., Raghunathan, A., Liang, P., Ma, T.: An explanation of in-context learning as implicit Bayesian inference. arXiv preprint arXiv:2111.02080 (2021)
52. Yang, J., et al.: Harnessing the power of LLMS in practice: a survey on ChatGPT and beyond. arXiv preprint arXiv:2304.13712 (2023)
53. Yao, Y., et al.: Docred: a large-scale document-level relation extraction dataset. In: Proceedings of the 57th Annual Meeting of the Association for Computational Linguistics, pp. 764–777 (2019)
54. Zhang, S., et al.: OPT: open pre-trained transformer language models. arXiv preprint arXiv:2205.01068 (2022)
55. Zhang, Y., Zhong, V., Chen, D., Angeli, G., Manning, C.D.: Position-aware attention and supervised data improve slot filling. In: Conference on Empirical Methods in Natural Language Processing (2017)
56. Zheng, L., et al.: Judging LLM-as-a-judge with MT-bench and chatbot arena. arXiv preprint arXiv:2306.05685 (2023)

Benchmarking Geospatial Question Answering Engines Using the Dataset GEOQUESTIONS1089

Sergios-Anestis Kefalidis[1]([✉]), Dharmen Punjani[2], Eleni Tsalapati[1],
Konstantinos Plas[1], Mariangela Pollali[1], Michail Mitsios[1],
Myrto Tsokanaridou[1], Manolis Koubarakis[1], and Pierre Maret[2]

[1] Department of Informatics and Telecommunications, National and Kapodistrian
University of Athens, Athens, Greece
{s.kefalidis,etsalapati,mpollali,kplas,cs2200011,mtsokanaridou,
koubarak}@di.uoa.gr
[2] Université St. Monnet, St. Etienne, France
dharmen.punjani@gmail.com, pierre.maret@univ-st-etienne.fr

Abstract. We present the dataset GEOQUESTIONS1089 for benchmarking geospatial question answering engines. GEOQUESTIONS1089 is the largest such dataset available presently and it contains 1089 questions, their corresponding GeoSPARQL or SPARQL queries and their answers over the geospatial knowledge graph YAGO2geo. We use GEOQUESTIONS1089 to evaluate the effectiveness and efficiency of geospatial question answering engines GeoQA2 (an extension of GeoQA developed by our group) and the system of Hamzei et al. (2021).

1 Introduction

Users are often interested in posing *geospatial questions* to search engines, question answering (QA) engines and chatbots. Examples of such geospatial questions are: "Which rivers cross London?", "Is there a Levi's store in Athens?" and "Which countries border Greece, have the euro as their currency and their population is greater than the population of Greece?". In this paper, we deal with the problem of answering such questions over *geospatial knowledge graphs* i.e., knowledge graphs (KGs) which represent knowledge about *geographic features* or simply *features* in the terminology of GIS systems [18,20]. Geospatial knowledge in KGs is encoded using latitude/longitude pairs representing the center of features (as e.g., in DBpedia and YAGO2), but also more detailed geometries (e.g., lines, polygons, multipolygons etc.) since these are more appropriate for

This work was supported by the first call for H.F.R.I. Research Projects to support faculty members and researchers and the procurement of high-cost research equipment grant (HFRI-FM17-2351). It was also partially supported by the ESA project DA4DTE (subcontract 202320239), the Horizon 2020 project AI4Copernicus (GA No. 101016798) and the Marie Skłodowska-Curie project QuAre (GA No. 101032307).

T. R. Payne et al. (Eds.): ISWC 2023, LNCS 14266, pp. 266–284, 2023.
https://doi.org/10.1007/978-3-031-47243-5_15

modeling the geometries of features such as rivers, roads, countries etc. (as in Wikidata [29], YAGO2geo [14], WorldKG [4] and KnowWhereGraph [12]).

The development of the above geospatial KGs has given rise to *geospatial QA engines* for them. Examples of such systems are the GeoQA engine developed by our group [24,25] and the systems of [1,9,17,28,31]. To evaluate the effectiveness and efficiency of these engines, there is currently only one benchmark: the GEOQUESTIONS201 dataset proposed by our group [25] and used in comparing GeoQA with the systems of [8,9] and [17]. In this paper we go beyond GEOQUESTIONS201 and make the following *original contributions*.

We present the benchmark GEOQUESTIONS1089, which contains 1089 triples of geospatial questions, their answers, and the respective SPARQL/GeoSPARQL queries. GEOQUESTIONS1089 is currently the largest geospatial QA benchmark and it is made freely available to the research community[1]. In addition to simple questions like those present in GEOQUESTIONS201, GEOQUESTIONS1089 contains semantically complex questions that require a sophisticated understanding of both natural language and GeoSPARQL to be answered. Furthermore, it expands the geographical area of interest, by including questions about the United States and Greece. This expanded list of countries of interest introduces additional challenges that QA engines must overcome. In this way, we contribute to a long-term research agenda towards QA systems with geospatial features.

We present the geospatial QA system GeoQA2 which is based on GeoQA [25] and its revised version [24]. GeoQA2 is available as open source[2]. It targets the union of the KG YAGO2 and the geospatial KG YAGO2geo, and improves GeoQA by having been optimized in various ways and being able to answer a greater variety of questions.

Using GEOQUESTIONS1089, we evaluate the effectiveness and efficiency of geospatial QA engines GeoQA2 and the engine of Hamzei et al. [9] and find that although GeoQA2 emerges victorious, mainly because of its disambiguation component, neither engine is able to process complex questions caused by both a limited vocabulary of geospatial relations and a template-based approach to query generation. We stress here that the competitor engine of Hamzei et al. has been designed to target YAGO2geo and therefore cannot answer questions such as "What is the length of the Awali river?" because the entity `yago:Awali_(river)` appears in YAGO2 but not in YAGO2geo meaning that it is lacking detailed geospatial information which is expected by the query generator of the engine.

We show that the pre-computation and materialization of entailed, but not stored explicitly, topological relations between entities in geospatial KGs can lead to substantial savings in geospatial query processing time. We show experimentally that this can speed up question answering for both engines studied.

---

[1] https://github.com/AI-team-UoA/GeoQuestions1089.
[2] https://github.com/AI-team-UoA/GeoQA2.

2   Related Work

We survey the state of the art in geospatial QA engines and the only dataset that exists for their evaluation (GEOQUESTIONS201). We also introduce the geospatial KG YAGO2geo since it is the only KG of interest to us in this paper.

YAGO2geo was developed by our group in [14]. It is based on the subset of YAGO2 [10] which includes only *geoentities* i.e., entities that have latitude/longitude co-ordinates associated with them (presumably, representing their center). YAGO2geo enriches the geospatial dimension of some of these geoentities with detailed geometries, namely lines, polygons and multi-polygons taken from official administrative datasets (for Greece, the United Kingdom and the Republic of Ireland) and the Global Administrative Areas dataset (GADM,[3]). Hence, YAGO2geo can be used to answer questions that could not be answered by YAGO2 because detailed administrative geospatial knowledge is required (e.g., "Which counties of England are crossed by river Thames?"). Additionally, for natural features such as lakes and rivers, the respective YAGO2 geoentities are enriched with detailed geometries from OpenStreetMap (OSM). Finally, YAGO2geo includes *new* geontities present in the above administrative datasets and OSM that were not present in YAGO2. In 2020, YAGO2geo was further extended with data of administrative divisions of the United States of America from the National Boundary Dataset[4]. YAGO2geo currently contains 703 thousand polygons and 3.8 million lines. YAGO2geo represents geographic knowledge by using the YAGO2 ontology, the GeoSPARQL ontology and the ontologies especially developed by the YAGO2geo developers for each dataset mentioned above.

The first QA engine over a KG has been a system for answering geospatial questions over DBpedia [31]. The system is based on a PostGIS database containing precise geospatial information of features in the United Kingdom provided by Ordnance Survey, a spatial index of DBpedia resources built using their point coordinates, and a SPARQL endpoint storing the DBpedia dataset. The three classes of questions considered are proximity (e.g., "Find churches within 1 km of the River Thames"), crossing (e.g., "Find the mouths of the rivers that cross Oxford") and containment (e.g., "Find churches in Manchester").

The next geospatial QA engine to be proposed was GeoQA [25] and its revised version [24]. GeoQA can answer geospatial questions over DBpedia interlinked with the parts of GADM and OSM for the United Kingdom and Ireland. GeoQA is implemented as a pipeline of six components (dependency parse tree generator, concept identifier, instance identifier, geospatial relation identifier, property identifier and query generator) using a template-based approach and the Frankenstein platform [27]. In addition to developing an engine, [25] proposed the dataset GEOQUESTIONS201 for its evaluation. This dataset consists of 201 questions, their answers and the corresponding SPARQL or GeoSPARQL queries. The questions GEOQUESTIONS201 have been categorized by [25] into

---

[3] https://gadm.org/.
[4] https://www.usgs.gov/.

seven categories. In this paper we develop a much larger dataset containing a larger variety of questions and we extend the categorization of [25] accordingly.

[17] use deep neural networks (LSTM networks and the large language model BERT) and a template-based approach like the one proposed by GeoQA for generating a GeoSPARQL query corresponding to an input geospatial question. They achieved better results than [25] in producing GeoSPARQL translations of input questions. However, they achieved worse results than [24] given that the GeoQuestions201 benchmark is very small to allow for the successful training of deep learning models. In contrast, neural approaches to non-spatial factoid question answering exhibit excellent results because the used deep learning models have been trained on very large question benchmarks [19].

Recently, [1] proposed a system for answering qualitative spatial questions based on deductive spatial reasoning. Initially, the system extracts toponyms and spatial relations from the question text using DeepPavlov [2]. Then, it creates triples based on these outputs and applies the crisp qualitative spatial reasoner of the SparQ toolbox [30]. A limitation of this approach is that it is focused on addressing only three types of spatial questions, two of those (Q-Type2, Q-Type3) are already addressed by GeoQA.

The most recent geospatial QA engine is that of Hamzei et al. [9], which presents an engine that extends the one originally presented in [8]. The system of Hamzei et al. will be discussed in more detail in Sect. 5.

3   The GeoQuestions1089 Dataset

The GeoQuestions1089 dataset consists of two parts, which we will refer to as GeoQuestions$_C$ (1017 questions) and GeoQuestions$_W$ (72 questions) both of which target the union of YAGO2 and YAGO2geo. GeoQuestions$_C$ is the union of the datasets GeoQuestions$_T$ and GeoQuestions$_F$.

To develop GeoQuestions$_T$, we asked each M.Sc. student of the 2020–2021 Knowledge Technologies course of our department to formulate 21 question-query-answers triples targeting YAGO2geo. We asked students to include in their questions one or more features and various kinds of geospatial relations: distance relations (e.g., near, at most 2km from), topological relations (e.g., in, borders, crosses) or cardinal directions (e.g., east of, northeast of). Also, they were asked to have questions for all four countries covered with official data by YAGO2geo: USA, Greece, United Kingdom and Ireland. Finally, one more constraint was that the generated GeoSPARQL queries for three of their questions should be with one, two and three aggregate functions, respectively. In at least one of these three cases, the students were asked to provide a question which can be mapped to an advanced GeoSPARQL expression like a nested query or a not-exists filter. In this way, we wanted to target questions that were more complex than the ones in GeoQuestions201. To obtain the answers, the students were asked to run their GeoSPARQL queries in a YAGO2geo endpoint that we provided. The questions gathered were factoid, simple/complex and, in some cases, with aggregations (e.g., counting), comparatives, or superlatives. The resulting dataset contained 615 questions targeting YAGO2geo.

To develop GeoQuestions$_F$, we asked third-year students of the 2020–2021 AI course in the same department to write 50 questions targeting the subset of OSM and the infoboxes of Wikipedia, imagining scenarios related to traveling or to generating geography questionnaires for students or TV games. The only constraint was that simple but also complex questions should be produced (examples of simple questions from GeoQuestions201 and complex questions from GeoQuestions$_T$ were given). In total, we gathered 9,335 questions. From this set, we randomly chose 1200 questions, for which we hired six M.Sc. students of the same course to clean them and translate them into SPARQL or stSPARQL/GeoSPARQL using YAGO2geo. Because this crowdsourcing effort was less restrictive than that of GeoQuestions$_T$, some questions didn't have answers in YAGO2geo alone. However, they could be answered using the union of YAGO2 and YAGO2geo KGs. After this, the students ran the queries in the YAGO2geo endpoint and stored the answers, when these existed. The resulting dataset contained 402 questions, 280 questions targeting YAGO2geo and 122 questions targeting the union of YAGO2 and YAGO2geo.

The dataset GeoQuestions$_C$ was checked by the authors of this paper. Each question (query) was checked both grammatically and syntactically, using Grammarly[5] and QuillBot[6]. When necessary, and because some queries required exorbitant compute resources to be answered in reasonable time, we rerun the queries against the endpoint using materialized relations (see Sect. 6). The resulting set contained 1017 question-query-answer triples.

GeoQuestions$_W$ consists of the elements of GeoQuestions$_C$ whose questions originally had spelling, grammar or syntax mistakes. In GeoQuestions$_W$, we include the original, incorrect questions with the end goal of benchmarking how capable QA engines are at handling incorrect input.

Extending the categorization of [25], we can see that the questions of dataset GeoQuestions1089 fall under the following categories:[7]

A. Asking for a thematic or a spatial attribute of a feature, e.g., *"Where is Loch Goil located?"*. In GeoQA2, these questions can be answered by posing a SPARQL query to YAGO2geo. Google and Bing both can also answer such questions precisely.

B. Asking whether a feature is in a geospatial relation with another feature or features, e.g., *"Is Liverpool east of Ireland?"*. The geospatial relation in this example question is a cardinal direction one (east of). Other geospatial relations in this category of questions include topological ("borders") or distance ("near" or "at most 2 km from"). In GeoQA2, these questions are answered by querying YAGO2geo using the detailed geometries of features for evaluating the geospatial relation of the question. Google and Bing both cannot answer such factoid questions, but can only return a list of relevant Web

---

[5] https://www.grammarly.com/.

[6] https://quillbot.com/.

[7] For comparison purposes, for each question category, we comment whether the search engines Google and Bing can answer such questions after having tried a few examples.

pages. The recently deployed chat feature of Bing gives more information by saying that "Liverpool ... is located on the eastern side of the Irish Sea".

C. Asking for features of a given class that are in a geospatial relation with another feature. E.g., *"Which counties border county Lincolnshire?"* or *"Which hotels in Belfast are at most 2km from George Best Belfast City Airport?"*. The geospatial relation in the first example question is a topological one ("border"). As in the previous category, other geospatial relations in this set of questions include cardinal or distance (as in the second example question). In GeoQA2, these questions can be answered by using the detailed geometries of features from YAGO2geo for evaluating the geospatial relations. Google and Bing can also answer such questions precisely in many but not all cases (e.g., they can answer the first question but not the second).

D. Asking for features of a given class that are in a geospatial relation with any features of another class, e.g., *"Which churches are near castles?"*. Arguably, this category of questions might not be useful unless one specifies a geographical area of interest; this is done by the next category of questions.

E. Asking for features of a given class that are in a geospatial relation with an unspecified feature of another class, and either one or both, is/are in another geospatial relation with a feature specified explicitly. E.g., *"Which churches are near a castle in Scotland?"* or *"In Greece, which beaches are near villages?"*. Google and Bing both cannot answer such questions precisely.

F. As in categories C, D and E above, plus more thematic and/or geospatial characteristics of the features expected as answers, e.g., *"Which mountains in Scotland have height more than 1000 m?"*. Google and Bing both give links to pages with lists of mountains of Scotland with their height.

G. Questions with quantities and aggregates, e.g., *"What is the total area of lakes in Monaghan?"* or *"How many lakes are there in Monaghan?"*. Google and Bing both can answer precisely the second question but not the first. For the first question both return pages with lists of lakes in Monaghan. The chat component of Bing attempts to answer the first question but fails.

H. Questions with superlatives or comparatives, e.g., *"Which is the largest island in Greece?"* or *"Is the largest island in France larger than Crete?"*. Google answers the first question accurately but Bing does not and instead gives a list of links to related pages. The chat component of Bing can answer the first question precisely (Crete). Both engines cannot answer the second question; they only give links to relevant Web pages. The chat component of Bing is able to answer the second question precisely. (Corsica is larger than Crete).

I. Questions with quantities, aggregates, and superlatives/comparatives, e.g., *"Which city in the UK has the most hospitals?"* or *"Is the total size of lakes in Greece larger than lake Loch Lomond in Scotland?"*. Google can answer the first question precisely but Bing fails and returns a list of best hospitals in cities of the UK. Both engines cannot answer the second question.

Table 1 describes GeoQuestions1089 giving numbers per type of question.

Table 1. GeoQuestions1089 statistics

Category	KG	Count in GeoQuestionsC	Combined in GeoQuestionsC	Count in GeoQuestionsW	Combined in GeoQuestionsW
A	YAGO2geo	144	175	14	17
	YAGO2geo + YAGO2	31		3	
B	YAGO2geo	134	139	11	11
	YAGO2geo + YAGO2	5		0	
C	YAGO2geo	155	178	12	14
	YAGO2geo + YAGO2	23		2	
D	YAGO2geo	25	25	0	0
	YAGO2geo + YAGO2	0		0	
E	YAGO2geo	134	135	7	7
	YAGO2geo + YAGO2	1		0	
F	YAGO2geo	21	24	1	2
	YAGO2geo + YAGO2	3		1	
G	YAGO2geo	146	174	8	11
	YAGO2geo + YAGO2	28		3	
H	YAGO2geo	114	142	7	8
	YAGO2geo + YAGO2	28		1	
I	YAGO2geo	22	25	2	2
	YAGO2geo + YAGO2	3		0	
All	YAGO2geo	895	1017	62	72
	YAGO2geo + YAGO2	122		10	

Comparison to GeoQuestions201. GEOQUESTIONS201 contains mostly simple questions that can be answered with simple queries. For that reason, the state of the art geospatial QA engines are able to answer a significant portion of it correctly, as was shown in [9] and confirmed by our own experience while developing GeoQA2.

GEOQUESTIONS1089 includes numerous complex questions that require both solid natural language understanding and advanced SPARQL features (nested queries, not-exists filters, arithmetic calculations) to be answered. For example: *"How many times bigger is the Republic of Ireland than Northern Ireland?"* or *"What is the population density of the municipality of Thessaloniki?"* or *"How much of the UK is woodland?"* or *"Is Belfast closer to the capital of the Republic of Ireland or the capital of Scotland?"* or *"Which islands don't have any lakes but have forests?"*. Additionally, GEOQUESTIONS1089 is targeted on YAGO2geo, enabling easier comparison of engines that target this KG. Furthermore, because YAGO2geo also includes data about the United States and Greece, new challenges arise that must be dealt with by a good QA engine. For instance, some Greek entities lack English labels, which makes disambiguation more difficult. All in all, GEOQUESTIONS1089 is a more varied and more challenging dataset that uses a much wider array of SPARQL functionality in its queries compared to GEOQUESTIONS201.

4   The QA Engine GeoQA2

GeoQA2 takes as input a question in English and the union of YAGO2 and YAGO2geo KGs, and produces a set of answers. QA is performed by translating the input question into a set of SPARQL/GeoSPARQL queries, ranking these queries, and executing the top-ranked query over a YAGO2geo endpoint.

The differences between GeoQA [25] and GeoQA2 can be summarized as follows. GeoQA was targeting DBpedia, GADM, and OSM for the United Kingdom and Ireland. GeoQA2 targets the union of YAGO2 and YAGO2geo. Most importantly, GeoQA2 can answer a greater variety of questions, including questions with quantities, aggregates, superlatives and comparatives thanks to the use of constituency parsing and the development of additional templates.

In Fig. 1 we present the GeoQA2 pipeline which contains the following components: dependency parse tree generator, concept identifier, instance identifier, geospatial relation identifier, property identifier and query generator. The functionality of these components will be discussed below using the question "Is the largest island in the United Kingdom larger than Crete by population?".

The *dependency parse tree generator* carries out part-of-speech (POS) tagging and generates a dependency parse tree for the input question using the Stanford CoreNLP toolkit [21].

The *concept identifier* identifies the *types of features (concepts)* present in the input question (e.g., "island") and maps them to the corresponding classes of the YAGO2 or YAGO2geo ontologies (e.g., `y2geoo:OSM_island`). These concepts are identified by the elements of the question that are tagged as nouns (POS tags

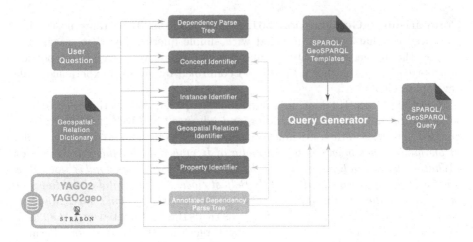

Fig. 1. The conceptual architecture of the GeoQA2 engine

NN, NNS, NNP and NNPS) during dependency parsing. Then, these elements are mapped to the ontology classes of YAGO2 and YAGO2geo using string matching based on n-grams.

The *instance identifier* identifies the *features* (*instances*) present in the input question (e.g., "United Kingdom" and "Crete"). The features are identified by the elements of the question that are tagged as proper nouns (POS tags NN, NNS and NNP) during dependency parsing. Then, these elements are mapped to YAGO2geo resources (e.g., `yago:United_Kingdom` and `yago:Crete`) using the TagMeDisambiguate tool [6]. In previous work [24] we tested a set of well-known tools on the task of named entity recognition and disambiguation for geographic entities in the dataset GEOQUESTIONS201. The tool of choice for GeoQA2 is TagMeDisambiguate, since it gave the best results in that study. The instance identifier also queries YAGO2geo to disambiguate the instances that are contained in YAGO2geo, but not in YAGO2.

The *geospatial relation identifier* first identifies the geospatial relations (e.g., "in") in the input question based on the POS tags VB, IN, VP, VBP and VBZ generated during dependency parsing. Then, it maps them to the respective spatial function of the GeoSPARQL or stSPARQL vocabulary (e.g., `geof:within`) according to a mapping between geospatial relations and stSPARQL/GeoSPARQL functions provided by a dictionary.

The *property identifier* identifies *attributes of features or types of features* specified by the user in input questions and maps them to the corresponding properties in YAGO2 or YAGO2geo. For instance, for the example question the property "population" of type of feature "island" will be identified and mapped to property `yago:hasPopulation`. The attributes in the input question are identified based on the POS tags NN, JJ, NNP and NP generated by the dependency parsing process and the concepts/instances identified by earlier steps.

The *query generator* produces the GeoSPARQL query corresponding to the input question using handcrafted query templates and the annotated parse tree. GeoQA2 has 10 templates while GeoQA [25] had 5 templates. For questions of types G, H and I (see Sect. 3), the query generator also constructs the constituency parse tree of the input question and uses it to modify the templates to support aggregates and superlatives (e.g., "largest").

5   The QA Engine of Hamzei et al.

Like GeoQA2, the engine of Hamzei et al. [9] takes as input a natural language question and translates it into a GeoSPARQL query targeting a version of YAGO2geo that has been extended with more data from OSM [9]. The engine uses a four-step workflow consisting of encoding extraction, grammatical parsing, intermediate representation generation and GeoSPARQL query generation. These steps are briefly described below using the question "How many pharmacies are in 200 m radius of High Street in Oxford?" as an example.

The step of *encoding extraction* extracts certain kinds of information from the question and encodes them using an extension of the *encoding classes* of [7]. These encoding classes offer a rich representational framework which can be used to classify a geospatial question according to what kind of question word it uses (e.g., "how many"), whether semantic categories such as placenames (e.g., "High Street" and "Oxford"), place types (e.g., "pharmacies"), geospatial relations (e.g., "in 200 m radius of" and "in") etc. are mentioned.[8] The encoding extraction step is implemented as a rule-based system but its POS tagging and named entity recognition components use the pre-trained neural network models of [13,16] and the large language model BERT [3].

In the *grammatical parsing* step, the engine of Hamzei et al. constructs a constituency parse tree and a dependency parse tree for the input question. In this step, the *intention* of the question is also computed (e.g., "How many pharmacies").

The *intermediate representation generation* step uses the information produced by the previous two steps to compute a first-order logic formula corresponding to the input question. For the example question, the formula is

$$Count(x) : Place(High\ Street) \land Place(Oxford) \land Pharmacy(x)$$
$$\land\ InRadiusOf(x, HighStreet, 200meter) \land In(HighStreet, Oxford)$$

where our notation for first-order logic is the usual note.

The step of *GeoSPARQL query generation* produces a GeoSPARQL query based on the first-order logic formula of the previous step by utilizing YAGO2geo and its ontology. Instead of doing place-name disambiguation, this step relies on string similarity search using an Apache Solr server for identifying instances. The

---

[8] The conceptual framework of Hamzei et al. [9] is much richer than the one of GeoQA2 and it includes concepts such as events, times etc. but it has not been tested with KGs or datasets involving these concepts.

resulting query is subsequently sent to an Apache Jena Fuseki endpoint where
YAGO2geo is stored to retrieve the answer(s).

The code for the Hamzei et al. engine is publicly available at[9] while a demo
is available at[10].

6   Improving the Performance of Geospatial QA Engines

One of the key challenges faced by GeoQA2 and the system of Hamzei et al.,
but also by any other geospatial query answering system, is the large number
of geometric calculations that it has to perform, which often leads to very long
response times. For instance, checking whether a geometry is within a large
administrative area with complex borders is computationally a very challenging
task. Hence, to improve the time performance of the two engines discussed previously, we *pre-computed and materialized* certain relations between entities in
the YAGO2geo KG that change infrequently. Materialization is an optimization
technique that has been widely used (e.g., see [26] for the case of geospatial
KGs).

During the evaluation process of Sect. 7, we observed that topological geospatial relations "within", "crosses", "intersects", "touches", "overlaps", "covers"
and "equals" require expensive computations, while "near", "north", "south",
"east" and "west" are easily computed. Hence, we decided to materialized the
above costly topological relations. This approach is particularly beneficial, since,
as shown below, it greatly boosts the performance of computationally demanding queries. To facilitate the evaluation of the QA engines using the materialized
relations and to maintain the integrity of the GeoSPARQL queries in GEO-
QUESTIONS1089, we developed a transpiler to automatically rewrite queries from
GeoSPARQL to SPARQL.

One of the major concerns related to materialization is the size of resulting
KG, and the overhead that this can cause to its processing. Overall, the materialized version of YAGO2geo had 17,210,176 more triples, which in terms of
system memory, amounts to about 3GB and 10.21% increased in total size, but
as shown below, it does not affect the performance of the QA system negatively.
The time required to calculate the implied geospatial relation was close to 5 d,
which can be considered negligible, as it happens offline, and it is being repeated
infrequently (only when the KG changes).

The calculation of the implied relations was facilitated by utilizing a distributed implementation of the algorithm GIA.nt [22], implemented in the system DS-JedAI [23][11]. GIA.nt is a holistic geospatial interlinking algorithm that
uses the DE-9IM topological model in order to discover all the topological relations between the geometries of two geospatial datasets. It employs a series

---

[9] https://github.com/hamzeiehsan/Questions-To-GeoSPARQL.
[10] https://tomko.org/demo/.
[11] https://github.com/GiorgosMandi/DS-JedAI.

of efficient techniques such as the dynamic space tiling, the minimum bounding rectangle intersection and the reference point technique to filter out redundant geometry verifications, and, therefore, to significantly reduce the default quadratic complexity of geospatial interlinking.

The geospatial part of YAGO2geo includes the datasets OS, OSI, OSNI, NBD, GAG, GADM and OSM. We used GIA.nt to discover the geospatial relations among the entities within the same dataset as well as all the other aforementioned geospatial datasets (Table 2).

Table 2. Number of materialized relations in YAGO2geo

Dataset	Number of discovered relations
OS	1,242,358
OSI	2,743,769
OSM	5,395,399
OSNI	522,221
GADM	2,773,983
GAG	25,695
NBD	4,506,751

Table 3. Average time performance of queries in YAGO2geo

Question Category	Number of questions	Average time	Average time materialized
B	12	< 1	<0.1
C	10	378	<1
D	13	**27237**	<2
E	9	262	<2
F	8	179	<1
G	3	100	<2
H	3	68	<2
I	2	245	<2

Table 4. Time performance in seconds of selected queries in YAGO2geo with and without materialized relations

Id	Question	Category	Execution time simple	Execution time materialized
1	What is the number of parks located within cities?	D	**70129**	<1
2	How many nature reserves contain forests?	D	11700	<1
3	Which counties border Donegal county?	C	1747	<1
4	Which is the largest county in the UK?	C	1609	<1
5	Which localities are south of lakes in County Cavan?	E	977	<1
6	Which forests are entirely within an Irish Barony?	E	501	<1
7	Which municipality in Crete region have population over 20000?	F	482	<1

We ran the experiments on a machine with the following specifications: Intel Xeon E5-4603 v2 @2.20 GHz, 128 Gb DDR3 RAM, 1.6 TB hard disk. YAGO2geo and the materialized relations were stored and configured in Strabon [15]. We selected Strabon due to our group's familiarity with its development, but also because it is one of the most efficient centralized geospatial RDF stores [11].

For the time-performance comparison of queries run against YAGO2geo with and without the materialization, we used 60 geospatial questions of GEOQUES-TIONS1089 that contain materialized relations. In Table 3 the average time difference to execute the GeoSPARQL and SPARQL queries using materialized relations is presented. The third and fourth column of this table show the average execution times for the queries in the second column. In Table 4 we display some of the queries for which we have significant time improvements. The reason for the slower execution of queries in category D is that they involve comparing complex geometries e.g., the geometries of all lakes and cities in a country. Hence, Strabon performs constly spatial joins involving the geometries that belong to these classes to get the final result. For the simple GeoSPARQL queries of category B, on the other hand, which needs to calculate a spatial relation only between two given geometries, it suffices to identify the triples representing this information, which has already been computed off-line.

7   Evaluation

In this section, we use the dataset GEOQUESTIONS1089 to benchmark the QA engines GeoQA2 and the one by Hamzei et al. [9]. The exact versions of the engines used are available in the repository of GEOQUESTIONS1089. We ran the experiments on a machine with the following specifications: Intel Xeon E5-4603 v2 @2.20GHz, 128 Gb DDR3 RAM, 1.6 TB HDD (RAID-5 configuration).

Methodology and Metrics. The question answering engine that is being evaluated attempts to generate a query for each natural language question in the dataset. If the generation is successful, the query is then processed by the transpiler that rewrites the query using materialized relations as mentioned in Sect. 6, and it is then sent to a geospatial RDF store that executes the query over our knowledge graph. The result is compared to the gold result included in GEOQUESTIONS1089. To accept an answer as correct, it must match the gold result exactly. We do not consider partially correct answers (e.g., when computed answers are a proper subset of the ones in the gold set) as correct. Likewise, we do not consider a superset of the answers in the gold set as correct. We chose to not use F-score because the correct number of returned answers/entities for each query varies greatly, which biases the metric towards certain kinds of questions.

Evaluating GeoQA2. To evaluate GeoQA2 we set up three Strabon endpoints. In the first two we store YAGO2 and YAGO2geo respectively. These endpoints are required by GeoQA2 to generate queries. In the third endpoint, which we use for retrieving the answers to our generated queries, we store YAGO2, YAGO2geo and its materialization.

Tables 5 and 6 show the results of the evaluation. The column "Generated Queries" gives the percentage of questions for which GeoQA2 was able to generate a query. The column "Correct Answers" gives the percentage of questions for which the query that was generated was able to retrieve the correct set of answers. Finally, the column "Correct Answers*" shows the same percentage computed over the set of questions for which a query was generated.

We observe that the complexity of the structure of the question affects significantly the performance of the system. For instance, GeoQA2 performed decently in answering rather simple questions (i.e., geospatial relation between two features), while it has difficulties in answering more structurally complex questions (i.e., questions with a combination of superlatives and quantities, questions with more sophisticated syntax or vocabulary). In addition, we see that GeoQA2 is a robust engine, meaning that it loses only a small percentage of its effectiveness when the input questions contain spelling, grammar or syntax mistakes.

Our benchmark showcases three core weaknesses of the GeoQA2 engine. First, a rule-based understanding of natural language, which falls apart for questions outside the specified rules. Second, the inherent difficulty of instance identification, especially for entities that have the same or extremely similar names (e.g., there are multiple places called Athens). Third, the limited array of GeoSPARQL queries that can be constructed using the existing templates, which are not enough to answer many of our more complex questions.

Table 5. Evaluation of GeoQA2 over GEOQUESTIONS$_C$.

Category	Generated Queries	Correct Answers	Correct Answers*
A	84%	47.42%	56.45%
B	76.25%	58.99%	77.35%
C	79.21%	44.38%	56.02%
D	56%	12%	21.42%
E	80%	31.85%	39.81%
F	66.66%	16.66%	25%
G	74.13%	32.18%	43.41%
H	71.12%	26.05%	36.63%
I	84%	20%	23.80%
Total	76.99%	38.54%	50.06%

Table 6. Evaluation of GeoQA2 over GEOQUESTIONS$_W$.

Category	Generate Questions	Correct Answers	Correct Answers*
A	82%	47.05%	57.14%
B	81.81%	54.54%	66.66%
C	85.71%	57.14%	66.66%
D	50%	33%	66.66%
E	88%	0.00%	0.00%
F	36.36%	0.00%	0%
G	50.00%	0.00%	0.00%
H	100.00%	0.00%	0.00%
I	50%	50%	100.00%
Total	72.22%	34.72%	48.07%

Evaluating the System of Hamzei et al. The engine of Hamzei et al. [9] requires two servers, an Apache Solr server, used for placename and place type identification, and an Apache Jena GeoSPARQL Fuseki server for executing the generated queries. Even though a Solr index is provided in the code repository of the engine, it is not suitable for our dataset. Hamzei et al. [9] use a modified version of YAGO2geo that does not include Greece and includes a number of additional entities from Open Street Map. We create a new Solr index that includes YAGO2 and YAGO2geo. We load the Fuseki endpoint with YAGO2, YAGO2geo, the materialized relations of YAGO2geo and the materialization of the surface area of every polygon in YAGO2geo. The last part is necessary because Fuseki does not have the ability to calculate the surface area of a polygon.

Table 7. Evaluation of the system of Hamzei et al. [9] over GEOQUESTIONS$_C$. Because the query generator of the engine was not designed to work with entities that do not have detailed geometries, we also provide statistics for the subset of questions that target YAGO2geo only.

Category	GEOQUESTIONS$_C$			GEOQUESTIONS$_C$ without YAGO2 Questions		
	Generated Queries	Correct Answers	Correct Answers*	Generated Queries	Correct Answers	Correct Answers*
Type-A	89.71%	10.85%	12.10%	88.88%	12.50%	14.06%
Type-B	95.68%	53.23%	55.63%	95.52%	55.22%	57.81%
Type-C	97.75%	30.33%	31.03%	97.41%	32.90%	33.77%
Type-D	100%	12%	12.00%	100%	12%	12.00%
Type-E	99.25%	7.40%	7.46%	99.25%	7.46%	7.51%
Type-F	79.16%	4.10%	5%	76.19%	4.76%	6%
Type-G	98.27%	11.49%	11.69%	97.94%	13.01%	13.28%
Type-H	97.18%	7.74%	7.97%	96.49%	7.89%	8.18%
Type-I	92%	0%	0.00%	95%	0%	0.00%
Total	95.77%	18.97%	19.81%	95.53%	20.67%	21.63%

In a similar vein to the evaluation of GeoQA2, the generated queries of the engine are processed by our transpiler before being sent to the Apache Jena Fuseki endpoint whose answer is compared to that included in GEOQUESTIONS1089. To communicate with the Fuseki endpoint we use Apache Jena's own SPARQL-OVER-HTTP scripts to make sure that queries are sent and results are returned correctly. Tables 7 and 8 show the results of the evaluation.

We make three main observations. First, we see that as questions become more complex, the effectiveness of the engine drops dramatically, as was the case in our evaluation of GeoQA. The more complex the question, the less likely it is that the query generator is able to construct the proper GeoSPARQL query, with the most extreme example being questions of type I. Second, the system severely underperforms in questions of Category A, which is one of the simpler categories. This is caused by the lack of a dedicated step for named entity disambiguation. For example, if given the input question *"Where is Dublin located?"* the engine of Hamzei et al. [9] will return the location of every place named "Dublin" in the KG, instead of the location of the capital of the Republic of Ireland. This leads to an explosive increase of returned answers. Moreover, there is no mechanism for ranking the returned answers in accordance to their relevance, so even taking the first 3 answers as candidates doesn't significantly change the picture. Instead of a dedicated disambiguation step, the engine relies on the automatic resolution of disambiguation during query execution, which is an approach that works well for category B questions. In the original evaluation of their system, the authors disregarded toponym disambiguation, but we consider it a core part of question answering. Third, the system can handle spelling, grammar, and syntax mistakes without performance loss.

The main weakness of the engine of [9] is the lack of a dedicated disambiguation step. This leads to answers that contain numerous irrelevant results, i.e.,

Table 8. Evaluation of the system of Hamzei et al. [9] over GEOQUESTIONS$_W$

Category	GEOQUESTIONS$_W$		
	Generated Queries	Correct Answers	Correct Answers*
A	88.23%	17.64%	20.00%
B	100.00%	54.54%	54.54%
C	100.00%	35.71%	35.71%
D	100.00%	0.00%	0.00%
E	87.50%	0.00%	0.00%
F	90.90%	0.00%	0.00%
G	100.00%	0.00%	0.00%
H	100.00%	0.00%	0.00%
I	100.00%	0.00%	0.00%
Total	94.44%	19.44%	20.58%

the system is lacking precision. The other significant weakness is the rule-based approach to query generation that is unable to deal with complex queries.

Engine Comparison. The results of our evaluation show that GeoQA2 significantly outperforms the QA engine of [9] by generating twice the amount of correct queries. The main factor of this performance gap is the existence of a dedicated named entity disambiguation step in GeoQA2 (instance identifier). Other than this main difference, the two engines are similar in a number of ways. Both utilize dependency and constituency parsing to understand the structure of the input question and the relations that exist among its tokens. Likewise, both engines have a rule-based query generator that uses a set of predefined templates that are filled in with instances and concepts to generate the final GeoSPARQL queries, although the engine of [9] uses a more dynamic of approach of combining smaller templates which allows it to generate queries for a significantly larger portion of the dataset. Considering these similarities, it follows that the engines must share some weaknesses. That is the case, with the inability of either engine to reliably answer complex questions being their most important weakness.

8   Conclusions and Future Work

We presented the dataset GEOQUESTIONS1089 and evaluated the QA engines GeoQA2 and Hamzei et al. [9] using it. We plan to extend the dataset by utilizing semi-automatic techniques as it has been done e.g., in LC-QuAD 2.0 [5]. This will allow us to train geospatial QA engines using deep learning techniques with the hope that they will be more effective than the ones evaluated in this paper.

References

1. Beydokhti, M.K., Duckham, M., Tao, Y., Vasardani, M., Griffin, A.L.: Qualitative spatial reasoning over questions (short paper). In: Ishikawa, T., Fabrikant, S.I., Winter, S. (eds.) Proceedings of the 15th International Conference on Spatial Information Theory, COSIT 2022, 5–9 September 2022, Kobe. LIPIcs, vol. 240, pp. 18:1–18:7. Schloss Dagstuhl - Leibniz-Zentrum für Informatik (2022). https://doi.org/10.4230/LIPIcs.COSIT.2022.18

2. Burtsev, M., et al.: Deeppavlov: open-source library for dialogue systems. ACL (4), 122–127 (2018). https://aclanthology.info/papers/P18-4021/p18-4021

3. Devlin, J., Chang, M., Lee, K., Toutanova, K.: BERT: pre-training of deep bidirectional transformers for language understanding. In: Burstein, J., Doran, C., Solorio, T. (eds.) Proceedings of the 2019 Conference of the North American Chapter of the Association for Computational Linguistics: Human Language Technologies, NAACL-HLT 2019, Minneapolis, 2–7 June 2019, Volume 1 (Long and Short Papers). pp. 4171–4186. Association for Computational Linguistics (2019). https://doi.org/10.18653/v1/n19-1423

4. Dsouza, A., Tempelmeier, N., Yu, R., Gottschalk, S., Demidova, E.: WorldKG: A world-scale geographic knowledge graph. In: CIKM '21: The 30th ACM International Conference on Information and Knowledge Management, Virtual Event, Queensland, 1–5 November 2021, pp. 4475–4484. ACM (2021)

5. Dubey, M., Banerjee, D., Abdelkawi, A., Lehmann, J.: LC-QuAD 2.0: a large dataset for complex question answering over wikidata and DBpedia. In: ISWC (2019)

6. Ferragina, P., Scaiella, U.: TAGME: on-the-fly annotation of short text fragments (by wikipedia entities). In: Huang, J.X., Koudas, N., Jones, G.J.F., Wu, X., Collins-Thompson, K., An, A. (eds.) Proceedings of the 19th ACM Conference on Information and Knowledge Management (CIKM 2010), Toronto, 26–30 October 2010, pp. 1625–1628. ACM (2010). https://doi.org/10.1145/1871437.1871689

7. Hamzei, E., Li, H., Vasardani, M., Baldwin, T., Winter, S., Tomko, M.: Place questions and human-generated answers: a data analysis approach. In: Kyriakidis, P., Hadjimitsis, D., Skarlatos, D., Mansourian, A. (eds.) AGILE 2019. LNGC, pp. 3–19. Springer, Cham (2020). https://doi.org/10.1007/978-3-030-14745-7_1

8. Hamzei, E.: Place-related question answering: from questions to relevant answers. Ph.D. thesis (2021)

9. Hamzei, E., Tomko, M., Winter, S.: Translating place-related questions to GeoSPARQL queries. In: Proceedings of the Web Conference (WWW) (2022)

10. Hoffart, J., Suchanek, F.M., Berberich, K., Weikum, G.: Yago2: a spatially and temporally enhanced knowledge base from wikipedia. Artif. Intell. **194**, 28–61 (2013)

11. Ioannidis, T., Garbis, G., Kyzirakos, K., Bereta, K., Koubarakis, M.: Evaluating geospatial RDF stores using the benchmark geographica 2. J. Data Semant. **10**(3–4), 189–228 (2021). https://doi.org/10.1007/s13740-021-00118-x

12. Janowicz, K., et al.: Know, know where, knowwheregraph: a densely connected, cross-domain knowledge graph and geo-enrichment service stack for applications in environmental intelligence. AI Mag. **43**(1), 30–39 (2022). https://doi.org/10.1609/aimag.v43i1.19120

13. Joshi, V., Peters, M.E., Hopkins, M.: Extending a parser to distant domains using a few dozen partially annotated examples. In: Gurevych, I., Miyao, Y. (eds.) Proceedings of the 56th Annual Meeting of the Association for Computational Linguistics, ACL 2018, Melbourne, 15–20 July 2018, Volume 1: Long Papers, pp. 1190–1199.

Association for Computational Linguistics (2018). https://doi.org/10.18653/v1/P18-1110

14. Karalis, N., Mandilaras, G., Koubarakis, M.: Extending the YAGO2 knowledge graph with precise geospatial knowledge. In: Ghidini, C., et al. (eds.) ISWC 2019. LNCS, vol. 11779, pp. 181–197. Springer, Cham (2019). https://doi.org/10.1007/978-3-030-30796-7_12

15. Kyzirakos, K., Karpathiotakis, M., Koubarakis, M.: Strabon: A semantic geospatial DBMS. In: Cudré-Mauroux, P., et al. (eds.) ISWC 2012. LNCS, vol. 7649, pp. 295–311. Springer, Heidelberg (2012). https://doi.org/10.1007/978-3-642-35176-1_19

16. Lample, G., Ballesteros, M., Subramanian, S., Kawakami, K., Dyer, C.: Neural architectures for named entity recognition. In: Knight, K., Nenkova, A., Rambow, O. (eds.) NAACL HLT 2016, The 2016 Conference of the North American Chapter of the Association for Computational Linguistics: Human Language Technologies, San Diego, 12–17 June 2016, pp. 260–270. The Association for Computational Linguistics (2016). https://doi.org/10.18653/v1/n16-1030 https://doi.org/10.18653/v1/n16-1030

17. Li, H., et al.: Neural factoid geospatial question answering. J. Spatial Inf. Sci. **23**, 65–90 (2021)

18. Longley, P.A., Goodchild, M.F., Maguire, D.J., Rhind, D.W.: Geographic Information Science and Systems, 4th edn. John Wiley and Sons (2015)

19. Lukovnikov, D., Fischer, A., Lehmann, J.: Pretrained transformers for simple question answering over knowledge graphs. In: Ghidini, C., et al. (eds.) ISWC 2019. LNCS, vol. 11778, pp. 470–486. Springer, Cham (2019). https://doi.org/10.1007/978-3-030-30793-6_27

20. Koubarakis, M. (ed.): Geospatial Data Science: A Hands-on Approach Based on Geospatial Technologies. ACM Books (2023)

21. Manning, C., Surdeanu, M., Bauer, J., Finkel, J., Bethard, S., McClosky, D.: The Stanford CoreNLP natural language processing toolkit. In: Proceedings of 52nd Annual Meeting of the Association for Computational Linguistics: System Demonstrations, pp. 55–60. Association for Computational Linguistics, Baltimore (2014). https://doi.org/10.3115/v1/P14-5010 https://aclanthology.org/P14-5010

22. Papadakis, G., Mandilaras, G.M., Mamoulis, N., Koubarakis, M.: Progressive, holistic geospatial interlinking. In: Leskovec, J., Grobelnik, M., Najork, M., Tang, J., Zia, L. (eds.) The Web Conference 2021, Virtual Event (WWW 2021)/Ljubljana, 19–23 April 2021, pp. 833–844. ACM/IW3C2 (2021). https://doi.org/10.1145/3442381.3449850

23. Papamichalopoulos, M., Papadakis, G., Mandilaras, G., Siampou, M.D., Mamoulis, N., Koubarakis, M.: Three-dimensional geospatial interlinking with jedai-spatial (2022). https://arxiv.org/pdf/2205.01905.pdf

24. Punjani, D., et al.: Template-based question answering over linked geospatial data. arXiv preprint arXiv:2007.07060 (2020)

25. Punjani, D., et al.: Template-based question answering over linked geospatial data. In: Purves, R.S., Jones, C.B. (eds.) Proceedings of the 12th Workshop on Geographic Information Retrieval, GIR@SIGSPATIAL 2018, Seattle, 6 November 2018, pp. 7:1–7:10. ACM (2018). https://doi.org/10.1145/3281354.3281362

26. Regalia, B.D.: Computational Time and Space Tradeoffs in Geo Knowledge Graphs. Ph.D. thesis, UC Santa Barbara (2020)

27. Singh, K., et al.: Why reinvent the wheel: let's build question answering systems together. In: Champin, P., Gandon, F.L., Lalmas, M., Ipeirotis, P.G. (eds.) Proceedings of the 2018 World Wide Web Conference on World Wide Web (WWW

2018), Lyon, 23–27 April 2018, pp. 1247–1256. ACM (2018). https://doi.org/10.1145/3178876.3186023

28. Stoilos, G., Papasarantopoulos, N., Vougiouklis, P., Bansky, P.: Type linking for query understanding and semantic search. In: Zhang, A., Rangwala, H. (eds.) The 28th ACM SIGKDD Conference on Knowledge Discovery and Data Mining (KDD 2022), Washington, 14–18 August 2022, pp. 3931–3940. ACM (2022). https://doi.org/10.1145/3534678.3539067

29. Vrandecic, D., Krötzsch, M.: Wikidata: a free collaborative knowledgebase. Commun. ACM **57**(10), 78–85 (2014). https://doi.org/10.1145/2629489

30. Wallgrün, J.O., Frommberger, L., Wolter, D., Dylla, F., Freksa, C.: Qualitative spatial representation and reasoning in the SparQ-toolbox. In: Barkowsky, T., Knauff, M., Ligozat, G., Montello, D.R. (eds.) Spatial Cognition 2006. LNCS (LNAI), vol. 4387, pp. 39–58. Springer, Heidelberg (2007). https://doi.org/10.1007/978-3-540-75666-8_3

31. Younis, E.M.G., Jones, C.B., Tanasescu, V., Abdelmoty, A.I.: Hybrid geo-spatial query methods on the semantic web with a spatially-enhanced index of DBpedia. In: Xiao, N., Kwan, M.-P., Goodchild, M.F., Shekhar, S. (eds.) GIScience 2012. LNCS, vol. 7478, pp. 340–353. Springer, Heidelberg (2012). https://doi.org/10.1007/978-3-642-33024-7_25

FedShop: A Benchmark for Testing the Scalability of SPARQL Federation Engines

Minh-Hoang Dang[1]([✉])(iD), Julien Aimonier-Davat[1](iD), Pascal Molli[1](iD), Olaf Hartig[2](iD), Hala Skaf-Molli[1](iD), and Yotlan Le Crom[1]

[1] Nantes Université, CNRS, LS2N, UMR 6004, 44000 Nantes, France
minh-hoang.dang@univ-nantes.fr
[2] Department of Computer and Information Science (IDA), Linköping University, Linköping, Sweden

Abstract. While several approaches to query a federation of SPARQL endpoints have been proposed in the literature, very little is known about the effectiveness of these approaches and the behavior of the resulting query engines for cases in which the number of federation members increases. The existing benchmarks that are typically used to evaluate SPARQL federation engines do not consider such a form of scalability. In this paper, we set out to close this knowledge gap by investigating the behavior of 4 state-of-the-art SPARQL federation engines using a novel benchmark designed for scalability experiments. Based on the benchmark, we show that scalability is a challenge for each of these engines, especially with respect to the effectiveness of their source selection & query decomposition approaches. FedShop is freely available online at: https://github.com/GDD-Nantes/FedShop.

Keywords: Federated Query Processing · Scalability · Source Selection · SPARQL

1 Introduction

Context and motivation: Several query engines for querying federations of SPARQL endpoints have been proposed in recent years [2,15,19]. In addition to different approaches to finding efficient query execution plans, these engines employ different source selection & query decomposition approaches. These approaches decompose any given query into subqueries associated with the federation members from which it is possible to retrieve relevant results for answering the given query. Any subquery for a federation member whose result will be either empty or cannot contribute to the overall result of the given query can be pruned in this step, reducing the effort and time needed to execute the query. Yet, the challenge is to identify such subqueries. The effectiveness of the approaches proposed for this task (and also of the query optimization approaches used by the engines) is typically evaluated using one of two benchmarks: FedBench [21] or

T. R. Payne et al. (Eds.): ISWC 2023, LNCS 14266, pp. 285–301, 2023.
https://doi.org/10.1007/978-3-031-47243-5_16

LargeRDFBench [18]. Both of these benchmarks are designed based on a fixed federation with a few hand-picked federation members.

Due to this design choice, these benchmarks cannot be used to study how the proposed approaches and engines behave if the number of federation members increases. Consequently, very little is known about this form of scalability of the proposed approaches and engines. While some authors have partitioned existing benchmark datasets to overcome this limitation [13,14,16,21,24], the resulting partitions do not resemble the characteristics of real-world datasets [9].

Contributions: Our main contribution in this paper is FedShop, a novel benchmark designed for scalability experiments. FedShop captures an e-commerce scenario with a scalable federation of online shops and rating sites, and with query workloads that simulate users who explore and search for products and offers across the federation. More specifically, the benchmark consists of the following:

- **10 pre-generated federations** ranging from 20 to 200 federation members,
- a schema-based **dataset generator** to generate further federations for which the scale factor is the number of federation members and for which the distribution law of every relationship of the data schema can be configured,
- **12 query templates** capturing different, use-case-specific types of queries,
- a collection of ten such queries per template (i.e., **120 queries** overall), and
- **reference source assignments** for each of these 120 queries over each of the ten pre-generated federations, as could be produced by a source selection approach that has provenance information about the complete query results.

Given the FedShop benchmark (as will be introduced in detail in Sect. 3), we make further contributions in this paper. In particular, we analyze the benchmark queries based on their Reference Source Assignments (cf. Sect. 4) and, then, present a comprehensive experimental study (cf. Sect. 5). In this study, we first show that, when using their reference source assignments, each of the 120 queries can be executed in less than 2 s over each of the 10 pre-generated federations. This illustrates that effective query decomposition and source selection can enable a customer to perform interactive queries on a federation of 200 endpoints. Thereafter, we use the benchmark to show novel experimental results that shed light on the scalability of four state-of-the-art SPARQL federation engines. The main takeaway of this study is that scalability is a challenge for the engines. None of the engines can deliver reasonable performance when querying the federation with 200 federation members. The reason for these performance issues is that the source selection approaches of the engines fail to produce source assignments that are even close to ideal. By uncovering these issues, we show that the benchmark provides an important new tool for evaluating the efficiency and scalability of approaches to query federations of RDF data sources.

The code source of the benchmark, as well as set-up instructions, further documentation and measurements of our experimental study are available online[1].

Furthermore, we provide access to the dataset, queries, and Virtuoso dump generated for experimentation.[2]

---

[1] https://github.com/GDD-Nantes/FedShop.
[2] https://doi.org/10.5281/zenodo.7919872.

In addition to using it for the experimental study presented in this paper, we contributed a more limited fragment of FedShop (only 12 queries and two federations) as a use case for a recent hackathon[3] on query federation. During the hackathon, developers of query federation engines used this fragment of FedShop to reveal several implementation issues and weaknesses in their engines.

2   Related Works

The benchmark FedBench [21] is mainly used for testing and analyzing the performance of SPARQL federation engines processing RDF hosted in SPARQL endpoints. The dataset of FedBench is a collection of 10 datasets from different domains: 4 datasets from life-sciences (Kegg, Chebi,...), 6 cross domains datasets (Dbpedia,Geonames,...), and 14 real queries. To add more datasets and queries, FedBench proposes a setup FedBench/SP2Bench with a collection of 16 datasets generated by clustering of the SP2Bench dataset [22] and 11 queries from SP2Bench. To transform SP2Bench into a federated benchmark, FedBench applied a clustering on the types of the SP2Bench dataset, i.e., each class of SP2Bench (Person, Article, Inproceedings,...) is assigned to different SPARQL endpoints, which generates 16 synthetic datasets. The main issue with this approach is that clustering on classes is limited to 16, and "the partitions do not resemble the characteristics of real-world datasets", as pointed out in [9].

LargeRdfBench [11,18] extends the dataset and workload of FedBench, respectively, to 13 datasets and 40 queries. However, FedBench, Fed-Bench/SP2Bench, and LargeRdfBench do not allow the evaluation of the behavior of the federated query engines when the number of federation members increases. It is also possible to add more federated queries as proposed in QFed [17]. However, having more federated queries does not address the issue of scalability with the number of federation members.

To scale on the federation size, Lusail [1], DARQ [16], LHD [24], LILAC [13] propose partitioning datasets into several datasets. The different techniques for partitioning a dataset is reported in [14]; it includes horizontal, vertical, and hybrid partitioning with or without replication. First, as highlighted in [8], synthetic benchmarks such as BSBM [6], LUBM [10], or SP2Bench [22] can be highly structured and do not correspond to more realistic data hosted on a public endpoint. Partitioning/clustering such synthetic data does not solve the problem of structuredness [8].

In LHD [24], BSBM [6] entities (products, offers, producers,...) have been hashed on their subjects and distributed over 10 SPARQL endpoints. Such partitioning is working but does not correspond to a real use-case. To evaluate DARQ [16], the LUBM benchmark [10] dataset has been partitioned with LUBM classes, generating the same issues as FedBench/SP2Bench. In Lusail [1], an evaluation has been conducted with 256 universities generated using the LUBM benchmark and distributed over 256 SPARQL endpoints. Interlinks come from professors who worked in different universities and students who graduated from

---

[3] https://github.com/MaastrichtU-IDS/federatedQueryKG.

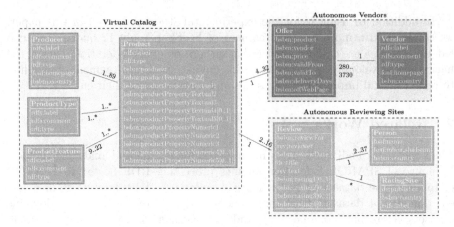

Fig. 1. The overall schema of BSBM extracted from [6]

different universities. Given these relations, 3 queries from the LUBM benchmark can be executed as federated queries (Q2, Q9, and Q13). In this setup, it is possible to increase the number of sources by adding new universities. Although this setup is interesting, the LUBM benchmark is designed for evaluating the reasoning capabilities of SPARQL engines, not with a real-use case in mind as with the explore use-case of Berlin Benchmark, for example. Consequently, a few queries make sense in a federated context and are not very challenging for a federated evaluation. In FedShop, we follow the same approach as Lusail, but we start from Berlin Benchmark and follow the explore use-case of BSBM.

3   The FedShop Benchmark

The FedShop use-case, inspired by the Berlin Benchmark (BSBM) use-case [6], involves a customer navigating through a virtual shop that comprises multiple autonomous shops, each with its own SPARQL endpoint. This exploration is powered by SPARQL queries executed across the federation, giving the illusion of one endpoint hosting all the different vendors as in the original BSBM. The SPARQL queries primarily aim to retrieve products based on certain criteria, obtain more product information, compare products, find similar products, and locate product reviews. Customers need to receive real-time feedback when using the FedShop use-case, which means all queries must processed quickly, within a few seconds.

The scalability of the benchmark is obtained by incorporating more shops (or reviewing sites) into the federated shop.

3.1   FedShop Data Generation

The overall schema of RDF data follows the schema described in Fig. 1. This schema is as close as possible to the schema of BSBM. We consider 3 different components in the schema. The virtual catalog comprises the products and their features, and it is shared by vendors and reviewing sites.

Each member of the federation (whether a vendor or a rating site) is considered autonomous and capable of operating independently of other members. Specifically, all product or review queries must generate results based solely on the vendor or rating site being queried. To ensure the autonomy of each member, we adhere to a straightforward guideline: *If a shop sells a product, it will have a local URI for that product, and all related information can be accessed via local URLs.* Essentially, this replicates how producers represent their products in the vendor domain. We follow the same approach for rating sites.

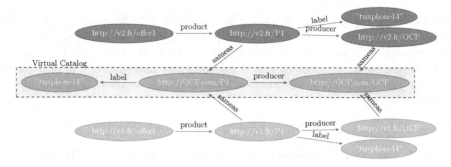

Fig. 2. Virtual catalog and replication of products across vendors

As entities of type Product, ProductType, Producer, and ProductFeature are replicated on many sites, all federation members have a `sameAs` link from local entities to the global entities of the virtual catalog. To illustrate, suppose two vendors $V1$ and $V2$ are selling the same product $P1$ named "tuxphone14" produced by the "OCP" company. Figure 2 describes the triples hosted by $V1$ on http://v1.fr and $V2$ on http://v1.fr. As we can see, products and their descriptions are replicated with local URLs by each vendor. `sameAs` links keep the connection with products of the virtual catalog. Following the FedShop data generation rules, we are sure that all the subjects of a vendor or a reviewing site are specific to its web domain, i.e., two different vendors cannot share the same subjects. We also know that all objects of `sameAs` predicates are global, i.e., potentially shared by all endpoints.

Generating a federated shop comprises two steps:

1. First, generate a virtual catalog of products shared by all vendors and rating sites. This catalog has a fixed size and will not be part of the final data.
2. Second, generate vendors and rating sites, each replicating products from the virtual catalog. The replication process follows a distribution law that decides how often the same product may appear on different vendors/rating sites.

To control the distribution laws when creating catalogs, vendors and rating sites, we rely on schema-based data generators such as WatDiv [4] or gMark [5]. As schema and distribution laws are declared as part of a specification, schema-generators allows to change the schema and distribution laws easily.

For the catalog, we chose to approximate the original BSBM configuration with 200,000 products. With this catalog, we generated a first federation of 20 sources $F(20)$ composed of 10 vendors and 10 rating sites. Next, we generated $F(40)$ just by adding 10 new vendors and 10 new rating sites; therefore, $F(40)$ includes $F(20)$. We continue this process until we reach $F(200)$. We described the overall size of the Federation in Table 1. It should be emphasized that the catalog itself does not constitute a component of the federation. Since all products are duplicated across all federation members, maintaining the catalog is unnecessary.

3.2   FedShop Query Generation

We follow the explore use-case of BSBM composed of 12 template queries. The explore use-case simulates a scenario where a customer is searching for products and reviews, e.g., *find products for a given set of generic features, retrieve basic information about a specific product, find products that are similar to a given product, retrieve in-depth information about a specific product, including offers and reviews.*

Table 1. Data Volume (#quads and storage) across FedShop sources. The bar chart breaks down the size of each federation by category.

	F(10)	F(20)	F(30)	F(40)	F(50)	F(60)	F(70)	F(80)	F(90)	F(100)
nquads (M)	5.167	11.821	17.852	24.335	30.374	37.080	43.827	50.764	56.883	63.079
size GB	0.98	2.21	3.35	4.57	5.71	6.97	8.25	9.56	10.71	11.88

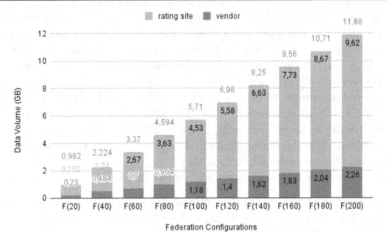

Template Federated Queries. We transformed the BSBM template queries to reflect the federated nature of the data in FedShop. For instance, the template query $Q1$ of BSBM allows a consumer to search for a product by knowing the product type and 2 product features. The template query $Q1$ has 4 placeholders: %ProductType%, %ProductFeature1%, %ProductFeature2%, %x%, which must be instantiated to be executed.

Listing 1 describes how we transformed the original Q1 template query of BSBM (Listing 3a) into the Q1 template query of FedShop (Listing 3b). Since local entities are linked to global entities, as shown in Sect. 3.1, we need to add a new **sameAs** triple pattern in the Q1 FedShop template query to link local products to global products. The principle of autonomy enables the execution of FedShop queries on SPARQL endpoints of any member, thereby returning results specific to that member. The same queries can also be executed in federation mode, thus transforming all vendors/rating sites into a virtual federated shop.

We applied this strategy to transform the 12 template queries of BSBM into 12 FedShop template queries.

Instantiate Template Federated Queries. To produce executable queries, we need to replace placeholders in template queries with real values. The objective is to find combinations of values with various selectivities that return results for all configurations of FedShop.

```
SELECT DISTINCT ?product ?label
WHERE {
  ?product rdfs : label  ?label  .
  ?product a %ProductType% .
  ?product bsbm:productFeature %ProductFeature1% .
  ?product bsbm:productFeature %ProductFeature2% .
  ?product bsbm:productPropertyNumeric1 ?value1 .
  FILTER (?value1 > %x%)
}
ORDER BY ?label
LIMIT 10
```

(a) Q1 BSBM query

```
SELECT DISTINCT ?product ?label
WHERE {
  ?product rdfs : label  ?label  .

  ?product rdf:type ?localProductType .
  ?localProductType owl:sameAs %ProductType% .

  ?product bsbm:productFeature ?localProductFeature1 .
  ?localProductFeature1 owl:sameAs %ProductFeature1% .

  ?product bsbm:productFeature ?localProductFeature2 .
  ?localProductFeature2 owl:sameAs %ProductFeature2% .
  ?product bsbm:productPropertyNumeric1 ?value1 .
  FILTER (?value1 > %x%)
}
ORDER BY ?label
LIMIT 10
```

(b) Q1 FedShop query

Lst. 1. Transformation of the Q1 BSBM template query into the Q1 FedShop template query

The overall process to instantiate template queries is as follows: (1) rewrite template queries as generic queries where placeholders are replaced with variables, (2) execute this queries on the $F(20)$ configuration, (3) chooses a distinct combination of values for placeholders randomly among the results of the execution.

For each of the 12 template queries, we generated 10 instances on the $F(20)$ configuration, each with a randomly selected combination of values We adopted this process for 2 reasons:

1. By instantiating on $F(20)$ we guarantee that the number of results of query instances can only grow when the number of sources increases, i.e., for configuration $> F(20)$.
2. By randomly selecting 10 combinations of values, we guarantee diversity w.r.t queries selectivity when the number of sources increases. For instance, the selectivity of a combination of placeholders can be different for $F(20)$ and $F(200)$. Since we do not know when generating $F(20)$ how the selectivity will evolve, we randomly choose 10 combinations of placeholders and observe experimentally how it evolves.

This entire process produces a workload of 120 queries that can run on 10 federations: $F(20)$ to $F(200)$. As in FedBench [21], we analyzed the structural features of our workload in Table 2. In sum, the FedShop queries comprise 1–18 triple patterns, with UNION, OPTIONAL, and many filters, including Regexp. Many queries use ORDER BY/LIMIT clauses along with DISTINCT projections.

4   FedShop Reference Source Assignment (RSA)

For each instantiated query, we generated a Reference Source Assignment (RSA) standard, i.e., an executable SPARQL 1.1 query with service clauses where source assignment has been precomputed [7]. Producing RSA queries follow two important objectives:

Table 2. Fedshop queries features: #tp: Number of triple patterns, #bgp: Number of BGP, #join: Number of joins, #union: Number of unions, #var: Number of variables in a query #nodes: Number of nodes in the graph representation of the query, #edge: Number of edges in the graph representation of the query, MJVD: mean join vertices degree, #OPT: Number of OPTIONAL, #regex: FILTER regexp, #filterR: FILTER relational, OB: order by.

query	#tp	#bgp	#join	#union	#var	#nodes	#edges	MJVD	#OPT	#regex	#filterR	OB	Distinct	Limit
q01	8	1	7	0	6	9	8	1,78	0	0	1	1	1	1
q02	16	4	12	0	16	17	16	1,88	3	0	0	0	0	0
q03	11	2	9	0	9	12	11	1,83	1	0	2	1	0	1
q04	18	2	16	1	9	13	12	1,85	0	0	2	1	1	1
q05	11	1	10	0	11	12	11	1,83	0	0	5	1	1	1
q06	2	1	1	0	2	3	2	1,33	0	1	0	0	0	0
q07	17	5	12	0	15	18	17	1,89	4	0	1	0	0	0
q08	11	5	6	0	11	12	11	1,83	4	0	0	1	0	1
q09	1	1	0	0	1	2	1	1,00	0	0	0	0	0	0
q10	7	1	6	0	6	8	7	1,75	0	0	2	1	1	1
q11	3	3	1	1	4	4	3	1,50	0	0	0	0	0	0
q12	10	1	9	0	10	11	10	1,82	0	0	0	0	0	0

1) Verifying that all FedShop queries can be executed with reasonable execution time, so the use-case of exploring a federated shop is realizable, and 2) observing the gap of performances of existing federated query engines.

To produce the Reference Source Assignment, we proceed in two steps:

(i) We perform query decomposition queries manually into SPARQL 1.1 subqueries with SERVICE clauses [2] and exhaustive source assignment, i.e., each subquery is initially assigned to all federation members. We perform query decomposition by analyzing the join variables of queries, i.e., variables used by at least 2 triple patterns. Because of the FedShop data generation rules described in Sect. 3.1, we know that join variables on subjects can only be resolved on one endpoint. This corresponds to the notion of local join variables in [1]. We also know that join variables that need to be resolved between two endpoints can only appear as objects of sameAs predicates or as an attribute. This corresponds to the concept of global join variables in [1]. As there is no query with join variables on attributes, global join variables can only appear as objects of sameAs predicates. Through the analysis of the join variables, we can find an efficient decomposition of template queries.

(ii) We compute the minimal source selection over decomposed queries with a simple query rewriting and an evaluation over the union of all data.

By analyzing the join variables of the 12 template queries, we observed three kinds of decomposition:

Single-domain Decomposition is applied to queries with no global join variables and where a subject of a triple pattern is bound as the query Q12 presented in Listing 3a (the bounded subject is v7:Offer858). For these queries, all triple patterns can be grouped into one service clause, and only one endpoint should return results. Consequently, such a query can be rewritten with only one service clause, as presented in Listing 3b. With no further informa-

```
prefix v7: <http://www.vendor7.fr>
SELECT * WHERE { #Q12
v7:Offer858 bsbm:product ?productURI .
?productURI owl:sameAs ?ProductXYZ .
?productURI rdfs: label ? productlabel .
v7:Offer858 bsbm:vendor ?vendorURI .
?vendorURI rdfs: label ?vendorname .
?vendorURI foaf:homepage ?vendorhomepage .
v7:Offer858 bsbm:offerWebpage ?offerURL .
v7:Offer858 bsbm:price ? price .
v7:Offer858 bsbm:deliveryDays ? deliveryDays .
v7:Offer858 bsbm:validTo ?validTo }
```

(a) Single Domain Query (Q12)

```
prefix v7: <http://www.vendor7.fr>
SELECT DISTINCT * WHERE { #Q12
VALUES ?bgp1 { <http://vendor1.fr> <...> }
SERVICE ?bgp1 {
<v7/Offer858> bsbm:product ?productURI .
?productURI owl:sameAs ?ProductXYZ .
?productURI rdfs: label ?productlabel .
<v7/Offer858> bsbm:vendor ?vendorURI .
?vendorURI rdfs: label ?vendorname .
?vendorURI foaf:homepage ?vendorhomepage .
<v7/Offer858> bsbm:offerWebpage ?offerURL .
<v7/Offer858> bsbm:price ?price .
<v7/Offer858> bsbm:deliveryDays ?deliveryDays .
<v7/Offer858> bsbm:validTo ?validTo }}
```

(b) Single Domain service query (Q12)

Lst. 2. Single Domain Queries

```
SELECT DISTINCT ?product ?label
WHERE {
  ?product rdfs : label  ? label .
  ?product rdf :type ?localProductType .
  ?localProductType owl:sameAs bsbm:ProductType647 .
  ?product bsbm:productFeature ?localProductFeature1 .
  ?localProductFeature1 owl:sameAs bsbm:ProductFeature8774 .
  ?product bsbm:productFeature ?localProductFeature2 .
  ?localProductFeature2 owl:sameAs bsbm:ProductFeature16935 .
  ?product bsbm:productPropertyNumeric1 ?value1 .
    FILTER (?value1 > "744"^^xsd:integer) }
ORDER BY ?label
LIMIT 10
```

(a) Multi Domain Query (Q1)

```
SELECT DISTINCT ?product ?label WHERE {
  VALUES ( ?bgp1 ) { <http://www.vendor1.fr/> <...> }
  SERVICE ?bgp1 {
  ?product rdfs : label  ? label .
  ?product rdf :type ?localProductType .
  ?localProductType owl:sameAs bsbm:ProductType647 .
  ?product bsbm:productFeature ?localProductFeature1 .
  ?localProductFeature1 owl:sameAs bsbm:ProductFeature8774 .
  ?product bsbm:productFeature ?localProductFeature2 .
  ?localProductFeature2 owl:sameAs bsbm:ProductFeature16935 .
  ?product bsbm:productPropertyNumeric1 ?value1 .
    FILTER (?value1 > "744"^^xsd:integer) }}
ORDER BY ?product ?label
LIMIT 10
```

(b) Multi Domain service query (Q1)

Lst. 3. Multi-domain Queries: Q1

tion, all endpoints have to be considered to find the one that contains results. Queries Q9, Q11, and Q12 belong to the single domain class of decomposition. **Multi-domain Decomposition** is applied to queries with no global join variables and no bounded subject in triple patterns as the query Q1 in Listing 3a. For these queries, all the triple patterns can be grouped into one service clause, but multiple endpoints may return results. Listing 3b describes the decomposition of query Q1. With no additional information, all endpoints have to be considered to find those that return results. Queries Q1, Q2, Q3, Q4, Q6, Q8, and Q10 belong to the multi-domain class of decomposition.

Cross-domain Decomposition is applied to queries with global join variables as the query Q5 described in Listing 3a. Q5 has 2 global join variables: **?product** and **?productFeature**. Following the decomposition algorithm of

```
SELECT DISTINCT ?product ?localProductLabel
WHERE {
  ?localProduct rdfs : label ?localProductLabel .
  ?localProduct bsbm:productFeature ?localProdFeature .
  ?localProduct bsbm:productPropertyNumeric1 ?simProperty1 .
  ?localProduct bsbm:productPropertyNumeric2 ?simProperty2 .
  ?localProduct owl:sameAs ?product .
  ?localProdFeature owl:sameAs ?prodFeature .
  ?localProductXYZ bsbm:productFeature ?localProdFeatureXYZ .
  ?localProductXYZ bsbm:productPropertyNumeric1 ?origProperty1 .
  ?localProductXYZ bsbm:productPropertyNumeric2 ?origProperty2 .
  ?localProductXYZ owl:sameAs bsbm:Product136030 .
  ?localProdFeatureXYZ owl:sameAs ?prodFeature .
    FILTER (bsbm:Product136030 != ?product)
    FILTER (?simProperty1 < (?origProperty1 + 20) &&
      ?simProperty1 > (?origProperty1 − 20))
    FILTER (?simProperty2 < (?origProperty2 + 70) &&
      ?simProperty2 > (?origProperty2 − 70))}
ORDER BY ?localProductLabel
LIMIT 5
```

(a) Cross Domain Query (Q5)

```
SELECT DISTINCT ?product ?localProductLabel WHERE {
  VALUES ( ?bgp1 ?bgp2 ) {
    ( <http://www.vendor1.fr/> <http://www.vendor1.fr/> )
    ( <http://www.vendor1.fr/> <http://www.vendor2.fr/> )
    # ... ) }
  SERVICE ?bgp1 {
  ?localProductXYZ owl:sameAs bsbm:Product136030 .
  ?localProductXYZ bsbm:productFeature ?localProdFeatureXYZ .
  ?localProdFeatureXYZ owl:sameAs ?prodFeature .
  ?localProductXYZ bsbm:productPropertyNumeric1 ?origProperty1 .
  ?localProductXYZ bsbm:productPropertyNumeric2 ?origProperty2} .
  SERVICE ?bgp2 {
  ?localProduct owl:sameAs ?product .
    FILTER (bsbm:Product136030 != ?product)
  ?localProduct rdfs : label ?localProductLabel .
  ?localProduct bsbm:productFeature ?localProdFeature .
  ?localProdFeature owl:sameAs ?prodFeature .
  ?localProduct bsbm:productPropertyNumeric1 ?simProperty1 .
  ?localProduct bsbm:productPropertyNumeric2 ?simProperty2} .
  FILTER(?simProperty1 < (?origProperty1 + 20) &&
    ?simProperty1 > (?origProperty1 − 20))
  FILTER(?simProperty2 < (?origProperty2 + 70) &&
    ?simProperty2 > (?origProperty2 − 70))}
ORDER BY ?product ?localProductLabel
LIMIT 5
```

(b) Cross-Domain service query (Q5)

Lst. 4. Cross-Domain Queries: Q5

[1], we generate two *exclusive groups* one related to `?localProductXYZ` and the second is related to `?localProduct`. For this decomposition, we generate 2 service clauses as described in Listing 3b. A filter push-down allows to push one filter into a service clause. In this decomposition, we consider that all combinations of pairs of endpoints should be contacted, i.e., all pairs of sources should be declared in the `VALUES` clause of the service query. Queries Q5 and Q7 belong to the cross-domain class of decomposition.

Until now, the query decomposition and source selection produce an exhaustive source assignment, i.e., all combinations of endpoints are considered. For computing minimal source assignment [7], we rewrite service queries into *provenance queries* by simply replacing `SERVICE` clauses with `GRAPH` clauses and changing the projection of the query as illustrated in Fig. 5 for the query Q5. The execution of the query Q5prov over the union of RDF data of all federation members returns the pairs of endpoints that effectively contribute to the results of query Q5. The results of provenance queries are used to update the `VALUES` clauses of RSA queries.

To validate our query decomposition and source selection, we verified that all RSA queries return correct and complete results, i.e., we obtain the same results as original queries evaluated over the union of all datasets. We also verified that RSA queries could be executed under 2 s for all configurations of FedShop (see Sect. 5).

```
SELECT DISTINCT ?product ?localProductLabel WHERE {
  VALUES ( ?bgp1 ?bgp2 ) {
    ( <http://www.vendor1.fr/> <http://www.vendor1.fr/> )
    ( <http://www.vendor1.fr/> <http://www.vendor2.fr/> )
    # ... ) }
  SERVICE ?bgp1 {
    ?localProductXYZ owl:sameAs bsbm:Product136030 .
    ?localProductXYZ bsbm:productFeature ?localProdFeatureXYZ .
    ?localProdFeatureXYZ owl:sameAs ?prodFeature .
    ?localProductXYZ bsbm:productPropertyNumeric1 ?origProperty1 .
    ?localProductXYZ bsbm:productPropertyNumeric2 ?origProperty2} .
  SERVICE ?bgp2 {
    ?localProduct owl:sameAs ?product .
    FILTER (bsbm:Product136030 != ?product)
    ?localProduct rdfs: label ?localProductLabel .
    ?localProduct bsbm:productFeature ?localProdFeature .
    ?localProdFeature owl:sameAs ?prodFeature .
    ?localProduct bsbm:productPropertyNumeric1 ?simProperty1 .
    ?localProduct bsbm:productPropertyNumeric2 ?simProperty2} .
  FILTER(?simProperty1 < (?origProperty1 + 20) &&
    ?simProperty1 > (?origProperty1 − 20))
  FILTER(?simProperty2 < (?origProperty2 + 70) &&
    ?simProperty2 > (?origProperty2 − 70))}
  ORDER BY ?product ?localProductLabel
  LIMIT 5
```

(a) Cross-Domain service query Q5

```
SELECT DISTINCT ?bgp1 ?bgp2 WHERE {
  graph ?bgp1 {
    ?localProductXYZ owl:sameAs bsbm:Product136030 .
    ?localProductXYZ bsbm:productFeature ?localProdFeatureXYZ .
    ?localProdFeatureXYZ owl:sameAs ?prodFeature .
    ?localProductXYZ bsbm:productPropertyNumeric1 ?origProperty1 .
    ?localProductXYZ bsbm:productPropertyNumeric2 ?origProperty2} .
  graph ?bgp2 {
    ?localProduct owl:sameAs ?product .
    FILTER (bsbm:Product136030 != ?product)
    ?localProduct rdfs: label ?localProductLabel .
    ?localProduct bsbm:productFeature ?localProdFeature .
    ?localProdFeature owl:sameAs ?prodFeature .
    ?localProduct bsbm:productPropertyNumeric1 ?simProperty1 .
    ?localProduct bsbm:productPropertyNumeric2 ?simProperty2} .
  FILTER(?simProperty1 < (?origProperty1 + 20) &&
    ?simProperty1 > (?origProperty1 − 20))
  FILTER(?simProperty2 < (?origProperty2 + 70) &&
    ?simProperty2 > (?origProperty2 − 70))}
  ORDER BY ?product ?localProductLabel
  LIMIT 5
```

(b) Provenance query for $Q5_{prov}$

Lst. 5. Source selection for an instance of $Q5$

5   Experimental Study

The experimental study aims to answer the following questions:

(1) What is the performance of the Reference Source Assignment (RSA) defined in Sect. 4? Is it possible to run a federated shop of 200 shops with federated queries? (2) How do the performances of existing federated query engines as the federation size increases? What is the gap with the RSA ?

Generating Data and Queries. We used the FedShop data generator to generate a catalog of 200 000 products following the schema of Fig. 1. Next, we generated 10 federations: F(20) to F(200), where each federation is composed of half of the vendors and half of the reviewing sites, i.e., F(200) is a federation of 100 vendors and 100 review sites. All instructions to install, configure, and run the FedShop benchmark are available on the FedShop GitHub repository. We used the FedShop query generator to instantiate a workload of 120 queries, where each template query is randomly instantiated 10 times. The 120 queries are to be executed on each of the 10 federations: F(20) to F(200). Detailed statistics on the generated data are available in the Jupyter Notebook of the repository.

Setting Up Federations. Setting up a federation of 200 endpoints raises serious questions about the tractability of the experiment. Starting one physical endpoint per vendor/reviewing as proposed in KOBE [12] is not realistic if one considers large federations. We take another approach based on Virtual Endpoints as proposed in Virtuoso. All endpoints are represented as Virtual Endpoints hosted in one Virtuoso server. Each endpoint is connected to a named RDF graph corresponding to one vendor or one reviewing site[4]. The monitored federated query engine is not aware that all endpoints are virtual. The number of threads of the Virtuoso server is 20, and those of the federated query engines are 20; they are defined so that all subqueries of a federated query engine are executed in parallel on the Virtuoso server. Each query in the workload has to be executed sequentially to get the correct measurement of execution times.

To run the FedShop benchmark, we developed the FedShop runner that automatically deploys the federations, runs the queries among the different configurations, and monitors the federated query engines under evaluation. All the instructions to run the benchmark and add a new federated query engine are available on the FedShop GitHub repository.

Evaluated Engines. To validate the benchmark's ability to analyze different engines and to reveal a new class of insights about these engines, we run the 10 configurations of FedShop on engines assessed in CostFed [20], namely: FedX [23], CostFed [20], ANAPSID [3] and SPLENDID [9]. Lusail [1] is not part of the evaluation because no implementation is available. We run the RSA queries with Apache Jena. All evaluated engines were integrated into the FedShop runner to ensure the reproducibility of results. We relaunch the federated query engine each time we run a query, i.e., federated query caches are not kept between the processing of 2 different queries.

---

[4] The Virtuoso database used at generation time is reused for execution.

Metrics. In our experiment, we mainly measure the evolution of 3 metrics when the number of sources increases: (1) The *Execution Time* is the total time spent by the federated query engine to produce the query results. Each query is executed 4 times, and the reported execution time is the average of the 4 execution time. (2) The number of queries that timeout. (3) The number of queries that terminate with errors.

We set the time out to 60 s per federated query. As the FedShop use-case corresponds to an interactive exploration of shops and reviews, we consider that a user does not wait for more than 60 s for the results of any queries of FedShop. In the worst case, testing a federated engine requires 4800*60 s = 80h, 3 d.

Since the number of sources increases, if a query timeout for a federation $F(i\text{-}1)$, it should also timeout for federation $F(i)$. To save experiment time, we execute a query in $F(i)$ only if it did not timeout in $F(i\text{-}1)$ and if there is no timeout in other attempts in $F(i)$.

A query engine may also produce errors when executing a query. These errors can be caused by unsupported query features or simple runtime exceptions as out-of-memory. In case of an error, we report the error, but when computing average execution times, we attribute the timeout value to the query execution time. This means that having errors when computing the average execution time degrades the average execution time.

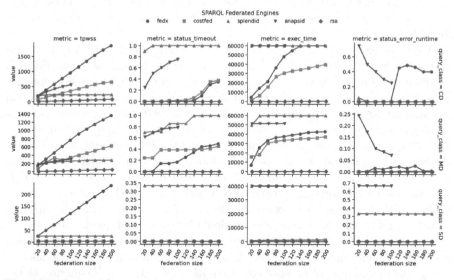

Fig. 3. Evolution of engine performance per query class. Each line of the plot corresponds to a class of queries from top to bottom: Cross-Domain (CD), Multi-Domain (MD), and Single Domain (SD). Columns correspond to evaluation metrics

5.1   Experimental Results

The overall results of the experimentation are displayed in Fig. 3. More detailed results per query and per engine are available in the Jupyter Notebook of the FedShop repository.

To improve the readability of the evaluation, we split the results according to the different classes of query decomposition detailed in Sect. 4, i.e., Single-Domain (SD) with 3 template queries and 30 instantiated queries, Multi-Domain (MD) with 7 template queries and 70 instantiated queries and Cross-Domain (CD) with 2 template queries and 20 instantiated queries.

For each class (CD/MD/SD), we computed the evolution of 3 metrics on the Y-axis as the size of the federation increases on the X-axis:

exec_time is the average execution time per query per class. The maximum value is 60 s as the timeout is set to 60 s.

error is the number of queries that finish with errors in the class. As there are 4 measurements per query, the maximum value for errors is respectively: $20 \times 4 = 80$ for the CD class, $70 \times 4 = 280$ for the MD class, and $30 \times 4 = 120$ for the SD class.

timeout is the number of queries that time out in the class. The maximum value per class is the same as for the error metric.

Since the size of the federation increases, source selection, execution times, and timeout should monotonically increase. The number of errors is not predictable.

We focus first on the execution time plot. We first see that RSA can execute all queries in less than 1 s on average with no errors. If we look at the detailed results in the Jupyter Notebook, the longest query of the RSA takes less than 2 s. This demonstrates that an adequate query decomposition and source selection can support interactive querying of a federation of 200 shops by a customer.

Regarding the execution time of evaluated federated engines, *we first observe that none can support interactive exploration of a federation of 200 shops.* Indeed, the best average execution time for Multi-domain queries is obtained by CostFed with more than 30 s. It goes up to 40 s for cross-domain queries. Only Single Domain queries are correctly processed by CostFed and FedX with performances similar to RSA queries. The execution times of Anapsid and Splendid increase quickly to reach the maximum average time of 60 s, i.e., all queries timeout.

We observe similar behavior on the timeout curves. No engine can terminate the workload without a timeout. FedX and CostFed process the SD queries correctly, but the number of timeouts grows quickly for MD and CD queries. Other engines have a high number of timeouts for the first configuration of FedShop.

Regarding the errors, as federated query engines are exposed for the first time to many endpoints with quite complex queries, they reveal some bugs in implementations. However, most errors come from out-of-memory errors. When federated queries are not properly decomposed, they generate significant data shipping from endpoints to federated query engines, and memory is quickly exhausted. We observe that the number of errors is decreasing for some engines.

The explanation is that the query timeouts before producing an error when the federation size increases.

Overall, we observe a significant performance gap between RSA and federated engines. Current federated engines fail to find the query decomposition of RSA. If triple patterns are not properly grouped, the number of subqueries sent to endpoints is high as the number of intermediate results transferred from endpoints to federated query engines. This seriously degrades performances. With RSA, the number of subqueries sent to endpoints is low as the number of intermediate results. This is the key to the high performance of RSA.

6   Concluding Remarks

FedShop is the first benchmark designed for studying the scalability of query federation engines. It is based on a well-known use-case of the semantic web community that makes sense in a federated context. The FedShop generator is highly configurable and generates a Reference Source Assignment standard (RSA) that can be used as an independent baseline. The FedShop runner allows running the experiment with reasonable resources in a reasonable time. It can be easily extended to integrate new federated query engines, as well as new use-cases (data and queries). We provided a smaller portion of FedShop (comprising only 12 queries and two federations) as a practical example of a recent query federation hackathon[5]. During the hackathon, the query federation engine developers utilized this FedShop fragment to identify various implementation problems and shortcomings in their engines[6]. In this paper, we presented a larger experiment highlighting the scalability issues for federated query engines and introduced the Reference Source Assignments (RSA). The RSA reveals ample opportunities for improvement in federated query engines.

As future work, considering its flexibility, FedShop can be improved in many different ways. Data generation can be customized to introduce diversity in shops where shops can have more products than others or shops are specialized in one category of product. We can also customize distribution laws per shop to control the structuredness of generated data [8]. It is also possible to introduce some noise during catalog replication to check semantic heterogeneity. For this paper, we keep BSBM queries and adapt them to the federated context. Adding new queries to have a more diversified query workload is possible. The last perspective of FedShop is beyond the benchmark. Current federation engines mainly targeted data integration use-case. A larger perspective for FedShop is to investigate how federation engines can be used to power federated applications.

Acknowledgments. This work is supported by the French ANR project DeKaloG (Decentralized Knowledge Graphs), ANR-19-CE23-0014, CE23 - Intelligence artificielle, the French CominLabs project MikroLog (The Microdata Knowledge Graph), and by Vetenskapsrådet (the Swedish Research Council, project reg. no. 2019-05655)

---

[5] https://github.com/MaastrichtU-IDS/federatedQueryKG.

[6] https://github.com/MaastrichtU-IDS/federatedQueryKG/blob/main/
UneditedReport.pdf.

References

1. Abdelaziz, I., Mansour, E., Ouzzani, M., Aboulnaga, A., Kalnis, P.: Lusail: a system for querying linked data at scale. Proc. VLDB Endow. **11**(4), 485–498 (2017)
2. Acosta, M., Hartig, O., Sequeda, J.: Federated RDF query processing. In: Sakr, S., Zomaya, A.Y. (eds.) Encyclopedia of Big Data Technologies, pp. 754–761. Springer, Cham (2019). https://doi.org/10.1007/978-3-319-77525-8_228
3. Acosta, M., Vidal, M.-E., Lampo, T., Castillo, J., Ruckhaus, E.: ANAPSID: an adaptive query processing engine for SPARQL endpoints. In: Aroyo, L., et al. (eds.) ISWC 2011. LNCS, vol. 7031, pp. 18–34. Springer, Heidelberg (2011). https://doi.org/10.1007/978-3-642-25073-6_2
4. Aluç, G., Hartig, O., Özsu, M.T., Daudjee, K.: Diversified stress testing of RDF data management systems. In: Mika, P., et al. (eds.) ISWC 2014. LNCS, vol. 8796, pp. 197–212. Springer, Cham (2014). https://doi.org/10.1007/978-3-319-11964-9_13
5. Bagan, G., Bonifati, A., Ciucanu, R., Fletcher, G.H.L., Lemay, A., Advokaat, N.: gmark: schema-driven generation of graphs and queries. In: 33rd IEEE International Conference on Data Engineering, ICDE 2017, San Diego, 19–22 April 2017, pp. 63–64. IEEE Computer Society (2017)
6. Bizer, C., Schultz, A.: The berlin SPARQL benchmark. Int. J. Semantic Web Inf. Syst. **5**(2), 1–24 (2009)
7. Cheng, S., Hartig, O.: Fedqpl: a language for logical query plans over heterogeneous federations of RDF data sources. In: Indrawan-Santiago, M., Pardede, E., Salvadori, I.L., Steinbauer, M., Khalil, I., Kotsis, G. (eds.) Proceedings of the 22nd International Conference on Information Integration and Web-Based Applications & Services, Virtual Event (iiWAS 2.20)/Chiang Mai, 30 November–2 December 2020, pp. 436–445. ACM (2020)
8. Duan, S., Kementsietsidis, A., Srinivas, K., Udrea, O.: Apples and oranges: a comparison of RDF benchmarks and real RDF datasets. In: Sellis, T.K., Miller, R.J., Kementsietsidis, A., Velegrakis, Y. (eds.) Proceedings of the ACM SIGMOD International Conference on Management of Data (SIGMOD 2011), Athens, Greece, 12–16 June 2011, pp. 145–156. ACM (2011)
9. Görlitz, O., Staab, S.: SPLENDID: SPARQL endpoint federation exploiting VOID descriptions. In: Hartig, O., Harth, A., Sequeda, J.F. (eds.) Proceedings of the Second International Workshop on Consuming Linked Data (COLD2011), Bonn, 23 October 2011, vol. 782 of CEUR Workshop Proceedings. CEUR-WS.org (2011)
10. Guo, Y., Pan, Z., Heflin, J.: LUBM: a benchmark for OWL knowledge base systems. J. Web Semant. **3**(2–3), 158–182 (2005)
11. Hasnain, A., Saleem, M., Ngonga Ngomo, A.-C., Rebholz-Schuhmann, D.: Extending largerdfbench for multi-source data at scale for SPARQL endpoint federation. In: Demidova, E., Zaveri, A., Simperl, E. (eds.) Emerging Topics in Semantic Technologies - ISWC 2018 Satellite Events [best papers from 13 of the workshops co-located with the ISWC 2018 conference], vol. 36 of Studies on the Semantic Web, pp. 203–218. IOS Press (2018)
12. Kostopoulos, C., Mouchakis, G., Troumpoukis, A., Prokopaki-Kostopoulou, N., Charalambidis, A., Konstantopoulos, S.: KOBE: Cloud-native open benchmarking engine for federated query processors. In: Verborgh, R., et al. (eds.) ESWC 2021. LNCS, vol. 12731, pp. 664–679. Springer, Cham (2021). https://doi.org/10.1007/978-3-030-77385-4_40

13. Montoya, G., Skaf-Molli, H., Molli, P., Vidal, M.-E.: Decomposing federated queries in presence of replicated fragments. J. Web Semant. **42**, 1–18 (2017)

14. Montoya, G., Vidal, M.-E., Corcho, O., Ruckhaus, E., Buil-Aranda, C.: Benchmarking federated SPARQL query engines: are existing testbeds enough? In: Cudré-Mauroux, P., et al. (eds.) ISWC 2012. LNCS, vol. 7650, pp. 313–324. Springer, Heidelberg (2012). https://doi.org/10.1007/978-3-642-35173-0_21

15. Oguz, D., Ergenc, B., Yin, S., Dikenelli, O., Hameurlain, A.: Federated query processing on linked data: a qualitative survey and open challenges. Knowl. Eng. Rev. **30**(5), 545–563 (2015)

16. Quilitz, B., Leser, U.: Querying distributed RDF data sources with SPARQL. In: Bechhofer, S., Hauswirth, M., Hoffmann, J., Koubarakis, M. (eds.) ESWC 2008. LNCS, vol. 5021, pp. 524–538. Springer, Heidelberg (2008). https://doi.org/10.1007/978-3-540-68234-9_39

17. Rakhmawati, N.A., Saleem, M., Lalithsena, S., Decker, S.: Qfed: query set for federated SPARQL query benchmark. In: Indrawan-Santiago, M., Steinbauer, M., Nguyen, H.-Q., Min Tjoa, A., Khalil, I., Anderst-Kotsis, G. (eds.) Proceedings of the 16th International Conference on Information Integration and Web-based Applications & Services, Hanoi, 4–6 December 2014, pp. 207–211. ACM (2014)

18. Saleem, M., Hasnain, A., Ngonga Ngomo, A.-C.: Largerdfbench: a billion triples benchmark for SPARQL endpoint federation. J. Web Semant. **48**, 85–125 (2018)

19. Saleem, M., Khan, Y., Hasnain, A., Ermilov, I., Ngonga Ngomo, A.-C.: A fine-grained evaluation of SPARQL endpoint federation systems. Semant. Web **7**(5), 493–518 (2016)

20. Saleem, M., Potocki, A., Soru, T., Hartig, O., Ngonga Ngomo, A.-C.: Costfed: cost-based query optimization for sparql endpoint federation. In: 14th International Conference on Semantic Systems (SEMANTICS), pp. 163–174. Elsevier (2018)

21. Schmidt, M., Görlitz, O., Haase, P., Ladwig, G., Schwarte, A., Tran, T.: FedBench: a benchmark suite for federated semantic data query processing. In: Aroyo, L., et al. (eds.) ISWC 2011. LNCS, vol. 7031, pp. 585–600. Springer, Heidelberg (2011). https://doi.org/10.1007/978-3-642-25073-6_37

22. Schmidt, M., Hornung, T., Meier, M., Pinkel, C., Lausen, G.: SP2Bench: a SPARQL performance benchmark. In: de Virgilio, R., Giunchiglia, F., Tanca, L. (eds.) Semantic Web Information Management: A Model-Based Perspective, pp. 371–393. Springer, Heidelberg (2010). https://doi.org/10.1007/978-3-642-04329-1_16

23. Schwarte, A., Haase, P., Hose, K., Schenkel, R., Schmidt, M.: FedX: a federation layer for distributed query processing on linked open data. In: Antoniou, G., et al. (eds.) The Semantic Web: Research and Applications, pp. 481–486. Springer, Heidelberg (2011). https://doi.org/10.1007/978-3-642-21064-8_39

24. Wang, X., Tiropanis, T., Davis, H.C.: LHD: optimising linked data query processing using parallelisation. In: Bizer, C., Heath, T., Berners-Lee, T., Hausenblas, M., Auer, S. (eds.) Proceedings of the WWW2013 Workshop on Linked Data on the Web, Rio de Janeiro, 14 May, 2013, vol. 996 of CEUR Workshop Proceedings. CEUR-WS.org (2013)

The Polifonia Ontology Network: Building a Semantic Backbone for Musical Heritage

Jacopo de Berardinis[1(✉)], Valentina Anita Carriero[2], Nitisha Jain[1],
Nicolas Lazzari[2], Albert Meroño-Peñuela[1], Andrea Poltronieri[2],
and Valentina Presutti[2]

[1] King's College London, 30 Aldwych, London, UK
jacopo.deberardinis@kcl.ac.uk
[2] University of Bologna, Bologna, Italy
andrea.poltronieri2@unibo.it

Abstract. In the music domain, several ontologies have been proposed to annotate musical data, in both symbolic and audio form, and generate semantically rich Music Knowledge Graphs. However, current models lack interoperability and are insufficient for representing music history and the cultural heritage context in which it was generated; risking the propagation of recency and cultural biases to downstream applications. In this article, we propose the Polifonia Ontology Network (PON) for music cultural heritage, centred around four modules: Music Meta (metadata), Representation (content), Source (provenance) and Instrument (cultural objects). We design PON with a strong accent on cultural stakeholder requirements and competency questions (CQs), contributing an NLP-based toolkit to support knowledge engineers in generating, validating, and analysing them; and a novel, high-quality CQ dataset produced as a result. We show current and future use of these resources by internal project pilots, early adopters in the music industry, and opportunities for the Semantic Web and Music Information Retrieval communities.

Keywords: Knowledge engineering · Ontology · Music Cultural heritage · Competency questions

1 Introduction

Musical heritage encompasses a diversity of human expressions and experiences leaving heterogeneous traces that are difficult to describe, connect, and preserve [30]. In Europe, music cultural heritage developed through varied sources: musical contents and objects (such as tunes, scores, melodies, notations, recordings, etc.) linked to tangible objects (theatres, conservatoires, churches, instruments, etc.) but also to their cultural and historical contexts, opinions and stories told by people with diverse social and artistic roles (scholars, writers, students, intellectuals, musicians, politicians, journalists, etc.), and facts expressed in different styles and perspectives (memoire, reportage, news, biographies, reviews)

© The Author(s) 2023
T. R. Payne et al. (Eds.): ISWC 2023, LNCS 14266, pp. 302–322, 2023.
https://doi.org/10.1007/978-3-031-47243-5_17

in different languages (English, Italian, French, Spanish, and German) and across centuries [10]. This diversity creates unique opportunities as well as challenges for researchers and practitioners attempting to study and preserve music heritage.

In the H2020 Polifonia project[1], various memory institutions, museums, music archives, scholars, commercial organisations, and citizens ask questions (e.g. *"Which tunes share melodic patterns and geographical origin?"*; *"How do libretto and music relate, e.g. in describing an emotion?"*; *"Can we trace the evolution of tonality and transition from modal to tonal?"*) across these multi-perspective and multi-modal sources. This demands the integration of musicological (notes, chords, modes, theories), historical (events, persons, places, objects) and archival/preservation (metadata, descriptors) data and perspectives. The project comprises 4 cultural institutions (CNAM, NISV, MiC, KNAW) and 10 pilots with a large variety and number of requirements. Ontologies and knowledge graphs (KGs) have the potential to overcome these challenges, and shed light on this wealth of resources by extracting, materialising and linking new music history knowledge that was previously overlooked and therefore missing [11,46].

Various ontologies and knowledge engineering methods have been proposed and applied to music industry and cultural heritage [13,48]. For example, Music Ontology [48] and DOREMUS [2] provide models to describe music metadata with a focus on discographic and classical music, respectively. Although these ontologies cover some aspects of musical heritage interest, they are individually insufficient to overcome the challenge of integrating the notation, metadata, and historical contexts needed for multi-perspective cultural analyses; thus leaving questions about the relationship between musical theory (melodies, tonalities, chords) and culture (historical events, architecture, geography) unanswered. To date, no available ontological framework integrates music metadata, notation, annotation, source provenance, and cultural heritage object descriptions. To the best of our knowledge, no toolkits exist to support knowledge engineering tasks around the lifecycle of competency questions, which is a central project requirement given the large number of variety of stakeholders, pilots and questions.

In this work, we describe the **Polifonia Ontology Network (PON), a set of new ontologies formalising the semantics of music representation, metadata, annotation, analysis, mediums of performance (instruments), and historical sources (provenance)**, enabling the creation of interoperable knowledge graphs from music datasets. To achieve this, we apply and extend eXtreme Design (XD) [9], a well-known ontology design methodology where ontological requirements are gathered from a comprehensive inventory of competency questions (CQs), and modularity is fostered through the reuse of Ontology Design Patterns (ODPs) [24,32]. We also release the PolifoniaCQ dataset, a collection of 361 competency questions on musical heritage. Further, we validate PON and provide evidence of its current and planned (re)use by three different types of users: (i) the Polifonia pilots, using them to generate musical culture KGs; (ii) a number of industrial and institutional stakeholders and early adopters, planning to use PON to annotate their in-house datasets;

---

[1] https://polifonia-project.eu/.

and (iii) a survey run in the Semantic Web and Music Technology communities showing intentions of use. More specifically, the contributions of this article are:

- *Extensions to XD* centred around CQ extraction and enhancement, including both methodological (a CQ-elicitation framework to mirror use cases from domain experts) and technological (a toolkit for assisted design and iterative improvement of CQs through language models) aspects (Sect. 3).
- *PolifoniaCQ*, a new dataset of competency questions driving the design and the evaluation of PON, with associated stories and personas (Sect. 3.1).
- The *Polifonia Ontology Network (PON v1.0)* resources, available on GitHub[2] and including 15 (CC-BY 4.0) ontology modules (Sect. 4).
- *Evidence of reuse* and impact from music stakeholders, applications within Polifonia, and interest from various research communities (Sect. 5).

2   Related Work

Ontologies play a fundamental role in the representation and management of knowledge, by providing common vocabularies to describe resources and queries. In the cultural heritage domain, there have been several efforts in this direction, such as the ArCo ontology, which pertains to the Italian cultural heritage [13], as well as others [11, 34]. Several ontologies exist in the music domain for addressing diverse applications, dealing with both symbolic notations and audio signal at different levels of specificity. MusoW [1] is a catalogue indexing online music resources, including ontologies and KGs. Here, we focus on music ontologies and categorise them according to their reference domain: (i) metadata; (ii) music theory; (iii) music notation; and (iv) audio features.

Multiple ontologies describe high-level music-related metadata, with the Music Ontology [48] and DOREMUS [41] being the most renowned. Other models focus on specific metadata: the OMAC Ontology describes musical works and claims about them [53]; the Performed Music Ontology[3] specialises on performances, and the OnVIE Ontology [55] describes mediums of performances. Similarly, the Musical Instrument Taxonomies [39] model instruments conceptually and terminologically, and the Smart Music Instrument Ontology [58] covers sensors and instruments within the realm of the Internet of Musical Things [57].

Some ontologies describe different elements ascribable to *music theory*. The Music Theory Ontology (MTO) [49] covers theoretical concepts of music theory, while the Functional Harmony Ontology [37] analyses harmonic sequences through reasoning. The Chord Ontology, Tonality Ontology, and Temperament Ontology [22] cover chords, tonal content, and instrument tuning, respectively.

Ontologies have also attempted to describe *musical notation*. For instance, the MIDI Linked Data Cloud [45] proposes a way to connect symbolic music descriptions that are encoded in the MIDI format. Meanwhile, the CHARM ontology [29] is focused on representing musical structures. The Music Theory

---

[2] https://github.com/polifonia-project/ontology-network.
[3] https://performedmusicontology.org/.

Ontology (MTO) [49] aims to capture the theoretical concepts related to music compositions, while the Music Score Ontology (Music OWL) [36] and the Music Annotation Ontology [17] represent the content of a music score.

Other works focus on audio signals or the procedures used to produce them. For example, The Audio Features Ontology [3], The Studio Ontology [21], and The Audio Effects Ontology [59] are dedicated to describing different aspects of audio production. The Computational Analysis of the Live Music Archive (CALMA) [4] project aims to link metadata of music tracks with computational analyses of recordings, through feature extraction, clustering, and classification. Additionally, ontologies have been used to model listeners' habits and music tastes, as well as similarities between different musical pieces [35,38,51,56].

Despite the numerous contributions, the scope of these ontologies is often too specific or ingrained in a genre, style, historical period – often addressing individual music stakeholders and/or datasets. Several ontologies were also developed independently, with little coordination across relevant contributions. In turn, this often hampers reuse and extension, while jeopardising interoperability – an essential requirement for the integration of music datasets [12].

3   The eXtreme Design Methodology in Polifonia

The Polifonia Ontology Network (PON) addresses the aforementioned challenges by integrating heterogeneous requirements related to musical content and contexts into a modular yet unified architecture. To develop PON, we rely on, and extend, the eXtreme Design [8,9] (XD) ontology engineering methodology. XD fosters the reuse of ontology design patterns (ODPs) [24,32] and provides support to incrementally address small sets of requirements formalised as competency questions (CQs). This minimises the impact of changes in future releases, which is beneficial to Polifonia (heterogeneous project requirements and participants). Moreover, XD has been successfully applied to the cultural heritage domain [14], and our ontology designers have relevant experience in using this methodology.

The application of XD iterates over a series of steps, for which we detail their process while highlighting our main extensions (see Fig. 1).

3.1   Requirements Collection

Ontological requirements are collected from *customers* in the form of *user stories* (e.g. "*Tosca* was performed in Rome on 14 January 2000"), which are then translated as competency questions (CQs) – the natural language counterpart of structured queries that the resulting KG should answer [26]. For instance, the previous story may become "*Where was a musical piece performed?*".

We borrow techniques from User eXperience design [25] to extend this framework with 3 new sections in the story template: persona, goal, and scenario. The *persona* is a research-based description of a typical user: name, age, occupation, skills and interests. The *goal* is a short textual description of what the persona

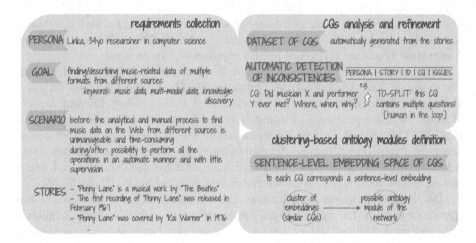

Fig. 1. Summary of the main Polifonia extensions to the eXtreme Design methodology.

aims to achieve in the story, complemented by a list of keywords (maximum 5) provided by the customers. The *scenario* describes how the persona's goals are currently solved, to contextualise the gap with the resource being developed.

In cooperation with the domain experts in Polifonia (music historians, librarians, computational musicologists, music analysts, archivists, data engineers, etc.), 22 personas have been created[4] from this step.

Iterative Refinement of CQs. Competency questions were then analysed to identify any inconsistencies that could create obstacles for ontology design. Common inconsistencies were due to vague concepts, for instance, the assertion of two compositions being *connected* without any specific context (in terms of the property) on which the connection can be established (e.g. similar melodies, rhythm). Other CQs were found to be overly complex or nested – entailing more than a single requirement as a result of nested logical operators articulating the question (e.g. "*How is track B connected to C to conclude D?*"). Such CQs needed to be conceptually simplified before being processed further.

To efficiently address these inconsistencies, we developed the *Infer, DEsign, CreAte* (IDEA) framework: analytical tools for CQ-driven ontology design based on language models[5]. IDEA automatically extrapolates and organises CQs from a source repository, analyses them to find inconsistencies and similarities, and visually projects them to a sentence-level embedding space [54]. The framework has enabled the iterative refinement and improvement of CQs through human-machine collaboration: questions are first extracted and preliminary validated by tagging them (complex, nested, ill-formed, passing), then brought to the attention of the corresponding ontology designer whenever their intervention is

---

[4] https://github.com/polifonia-project/stories.
[5] https://github.com/polifonia-project/idea.

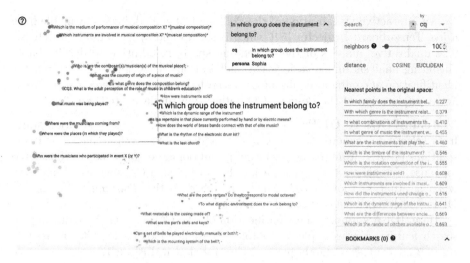

Fig. 2. Visualisation of the Polifonia CQ embeddings using TensorBoard.

needed. To date, 3 cycles of CQ improvement have been completed with IDEA. Instead, the analysis of CQ embeddings through similarity facilitated the identification of overlapping requirements from the pilots (beyond the syntactic level); which in turn enabled and fuelled discussion from various experts and pilots during our ontology design meetings (e.g. 2 CQs may have similar interpretation or semantics for OD, but entail different semantics across pilots).

The PolifoniaCQ Dataset. At the end of this process, we obtained 361 CQs, which are systematically collected in the PolifoniaCQ dataset with pointers to their personas and stories. We make this dataset available under CC-BY 4.0[6].

3.2 Ontology Network Design and Development

Clustering CQs as Ontology Modules. The refined CQs could then be translated in clear, atomic and consistent ontological requirements. Given the wide diversity of CQs – ranging from general events to musicological interpretations of specific passages in compositions, the first step was to achieve a meaningful categorisation into thematic clusters. This step led to the definition of the ontology modules shaping the architecture of the Polifonia Ontology Network.

To streamline this process, we analysed the CQ embedding space generated and projected by IDEA. This is done by computing the sentence-level embeddings (a feature vector of fixed size) for each CQ in the PolifoniaCQ dataset. The latter can be considered as a point in a high dimensional space – providing a numerical summary of the question's meaning [18]. Embeddings are computed via Sentence-BERT [50] due to its state of the art performance on a number of question-related tasks, including multi-lingual search and paraphrase detection.

---

[6] https://github.com/polifonia-project/polifoniacq-dataset.

An interactive visualisation of the PolifoniaCQ embeddings is available from a live Tensorboard Projector [54] which is set up and synchronised via IDEA[7]. The qualitative analysis of the embedding space, in addition to density-based clustering analysis under various parametrisations, have jointly facilitated the identification of common requirements (as nested clusters) and enabled the interactive exploration of the PolifoniaCQ dataset via similarity (c.f. Fig. 2).

Matching CQs to ODPs. For each module/ontology, an XD iteration starts from selecting a coherent set of CQs. To address those requirements, existing solutions (ODPs) from ontologies or online catalogues of patterns are considered for reuse, extension, and specialisation. For instance, a CQ such as "Where and when a situation took place?" can be matched to the *TimeIndexedSituation*[8] ODP, which represents temporal situations.

Here, IDEA supports the identification of "the CQ set" via the multi-lingual search feature. For example, an ontology designer looking for CQs related to places may express a search query as shown below in Listing 1.1.

Listing 1.1. Search results for query "*questions related to places*" with similarity score.

```
1    0.377   Where were the places in which musicians played?
2    0.368   Which are all organs near to geographic coordinates x, y?
3    0.341   What are geographically distinct features of organs from a region?
4    0.287   Where is the church/bell tower?
5    0.285   What is the provenance of the event attendees?
6    0.275   Which tunes which share melodic patterns or geographical origin?
7    0.265   What places did a musician visited in her career?
8    0.263   Where is the Bell Tower?
9    0.246   Where was a musical composition performed?
10   0.238   In which buildings was a musical composition performed?
```

Direct/Indirect Ontology Reuse. Depending on the project's requirements, reuse of ontologies and ODPs is direct and/or indirect [15]. The former approach directly includes/imports ontologies or part of them (e.g. individual entities, relations) thus introducing a dependency to any possible changes and availability. In indirect reuse, relevant entities and patterns from other ontologies are used as templates (replicated and extended) while being aligned to ensure interoperability. In Polifonia, we follow a hybrid approach: ArCo ontology [13] is directly reused since its development and maintenance involves one of the project's partners (MiC), while others (such as DOREMUS) are indirectly reused and aligned.

Validation and Testing. Ontology modules have been developed in close collaboration with domain experts and pilot leaders throughout the whole development cycle. This has allowed the ontology design team to leverage the domain expertise in Polifonia to technically validate our modules at different stages: from the collection and analysis of requirements, to iterations of ontology designs. Validation was facilitated by IDEA (at the CQ-level), and, at the modelling level, by the Graphical Framework For OWL Ontologies (Graffoo) notation [20] – providing a powerful visual language for coproduction activities. This has also been

---

[7] https://polifonia-project.github.io/idea/category/competency-questions.

[8] http://ontologydesignpatterns.org/wiki/Submissions:TimeIndexedSituation.

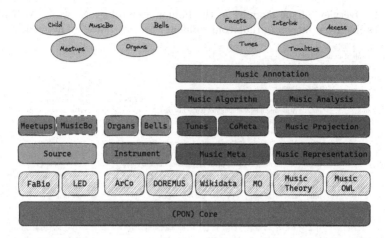

Fig. 3. Overview of the main modules in the Polifonia Ontology Network, with Polifonia's pilots as early adopters (grey circles). Foundational models (`Source`, `Instrument`, `Music Meta`, `Music Representation`) provide the backbone of PON, built on top of the `Core` module while leveraging the main ontologies reused directly or indirectly.

achieved through data snippets provided by the pilots, which have been modelled by our ontologies and triggered further iterations of improvements.

Overall, the involvement of domain experts from different institutions and background (complementary views and notions), the 10 pilots in the Polifonia project (reasonable diversity of application domains), and the use of collaborative workflows have also contributed to mitigate bias in the development of PON.

4   The Polifonia Ontology Network

The Polifonia Ontology Network (PON) provides a modular backbone of music ontologies to address both cultural heritage and more general queries in the music domain. As illustrated in Fig. 3, PON v1.0 comprises 15 ontology modules that are organised thematically (colours, horizontal view) and hierarchically, to highlight their dependencies (vertical view). At the bottom of the architecture lies our `Core` module (providing general-purpose elements of design, ODPs, and alignments) and the reused ontologies. Four foundational models provide interoperability across PON through their abstract design: `Source`, `Instrument`, `Music Meta`, and `Music Representation`. These are specialised and extended in the upper levels to add functionalities and contextualise specific domains.

A summary of PON modules is given in Table 1, with links to the repositories storing the modules with documentation, diagrams, and examples. Through our foundational models, PON ontologies can be applied to a wide set of music projects, and the modular design simplifies extensibility and maintenance. To facilitate this process, further documentation and tutorials are also being made available at https://polifonia-project.github.io/ontology-network/. An example of use involving 5 PON modules (besides `Core`) is shown in Fig. 4.

Table 1. Overview of the modules in the Polifonia Ontology Network. All URIs are also accessible from https://github.com/polifonia-project/ontology-network.

de Berardinis, J. et al. (2023).
The Polifonia Ontology Network: Building a Semantic Backbone for Musical Heritage.
10.5281/zenodo.7919970

Module	Prefix	Outline	Repository
Core	core:	Elements of general reuse and ontology design patterns	/core-ontology
Music Meta	mm:	Achieving interoperability of music metadata	/music-meta-ontology
Music Representation	mr:	Foundational model to describe arbitrary musical content	/music-representation-ontology
Music Instrument	mop:	Instruments and their evolution through time and space	/music-instrument-ontology
Source	src:	Musical sources and their context of production	/source-ontology
Tunes	tunes:	A specialisation of Music Meta for folk music	/tunes-ontology
CoMeta	com:	An extension of Music Meta to represent music corpora	/cometa-ontology
Music Projection	mp:	Achieving interoperability of music notation systems	/music-projection-ontology
Organs	organ:	A rich descriptive model of organs and building methods	/organs-ontology
Bells	bell:	Describing bells, bell towers and bell ringers	/bell-ontology
Music Algorithm	mx:	Computational methods for music and their parametrisation	/music-algorithm-ontology
Music Analysis	ma:	Music analysis through reasoning using modal-tonal theories	/music-analysis-ontology
Music Annotation	ann:	A wrapper of ontologies for music annotations (audio, symbolic)	/music-annotation-ontology
PON (full)	pon:	The whole Polifonia Ontology Network (imports all modules).	**/ontology-network**

4.1 Foundational Models and Their Extensions and Specialisations

The Music Meta module provides a rich and flexible ontology to describe music metadata related to artists, compositions, performances, recordings, broadcasts, and links. Music Meta focuses on provenance and interoperability – essential requirements for the integration of music datasets, which is currently hampered by the specificity of existent ontologies. The model is based on the Information-Realisation ODP [23], allowing to reduce complexity of FRBR-based models, whose application in the music domain has raised concerns [52].

To enable data integration from existing knowledge bases and datasets, we also align Meta to Music Ontology [48], DOREMUS [3], and Wikidata. To facilitate the reuse of Music Meta and its data conversion into OWL/RDF Knowledge Graphs, we developed a library to map arbitrary music metadata into RDF triples. This enables a practical and scalable workflow for data lifting to create Music Knowledge Graphs without expert knowledge of our ontological model.

The Tunes module extends and specialises Music Meta for folk music. The main novelty consists in grouping and describing *tunes* into *"tune families"* depending on their melodic similarity (an association requiring rich provenance description of the musicological analysis on the source); which also extends to lyrics families.

CoMeta reuses and extends Music Meta to describe arbitrary music collections, corpora, and datasets. Here, metadata is described at the *collection-level* (data curator, annotations provided, availability of audio music, etc.), and at the *content-level*, (e.g., the title, artist, release of each piece in a dataset). The design of CoMeta is informed by a survey of Music Information Retrieval datasets [44].

The Music Representation module provides a comprehensive schema to describe the analysis of musical objects (a score, an audio track, etc.) interpreted according to a theory. Fragments of a musical object (elements of a music object whose temporal location is uniquely identifiable) are described by annotations provided by an agent (e.g. expert annotator, algorithm). An annotation is either the subjective result of an analysis (e.g. a chord played in a specific section) or objective in nature (e.g. a note in a digital score). Each annotation describes some music content (e.g. notes, chords, etc.), which we refer to as a *musical projection* [42]. Annotations are formalised via our Music Annotation Pattern [5]. whereas the definition of music projections is delegated to the Music Projection module. The generality of the module and its abstraction over the represented content enables the interoperability of different music annotation schemas. The module is aligned to MusicOWL [36], Music Notation Ontology [16], Music Note Ontology [47], and our JAMS ontology (c.f. Sect. 4.2).

The Music Projection module formalises musical entities that can be subject of an annotation. This ranges from traditional musical notation (e.g. note, chords) to informal annotations (e.g. mood, danceability). The module is aligned with MusicOWL, Music Notation Ontology, Music Note Ontology, Music Theory Ontology [49], Chord Ontology [22], and Roman Chord Ontology[9]. This allows to integrate existing domain ontologies. Notably, we also harmonise different chord representations (Chord Ontology, the Roman Chord Ontology and the Tonality Ontology) based on the Unified Model of Chords in Western Harmony [31].

The Instrument Module describes musical instruments as mediums of performance and their technical properties. Given that numerous taxonomies of instruments into *groups* and *families* exist (e.g. Hornbostel-Sachs, MIMO, MusicBrainz) and finding common categorisations is an open problem [39], our module provides an abstraction capable to express arbitrary classifications. This is achieved by leveraging the Information-Realisation and the Collection ODPs. Overall, the module allows to: (i) refer to instruments as entities (an instrumentation of a piece for "piano" and "viola") as well as conceptually (e.g. a viola has 4 strings); (ii) support the integration with different taxonomies and vocabularies, such as [40]; (iii) describe the evolution of instruments in time and space (e.g. a viola as a cultural heritage object being relocated). This provides a foundational level where contributors can "plug" their instrument-specific ontologies [60].

The Bells module extends Instrument to describe bells by means of measurable, intrinsic aspects such as weight, materials, conservation status. The main entities contextualising bells are: (i) the author(s), such as the foundry who built the bell; (ii) the agencies that played some role e.g. the agency that took care of cataloguing the bell; (iii) the place(s) where it has been located; (iv) the tower(s) where the bell has been included; (v) the tools that the set of bells is played with; (vi) documents related to the bells, e.g. bibliographies, protective measures.

The Organs module extends Instrument to describe organs as (i) a musical instrument consisting of parts; and (ii) as a focal point of *projects* detailing its

---

[9] https://github.com/polifonia-project/roman-chord-ontology.

changes throughout time. To address the former, we used the Parthood pattern from the DOLCE ontology[10]. The entities of the ODP, `Whole` and `Part` make possible the specification of the whole instrument and its parts. In the ontology, the `Whole` entity refers to the organ instrument, and the `Part` entity refers to the parts of the organ that are `Console`, `WindSystem`, `Case`, `Division`, and `Action`.

The Source module represents various sources of music-related information. These include manuscripts, textbooks, articles, interviews, reviews, comments, memoirs, etc. of different scope and format (physical, digital). The module aims to provide general support to describe information related to the *creator* and *type* of the source, the *time* and *place* when/where it was created, the *context of production* and *usage*, and the *subject* and *goals*. Although this conceptualisation leans towards bibliographical sources, the module provides expressivity to indicate multimedia documents (e.g. images of scores, audio recording, video). For example, a video recording of a performance can be considered as a musical source – providing documentary evidence of a composition e.g. during an event.

The Meetups module describes encounters between people in the musical world in Europe from c. 1800 to c. 1945. Historical meetups, which are the main subject of this module, are described by means of four main components: the people involved in the meetup, for instance, the person that is the subject of interest and the people interacting in the event, the place where the encounter took place (e.g., city, country, venue), the type of event, the reason (e.g., music making, personal life, business, among others) and the date when it took place.

The MusicBO module is developed by following a *KG-to-ontology* process [43]. Ontological axioms, grouped into *patterns*, are empirically generated from the MusicBO knowledge graph – which is built from a textual corpus on music performances and encounters between music-related agents in Bologna since the 17th century. Such patterns include information about the probability of axioms to *happen* (as they are derived from the data). For instance, the probability of instances of the pattern *compose* situation (the process of creating art) to have `NaturalPerson` as range of the `artist` property, is higher than the probability of having an `Organisation` as a composer. In sum, the content of the ontology module is highly dependent on the KG, and the most populated and described entities are: persons, places, organisations, works of art, theatres, and books.

4.2 Modules for Analysis and Annotation of Music

The Music Algorithm module formalises algorithms that can operate on music metadata (using the Meta module), and musical content (via the representation module). The module commitments are similar to those defined by Diamantini et al. in [19]. Indeed, an algorithm is characterised by three main components: a *formalisation*, which can be theoretical (e.g. pseudocode) or executable (e.g.

---

[10] http://www.ontologydesignpatterns.org/ont/dul/DUL.owl.

using a programming language); a *parametrisation* (e.g. input data); and the kind of *task* it solves. The latter defines a set of entities that are processed alongside the input and output data requirements and the final goal achieved. The module allows theoretical and quantitative performances to be represented in the context of the algorithm's parametrisation. Through an abstract and general definition, the formalisation in Music Algorithm can be seen as a general pattern, capable of representing any algorithm regardless of the domain of application. In the context of music, the output of the algorithm is considered an analysis, which is then represented via the **Representation** module.

The Music Analysis module allows for the analysis of musical pieces using historical and present-day established musical theories: the *modal* and *tonal* theories. Through the use of this framework, different subjective analyses can be unified – overcoming the limitations imposed by a "global" theoretical perspective. Different theoretical viewpoints can be used for the interpretation of the same piece. Currently, two historical theories are implemented: Zarlino (1558) and Praetorius (1619) [27,28]. Through the use of formal reasoning and a comprehensive axiomatisation, the ontology is able to automatically infer the theoretical interpretations of a musical piece and its evolution in time and space.

The Music Annotation module provides different music annotation models to accommodate musicological and information retrieval use cases. The primary objective of this module is to enhance support for other descriptional systems, thus increasing interoperability and conversion possibilities from various music annotation formats. Indeed, all our models are logically interconnected through **Music Representation**. A fully fledged annotation model here is the JAMS Ontology [7][11]. This ontology mimics the structure of a JAMS (JSON Annotated Music Specification for Reproducible MIR Research) document [33]. It semantically describes and connects all the elements of the JAMS specification (**Annotation, Observation**, etc.), including the music metadata and the annotation contents using the **Music Meta** and **Representation** modules, respectively.

5   Adoption and Impact

We provide evidence of PON use by Polifonia pilots (Interlink, Tonalities, Meetups, Bells, and MusicBO), which have contributed 6 musical heritage KGs (Sect. 5.1); potential interest of reuse and opportunities for the Semantic Web and Music Technology communities collected from an online survey (Sect. 5.2); early adopters and ongoing synergies from the Polifonia Stakeholder Network for PON validation and annotation of cultural and industrial datasets (Sect. 5.3).

5.1   Current Use by Polifonia Pilots

Interlink has released ChoCo and Harmory KGs. Choco [7] provides 20K+ harmonic annotations of scores and tracks, that were integrated from 18 chord

---

[11] https://github.com/polifonia-project/jams-ontology.

datasets[12]. The KG uses the JAMS ontology in `Music Annotation`, and the `Roman` ontology from the `Music Projection` module. Harmory [6] is a KG of interconnected harmonic patterns derived from ChoCo, and aimed at human-machine creativity (pattern discovery, chord generation, harmonic similarity).

Tonalities KG includes data[13] from 377 MEI scores and their annotations w.r.t. theoretical concepts (roots, harmonic progressions, dissonant patterns, cadences, etc.), using the 2 theoretical models in the `Music Analysis` module.

Meetups KG describes 74K+ historical meetups from c.1800 to 1945, mentioning 51K+ people from 5K+ places in Europe[14]. It uses the `Meetups` ontology and is extracted from 1K artists' biographies on open-access digital sources.

Bells KG describes 88 bells catalogued by the Italian Ministry of Culture[15]. It relies on the `Bells` module and is part of the ArCo KG – the largest Italian cultural heritage KG from the Italian General Catalogue of Cultural Heritage.

MusicBO KG is built via text-to-KG methods [43] on a collection of 137 documents[16] on performances and encounters between musicians, composers, and critics happened in Bologna from the 17th century. As mentioned in Sect. 4, the KG[17] is used as input to the *bottom-up* modelling of the `MusicBO` ontology.

5.2 Survey of Interest for Future Applications

To gather interest of adoption, we conducted an online survey in which we ask potential adopters 14 questions regarding their background, relevance, and interest in using music ontologies. The survey was conducted via Google Forms, and distributed in the Semantic Web (SW), Music Information Retrieval (MIR), and Digital Humanities mailing lists – gathering a total of $N = 61$ responses. Among our respondents, 25 work in Semantic Web, 23 in MIR, 26 in Musicology. Most of them have encountered the need for modelling music related data and resources with ontologies (65.6%), focusing primarily on music metadata (45) theory and notation (29), annotations (25) and instruments (28); with 75% doing research or project work related to music data with multiple stakeholders.

Participants were asked to quantify the agreement with statements from 1 (absolutely disagree) to 5 (absolutely agree), 3 being a neutral response (NR; neither agree nor disagree). Results are illustrated in Fig. 5. From questions 6–14 we found that: 49.2% find the reuse of existing music ontologies to be challenging (with 42.6% NR), and the same can be said about the interoperoperability of existing ontologies (57%; 36% NR), their lack of coverage of concepts related to music history and music cultural heritage (57.3%; 32.8% NR); and the lack of large datasets of competency questions for this domain (63%; 34% NR). We also

---

[12] https://polifonia.disi.unibo.it/choco/.

[13] https://data-iremus.huma-num.fr/sparql.

[14] http://data.open.ac.uk/context/meetups.

[15] https://dati.cultura.gov.it/sparql.

[16] https://doi.org/10.5281/zenodo.6672165.

[17] https://polifonia.disi.unibo.it/musicbo/.

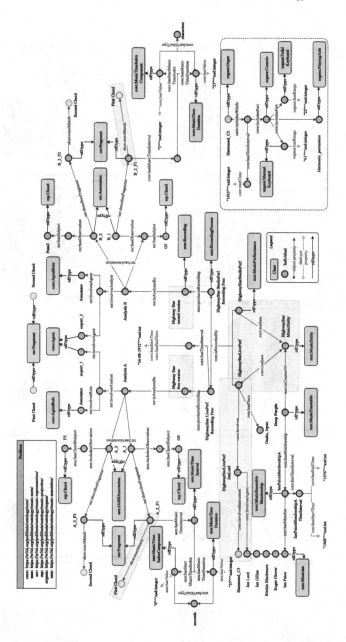

Fig. 4. Graffoo [20] example of "Highway Star" by Deep Purple using 5 PON modules to describe: metadata information (Music Meta, *bottom*), instrument (Organs, *bottom-right*) and annotation of musical content on two audio recordings via the Music Representation, Projection, and Annotation modules, either related to a studio (*top-right*) or a live (*top-left*) performance of the same piece. We remark how the two musical annotations are made interoperable via PON despite their profound differences (JAMS [33] and text, respectively) as they refer to the same fragment.

316   J. de Berardinis et al.

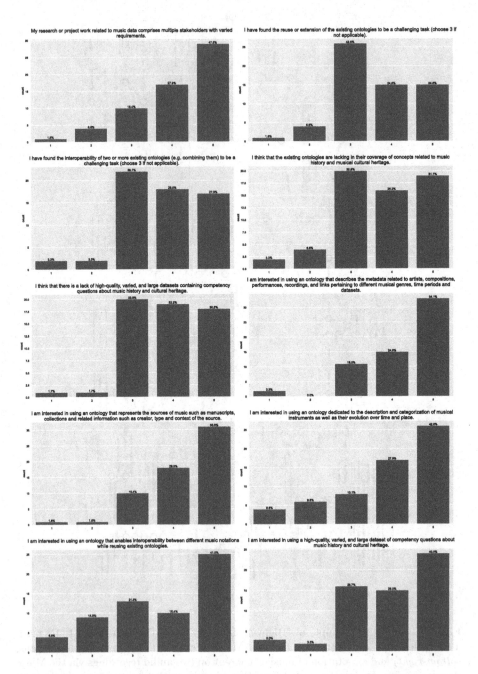

Fig. 5. Selection of questions 4, 6, 7–14 from the online survey, where responses are expressed on a Likert scale ranging from 1 (*strongly disagree*) to 5 (strongly agree).

find strong evidence for potential reuse of PON, as participants would be interested in using ontologies for music metadata (78.7%), sources (80.3%), musical instruments (70.5%), and music content (57.4%; 21.3% NR), as well as a CQ dataset for musical heritage (65%; 26.7% NR).

5.3   Adoption by Polifonia Stakeholders

In addition to internal and potential adopters, industrial and institutional stakeholders in the Polifonia Stakeholder Network have also expressed interest to use PON resources. These include the **Digital Music Observatory**, concerning the use of Music Meta and Source to annotate the numerous music resources of the consortium; and the **Université Catholique de Louvain** where Anne-Emmanuelle Ceulemans uses the Music Anlysis module for studying the annotation of cadences in Josquin des Prez (composer of High Renaissance music).

We have also planned work with **Deezer**, **Songfacts**, and **MusicID** for the evaluation, extension, and reuse of Music Meta driven by their resources; and collaborations with the EU H2020 **MuseIT**[18] project to extend the ChoCo KG.

6   Availability, Sustainability, and FAIRness

PON namespaces are introduced in Sect. 4, and permanent URIs were created with the W3C Permanent Identifier Community Group. PON is under version control on public GitHub repositories (c.f. Table 1), and all repositories are also published on Zenodo (with associated DOIs) under the CC-BY 4.0 licence. The storage of all resources on GitHub guarantees their persistence beyond the project, with the University of Bologna and the Italian Ministry of Culture (MiC) committed to host and maintain PON on the long term. We also remark that PON is reused as a sibling ontology project of ArCo by MiC [13].

7   Conclusions

This article addresses the creation of the Polifonia Ontology Network (PON), a collection of *expressive* ontologies for musical cultural heritage that enable *interoperability* of existent semantic models for music content and contexts (MusicOWL, Music Notation, Music Ontology, DOREMUS, etc.). Departing from multidisciplinary and domain-expert based requirements in the Polifonia project, we applied and extended the XD methodology for ontology engineering both methodologically (persona/story framework) and technologically (IDEA framework for NLP-assisted co-design). We release 15 new ontologies in PON (v1.0) and the PolifoniaCQ dataset of 361 competency questions under CC-BY 4.0; and provide strong evidence of current and potential reuse by institutional and industrial stakeholders. As next steps, we are planning to perform an extensive CQ-driven evaluation of PON modules; and support our stakeholders and early adopters in the reuse, extension and long term maintenance of our resources.

---

[18] https://www.muse-it.eu/.

Acknowledgements. This project has received funding from the European Union's Horizon 2020 research and innovation programme under grant agreement No 101004746. The authors also acknowledge everyone who contributed to the development of the Polifonia Ontology Network.

References

1. MusoW: Music data on the Web. https://projects.dharc.unibo.it/musow/
2. Achichi, M., Bailly, R., Cecconi, C., Destandau, M., Todorov, K., Troncy, R.: Doremus: doing reusable musical data. In: ISWC: International Semantic Web Conference (2015)
3. Allik, A., Fazekas, G., Sandler, M.B.: An ontology for audio features. In: Proceedings of the 17th International Society for Music Information Retrieval Conference, ISMIR 2016, New York City, United States, 7–11 August 2016 (2016)
4. Bechhofer, S., Dixon, S., Fazekas, G., Wilmering, T., Page, K.: Computational analysis of the live music archive. In: ISMIR2014, 15th International Society for Music Information Retrieval Conference (2014)
5. de Berardinis, J., Meroño-Peñuela, A., Poltronieri, A., Presutti, V.: The music annotation pattern. In: Svátek, V., Carriero, V.A., Poveda-Villalón, M., Kindermann, C., Zhou, L. (eds.) Proceedings of the 13th Workshop on Ontology Design and Patterns (WOP 2022) co-located with the 21th International Semantic Web Conference (ISWC 2022), Online, 24 October 2022. CEUR Workshop Proceedings, vol. 3352. CEUR-WS.org (2022). https://ceur-ws.org/Vol-3352/pattern2.pdf
6. de Berardinis, J., Meroño-Peñuela, A., Poltronieri, A., Presutti, V.: The harmonic memory: a knowledge graph of harmonic patterns as a trustworthy framework for computational creativity. In: Proceedings of the ACM Web Conference 2023, pp. 3873–3882 (2023)
7. de Berardinis, J., Meroño-Peñuela, A., Poltronieri, A., Presutti, V.: Choco: a chord corpus and a data transformation workflow for musical harmony knowledge graphs (2023, manuscript under review)
8. Blomqvist, E., Hammar, K., Presutti, V.: Engineering ontologies with patterns - the extreme design methodology. In: Ontology Engineering with Ontology Design Patterns - Foundations and Applications, Studies on the Semantic Web, Amsterdam, vol. 25. IOS Press (2016). https://doi.org/10.3233/978-1-61499-676-7-23
9. Blomqvist, E., Presutti, V., Daga, E., Gangemi, A.: Experimenting with eXtreme design. In: Cimiano, P., Pinto, H.S. (eds.) EKAW 2010. LNCS (LNAI), vol. 6317, pp. 120–134. Springer, Heidelberg (2010). https://doi.org/10.1007/978-3-642-16438-5_9
10. Bottini, T., et al.: D1.1 roadmap and pilot requirements 1st version. Technical report, EU Commission, The Polifonia consortium (2021)
11. Bruseker, G., Carboni, N., Guillem, A.: Cultural heritage data management: the role of formal ontology and CIDOC CRM. Heritage and archaeology in the digital age: acquisition, curation, and dissemination of spatial cultural heritage data, pp. 93–131 (2017)
12. Carriero, V.A., et al.: Semantic integration of MIR datasets with the polifonia ontology network. In: Proceedings of the International Society for Music Information Retrieval Conference, ISMIR (2021)
13. Carriero, V.A., et al.: ArCo: the Italian cultural heritage knowledge graph. In: Ghidini, C., et al. (eds.) ISWC 2019. LNCS, vol. 11779, pp. 36–52. Springer, Cham (2019). https://doi.org/10.1007/978-3-030-30796-7_3

14. Carriero, V.A., Gangemi, A., Mancinelli, M.L., Nuzzolese, A.G., Presutti, V., Veninata, C.: Pattern-based design applied to cultural heritage knowledge graphs. Semant. Web **12**(2), 313–357 (2021). https://doi.org/10.3233/SW-200422

15. Carriero, V.A., et al.: The landscape of ontology reuse approaches. In: Applications and Practices in Ontology Design, Extraction, and Reasoning, vol. 49, p. 21 (2020)

16. Cherfi, S.S., Guillotel, C., Hamdi, F., Rigaux, P., Travers, N.: Ontology-based annotation of music scores. In: Corcho, Ó., Janowicz, K., Rizzo, G., Tiddi, I., Garijo, D. (eds.) Proceedings of the Knowledge Capture Conference, K-CAP 2017, Austin, TX, USA, 4–6 December 2017, pp. 10:1–10:4. ACM (2017). https://doi.org/10.1145/3148011.3148038

17. Cherfi, S.S.S., Guillotel, C., Hamdi, F., Rigaux, P., Travers, N.: Ontology-based annotation of music scores. In: Proceedings of the Knowledge Capture Conference. K-CAP 2017. Association for Computing Machinery, New York (2017). https://doi.org/10.1145/3148011.3148038

18. Church, K.W.: Word2vec. Nat. Lang. Eng. **23**(1), 155–162 (2017)

19. Diamantini, C., Potena, D., Storti, E.: Ontology-driven KDD process composition. In: Adams, N.M., Robardet, C., Siebes, A., Boulicaut, J.-F. (eds.) IDA 2009. LNCS, vol. 5772, pp. 285–296. Springer, Heidelberg (2009). https://doi.org/10.1007/978-3-642-03915-7_25

20. Falco, R., Gangemi, A., Peroni, S., Shotton, D., Vitali, F.: Modelling OWL ontologies with Graffoo. In: Presutti, V., Blomqvist, E., Troncy, R., Sack, H., Papadakis, I., Tordai, A. (eds.) ESWC 2014. LNCS, vol. 8798, pp. 320–325. Springer, Cham (2014). https://doi.org/10.1007/978-3-319-11955-7_42

21. Fazekas, G., Sandler, M.B.: The studio ontology framework. In: Proceedings of the 12th International Society for Music Information Retrieval Conference, ISMIR 2011, Miami, Florida, USA, 24–28 October 2011. University of Miami (2011)

22. Fazekas, G., Raimond, Y., Jacobson, K., Sandler, M.: An overview of semantic web activities in the omras2 project. J. New Music Res. **39** (2010). https://doi.org/10.1080/09298215.2010.536555

23. Gangemi, A., Peroni, S.: The information realization pattern. In: Hitzler, P., Gangemi, A., Janowicz, K., Krisnadhi, A., Presutti, V. (eds.) Ontology Engineering with Ontology Design Patterns - Foundations and Applications. Studies on the Semantic Web, vol. 25, pp. 299–312. IOS Press (2016). https://doi.org/10.3233/978-1-61499-676-7-299

24. Gangemi, A., Presutti, V.: Ontology design patterns. In: Staab, S., Studer, R. (eds.) Handbook on Ontologies. IHIS, pp. 221–243. Springer, Heidelberg (2009). https://doi.org/10.1007/978-3-540-92673-3_10

25. Gruen, D., Rauch, T., Redpath, S., Ruettinger, S.: The use of stories in user experience design. Int. J. Hum.-Comput. Interact. **14**(3–4), 503–534 (2002)

26. Grüninger, M., Fox, M.S.: The role of competency questions in enterprise engineering. In: Rolstadås, A. (ed.) Benchmarking — Theory and Practice. IAICT, pp. 22–31. Springer, Boston, MA (1995). https://doi.org/10.1007/978-0-387-34847-6_3

27. Guillotel-Nothmann, C.: Knowledge extraction and modelling in the project thesaurus musicarum germanicarum. In: Prague DH Workshops Session III: Editions (2020)

28. Guillotel-Nothmann, C., Ceulemans, A.E.: Das diatonisch-chromatische system zur zeit des michael praetorius. eine digitale neuerschließung des syntagma musicum (1619) in verbindung mit dem tanzzyklus terpsichore (1612). In: Musik im Umbruch. Michael Praetorius zum 400. Todestag, Harrassowitz (2021)

29. Harley, N., Wiggins, G.: An ontology for abstract, hierarchical music representation. In: Demo at the 16th International Society for Music Information Retrieval Conference (ISMIR 2015), Malaga, Spain (2015)
30. Hart, M.: Preserving our musical heritage: a musician's outreach to audio engineers. J. Audio Eng. Soc. **49**(7/8), 667–670 (2001)
31. Hentschel, J., Moss, F.C., McLeod, A., Neuwirth, M., Rohrmeier, M.: Towards a unified model of chords in western harmony. In: Münnich, S., Rizo, D. (eds.) Music Encoding Conference Proceedings 2021, pp. 143–149. Humanities Commons (2022). https://doi.org/10.17613/4crx-fr36
32. Hitzler, P., Gangemi, A., Janowicz, K., Krisnadhi, A., Presutti, V. (eds.): Ontology Engineering with Ontology Design Patterns - Foundations and Applications. Studies on the Semantic Web, vol. 25. IOS Press, Amsterdam (2016)
33. Humphrey, E., Salamon, J., Nieto, O., Forsyth, J., Bittner, R., Bello, J.: Jams: a json annotated music specification for reproducible MIR research. In: Proceedings of the 15th International Society for Music Information Retrieval Conference, ISMIR 2014, Taipei, Taiwan, 27–31 October 2014, pp. 591–596 (2014)
34. Isaac, A., Haslhofer, B.: Europeana linked open data-data. europeana. eu. Semant. Web **4**(3), 291–297 (2013)
35. Jacobson, K., Raimond, Y., Sandler, M.B.: An ecosystem for transparent music similarity in an open world. In: Proceedings of the 10th International Society for Music Information Retrieval Conference, ISMIR 2009, Kobe International Conference Center, Kobe, Japan, 26–30 October 2009. International Society for Music Information Retrieval (2009)
36. Jones, J., de Siqueira Braga, D., Tertuliano, K., Kauppinen, T.: Musicowl: the music score ontology. In: Proceedings of the International Conference on Web Intelligence, pp. 1222–1229 (2017)
37. Kantarelis, S., Dervakos, E., Kotsani, N., Stamou, G.: Functional harmony ontology: musical harmony analysis with description logics. Web Semant. **75**(C) (2023). https://doi.org/10.1016/j.websem.2022.100754
38. Kim, H.H.: A semantically enhanced tag-based music recommendation using emotion ontology. In: Selamat, A., Nguyen, N.T., Haron, H. (eds.) ACIIDS 2013. LNCS (LNAI), vol. 7803, pp. 119–128. Springer, Heidelberg (2013). https://doi.org/10.1007/978-3-642-36543-0_13
39. Kolozali, S., Barthet, M., Fazekas, G., Sandler, M.B.: Knowledge representation issues in musical instrument ontology design. In: ISMIR, pp. 465–470 (2011)
40. Lisena, P., et al.: Controlled vocabularies for music metadata. In: ISMIR: International Society for Music Information Retrieval (2018)
41. Lisena, P., Troncy, R.: Doing reusable musical data (DOREMUS). In: Proceedings of Workshops and Tutorials of the 9th International Conference on Knowledge Capture (K-CAP2017), Austin, Texas, USA, 4 December 2017. CEUR Workshop Proceedings, vol. 2065. CEUR-WS.org (2017)
42. Marsden, A.: Music analysis by computer: ontology and epistemology. In: Meredith, D. (ed.) Computational Music Analysis, pp. 3–28. Springer, Cham (2016). https://doi.org/10.1007/978-3-319-25931-4_1
43. Meloni, A., Reforgiato Recupero, D., Gangemi, A.: AMR2FRED, a tool for translating abstract meaning representation to motif-based linguistic knowledge graphs. In: Blomqvist, E., Hose, K., Paulheim, H., Ławrynowicz, A., Ciravegna, F., Hartig, O. (eds.) ESWC 2017. LNCS, vol. 10577, pp. 43–47. Springer, Cham (2017). https://doi.org/10.1007/978-3-319-70407-4_9
44. Meroño-Peñuela, A., et al.: D2.1: Ontology-based knowledge graphs for music objects (v1.0) (2021)

45. Meroño-Peñuela, A., et al.: The MIDI linked data cloud. In: d'Amato, C., et al. (eds.) ISWC 2017. LNCS, vol. 10588, pp. 156–164. Springer, Cham (2017). https://doi.org/10.1007/978-3-319-68204-4_16

46. Moraitou, E., Christodoulou, Y., Caridakis, G.: Semantic models and services for conservation and restoration of cultural heritage: a comprehensive survey. Semant. Web **14**(2), 261–291 (2023). https://doi.org/10.3233/SW-223105

47. Poltronieri, A., Gangemi, A.: The music note ontology. In: Hammar, K., Shimizu, C., Küçük McGinty, H., Asprino, L., Carriero, V.A. (eds.) Proceedings of the 12th Workshop on Ontology Design and Patterns (WOP 2021), Online, 24 October 2021 (2021)

48. Raimond, Y., Abdallah, S., Sandler, M., Giasson, F.: The music ontology. In: Proceedings of the 8th International Conference on Music Information Retrieval (ISMIR 2007), Vienna, Austria (2007)

49. Rashid, S.M., De Roure, D., McGuinness, D.L.: A music theory ontology. In: Proceedings of the 1st International Workshop on Semantic Applications for Audio and Music, SAAM 2018, pp. 6–14. Association for Computing Machinery, New York (2018). https://doi.org/10.1145/3243907.3243913

50. Reimers, N., Gurevych, I.: Sentence-BERT: sentence embeddings using siamese BERT-networks. arXiv preprint arXiv:1908.10084 (2019)

51. Rho, S., Song, S., Hwang, E., Kim, M.: COMUS: ontological and rule-based reasoning for music recommendation system. In: Theeramunkong, T., Kijsirikul, B., Cercone, N., Ho, T.-B. (eds.) PAKDD 2009. LNCS (LNAI), vol. 5476, pp. 859–866. Springer, Heidelberg (2009). https://doi.org/10.1007/978-3-642-01307-2_89

52. Riley, J.: Application of the Functional Requirements for Bibliographic Records (FRBR) to Music. In: ISMIR, pp. 439–444 (2008)

53. Sanfilippo, E.M., Freedman, R.: Ontology for analytic claims in music. In: Chiusano, S., et al. (eds.) ADBIS 2022, pp. 559–571. Springer, Cham (2022). https://doi.org/10.1007/978-3-031-15743-1_51

54. Smilkov, D., Thorat, N., Nicholson, C., Reif, E., Viégas, F.B., Wattenberg, M.: Embedding projector: interactive visualization and interpretation of embeddings. arXiv preprint arXiv:1611.05469 (2016)

55. Szeto, K.: Ontology for voice, instruments, and ensembles (ONVIE): revisiting the medium of performance concept for enhanced discoverability. Code4Lib J. (54) (2022)

56. Thalmann, F., Carrillo, A.P., Fazekas, G., Wiggins, G.A., Sandler, M.: The mobile audio ontology: experiencing dynamic music objects on mobile devices. In: 2016 IEEE Tenth International Conference on Semantic Computing (ICSC), pp. 47–54. IEEE (2016)

57. Turchet, L., Antoniazzi, F., Viola, F., Giunchiglia, F., Fazekas, G.: The internet of musical things ontology. J. Web Semant. **60**, 100548 (2020)

58. Turchet, L., Bouquet, P., Molinari, A., Fazekas, G.: The smart musical instruments ontology. J. Web Semant. **72**, 100687 (2022). https://doi.org/10.1016/j.websem.2021.100687. https://www.sciencedirect.com/science/article/pii/S1570826821000573

59. Wilmering, T., Fazekas, G., Sandler, M.B.: The audio effects ontology. In: Proceedings of the 14th International Society for Music Information Retrieval Conference, ISMIR 2013, Curitiba, Brazil, 4–8 November 2013 (2013)

60. Zanoni, M., Setragno, F., Sarti, A., et al.: The violin ontology. In: Proceedings of the 9th Conference on Interdisciplinary Musicology (CIM 2014). Citeseer (2014)

In-Use Track

Solving the IoT Cascading Failure Dilemma Using a Semantic Multi-agent System

Amal Guittoum[1,2]([✉]) [iD], François Aïssaoui[1] [iD], Sébastien Bolle[1] [iD],
Fabienne Boyer[2] [iD], and Noel De Palma[2] [iD]

[1] Orange Innovation, Meylan, France
{amal.guittoum,francois.aissaoui,sebastien.bolle}@orange.com
[2] University of Grenoble Alpes - LIG, Grenoble, France
{fabienne.boyer,noel.palma}@univ-grenoble-alpes.fr
https://www.orange.fr,https://www.liglab.fr/en

Abstract. Managing interdependent Internet of Things (IoT) devices can be challenging because different actors, e.g., operators and service providers, propose siloed Device Management (DM) solutions that are unable to handle cascading failures across multiple devices. To address this issue, we propose a novel approach based on a cooperative Multi-agent System (MAS) allowing siloed DM solutions to manage IoT cascading failures automatically and coordinately. The proposed MAS leverages Semantic Web standards to establish a common understanding of device dependencies and failures. It relies on the Digital Twin technology to represent dynamic device dependencies accurately for failure root cause identification. Our approach has been effective in handling cascading failures in Smart Home scenarios, reducing time to repair failure, saving Customer Care costs, and minimizing resource consumption in IoT infrastructure such as energy consumption.

Keywords: IoT Failure Management · Multi-agent system ·
Ontology · Semantic Digital Twin · Interoperability · Collaboration

1 Introduction

The Internet of Things (IoT) is gaining widespread popularity across multiple domains, such as healthcare and transportation. The pivotal factor for creating value in IoT is IoT devices that can perform tasks with minimal human intervention. To ensure smooth IoT operations, monitoring and managing these devices is essential. This is referred to as IoT Device Management (DM).

In today's IoT systems, DM is provided by siloed DM platforms, e.g., *Amazon Web Service (AWS)*[1], *Orange Live Objects*[2], governed by different actors, which can be operators, service providers, or device manufacturers [1,19,37]. These

---

[1] https://aws.amazon.com/fr/iot-device-management/.
[2] https://liveobjects.orange-business.com/.

© The Author(s), under exclusive license to Springer Nature Switzerland AG 2023
T. R. Payne et al. (Eds.): ISWC 2023, LNCS 14266, pp. 325–344, 2023.
https://doi.org/10.1007/978-3-031-47243-5_18

DM platforms integrate devices built by different manufacturers to perform key DM functions such as firmware updates and Failure Management (FM). However, they are facing a strong limitation regarding the management of *Cascading Failure dilemmas* that arise when the failure of one device instigates the failure of dependent devices and applications managed by different DM actors [44].

Cascading failures are particularly problematic because they generate more customer calls to customer care applications of DM actors. Their mitigation usually requires human intervention, which increases the cost of Customer Care. For example, the Orange company reports a cost of *20€* for one customer call and *100€* for sending a technician, where customers perform *100 calls per week* to request IoT device recovery. Moreover, failures are one of the main causes of energy waste in connected environments. Studies show that 25–45% of HVAC energy consumption is wasted due to failures [25]. Despite cascading failures leading to business and environmental damages, there is no existing solution for managing them in multi-actor IoT systems, to the best of our knowledge.

In this paper, we address this open research challenge and propose a practical solution allowing siloed DM actors to manage cascading failures in an automatic and coordinated manner. This solution relies on a cooperative Multi-Agent System (MAS)[3]empowered by Semantic Web and Digital Twin technologies. More precisely, we rely on *cOllaborative caScading fAilure Management Agent (OSAMA)*, a semantic agent to be integrated into the legacy DM platforms in order to help them understand, collaborate and make effective decisions regarding Cascading Failure Management (CFM). OSAMA exploits a set of Semantic Web standards, such as ontologies, in order to simplify failure information exchange and enhance the interoperability among siloed DM platforms. It leverages the Semantic Digital Twin technology[4], modeling dynamic dependency relationships among IoT devices for failure root cause identification. Upon failure, OSAMA agents start a collaborative protocol that allows them to automatically identify the roots of the failures and recover the failed devices.

The contribution of this work includes (i) The IoT-F ontology describing IoT device failures and their recovery actions; (ii) The OSAMA agent leveraging the Belief-Desire-Intention model (BDI) [32] to enable collaborative CFM; (iii) A collaborative CFM protocol; (iv) A proof of concept for the proposed solution demonstrating its potential impact in reducing time to repair failure, saving Customer Care costs and minimizing resource consumption in IoT infrastructures. Moreover, we provide plans for large adoptions of our solution in the DM market.

This paper is organized as follows: We begin by providing the necessary background information to facilitate comprehension of our work. Next, we present a motivating use case. Then, we detail our proposed solution for CFM. Finally, we discuss the evaluation results, related work, and avenues for future research.

A table of acronyms (see Table 1) has been provided to enhance readability.

---

[3] MAS refers to a network of software agents that operate independently while being loosely connected to address complex problems that are beyond the individual capacities or knowledge of each agent.

[4] A Semantic Digital Twin is a virtual and synchronized representation of real-world entities and processes built using a semantic description.

Table 1. Acronyms used in this paper

Acronym	Meaning
BDI	Belief Desire Intention
CFM	Cascading Failure Management
DKG	Dependency Knowledge Graph
DM	IoT Device Management
DMP	Device Management platform Provider
FKB	Failure Knowledge Base
FM	Failure Management
FMEA	Failure Mode Effect Analysis
MAS	Multi-Agent System
MN	device MaNufacturer
OSAMA	cOllaborative caScading fAilure Management Agent
SP	Service Provider

2 Background

2.1 Overview of Legacy Solutions

Current IoT systems are managed by multiple actors, each having its legacy solution for managing failures on its IoT devices as part of its customer care services. We have conducted a market-based study[5] on the FM capabilities of these siloed DM actors. As a result, we identify the following profiles with distinct FM capabilities, including Device Manufacturers (MN), DM Platform Providers (DMP), and Service Providers (SP).

MNs build and deliver IoT devices to end users and IoT suppliers. Mostly, MNs do not have DM platforms to perform DM operations on their IoT devices. However, they may propose a mobile application-based solution in order to allow end users to perform basic DM operations on IoT devices such as *firmware update*. Moreover, they may acquire information about IoT device failures, their causes, effects, and recovery actions. This failure information is usually identified during the design and test stage for risk assessments using several approaches such as *Failure Mode Effect Analysis* (FMEA) [13]. It may be represented in tables used by customer care services to recover failures manually or build support pages to help end users manage failures on their devices [40]. DMPs propose a DM platform that allows several DM operations such as *firmware update and device reboot*. These DM platforms propose DM as a service solution for end users and enterprises to help them manage their IoT devices. They integrate IoT devices built by different MNs. Some of these DM platforms propose failure detection features using Machine Learning (ML)[6] or alarm-based system[7].

---

[5] This study is limited by the information available online.

[6] https://www.avsystem.com.

[7] https://aws.amazon.com/fr/iot-device-management/.

They may recover elementary failures on IoT devices remotely using DM operations. However, they do not acquire end-to-end solutions for automatic FM and are limited when the failure spreads across IoT devices managed by different DM platforms. SPs ensure IoT connectivity and provide IoT services via various devices such as Orange's *LiveBox* for connectivity and Samsung's *SmartThings hub* for home automation services. Each SP proposes its own proprietary DM platform for managing its devices. Proprietary DM platforms proposed by SP allow similar features as the DMP DM platform. Moreover, SPs own failure information on their provided devices.

2.2   Complex IoT Device Dependency

Dependency relationships between IoT devices cause failures to propagate across them. In our previous work [17], we provided a taxonomy for dependencies between IoT devices that exacerbate cascading failure propagation, including *(1)Direct dependencies* when IoT devices utilize each other's services (service dependency), and *(2)Indirect dependencies* that are generated due to interactions between sensors and actuators via the physical environment (environment-based dependency), or created by applications running on top of IoT devices, even when an application acts on a set of devices based on the state of other devices (state-based dependency) or when it forwards data flows between them (data-based dependency). These dependency relationships are abundant and dynamic.

2.3   IoT Failures

IoT integrates physical processes with digital connectivity, often using three components represented by devices, connectivity protocols, and cloud platforms [8]. While failures may occur in any of these components, IoT device failures are more common due to several factors, such as their minimal computational resources [28]. Failures on IoT devices are divided into two main classes: (1) *Fail-stop failure* when an IoT device becomes unresponsive to external requests; (2) *Non-fail stop failure* occurs when IoT device response diverges from the correct response, such failed responses are classified in the literature [9,27,28,36] into five categories: *High Variance*: when a device oscillates between states faster than the environment dictates; *Stuck-at*: when a device is expected to change its state, but it fails to do so; *Spike*: when the numeric state of a device increases or decreases at a faster rate than what is determined by the environment; *Outlier*: when a device reports incorrect state for a single poll; *Calibration*: when sensor data shows an offset, i.e., it has a different gain than the actual ground truth value. Cascading failures occur when one device's failure (fail or non-fail stop) spreads to other devices through dependencies.

3   Motivating Use Case

We consider a smart home managed by five DM actors. It illustrates the cascading failure scenarios that are difficult to overcome with market DM solutions.

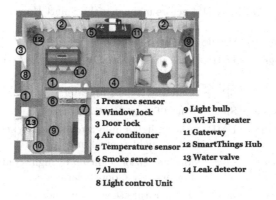

1 Presence sensor
2 Window lock
3 Door lock
4 Air conditoner
5 Temperature sensor
6 Smoke sensor
7 Alarm
8 Light control Unit
9 Light bulb
10 Wi-Fi repeater
11 Gateway
12 SmartThings Hub
13 Water valve
14 Leak detector

Fig. 1. Smart home architecture

3.1 Smart Home Scenario Architecture

The smart home scenario (see Fig. 1) consists of three intelligent systems deployed in a home consisting of a living room and a kitchen: **1) Light management system:** Relies on a *light sensor, presence detection sensors, light bulbs* installed in the living room and the kitchen, and a *light control unit*. The latter controls light using the light measurement service supplied by *the light sensor*, the presence detection services of *the presence sensors*, and the light bulbs' services. **2) Temperature management system:** Controls the home temperature using a *temperature sensor* and an *air conditioner*. It is mainly based on automation rules[8] 1–3 described in Table 3. **3) Security control system:** Launches *an alarm* when intruders, fires, or leaks are detected. It consists of *an alarm* that uses the presence detection services provided by *the presence sensors* to detect intruders. *The alarm* also uses temperature, smoke, and leak sensors' services for fire and leak detection. This system is reinforced by rules 4–7.

A gateway connects devices in the living room to the Internet, while a Wi-Fi repeater connects the kitchen devices. The SmartThings platform[9] [33] enables automation rules described in Table 3 using a *SmartThings Hub*. Devices in the smart home are managed by five DM actors with different profiles each proposing its own solution for managing devices integrated into its system (see Table 2).

3.2 Illustration of Cascading Failure Dilemma

Due to the dependencies among IoT devices, a failure of one of them can generate multiple cascading failures. Take Scenario 01 (see Table 4) as an example, in which a cascading failure occurs due to a high variance failure on the leak detector. The failure affects the alarm and the water valve, which are state-dependent

---

[8] Automation rules allow the automated composition of IoT services in a connected environment.

[9] SmartThings is Samsung's IoT platform that enables automation rules across IoT devices in Smart Homes.

Table 2. DM actors managing the Smart Home

DM actors	Profile	Managed devices
Orange	DMP	Leak detector, water valve, temperature sensor, windows door
	SP	Gateway, WI-FI repeater
Samsung	SP	SmartThings Hub
Amazon	DMP	Alarm, lights bulb airconditioner, smoke sensor, light control unit
Philips	MN	Motion sensor, light bulbs, light control unit windows, door, alarm
Kelvin	MN	Temperature sensor, airconditioner, leak detector, water valve

Table 3. The smart home automation rules

No	Type	Automation Rule
1	Comfort	Adjust the air conditioner regarding the temperature returned by the temperature sensor
2	Comfort	Open the two windows when the air conditioner is deactivated
3	Comfort	Close the two windows and turn on the air conditioner when the temperature exceeds a threshold
4	Security	Turn on the alarm and unlock the door and both windows upon detection of fire
5	Security	Turn on the alarm and close the water valve when leak is detected
6	Security	Notifies the User, closes the windows, closes the door, and turns on the alarm when detecting an intruder while the User is out of the home
7	Security	Set light bulbs to red when the alarm is activated

Table 4. Cascading Failure scenarios

Scenario	Root cause	Impacted devices	Detected at
1	High Variance on the leak detector	Alarm Water Valve Light bulbs	Light bulbs
2	High Variance on Smoke sensor	Alarm Light bulbs door windows	Door
3	Stuck at no motion on the motion sensor	Light control unit Light bulb	Light bulbs
4	Outlier on the temperature sensor	Window Airconditioner	Airconditioner
5	Stuck at smoke detected on the smoke sensor	Alarm Light bulbs Door Windows	Alarm
6	Spikes on the temperature sensor	Window Airconditioner	Airconditioner
7	Fail stop on the WIFI repeater	Alarm, light bulb smoke sensor, water valve	Alarm
8	Stuck at leak detected on the leak detector	Alarm Water Valve Light bulbs	Water valve

on the leak detector (see Rule 5 in Table 3). Additionally, the light bulbs are affected as they are state-dependent on the alarm, as per Rule 7. Such cascading failures pose a significant challenge for DM actors. In this case, the alarm and light bulbs are managed by the *Amazon* DM platform, whereas the water valve and leak detector are managed by the *Orange* DM platform (see Table 2). As a result, these siloed DM actors cannot identify the failure's root cause. Furthermore, the failure recovery information is distributed across different device manufacturers: *Kelvin* and *Philips*, which further complicates the situation.

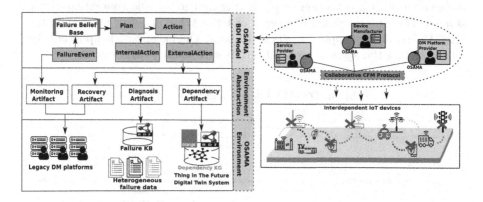

Fig. 2. Overview of Semantic Multi-OSAMA For Collaborative CFM

4 Semantic Multi-OSAMA for Collaborative CFM

MAS enables the integration of multiple legacy systems by developing an agent wrapper around them, enabling their participation in collaborative problem-solving and decision-making processes [42]. Relying on this advantage, we propose a MAS to help legacy DM solutions automatically manage cascading failure dilemmas. Our solution consists of a set of cooperative agents called *OSAMA* to be integrated by DM actors in their legacy solutions. These *OSAMAs* adopt a BDI model to handle cascading failures. They collaborate according to a *collaborative CFM protocol* to recover from cascading failures that spread across devices managed by different actors.

Within their shared environment, OSAMAs are provided by four (04) *Artifacts* encapsulating external services that they can explore at runtime to ease CFM (see Fig. 2): 1) *Monitoring Artifact*: Allows to monitor IoT devices and detect failures using legacy DM platforms; 2) *Diagnosis Artifact*: Allows to identify failure type and its compensatory actions using Failure Knowledge Base (FKB); 3) *Dependency Artifact*: Thanks to Semantic Digital Twins, this artifact allows to automatically access an accurate view of dynamic dependency relationships between IoT devices in order to ease cascading failure root cause identification; 4) *Recovery Artifact*: Allows to execute recovery actions on IoT devices using legacy DM platforms. In the following, we discuss the *OSAMA* BDI model, artifacts, and the *Collaborative CFM Protocol*.

4.1   OSAMA BDI Model

The *OSAMA* design follows a BDI model, which is helpful in developing autonomous agents in various domains thanks to its flexibility, robustness, and transparency [38]. The BDI agent model aims at programming rational agents based on human mental attitudes of beliefs, desires, and intentions [7,38]. Beliefs correspond to an agent's understanding of its surroundings, other agents, and itself. Desires refer to the conditions an agent wants to achieve, and intentions are the commitments to achieving those desires. In order to accomplish its desires, an agent utilizes a collection of plans executed in specific contextual circumstances. These plans consist of a series of actions that an agent must undertake, given the conditions implied by its belief base. The belief base is updated based on events that the agent perceives from its surrounding environment.

Table 5. OSAMA Internal and External Actions

Action	Type	Description
$sendCFMRequest(device_i, OSAMA_k)$	Internal	Send by the $OSAMA$ that initiates the recovery of a detected cascading failure scenario requesting the $OSAMA_k$ to check and recover the $device_i$.
$responseCFMRequest(device, OSAMA_k)$	Internal	Send by the $OSAMA$ that participates in the recovery of a cascading failure scenario involving $device_i$, to the $OSAMA_k$, the initiator of the cascading failure recovery.
$requestDiagnosis(OSAMA_k, device_i, S)$	Internal	Send by the $OSAMA$ to request diagnosis information from the $OSAMA_k$ for $device_i$ having the symptoms[a] S, when it could not perform diagnosis by itself.
$getDiagnosisAgent(device_i)$	External	Allows an $OSAMA$ to get candidate $OSAMA_d$ able to perform diagnosis on device $device_i$ when it could not perform diagnosis by itself.
$getDeviceState(device_i)$	External	Allows an $OSAMA$ to check whether the $device_i$ is failed or not by accessing the monitoring artifact.
$getDeviceSymptoms(device_i)$	External	Allows an $OSAMA$ to get symptoms of the $device_i$ by accessing the monitoring artifact.
$getDependency(device_i)$	External	Allows an $OSAMA$ to get a list of devices to which the $device_i$ depends on by accessing the dependency artifact.
$recover(recoveryAction, device_i)$	External	Allows an $OSAMA$ to perform the $recoveryAction$ on the $device_i$ by accessing the recovery artifact.
$diagnosis(device_i, symptoms)$	External	Allows an $OSAMA$ to get diagnosis information such as proposed recovery action for the failed $device_i$ based on a set of $symptoms$ by accessing the diagnosis artifact.

[a] Symptoms refers to device characteristics describing device failed states such as memory usage.

Based on the explained BDI model terminology, we define the *OSAMA* as a tuple $<Evt, Blf, Pl, Act>$, where: $Evt = \{evt_1, evt_2, ..., evt_n\}$ represents a set of failure events perceived by the *OSAMA* through the monitoring artifact or reported by other *OSAMAs* during CFM. A failure event

$evt_i = (device_k, sourceType, source)$, where $sourceType$ indicates the failure is detected by monitoring artifact or other $OSAMA$ specified by $source$. Failure events allow the $OSAMA$ to update its *Belief Base* and take actions to handle failures; $Blf = \{blf_1, blf_2, ..., blf_n\}$ represents positive ground literals in a first-order logical language describing IoT devices state such as $blf_j^i = failed(device_i)$ if $device_i$ is failed, $recovered(device_i)$ otherwise. It is updated when receiving failure events or recovering a failed device; Act represents a set of internal and external actions that the $OSAMA$ performs for CFM. Internal actions are executed by the $OSAMA$, while external actions access shared artifacts that abstract external services deployed in the $OSAMA$ environment (See Table 5); $Pl = \{p_1, p_2, ..., p_n\}$ represents $OSAMA$ plans. A plan $p_i \equiv evt \rightarrow Act_i$ has an event evt, including adding or deleting failure beliefs and receiving CFM requests. Such an event triggers a subset of $OSAMA$ actions Act_i to handle failures and CFM requests.

4.2 Diagnosis Artifact

This artifact embeds a Failure Knowledge Base (FKB) that allows $OSAMAs$ to get failure information such as possible compensatory actions, given a set of failure symptoms provided by the monitoring artifact, thanks to the SPARQL queries. We assume that each DM actor generates an FKB involving its governed failure information (see Sect. 2.1). These FKBs are built using an ontology called IoT-F^{10} [14] (see Fig. 3) that we developed using the ontology engineering methodology NeOn [41]. The main purpose of the IoT-F ontology is to allow $OSAMAs$ to share a global understanding of heterogeneous and distributed failure information. However, it has other intended usages such as assisting DM

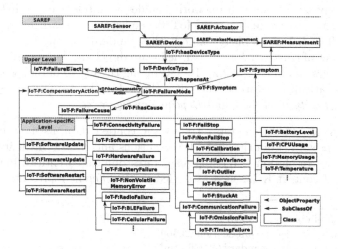

Fig. 3. IoT-F: IoT Failure Ontology

---

[10] https://iotfontology.github.io/.

actors in structuring their failure information, characterized by heterogeneity, incompleteness, and ambiguity [40]. The IoT-F ontology **reuses** the standardized ontology $SAREF^{11}$. Its architecture is based on two levels inspired by the work [13]: 1) The top level is based on the FMEA concepts, which provide a generic model for failure description in any domain of interest. We reused FMEA concepts proposed in [13], which have been inspired by relevant standards such as IEC60812[12] and ISO13372[13]; 2) The application-specific level represents failures in IoT systems. To build the application-specific level, we reused a set of non-ontological resources that describe relevant information about IoT failure, such as literature taxonomies [9,28,29,36] for IoT failure, failure cause, and recovery actions taxonomies, and market DM models mainly $Matter^{14}$ and TR-181[15]. The main concept of the IoT-F ontology is *IoT-F:FailureMode* representing IoT failures associated with an IoT device type *IoT-F:DeviceType*, described by: a set of symptoms *IoT-F:Symptom* representing failure symptoms, causes *IoT-F:FailureCause*, effects *IoT-F:FailureEffect*, and possible compensatory actions *IoT-F:CompensatoryAction*. Each of these classes is specialized at the application-specific level to describe IoT failures.

4.3 Dependency Artifact

This artifact allows *OSAMAs* to identify failure root causes through the analysis of dependency relationships among IoT devices. It incorporates a framework, developed in our previous work [17], that enables automatic inference and analysis of dynamic dependency relationships among IoT devices using *Semantic Digital Twins*. Namely, the dependency relationships are represented as an IoT Dependency Knowledge Graph (DKG). The DKG serves as a Digital Twin view, representing the current devices and their dependencies.

In conceptual terms, the framework includes an ontology called IoT-D[16] that enables a shared representation of IoT dependencies across heterogenous DM solutions. The IoT-D ontology extends the standardized ontology *SAREF* to describe a set of contextual data that delineate direct and indirect dependencies among devices (refer to Sect. 2.2). By leveraging the IoT-D ontology, the framework automatically constructs the DKG through a three-step process: *Context extraction*, *Entity resolution*, and *Dependency inference*.

1. The context extraction step retrieves the context data, as described in the IoT-D ontology, from the siloed DM solutions and transforms it into KGs.
2. The entity resolution (ER) step aggregates duplicated entities found in the extracted context KGs, such as devices with different representations. This

---

[11] https://saref.etsi.org/core/v3.1.1/.
[12] https://webstore.iec.ch/publication/26359.
[13] https://www.iso.org/standard/52256.html.
[14] https://csa-iot.org/all-solutions/matter/.
[15] https://usp-data-models.broadband-forum.org/.
[16] https://iotdontology.github.io/.

step relies on the advanced features of the *SHACL standard*[17], namely SHACL rules and SHACL functions. The idea is to use a SHACL rule to infer the *owl:sameAs* relationships between duplicated entities in the extraction KGs. This SHACL rule uses SHACL functions to compute similarity metrics between attributes of two entities and then decide on the inference of the *owl:sameAs* relationships between them. SHACL functions may embed several similar functions. In our work, we used string similarity functions.

3. The dependency inference step builds the DKG by inferring dependency relationships in the aggregated KGs. It leverages a set of SHACL rules to infer dependency relationships among IoT device representations by reasoning on their contextual relationships provided in the aggregated context KGs.

In the DKG, IoT device representations are annotated with information about the OSAMAs that manage them, such as the *OSAMA communication modality*, using the *FOAF:Agent* class. This annotation allows OSAMAs to communicate with each other while exploring the DKG for failure root cause identification.

From a technical standpoint, the dependency artifact is integrated into the Orange Digital Twin platform *Thing in the future*(Thing'in)[18], which provides a set of APIs for OSAMAs to query the DKG when identifying failure root causes.

4.4 Monitoring and Recovery Artifacts

These artifacts embed monitoring and recovery functions of the legacy DM platform to allow *OSAMA* to monitor IoT devices, detect failures, and execute recovery actions. The monitoring artifact proactively sends failure events to its associated *OSAMA*. The recovery artifact allows *OSAMA* to execute recovery actions remotely, thanks to the remote management capabilities of legacy DM platforms. Note that we have chosen to reuse legacy DM platforms for monitoring and recovery as most of them provide such capabilities [39]. This could boost usability and save integration costs by avoiding the development of a solution from scratch, which consists in integrating heterogenous IoT devices through APIs to be accessed by *OSAMAs* for monitoring and recovery.

4.5 Collaborative CFM Protocol

Using the artifacts mentioned above, the *OSAMAs* collaborate with each other to solve cascading failure dilemmas according to a collaborative CFM protocol. We specialized the *OSAMA* into three different profiles, including *OSAMA-SP*, *OSAMA-DMP*, and *OSAMA-MN*, each having specified missions and artifacts according to their FM capabilities (see Sect. 2.1): *OSAMA-SP* and *OSAMA-DMP* are responsible for managing cascading failure requests. The first has full FM capabilities to manage failure on its devices. It collaborates with other *OSAMA-SPs* and *OSAMA-DMPs* for CFM. The latter manages failures collaboratively with *OSAMA-MNs* by requesting failure information owned by them.

---

[17] https://www.w3.org/TR/shacl-af/.
[18] https://tech2.thinginthefuture.com/.

Based on these profiles, the collaborative CFM protocol is described in Algorithm 1. The protocol is executed by *OSAMA-SP* and *OSAMA-DMP* when a failure event is reported on a device (line 2). *OSAMA* starts by updating the *belief base* in order to activate *failure plans* (line 3). Then, it requests device symptoms from the monitoring artifact (line 5). Next, depending on its profile, it either performs the diagnosis by itself (lines 6–8) or requests a diagnosis from other OSAMAs (lines 9–13) to get possible recovery actions. Next, it recovers the IoT device by executing the proposed compensatory action using the recovery artifact (line 14). If the device is still in a failed state (line 15), the *OSAMA* launches the plan for CFM: it queries the DKG of the failed device (line 17); for each device in the DKG, it requests cascading failure check from *OSAMA* managing it (line 18–21). Requested OSAMA deals with requests following the same algorithm by propagating on their turn the CFM request if they could not recover the failure. They respond when no more devices exist to explore (lines 27–29). After receiving all the responses, the *OSAMA* initiating the CFM request recovers the device (line 22) and notifies the customer care service if it is still in a failed state (lines 23–25). Then, it updates its *belief base* considering the device as recovered (line 26).

Algorithm 1. Collaborative CFM Protocol

```
 1: BEGIN
 2: if failure event evt = (device_i, sourceType, source) arrives then
 3:    Update the belief base Blf with predicate failed(device_i)
 4:    [Local Failure Plan]
 5:    S ← getDeviceSymptoms(device_i)
 6:    if Profile=SP then
 7:       recovery ← diagnosis(device_i, S)
 8:    end if
 9:    if Profile=DMP then
10:       OSAMA_d ← getDiagnosisAgent(device_i)
11:       requestDiagnosis(OSAMA_d, device_i, S)
12:       Wait for proposed recovery action recovery from OSAMA_d.
13:    end if
14:    recover(recovery, device_i)
15:    if getDeviceState(device_i) = failed then
16:       [Cascading Failure Plan]
17:       DKG ← getDependency(device_i)
18:       for (device_k, OSAMA_k) in DKG do
19:          sendCFMRequest(device_k, OSAMA_k)
20:          Wait for response OSAMA_k
21:       end for
22:       recover(recovery, device_i)
23:       if getDeviceState(device_i) = failed then
24:          Notify customer care service
25:       end if
26:       Update the belief base Blf with predicate recovered(device_i)
27:       if sourceType = OSAMA then
28:          responseCFMRequest(device_i, source)
29:       end if
30:    end if
31: end if
32: END
```

Let us illustrate the CFM protocol in Scenario 01 (see Table 4). In this scenario, a high variance failure is detected in the light bulbs by Amazon's OSAMA. To address this issue, Amazon OSAMA requests assistance from Philips OSAMA, the MN of the light bulbs, to diagnose and obtain recovery actions. Subsequently, Amazon OSAMA executes the proposed recovery plan; however, the light bulbs still report a high variance failure. The Amazon OSAMA assumes that the failure is due to a cascading failure and initiates the CFM, which involves retrieving the DKG describing devices that the light bulbs depend on. The DKG refers to the alarm device, which is managed by Amazon OSAMA. Collaboratively, Amazon OSAMA and Philips OSAMA diagnose the alarm device and execute the recovery plan. However, the alarm device still reports a high variance failure. Amazon OSAMA continues the CFM approach by retrieving the DKG of the alarm device, which refers to the leak detector managed by Orange OSAMA. Amazon OSAMA requests assistance from Orange OSAMA, which collaboratively diagnoses the leak detector with the assistance of Kelvin OSAMA, the MN of the leak detector. After diagnosing and recovering the leak detector, Orange OSAMA notifies Amazon OSAMA, which notices that the alarm and light bulbs have returned to normal, successfully concluding the CFM request.

5   Evaluation

We implemented the *OSAMAs* with the *JaCaMo* framework (version 1.1)[19], which allows adaptable and scalable MAS management and coordination in complex environments [5]. Within the JaCaMo framework, the CFM protocol described in Algorithm 1 is implemented using the *Jason*[20] BDI technology allowing OSAMA agent to handle failure events in a parallel and coherent manner. The OSAMAs artifacts are implemented with the *Cartago*[21] technology that allows agents to access resources and services within their shared environment.

Reasoning in the diagnosis artifact is implemented with *Apache Jena* (version 3.4.0)[22]. To better represent a multi-actor deployment, we deployed the *OSAMAs* associated with the motivating use case in an Orange cloud infrastructure with the following resource: 1000 MIPS as CPU and 2GB as requested memory.

Based on these experimentation settings, we performed qualitative and quantitative evaluations of the proposed solution: The qualitative evaluation has been performed on the smart home use case presented in Sect. 3, by checking how our *OSAMAs* perform regarding cascading failure scenarios presented in Table 4. As described above, the smart home includes *17 IoT devices* managed by five DM actors and interconnected through *46 dependencies* described by the DKG. Each DM actor was associated with an OSAMA agent. The experiment has consisted in injecting failures in OSAMA agents' belief bases and letting them collaboratively perform CFM. Regarding the quantitative evaluation, it consisted of 1) measuring the completion time of the collaborative CFM protocol and 2) comparing our solution with the Orange legacy one based on simulated IoT infrastructures using our extension of the simulator *iFogSim* [18] that we refer to as *FMSim*. The result is discussed in the following.

Performance Evaluation. We evaluate the performance of the collaborative CFM protocol performed by the use case OSAMAs (see Table 2) in a cloud-based

---

[19] https://github.com/jacamo-lang/jacamo.
[20] https://jason.sourceforge.net/wp/.
[21] https://cartago.sourceforge.net/.
[22] https://github.com/apache/jena.

deployment. We measured the completion time of the collaborative CFM protocol on cascading failure scenarios involving devices with different dependency depths since this latter is the parameter that impacts the number of message exchanges between the OSAMAs during the collaborative CFM. We found that it takes, on average 5 s (see Fig. 5a), which we consider acceptable compared to the Orange legacy solution taking *from 15 to 20 min*.

Moreover, this performance can be enhanced more by reducing message exchange between *OSAMAs* using ML capabilities such as predicting the root cause of a cascading failure or offloading them to the edge to reduce latency. The DKG could also be deployed at the edge, as *Thing'in platform* allows this feature.

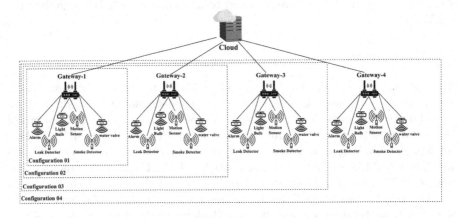

Fig. 4. Simulation Topology

Resource Consumption. Failures in IoT infrastructures can result in a significant loss of resources, as they make the infrastructure circulate useless and failed data and execute failed tasks. To show the impact of OSAMA in reducing such resource loss, we compared the resource consumption of IoT infrastructures managed by *OSAMAs* with those managed by the Orange legacy DM solutions using the simulator *FMSim*, our extension for the iFogSim simulator. The latter is a widely used Discrete Event Simulator for Fog and IoT because of its flexibility, scalability, and accessibility [30]. It uses a Sense-Process-Act model based on sensors, application modules, and actuators. Sensors send data to application modules deployed in Fog devices, which send actions as events to actuators according to a defined application logic. However, *iFogSim* does not support failure simulation on IoT devices. To this end, we developed *FMSim* [16], an extension for *iFogSim* allowing failure injection and recovery simulation on IoT devices. FMSim allows us to inject cascading failures (scenarios 1–6 described in Table 4) in simulated IoT infrastructures with different configurations (see Fig. 4), and measure resource consumption in the two cases: 1) The time to delete failure is set to OSAMA recovery time, and 2) The time to delete failure is set to legacy solution recovery time, represented by the average of failure recovery time of the Orange legacy solution taking *from 15 to 20 min*. Resource consumption is represented by energy consumption, network usage, IoT application execution time, and the cost of executing IoT applications in the cloud. We report in Fig. 5b the relative resource gain achieved by our approach compared to legacy approaches deployed within the Orange organization. Specifically, in Configuration 4, we observed resource gains of *16 Mjoule, 650 bytes* in terms of energy consumption and network usage respectively, which indicates that managing failures on IoT infrastructure using our solution instead of the legacy solution saves 16 Mjoule in energy consumption and 650 bytes in network usage. These gains can be attributed to the faster repair time achieved by *OSAMAs* compared to legacy solutions. As a result, *OSAMAs* enable swift recovery from resource-intensive failures, such as *High Variance*, thereby reducing resource loss in IoT infrastructure.

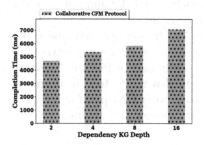 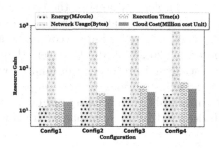

(a) CFM completion time as a function of the DKG depth   (b) Resources gain of using *OSAMA* instead of legacy solution

Fig. 5. Experiment Results

6   Related Work

IoT failure management consists of three steps: failure detection, failure diagnosis for failure type and root cause identification, and failure recovery. IoT failure management is only partly treated in the literature, as most efforts focus on IoT failure detection [20,21,24], often notifying users to act themselves [28]. Few works have been proposed for IoT failure diagnosis. Early solutions propose a model-based approach, which consists of a mathematical model that describes the running behavior of devices [25]. Then, this model is used to estimate device output. The differences between the estimated and measured outputs are monitored to detect failures and determine their type [22]. Despite model-based approaches providing high accuracy models with low computation [3], they still need to be adapted for complex systems such as IoT [11]. To fill this gap, failure diagnosis techniques have evolved into data-driven approaches that analyze failure from signals or operational data using machine learning methods. These approaches leverage sensor device data to build models for fault identification and characterization [23]. Several algorithms were proposed for IoT fault diagnosis to detect and determine faulty devices and the type of fault [6,10,23,46].

However, the availability and quality of learning data of all possible fault types of large-scale systems such as IoT could be impossible [43].

The work [11] argues that knowledge-based failure diagnosis is especially well-suited for complex or multi-actor systems for which detailed mathematical models are unavailable, and diagnosis learning data are governed by different actors. These approaches rely on an FKB that contains failure diagnosis information provided by experts at the design or the operational level of devices. Experts-based fed of FKB ensures more accurate diagnosis results [12]. Several ontologies to generate FKB have been proposed for a range of assets such as Loaders [45], Cyber-physical system [2,34,35], Wireless Sensor Network [4], and Folio ontology for IoT systems [40]. To the best of our knowledge, the latter is the only proposed work to describe IoT failures. However, expressive classification for IoT failure behaviors, recovery actions, and failure symptoms is missing in this ontology. Moreover, the proposed approaches for IoT failure diagnosis do not address automatic failure root cause identification.

Regarding the failure recovery, some technical frameworks have been proposed in [26,28,29,31]. However, they rely mainly on device replication and replacement to recover from failure, which is costly and ineffective. Moreover, all existing solutions do not consider the practical reality: **IoT is managed by multiple actors using siloed and heterogenous DM platforms**, where devices and failure information are governed by different DM actors.

7   Conclusion and Future Work

In this paper, we presented our practical solution to help market DM actors address the dilemma of IoT cascading failures. It consists of a set of cooperative agents called OSAMAs, allowing siloed DM actors to manage cascading failures in an automatic and coordinated manner.

Our solution has shown how Semantic Web standards, e.g., ontologies and SHACL, unlock several challenges to solve the IoT cascading failure dilemma, such as efficiently storing, querying, and reasoning on abundant and heterogenous data related to IoT device dependencies and failures.

The evaluation results showed the significant impact and potential business savings of the proposed solution by reducing time to repair failures and minimizing resource waste in connected environments. We considered several design choices to ease and accelerate the adoption of the proposed solution by market DM actors, such as 1) the adoption of the BDI model that reflects human-like behavior, which eases the integration of the proposed solution by the DM actors, 2) the use of the FMEA model to design the IoT-F ontology, which has shown its usability in the literature based on a System Usability Scale (SUS) tests [13], and 3) the reuse of legacy platform features within the OSAMA agent for monitoring and recovery to save costs and accelerate integration efforts.

We have several plans for large-scale deployment and adoption of our solution in the device management market: The main plan consists in refining our solution based on further experimentation and user feedback within our device management team in the Orange company, but also with Orange partners and relevant stakeholders to ensure the practical applicability and adoption of our approach, since it involves the collaborative effort of all device management actors. Another potential plan is to submit our solutions as a standard draft to standardization organizations in which Orange is involved, such as the European Telecommunications Standards Institute (ETSI) or the Connectivity Standards Alliance (CSA), to enable collaborative improvement and widest adoption of the proposed solution by several device management actors and experts.

Supplemental Material Availability. Source Code for IoT-F ontology [14], OSAMA agents [15], and FMSim simulator [16] is available from GitHub.

References

1. Aïssaoui, F., Berlemont, S., Douet, M., Mezghani, E.: A semantic model toward smart IoT device management. In: Barolli, L., Amato, F., Moscato, F., Enokido, T., Takizawa, M. (eds.) Web, Artificial Intelligence and Network Applications, pp. 640–650. Springer, Cham (2020). https://doi.org/10.1007/978-3-030-44038-1_59

2. Ali, N., Hong, J.E.: Failure detection and prevention for cyber-physical systems using ontology-based knowledge base. Computers **7**(4) (2018). https://doi.org/10.3390/computers7040068. https://www.mdpi.com/2073-431X/7/4/68

3. Alsabilah, N., Rawat, D.B.: Anomaly detection in smart home networks using Kalman filter. In: IEEE INFOCOM 2021 - IEEE Conference on Computer Communications Workshops (INFOCOM WKSHPS), pp. 1–6 (2021). https://doi.org/10.1109/INFOCOMWKSHPS51825.2021.9484507

4. Benazzouz, Y., Keir Aktouf, O.E., Parissis, I.: A fault fuzzy-ontology for large scale fault-tolerant wireless sensor networks. Procedia Comput. Sci. **35**, 203–212 (2014). https://doi.org/10.1016/j.procs.2014.08.100. Knowledge-Based and Intelligent Information & Engineering Systems 18th Annual Conference, KES-2014 Gdynia, Poland, September 2014 Proceedings

5. Boissier, O., Bordini, R., Hubner, J., Ricci, A.: Multi-Agent Oriented Programming: Programming Multi-Agent Systems Using JaCaMo. Intelligent Robotics and Autonomous Agents Series. MIT Press (2020)

6. Borhani, A., Zarandi, H.R.: Thingsdnd: IoT device failure detection and diagnosis for multi-user smart homes. In: 2022 18th European Dependable Computing Conference (EDCC), pp. 113–116 (2022). https://doi.org/10.1109/EDCC57035.2022.00028. Fault detection on sensors in smart home settings

7. Bratman, M.: Intention, Plans, and Practical Reason. Harvard University Press, Cambridge (1987)

8. Celik, Z.B., Tan, G., Mcdaniel, P.: Iotguard: dynamic enforcement of security and safety policy in commodity IoT. In: Proceedings 2019 Network and Distributed System Security Symposium (2019)

9. Chakraborty, T., et al.: Fall-curve: a novel primitive for IoT fault detection and isolation. In: Proceedings of the 16th ACM Conference on Embedded Networked Sensor Systems, SenSys 2018, pp. 95–107. Association for Computing Machinery, New York (2018). https://doi.org/10.1145/3274783.3274853

10. Chen, Y., Zhen, Z., Yu, H., Xu, J.: Application of fault tree analysis and fuzzy neural networks to fault diagnosis in the internet of things (IoT) for aquaculture. Sensors **17**(1) (2017). https://doi.org/10.3390/s17010153

11. Chi, Y., Dong, Y., Wang, Z.J., Yu, F.R., Leung, V.C.M.: Knowledge-based fault diagnosis in industrial internet of things: a survey. IEEE Internet Things J. **9**(15), 12886–12900 (2022). https://doi.org/10.1109/JIOT.2022.3163606
12. Chi, Y., Wang, Z.J., Leung, V.C.M.: Distributed knowledge inference framework for intelligent fault diagnosis in IIoT systems. IEEE Trans. Netw. Sci. Eng. **9**(5), 3152–3165 (2022)
13. Emmanouilidis, C., Gregori, M., Al-Shdifat, A.: Context ontology development for connected maintenance services. IFAC-PapersOnLine **53**(2), 10923–10928 (2020). https://doi.org/10.1016/j.ifacol.2020.12.2833. 21st IFAC World Congress
14. Guittoum, A.: IoT-F ontology documentation. https://github.com/Orange-OpenSource/collaborativeDM-IoTF-ontology-documentation
15. Guittoum, A.: OSAMA agents in the Smart home use case. https://github.com/Orange-OpenSource/collaborativeDM-OSAMA-agent
16. Guittoum, A.: The FMSim simulator. https://github.com/Orange-OpenSource/collaborativeDM-FM-Simulator
17. Guittoum, A., et al.: Inferring threatening IoT dependencies using semantic digital twins toward collaborative IoT device management. In: Proceedings of the 38th ACM/SIGAPP Symposium on Applied Computing. SAC 2023. Association for Computing Machinery, New York (2023). https://doi.org/10.1145/3555776.3578573
18. Gupta, H., Dastjerdi, A.V., Ghosh, S.K., Buyya, R.: iFogSim: a toolkit for modeling and simulation of resource management techniques in internet of things, edge and fog computing environments (2016)
19. Jia, Y., et al.: Who's in control? On security risks of disjointed IoT device management channels. In: Proceedings of the 2021 ACM SIGSAC Conference on Computer and Communications Security, CCS 2021, pp. 1289–1305. Association for Computing Machinery, New York (2021)
20. Kapitanova, K., Hoque, E., Stankovic, J.A., Whitehouse, K., Son, S.H.: Being smart about failures: assessing repairs in smart homes. In: Proceedings of the 2012 ACM Conference on Ubiquitous Computing, UbiComp 2012, pp. 51–60. Association for Computing Machinery, New York (2012). https://doi.org/10.1145/2370216.2370225
21. Kodeswaran, P., Kokku, R., Sen, S., Srivatsa, M.: Idea: a system for efficient failure management in smart IoT environments. In: MobiSys 2016 - Proceedings of the 14th Annual International Conference on Mobile Systems, Applications, and Services pp. 43–56 (2016). https://doi.org/10.1145/2906388.2906406
22. Lazarova-Molnar, S., Shaker, H.R., Mohamed, N., Jorgensen, B.N.: Fault detection and diagnosis for smart buildings: state of the art, trends and challenges. In: 2016 3rd MEC International Conference on Big Data and Smart City (ICBDSC), pp. 1–7 (2016). https://doi.org/10.1109/ICBDSC.2016.7460392
23. Li, J., Guo, Y., Wall, J., West, S.: Support vector machine based fault detection and diagnosis for HVAC systems. Int. J. Intell. Syst. Technol. Appl. **18**, 204 (2019)
24. Najari, N., Berlemont, S., Lefebvre, G., Duffner, S., Garcia, C.: Robust variational autoencoders and normalizing flows for unsupervised network anomaly detection. In: Barolli, L., Hussain, F., Enokido, T. (eds.) AINA 2022. LNNS, vol. 450, pp. 281–292. Springer, Cham (2022). https://doi.org/10.1007/978-3-030-99587-4_24
25. Najeh, H.: Diagnosis in building: new challenges. Theses, Université Grenoble Alpes; École nationale d'ingénieurs de Gabès (Tunisie) (2019)
26. Nishiguchi, Y., Yano, A., Ohtani, T., Matsukura, R., Kakuta, J.: IoT fault management platform with device virtualization. In: IEEE World Forum on Internet of Things, WF-IoT 2018 - Proceedings 2018-January, pp. 257–262 (2018)

27. Norris, M., et al.: Iotrepair: systematically addressing device faults in commodity IoT. In: 2020 IEEE/ACM Fifth International Conference on Internet-of-Things Design and Implementation (IoTDI), pp. 142–148 (2020)

28. Norris, M., et al.: Iotrepair: flexible fault handling in diverse IoT deployments. ACM Trans. Internet Things **3**(3) (2022). https://doi.org/10.1145/3532194

29. Ozeer, U.I.Z.: Autonomic resilience of distributed IoT applications in the Fog. Theses, Université Grenoble Alpes (2019)

30. Perez Abreu, D., Velasquez, K., Curado, M., Monteiro, E.: A comparative analysis of simulators for the cloud to fog continuum. Simul. Model. Pract. Theory **101**, 102029 (2020)

31. Power, A.: A predictive fault-tolerance framework for IoT systems. Ph.D. thesis, Lancaster University (2020). https://doi.org/10.17635/lancaster/thesis/1063

32. Rao, A.S.: AgentSpeak(L): BDI agents speak out in a logical computable language. In: Van de Velde, W., Perram, J.W. (eds.) MAAMAW 1996. LNCS, vol. 1038, pp. 42–55. Springer, Heidelberg (1996). https://doi.org/10.1007/BFb0031845

33. Samsung: SmartThings rule. https://developer-preview.smartthings.com/docs/automations/rules/. Accessed 6 Avril 2022

34. Sanislav, T., Mois, G.: A dependability analysis model in the context of cyber-physical systems. In: 2017 18th International Carpathian Control Conference (ICCC), pp. 146–150 (2017)

35. Sanislav, T., Zeadally, S., Mois, G.D., Fouchal, H.: Reliability, failure detection and prevention in cyber-physical systems (CPSS) with agents. Concurr. Comput. Pract. Exp. **31**(24), e4481 (2019). https://doi.org/10.1002/cpe.4481

36. Sharma, A.B., Golubchik, L., Govindan, R.: Sensor faults: detection methods and prevalence in real-world datasets. ACM Trans. Sen. Netw. **6**(3) (2010)

37. Shibuya, M., Hasegawa, T., Yamaguchi, H.: A study on device management for IoT services with uncoordinated device operating history. In: ICN 2016, p. 84 (2016)

38. Silva, L.D., Meneguzzi, F., Logan, B.: BDI agent architectures: a survey. In: Bessiere, C. (ed.) Proceedings of the Twenty-Ninth International Joint Conference on Artificial Intelligence, IJCAI 2020, pp. 4914–4921. International Joint Conferences on Artificial Intelligence Organization (2020)

39. Sinche, S., et al.: A survey of IoT management protocols and frameworks. IEEE Commun. Surv. Tutor. **22**(2), 1168–1190 (2020)

40. Steenwinckel, B., et al.: Towards adaptive anomaly detection and root cause analysis by automated extraction of knowledge from risk analyses. In: SSN@ISWC (2018)

41. Suárez-Figueroa, M.C., Gómez-Pérez, A., Fernández-López, M.: The NeOn methodology for ontology engineering. In: Suárez-Figueroa, M.C., Gómez-Pérez, A., Motta, E., Gangemi, A. (eds.) Ontology Engineering in a Networked World, pp. 9–34. Springer, Heidelberg (2012). https://doi.org/10.1007/978-3-642-24794-1_2

42. Carnegie Mellon University: Intelligent Software Agents. https://www.cs.cmu.edu/~softagents/multi.html

43. Wilhelm, Y., Reimann, P., Gauchel, W., Mitschang, B.: Overview on hybrid approaches to fault detection and diagnosis: combining data-driven, physics-based and knowledge-based models. Procedia CIRP **99**, 278–283 (2021). https://doi.org/10.1016/j.procir.2021.03.041. 14th CIRP Conference on Intelligent Computation in Manufacturing Engineering, 15–17 July 2020

44. Xing, L.: Cascading failures in internet of things: review and perspectives on reliability and resilience. IEEE Internet Things J. **8**(1), 44–64 (2021)

45. Xu, F., Liu, X., Chen, W., Zhou, C., Cao, B.: Ontology-based method for fault diagnosis of loaders. Sensors **18**(3) (2018). https://doi.org/10.3390/s18030729
46. Zhang, H., Zhang, Q., Liu, J., Guo, H.: Fault detection and repairing for intelligent connected vehicles based on dynamic Bayesian network model. IEEE Internet Things J. **5**(4), 2431–2440 (2018)

Aviation Certification Powered by the Semantic Web Stack

Paul Cuddihy[1]([✉]), Daniel Russell[2], Eric Mertens[3], Kit Siu[1], Dave Archer[3], and Jenny Williams[1]

[1] GE Aerospace Research, Niskayuna, NY 12309, USA
{cuddihy,siu,weisenje}@ge.com
[2] GE Aerospace, Grand Rapids, MI 49512, USA
daniel.russell@ge.com
[3] Galois, Portland, OR 97204, USA
{emertens,dwa}@galois.com

Abstract. Every deployed DoD system undergoes certification (or qualification, for military) to assess the software system's fitness for use. Certification requires that human subject matter expert look over evidence and evaluate its conformance to standards such as DO-178C or the Risk Management Framework (RMF). Current practices are not keeping pace with the ever-increasing size of software systems and the amount of evidence required for their certification. This problem is further exasperated when platforms are comprised of systems of systems developed by multiple suppliers, each providing data generated by different tools, in different formats, and captured with different granularity. We demonstrate the application of W3C Semantic web technologies to perform efficient evidence curation under a military research program. This tech stack offers the right solutions for integrating data from heterogeneous sources and for performing graph-traversal queries across data that changes at a regular frequency.

Keywords: Recursive graph traversal · certification · curation

1 Introduction

Every deployed aviation system undergoes certification (or qualification, for military) to assess the software system's fitness for use; whether it's following DO-178C guidance, a Certification and Accreditation (C&A) process, Risk Management Framework (RMF), or Assessment and Authorization (A&A). Certification requires that a human subject matter expert look over evidence and evaluate its conformance to standards. With evidence consisting of ever-increasing numbers of requirements, architecture components, test cases, and additional data, the current practices are not able to scale. This problem is further exasperated when platforms are made up of systems of systems developed by multiple suppliers, each providing data generated by different tools, in different formats, and captured with different levels of granularity.

One way to solve this problem is through efficient evidence curation. Curation normalizes the data by defining a schema and organizing the artifacts against it. It must then

© The Author(s) 2023
T. R. Payne et al. (Eds.): ISWC 2023, LNCS 14266, pp. 345–361, 2023.
https://doi.org/10.1007/978-3-031-47243-5_19

provide easy access to the data so that it can be used to develop a certification compliance report or to assemble an assurance case with a structured argument showing how the system meets the goals of safe and secure operation. These reports and assurance cases may require updating at a regular frequency to reflect software updates and bug fixes.

The W3C Semantic Web stack offers the right solution for integrating data from heterogeneous sources. An ontology provides the means to reify a schema – it provides the rigidity needed to define an ontology with common subjects and predicates universally applicable to certification evidence. Inference and ingestion tools provide the means to check the dataset's compliance to the ontology either during or post ingestion. SPARQL is an excellent match for the inherently recursive graph structure of assurance case evidence and can provide results for a certification report.

In this paper, we describe how we curate certification evidence into our opensource Rapid Assurance Curation Kit (RACK), which consists of a semantic triplestore backed by an ontology. This curation platform is developed under DARPA Automated Rapid Certification of Software (ARCOS) [1]. There are three performer teams on this research program that generate evidence (known as Technical Area 1—TA1) and three other performer teams that use the evidence to assemble assurance cases (known as TA3). The development of RACK and the curation effort is known as TA2; the authors of this paper are part of this sole performer team on the program. RACK is used by all performer teams on ARCOS.

2 Background

2.1 Definition of Data Curation

Curation means organizing the data, assessing its quality, and providing easy access to it. A system development process produces artifacts in a multitude of formats, some of which we will illustrate in the next subsection. To make use of these artifacts, the data within must be identified, extracted, and organized. To ensure that the data is curated correctly, data verification is performed at various stages. Verification is done at ingestion time to make sure that all incoming data matches the types specified by the ontology and that all properties and classes are correct. The next level of verification is performed after ingestion of the complete dataset to ensure that it adheres to any specified ontology constraints such as cardinality. The final verification step is domain specific. In airborne system certification, for example, we perform a query that counts how many tests do not trace to requirements.

2.2 Diversity of Tools and Artifacts

The system development process is typically defined in a series of planning documents that describe how the development team will conform to the certification guidelines. Examples are PSAC (Plan for Software Aspects of Certification), SDP (Software Development Plan), SVP (Software Verification Plan), SCMP (Software Configuration Management Plan), and SQAP (Software Quality Assurance Plan). These plans are freeform text documents; an example template can be found here [2]. Planning documents describe how the development team will generate artifacts through a series of development activities and how those artifacts will be used as evidence that the team has followed the plan. A system development process often uses multiple tools that produce a diversity of artifacts in various formats. RACK would curate the elements of the plans and the evidence produced by development activities, and show how evidence is related, revealing where the development process may have deficiencies or errors.

IBM Rational® DOORS® is a requirements management tool [3] where members of an organization can access, author, and modify requirements. The tool provides links to other DOORS® objects, but the plans dictate traceability to design items such as source code or testing. In this work, RACK would curate from DOORS® the requirement identifier, the requirement text, and any traceability information (Fig. 1).

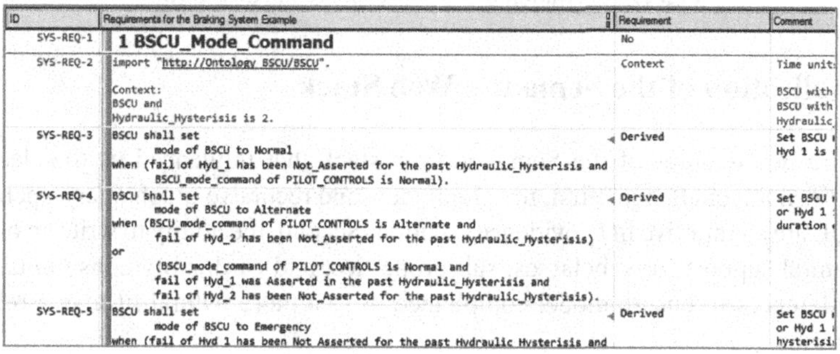

Fig. 1. Illustration of requirements captured in DOORS®[1]

Developing requirements-based tests is an important verification step, often captured in XML. Figure 2 illustrates a test procedure file that would be created for each requirement. In this work, RACK would curate evidence information such as test identifier and the requirement that this test verifies. After tests are run, results could be saved in a myriad of possible formats depending on the platform. Since it's commonplace for test procedures to define expected outputs, RACK would curate the pass/fail result from each test output file.

Many other tools exist that aid in developing artifacts within the development process. RACK is a common repository for evidence from all tools. By combining evidence produced from the multitude of tools, a knowledge graph can be assembled that allows for the analysis of the entire development process from one place.

---

[1] Requirements are textual in nature. This illustrative example is from our 2019 SAE paper [4] where we introduced a tool to capture requirements in a more formal and structural way.

```
<ctpm:TestStep>
    <ctpm:UniqueId>SYS-REQ-6_Context_1_TS026</ctpm:UniqueId>
    <ctpm:RequirementId>SYS-REQ-6</ctpm:RequirementId>
    <ctpm:ContextId>Context_1</ctpm:ContextId>
    <ctpm:TestCaseId>SYS-REQ-6-TC014_1</ctpm:TestCaseId>
    <ctpm:TestStepId>TS026</ctpm:TestStepId>
    <ctpm:InputData>
        <ctpm:SpecificationName>BSCU__pressure__BSCU__Hyd_1__Properties__h
        <ctpm:TestData>0</ctpm:TestData>
    </ctpm:InputData>
    <ctpm:InputData>
        <ctpm:SpecificationName>BSCU__threshold__BSCU__Hyd_1__Properties__h
        <ctpm:TestData>2000</ctpm:TestData>
    </ctpm:InputData>
```

Fig. 2. Illustration of a test procedure in XML format

3 Application of the Semantic Web Stack

There are two features of the Semantic Web stack that influenced us to select it for this certification challenge. First, the graph view and recursive graph query operators in SPARQL are an intuitive fit to evidence curation. Second, the ability to write an ontology with natural support for subclasses, sub-properties, and cardinality constraints, and to write inferences to ensure model compliance were a more natural fit than a relational schema.

3.1 Graph Databases and SPARQL

Common to all certification guidance is the need to define requirements with success and failure criteria. A graph display of a subset of curated evidence is shown in Fig. 3. In this example, a SYSTEM component is governed by a PIDS_Req (Prime Item Development requirement) which is satisfied by additional requirements such as SRS_Req (Software Requirements Specification). Some requirements are verified by tests, which may also verify other types of requirements. Some tests are confirmed by test results. Both the subclassing of REQUIREMENT and the visual graph structure are very intuitive to the certification community. Importantly, this type of graph display is very close to the natural state of the data in a triplestore, indicating a strong fit.

In most examples, system components are arranged in a tree-like network of *partOf* relationships and requirements can *satisfy* layers of additional requirements, creating a need for straight-forward ways to write recursive graph queries. SPARQL's graph structure and recursive operators such as * and + are a natural fit. Take for example this simple query:

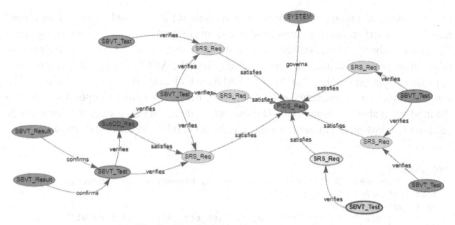

Fig. 3. Graph view of curated evidence

```
prefix TESTING:<http://arcos.rack/TESTING#>
prefix SYSTEM:<http://arcos.rack/SYSTEM#>
prefix REQUIREMENTS: <http://arcos.rack/REQUIREMENTS#>

select distinct ? testStatus where {{
        ? testStatus a TESTING:TEST_STATUS .
        <SOME_URI> (^(SYSTEM:partOf) |
                    ^(REQUIREMENTS:governs) |
                    ^(REQUIREMENTS:satisfies) |
                    ^(TESTING:verifies) |
                    ^(TESTING:confirms) |
                      TESTING:result     )+ ?testStatus .
    }}
```

The URI of any instance of any subclass* of SYSTEM, REQUIREMENT, TEST, or TEST_RESULT may be substituted in for *<SOME_URI>* and the query will return a list of test statuses (*Passed, Failed, Indeterminate*) that roll up the piece of evidence. This SPARQL query will find the test status through layers of subsystems, layers of requirements, and all associated tests. The ability of such a relatively simple SPARQL query to deliver powerful results for a variety of types of evidence is a clear indication that the W3C Semantic Web stack is a great fit for our domain.

3.2 Authoring the Ontology

The ontology is written using the Semantic Application Design Language (SADL) [5, 6]. SADL is an open-source, controlled-English language that is automatically converted to OWL [7]. Besides being an ontology language, SADL is an Eclipse-integrated development environment (IDE) with Xtext [8]. This environment provides semantic coloring of different types of concepts in models, hyperlinking of concepts to their definitions and usage, graphical visualization of models, type checking, content assist, and other functionality useful for authoring models. Below is a snippet of the ontology written in SADL with the OWL translation below. Notice how SADL is very natural for humans to read and write as compared to OWL, even with its standard serializations. This allows non-semantic experts to read, write, and contribute to the data model, which is important for maintainability, as we will describe in the next section on the participative process of updating and maintaining this model throughout the ARCOS program. Our ontology consists of approximately 7,800 lines of SADL, which compiles into 7,400 triples. The semantic model in its entirety can be found on GitHub[2]. A more in-depth discussion of the model can also be found in [9]. The snippet we included below does not demonstrate cardinality constraints but note that this can be done inline in the SADL model.

```
REQUIREMENT
    (note "Captures (both high- and low-level) properties of a process or arti-
    fact that are to be assessed")
    is a type of ENTITY.
    governs (note "ENTITY(s) that are the subject of the requirement")
    describes REQUIREMENT with values of type ENTITY.
    governs is a type of wasImpactedBy.
    satisfies (note "Parent ENTITY(s) (e.g. REQUIREMENT) that this REQUIREMENT
    is derived from")
    describes REQUIREMENT with values of type ENTITY.
    satisfies is a type of wasImpactedBy.
    Rq:mitigates (note "ENTITY(s) (e.g. HAZARD) that is being mitigated by this
    REQUIREMENT")
    describes REQUIREMENT with values of type ENTITY.
    Rq:mitigates is a type of wasImpactedBy.
    wasGeneratedBy of REQUIREMENT only has values of type
    REQUIREMENT_DEVELOPMENT.
REQUIREMENT_DEVELOPMENT
    (note "ACTIVITY that produces REQUIREMENTs") is a type of ACTIVITY.

<owl:Class rdf:about="http://arcos.rack/REQUIREMENTS#REQUIREMENT">
 <rdfs:subClassOf>
  <owl:Restriction>
   <owl:allValuesFrom>
    <owl:Class
       rdf:about="http://arcos.rack/REQUIREMENTS#REQUIREMENT_DEVELOPMENT"/>
   </owl:allValuesFrom>
   <owl:onProperty rdf:resource="http://arcos.rack/PROV-S#wasGeneratedBy"/>
  </owl:Restriction>
 </rdfs:subClassOf>
 <rdfs:comment xml:lang="en">Captures (both high- and low-level) properties of
  a process or artifact that are to be assessed</rdfs:comment>
 <rdfs:subClassOf rdf:resource="http://arcos.rack/PROV-S#ENTITY"/>
</owl:Class>
<owl:Class rdf:about="http://arcos.rack/REQUIREMENTS#REQUIREMENT_DEVELOPMENT">
```

3.3 Maintaining the Ontology

To sustain the ontology, we formed a participative process where all ARCOS performers are stakeholders in evolving the model. The Data Model Decision Team (DMDT) is made up of one representative from each performer team. The group meets regularly

---

(bi-weekly) and any member of the DMDT can propose a change. We follow a RAPID process as shown in Fig. 4. The TA2 team administers the meetings, implements agreed changes, and maintains the ontology. SADL's role as the key enabler to bringing the Semantic Web stack to this DARPA community cannot be overemphasized. We could not have had as deep discussions, or achieved as good of a consensus, if we were looking at relational schemas, or OWL for that matter.

Fig. 4. We use a participative RAPID approach to maintain the ontology.

4   Evidence Ingestion Pipeline

Ingesting thousands of pieces of various types of evidence from multiple providers across large teams requires a rich set of tools layered over the triplestore and organized into an ingestion pipeline. Figure 5 provides a simplified view of this pipeline.

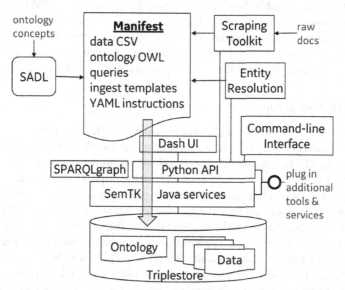

Fig. 5. High-level view of the rich pipeline of tools used in RACK.

At the bottom is a SPARQL 1.1 compliant triplestore. For practical and programmatic reasons, we use Apache Fuseki [10] for this stage of the program. Over that is the

Semantics Toolkit (SemTK) service layer [11, 12]. A suite of semantics tools that has been in development at GE for several years, SemTK is based upon the concept of "node-groups" [13] which are graphical depictions of a subgraph of interest, with additional annotations for automatic generation of queries including ingestion. SemTK includes the SPARQLgraph interface for visually editing nodegroups and ingestion mapping templates, running queries, and performing various utility functions. It also provides Java and REST APIs for asynchronous queries, ingestion, and utility functions. Then there is a Python API [14] upon which several other tools are built, including a user interface, RACK UI, which supports basic data loading and links to SPARQLgraph, and a command-line interface.

The manifest format defines the large and complex data packages that are used to populate RACK. It is comprised of sub-folders of OWL ontology files, CSV data files, nodegroup queries, ingestion templates, SemTK reports, and YAML files that describe the manifest's components and loading sequence.

As described in the previous section, SADL is used to compose the ontology, and the SADL tools compile into OWL, which is then loaded via the manifest. Other important tools include the Scraping Toolkit, which accesses the ontology through the semtk-python layer and is then used to build document scrapers which output CSV and YAML files for the manifest. The Entity Resolution Tool uses semtk-python to access both the ontology and previously loaded data to create CSV files that describe entities which can be combined in an additional, cleaner copy of the data.

Curation of data from multiple sources involves the orchestration of many complex processes. The pipeline introduced above allows us to load large ingestion packages successfully and repeatably. RACK can ingest a data package of 2.5M triples in under 15 min, inclusive of type checking, URI lookup and linking, and verification of the domains and ranges of all properties. The APIs allow other ARCOS performer teams to build and integrate RACK features and capabilities into their own tools. The following sections of this paper will describe key components of RACK in more details.

4.1 SemTK Nodegroups

The "nodegroup" is a fundamental concept of the SemTK layer upon which RACK's data ingestion and querying is built. A simple example is shown in Fig. 6. The nodegroup is edited using SPARQLgraph by dragging classes from the ontology onto the canvas and selecting desired properties. It represents a subgraph of interest for a particular query or queries. Pathfinding assists the editing process and may be based either solely upon the ontology or account for existing instance data when choosing likely paths. By default, a node represents not only the class shown, but all subclasses. Data properties appear by name only, and object properties as links to additional nodes. The graphical editor provides a rich set of annotations that allow properties to be selected for return, labeled optional or minus, filtered, and have functions applied. Object properties may have operators such as * and + applied. Unions are supported. Although a very useful subset of SPARQL is supported, nodegroups have yet to support the full expressivity of SPARQL.

The right side of Fig. 6 shows SPARQL for a "select distinct" query that is auto-generated by SemTK, with some prefixes removed and edits made for readability. Query types such as count, construct, ask, and delete are all supported. Nodegroups are stored in a "nodegroup store" and referenced by id. When applied to a different SPARQL connection, "FROM" or "USING" clauses are updated appropriately. Stored nodegroups support the concept of "runtime constraint," which allow the APIs to assist in sending along constraints such as *?requirement_id = "Req1"* when a query is executed. It should be noted that since the SPARQLgraph editor is ontology-driven, all SPARQL-generated queries (and more importantly, the ingestion process described below) are consistent with the ontology.

Fig. 6. Simple nodegroup and auto-generated SPARQL

4.2 SemTK Ingestion Templates

Building upon the nodegroup concept are ingestion templates. A template consistent with the nodegroup in Fig. 6 is shown in Fig. 7. A template maps the data in each line of a CSV file to a nodegroup such that the triples representing one nodegroup subgraph will be inserted for each line of the CSV.

The right side of the template shows the names of four columns in a target CSV file. The left shows where each maps to the nodegroup. With certain exceptions related to lookup and CSV validation features, empty or missing values are pruned from the node-group before the line of CSV data is inserted.

The ingestion process supports many features beyond the scope of this paper. However, a few of them are critical to the RACK ingestion process. Most importantly is the *URI Lookup* feature. Note that all the bolded rows in the ingestion template (which represent classes) are set to "—Generate UUID," meaning that random URI's will be generated during ingestion and not built from strings in the CSV. The darkened boxes near *?SYSTEM* and *?system_id* indicate the instance of the class SYSTEM will be looked up in the target graph using the property *identifier* (the property with object *?system_id*) and the value from the column *system_id*.

When looking up URIs, the template provides the options of *create-if-missing*, *error-if-missing*, and *error-if-exists*. For the first two more commonly used options, once the URI is found, other properties will be added to the existing data. RACK uses these features to store all data with random URIs and avoid the need to publish and enforce standards for URI construction across different program performers. Instead, data is looked up by identifier.

In addition to *error-if-missing*, the ingestion process also checks the format of all data presented as URIs, dates, times, numbers, etc. and prevents ingestion of any data that is not properly formatted. This works alongside the ontology-driven nodegroup used to ingest each row, which guarantees that the types, properties, domains, and ranges in all the triples conform to the ontology. These represent RACK's first level of data verification on incoming data before it enters the triplestore.

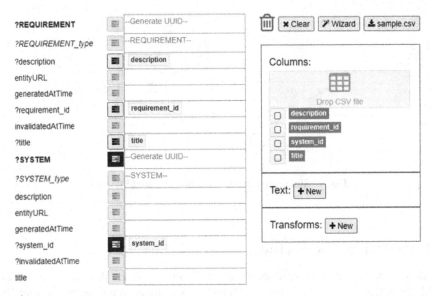

Fig. 7. An ingestion template.

4.3 Automatic Ingestion Templates ("Ingest by Class")

The SemTK nodegroup and template-based ingestion process described above is both powerful and very flexible. We determined that a less flexible standardized ingestion template would speed understanding and adoption of ingestion across the many performers on the program. To this end, a standard ingestion template can be automatically generated for any given class.

RACK's auto-generated class ingestion templates have the following attributes. There is one instance of the target class that is looked up by *?identifier* in the mode *create-if-missing*. This means that an instance of the target class will be created if needed, but if one already matches the *?identifier*, then the data from the row will be added to the existing instance. Each data property has a corresponding column in the CSV. Each outgoing object property's object will also be looked up by its identifier, using a column name of the format: *<propertyShortName>_identifier*. The objects of object properties are looked up in the mode *error-if-missing*. This has the positive effect of preventing ingestion of links to non-existent instances. It does, however, force data to be ingested in a specific order such that object property objects always exist. In cases where circularities exist, custom templates must be used instead of these auto-generated versions.

RACK provides additional features to ease the use of auto-generated templates. There are API calls to get a copy of the nodegroup for inspection, and to get sample CSV files compatible with the template. Nodegroups have all properties set to optional so they may also be used to generate SELECT or CONSTRUCT queries to explore ingested data.

Despite the loss of expressivity, the forced ordering of loading, and in many cases loss of performance compared to customized ingestion templates, these auto-generated templates have proven very easy to understand and use. Most of the data ingestion in RACK to date has leveraged this feature.

4.3.1   Checking Quantified Cardinality.

SemTK has a copy of the ontology including cardinality constraints available to it during ingestion, but it is not practical to enforce quantified cardinality during the ingestion process. Actual counts will be lower than cardinality limits while ingestion is incomplete. With multiple-step ingestion packages, it is not possible to report such errors during a single ingestion. Actual counts exceeding cardinality limits would be possible but inefficient.

We chose instead to provide a SemTK REST function for checking quantified cardinality that can be run after ingestion of the entire dataset is complete. This is available in the reports feature, described in a later section, and accessible through various APIs. The cardinality check reads through the ontology and runs a SPARQL query for each cardinality restriction. It returns a table of violations consisting of the following fields:

- class – the class with the restricted property
- property – the property being restricted
- restriction – type of restriction (max, min, qualified)
- limit – cardinality limit declared in the model and violated in the data
- subject – the instance of the class that violates the restriction
- actual_cardinality – the actual cardinality of the property for this subject

4.4   Ingestion Packages

To maintain a clean separation of data curation and data exploration, and to conform to the data owner's specification that data be stored locally, RACK supports an archive format that contains a complete copy of the ontology, datasets, queries, and reports. These "ingestion packages" can be generated using our data curation tools and ensure that the resulting RACK state is easy to reproduce for multiple users and across multiple reloads.

This reproducibility has been important for enabling us to make sweeping changes as the ontology and dataset evolved without sacrificing the ability for users to work with past versions of the data. Each ingestion package comes complete with the appropriate version of the ontology. Internally the ingestion packages are structured as zip files containing the various component OWL, CSV, and JSON files indexed by YAML files. Manifest files indicate how the content should be loaded into RACK. Model and data manifest files describe the sequence in which OWL or CSV files are loaded, which triplestore graphs to load them to, and which ingestion templates to use for each. Manifests may also specify nodegroups (for queries or custom ingestion templates) to be loaded to the nodegroup store. Beyond the data and ontology, an ingestion package contains enough information to indicate target graphs, clear data, perform entity resolution and other maintenance tasks performed at load-time.

Significant support has been built to facilitate the use of ingestion packages within our program. The RACK command line interface[3] supports automatically building ingestion package zip files given a set of manifest files. Ingestion packages may be loaded into RACK using the command line interface or a simple RACK user interface page (highlighted later in Sect. 6). Further, as zip files, ingestion packages may be easily shared between users and reliably reproduced into any given RACK installation. Notably, these operations require no semantic expertise and therefore lower the barrier to entry for using RACK.

4.5 Scraping Toolkit

The norm for system development is for a multitude of tools and methodologies to be used, each creating evidence supporting certification. Generically, data curation must extract raw data from source material, perform data transformation on that raw data to define it per the ontology, and format it as an ingestion package. One of the support tools provided with RACK is the Scraping Toolkit (STK)[4] that facilitates the collection of evidence into ingestible packages. Fundamentally, the STK is a Python library that is auto-generated from the ontology. The STK provides methods for collecting the evidence that are automatically curated into fully formed ingestion packages from raw evidence using the ingestion templates.

Raw sources of evidence are processed by creating a Python script that identifies the individual pieces of evidence. Scripts start with "CreateEvidenceFile", a method that initializes a RACK-DATA.xml file that is used to collect bits of evidence as they are found while processing the source material. When evidence is found, there are "Add" methods that append evidence to the RACK-DATA.xml file. Each data class has its own "Add" method that is customized to its ontological definition, with optional parameters for each property. As additional evidence is found while processing the source material, the RACK-DATA.xml is continually expanded until the end of the script at which time the "createCDR" method processes the RACK-DATA.xml to create a fully formed ingestion package. This process simplifies the creation of the transformation scripts by not requiring the data provider to have to sort and manage interspersed data, but rather can just record all information that is found as it comes while processing the source material—the processing in "createCDR" curates and combines evidence.

Python works well as it is an easy, well known programming language and there is a large library of existing modules that can be used. Regular Expressions in Python

---

[3] https://github.com/ge-high-assurance/RACK/tree/master/cli.

[4] https://github.com/ge-high-assurance/RACK/tree/master/ScrapingToolKit.

are easy to use and libraries for XML, DOCX, and even source code exist that can be combined with the STK to make data extraction from nearly any source relatively simple.

4.6 Entity Resolution

Any time data is collected from multiple sources there's a possibility of creating different instances within the same data graph even though it's meant to be the same piece of evidence. Small inconsistencies that a human might miss are inconsistent capitalization or the use of different types of dashes. While it is generally preferable to have all these disconnects addressed as part of the scraping process this is not always possible.

To accommodate this inevitability within RACK, we perform entity resolution to resolve these issues without modifying the source data graphs. In the RACK ontology, a SAME_AS class is defined with two object properties: *primary* and *secondary*. When a user identifies instances within the data graph that should be combined, a new SAME_AS instance is created that connects the two instances. To aid in this process, we created an Entity Resolution Tool that evaluates the likelihood of possible matches based on a set of rules guided by the ontology. For example, two instances that have the same identifier, and one's type is a super class of the other would have a high likelihood representing the same evidence, as would two instances with the same class with identifiers that only differ by a hyphen. Alternatively, two instances that represent evidence from the same source material with nearly identical identifiers (for example, SRS_Req*1*, SRS_Req*2*) will have a lower probability of representing the same evidence. These rules can be customized, and the Entity Resolution Tool will extract possible matches from the data based on class compatibility, score them based on the defined rules, and present the results to a user for final determination.

While this creates a relationship within the data graph, usage of this relationship in queries would be complicated as now every node within the search would have to allow for this potential. Rather than leave this complication to the user to deal with, we collapse these SAME_AS relationships into a single, additional resolved data graph. This cleaner copy of the data graph has all the instance data from the source graphs except any object that was identified as a secondary is merged into the primary. Any conflicts related to this merge is resolved by using the primary's data. This new graph allows queries to be run that do not have to account for the SAME_AS complexities while leaving the original source graphs untouched and available for review. Maintaining the source graph is still necessary for providing providence of the evidence—from source material to the final evidence graph a clear line can still be drawn.

5 Evidence Exploration

Our vision for RACK is that data exploration will be accomplished with tools built by users on top of the RACK APIs. We have built query nodegroups that serve both as stand-alone data verification tools, and as samples for data retrieval that is performed by such tools. Further, RACK includes a generic reporting tool that allows queries to be organized into sets that are of interest to a particular role, and repeatedly executed in bulk into a summary page.

5.1 Queries

The RACK tool includes over 30 pre-defined queries[5] in the form of nodegroups that are pre-loaded into the SemTK nodegroup store during ingestion of manifests.

A dozen of these queries are meant as follow-ups to cardinality checking. They query instances of and give additional information about data that has violated a particular cardinality constraint such as a REQUIREMENT without a *description*. This additional information proves useful in troubleshooting ingestion problems. But other queries that check constraints are slightly more complex than can be easily expressed in SADL. In one example, the REQUIREMENT was intended as an abstract superclass, so a query is provided to check for instances of this class. Pre-defined data verification queries can check for OR conditions, such as finding requirements that do not either satisfy another requirement or govern a system component.

Other queries show structure of the evidence. They take a runtime constraint of an entity such as a REQUIREMENT, SYSTEM, or HAZARD and produce tree or table output showing how requirements or systems roll up to each other. In the case of HAZARDs, the sample query shows the entity from which the hazard was derived, and the requirement tree that attempts to mitigate it, if any.

Finally, there are queries that demonstrate how to check the evidence in an assurance case. Examples include finding requirements with no passed tests, or those specifically with failures, or those with no tests at all. These query nodegroups are intended to be useful as well as demonstrative of how users can write their own as they manually explore the data or build tools on top of RACK APIs.

5.2 Reports

Nodegroups can be assembled—along with a few special functions—into reports, which can be stored as JSON files and drag-and-dropped into SPARQLgraph, or in the node-group store and accessed by id. A simple editor using *jsoneditor* [15] inside of SPAR-QLgraph allows users to assemble the queries that impact their specific role (i.e., was the data loaded properly vs. is the evidence complete vs. are all systems governed by REQUIREMENTs with passing TESTs) and re-run the group of queries in a single step.

The "special functions" include the cardinality checker described earlier, and a simple count of the number of instances of each class. Each nodegroup may be executed as SELECT DISTINCT to tables, or as CONSTRUCT queries to network graphs. For tables, success or failure may be defined with simple row count constraints. So, a query for bad data (e.g., an INTERFACE without a source) that returns no rows simply shows up as *success*, whereas one that finds rows is labelled *failure* and the table of results included.

Although not intended to replace evidence-checking applications that may be built on RACK, the report provides a powerful ability to run a large number of queries in one step and produce pages of output which are easy to scan for issues, and which provide some level of interaction (such as sorting and filtering tables).

---

[5] https://github.com/ge-high-assurance/RACK/tree/master/RACK-Ontology/nodegroups.

6 Impact and Lessons Learned

RACK has broad adaptation in the ARCOS research community, including teams at Lockheed Martin, SRI, GrammaTech, STR, RTX, Honeywell, and more. The communal ontology allows data providers (TA1 teams) to ingest their evidence, and in some cases, to extend the ontology with subclasses and sub-properties germane to their tools.

Lockheed Martin's tool called CertGATE produces Evidential Assurance Case Fragments (EACFs), which are structured arguments linked to pieces of evidence that are ingested into RACK. Similarly, SRI's DesCert team created an extensive ontology extension[6] to capture the evidence produced by their multitude of tools [16]. The evidence "interface" in RACK enabled software and documentation analysis tools, like the one developed by the A-CERT[7] team lead by GrammaTech, to uniformly capture evidential claims: claim that a certain property holds about the system, link the claim to the relevant design and implementation elements, and supply raw evidence supporting the claim. The assurance case research teams (TA3s) have also broadly integrated RACK into their tools. STR's ARBITER currently automates the harvesting of data from RACK, organizes it as guided by assurance reasoning strategies, and presents a candidate assurance case for review by an end user via a browser-based GUI. Similarly, RTX's AACE, an Automatic Assurance Case Framework, instantiates security case patterns using data provided by its evidence manager, which is informed by RACK [17, 18]. Honeywell's Clarissa tool maps RACK evidence into logic programming, which led to research breakthroughs such as target constrained natural query language built on top of the RACK ontology within a principled, structured case adhering to Assurance 2.0 methodology [19].

One lesson learned in working on the ARCOS program and serving as the evidence curator and ontology maintainer is that users need help with triplification. Non-semantic experts need help getting data into the triplestore. Requesting RACK users provide their certification evidence in the form of triples would have required extensive training and subsequent debugging and may have jeopardized the approach. So, we introduced the performer teams to SemTK and default class ingestion templates, which use the ontology to map CSV files to triples while performing significant verification. To make the tool programmatically interactive, we provided Java and REST APIs, and we also provided Python-based command line interfaces. These interfaces helped, but still some users struggled with installation. The game changer was a Dash[8]-based RACK UI web page that lessened the friction for end users to load data into RACK (Fig. 8). By turning data ingestion into a 1-click process, data providers can focus on delivering high quality data instead of agonizing over multi-step installation. Data consumers indirectly reap these benefits because the easier it is to ingest high quality data into RACK, the bigger the treasure trove of information to mine to show certification standards compliance. The user simply zips up the ontology files and data files into an ingestion package, along with the manifest that lists the underlying model footprint and load steps. On ARCOS, the target DoD system contained approximately 170 CSV data files. We are also developing

---

[6] https://github.com/ge-high-assurance/RACK/blob/master/overlays/SRI-Ontology/ontology.

[7] https://grammatech.github.io/prj/acert/

[8] https://dash.plotly.com/

an integrated environment called RITE (**RACK** **I**ntegrated cer**T**ification Environment)[9], which integrates SADL and RACK. This will allow users to write or modify an ontology and quickly prove its usability via sample data. It will also assist users in composing ingestion packages, which as noted, can contain hundreds of data files.

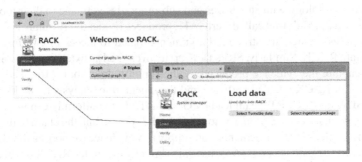

Fig. 8. RACK UI page with 1-click data load and 1-click data verification.

7 Conclusions

In this paper we described how we were able to bring the Semantic Web stack into the aviation certification domain. The graph view and recursive graph query operators in SPARQL are an intuitive fit to evidence curation. The ability to write an ontology with natural support for subclasses, sub-properties, and cardinality constraints, and to write inferences to ensure model compliance were a natural fit. Our most recent ingestion package consists of approximately 2.5M triples. RACK has been integrated into the tools of at least six other performer teams.

Acknowledgement and Disclaimer. Distribution Statement A. Approved for public release: distribution unlimited. This research was developed with funding from the Defense Advanced Research Projects Agency (DARPA). The views, opinions and/or findings expressed are those of the authors and should not be interpreted as representing the official views or policies of the Department of Defense or the U.S. Government.

References

1. ARCOS. https://www.darpa.mil/program/automated-rapid-certification-of-software.html. Accessed 14 Apr 2023
2. psac-template. https://studylib.net/doc/26041621/psac-template. Accessed 28 July 2023
3. Overview of Rational® DOORS®. https://www.ibm.com/docs/en/engineering-lifecycle-man agement-suite/doors/9.6.0?topic=overview-rational-doors. Accessed 28 July 2023

---

[9] https://github.com/ge-high-assurance/RITE.

4. McMillan, C., Crapo, A., Durling, M., Li, M., et al.: Increasing development assurance for system and software development with validation and verification using ASSERT™. SAE Technical Paper 2019-01-1370 (2019). https://doi.org/10.4271/2019-01-1370
5. Crapo, A., Moitra, A.: Toward a unified English-like representation of semantic. Int. J. Semant. Comput. **7**(3), 215–236 (2013)
6. SADL   GitHub   Page.   https://github.com/SemanticApplicationDesignLanguage/sadl. Accessed 14 Apr 2023
7. OWL. https://www.w3.org/OWL. Accessed 14 Apr 2023
8. Xtext. http://www.eclipse.org/Xtext/. Accessed 14 Apr 2023
9. Moitra, A., et al.: A semantic reference model for capturing system development and evaluation. In: International Conference on Semantic Computing (ICSC), Laguna Hills (2022)
10. Fuseki. https://jena.apache.org/documentation/fuseki2. Accessed 18 Apr 2023
11. Cuddihy, P., McHugh, J., Williams, J.W., Mulwad, V., Aggour, K.S.: SemTK: a semantics toolkit for user-friendly SPARQL generation and semantic data management. In: 17th International Semantic Web Conference (ISWC), Industry and Blue Sky Ideas Track, Monterey, CA (2018)
12. Semantics Toolkit GitHub age. https://github.com/ge-semtk/semtk. Accessed 18 Apr 2023
13. Kumar, V.S., Cuddihy, P., Aggour, K.S.: NodeGroup: a knowledge-driven data management abstraction for industrial machine learning. In: Proceedings of the 3rd International Workshop on Data Management for End-to-End Machine Learning, pp. 1–4. (2019)
14. Semtk-python GitHub Page. https://github.com/ge-semtk/semtk-python3. Accessed 18 Apr 2023
15. Jsoneditor GitHub Page. https://github.com/josdejong/jsoneditor. Accessed 13 Apr 2023
16. Shankar, N., et al.: DesCert: design for Certification. arXiv preprint arXiv:2203.15178 (2022)
17. Wang, T.E., Daw, Z., Nuzzo, P., Pinto, A.: Hierarchical contract-based synthesis for assurance cases. In: Proceedings of NASA Formal Methods: 14th International Symposium, NFM 2022, Pasadena, CA, pp. 175–192 (2022)
18. Oh, C., Naik, N., Daw, Z., Wang, T. E., & Nuzzo, P: ARACHNE: automated validation of assurance cases with stochastic contract networks. In: Proceedings of Computer Safety, Reliability, and Security: 41st International Conference (SAFECOMP 2022), Munich, Germany, pp. 65–81 (2022)
19. Bloomfield, R., Rushby, J.: Assurance 2.0: a manifesto. arXiv preprint arXiv:2004.10474 (2020)

The Holocaust Archival Material Knowledge Graph

Herminio García-González[1](✉)(iD) and Mike Bryant[2,3](iD)

[1] Kazerne Dossin, Goswin de Stassartstraat 153, 2800 Mechelen, Belgium
herminio.garciagonzalez@kazernedossin.eu
[2] King's College London, Strand, London WC2R 2LS, UK
michael.bryant@kcl.ac.uk
[3] NIOD Institute for War, Holocaust and Genocide Studies, Herengracht 380,
1016 CJ Amsterdam, Netherlands

Abstract. Research into the Holocaust faces particular challenges due to the diversity and dispersal of its sources. The EHRI Portal, one of the main outputs of the EHRI project, is a platform for contextualising and integrating metadata about Holocaust-related archival material. In this work we undertake to deliver the EHRI Portal's archival metadata as Linked Open Data in order to explore the benefits that this model can provide to the field in terms of decentralised data access and integration with the wider Semantic Web. We describe the process of transforming the existing data to a Knowledge Grah aligned with the new ICA conceptual model, Records in Contexts (RiC). As part of this process we describe the challenges and limitations of this alignment, along with future developments that could result in a better fit with our use-case. We envision this work as the first step in delivering Holocaust data to the Semantic Web, allowing partner institutions to evaluate its capabilities and potentially adopt it for their own solutions, making the field more interconnected.

Keywords: Holocaust · Knowledge Graph · Shoah · Data transformation · Linked Open Data · Records in Contexts

1 Introduction

The creation of accessible, coherent and well integrated datasets has been demonstrated to be an important catalyst in enabling researchers to produce innovative and groundbreaking research [19]. In the Humanities, even before consideration is given to the interpretation of sources, their accessibility and complex provenances often present researchers with considerable logistical, organisational, and accessibility challenges [22]. In research pertaining to the Holocaust and its historical legacy these challenges are particularly acute. For numerous reasons, including the intentional destruction of evidence [26] and the widespread dislocation of people and administrative bodies following the Second World War,

© The Author(s) 2023
T. R. Payne et al. (Eds.): ISWC 2023, LNCS 14266, pp. 362–379, 2023.
https://doi.org/10.1007/978-3-031-47243-5_20

Holocaust-related material and archival sources are highly fragmented and dispersed. In practice, this means that researchers seeking to access important Holocaust sources must in many cases navigate a complex trans-national patchwork of archives with different mandates, cataloguing practices, and systems of arrangement.

Overcoming barriers to effective trans-national Holocaust research is one of the principal goals of the European Holocaust Research Infrastructure (EHRI)[1], an EU-funded research project, now in its third 4-year phase and soon to transition into a permanent organisation as a European Research Infrastructure Consortium (ERIC). For over a decade, EHRI has built tools to help researchers understand and navigate the complex landscape of Holocaust research [25], cataloguing sources across many hundreds of institutions and working with numerous archives, large and small, to integrate and contextualise their collection descriptions. A major part of these efforts is the EHRI Portal [5][2], an online database of Holocaust-related archival sources, which enables the integration and interlinking of archival descriptions and their associated metadata from around the world.

The development of the EHRI Portal, its technologies and APIs, along with various initiatives aimed at increasing the interconnectedness of its metadata have been described elsewhere [3]. In this paper we focus on our efforts to expose the rich metadata contained in the EHRI Portal, derived from institutions around the world as well as EHRI's own archival specialists, in a manner compatible with the Semantic Web and capable of better integrating with the emerging network of Linked Open Data (LOD) sources.[3] Semantic Web technologies offer a unique means by which entities can be identified unambiguously, linked across databases, and where new data can be automatically inferred [4], capabilities which have been demonstrated to effectively support Digital Humanities activities [27]. The Knowledge Graph (KG) of Holocaust-related descriptions presented below, based on the EHRI Portal data, serves as a first step to increasing the visibility of this kind of material and facilitate other LOD publishers to link to EHRI's entities.

Producing and publishing LOD is a challenge common to many GLAM institutions [1,10], where datasets of research interest are frequently siloed in legacy databases and intermingled with more closely-held administrative data, not amenable to being made public. As described in [5], the EHRI Portal, while developed under an "open-first" approach, also includes many affordances for restricting the visibility and accessibility of material that is private to individual users, concealed from view for copyright reasons, or otherwise sensitive. We believe that the approaches described in this paper therefore have wide applicability to other practitioners who have an interest in expanding the openness of their data, particularly archival institutions. In addition, many archival institutions present a technological deficit making it very hard for them to adapt

---

[1] https://www.ehri-project.eu/.

[2] https://portal.ehri-project.eu/.

[3] https://lod-cloud.net/.

to new technologies and migrate old data [32]. This KG, therefore, could serve as an example for Holocaust-related institutions that wish to experiment with Semantic Web technologies, and their possibilities, without being required to make more costly and disruptive technical investments. In the future, if more institutions decide to expose their data as LOD, connections could be made both to and from this KG, allowing it to act as an authority hub for Holocaust-related material and facilitating connections between different holding institutions (see Sect. 5.3).

The rest of this paper is structured as follows: Sect. 2 describes related work; in Sect. 3 we outline EHRI's data and services and how the transformation was carried out; Sect. 4 introduces the KG and its main characteristics; in Sect. 5 we enumerate the challenges that arise from this work and how we intend to solve them in future. Finally, in Sect. 6 we draw the conclusions obtained from this work.

2   Related Work

Many works have addressed the modelling of historical data as KGs. One widely-cited example is Europeana [21], which offers metadata about different types of cultural heritage material. The level of detail offered by Europeana could, however, be considered insufficient for many researchers [30] and it does not seek to contextualise subject-specific material as EHRI does. With regard to the Second World War as a whole, in [6] the authors investigated a linking algorithm to enrich WWII collections with events information modelled as LOD. Similarly, WarSampo [23] offers a Finnish KG for WWII integrating many different data sources[4] and offering them through a single web interface.[5] This KG models different perspectives such as events, persons, army units, places, etc. To the best of our knowledge, however, no KG has sought to model the archival landscape of Holocaust-related sources.

Even though no KG has yet taken a holistic view of Holocaust-related archival material, a number of relevant initiatives have appeared in recent years focused on a particular region or country.[6] Others, with a more trans-national perspective that address similar topics (e.g., Jewish material) do inevitably overlap with EHRI's scope, such as the Yerusha platform which offers a centralised access for Jewish archival heritage.[7] To date, however, there is a dearth of linkages between these platforms, complicating both users' access to the information in navigating many overlapping sources, and the task of the holding institutions in keeping their metadata up-to-date in multiple places. This plethora of siloed alternatives gives traction to an alternative semantic landscape where data could be more interoperable and authority hubs (today's aggregators) could act as linking facilitators (see Sect. 5.3.)

---

[4] https://seco.cs.aalto.fi/projects/sotasampo/en/#datasets.

[5] https://www.sotasampo.fi/en/.

[6] https://www.oorlogsbronnen.nl/.

[7] https://yerusha.eu/.

In Cultural Heritage a number of conceptual models, vocabularies and ontologies (some of them related to a conceptual model) have emerged aiming to cover different aspects of the field, e.g., CIDOC-CRM [12], PROV-O [24], FRBR[8], NIE-INE[9], ROAR[10] or ARKIVO [29], among others. As relates specifically to archives, a number of attempts have been made to address the mapping from the Encoded Archival Description (EAD) XML schema to these aforementioned ontologies. For example, converting from EAD to CIDOC-CRM has been addressed, among others, by [7,15,35,36] with different levels of EAD semantic coverage. CIDOC-CRM, however, was originally intended for interoperability of museum objects, with some links to archives or libraries, which limits the establishment of metadata equivalents. Moreover, due to these differences in scope, domain experts will always be more comfortable with a domain-specific model capable of integrating with a broader scope and which, for archives, effectively unifies the widely-adopted International Council of Archives (ICA) standards [18]. More recently, a transformation tool from EAD to Records in Contexts Ontology (RiC-O) has been released [14], using XSLT stylesheets as the base for the mapping. As explained later, EHRI expands ICA standards to fit some specific needs making us opt for a domain specific conversion which can be later shared as an EAD to RiC-O mapping for the whole community based on the shared commonalities.

Inside the EHRI project there have been a number of existing cases where semantic and/or RDF technologies were employed, in addition to those mentioned below relating to EHRI's data model. As we have written about previously [5], EHRI uses a graph database (Neo4j) as its underlying data store, and while it functions as a "property graph" rather than a native triplestore, it has some common characteristics. We have on two occasions experimented with automatic mapping from the internal Neo4j schema to a LOD format, one using an interface to the SAIL (Storage and Inference Layer) API[11], and the other using the NeoSemantics (n10s) Neo4j plugin.[12] While both approaches showed promise in some respects, we did not put them into production due to either compatibility issues stemming from tightly-coupled dependencies, or limitations in query performance and scalability resulting from the on-the-fly translation approach.

A more recent undertaking aimed to enrich data already in the portal relating to controlled vocabularies for camps and ghettos, linking them with Wikidata and georeferencing them against GeoNames [2]. Although the goal of this work was not to fully convert EHRI Portal data to RDF it established some of the foundations that we build on here. Inside the wider EHRI consortium we

---

[8] https://repository.ifla.org/bitstream/123456789/811/2/ifla-functional-requirements-for-bibliographic-records-frbr.pdf.

[9] https://github.com/nie-ine/Ontologies.

[10] https://leonvanwissen.nl/vocab/roar/docs/.

[11] https://rdf4j.org/documentation/reference/sail/.

[12] https://neo4j.com/labs/neosemantics/.

also want to highlight the Holocaust Victims Names database[13] hosted by the Fondazione Centro di Documentazione Ebraica Contemporanea (CDEC) [8] for which they developed a Shoah ontology[14] reusing and extending existing ontologies like FOAF[15] and BIO[16] (extended in bio-ext[17]) and using it to model the information about these victims. This example motivated us to offer EHRI Portal data as LOD so initiatives such as this from partner institutions could be linked and jointly queryable by users.

3   EHRI's Data and Transformation

3.1   EHRI's Data Model

Data in the EHRI Portal is based around three main entities: countries; archival institutions; and archival descriptions. Countries constitute an entry point and provide information on the situation of Holocaust research in a relevant country. Collection-holding institutions (CHIs)—typically archives or bodies with similar mandates—are grouped within their host country and include relevant contact details along with additional context and information pertaining to their holdings-as described in the International Standard for Describing Institutions with Archival Holdings (ISDIAH).[18] Archival descriptions are contained within their holding institution and store the information aligned with the General International Standard Archival Description (ISAD(G)).[19] One notable characteristic of archival descriptions is that they can be nested to arbitrary depth to form a hierarchy, modelling the physical arrangement of the described materials (e.g., fonds, series, subseries, item, etc.)

In addition to these three main entities, the EHRI Portal also employs entities for enriching and indexing archival metadata. Authority sets are collections of people, families, or corporate bodies—as defined in the International Standard Archival Authority Record for Corporate Bodies, Persons and Families (ISAAR (CPF))[20]—whilst a set of controlled vocabularies[21] hold content-specific terms defined by the project for, at present, subject headings and historical places. These authoritative entities are linked from the access points and creators sections of the archival description, serving as a connecting point between collections and facilitating thematic search.

---

[13] http://dati.cdec.it/.

[14] http://dati.cdec.it/lod/shoah/shoah.rdf.

[15] http://xmlns.com/foaf/0.1/.

[16] https://vocab.org/bio/.

[17] http://dati.cdec.it/lod/bio-ext/.

[18] https://www.ica.org/en/isdiah-international-standard-describing-institutions-archival-holdings.

[19] https://www.ica.org/en/isadg-general-international-standard-archival-description-second-edition.

[20] https://www.ica.org/en/isaar-cpf-international-standard-archival-authority-record-corporate-bodies-persons-and-families-2nd.

[21] https://portal.ehri-project.eu/vocabularies.

Finally, this structure is augmented by *annotations* and *links*, both modelled as first-class entities that can connect and add additional information to those discussed above. In the current EHRI Portal, vocabularies, annotations, and links are the only parts of the data model derived from and partially aligned with RDF, namely the Simple Knowledge Organisation System (SKOS) [28] in the case of vocabularies, and the Web Annotation Data Model [33] framework for annotations and links. EHRI's use of the relevant standards for linking and indexing metadata records is discussed further in [3].

3.2   Ontology Alignment

As noted above, EHRI's data is primarily aligned with the conceptual standards from the International Council on Archives (ICA). As a result, import and export of metadata pertaining to archival descriptions from the EHRI Portal was designed around EAD [31], the most well established format derived from ISAD(G).[22] However, while EAD is widely adopted in the archival field, it inherits the limitations that non-semantic XML technologies present, as discussed in [17], along with other issues stemming from its flexibility as an encoding medium [34].

Seeking to address said limitations, the ICA has been working on a new conceptual model of the archival domain, using a graph as data model. Dubbed Records in Contexts-Conceptual Model (RiC-CM) [20], it is currently on its second draft version, v0.2, released in 2021, and offers a companion ontology for modelling the data in RDF, called RiC-O.[23] As this specification is intended to supersede EAD in the future, we have used it as our base ontology for the transformation of EHRI's data into semantic form.

Using RiC-O 0.2 as a foundation has distinct benefits. It allows us to implement a version of EHRI's data using Records in Contexts (RiC) on top of the existing implementation, letting us test the new data model before the stable version is released. It presents a future common alignment point for other institutions that are currently using ISAD(G) (and/or ISAAR) for data publication and will likewise, in future, seek to make a similar transition, potentially building on EHRI's mapping rules for their own use cases. And it constitutes a zero-cost demonstration for EHRI partner institutions of how RiC works and its potential benefits, without them having to make a substantial investment themselves in mapping or adapting their in-house data sources.

Since not all of our required semantics are covered by the current RiC-O draft, however, it has been necessary for us to extend the ontology in some respects. Following best practice in ontology modelling we have tried to reuse other ontologies or vocabularies as much as possible, using schema.org[24] to complete some fields missing from RIC-O. Schema.org offers a set of classes dedicated

---

[22] In addition to its counterpart schema for authority information, the Encoded Archival Context (EAC).

[23] https://www.ica.org/en/records-in-contexts-conceptual-model.

[24] https://schema.org/.

to archives since its version 3.5. These classes and their fields complement and align very well to those in RiC-O. For those fields still missing, but necessary from our data perspective, we have included them as properties of a future EHRI ontology (e.g., https://lod.ehri-project-test.eu/ontology#).

3.3   Data Transformation

Construction of the KG consists of two main processes: harvesting and transformation. For the harvesting process we have made use of the existing (JSON-based) EHRI API endpoints as a more open and reproducible alternative to requiring privileged access to the internal database. Specifically, we have used the REST-style EHRI Search API[25] for harvesting information about countries, archival institutions and archival descriptions, and the GraphQL API [9][26] for extracting additional metadata such as links between entities. For controlled vocabularies we use the existing RDF-format data[27] but incorporate additional harvested links in the process of building the complete KG.

To process the harvested data we make use of the ShExML language [16] and engine,[28] executing mapping rules for each entity in succession, following the paginated structure of responses from the EHRI APIs. This permits resumption of the transformation if required and was further deemed necessary given the amount of data present in the EHRI Portal, exceeding 400,000 archival descriptions.[29] The execution of these mapping rules produce several Turtle files that are then merged together, using the RDF compositional property, along with the pre-existing SKOS-format vocabularies. All the materials and resources used for the harvesting and transformation process are open source and can be consulted on Github.[30]

4   Dataset

4.1   Approximate Size and Characterisation

The KG consists of 6,571,095 triples that in Turtle format comprise 767MB of data[31]. We have published this KG using Apache Jena Fuseki as the triple store[32] and the LodView viewer[33] in order to allow exploration of the data.[34] The KG also provides a SPARQL endpoint for more complex queries.[35]

---

[25] https://portal.ehri-project.eu/api/v1/.
[26] https://portal.ehri-project.eu/api/graphql/.
[27] See for an example: https://portal.ehri-project.eu/vocabularies/ehri_terms/export.
[28] https://github.com/herminiogg/ShExML.
[29] Consulted on 04/04/2023.
[30] https://github.com/herminiogg/EHRI2LOD.
[31] Statistics consulted on 04/04/2023.
[32] https://jena.apache.org/documentation/fuseki2/.
[33] https://github.com/LodLive/LodView.
[34] https://lod.ehri-project-test.eu/.
[35] https://lod.ehri-project-test.eu/query/.

As mentioned above, we have used RiC-O as the primary modelling ontology, with some additional fields aligned to schema.org. In these cases, we have double-classed the instances that combine predicates from both specifications, allowing for better discoverability and data completeness. These double typed classes are country (`rico:Place` and `schema:Country`) and archival institution (`rico:CorporateBody` and `schema:ArchiveOrganization`).[36] In the future EHRI ontology this will be made explicit with a dedicated class that inherits from both super classes. At the same time, and following the same principle, we have added the three possible name predicates, i.e., `rdfs:label`, `schema:name` and `rico:name`, allowing for a more standardised access from existing agents.

Inverse relations are always provided where possible as the RiC-O specification suggests, letting users navigate the graph in bidirectional fashion and making the graph more predictable. Examples of this are `rico:hasOrHadHolder` and `rico:isOrWasHolderOf` or `rico:hasInstantiation` and `rico:isInstantiationOf`.

In order to better interconnect with existing or future KGs and to allow users explore beyond just our dataset we have provided the following links. For countries we have connected each country to its DBpedia instance (e.g., `ehri-country:gb owl:sameAs dbr:United_Kingdom`). In the case of archival institutions we have linked them to the main institution webpage which could, potentially, provide additional information in semantic format. In addition, for controlled vocabularies concerning camps and ghettos (that were already in RDF), many entities provide a link to Wikidata [13] (using `rdfs:seeAlso`) pointing to the equivalent entity [11]. A class diagram can be consulted in Fig. 1.

4.2   Post-transformation Enrichment

In addition to the triples and links generated from the batch process, there are other kinds of links that can be included per case, and that are out of the scope of the batch transformation due to potentially requiring manual verification and update. For now, we perform two post-tranformation enrichments: language links with their counterparts in DBpedia; and links of EHRI authorities (persons and corporate bodies) to their counterparts in the CDEC dataset.

In the case of DBpedia, languages are easily linked based on the label similarity against `dbo:Language` instances. For this purpose a federated `CONSTRUCT` SPARQL query is run on the resulting KG[37] and the results are supervised by content experts. For CDEC person database links we run another federated query that, similar to that used with DBPedia, establishes the links between

---

[36] Two types of corporate bodies exist in the EHRI portal data: contemporary collection-holding institutions and (often historical) authorities relating to archival materials. RiC-O does not make a distinction between them, therefore, for the conversion of collection-holding institutions we use some additional properties from `schema:ArchiveOrganization` leaning us towards double typing its instances. For authorities we only use the `rico:CorporateBody` properties.

[37] https://github.com/herminiogg/EHRI2LOD/blob/main/src/auxFiles/linksLanguagesDBpedia/linksLanguagesDBpediaFederatedQuery.rq.

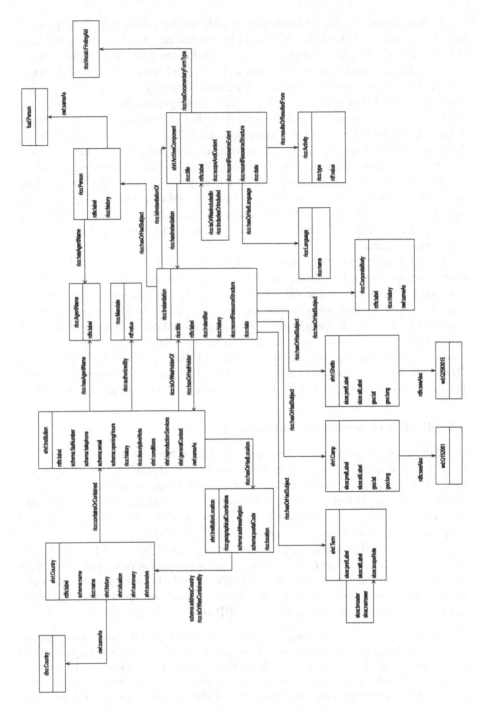

Fig. 1. Class diagram representing the data model followed in the conversion to RDF using RiC-O and schema.org as the base ontologies.

```
PREFIX foaf: <http://xmlns.com/foaf/0.1/>
PREFIX owl: <http://www.w3.org/2002/07/owl#>
PREFIX rdfs: <http://www.w3.org/2000/01/rdf-schema#>
PREFIX rico: <https://www.ica.org/standards/RiC/ontology#>
PREFIX schema: <http://schema.org/>
PREFIX ehri_institutions: <http://lod.ehri-project-test.eu/institutions/>
PREFIX shoah: <http://dati.cdec.it/lod/shoah/>

SELECT ?record WHERE {
    ehri_institutions:it-002845 rico:isOrWasHolderOf ?instantiation .
    ?instantiation rico:isInstantiationOf ?record .
    ?record rico:hasOrHadSubject ?personEHRI .
    ?personEHRI owl:sameAs ?person .
    SERVICE <http://lod.xdams.org/sparql> {
        ?person a foaf:Person ;
                shoah:persecution ?persecution .
        ?persecution shoah:toNaziCamp ?camp .
        ?camp rdfs:label "Auschwitz" .
    }
}
```

Listing 1: SPARQL Federated query to get the records referring to people deported to Auschwitz.

EHRI and CDEC authority files.[38] These triples are verified by CDEC staff and then are retained for future use, such that only previously unseen relations are required to be validated. Both generated links datasets are uploaded to the main triple store and added to the KG. These post-transformation enrichments allow executing SPARQL Federated queries over multiple KGs letting users answer more complex questions like the example given in Listing 1. More examples can be found in the EHRI KG landing page.[39]

5 Challenges and Future Work

5.1 Mapping Copies and Originals

Even though the majority of the data in the EHRI Portal is mapped using the techniques described in this paper there are still some aspects where the available ontologies do not provide us with satisfactory solutions. In other cases, solutions will require further consensus from the community.

One significant challenge pertaining to Holocaust-related material is the amount of copying of material that has been carried out by different archives

---

[38] https://github.com/herminiogg/EHRI2LOD/blob/main/src/auxFiles/linksToCDEC/queryToMatchToCDEC.rq.

[39] https://lod.ehri-project-test.eu/.

around the world, who have proceeded to describe the same underlying material using their own specific in-house style. From the very beginning, the EHRI Portal has had, as one of its main goals, the recontextualisation of Holocaust sources. In the project's second phase a system was introduced allowing descriptions of copied material to link to the holder of the original sources and/or those sources directly [3]. Users can now have a clearer view, where these connections are made, of the different versions of original archival material that is available to them in various holding institutions.[40]

The EHRI Portal supports four types of links depending on the specificity of the available information: 1) copy archival unit to original archival unit (the archival unit was copied from this specific original archival unit); 2) copy archival institution to original archival institution (the institution holds copies from another institution without specifying which); 3) copy archival unit to original archival institution (the archival unit was copied from the mentioned archival institution, without knowing from which exact collection it was copied); and 4) copy archival institution to original archival unit (the archival institution holds copies of this original archival unit without knowing which copied archival unit holds the copies.) All links can be interpreted bidirectionally, for example, X archival unit was copied from Y original archival unit or Y original archival unit was copied into X archival unit.

Looking into the current RiC-O draft, the properties `rico:hasCopy`, `rico:isCopyOf`, `rico:hasOriginal` and `rico:isOriginalOf` seem to cover the same semantics explained above. However, if we look at the domain and range of these properties we see that they are bound to `rico:RecordResource` meaning that the relation can only be established between two entities of this type or its descendants. Ultimately, this translates to being able to map only one out of the four supported link types in the EHRI Portal. A potential future solution will be to introduce these custom properties used in the EHRI Portal as properties of the planned EHRI ontology.

In addition, the RiC-CM puts the emphasis on the distinction between a Record Resource and an Instantiation, the latter being the representation of the record in a digital or physical form. In this sense, we can see copies as different instantiations of the same record where, for example, the original may be a deed and the copy a microfilm, but in essence both refer to the same original material. Looking at the data already mapped, however, this presents an issue, as archival units (Record Resources in RiC-CM) are assumed to be held by only one institution in the EHRI Portal, with identifiers derived from this hierarchy. In order to maintain this information, therefore, we are compelled to continue creating only one instantiation per Record Resource and make the links between them.

One alternative would be to use the `owl:sameAs` property to indicate that in fact the resource is the same. Unfortunately, this creates some additional verbosity in our mapped data, hindering the clarity of the graph and potentially affecting how users navigate it. While it does not constrain the use of the ontology

---

[40] See for an example: https://portal.ehri-project.eu/units/us-005578-irn524242.

for our mapped data, it is true that clarifying the semantics for these cases when using RiC-O will benefit data producers and consumers as exposed with this case. Thus, we will follow the development of RiC-O closely to adapt our conversion process if this point becomes clearer in future revisions.

5.2 Incremental Updates

As mentioned in Sect. 3.3, we opted for a batch approach for the conversion of data from the EHRI APIs to the KG. This means that at some point data could be added, updated or deleted in the EHRI Portal making parts of the KG obsolete or incomplete. In order to cope with this issue many strategies could be taken. One possible approach would be to execute the batch process as a nightly task and exchange the old KG for the newly generated one. However, given the size of the dataset this process would be time consuming and fairly inefficient. We have therefore designed a workflow that, while based on the batch approach, incorporates only updates that took place since the previous harvesting operation without impacting the overall performance. Our envisioned solution is to process change events from the EHRI Portal as a stream that are incorporated into an append-only historic log where all changes since the creation of the KG can be tracked. This would facilitate not only processing the changes as they arrive, but also reconstructing update events in cases where it is needed to replicate them for further migrations or installations, or recover from down time. From each of these events it is possible to download the new contents from the harvesting source (Search API or GraphQL API) and, depending on the type of event (creation, deletion, update), run the necessary INSERT and/or DELETE SPARQL queries against the SPARQL endpoint. This workflow can be seen in Fig. 2. We will undertake the implementation of the proposed data update architecture as future work in order to more efficiently keep the KG up-to-date in a timely manner.

5.3 EHRI KG as an Authority Hub

The EHRI Portal acts as an aggregator for information about Holocaust documentation, allowing users to seamlessly access metadata about collections, and institutions to contextualise their own records in a larger, trans-national landscape. This enhanced contextualisation happens in the EHRI Portal, where researchers can benefit from it, but the metadata providers themselves are not able to easily reflect it in their own data. In this sense, this centralised approach presents challenges when it comes to improving agents' access, and the reusability of data contributed by the institutions themselves.

Federated approaches, however, pose other challenges, such as how to actively manage the links between different nodes, how to manage widely-used persistent and unique identifiers, and how to foster node discoverability. These challenges, however, can be mitigated by an aggregator which can promote visibility, link an institution's data to other data in the network, and is able to manage coherent and consistent identifiers across the network. We should, therefore, take those

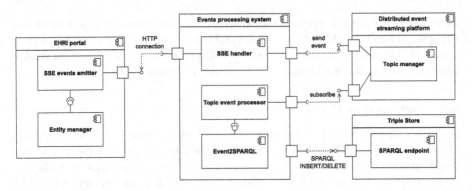

Fig. 2. Architecture of the envisioned stream-based incremental update system to align the KB with the EHRI Portal's live dataset where the EHRI portal will emit events in the form of Server-Sent Events (SSE). A SSE handler will process and send them to a topic in a distributed event streaming platform (e.g., Apache Kafka). Finally, an event processor will be subscribed to the event streaming platform and will create (and post to the SPARQL endpoint of the triple store) the corresponding SPARQL INSERT and/or DELETE queries based on the events contents.

advantages and put them to work in a federated manner. In this regard, we see this KG as a first step in establishing an authority hub (as opposed to a data aggregator) where the source of truth is the institutions' own data. This allows for a more lightweight KG where only general metadata information about collections is served, with the rest being available on-demand (via Semantic Web technologies) based on users' requirements. The authority hub, then, would have the responsibility to maintain the links among different providers' items, allowing institutions to search across the network throughout the hub or even re-utilising the data for their own systems.

Moreover, as more institutions start to work following these principles, fewer data integration procedures will be required, reducing the social, technical, and institutional challenges of keeping aggregated metadata sufficiently up-to-date.

5.4 Engaging User Communities

Institutions dealing with Holocaust-related material present a varying degree of technical capacity, ranging from those that already offer data as LOD, like CDEC, to others where data is either not sharable or is available only as PDF files or some other form similarly unsuitable for machine processing. In addition, technical investments typically come with a high cost for these institutions, both financially and in terms of staff training. Advancements in this area, therefore, will not be made lightly, and we envisage the KG presented here as a way to showcase the benefits that Semantic Web technologies can deliver to Holocaust-related institutions without requiring them to make financial commitments.

We anticipate that users of the KG will be as varied as users of the EHRI Portal itself, which currently counts around 35,000 monthly user sessions, growing at over 20% per year for the past four years. Among these we find researchers and educators who are engaged with digital methods and for whom this KG could give answers to new research questions. We also find archivists and other knowledge professionals who see in the EHRI portal an opportunity to increase their collections visibility, discoverability and outreach. For the latter, the greater interconnectedness in archival descriptions explored in this paper would allow them to better contextualise their work with that of other institutions handling similar material, thereby increasing the aforementioned visibility and discoverability of sources. This should encourage Semantic Web technologies to be a stronger consideration in driving technical choices within these organisations.

It is also worth noting that while this KG is focused on Holocaust-related material (the scope of the EHRI project), the approach taken here is subject-matter agnostic and therefore just as applicable to the wider archival field, and indeed any users of ICA conceptual standards such as ISAD(G). If we can encourage more institutions within the EHRI consortium and the wider archival space to publish their data as LOD, connected to this KG, we will be able to offer more information (e.g., via SPARQL Federated queries) in the EHRI Portal, improving its completeness and usefulness to users of all stripes. During the last months this work has been presented within the consortium[41] where feedback has been positive, particularly in regard to EHRI seeking an enlarged role as an authority hub and strengthening connections with platforms like Wikidata and other KG projects in overlapping domains.

As a result of these specific circumstances, the EHRI KG is currently available for public use in a testing capacity in order to gain feedback on the data representation and experience in running the services. This is made explicit by the use of a placeholder domain name for URIs containing the "-test" suffix, which will be replaced by the permanent "ehri-project.eu" domain in use elsewhere for EHRI's production services. When this migration takes place, web redirections will be put in place from the test to production domains in order to ensure that early adopters can straightforwardly migrate to the production platform.

6   Conclusions

Given that the RiC conceptual model has not yet reached its first non-draft release, the work described here is also evolving. We have described in Sect. 3 the general shape of EHRI's data and how we have approached schema alignment, and where it has been necessary to extend or work around limitations with the ontology. Likewise we have described how the transformation is implemented, using EHRI's existing APIs and the ShExML mapping language. The resulting dataset, described in Sect. 4, is further enriched with connections to more general KBs, such as DBpedia, or others within the same domain, such as CDEC's person database. In Sect. 5 we described a number of planned advancements to the EHRI

---

[41] See for example: https://docs.google.com/presentation/d/1bha1C0cy1TpZp_ighCaZ 1Sxohy23QizEkamk5hEuk-E/edit?usp=sharing.

KB, including the incorporation of more information about the provenance of Holocaust sources.

The vision described above in Sect. 5.3-of a distributed LOD environment where each custodian of Holocaust-related material can publish its own metadata, integrating with a common set of vocabularies and authorities that are curated by domain-specific entities like EHRI, or more general ones like Wikidata-is appealing for many reasons. Researchers can benefit enormously from efforts to bring coherence and a deeper level of contextualisation to domains like Holocaust research which are, as discussed in the introduction to this paper, fraught with historical and organisational complexity. Centralised approaches to data integration, whilst necessary with today's level of LOD adoption in the archival domain, are complex to administer and invariably compromised in how up-to-date and comprehensive they can manage to be.

By expanding EHRI's LOD capabilities, building on efforts by the creators of RiC and other such systems, we can hope to foster a greater degree of knowledge interoperability in the domain of Holocaust research. If more data providers can justify the necessary technical investments to eventually publish their own linked datasets, perhaps using the techniques described here as a blueprint with which to do so, this will correspondingly benefit EHRI's goals in contextualising Holocaust sources and bringing greater clarity to the domain.

Supplemental Material Availability: The presented Knowledge Graph and the accompanying documentation are available for consultation on: https://lod.ehri-project-test.eu/. The source code for the conversion can be openly consulted on https://github.com/herminiogg/EHRI2LOD and a persistent version of the code used for this paper can be found on https://doi.org/10.5281/zenodo.8185859.

Acknowledgements. This work has been carried out in the context of the EHRI-3 project funded by the European Commission under the call H2020-INFRAIA-2018–2020, with grant agreement ID 871111 and DOI 10.3030/871111.

The authors would like to thank the NIOD Institute for War, Holocaust and Genocide studies for financial support in the Open Access publication of this work.

References

1. Alexiev, V.: Museum linked open data: ontologies, datasets, projects. Digital Present. Preser. Cult. Sci. Herit. **8**, 19–50 (2018). https://doi.org/10.55630/dipp. 2018.8.1
2. Alexiev, V., Nikolova, I., Hateva, N.: Semantic archive integration for holocaust research: the EHRI research infrastructure. Umanistica Digitale **3**(4) (2019). https://doi.org/10.6092/issn.2532-8816/9049
3. Arie Erez, S., Blanke, T., Bryant, M., Speck, R., Rodriguez, K., Vanden Daelen, V.: Record linking in the EHRI portal. Rec. Manag. J. **30**(3), 363–378 (2020). https://doi.org/10.1108/RMJ-08-2019-0045
4. Berners-Lee, T., Hendler, J., Lassila, O.: The semantic web. Sci. Am. **284**(5), 34–43 (2001)
5. Blanke, T., et al.: The European holocaust research infrastructure portal. J. Comput. Cult. Herit. (JOCCH) **10**(1), 1–18 (2017). https://doi.org/10.1145/3004457

6. Both, J., de Hooge, D., IJff, R., Inel, O., de Boer, V., Aroyo, L.: Linking dutch world war II cultural heritage collections with events extracted by machines and crowds. In: Joint Proceedings of SEMANTiCS 2017 Workshops co-located with the 13th International Conference on Semantic Systems (SEMANTiCS 2017), Amsterdam, Netherlands, 11–14 September 2017. CEUR-WS (2017). https://ceur-ws.org/Vol-2063/events-paper3.pdf

7. Bountouri, L., Gergatsoulis, M.: The semantic mapping of archival metadata to the CIDOC CRM ontology. J. Arch. Organ. **9**(3–4), 174–207 (2011). https://doi.org/10.1080/15332748.2011.650124

8. Brazzo, L., Mazzini, S.: From the holocaust victims names to the description of the persecution of the European jews in nazi years: the linked data approach and a new domain ontology. In: Book of Abstract of DH (2015)

9. Bryant, M.: GraphQL for archival metadata: an overview of the EHRI GraphQL API. In: 2017 IEEE International Conference on Big Data (Big Data), pp. 2225–2230. IEEE (2017). https://doi.org/10.1109/BigData.2017.8258173

10. Candela, G., Sáez, M.D., Escobar Esteban, M., Marco-Such, M.: Reusing digital collections from GLAM institutions. J. Inf. Sci. **48**(2), 251–267 (2022). https://doi.org/10.1177/0165551520950246

11. Cooey, N.: Leveraging Wikidata to enhance authority records in the EHRI portal. J. Libr. Metadata **19**(1–2), 83–98 (2019). https://doi.org/10.1080/19386389.2019.1589700

12. Doerr, M.: The CIDOC conceptual reference module: an ontological approach to semantic interoperability of metadata. AI Mag. **24**(3), 75–75 (2003). https://doi.org/10.1609/aimag.v24i3.1720

13. Erxleben, F., Günther, M., Krötzsch, M., Mendez, J., Vrandečić, D.: Introducing wikidata to the linked data web. In: Mika, P., et al. (eds.) ISWC 2014. LNCS, vol. 8796, pp. 50–65. Springer, Cham (2014). https://doi.org/10.1007/978-3-319-11964-9_4

14. Francart, T., Clavaud, F., Charbonnier, P.: RiC-O converter: a software to convert EAC-CPF and EAD 2002 XML files to RDF datasets conforming to records in contexts ontology. In: Proceedings of Linked Archives International Workshop 2021 co-located with 25th International Conference on Theory and Practice of Digital Libraries (TPDL 2021), pp. 30–36 (2021). https://ceur-ws.org/Vol-3019/LinkedArchives_2021_paper_14.pdf

15. Gaitanou, P., Bountouri, L., Gergatsoulis, M.: Automatic generation of crosswalks through CIDOC CRM. In: Dodero, J.M., Palomo-Duarte, M., Karampiperis, P. (eds.) MTSR 2012. CCIS, vol. 343, pp. 264–275. Springer, Heidelberg (2012). https://doi.org/10.1007/978-3-642-35233-1_26

16. García-González, H., Boneva, I., Staworko, S., Labra-Gayo, J.E., Lovelle, J.M.C.: ShExML: improving the usability of heterogeneous data mapping languages for first-time users. PeerJ Comput. Sci. **6**, e318 (2020). https://doi.org/10.7717/peerj-cs.318

17. Gartner, R.: An XML schema for enhancing the semantic interoperability of archival description. Arch. Sci. **15**(3), 295–313 (2015). https://doi.org/10.1007/s10502-014-9225-1

18. Gueguen, G., da Fonseca, V., Pitti, D., Grimoüard, C.: Toward an international conceptual model for archival description: a preliminary report from the International Council on Archives' Experts Group on archival description. Am. Arch. **76**(2), 567–584 (2013). https://doi.org/10.17723/aarc.76.2.p071x02401282qx2

19. Hyvönen, E.: Using the semantic web in digital humanities: shift from data publishing to data-analysis and serendipitous knowledge discovery. Semant. Web **11**(1), 187–193 (2020). https://doi.org/10.3233/SW-190386

20. International Council on Archives (ICA): Records in Contexts-Conceptual model (RiC-CM) 0.2 (2021). https://www.ica.org/sites/default/files/ric-cm-02_july2021_0.pdf. Accessed 03 Apr 2023

21. Isaac, A., Haslhofer, B.: Europeana Linked Open Data - data.europeana.eu. Semant. Web **4**(3), 291–297 (2013). https://doi.org/10.3233/SW-120092

22. Khan, N.A., Shafi, S., Ahangar, H.: Digitization of cultural heritage: global initiatives, opportunities and challenges. J. Cases Inf. Technology (JCIT) **20**(4), 1–16 (2018). https://doi.org/10.4018/JCIT.2018100101

23. Koho, M., Ikkala, E., Leskinen, P., Tamper, M., Tuominen, J., Hyvönen, E.: WarSampo knowledge graph: Finland in the second world war as linked open data. Semant. Web **12**(2), 265–278 (2021). https://doi.org/10.3233/SW-200392

24. Lebo, T., et al.: Prov-o: the prov ontology (2013). https://www.w3.org/TR/prov-o/

25. de Leeuw, D., Bryant, M., Frankl, M., Nikolova, I., Alexiev, V.: Digital methods in holocaust studies: the European holocaust research infrastructure. In: 2018 IEEE 14th International Conference on e-Science (e-Science), pp. 58–66. IEEE (2018). https://doi.org/10.1109/eScience.2018.00021

26. Malka, T.D.: Missing persons and World War II: between personal and national loss. War Hist. **29**(3), 641–663 (2022). https://doi.org/10.1177/09683445211038600

27. Meroño-Peñuela, A., et al.: Semantic technologies for historical research: a survey. Semant. Web **6**(6), 539–564 (2015). https://doi.org/10.3233/SW-140158

28. Miles, A., Bechhofer, S.: SKOS simple knowledge organization system reference (2009). https://www.w3.org/TR/skos-reference/

29. Pandolfo, L., Pulina, L., Zielinski, M.: Towards an ontology for describing archival resources. In: Proceedings of the Second Workshop on Humanities in the Semantic Web (WHiSe II) co-located with 16th International Semantic Web Conference (ISWC 2017), pp. 111–116 (2017). https://ceur-ws.org/Vol-2014/paper-12.pdf

30. Peroni, S., Tomasi, F., Vitali, F.: Reflecting on the Europeana data model. In: Agosti, M., Esposito, F., Ferilli, S., Ferro, N. (eds.) IRCDL 2012. CCIS, vol. 354, pp. 228–240. Springer, Heidelberg (2013). https://doi.org/10.1007/978-3-642-35834-0_23

31. Pitti, D.V.: Encoded archival description: an introduction and overview. New Rev. Inf. Netw. **5**(1), 61–69 (1999). https://doi.org/10.1080/13614579909516936

32. Ruest, N., Lin, J., Milligan, I., Fritz, S.: The archives unleashed project: technology, process, and community to improve scholarly access to web archives. In: Proceedings of the ACM/IEEE Joint Conference on Digital Libraries in 2020, pp. 157–166 (2020). https://doi.org/10.1145/3383583.3398513

33. Sanderson, R., Ciccarese, P., Young, B.: Web Annotation data model (2017). https://www.w3.org/TR/annotation-model/

34. Shaw, E.J.: Rethinking EAD: balancing flexibility and interoperability. New Rev. Inf. Netw. **7**(1), 117–131 (2001). https://doi.org/10.1080/13614570109516972

35. Stasinopoulou, T., et al.: Ontology-based metadata integration in the cultural heritage domain. In: Goh, D.H.-L., Cao, T.H., Sølvberg, I.T., Rasmussen, E. (eds.) ICADL 2007. LNCS, vol. 4822, pp. 165–175. Springer, Heidelberg (2007). https://doi.org/10.1007/978-3-540-77094-7_25

36. Theodoridou, M., Doerr, M.: Mapping of the encoded archival description DTD element set to the CIDOC CRM (2001). https://cidoc-crm.org/sites/default/files/ead.pdf

Scaling Data Science Solutions with Semantics and Machine Learning: Bosch Case

Baifan Zhou[1,2(✉)], Nikolay Nikolov[1,3], Zhuoxun Zheng[1,4], Xianghui Luo[5], Ognjen Savkovic[6], Dumitru Roman[1,3], Ahmet Soylu[2], and Evgeny Kharlamov[1,4]

[1] Department of Informatics, University of Oslo, Oslo, Norway
baifanz@ifi.uio.no
[2] Department of Computer Science, Oslo Metropolitan University, Oslo, Norway
[3] SINTEF AS, Trondheim, Norway
nikolay.nikolov@sintef.no
[4] Bosch Center for Artificial Intelligence, Renningen, Germany
[5] ACM Member, Berlin, Germany
[6] Department of Computer Science, Free University of Bozen-Bolzano, Bozen-Bolzano, Italy

Abstract. Industry 4.0 and Internet of Things (IoT) technologies unlock unprecedented amount of data from factory production, posing big data challenges in volume and variety. In that context, distributed computing solutions such as cloud systems are leveraged to parallelise the data processing and reduce computation time. As the cloud systems become increasingly popular, there is increased demand that more users that were originally not cloud experts (such as data scientists, domain experts) deploy their solutions on the cloud systems. However, it is non-trivial to address both the high demand for cloud system users and the excessive time required to train them. To this end, we propose Sem-Cloud, a semantics-enhanced cloud system, that couples cloud system with semantic technologies and machine learning. SemCloud relies on domain ontologies and mappings for data integration, and parallelises the semantic data integration and data analysis on distributed computing nodes. Furthermore, SemCloud adopts adaptive Datalog rules and machine learning for automated resource configuration, allowing non-cloud experts to use the cloud system. The system has been evaluated in industrial use case with millions of data, thousands of repeated runs, and domain users, showing promising results.

Keywords: ontology engineering · knowledge graph · semantic ETL · machine learning · cloud computing · welding · quality monitoring · Industry 4.0 · rule-based reasoning · Datalog

---

B. Zhou and N. Nikolov—Contributed equally to this work as first authors.

T. R. Payne et al. (Eds.): ISWC 2023, LNCS 14266, pp. 380–399, 2023.
https://doi.org/10.1007/978-3-031-47243-5_21

1 Introduction

Background. Industry 4.0 [1] aims at highly automated smart factories that rely on IoT technology [2], spanning across data acquisition, communication, information processing and actuation. This has unlocked unprecedented amounts of data that are generated by production systems [3] and, thus, drastically increased the demand for data-driven analytical solutions and cloud technology. We illustrate a common industrial scenario of development and deployment of data-driven solutions on cloud with a Bosch welding case[1] of quality monitoring in Fig. 1: The data from a production environment such as welding machines (a) has first to be acquired in different formats, e.g., CSV, JSON, XML (b); then they should be integrated into a uniform format (c); After that, the project team (including welding experts, data scientists, managers. etc.) wants to run data analysis on cloud infrastructures on top of the large data volumes from many factories (d); After data analysis, these users need to discuss and log the results (e); The whole process involves iterative and cross-domain communication between the stakeholders (f).

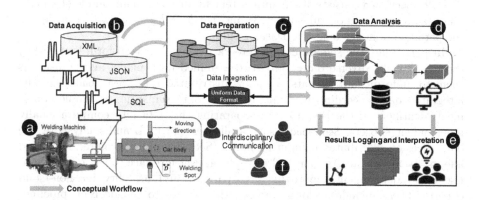

Fig. 1. Data analytics development cycle exemplified on the Bosch case of welding condition monitoring. In industrial data science projects, many users are non-cloud experts (e.g., welding experts, ML experts) and want to scale their solutions on the cloud.

Challenges. From the scenario, we see that scaling data science solutions poses challenges related to dealing with the high data *volume*, *variety*, and more *users*, namely enabling non-cloud experts to leverage cloud systems. Indeed, industries equipped with IoT technologies produce huge volumes of production data. In the

---

[1] Automated welding is an impactful manufacturing process that is involved in the production of millions of cars annually, deployed world-wide at many factories. Data-driven analytics solutions for welding can greatly help in reducing the cost and waste in production quality. Errors in production can only be resolved by destroying newly produced cars in samples.

Bosch case, one factory alone produces more than 1.9 million welding records per month. The data generated by different software versions, locations, customers have a variety of data formats, feature names, available features, etc. Meanwhile, many users that are not cloud experts, such as domain experts and data scientists, want to deploy the data science solutions on the cloud. In a standard implementation of the workflow in Fig. 1, the project team requires extensive assistance from cloud experts, whenever they want to deploy solutions or make small changes to their solutions deployed on the cloud. To facilitate the adoption of cloud systems for more projects and users, one can equip all projects with some cloud experts, or launch training programs about cloud technology for all users. Both require careful planing to balance time, cost, and benefits.

Our Approach. To address these scalability challenges in terms of data volume, data variety, and democratising cloud systems, we propose SemCloud: a semantics-enhanced cloud system, that scales semantic data integration and data analysis on the cloud with distributed computing, and allows non-cloud experts to deploy their solutions. Our system is motivated by a use case at Bosch aiming at scaling data science solutions in welding condition monitoring (Sect. 2). SemCloud consists of semantic artefacts such as domain ontologies, mappings, adaptive Datalog rules (Sect. 3) and *machine learning* (ML) that learns the parameters in the adaptive Datalog rules.

In particular, the semantic data integration (extract-transform-load, ETL) (Sect. 3.2) maps diverse data sources to a unified data model and transforms them to uniform data formats. To allow distributed ETL, SemCloud slices the integrated data according to domain-specific data semantics (machine equipment identifiers in the Bosch case), separating the data into computationally independent subsets. SemCloud then parallelises the ETL and analysis of the data slices on distributed computing nodes (Sect. 3.3). Furthermore, SemCloud adopts a semantic abstraction and a graphical user interface (GUI) to democratise cloud deployment, improving transparency and usability for non-cloud experts. These include a cloud ontology that allows to encode ETL pipelines in knowledge graphs (Sect. 3.4), and a set of adaptive Datalog rules (Sect. 3.5) for automatically finding optimal resource configurations. These rules are adaptive because some of their predicates are functions learnt with machine learning (ML) (Sect. 3.6).

We note that the existing work on this topic addressed the cloud deployment issues only to a limited extent [4,5], whereby they either only focus on the formal description of cloud, or on the limited adaptability of cloud systems. SemCloud exploits and significantly extends our previous works on ML in the context of Industry 4.0 [6,7], and container-based big data pipelines [8] (Fig. 4) by enhancing the framework with semantic artefacts and modules for specifying container-based pipelines, including pipeline step templates for containerisation and management of inter-step communication and data transmission (Sect. 3.3).

We evaluated (Sect. 4) SemCloud extensively: the cloud deployment report to verify SemCloud performance on reducing computational time, with an industrial datasets of about 3.1 million welding spots; the performance of rule parameter learning and inference based on 3562 times of repeated runs of the system.

2   Motivating Use Case: Welding Quality Monitoring

In this section we discuss our motivating use case in more details, explain why scaling data science solution to large data sets and more users is critical and discuss requirements for the cloud system.

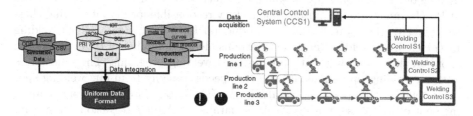

Fig. 2. (a) The data variety issue. (b) The data volume issue exemplified with the production data.

Condition Monitoring for Automated Welding. Condition monitoring refers to a group of technologies for monitoring condition parameters in production machinery to identify potential developing faults [9]. The use case addresses one type of condition monitoring, quality monitoring (another type is machine health monitoring), for resistance spot welding at Bosch, which is a fully automated welding process that is essential for producing high-quality car bodies globally in the automotive industry. During the welding process (Fig. 1a), two welding gun electrodes press two or three worksheets (car body parts) with force, an electric current flows through the electrodes and worksheets, generating a large amount of heat due to electric resistance. The materials in a small area between the two worksheets melt and then congeal after cooling, forming a weld nugget (or welding spot) connecting the worksheets. The core of quality monitoring is to measure, estimate or predict some categorical or numerical quality indicators. The diameter (Fig. 1a) of welding spots is typically used as the quality indicator of a single welding act according to industrial standards [9, 10]. Conventional practice adopts destructive methods to tear the welded car bodies apart, although they can only be applied to a small sample of car bodies, and the destroyed samples are waste and cannot be reused. Bosch is developing data-driven solutions to predict the welding quality, to reduce the waste and improve the coverage of quality monitoring.

Bosch Big Data. Welding condition monitoring faces big data challenges of variety and volume. In terms of *data variety*, Bosch has many data sources of different locations and conditions (Fig. 2a). The production data alone are collected from at least four locations and three original equipment manufacturers

(OEMs). These data differ in semantics and formats because of software versioning, customer customisation, as well as sensor and equipment discrepancy based on the concrete needs in the location. For example, they may be stored in various formats such as CSV, JSON, XML, etc., and may have different names for the same variables, have some variables missing in one source but present in another, or data may be measured with different sampling rate, etc.

In terms of *data volume*, data science models need a reasonably large amount of data to make the training meaningful and representative for the given data science tasks. For simplicity, we consider a representative example, whereby we assume one month data are meaningful, which was confirmed by data scientists at Bosch. In an example automobile factory responsible for manufacturing chassis (Fig. 2b), there are 3 running production lines with a total of 45 welding machines. Each welding machine is responsible for a number of types of welding spots on the car bodies, with pre-designed welding programs. These machines perform welding operations at different speeds, ranging from one welding spot per second, to one spot per several minutes. The data related to one single welding spot consist of several protocols or databases. After integration, these data become to a set of relational tables with 263 attributes, and a simplified estimation gives that one factory produces 64.8k spots every day, and 1.944 million spots per months, which account for the production of about 432 cars. Considering an average of 125 KB data for one welding operation gives the estimation of data volume meaningful for training as 243 GB (The real amount varies and can be larger, e.g., it was estimated as 389.32 GB in one real case. Here we adopt the simplification with a similar magnitude.).

Cloud Deployment Requirements. Considering the challenges, the welding quality monitoring system should give quality estimation/prediction not with excessive response time, although the data volume is large. In addition, the data come from various sources with diverse formats. Moreover, industrial data science projects involve many users that are non-cloud experts (Fig. 1). They should be equipped with tools to help deploy their data science solutions without extensive cloud expertise. The cloud infrastructure has resources of computing, memory, storage, network, etc. which need to be configured for optimised performance. Based on the information, we derive the following requirements for the system:

– *R1, Scalability on Data Volume:* The system should be able to reduce the computational time significantly when processing large data volumes.
– *R2, Scalability on Data Variety*: The system should be able to handle data variety, integrating heterogeneous data to uniform data formats.
– *R3, Scalability on Users:* The system should improve the *transparency* of the cloud system, automate resource configuration, and allow good *usability* for users, especially non-cloud experts,

3   SemCloud: Semantics-Enhanced Cloud System

To address the challenges and requirements, we propose our SemCloud system. We first give an architectural overview (Fig. 3) and then elaborate on the components.

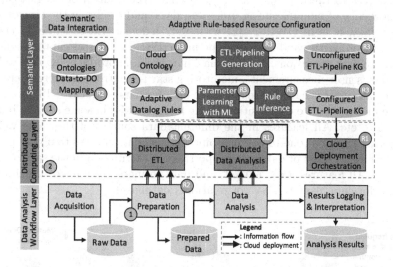

Fig. 3. Architectural overview of SemCloud including (1) semantic data integration; (2) distributed computing; (3) adaptive rule-based reasoning; each of which consists of a set of semantic artefacts (barrels) or modules (boxes). Ⓡ indicates the requirements the artefacts or modules intended to address.

3.1   Architectural Overview

The architecture of SemCloud is shown in Fig. 3. The *Data Analysis Workflow Layer* adopts a common workflow: data acquisition, data preparation, data analysis, results logging and interpretation; the raw data are first acquired, then prepared for data analysis, and, finally, the analysis results are generated, including models, predictions and human interpretation. In the data preparation stage, we employ *Semantic Data Integration* (Fig. 3.1) that relies on domain ontologies and semantic mappings to transform diverse data sources into uniform data formats. SemCloud scales the data analysis workflow to the cloud by with the *Distributed Computing* (Fig. 3.2), which includes the distributed ETL, distributed data analysis, and deployment orchestration that allocates cloud resources to the previous two modules. *Adaptive Rule-based Resource Configuration* (Fig. 3.3) provides a cloud ontology and GUI for the users to encode ETL pipelines in KGs, which contain resource configuration information that is automatically reasoned by a set of adaptive Datalog rules. These rules consist of aggregation operations and parameterised functions, where the parameters in the functions are learned via ML.

3.2   Semantic Data Integration

To accommodate the diverse data sources/formats and convert all data to uniform data formats [6,7], we employ domain ontologies as the data models and the semantic mappings (Data-to-DO, data to domain ontology) that map diverse data sources to the data models. In particular, the domain ontologies capture the knowledge of manufacturing processes, data, and assets. In the case of welding ontology, it is in OWL 2 QL, with 1542 axioms, which define 84 classes, 123 object properties and 246 datatype properties. The classes capture concepts such as welding operations, welding machines, welding products (spots), welding programs, sensor measurements, monitoring status, control parameters, etc. The diverse data sources have discrepancies in data formats (e.g., CSV, JSON, XML), feature names, feature composition (some features exist in some sources but not in others), etc. All features in the different data sources of the same welding process are mapped (one-to-one mapping for each data source) to object properties (for foreign keys) or datatype properties (for attributes) in the same domain ontology. All features are renamed, and data formats are unified in one of the selected formats, usually CSV (or relational database).

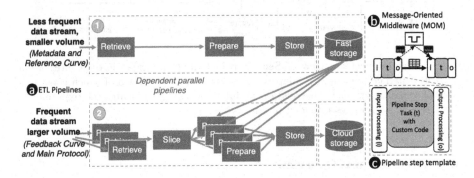

Fig. 4. (a) Dependent parallel ETL pipelines that break down ETL into four steps: *Retrieve, Slice, Prepare, Store*; (b) The cloud deployment of one step in the ETL pipeline as a container, where the MOM is responsible for the communication between steps of the ETL pipeline. (c) Zoom in one step, we see the three parts: *Input Processing, Output Processing* and *Pipeline Step Task*.

3.3   Distributed ETL and Data Analysis

Distributed ETL. To enable distributed ETL, we need to find a strategy that makes the ETL parallelisable, treat data streams with different updating frequencies, and handle data dependencies. SemCloud achieves this by breaking down the ETL into pipelines of four steps: *retrieve, slice, prepare*, and *store* (Fig. 4). Data retrieval constitutes the process of retrieving data from databases or online streams present in different factories and can normally be handled by a single computing node. These data are then split into subsets by the step *slice* to achieve parallel processing according to data semantics that make the splitting meaningful and each subset independently processable. In the welding use case, each subset only belongs to one welding machine, because the data analysis of welding quality monitoring of one machine can be safely assumed to be observable or predictable with data from this particular machine, without considering other machines. In this way, the datasets are separated into subsets that are computationally independent. We then deploy the ETL stage and the subsequent two stages on the cloud system that has resources for computing, storage and networking, to reduce the overall computational time.

An important strategy here is the hierarchically dependent parallel pipelines. We consider two types of data streams: the less frequently updated one with usually smaller volume, and the (more) frequently updated one with usually larger volume. (1) The former one has only three ETL steps: retrieve, prepare and store, because it requires resource (computing, storage, network) of one single cloud node and does not need slicing to parallelise. The intermediate results of this ETL pipeline are stored in a database using in-memory storage for fast query access. In the welding case, the metadata and reference curves follow this ETL pipeline. (2) The latter one has four ETL steps because it involves the application of slicing for parallelising. The results of this ETL pipeline are stored on dedicated cloud storage. In the welding case, the processing of feedback curves and main protocol requires more resources and is implemented through this pipeline. The ETL of these two data streams are dependent because the *prepare* step of the frequent data stream must pull intermediate results of less frequent data stream.

Distributed Data Analysis. The key of distributed data analysis is to make assumptions of what computation is parallelisable, and split the computations into independent computing tasks. Here the target of data analysis is to predict the welding quality quantified by quality indicators such as spot diameters or Q-Values [7,11]. The tasks include both classification (good or bad quality), regression (diameter values [12] or Q-Values), and forecasting [13] (predicting quality in the future). In practice, the latter two are preferred by domain experts because they provide more insights than a simple classification.

Both classic methods (feature engineering with e.g., linear regression) and deep learning (LSTM networks) are employed. We developed and tested various ML models [11,13]. We used model performance for tuning the hyper-parameters and considered both model performance and adoption difficulty for selecting the best models [7]. These models take input features such as sensor measurements, monitoring status and control parameters and predict the quality indicators. The training was done with various regimes [14]: the ground truth training data included simulation data, lab data, historical production data; the validation data were subsets of the training data for selecting hyper-parameters; test data were both of the same welding machines or different machines (testing transferability). According to domain knowledge, we assume that the interplay between welding machines to be only marginally significant and that it is safe to predict the welding quality of one welding machine only by using information of this welding machine. This assumption has been verified and obtained a prediction error of about 2% [11]. Thus, the data analysis on data of each welding machine can be performed independently if each subset contains all data of one machine.

Cloud Deployment Orchestration. To orchestrate the distributed computation, SemCloud encapsulates ETL steps or data analysis as containers and runs the containers independently and in parallel, allowing for deploying multiple instances of the same ETL step or data analysis [8]. Each instance is implemented by a template composed of three main parts: *Input Processing, Pipeline Step Task*, and *Output Processing* (Fig. 4c). The *Input Processing* fetches data from remote sources and moves the data to the step workspace. The *Pipeline Step Task* wraps custom code to process the fetched data. The *Output Processing* component delivers the processed data to a specific destination, notifies that they are available for the next steps, and clears up temporary and input data from the step workspace. Configuration and attributes of a pipeline step can be expressed as parameters and injected at deployment time. The communication between the steps is handled by Message-oriented Middleware (MOM) [15] (Fig. 4b), so that the consecutive steps do not need to run simultaneously for interaction, ensuring temporal decoupling. None of the sequential steps needs to know about the existence of other steps or their scaling configuration, thus achieving space decoupling. Therefore, it is possible to assign more instances to bottlenecked pipeline steps that are more computationally heavy and reduce the overall processing time.

3.4 ETL Pipeline Generation

Cloud Ontology. SemCloud provides the users GUI to construct ETL pipelines and encode them into knowledge graphs, based on a SemCloud ontology (Fig. 5a). The ontology *SemCloud* is written in OWL 2, and consists of 20 classes and 165 axioms. It has three main classes: *DataEntity, Task, Requirement*. *DataEntity* refers to any dataset to be processed; *Task* has sub-classes that represents the four types of tasks in the data preparation: *retrieve, slice, prepare*, and *store*; and *Requirement* that describes the requirements for computing, storage and networking resources.

ETL Pipeline Generation in KGs. We now illustrate the generation of ETL pipelines in knowledge graphs with the example in Fig. 5b. The data for welding condition monitoring have multiple levels of updating frequencies, which should be accommodated by the ETL pipelines. For example, data that are generated for each welding operation are updated after each welding operation, and thus are updated very frequently (about one second for one operation). For these data, the users construct an ETL pipeline p1 with four layers (via GUI). Firstly, data are "retrieved" from the welding factories. Thus, the layer l1 is of type *RetrieveLayer*, and has the task t1 of type *Retrieve*. The task t1 has an IO handler io, which has an output d1 of type *DataEntity*. Then the data are read in by a task t2 of type *Slice*, and "sliced" into smaller pieces d2, d3. These slices are input to different computing nodes to do tasks t3 and t4 of type *Prepare*. Finally, all prepared data entities are stored by t5 of type *Store*.

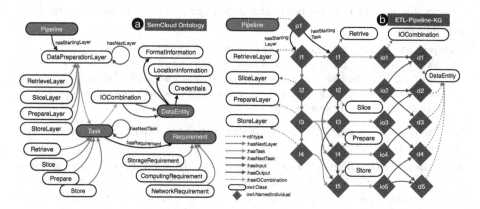

Fig. 5. (a) Schematic illustration of the SemCloud ontology. (b) Partial illustration of a KG for ETL-Pipeline.

3.5 Adaptive Datalog Rules Inference for Resource Configuration

Obtaining an optimised cloud configuration is not a trivial task. Cloud experts typically try different configurations by testing the system with various settings and use the system performance under these test settings as heuristics to manually decide the cloud configurations. In SemCloud, we design a set of declarative adaptive rules written using logical programming to make the cloud configurations explicit, automated, less error-prone where the system optimisation is done with help of external functions learned with ML, such that the rules can be also used by non-cloud experts.

To this end, SemCloud uses adaptive rules in Datalog with aggregation and calls to external predicates learned by ML (they are adaptive because the function parameters are learned, see Sect. 3.6). In particular, we consider non-recursive rules of the form $A \leftarrow B_1, \ldots, B_n$ where A is a head of rule (the consequence of the rule application) and $B_1, \ldots, B_n$ are either predicates that apply join or aggregate function that filters out the results. For the theouploary of Datalog we refer to [16–19]. In the following we provide some example rules and explain their logic.

We have six different Datalog programs (set of rules) that run independently and that are divided into three steps: (i) graph extraction rules that populate rule predicates by extracting information from the ETL-pipeline KGs (e.g., $rule_0$) (ii) resource estimation rules that estimate the resource consumption for the given pipeline if there is only one computing node (assuming infinitely large nodes, e.g.,

$rule_2$) (iii) resource configuration rules that find the optimal resource allocation in distributed computing the given pipeline (e.g., $rule_3$).

Graph Extraction Rules. These rules populate the predicates so that these predicates will be used for the resource estimation and configuration. The $rule_0$ exemplifies populating the predicate `subgraph1` that is related to the ETL pipeline p.

```
subgraph1(p,n,v,ms,mp,ssl,spr,sst)  ←  ETLPipeline(p),
    hasInputData(p,d), hasVolume(d,v), hasNoRecords(d,n)
    hasEstSliceMemory(p,ms), hasEstPrepareMemory(p,mp)
    hasEstSliceStorage(p,ssl), hasEstPrepareStorage(p,spr)
    hasEstStoreStorage(p,sst)                              (rule₀)
```

Similarly, we have rule $rule_1$ that creates `subgraph2(p,n,v,ms,mp,ts,tp, nc,ns,mrs,mrp,mode)`.

Resource Estimation Rules. These rules are used to estimate required resources assuming one computing node. For example, $rule_2$ estimates the required slice memory (`ms`), prepare memory (`mp`), slice storage (`ssl`), prepare storage (`spr`), and the store storage (`sst`). The rule then stores these estimations in the predicate `estimated_resource`.

```
estimated_resource(p,ms,mp,ssl,spr,sst) ←
    subgraph1(p,n,v,ms,mp,ssl,spr,sst),
    ms=@func_ms(n,v), mp=#avg{@func_mp(n,v,ms,i):range(i)},
    spr=#avg{@func_spr(n,v,ssl,i):range(i)},
    ssl=@func_ssl(n,v), sst=@func_sst(n,v,ssl,spr)      (rule₂)
```

where `@func_ms`, `@func_ssl`, `@func_sst`, etc. are parameterised ML functions whose parameters are learnt in the *rule parameter learning* (Sect. 3.6). In the implementation, those are defined as external built-in functions that are called in the grounding phase of the program and then are replaced by concrete values [16, 17]. We also have other resource estimation rules that estimate other resources, such as CPU consumption.

Resource Configuration Rules. These rules find the optimal cloud configurations based on the estimated cloud resource. $rule_3$ is an example for deciding the slicing strategy and the storage strategy, and finding the optimal resource configuration such as the chuck size (`nc`), slice size (`ns`), memory reservation for *slice* (`mrs`) and for *prepare* (`mrp`). In essence, $rule_3$ stipulates that if the maximum of estimated slice memory (`ms`) and prepare memory (`mp`) is greater than a given threshold (`c1*nm`), and the maximum of estimated slice storage (`ssl`), prepare storage (`spr`), and store storage (`sst`) is smaller than (or equal to) another threshold (`c2*ns`), then the chosen strategy for the given pipeline is *slicing* (thus `nc` and `ns` are computed), and *fast storage* (`fs`, where the thresholds are calculated from cloud attributes.

```
configured_resource(p,nc,ns,fs,mrs,mrp) ←
    subgraph2(p,n,v,ms,mp,ts,tp,nc,ns,mrs,mrp,mode),
    estimated_resource(p,ms,mp,ssl,spr,sst),
    CloudAttributes(c,c1,c2,c3,nm,ns,fs,cs),
```

```
#max{ms,mp} > (c1 * nm), #max{ssl,spr,sst} <= (c2 * ns),
nc = @func_fs_1(n,v,ts,tp), ns = @func_fs_2(n,v,ts,tp),
mrs = #min{ms, #max{@func_ss(n,v,nc,ns), c3*ms}},
mrp = #min{mp, #max{@func_pn(n,v,nc,ns), c3*mp}}        (rule_3)
```

3.6 Rule Parameter Learning with Machine Learning

The functions in the adaptive rules are in the form of ML models. The *resource estimation rules* are selected from the best model resulting from training three ML methods and the pilot running statistics. These three ML methods are *Polynomial Regression (PolyR)* (Eq. 1), *Multilayer Percetron (MLP)* (Eq. 2), and *K-Nearest Neighbours (KNN)*. (Eq. 3). We selected these three methods because they are representative classic ML methods suitable for the scale of the pilot running statistics. PolyR transfers the input features $(x_i, i \in \{1, 2, ..., n\}$, n is the number of input features) to a series of polynomial vectors $([1, x_i, x_i^2, ...x_i^m]$, m is the highest degree), and then constructs a predictor by multiplying a weight matrix $(\mathbf{W} \in \mathbb{R}^{m \times n})$. MLP consists of multiple layers of perceptrons, where each perceptron applies the *ReLu* function to the weighted sum of all neuron outputs of the previous layer plus the bias terms $\mathbf{W}^{(l-1)}\mathbf{h}^{(l-1)} + \mathbf{b}^{(l-1)}$. For a given data i whose output feature y_i is to be predicted, KNN finds its k samples (s, consisting of pairs of input $\mathbf{x}_s$ and output y_s) that are most similar to i (the k nearest neighbours $\mathcal{N}_k$) in the training data, and uses a weighted sum (the reciprocal of distance $d(s, i)$) of the output features y_s in $\mathcal{N}_k$ as the estimation.

The *resource configuration rules* are trained with the same three ML methods and with optimisation techniques such as Bayesian optimisation or grid search. For example, the functions @func_fs_1 and @func_fs_2 that find the optimal chuck size (nc) and slice size (ns) are trained by finding the arguments of (nc, ns) for the minimal total computing time (t_{total})

$$\text{nc, ns} = \underset{\text{nc,ns}}{\arg\min}\; t_{\text{total}} = \underset{\text{nc,ns}}{\arg\min}\; f(\text{v}, \text{n}, \text{nc}, \text{ns}, t_{\text{slice}}, t_{\text{prepare}})$$

$$\mathbf{x}_i = [1, x_i, x_i^2, ...x_i^m]^\mathbf{T} \quad \mathbf{h}^{(0)} = \mathbf{x} = [x_1, x_2, ..., x_n]^\mathbf{T} \quad\quad s = (\mathbf{x}_s, y_s)$$
$$\hat{y}_i = \sum_i \mathbf{W}\mathbf{x}_i \quad\quad \mathbf{h}^{(l)} = ReLu(\mathbf{W}^{(l-1)}\mathbf{h}^{(l-1)} + \mathbf{b}^{(l-1)}) \quad \mathcal{N}_k = \{s | d(s, i) \le d_k\}$$
$$err = ||\hat{\mathbf{y}} - \mathbf{y}||^2 \quad\quad \hat{y} = ReLu(\mathbf{W}^{(L-1)}\mathbf{h}^{(L-1)} + b^{(L-1)}) \quad d(s, i) = ||\mathbf{x}_s - \mathbf{x}_i||$$
$$(1) \quad\quad\quad\quad\quad (2) \quad\quad\quad\quad \hat{y}_i = \mathbf{w}\mathbf{y}_s, s \in \mathcal{N}_k$$
$$(3)$$

4 Implementation and Evaluation

We implemented our system with a front-end GUI based on Angular, HTML/CSS, and a back-end system based on ASP.NET Core, JavaScript, Python and DLV system [20,21]. The GUI adopts the common design pattern of Model-View-Controller and has a RESTful API that handles the requests and responses between the front-end and back-end.

The evaluation consists of (4.1) cloud deployment report, verifying to what extent SemCloud reduces computational time for semantic ETL (R1, R2); and (4.2) rule parameter learning and inference, validating whether the rule parameter learning and inference is scalable (R1) and accurate, so that the non-cloud experts can use SemCloud with confidence (R3).

4.1   Cloud Deployment Report

Data Description. To determine whether SemCloud reduces computational time, we use a dataset of 3 production lines for one month. The dataset is anonymised and simulated based on a welding factory in Germany. We simulated the dataset because it allows the freedom of evaluating settings and the information of real data is subject to a non-disclosure agreement. One production line has 10–20 machines, amounting to 45 machines in total. Each machine performs welding operations at a different speed, ranging from 1 spot/second, to 1 spot per several minutes (due to maintenance time, delay time, and various situations). The total amount of data are 389.42 GB, which represent 3.1 million spots, estimated to be related to 692.3 cars

Deployment Setting. We deployed the SemCloud system on an infrastructure of 7 computing instances connected by a network that were managed by a Rancher container orchestrator [22]. We adopt the automatic setting, whereby resource configurations are provided via adaptive Datalog rules and the Rancher system automatically assigns containers to resources according to the configuration.

Performance Comparison. We demonstrate the performance comparison between the ETL processing with the legacy system (without SemCloud) and with our SemCloud system (Fig. 6). The legacy system is comprised of a integrated software that performs both the preparation of the metadata/reference curves and the processing of the feedback curve and main protocol data. The legacy system was deployed in a node that meets the total requirements for the experimental data to monitor the resource usage.

It can be seen that the memory usage of the computing instance for the legacy solution increases monotonously along the processed input data volume, while SemCloud requires almost zero increase of memory allocation, which means SemCloud can deploy the ETL process on many computing instances with no extra memory demand. Figure 6b shows SemCloud requires slightly more CPU power. This is expected and understandable, because the distributed deployment consumes more computing power per unit of time, but decreases the overall computing time. The latter is confirmed by Fig. 6c: as the input data volume increases the reduced computing time brought by SemCloud becomes increasingly significant (R1).

4.2   Evaluation of Rule Parameter Learning and Inference

Pilot Running Statistics. To verify the scalability and accuracy of the rule parameter learning and inference, we gather pilot running statistics, train and

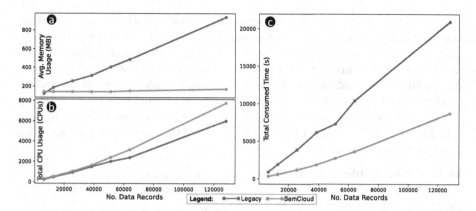

Fig. 6. (Performance comparison by (a) memory usage, (b) total CPU usage (integrated over time), (c) consumed time: SemCloud significantly reduces the memory usage and consumed time (by about 50%), and uses slightly more total CPU, compared to the *legacy* solution (Without SemCloud). X-axis: processed input data volume.

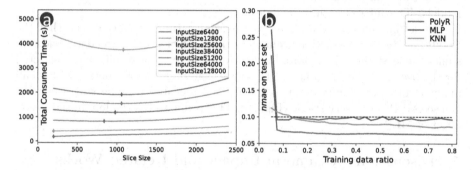

Fig. 7. (a) Optimisation to find the best slice size for the least time, when chunk size is fixed. (b) Comparing ML methods to find the minimal training data

test the ML functions in SemCloud. We run SemCloud repeatedly 3562 times with different sizes of subsets of the welding dataset in Sect. 4.1 and gather pilot running statistics. These statistics include data information, e.g., input data size, different configurations, e.g., slice size, and recorded resource consumption e.g., memory consumption, mCPU consumption.

Experiment Setting. We split the pilot running statistics so that 80% are for rule parameter training and 20% for rule testing and inference. Three ML models are trained and tested: *PolyR*, *MLP*, and *KNN*. We adopt a grid search strategy for hyper-parameter tuning. The final hyper-parameter are, PolyR: $4^c irc$; MLP: 2 hidden layers with neurons 10 and 9; KNN: 2 neighbours.

Performance Metrics. We use several performance metrics: *normalised mean absolute error (nmae)* [23] to measure prediction accuracy, minimal training data amount (Min. $|\mathcal{D}_{train}|$ for yielding satisfactory results, optimisation time (Opt. time), learning time and inference time. Intuitively, $nmae$ reflects the scale-independent average prediction error. It is computed as *mean absolute error* normalised by the mean value of the configuration $\bar{c}$: $nmae = mae/\bar{c}$. $nmae$ reflects the mean absolute error between the ground truth configuration c and the predicted configuration $\hat{c}$: $mae = \frac{1}{|\mathcal{D}_{test}|} \sum_{\mathcal{D}_{test}} |c - \hat{c}|$, and $\bar{c} = \sum_{\mathcal{D}_{test}} c/|\mathcal{D}_{test}|$. We normalise mae because its scale is dependent on the variable for which we calculate mae. If it is divided by the mean value of the variable, it becomes $nmae$ which is scale-independent.

Learning and Inference Results. The optimisation results of *slice size* shows we can configure it to find a "sweet spot" to minimise the total consumed time (Fig. 7a). The performance of rule learning and inference is shown in Table 1 (R3). The learning time is the time it takes to train the models. The inference time includes

Table 1. Parameter learning and reasoning results, recorded on Intel Core i7-10710U.

Metric	PolyR	MLP	KNN
$nmae$	0.0671	0.0947	0.0818
Min. $|\mathcal{D}_{train}|$	7.42%	50.97%	10.00%
Opt. time	1.12 s	174.32 s	7.25 s
Learning time	20.82 ms	120.31 ms	27.52 ms
Inference time	<1.00 ms	<1.00 ms	<5.00 ms

the model inference time and the rule reasoning time. It can be seen that the PolyR has the best prediction accuracy, requires the least training data, and consumes the least time. Therefore, PolyR generates the best results and is selected for the use case. We presume the reason is that PolyR works better with small amounts of and not very complex data (3562 repeated running statistics). We can see MLP is not very stable (Fig. 7b). This is due to the random initialisation effect of MLP.

5   Discussion on General Impact and Related Works

Uptake for the Cloud Community. SemCloud is an attempt for democratising cloud systems for non-cloud experts. We hope to inspire research and a broad range of users who are pursuing scaling data science solutions on the cloud, but are impeded by the long training time for acquiring cloud expertise. Providing a dynamically scalable (on a step and pipeline level), general-purpose solution for big data pipelines on heterogeneous resources that a broad audience can use is an open research topic [24,25]. The currently available multitude of tools for big data pipeline management only partially addresses these issues as shown in [26]. Data pipeline management approaches in literature such as [27–29] also partially address the issue but either specifically support a knowledge domain (scientific workflows, ad-hoc languages), fail to address issues related to individual step scalability, or are not well-suited for dynamic long-running jobs. Other works that touch that topic [30–33] also do not address the automatic resource allocation issue and are not designed for non-cloud experts. Our approach tackles these issues and the presented principles should be easy to reproduce.

Uptake in Terms of Semantic Technology. We open-source our cloud ontology [34]. We hope this ontology can facilitate research of semantic technology

in the scalability challenges, that the tenets of explicit, transparent, and shared knowledge can advance in the practice in academia and industry. We developed it as we did not find a suitable ontology for our challenges. Past works about cloud ontologies focus more on describing the different layers and components [4,5], services [35], functional or non-functional features and the interaction between the layers [36]. They cover the cloud tasks and resource allocation, but to a limited extent. There exist other works about the resource management topic [37–39], but they do not provide mechanism or reasoning for adaptive and automatic resource configuration. Works about cloud reasoning are focused on other aspects like security attacks [40], minimising sources like computing nodes [41], computational requirements [42], service placement [43], verifying policy properties [44], deploying semantic reasoning on the cloud [45]. There is insufficient discussion on helping users to automate the cloud resource configuration.

Uptake by Stakeholders and Benefits. Semantic technologies play an increasingly important role in modern industrial practice. Ontologies, as a good way for formal description of knowledge, offer unambiguous "lingua franca" for cross-domain communication. They can help users to perform tasks of a remote domain that otherwise would be error-prone, time-consuming and cognitively demanding. We incorporated rule-based reasoning, falling in the category of symbolic reasoning, with machine learning, which is a type of sub-symbolic reasoning. The combination takes benefits from both: SemCloud becomes more agnostic of cloud infrastructure and adapts to the resource conditions, thus exploiting explicit domain knowledge via semantics and learning implicit relationship via ML.

In addition, we tested SemCloud with users of various backgrounds (welding experts, data scientists, semantic experts). SemCloud could improve their working efficiency. Before using SemCloud, users that are the non-cloud experts have very limited understanding of the cloud system, and did not use the cloud system. Through SemCloud, these users could obtain better understanding of the cloud system, start using the cloud system, and rely on the SemCloud to automatically configure the resource allocation. We tested the GUI with the users to collected feedback for improving the usability and expanding the functionalities.

Lessons Learnt on Costs and Risks. The main costs for development of such systems comprise the early development time for the semantic infrastructure that mediates between the cloud resources, data analysis solutions and users. Naturally, these costs vary depending on the specific project. It was manageable in our case, but should be carefully evaluated for each project individually. The key lessons learnt for reducing costs is that a good cross-domain communication framework is essential, where experts of different backgrounds can speak a common language and reduce misunderstanding and communication time. A possible and important risk is that the assumption could be wrong as to whether and to what extent the ETL and data analysis can be parallelised. It is recommended to verify the assumption early to avoid further costs.

6   Conclusion, and Outlook

Conclusion. This work presents our SemCloud system motivated by a Bosch use case of welding monitoring, for addressing the scalability challenges in terms of *data volume, variety,* and more *users*. SemCloud provides semantic abstraction that mediates between the users, ETL and data analysis, as well as cloud infrastructure. The scalability in terms of data variety is addressed by semantic data integration, data volume by distributed ETL and data analysis, and scalability to more users by adaptive Datalog rule-based resource configuration. These Datalog rules are adaptive because they have parameterised functions learnt from pilot running statistics via ML, a combination of symbolic and sub-symbolic approaches. We evaluated SemCloud extensively through cloud deployment with large volume of industrial data, and rule learning from thousands of pilot runs of the system, showing very promising results.

Outlook. SemCloud is under the umbrella of Neuro-Symbolic AI for Industry 4.0 at Bosch [46] that aims at enhancing manufacturing with both symbolic AI (such as semantic technologies [47]) for improving transparency [48], and ML for prediction power [49]. Bosch is developing user-friendly cloud technology in the framework of EU project DataCloud with many EU partners [50]. SemCloud is partially developed with production end-users and current deployed in a Bosch evaluation environment. We plan to push it into the production to test with more users and collect feedback, and work together with EU partners for transferring the knowledge and experience to other manufacturing domains to increase the wide adoption. We also plan to develop formal theories for knowledge representation and reasoning for cloud technology and automatic resource configuration, e.g., better modelling framework, advanced reasoning rules, and deeper integration of symbolic and sub-symbolic reasoning.

Acknowledgements. The work was partially supported by the European Commission funded projects DataCloud (101016835), enRichMyData (101070284), Graph-Massivizer (101093202), Dome 4.0 (953163), OntoCommons (958371), and the Norwegian Research Council funded projects (237898, 323325, 309691, 309834, and 308817).

References

1. Kagermann, H.: Change through digitization—value creation in the age of industry 4.0. In: Albach, H., Meffert, H., Pinkwart, A., Reichwald, R. (eds.) Management of Permanent Change, pp. 23–45. Springer, Wiesbaden (2015). https://doi.org/10.1007/978-3-658-05014-6_2
2. ITU, Recommendation ITU - T Y.2060: Overview of the internet of things, Technical report, International Telecommunication Union (2012)
3. Chand, S., Davis, J.: What is smart manufacturing. Time Magazine Wrapper **7**, 28–33 (2010)
4. Youseff, L., Butrico, M., Da Silva, D.: Toward a unified ontology of cloud computing. In: 2008 Grid Computing Environments Workshop, pp. 1–10. IEEE (2008)

5. Ageed, Z.S., Ibrahim, R.K., Sadeeq, M.A.: Unified ontology implementation of cloud computing for distributed systems. Curr. J. Appl. Sci. Technol., 82–97 (2020)

6. Svetashova, Y., et al.: Ontology-enhanced machine learning: a Bosch use case of welding quality monitoring. In: Pan, J.Z., et al. (eds.) ISWC 2020. LNCS, vol. 12507, pp. 531–550. Springer, Cham (2020). https://doi.org/10.1007/978-3-030-62466-8_33

7. Zhou, B., et al.: SemML: facilitating development of ml models for condition monitoring with semantics. J. Web Semant. **71**, 100664 (2021)

8. Nikolov, N., et al.: Conceptualization and scalable execution of big data workflows using domain-specific languages and software containers. Internet Things **16**, 100440 (2021)

9. DIN, Maintenance-maintenance terminology, Trilingual Version EN 13306:2017 13306 (2018) 2017

10. ISO, Resistance welding - procedures for determining the weldability lobe for resistance spot, projection and seam welding, Standard, International Organization for Standardization, Geneva, CH (2004)

11. Zhou, B., Svetashova, Y., Byeon, S., Pychynski, T., Mikut, R., Kharlamov, E.: Predicting quality of automated welding with machine learning and semantics: a bosch case study. In: CIKM '20: The 29th ACM International Conference on Information and Knowledge Management, Virtual Event, Ireland, 19–23 October 2020, pp. 2933–2940. ACM (2020)

12. Zhou, B., Pychynski, T., Reischl, M., Mikut, R.: Comparison of machine learning approaches for time-series-based quality monitoring of resistance spot welding (RSW). Arch. Data Sci. Ser. A (Online First) **5**(1), 13 (2018)

13. Zhou, B., Pychynski, T., Reischl, M., Kharlamov, E., Mikut, R.: Machine learning with domain knowledge for predictive quality monitoring in resistance spot welding. J. Intell. Manuf. **33**(4), 1139–1163 (2022). https://doi.org/10.1007/s10845-021-01892-y

14. Zhou, B.: Machine learning methods for product quality monitoring in electric resistance welding, Ph.D. thesis, Karlsruhe Institute of Technology, Germany (2021)

15. Albano, M., Ferreira, L.L., Pinho, L.M., Alkhawaja, A.R.: Message-oriented middleware for smart grids. Comput. Stan. Interfaces **38**, 133–143 (2015)

16. Leone, N., et al.: The DLV system. In: Flesca, S., Greco, S., Ianni, G., Leone, N. (eds.) JELIA 2002. LNCS (LNAI), vol. 2424, pp. 537–540. Springer, Heidelberg (2002). https://doi.org/10.1007/3-540-45757-7_50

17. Ianni, G., Calimeri, F., Pietramala, A., Santoro, M.C.: Parametric external predicates for the DLV system, CoRR cs.AI/0404011. http://arxiv.org/abs/cs/0404011

18. Abiteboul, S., Hull, R., Vianu, V.: Foundations of Databases, vol. 8. Addison-Wesley Reading, Boston (1995)

19. Paramonov, S., Werner, N., Ognjen, S.: An asp approach to query completeness reasoning. Theory Pract. Logic Program. **13**(4), 1–10 (2013)

20. DLVHEX, DLVHEX source documentation. URL: http://www.kr.tuwien.ac.at/research/systems/dlvhex/doc2x/index.html. Accessed 31 July 2023

21. Eiter, T., et al.: The DLVHEX system. KI-Künstliche Intelligenz **32**, 187–189 (2018)

22. Rancher, Rancher kubernetes clusters. https://rancher.com/products/rancher. Accessed 14 Mar 2022

23. Chai, T., Draxler, R.R.: Root mean square error (RMSE) or mean absolute error (MAE)?-Arguments against avoiding RMSE in the literature. Geosci. Model Dev. **7**(3), 1247–1250 (2014)

24. Barika, M., Garg, S., Zomaya, A.Y., Wang, L., Moorsel, A.V., Ranjan, R.: Orchestrating big data analysis workflows in the cloud: research challenges, survey, and future. ACM Comput. Surv. **52**(5), 1–41 (2019)

25. Buyya, R., et al.: A manifesto for future generation cloud computing: research directions for the next decade. ACM Comput. Surv. **51**(5), 1–38 (2018)

26. Matskin, M., Tahmasebi, S., Layegh, A., Payberah, A.H., Thomas, A., Nikolov, N., Roman, D.: A survey of big data pipeline orchestration tools from the perspective of the datacloud project. In: Supplementary Proceedings of the XXIII International Conference on Data Analytics and Management in Data Intensive Domains, Moscow, Russia, vol. 3036 (2021)

27. Gerlach, W., et al.: Skyport-container-based execution environment management for multi-cloud scientific workflows. In: 2014 5th International Workshop on Data-Intensive Computing in the Clouds, pp. 25–32. IEEE (2014)

28. Qasha, R., Cala, J., Watson, P.: Dynamic deployment of scientific workflows in the cloud using container virtualization. In. IEEE International Conference on Cloud Computing Technology and Science (CloudCom) 2016, 269–276 (2016)

29. Alaasam, A.B., Radchenko, G., Tchernykh, A., Borodulin, K., Podkorytov, A.: Scientific micro-workflows: where event-driven approach meets workflows to support digital twins. In: Russian Supercomputing Days, pp. 489–495 (2018)

30. Tan, Q.W., Goh, W., Mutwil, M.: LSTrAP-cloud: a user-friendly cloud computing pipeline to infer coexpression networks. Genes **11**(4), 428 (2020)

31. Zhao, M., Li, Z., Liu, W., Chen, J., Li, X.: Ufc2: user-friendly collaborative cloud. IEEE Trans. Parallel Distrib. Syst. **33**, 2163–2182 (2021)

32. Kumar, P.S., Kumar, A., Rathore, P.S., Chatterjee, J.M.: An on-demand and user-friendly framework for cloud data centre networks with performance guarantee. Cyber Secur. Parallel Distrib. Comput.: Concepts, Tech., Appl. Case Stud., 149–159 (2019)

33. Mulfari, D., Celesti, A., Villari, M.: A computer system architecture providing a user-friendly man machine interface for accessing assistive technology in cloud computing. J. Syst. Softw. **100**, 129–138 (2015)

34. Zhou, B., Zheng, Z., Kharlamov, E.: The SemCloud ontology, open source under (2023). https://github.com/nsai-uio/SemCloud

35. Tahamtan, A., Beheshti, S.A., Anjomshoaa, A., Tjoa, A.M.: A cloud repository and discovery framework based on a unified business and cloud service ontology. In: 2012 IEEE Eighth World Congress on Services, pp. 203–210. IEEE (2012)

36. Al-Sayed, M.M., Hassan, H.A., Omara, F.A.: CloudFNF: an ontology structure for functional and non-functional features of cloud services. J. Parallel Distrib. Comput. **141**, 143–173 (2020)

37. Castañé, G.G., Xiong, H., Dong, D., Morrison, J.P.: An ontology for heterogeneous resources management interoperability and HPC in the cloud. Futur. Gener. Comput. Syst. **88**, 373–384 (2018)

38. Ma, Y.B., Jang, S.H., Lee, J.S.: Ontology-based resource management for cloud computing. In: Nguyen, N.T., Kim, C.-G., Janiak, A. (eds.) ACIIDS 2011. LNCS (LNAI), vol. 6592, pp. 343–352. Springer, Heidelberg (2011). https://doi.org/10.1007/978-3-642-20042-7_35

39. Zhang, C., Yang, Y., Du, Z., Ma, C.: Particle swarm optimization algorithm based on ontology model to support cloud computing applications. J. Ambient. Intell. Humaniz. Comput. **7**(5), 633–638 (2016)

40. Choi, C., Choi, J.: Ontology-based security context reasoning for power IoT-cloud security service. IEEE Access **7**, 110510–110517 (2019)

41. Ghetas, M., Yong, C.H.: Resource management framework for multi-tier service using case-based reasoning and optimization algorithm. Arab. J. Sci. Eng. **43**(2), 707–721 (2018)

42. Rakib, A., Uddin, I.: An efficient rule-based distributed reasoning framework for resource-bounded systems. Mob. Netw. Appl. **24**(1), 82–99 (2019)

43. Forti, S., Bisicchia, G., Brogi, A.: Declarative continuous reasoning in the cloud-IoT continuum. J. Log. Comput. **32**(2), 206–232 (2022)

44. Backes, J., et al.: Semantic-based automated reasoning for AWS access policies using SMT. In: 2018 Formal Methods in Computer Aided Design (FMCAD), pp. 1–9. IEEE (2018)

45. Su, X., et al.: Distribution of semantic reasoning on the edge of internet of things. In: 2018 IEEE International Conference on Pervasive Computing and Communications (PerCom), pp. 1–9. IEEE (2018)

46. Zhou, B., et al.: Neuro-symbolic AI at bosch: data foundation, insights, and deployment. In: Proceedings of the ISWC 2022 Posters, Demos and Industry Tracks of CEUR Workshop Proceedings, vol. 3254 (2022)

47. Yahya, M., Zhou, B., Breslin, J.G., Ali, M.I., Kharlamov, E.: Semantic modeling, development and evaluation for the resistance spot welding industry. IEEE Access (2023)

48. Zheng, Z., Zhou, B., Zhou, D., Soylu, A., Kharlamov, E.: Executable knowledge graph for transparent machine learning in welding monitoring at Bosch. In: Proceedings of the 31st ACM International Conference on Information & Knowledge Management, pp. 5102–5103 (2022)

49. Tan, Z., et al.: Literal-aware knowledge graph embedding for welding quality monitoring: a bosch case. In: ISWC. Springer, Cham (2023)

50. DataCloud, Enabling the big data pipeline lifecycle on the computing continuum (2022). https://datacloudproject.eu/. Accessed 14 Mar 2022

AIDA-Bot 2.0: Enhancing Conversational Agents with Knowledge Graphs for Analysing the Research Landscape

Antonello Meloni[1], Simone Angioni[1], Angelo Salatino[2], Francesco Osborne[2,3], Aliaksandr Birukou[4], Diego Reforgiato Recupero[1(✉)], and Enrico Motta[2]

[1] Department of Mathematics and Computer Science, University of Cagliari, Cagliari, Italy
{antonello.meloni,simone.angioni,diego.reforgiato}@unica.it
[2] Knowledge Media Institute, The Open University, Milton Keynes, UK
{angelo.salatino,francesco.osborne,enrico.motta}@open.ac.uk
[3] Department of Business and Law, University of Milano Bicocca, Milan, Italy
[4] Springer-Verlag GmbH, Tiergartenstrasse 17, 69121 Heidelberg, Germany
aliaksandr.birukou@springer.com

Abstract. The crucial task of analysing the complex dynamics of the research landscape and uncovering the latest insights from the scientific literature is of paramount importance to researchers, governments, and commercial organizations. Springer Nature, one of the leading academic publishers worldwide, plays a significant role in this domain and regularly integrates and processes a variety of data sources to inform strategic decisions. Since exploring the resulting data is a challenging task, in 2021 we developed AIDA-Bot, a chatbot that addresses inquiries about the research landscape by utilising a large-scale knowledge graph of scholarly data. This paper presents the novel AIDA-Bot 2.0, which can both 1) support a set of predetermined question types by automatically translating them to formal queries on the knowledge graph, and 2) answer open questions by summarising information from relevant articles. We evaluated the performance of AIDA-Bot 2.0 through a comparative assessment against alternative architectures and an extensive user study. The results indicate that the novel features provide more accurate information and an excellent user experience.

Keywords: Conversational Agents · Knowledge Graphs · Scholarly Data · Science of Science · Scholarly Analytics

1 Introduction

The challenging task of analysing the dynamics of the research landscape and uncovering the latest insights from the scientific literature is of paramount importance to researchers, governments, and commercial organizations. Springer Nature (SN), one of the leading academic publishers worldwide, plays a significant role in this domain. Their Computer Science portfolio comprises over 170

T. R. Payne et al. (Eds.): ISWC 2023, LNCS 14266, pp. 400–418, 2023.
https://doi.org/10.1007/978-3-031-47243-5_22

journals and provides extensive coverage of the top conferences, resulting in approximately 900 proceedings volumes per year. Therefore, SN needs to continuously monitor the academic landscape to inform short- and long-term strategic decisions. For instance, editorial teams must regularly assess the quality of research venues, discover emerging communities and research areas, identify key researchers that could organise special issues or edit books on strategic topics, and evaluate the potential impact of new technologies on the industrial sectors. To this end, SN relies on a robust data pipeline that combines various large-scale academic datasets and provides analytical functionalities based on cutting-edge data mining and machine learning solutions. Semantic Web and Knowledge Graph technologies play a pivotal role in this infrastructure as they enable the integration and querying of diverse information from heterogeneous data sources [33]. Since 2014, SN and The Open University have collaboratively explored the application of semantic technologies in this space, resulting in numerous tools that have been integrated into the SN workflow [30,41–43]. In 2020, this collaboration led to the development of the AIDA Dashboard [4], a web application that allows users to assess and compare journals and conferences according to a comprehensive range of analytics. The AIDA Dashboard relies on the Academia/Industry DynAmics (AIDA) Knowledge Graph[1] [3], a knowledge base which integrates multiple data sources (e.g., OpenAlex, DBLP, DBpedia, CSO) and describes over 25 million scientific papers. A freely available version of the AIDA Dashboard was first launched at ISWC 2022 [2].

The AIDA Dashboard proved to be an excellent way to explore the multifaceted data in AIDA KG. However, it also suffers from two inherent limitations: 1) it mainly focuses on venues (journals and conferences), and 2) it only reports a fixed set of precomputed analytics. Therefore, it does not allow users to exploit the full range of information in the AIDA KG by formulating specific queries over all the described entities, including researchers, articles, organisations, countries, venues, and research topics. For example, an editor cannot retrieve the top researchers in a certain field, compare the academic impact of two organizations, or find all the articles in a journal that focus on a combination of topics. Implementing an interface based on a formal query language, such as SPARQL or SQL, was also not an option, as most users would not be comfortable with this solution. We thus decided to develop an alternative solution based on a conversational agent. The first prototype of this system was presented as a demo at ISWC 2021 [21].

In this paper, we introduce AIDA-Bot 2.0, a chatbot able to answer various questions about the research landscape and the scientific literature. This conversational agent has been designed to both 1) support a set of predetermined question types (e.g., "List all entities with a certain characteristic", "Compare two entities") by automatically translating them to formal queries on the knowledge graph, and 2) answer open questions (e.g., "What is a convolutional neural network?", "Define knowledge graph") by summarising information from relevant articles in the knowledge graph. This hybrid approach ensures that the

---

[1] Academia/Industry DynAmics Knowledge Graph - http://w3id.org/aida/.

responses provided are grounded in factual information that can be easily verified and, if necessary, corrected by updating the knowledge graph.

Recent advancements in natural language processing have led to the development of large language models, such as GPT 4.0 [29], which can generate
coherent and eloquent responses to user queries. However, these models have
raised concerns about the accuracy and reliability of the generated content, as
they may produce text that is not based on factual knowledge, leading to what
is known as hallucinations. For instance, asking the current version of ChatGPT
for a list of prominent papers in Blockchain will result in a set of mostly fictional articles, typically generated by combining keywords and authors of real
papers. Furthermore, recent studies suggest that recent GPT models exhibit
limited accuracy in generating consistent responses to inquiries in the scientific
domain [6]. In contrast, our aim in building AIDA-Bot 2.0 was to ensure that
the system produces only accurate and verifiable information within a specific
domain.

AIDA-Bot 2.0 boasts several significant improvements over its predecessor,
AIDA-Bot 1.0 [22]. These include: i) a novel grammar-based approach for identifying question types, ii) the capacity to accommodate up to three filters in a
query, and iii) the ability to respond to open queries by providing summaries of
relevant articles.

We evaluated AIDA-Bot 2.0 in terms of both accuracy and usability. We
first conducted a comparative evaluation in which ten researchers posed 15 questions to AIDABot 2.0 and three alternative solutions and ranked the responses.
We then performed a user study that involved five senior computer science
researchers to obtain an in-depth evaluation of AIDABot 2.0 usability and usefulness.

In summary, the main contributions of this paper are the following:

- AIDA-Bot 2.0, a novel conversational agent that takes advantage of a large-
  scale knowledge graph to produce reliable answers in the research domain;
- a new hybrid architecture for addressing both pre-determined and open questions that greatly improves on AIDA-Bot 1.0;
- an evaluation comparing AIDA-Bot 2.0 against three alternative architectures;
- a user study further assessing AIDA-Bot 2.0's user experience;
- a discussion of the impact and uptake of this tool.

The remainder of this manuscript is structured as follows. Section 2 describes
the pipeline for data integration and AIDA KG. Section 3 presents the AIDA-
Bot 2.0 architecture. Section 4 reports the outcome of the evaluations. Section 5
describes the uptake and impact of AIDA-Bot and Sect. 6 discusses the development plans. Section 7 presents the related work on conversational agents. Finally,
Sect. 8 concludes the paper and outlines future research directions.

2   The AIDA Knowledge Graph Pipeline

The SN Data Cloud Infrastructure, based on Google BigQuery[2] and Google Vertex AI Workbench[3], enables us to define complex data pipelines to integrate different data sources, update them regularly, and enrich them by applying machine learning models for classification and information extraction. It is also employed to facilitate data exchange between different systems within SN, ensuring that data and analytics are consistent.

In an effort to obtain a more comprehensive and detailed representation of research dynamics in Computer Science, we adopted this system to create and maintain the Academia/Industry DynAmics Knowledge Graph (AIDA KG) [3]. AIDA KG is a large-scale knowledge base that describes publications and patents in Computer Science according to their research topics, authors, conferences, journals, organisations, types of organisations (i.e., academia, industry, or collaborative), and industrial sectors (e.g., automotive, financial, semiconductors, manufacturing). It is generated by integrating data sources such as OpenAlex[4], DBLP, Research Organization Registry[5] (ROR), DBpedia, the Computer Science Ontology[6] (CSO), and the Industrial Sectors Ontology[7] (INDUSO).

The current version of AIDA KG describes 25M publications and 8M patents.

AIDA KG focuses on eight main classes: *paper, patent, author, affiliation, journal, conference, topic,* and *industrialSector*. All entities from these classes are interlinked via 22 unique relationships such as: i) *hasAffiliation*, to indicate the affiliations of the authors of a paper, ii) *hasTopic* to identify the topics of papers and patents, iii) *schema:creator* to indicate the author of a paper. The complete schema of AIDA KG is available at https://w3id.org/aida.

The pipeline used to generate AIDA KG comprises different stages. First, it downloads and prepares all the relevant data sources. Then, it integrates research papers from the OpenAlex and DBLP, unifying them using DOIs and title similarity. Next, it leverages the CSO Classifier [43] to annotate all research documents according to their relevant topics, drawn from the Computer Science Ontology [44]. It then uses the ROR IDs from OpenAlex, to determine whether documents are written by academic institutions, industrial organizations, or through a collaborative effort. To provide additional context to the AIDA KG, all documents created by industrial authors, including those resulting from collaboration with academia, are also annotated with information regarding the relevant industrial sectors from INDUSO. This is accomplished by utilising the description of the affiliation available on DBPedia. For example, to characterise the company 'Samsung', we retrieve the relevant entity in DBpedia[8], extract information about their products, and map them to relevant sectors

---

2   Google BigQuery - https://cloud.google.com/bigquery.

3   Google Vertex AI Workbench - https://cloud.google.com/vertex-ai-workbench.

4   OpenAlex - https://openalex.org/.

5   ROR - https://ror.org/.

6   CSO - https://w3id.org/cso.

7   INDUSO - https://w3id.org/aida/#induso.

8   https://dbpedia.org/page/Samsung.

in INDUSO, in this case: "semiconductor", "telecommunications", and "home appliances".

The AIDA Knowledge Graph is publicly available[9] and distributed under the CC-BY 4.0 license. In addition, it can be queried using SPARQL from the main triplestore https://w3id.org/aida/sparql/. While the current version focuses on Computer Science, we are now expanding it to cover additional disciplines.

3   The Architecture of AIDA-Bot 2.0

The architecture of AIDA-Bot 2.0 consists of two main modules: Question Understanding and Response Generator.

The Question Understanding module analyses the user input with the aim of recognising one of the four predefined query types (count, list, describe, and compare) and converting the question into a formal query on the knowledge graph. AIDA-Bot 2.0 supports complex queries using up to three filters (e.g., "List the top five papers about *computer vision* and *machine learning* written by researchers from the *University of Cambridge*"), in contrast with the previous version, which allowed only one condition.

The module extracts a set of key terms and searches them in AIDA KG to identify the relevant entities and their types.

It then uses the resulting entities to generate all pertinent questions the system can automatically translate to queries over the knowledge graph. Finally, it computes the similarity between the user's input question and the set of generated questions. This solution allows us to detect an extensive array of formulations associated with each supported question, encompassing different linguistic expressions.

If the similarity score between the user input and the most similar generated question exceeds a threshold, the Response Generator module uses a template to translate the latter to a query on AIDA KG and retrieves the relevant information. Otherwise, the system retrieves from AIDA KG the set of articles containing in the title or the abstract the key terms extracted from the user question. It then applies a question-answering model to produce a response based on the articles.

In the following, we describe the two modules in detail and provide more information on the adopted transformer models.

3.1   Question Understanding

The Question Understanding module analyses the input query and uses named-entity recognition (NER) to identify the key terms, which include nouns, noun phrases, named entities, and compound expressions in quotes. This information extraction step employs spaCy[10], an open-source Python library for Natural Language Processing[11].

---

[9] AIDA Knowledge Graph Download - https://w3id.org/aida.

[10] Spacy - https://spacy.io/.

[11] Specifically, we adopted the "en_core_web_sm" model.

We allow users to employ compound expressions in quotes to specify an exact match, similar to search engines. To avoid redundancy, nouns and noun phrases that appear in a named entity or an expression enclosed in quotation marks, are removed from the key terms. We also discard from key terms words that suggest questions (e.g., "who", "what") and terms that indicate an entity type (e.g., "papers", "articles", "citations"). For instance, the request *"Count papers about mathematics and matrix algebra written by authors from 'French Institute for research in computer science and automation' "*, contains the nouns *papers, mathematics, matrix, algebra, authors, French, Institute, research, computer, science, automation*, which are also included in the noun phrases *'mathematics', 'matrix algebra', 'authors', 'French Institute', 'research', 'computer science', 'automation'* and, therefore, are discarded. The words *papers* and *authors* are removed as they are types in AIDA KG. All the terms which appear in the quoted expression are also discarded. Therefore, the resulting key terms would be: *'mathematics', 'matrix algebra'* and *"French Institute for research in computer science and automation"*.

The key terms are searched in AIDA KG to retrieve the relevant entities and their types. In the previous example, all key terms would be found in AIDA KG: the "French Institute for research in computer science and automation" as *organization* while 'mathematics' and 'matrix algebra' as *topic*.

The Question Understanding module uses the resulting entities to generate a grammar for producing all compatible requests that can be translated to queries on the knowledge graph. A grammar is a set of production rules that describe how to generate valid sentences. These rules specify the allowable combinations of symbols or tokens and the order in which they appear.

In our system, the grammar is dynamically generated by using templates that include placeholders that are populated with the entities and their types. In the following, we report an example of a simple template for each query type.

1. count < sub_c > {}
2. list the <super> {num} <sub_l> {}
3. describe {}
4. compare {} vs {}

where:

- <sub_c> = papers | authors | conferences | organizations | citations | journals
- <super> = top | most important | main | most cited
- <sub_l> = papers | authors | conferences | organizations | topics | journals

Curly parentheses can only be filled with instances from the AIDA KG. Variables in angular parenthesis (e.g., <sub_c>) can only be filled with the previously defined items (e.g., papers, authors, conferences, and so on). Additionally, synonyms for these items, as pre-defined in a list, may also be employed. For example, <sub_c> would match both the words "papers" and "articles".

During the generation of the grammar, the system will produce all questions compatible with the set of detected entities. When considering the four templates defined above, if the system detects entities of type ["topics", "conferences", "organizations", "authors", "journals"], it will produce a range of questions of types 1 and 2. The module produces types 1 and 2 queries with up to three identified instances, allowing users to specify queries with three filters. Whenever at least one element from ["authors", "conferences", "organizations"] is found, the system will produce queries of type 3. Whenever it detects two items of the same class, it will generate queries of type 4.

In practice, each question type is supported by multiple templates since the same type of question can appear in several forms. For example, *how many* <*sub_c*> {} is another template for the query type *count* and would support questions such as "How many papers are there about the semantic web and machine learning?". Therefore, from a modest number of initial templates covering the four query types (15 in the current implementation) and a set of identified entities, AIDA-Bot can generate a large number of candidate questions. Current templates were derived from use cases specific to SN and further improved through iterative refinement based on user feedback. Since developing new templates requires limited effort, the system can be easily adapted to other domains.

Next, the system computes the similarity between the original user request and the questions generated by the grammar. This step enables us to recognise a wide variety of formulations pertaining to the same question. In practice, we encode both the user's input and the generated questions as sentence embeddings and then compute their cosine similarity. If the similarity score between the user input and the most similar generated question exceeds an empirically established threshold, the module designates the latter as the representative of the user query. As this question was derived from a template, the system knows how to translate it into a query on the knowledge graph.

Finally, the Question Understanding module sends all pertinent information for the next phase to the Response Generator, including key terms, entities, entity types, and query types.

3.2   Response Generator

The Response Generator distinguishes two main cases. If the user request matched one of the generated queries, it produces the equivalent query, runs it over AIDA KG, and retrieves the relevant data. To produce a natural language response, the module employs a response template tailored to each specific query type. These templates are populated with relevant data and further refined through the adjustment of singular and plural terms, ensuring grammatical correctness and coherence in the answer.

When the user question fails to match one of the generated queries, the module handles the user's request as an 'open question'. In such cases, the module endeavours to generate a response by employing a question-answering model that operates on both the user request and the abstracts of relevant articles. To this end, it retrieves from AIDA KG the set of papers containing relevant key terms. If the query returns no paper, typically because the user request was out of scope, AIDA-Bot asks the user to reformulate or modify the request. Otherwise, the module selects the papers whose abstracts exhibit the highest similarity to the user query. This selection process utilises a transformer model designed for assessing sentence similarity. Subsequently, a summarisation model is applied to condense the abstracts into a more concise text. Finally, the module employs a question-answering model to generate a response to the user question based on the resulting information. The answer is further enhanced by providing a brief bibliography that lists the relevant articles. When feasible, the bibliography includes the Digital Object Identifiers (DOIs) and links to the open-access versions of the articles.

3.3   Transformer Models

AIDA-Bot 2.0 relies on transformer models for three main tasks: i) assessing the similarity between two texts, ii) summarising a text, and iii) question-answering.

The transformer model employed for measuring sentence similarity is the 'all-MiniLM-L6-v2', sourced from the Sentence-Transformers library[12]. This model was chosen due to its efficiency and compact size. Widely recognised as state-of-the-art technology, it is highly regarded for its effectiveness in addressing tasks pertaining to Semantic Textual Similarity [37]. To utilise this model, we leveraged the SentenceTransformers framework[13], which provides a convenient package for accessing BERT-based models and their variants, such as RoBERTa, MPNet, and ALBERT.

The question-answering and the summarisation models are 'distilbert-base-cased-distilled-squad'[14] and 'sshleifer/distilbart-cnn-12-6'[15] from Huggingface.

Their performances are comparable to those of BERT, but they use less computing power. The question-answering transformer, in particular, runs 60% quicker while retaining 95% of BERT's performance. It was developed by distilling the BERT base with 40% fewer parameters than the standard *textitbert-base-uncased*.

The summarisation model is based on DistilBART models, which are models created by removing the decoder layers from a Seq2Seq transformer and then producing high-quality student models through fine-tuning. We evaluated various BART models and observed that bart-large-cnn and distilbart-cnn-12-6 consistently generated superior summaries for our use cases. We adopted distilbart-cnn-12-6 since it is significantly lighter.

4   Evaluation

In this section, we present a systematic evaluation of the AIDA-Bot 2.0 against three alternative architectures (Sect. 4.1), which involved the participation of

---

[12] https://www.sbert.net/docs/pretrained_models.html.
[13] https://www.sbert.net/.
[14] https://huggingface.co/distilbert-base-cased-distilled-squad.
[15] https://huggingface.co/sshleifer/distilbart-cnn-12-6.

10 users. Furthermore, we present the findings of a user study conducted with five researchers in Computer Science (Sect. 4.2). The data produced during the evaluation and the user study are available online[16].

4.1 Comparative Evaluation

As previously discussed, AIDA-Bot 2.0 incorporates three main key enhancements over AIDA-Bot: i) the grammar-based method for detecting query types, ii) the ability to support queries with up to three filters, and iii) the capability to answer open queries by summarising relevant articles. To validate the efficacy of these improvements, we conducted a formal evaluation that compared AIDA-Bot 2.0, as described in Sect. 3, with three baselines:

- **AB** (AIDA-Bot, version 1.0) as originally presented at ISWC 2021 [21] and described in the subsequent journal paper [22]. This version adopts a simple token-aware approach to match user input with query types;
- **AB-G** (AIDA-Bot 1.0 with the grammar-based approach), a more advanced version of AB that employs the novel grammar-based approach;
- **AB-GF** (AIDA-Bot 1.0 with the grammar-based approach and filters), a further extension that also supports complex queries incorporating up to three filters.

To compare these four approaches, we organised individual sessions with ten researchers in Computer Science with an average of 12 years of academic experience. We instructed each researcher to generate 15 questions covering the five query types supported by our system: count, list, describe, compare, and open. Regarding the open-ended question, the researchers were requested to formulate queries that could realistically be covered in research articles. For each query, we listed the answers produced by the four chatbots in random order. The researchers were asked to rate their satisfaction with the responses on a Likert Scale ranging from 1 (very dissatisfied) to 5 (very satisfied).

Table 1. Average score of the four chatbots per query type. In bold, the best results.

Chatbot	Count	List	Describe	Compare	Open	Average
AB	2.33	1.37	1.62	2.60	1.00	1.79
AB-G	3.48	3.49	4.05	3.13	1.20	3.07
AB-GF	4.11	3.91	4.05	3.13	1.20	3.28
AIDA-Bot 2.0	**4.15**	**4.04**	**4.81**	**3.20**	**4.30**	**4.10**

Table 1 reports the average scores obtained by the four chatbots across the query types. The findings indicate that the implementation of the three new

---

[16] AIDA-Bot 2.0 evaluation data - https://w3id.org/aida/downloads#evaluation.

features has a favourable impact on the overall mean rating, which increases from 1.79 to 4.10. Furthermore, the average rating for each query type shows a steady increase when the new methods are integrated. Notably, users exhibited the highest level of satisfaction with 'describe' type queries, commonly utilized for zooming on researchers or topics, and 'open' type queries, indicating AIDA-Bot 2.0's substantial proficiency in handling non-predefined queries.

4.2   User Study

We performed a user study involving five computer scientists in order to assess the usability of the system and collect additional feedback. The users were selected among researchers in Computer Science at the University of Cagliari (IT), Gesis - Leibniz Institute for Social Science (DE), and The Open University (UK). Their areas of expertise include Artificial Intelligence, Natural Language Processing, Semantic Web, Complex Networks, Data Science, and Big Data.

We began each session with a 15-minute presentation of AIDA-Bot 2.0 and its capabilities. Then, we instructed the users to engage in an interactive session of about 45 min.

We asked them to complete a two-part survey describing their overall experience. The first section uses the standard *System Usability Scale* (SUS) questionnaire to assess the usability of AIDA-Bot 2.0. The second section includes five open questions regarding the strengths, weaknesses, and general feedback about AIDA-Bot 2.0. In what follows, we describe the outcome of these surveys.

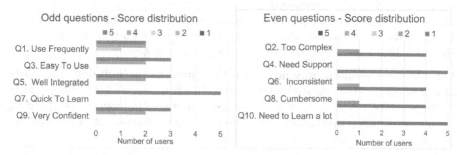

(a) Odd questions. The higher the score, the better the system.

(b) Even questions. The lower the score, the better the system.

Fig. 1. SUS Questionnaire results.

SUS Questionnaire. The SUS questionnaire[17] provided excellent results, scoring 93.5/100, which is equivalent to an A grade, placing the AIDA-Bot 2.0 in the 95 percentile rank[18].

---

[17] SUS   Questionnaire   Questions: https://www.usability.gov/how-to-and-tools/methods/system-usability-scale.html.

[18] Interpreting a SUS score - https://measuringu.com/interpret-sus-score/.

Figures 1a and 1b show the score distribution of the users. Specifically, Fig. 1a focuses on the odd questions (the positive ones, which should obtain a high score), while Fig. 1b reports on the even ones (the negative ones, which should obtain a low score). According to the users' feedback, the AIDA-Bot 2.0 was found to be easy to use (with an average rating of 4.6 ± 0.5[19]) and its features were well-integrated (4.6 ± 0.5). They stated that it was not complex to use (1.2 ± 0.4) and that they would not require any assistance to use it in the future (1.0 ± 0.0). Additionally, the SUS results indicated that most users felt highly confident while using our system (4.6 ± 0.5) and would be willing to use it frequently (4.2 ± 0.8).

Open Questions. In this section, we summarise the answers to the open questions.

Q1. What are the main strengths of AIDA-Bot 2.0? Three users stated that the main strength is the simplicity of the system in quickly providing all the information needed. One user considered the main strength the possibility to retrieve and explore scholarly information without having to search internal databases or the Web. The last user identified the primary strength of AIDA-Bot 2.0 as its capability to compare entities according to predefined metrics.

Q2. What are the main weaknesses of AIDA-Bot 2.0? The main weakness pointed out by most evaluators is the response time, as the current prototype can take several seconds to produce an answer. Two users expressed reservations about the quality of the open-ended responses, noting occasional instances where the formulation appeared peculiar. This issue can be attributed in part to the heightened expectations of users in light of the recent release of advanced GPT models, which have raised the bar for text generation quality.

Q3. Can you think of any additional features to be included in AIDA-Bot 2.0? The users suggested several interesting features, such as i) the possibility to generate a bibliography based on user inputs, ii) improving the approach for answering open questions by including GPT-like models, and iii) the ability to remember what the user said earlier in the conversation.

Q4. Can you think of any additional types of queries for AIDA-Bot 2.0? The users put forward several suggestions to enhance the system's functionality. First, they suggested the possibility to answer arbitrary questions about the content of a specific paper. They also recommended augmenting the system's ability to compare entities by allowing the definition of arbitrary metrics for comparison. Finally, they suggested incorporating a feature that enables the identification of articles referencing particular analysis techniques, algorithms, or datasets.

Q5. What would you add to increase the accuracy/comprehensiveness of the information returned by AIDA-Bot 2.0? Two users proposed

---

[19] With the notation $X \pm Y$, we specify that X is the average score and Y the standard deviation.

enhancing the entity detection methodology by incorporating the complete conversational context, encompassing previous messages as well as a user model. One user recommended utilizing the full text of research papers instead of just abstracts to improve the precision and comprehensiveness of the extracted information.

In summary, the user study demonstrated that AIDA-Bot 2.0 is highly usable and perceived as a valuable tool for providing accurate information about the research landscape. However, the emergence of modern GPT models has raised user expectations regarding the utilization of contextual information to comprehensively comprehend queries and generate highly coherent open-domain responses in real time. Although AIDA-Bot 2.0 is designed specifically for answering questions about the research landscape, it may be beneficial to integrate some of these new solutions. The primary challenge going forward is to do so without compromising the accuracy of the resulting analytics or deviating from the verifiable information in the knowledge graph.

5   Uptake and Impact

Since 2014, the collaboration between The Open University and SN has produced a wide range of tools based on AI and semantic technologies that have had a transformative effect on SN workflow, reducing the cost, improving the quality of the metadata, and supporting decision-making. These include intelligent services for automatically classifying articles [43] and proceeding books [41], recommending publications [48], evolving domain ontologies [30], and predicting the emergence of research topics [42].

In 2020, we generated AIDA KG by integrating multiple data sources in order to offer a very granular representation of research articles in terms of both research topics and the industrial sectors. The AIDA Dashboard, a web application to assess and compare journals and conferences, was the first tool to take advantage of this new resource [2].

In 2021, we released the first prototype of AIDA-Bot with the aim of allowing editors, analysts, and ultimately researchers to formulate complex natural language queries over AIDA KG. In 2023, we released AIDA-Bot 2.0, which marked a significant advancement over its predecessor, mainly due to its enhanced capacity to process complex queries and deliver responses to open-ended inquiries using information from the scientific literature. AIDA-Bot 2.0 was designed to cater to a range of specific use cases. Specifically, editors need to identify, assess, and compare the key researchers, organizations, venues, and trends within a certain field in order to evaluate the scope of the SN catalogue and initiate new editorial endeavours. The resulting information needs to be reliable but also verifiable, in order to be included in relevant reports. This process typically requires time-consuming analyses conducted by senior professionals in tandem with data analysts who must repeatedly procure accurate data from databases, resulting in delays and substantial expenses. A task such as identifying the key researchers at the intersection of deep learning and human-computer interaction would then take several days. AIDA-Bot 2.0 overcomes this bottleneck by allowing users to directly formulate natural language queries and receive real-time verifiable answers that refer to the internal KG or specific research articles.

The adoption of these solutions within SN is a testament to the advantages of incorporating knowledge graph technologies in this domain, yielding notable improvements in several key aspects and providing numerous benefits to the organization. Specifically, our technology has considerably reduced the amount of time required for performing complex analyses, leading to enhanced operational efficiency and reduced costs. Moreover, it has contributed to a reduction in the number of personnel involved in the analysis process. This, in turn, has freed up the time of analysts, enabling them to focus on other critical tasks. Finally, our system's ability to efficiently assess pertinent information has greatly enhanced the reliability and accuracy of the analyses, positively impacting the velocity and quality of the decision-making process.

6   Continuous Development Plan

We aim to keep developing and expanding AIDA-Bot 2.0 in the following years and we have several exciting developments in the works.

One of the key objectives is to integrate AIDA-Bot 2.0 with other tools at SN to provide a seamless and more comprehensive data exploration experience. For instance, AIDA-Bot 2.0 will be fully integrated into the AIDA Dashboard [2], which currently allows editors to explore and compare research venues. The main objective is to foster more contextual and refined data explorations by allowing users to ask additional questions to expand or clarify the analytics. For example, when visualising the list of researchers active in a conference, the user will be able to ask the system to describe a researcher in detail or report their paper in a specific field.

Similarly, we are also planning to integrate the AIDA-Bot 2.0 with other internal dashboards, such SN Insights[20], a tool for exploring and aggregating their own published content. We aim to assist the editor by allowing them to formulate more specific questions on SN Insight's large set of analytics.

To further improve AIDA-Bot 2.0's functionalities, we are exploring the use of GPT 4.0 APIs to replace the local question-answering model. We are also investigating the possibility of developing an internal model based on LLaMA [49] or similar solutions. These deployments will allow for even more accurate and effective information retrieval while reducing response time. We also plan to switch the NER pipeline to a more robust transformer-based model, in order to solve occasional inaccuracies.

Finally, a substantial avenue for large-scale deployment is expanding AIDA-Bot 2.0 toward other disciplines. This is especially important given that research endeavours are becoming increasingly multidisciplinary, and the most compelling insights and potential for new editorial initiatives are often found at the intersections of two or more fields. In light of this, we are presently engaged in efforts

---

[20] SN Insights - https://sn-insights.dimensions.ai/.

to integrate Engineering, Material Science, and Biomedical Science, which are other fields with a high presence of conference proceedings.

7 Related Work

Chatbots are often classified into two main classes, based on their objectives: task-oriented [36] and non-task-oriented [11]. Task-oriented chatbots are made to perform certain tasks, such as booking a hotel room, airfare, or other travel-related accommodations, putting an order for goods, planning events, or helping users find information [19]. Despite their limited scope, they are designed to help users accomplish a certain task within a specific scope. On the other hand, non-task-oriented chatbots operate in the open domain and aim to emulate the characteristics of human-human unstructured dialogue [38].

Additionally, chatbots can be categorized according to their engine (AI-based vs. rule-based). Rule-based chatbots employ a structured flow, reminiscent of a tree structure, to address user queries and provide appropriate responses [46]. This flow-based approach involves organizing a set of predefined rules or decision nodes that guide the chatbot's conversational path. They typically lead the user with more inquiries in order to eventually get the proper response. Conversely, AI-based chatbots seek to deduce the user's intent directly from the input text by employing artificial intelligence (AI) and natural language processing techniques [23].

Chatbots are often designed to focus on specific domains, such as i) education [28], ii) business [7], and iii) healthcare [18]. In the education domain, chatbots help teachers in a variety of disciplines, such as English [45], Medicine [8], and Business [39]. Other chatbots are capable of responding to questions concerning institutions that are typically covered in FAQs [35]. The reader is directed to [28] for a survey of articles on the use of chatbots in education. In the business domain, several chatbots assist enterprises with routine tasks [7]. For example, chatbots were developed to support commercial customer service and e-commerce [12]. In the health domain, chatbots often focus on specific health-related questions in domains such as mental health [27] and child health [50]. For instance, Divya et al. [14] developed a medical chatbot that allows users to self-diagnose illnesses and get comprehensive descriptions of the problems. Two more healthcare chatbots are Mandy [26] and MedChatbot [8]. The former is used by healthcare practitioners to automate patient intake. The latter supports medical students financially. Some chatbots also collect information on users' eating habits or provide businesses with a way to access allergy data based on the users' allergies [17].

Recent years have seen the emergence of a number of conversational agents and question-answering systems based on knowledge graphs and semantic web technologies [1,5,16,31,47]. These systems are capable to run complex queries on heterogeneous data from a variety of sources [15], including big general knowledge bases like Wikidata [24] and DBpedia [5], yielding a competitive advantage. Furthermore, it is possible to continuously update and improve these knowledge graphs by applying a variety of techniques for link prediction [25,40] and information integration [13,32]. As a result, a number of well-known conversational agents now utilise extensive knowledge graphs such as the Google Knowledge Graph [9] and the Alexa Knowledge Graph [51].

Recently, the focus shifted to the creation of sophisticated conversational agents that took advantage of transformers. GPT-2 (Generative Pre-trained Transformer) [34], GPT-3 [10], and the recent GPT-4 [29] are three examples in this field. GPT-3 was released in 2020 and became one of the largest language models to date, with 175 billion parameters. It was trained on a large corpus of 45 terabytes of text data from the internet, including books, articles, and websites, and can perform a wide range of natural language tasks, such as language translation, summarisation, and question-answering. GPT-4, is the next iteration of the GPT that is used in ChatGPT, but the exact details of its architecture and training data have not been disclosed. For a more thorough summary of relevant literature, we refer to Mariani et al. [20].

In the last few months, GPT models have been used to power several prototypical chatbots targeted at the scholarly domain, such as Scite[21], Elicit[22], and CoreGPT[23]. These systems aim to assist users with a variety of tasks, such as identifying trends in the literature, choosing a venue for sharing their work, finding suitable collaborators, searching relevant articles, and more. However, it is not clear yet to what extent these new solutions can produce accurate answers about the academic landscape.

AIDA-Bot 2.0 adopts a hybrid architecture that combines easily extendable templates to translate user requests to queries over a knowledge graph and question-answering models for answering open questions with information from the literature. The main objective is to avoid hallucinations and provide verifiable and accurate information about the scholarly domain.

8   Conclusions

In this paper, we presented AIDA-Bot 2.0, a novel conversation agent designed to provide accurate and factual information about the research landscape, and discussed its role within Springer Nature workflow. AIDA-Bot 2.0 builds on top of the Academia/Industry Dynamics Knowledge Graph (AIDA KG), a large knowledge graph containing over 1.5B triples obtained by integrating data about 25M papers from OpenAlex, DBLP, DBpedia, ROR, CSO, and INDUSO. It offers two main capabilities: 1) the ability to identify a set of pre-determined question types and translate them to formal queries over the knowledge graph, and 2) the ability to answer open questions by summarising relevant information from articles. We conducted two evaluations that demonstrated the benefits of AIDA-Bot 2.0's new features and proved its excellent usability.

---

[21] Scite - https://scite.ai/.

[22] Elicit - https://elicit.org/.

[23] CoreGPT - https://tinyurl.com/mvrk2z4x.

In future work, we aim to incorporate the valuable user feedback received from the evaluations into the development of AIDA-Bot 2.0. Furthermore, we will explore the integration of other knowledge sources and research fields to improve the quality and coverage of the information provided. We also plan to produce a lightweight version that will be made freely available to the research community, similar to what we did for the AIDA Dashboard. Finally, we plan to further investigate how modern language models can be integrated with knowledge graphs in order to produce verifiable information in the scientific domain.

References

1. Expert System for Question Answering on Anomalous Events and Mitigation Strategies Using Bidirectional Transformers and Knowledge Graphs, Abu Dhabi International Petroleum Exhibition and Conference, vol. Day 3 Wed, 02 November 2022 (2022). https://doi.org/10.2118/211855-MS, d031S084R002
2. Angioni, S., Salatino, A., Osborne, F., Birukou, A., Recupero, D.R., Motta, E.: Leveraging knowledge graph technologies to assess journals and conferences at springer nature. In: Sattler, U., et al. (eds.) The Semantic Web - ISWC 2022. LNCS, pp. 735–752. Springer, Cham (2022). https://doi.org/10.1007/978-3-031-19433-7_42
3. Angioni, S., Salatino, A., Osborne, F., Recupero, D.R., Motta, E.: Aida: a knowledge graph about research dynamics in academia and industry. Quant. Sci. Stud. **2**(4), 1356–1398 (2021)
4. Angioni, S., Salatino, A.A., Osborne, F., Recupero, D.R., Motta, E.: Integrating knowledge graphs for analysing academia and industry dynamics. In: Bellatreche, L., et al. (eds.) TPDL/ADBIS -2020. CCIS, vol. 1260, pp. 219–225. Springer, Cham (2020). https://doi.org/10.1007/978-3-030-55814-7_18
5. Athreya, R.G., Ngonga Ngomo, A.C., Usbeck, R.: Enhancing community interactions with data-driven chatbots-the dbpedia chatbot. In: Companion Proceedings of the The Web Conference 2018, Lyon, France, pp. 143–146 (2018)
6. Auer, S., et al.: The SciQA scientific question answering benchmark for scholarly knowledge. Sci. Rep. **13**(1), 7240 (2023). https://doi.org/10.1038/s41598-023-33607-z
7. Bavaresco, R., et al.: Conversational agents in business: a systematic literature review and future research directions. Comput. Sci. Rev. **36**, 100239 (2020)
8. Bharti, U., Bajaj, D., Batra, H., Lalit, S., Lalit, S., Gangwani, A.: Medbot: conversational artificial intelligence powered chatbot for delivering tele-health after covid-19. In: 2020 5th International Conference on Communication and Electronics Systems (ICCES), Budva, Montenegro, pp. 870–875 (2020). https://doi.org/10.1109/ICCES48766.2020.9137944
9. Bollacker, K., Evans, C., Paritosh, P., Sturge, T., Taylor, J.: Freebase: a collaboratively created graph database for structuring human knowledge. In: Proceedings of the 2008 ACM SIGMOD International Conference on Management of Data, SIGMOD 2008, New York, NY, USA, pp. 1247–1250. Association for Computing Machinery (2008). https://doi.org/10.1145/1376616.1376746

10. Brown, T., et al.: Language models are few-shot learners. In: Larochelle, H., Ranzato, M., Hadsell, R., Balcan, M., Lin, H. (eds.) Advances in Neural Information Processing Systems, vol. 33, pp. 1877–1901. Curran Associates, Inc. (2020). https://proceedings.neurips.cc/paper_files/paper/2020/file/1457c0d6bfcb4967418bfb8ac142f64a-Paper.pdf

11. Chen, H., Liu, X., Yin, D., Tang, J.: A survey on dialogue systems: recent advances and new frontiers. SIGKDD Explor. Newsl. **19**(2), 25–35 (2017). https://doi.org/10.1145/3166054.3166058

12. Cui, L., Huang, S., Wei, F., Tan, C., Duan, C., Zhou, M.: SuperAgent: a customer service chatbot for E-commerce websites. In: Proceedings of ACL 2017, System Demonstrations, Vancouver, Canada, pp. 97–102. Association for Computational Linguistics (2017). https://aclanthology.org/P17-4017

13. Dessí, D., Osborne, F., Recupero, D.R., Buscaldi, D., Motta, E.: Scicero: a deep learning and NLP approach for generating scientific knowledge graphs in the computer science domain. Knowl.-Based Syst. **258**, 109945 (2022)

14. Divya, S., Indumathi, V., Ishwarya, S., Priyasankari, M., Devi, S.K.: A self-diagnosis medical chatbot using artificial intelligence. J. Web Dev. Web Des. **3**(1), 1–7 (2018)

15. Fensel, D., et al.: Knowledge graphs methodology, tools and selected use cases (2020). https://lib.ugent.be/catalog/ebk01:4100000010122122

16. Höffner, K., Walter, S., Marx, E., Usbeck, R., Lehmann, J., Ngonga Ngomo, A.C.: Survey on challenges of question answering in the semantic web. Semantic Web **8**(6), 895–920 (2017)

17. Hsu, P., Zhao, J., Liao, K., Liu, T., Wang, C.: Allergybot: a chatbot technology intervention for young adults with food allergies dining out. In: Proceedings of the 2017 CHI Conference Extended Abstracts on Human Factors in Computing Systems, Denver, Colorado, pp. 74–79 (2017)

18. Laranjo, L., et al.: Conversational agents in healthcare: a systematic review. J. Am. Med. Inform. Assoc. **25**(9), 1248–1258 (2018)

19. Li, L., Lee, K.Y., Emokpae, E., Yang, S.B.: What makes you continuously use chatbot services? evidence from Chinese online travel agencies. Electron. Mark. (2021). https://doi.org/10.1007/s12525-020-00454-z

20. Mariani, M.M., Hashemi, N., Wirtz, J.: Artificial intelligence empowered conversational agents: a systematic literature review and research agenda. J. Bus. Res. **161**, 113838 (2023). https://doi.org/10.1016/j.jbusres.2023.113838

21. Meloni, A., Angioni, S., Salatino, A., Osborne, F., Reforgiato Recupero, D.: Aidabot: a conversational agent to explore scholarly knowledge graphs. CEUR-WS (2021). https://ceur-ws.org/Vol-2980/paper310.pdf

22. Meloni, A., Angioni, S., Salatino, A.A., Osborne, F., Recupero, D.R., Motta, E.: Integrating conversational agents and knowledge graphs within the scholarly domain. IEEE Access **11**, 22468–22489 (2023). https://doi.org/10.1109/ACCESS.2023.3253388

23. Mohan, S., Chowdhary, C.: An AI-based chatbot using deep learning. In: Intelligent Systems: Advances in Biometric Systems, Soft Computing, Image Processing, and Data Analytics, chap. 12, London, UK, pp. 231–242. Apple Academic Press (2019). https://doi.org/10.1201/9780429265020-12

24. Mora-Cantallops, M., Sánchez-Alonso, S., García-Barriocanal, E.: A systematic literature review on wikidata. Data Technologies and Applications (2019)

25. Nayyeri, M., et al.: Trans4e: link prediction on scholarly knowledge graphs. Neurocomputing **461**, 530–542 (2021)

26. Ni, L., Lu, C., Liu, N., Liu, J.: MANDY: towards a smart primary care chatbot application. In: Chen, J., Theeramunkong, T., Supnithi, T., Tang, X. (eds.) KSS 2017. CCIS, vol. 780, pp. 38–52. Springer, Singapore (2017). https://doi.org/10.1007/978-981-10-6989-5_4

27. Oh, K.J., Lee, D., Ko, B., Choi, H.J.: A chatbot for psychiatric counseling in mental healthcare service based on emotional dialogue analysis and sentence generation. In: 2017 18th IEEE International Conference on Mobile Data Management (MDM), KAIST, Daejeon, pp. 371–375. IEEE (2017)

28. Okonkwo, C.W., Ade-Ibijola, A.: Chatbots applications in education: a systematic review. Comput. Educ. Artif. Intell. **2**, 100033 (2021). https://doi.org/10.1016/j.caeai.2021.100033

29. OpenAI: Gpt-4 technical report (2023)

30. Osborne, F., Motta, E.: Pragmatic ontology evolution: reconciling user requirements and application performance. In: Vrandečić, D., et al. (eds.) ISWC 2018. LNCS, vol. 11136, pp. 495–512. Springer, Cham (2018). https://doi.org/10.1007/978-3-030-00671-6_29

31. Pang, R.Y., et al.: QuALITY: question answering with long input texts, yes! In: Proceedings of the 2022 Conference of the North American Chapter of the Association for Computational Linguistics: Human Language Technologies, Seattle, United States, pp. 5336–5358. Association for Computational Linguistics (2022). https://doi.org/10.18653/v1/2022.naacl-main.391, https://aclanthology.org/2022.naacl-main.391

32. Paulheim, H.: Knowledge graph refinement: a survey of approaches and evaluation methods. Semantic web **8**(3), 489–508 (2017)

33. Peng, C., Xia, F., Naseriparsa, M., Osborne, F.: Knowledge graphs: opportunities and challenges. Artif. Intell. Rev. **56**, 1–32 (2023)

34. Radford, A., Wu, J., Child, R., Luan, D., Amodei, D., Sutskever, I.: Language models are unsupervised multitask learners (2019)

35. Ranoliya, B.R., Raghuwanshi, N., Singh, S.: Chatbot for university related FAQs. In: 2017 International Conference on Advances in Computing. Communications and Informatics (ICACCI), Manipal, India, pp. 1525–1530. IEEE (2017)

36. Rastogi, A., Zang, X., Sunkara, S., Gupta, R., Khaitan, P.: Towards scalable multi-domain conversational agents: the schema-guided dialogue dataset. In: Proceedings of the AAAI Conference on Artificial Intelligence, New York, USA, vol. 34, pp. 8689–8696 (2020)

37. Reimers, N., Gurevych, I.: Sentence-Bert: sentence embeddings using SIAMESE Bert-networks. In: Proceedings of the 2019 Conference on Empirical Methods in Natural Language Processing. Association for Computational Linguistics (2019). https://arxiv.org/abs/1908.10084

38. Roller, S., et al.: Recipes for building an open-domain chatbot. In: EACL. Online (2021)

39. Rooein, D., Bianchini, D., Leotta, F., Mecella, M., Paolini, P., Pernici, B.: achatwf: generating conversational agents for teaching business process models. Softw. Syst. Model. (2021). https://doi.org/10.1007/s10270-021-00925-7

40. Rossi, A., Barbosa, D., Firmani, D., Matinata, A., Merialdo, P.: Knowledge graph embedding for link prediction: a comparative analysis. ACM Trans. Knowl. Disc. Data (TKDD) **15**(2), 1–49 (2021)

41. Salatino, A.A., Osborne, F., Birukou, A., Motta, E.: Improving editorial workflow and metadata quality at springer nature. In: Ghidini, C., et al. (eds.) ISWC 2019. LNCS, vol. 11779, pp. 507–525. Springer, Cham (2019). https://doi.org/10.1007/978-3-030-30796-7_31

42. Salatino, A.A., Osborne, F., Motta, E.: Augur: Forecasting the emergence of new research topics. In: Proceedings of the 18th ACM/IEEE on Joint Conference on Digital Libraries. JCDL 2018, pp. 303–312, New York, NY, USA. ACM (2018). https://doi.org/10.1145/3197026.3197052

43. Salatino, A.A., Osborne, F., Thanapalasingam, T., Motta, E.: The CSO classifier: ontology-driven detection of research topics in scholarly articles. In: Doucet, A., Isaac, A., Golub, K., Aalberg, T., Jatowt, A. (eds.) TPDL 2019. LNCS, vol. 11799, pp. 296–311. Springer, Cham (2019). https://doi.org/10.1007/978-3-030-30760-8_26

44. Salatino, A.A., Thanapalasingam, T., Mannocci, A., Osborne, F., Motta, E.: The computer science ontology: a large-scale taxonomy of research areas. In: Vrandečić, D., et al. (eds.) ISWC 2018. LNCS, vol. 11137, pp. 187–205. Springer, Cham (2018). https://doi.org/10.1007/978-3-030-00668-6_12

45. Sarosa, M., Kusumawardani, M., Suyono, A., Wijaya, M.H.: Developing a social media-based chatbot for English learning. IOP Conf. Ser. Materials Sci. Eng. **732**(1), 012074 (2020). https://doi.org/10.1088/1757-899x/732/1/012074

46. Singh, J., Joesph, M.H., Jabbar, K.B.A.: Rule-based chabot for student enquiries. J. Phys. Conf. Ser. **1228**(1), 012060 (2019). https://doi.org/10.1088/1742-6596/1228/1/012060

47. Stasaski, K., Hearst, M.: Semantic diversity in dialogue with natural language inference. In: Proceedings of the 2022 Conference of the North American Chapter of the Association for Computational Linguistics: Human Language Technologies, United States, pp. 85–98. Association for Computational Linguistics, Seattle (2022). https://doi.org/10.18653/v1/2022.naacl-main.6 , https://aclanthology.org/2022.naacl-main.6

48. Thanapalasingam, T., Osborne, F., Birukou, A., Motta, E.: Ontology-based recommendation of editorial products. In: Vrandečić, D., et al. (eds.) ISWC 2018. LNCS, vol. 11137, pp. 341–358. Springer, Cham (2018). https://doi.org/10.1007/978-3-030-00668-6_21

49. Touvron, H., et al.: Llama: open and efficient foundation language models. arXiv preprint arXiv:2302.13971 (2023)

50. Vaira, L., Bochicchio, M.A., Conte, M., Casaluci, F.M., Melpignano, A.: Mamabot: a system based on ml and NLP for supporting women and families during pregnancy. In: Proceedings of the 22nd International Database Engineering & Applications Symposium, Villa San Giovanni, Italy, pp. 273–277 (2018)

51. Zhu, Q., et al.: Collective knowledge graph multi-type entity alignment. In: The Web Conference 2020 (2020). https://www.amazon.science/publications/collective-knowledge-graph-multi-type-entity-alignment

The Wikibase Approach to the Enslaved.Org Hub Knowledge Graph

Cogan Shimizu[1]([✉]), Pascal Hitzler[2], Seila Gonzalez-Estrecha[3],
Jeff Goeke-Smith[3], Dean Rehberger[3], Catherine Foley[3], and Alicia Sheill[3]

[1] Wright State University, Dayton, Ohio, USA
cogan.shimizu@wright.edu
[2] Kansas State University, Manhattan, USA
[3] Michigan State University, East Lansing, USA

Abstract. Many methodologies and platforms for creating, deploying, and defining the manner of knowledge graphs are available. For this paper, we single out the platform, Wikibase. Using Wikibase comes with many advantages: out-of-the-box software for de-referencing, a convenient user interface, a consistent way to track and record provenance and lineage, and the ability to execute SPARQL queries against an RDF representation of the knowledge graph. However, the provenance mechanism and the exact nature of the structure of the Wikibase representation can complicate developing a principled schema for knowledge graphs, as well as the approach to the materialization of the data for upload to the platform. In this paper, we detail the methodology used to design, implement, and deploy the Enslaved.Org Hub, a nationally recognized knowledge graph for documenting the peoples of the historical slave trade.

1 Introduction

There are many methodologies and platforms for creating, deploying, and defining the manner of knowledge graphs now available, which emphasize different characteristics or use-cases for a particular knowledge graph (KG). Of particular interest, are *community-driven knowledge graphs* (CKGs). That is, a KG that accepts community data from community sources (i.e., data that comes from outside the original development team) and, in general, have a focus on modeling and presenting provenance and lineage of the constituent data. With the growth of the use of KGs, some communities and larger constituencies are being left behind because many of the human-machine interfaces for KGs require more advance technical skills. To address this, the platform, Wikibase, can be deployed to mitigate issues of access for less technically practiced community members.

Using the Wikibase platform has many advantages: an out of the box software for de-referencing, a convenient user interface for the less technically practiced, a consistent way to track and record provenance and lineage of data, and the option

T. R. Payne et al. (Eds.): ISWC 2023, LNCS 14266, pp. 419–434, 2023.
https://doi.org/10.1007/978-3-031-47243-5_23

to execute SPARQL queries against an RDF representation of the knowledge graph. However, the provenance mechanism and the exact nature of the structure of the Wikibase representation can complicate developing a principled schema for knowledge graphs, as well as the approach to the materialization of the data for upload to the platform.

Indeed, other institutions, such as the European Union (EU), have also come to the conclusion that utilizing Wikibase can serve as the foundation for a community-driven knowledge graph. For instance, the EU Knowledge Graph[1] [6] is deployed on a Wikibase installation, as is the Disability Wiki that serves as an metadata knowledge graph for community documents [3]. There is also growing interest in a methodology (e.g., [1]) for deploying to Wikibase, but the process is, as of yet, nascent. Furthermore, the Wikibase platform does offer up data modeling problems for the accurate deployment of ontologies, which still need to be addressed.

This paper reports on the lessons learned using Wikibase while developing the Enslaved.Org Hub,[2] which is a very visible[3] community-driven knowledge graph for documenting the stories of peoples of the historical slave trade, with a focus on North America and the Caribbean [8,9].

Concretely, this paper describes the overall approach that was taken for developing and deploying a CKG to Wikibase, using the Enslaved.Org Hub knowledge graph as a case study. The purpose of this paper is to (a) report on the approach taken for the Enslaved.Org Hub knowledge graph design and deployment and (b) demonstrate how traditional ontology engineering can be applied to deploying to the Wikibase platform. Our approach consists of three top-level steps, as follows. We provide a finer grained detailing of the steps in Sect. 3.

1. **Develop the schema:** details how the Modular Ontology Modeling (MOMo) [13] methodology can be used to create a reusable and extendable schema for a CKG that takes into account both learned lessons while developing the Enslaved.Org Hub, and reports on recent work that can improve the process.
2. **Populate the KG:** encapsulates exactly how raw data is translated into a format that can be ingested by the Wikibase platform, a process that includes the strategies taken for both de-duplication and validation of the data.
3. **Deploy the KG:** includes both the processes taken to make the data FAIR [15], and the documentation strategy.

In Sect. 2, we introduce the Enslaved.Org Hub mission and motivate the use of both Wikibase and a knowledge graph for tackling the described obstacles. In Sect. 3, we provide additional detail regarding each of the sub-steps which compose the overall approach. Finally, in Sect. 4, we conclude with future work.

---

[1] https://linkedopendata.eu/wiki/The_EU_Knowledge_Graph.

[2] https://enslaved.org/.

[3] It made U.S. national news upon launch, e.g. [9].

2   Case Study: The Enslaved.Org Hub

The scourge of African enslavement was fundamental to the making of Europe, Africa, the Americas, and Middle East and parts of the Asian subcontinent. The enduring legacies of black bondage shape the moral questions of humanity in our times. We have seen in the past decade a growth in interest in the subject in film, on television, and in historical fiction. Historians have spilled much ink writing monographs aimed primarily at other scholars. At the same time, however, it is a worthy goal to expand the production of scholarly output and to bring what historians do to the general public.

Recently, there has been a significant shift in perceptions about what we can know about Enslaved Africans, their descendants, and those who asserted ownership over them throughout the world. As a result, a growing number of collections of scanned original manuscript documents, digitized material culture, and databases, that organize and make sense of records of enslavement, are free and readily accessible for scholarly and public consumption. Although this data is available through individual data silos, this proliferation of different projects and databases presents scholars, students, and the interested public with a number of challenges:

- Most of these databases focus on the individuals of the slave trade, but data is often limited to the focus of the project. Further, the task of disambiguating (or merging) individuals across multiple datasets is nearly impossible given the current, silo-ed nature of all databases about slavery and the enslaved;
- There is no central, universally recognized clearinghouse for slave data. As such, it is difficult to find projects and databases;
- Individual projects and databases are isolated, preventing federated and cross project searching, browsing, and quantitative analysis;
- There are no best practices for digital data creation collectively agreed upon by the scholarly community;
- Important data is often lost or remain locked away in scholars' files, completely inaccessible to other scholars, students, descent communities, and the general public;
- Project participants rarely get scholarly credit for the work that goes into creating and releasing digital data;
- and Humanists have little incentive to deposit datasets.

To address these challenges, the Enslaved.Org project, has pioneered a new model for humanities scholarship. Enslaved.Org brings together programmers, project managers, archivists, librarians, and historians in a collective endeavor and, over the years, with an expanding consortium of contributors. This collaborative approach challenges humanists to broaden their thinking about the production of knowledge; the sharing, as opposed to guarding, of research materials; and the benefits of collaboration. In sum, the model of Enslaved.Org disrupts conventions of humanities scholarship in much the way it attempts to disrupt – for the better – historical perspectives on slavery and the individual lives of those enslaved.

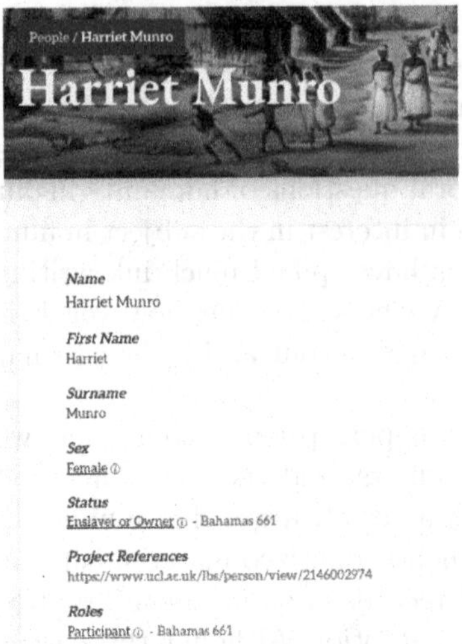

People / Harriet Munro

Harriet Munro

Name
Harriet Munro

First Name
Harriet

Surname
Munro

Sex
Female ①

Status
Enslaver or Owner ① - Bahamas 661

Project References
https://www.ucl.ac.uk/lbs/person/view/2146002974

Roles
Participant ① - Bahamas 661

(a) This view shows a *knowledge box*, which provides a friendly user interface for displaying the data about a particular entity (Harriet Munro) from the Enslaved.Org Hub knowledge graph.

James Connelly (Q1087828)

LVA-PER-ENS.1186850._0007_0005_0001-0010.JamesConnelly.24257
LVA-PER-ENS.1186850._0007_0005_0001-0010.JamesConnelly.24257

▼ In more languages
Configure

Language	Label	Description	Also known as
English	James Connelly	LVA-PER-ENS.1186850._0007_0005_0001-0010.JamesConnelly.24257	LVA-PER-ENS.1186850._...

Statements

instance of	⋮ Person		
	▸ 0 references		

hasName	⋮ James Connelly		
	recordedAt	Registration of James Connelly	
	▸ 1 reference		

(b) This view shows the standard Wikibase view of the data about an entity (James Connelly), which provides a more granular detail (including provenance and lineage) for each assertion at a slight cost to readability and usability.

Fig. 1. Snapshots of the user interfaces for the Enslaved.Org Hub knowledge graph.

The technical goal of Enslaved.Org established the Enslaved.Org Hub,[4] a website that provides one-stop querying and inspection capabilities for integrated historic data on the slave trade, originating from a diverse set of data sources and contributors, thereby allowing students, researchers and the general public to search over numerous databases to understand and reconstruct the lives of individuals who were part of the historical slave trade (see Fig. 1 for screenshots of interfaces provided by the Hub). To address the underlying data integration issues, Enslaved.Org opted to follow the state of the art by establishing a knowledge graph, expressed in RDF, with an underlying schema in form of an OWL ontology, called the Enslaved.Org Ontology; the modeling approach and its core concepts are detailed in [14].

The Enslaved.Org Ontology expresses metadata record types and core fields that the Enslaved.Org research team identified as frequently occurring in historic slave trade data projects. This paper focuses on conveying the development process used to make the raw data accessible on the Wikibase platform and navigable against a schema.

---

[4] http://enslaved.org/.

Availability

The Enslaved.Org Hub can be found and explored at https://enslaved.org/. Documentation for Enslaved.Org metadata, ontology, and controlled vocabularies is available at https://docs.enslaved.org/. The source code is available at https://github.com/matrix-msu/Enslaved-Hub, shared under the GPL 3.0.[5] The data itself is shared under the CC BY-NC-SA 4.0 license.[6]

Uptake and Usage

Enslaved.Org has had significant public uptake [9], as well as the voluntary submission of additional historical databases.[7] Additionally, in the last year, the platform has 3.5K unique monthly users and, over that time period, has had 334K page views over 53K visits. In the last six months, the dataset has been downloaded 54 times for large scale analytical purposes (by users outside of the team).

3   The Approach

This section comprises a total of seven sub-steps, aligned with the three steps of the approach, as depicted in Fig. 2 (middle and right): developing and transferring the schema (Sect. 3.1); materializing, validating, and resolving co-references in the knowledge graph (Sect. 3.2); and deploying the knowledge graph to the Wikibase platform (Sect. 3.3), as well as engaging bespoke interfaces for data discoverability, navigability, and visualization.

3.1   Developing the Schema

This top-level step in our approach comprises two distinct sub-steps: develop a schema for the use-case according to best practices and adjust the schema as necessary to fit to the semantics or technological idiosyncrasies of where the knowledge graph will be deployed.

---

[5] https://opensource.org/licenses/GPL-3.0/.

[6] https://creativecommons.org/licenses/by-nc-sa/4.0/.

[7] https://institute.enslaved.org/schedule/.

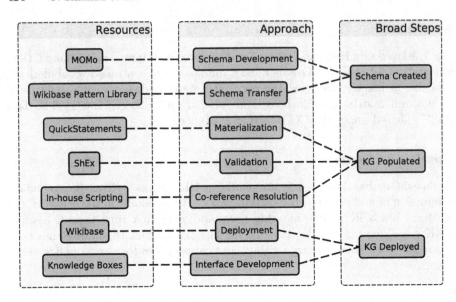

Fig. 2. This diagram displays the resources used (left) to implement our approach (middle) for creating and deploying the Enslaved.Org Hub knowledge graph. These steps are broadly categorized (right) for simplicity.

Schema Development with Best Practices The development of the Enslaved.Org Ontology – which serves as the schema for the Enslaved.Org Hub Knowledge Graph – was originally accomplished by executing the Modular Ontology Modeling (MOMo) methodology [13]. The steps of this nine-step process is shown in Fig. 3. MOMo was designed to create reusable and extendable schemas. These characteristics are driven by its modular nature, which in turn, leverage underlying best-practices encapsulated within re-used ontology design patterns. The process taken for developing the schema is in deeper detail described in [14], and it is essentially a further development of the eXtreme Design Methodology [4] emphasizing modularity, ontology design pattern *libraries*, use of certain types of schema diagrams, and a systematic approach to axiomatization in OWL.

For the context of our discussion herein, it is important to emphasize that MOMo has been designed to create ontologies capable of capturing complex relationships between ontology entities in a flexible manner akin to human expert conceptualizations, without overemphasizing formal logical aspects. One of the results of this is that MOMo often naturally leads to ontologies with plenty of reification (and sometimes even reification involving other reification). This would usually make a large ontology harder to understand, however in MOMo this is balanced out by the highly modular structure which, in a divide-and-conquer fashion, compartmentalizes the ontology into much easier to understand modules each of which focuses on a single key term that is part of the human expert's way of conceptualizing the application domain. Central and systematic

---

1. Identify and scope the use-case;
2. Identify key notions from the use-case and data sources;
3. Make or collect competency questions;
4. Match the key notions to patterns;
5. Instantiate the patterns into modules;
6. Systematically axiomatize the modules;
7. Assemble the modules and fill inter-module gaps, as necessary;
8. Review the final product for consistency; and
9. Produce the artifacts (e.g., documentation and serialization).

Fig. 3. This listing shows the nine steps that comprise the Modular Ontology Modeling (MOMo) [13] methodology.

use of simplified schema diagrams throughout the collaborative (with domain and data experts) development process furthermore provide a means to bridge (inter)disciplinary gaps without burdening domain experts with technical ontology engineering details.

Transferring the Schema. On the outset of the project, it was unknown exactly which platform would be used to deploy the knowledge graph. There were several options discussed, such as the use of a triplestore (e.g., Apache Jena Fuseki[8]), a property graph (e.g., Neo4j[9]), and Wikibase). It was our (naïve) thought that it would be relatively straightforward to map the ontology produced from following MOMo into a new version, as necessary, based on the future platform. That is, by possibly providing mappings between the patterns and modules that composed the resultant ontology to whichever new form was needed.

In the end, for the reasons stated above, Wikibase was chosen. This choice, while having many positives regarding its data management, transparency, and navigability support, was – unfortunately – not nearly as straightforward when mapping a traditionally designed ontology into the underlying Wikibase model [16]. As such, we point to two recent works [7,12] which report on improved processes for mapping traditional ontological formalisms into the Wikibase structure, where we seek to side-step the issue by providing ontological primitives (i.e., patterns) that are directly mappable into Wikibase, but still retaining their ability represent other common ontological formalisms that are present in other (non-Wikibase) ontologies and knowledge graph schemas.

---

[8] https://jena.apache.org/documentation/fuseki2/.
[9] https://neo4j.com/.

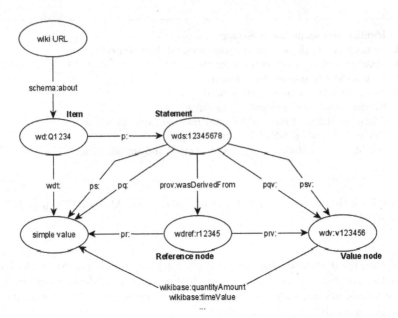

Fig. 4. This diagram shows the Wikibase RDF structure. Essentially all assertional triples are reified as "Statements," where all qualifications and provenance (references) on the assertion are linked as context to the Statement node. The different namespaces originate from Wikibase, and they are used to differentiate the role of a predicate in the reification process (i.e., turning a fact into a **Statement**) without necessitating changing the name of the predicate.

In particular, the Wikibase RDF structure is shown in Fig. 4. Essentially, Wikibase reifies all assertional triples into Statements, which can then have *qualifiers* and *references* attached to them, which provide contextual information about the statement. For example, a *qualifier* might be the temporal extent of the fact (i.e., when the statement was valid) and a *reference* might indicate from whence the data was derived (e.g., a publication). This sort of structure is easily modeled in labeled property graphs or the forthcoming RDF*, but is a bit less straightforward in traditional RDF graphs. Figure 5 shows how the patterns developed in [7,12] can still result in a coherent (graphical) depiction of the ontology or schema (see [12] for a detailed discussion).

By starting with these patterns (as laid out in detail in [12]), it is possible to develop a modular ontology in the spirit of the MOMo methodology, that is then seamlessly translateable into the Wikibase RDF structure. Thus, the next steps of the Wikibase process become streamlined, and some validation tasks become less onerous.

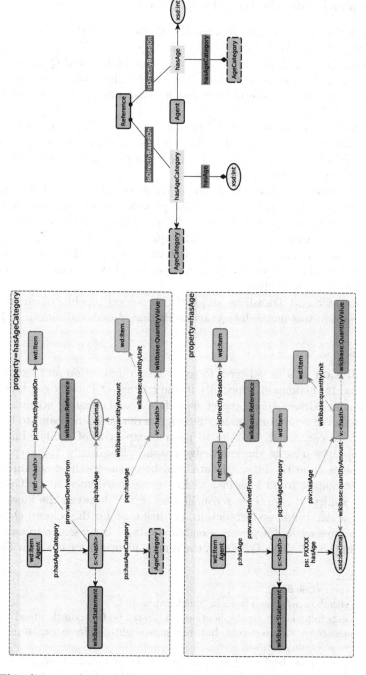

Fig. 5. This diagram shows three schema diagrams, which indicate how to model a record of a person's age according to the underlying Wikibase structure (on the left). The intent is to use only the right diagram, with the Wikibase model implicit. See [12] for elaborations.

3.2   Implementing the Knowledge Graph

In many ways, the materialization of the Enslaved.Org Hub knowledge graph is a classic Extract, Transform, Load (ETL) operation. Two pieces of software were primarily used to perform these steps: OpenRefine and QuickStatements. While we do not recommend the exclusive use of these two pieces of software, they do come with very useful functionality that aids in the development of a CKG.

OpenRefine[10] provides powerful mechanisms for cleaning up dirty or noisy data. It also provides analytical tools that can help understand the nature of ingested (or *refined*, even) data. This tool is the core piece of software for performing the Extract and Transform steps.

QuickStatements[11] is an open-source Wikibase software tool that performs ingest operations from a browser. It also provides an interface for editing the items that are to be ingested. To ingest into Wikibase, the data must be transformed into statements to be digested by QuickStatements. To this end, OpenRefine can output triples in the QuickStatements format. This tool is primarily used for the Load aspect of the ETL pipeline; it and extensions for usability, are discussed in the next section.

The Extract and Transform steps of the general pipeline occur over three discrete steps in this methodology: reconciliation,[12] materialization, and validation.

Reconciliation is a broad term for co-reference resolution and semantic harmonization. It is common, especially in the context of knowledge graphs which are community-driven (e.g., expect new data – and possibly schemas – to be contributed over time from outside the original development team) to hold some data fields as controlled, in order to prevent explosion of similar, but distinct terms from appearing in the knowledge graph.[13] Essentially, this step will take data elements from the ingested data, and based on specified column headers, attempt to map it to an identifier within a controlled vocabulary. OpenRefine offers the ability to connect a reconciliation service between the ingested data and a particular Wikibase installation. For instance, for the column *Occupation*, an occupation such as *Carpenter* is matched using a fuzzy search to an identifier of the form Q###. This Q### is the unique identifier for the item *Carpenter*

---

[10] https://openrefine.org/.

[11] https://github.com/magnusmanske/quickstatements.

[12] The terms reconciliation, de-duplication, and co-reference resolution tend to be used interchangeably within our field, but may have slightly different semantics in other disciplines (e.g., linguistics).

[13] This can, of course, backfire. For example, the oft-used example of *partOf* in Wikidata is extremely overloaded having many "flavors" of usage. However, the use of controlled vocabularies as a type can be used to neatly cluster terms to make querying easier (e.g., Carpenter and Woodworker can both be easily found with the same query).

in the connected Wikibase installation, and it will carry all the content associated with the term.

Materialization is the formulation of triples (i.e., text of the form *subject predicate object*, where each element of the triple is a URI). After all the vocabularies are reconciled, the schema of the data model can be uploaded using OpenRefine's Wikibase extension.[14] Within the context of OpenRefine, the schema is a list of edits that a prospective user would take to add the entry manually. As a result, this is merely a mapping of tabular data to Wikibase fields. The exact steps to fill out this form would be directly informed by the schema, as developed in Sect. 3.1. The process of transforming ontological axioms into Wikibase structures is an open question. This is partially informed by [7,12], but a principled approach has not yet been developed. For the Enslaved.Org Hub, the process was done manually by experts with an intuition for the state of the data (rather than the optimistic view an ontology would take). After the materialization process has completed, the extension provides the option to download all the statements.

Validation is a straightforward check that the data has been materialized correctly, as well as checking for holes or gaps in the data. The recommended method for doing so is via *data shapes*.[15] The W3C recommends the use of SHACL [11], but this is not required. For example, against the Enslaved.Org Ontology using ShEx [2],the Enslaved.Org Project formulated four shape expressions (one for people, one for events, one for places, and one for sources). The validation itself was accomplished via the JavaScript ShEx library.[16]

To accelerate the process, validation should be part of a CI/CD (continuous integration/continuous development) pipeline. Based on the size of the KG, ample time should be budgeted for this iterative step. Neither SHACL (via e.g., pySHACL[17] nor ShEx run quickly. Validating the Enslaved.Org KG required an overnight execution. Fixes, unfortunately, require manual intervention; and thus QuickStatements (described further in the next section) can be used to fix outstanding errors before the data is validated against the shape expressions again.

3.3 Deploying the Knowledge Graph

For this step of the methodology, we define *deploying* to mean less the configuration of the Wikibase installation, and more both the ingestion of data into Wikibase, and the considerations (within the context of the Enslaved.Org Project's context) in managing the installation over the (C)KG life cycle.

---

[14] https://openrefine.org/docs/technical-reference/wikibase/architecture.
[15] Essentially, validation occurs by checking the data under the closed world assumption, rather than the open world assumption.
[16] https://github.com/shexjs/shex.js.
[17] https://github.com/RDFLib/pySHACL.

As the choice of using Wikibase was largely motivated by community (data) accessibility, it is also important that updating and maintaining the CKG are approachable and accessible tasks. For the Enslaved.Org Project (i.e., Digital Humanities), it is very common to encounter people who are not technically trained. For example, Wikibase provides a Python library, Pywikibot,[18] for ingesting data, however this is only useful to those who have the requisite training.

As such, the ingestion tool of choice is another provided by Wikibase, Quick-Statements, as introduced in the previous section. For the Enslaved.Org Project, however, it was necessary to improve the QuickStatements tool, and resulted in the Enslaved.Org QuickStatements.[19] In particular, some performance issues were encountered when thousands of records (items) were ingested. The tool had excessive execution time and relied heavily on the browser. Thus, if a new addition into a Wikibase installation was slow, then editing existing records was even slower because of the nature of the operation. Enslaved.Org QuickState-ments tries both to fix some of these performance issues and to enhance the user experience (UX) so non-programmers feel comfortable utilizing the tool.

Briefly, some of the key improvements to Quickstatement are

- removed reliance on the browser for execution: all ingestion and editing happens server side;
- improved concurrency: parallel execution with 40 bots to ingest hundreds or thousands of records within minutes;
- restructured the database: one table per batch is used instead of having all the batches in one monolithic table, allowing access to individual batches more quickly;
- added pagination to the batches page;
- improved the general UX;
- pruned unnecessary third-party and external libraries;
- added file ingestion for statements instead of browser-only ingestion;
- ameliorated error reporting;
- and modified the tool so it relies on a different API call to edit items as a whole: a new feature that is critical for including a large number of sources and/or qualifiers per statement.

The systems environment does include additional challenges when running a Wikibase at beyond a small test environment for development. While foreseen challenges included normal concerns over maintenance, backup, and restoration, the key concerns come with the growth of the community data. Substantial growth in the items stored in Wikibase was expected. Yet, less anticipated was that Mediawiki,[20] and thus Wikibase, retain the history of every page, which in the context of Wikibase is every Item or Property. Preserving the edit history of the data we are presenting is an important function for the community, yet,

---

[18] https://pypi.org/project/pywikibot/.

[19] https://github.com/matrix-msu/QuickStatements.

[20] Mediawiki is the foundation to all Wikimedia software, including Wikipedia and Wikidata.

simultaneously, it is crucial to minimize the total number of edits on the data set, both for semantic reasons (edits imply something changed, and the reason for the change should be recorded), and for space reasons (every edit potentially is a full copy of the Item that must be stored). To manage this, a method was developed to create a full running second copy of the database, starting at a given point in time, for testing edits and additions. In doing so, the iterative process of testing and of building the additions and changes to a data set can be attempted and refined without adding edits to the primary repository.

Another key challenge involved in running a Wikibase is that a project like Enslaved.Org regularly requires reprocessing data – if not the whole data set, then a substantial fraction of it. Wikibase, as extension of Mediawiki, is optimized for single page viewing as the primary interactive mechanism (see Fig. 1b). Thus, free text search, which effectively requires an index of all text in the system, requires updating and maintaining that index as an ongoing process, often requiring regular sweeps of every item in the system. At the same time, for graph databases, the system often maintains a constant stream of requests for the latest changes. With these system heavy processes, if they get too far behind, the system will stop doing interactive updates and requests, and the systems operator must reload the data from scratch, from a bulk export operation. These system problems match the sort that David Rosenthal outlines in his discussion of using cloud systems for community archival work: [5] "Traditionally, access to archived content has been on an item-by-item basis. ... Each scholar accessing the collection will access a substantial proportion of it in a short time". To help alleviate this tax on systems, Enslaved.Org provides monthly dumps of all content as a downloadable dataset, as well as the same dumps that are used to load the free text and graph search tools. It is also encouraged to use these dumps for analysis.

Developing Bespoke Visualizations. How a knowledge graph is used, especially a *community-driven* knowledge graph, is greatly influenced by the interests, expertise, and backgrounds of those expected to interact with it. In particular and as stated in Sect. 2, the end-users might range from elementary school students to (amateur) genealogists to historians. Thus, we expect a wide range of socio-technical competencies and interests. As such, the Enslaved.Org Hub supports many modes of interaction: dumps of all content (supra), a traditional Wikibase view (Fig. 1b), and a knowledge box view (Fig. 1a). While the provision of the first two of these services comes easily with the use of the Wikibase platform, the latter requires additional software and UI/UX development.

The exact description of the development is outside of the scope of the paper; we, instead, mention it here as an important consideration in the deployment of any knowledge graph, but in particular those that are expected to engage with non-technical users or laypeople.

4   Conclusion

In this paper, we have outlined our approach for developing a community-driven knowledge graph that will be deployed on the Wikibase platform, as demonstrated by the Enslaved.Org Hub, which is publicly available online at https://enslaved.org/.
The approach taken comprises:

1. develop the knowledge graph schema (i.e., the ontology) according to best practices;
2. adjust the schema to the underlying semantics and technology stack which will deploy the knowledge graph;
3. de-duplicate (or resolve co-references), materialize, and validate the contents of the knowledge graph; and
4. deploy the knowledge graph, including any bespoke tools for discovery, navigation, and visualization.

Step 1 is motivated and described in detail in [14]. For Step 2, we provide updates to that process by including recent work on mapping traditional ontological structures into Wikibase much more seamlessly. Step 3 was described via its smaller tasks, and Step 4 was discusses lessons learned through the deployment of the Enslaved.Org Hub.

Finally, while this paper reports the development and deployment of the Enslaved.Org Hub, the steps taken are largely generalizable and will be helpful to those in the wider community that are interested in creating, deploying, and maintaining a knowledge graph on Wikibase.

Future Work

We have identified two particularly important next steps, which will improve the outcomes of taking our approach.

– Ontology to Shapes: This methodology does not specifically subscribe to a particular methodology for creating shape expressions from an ontology. While the process taken for the Enslaved.Org project was manual, a generalized methodology for interpreting ontological axioms into shape expressions would be useful. In particular, we will also examine the WShex [10] for applicability in this case.
– Configurable reconciliation: this methodology recommended the use of the fuzzy search functionality of OpenRefine, as it is conveniently packaged within the ingestion software. However, co-reference resolution is a relatively open field. Focusing efforts on de-duplication methods within the tighter bounds of mapping to a controlled vocabulary may be easier.

Supplemental Material Statement: Throughout the paper, references are given to enslaved.org sources, which are publicly available and relevant to assessing the paper's contributions. In particular, please see the Availability paragraph at the end of Sect. 2.

Acknowledgement. This work was supported by The Andrew W. Mellon Foundation through the Enslaved.Org Hub project.

References

1. Alemayehu, S.A., et al.: Methodology for creating a community corpus using a Wikibase knowledge graph. In: Villazón-Terrazas, B., Ortiz-Rodriguez, F., Tiwari, S., Sicilia, M.A., Martín-Moncunill, D. (eds.) KGSWC 2022. CCIS, pp. 285–297. Springer, Cham (2022). https://doi.org/10.1007/978-3-031-21422-6_21
2. Baker, T., Prud'hommeaux, E. (eds.): Shape Expressions (ShEx) 2.1 Primer. Final Community Group Report 09 October 2019 (2019). https://shex.io/shex-primer/index.html
3. Bisen, K.S., et al.: Wikibase as an infrastructure for community documents: The example of the Disability Wiki platform. In: Simsek, U., Chaves-Fraga, D., Pellegrini, T., Vahdat, S. (eds.) Proceedings of Poster and Demo Track and Workshop Track of the 18th International Conference on Semantic Systems co-located with 18th International Conference on Semantic Systems (SEMANTiCS 2022), Vienna, Austria, September 13th to 15th, 2022. CEUR Workshop Proceedings, vol. 3235. CEUR-WS.org (2022). https://ceur-ws.org/Vol-3235/paper14.pdf
4. Blomqvist, E., Hammar, K., Presutti, V.: Engineering ontologies with patterns - the eXtreme Design methodology. In: Hitzler, P., Gangemi, A., Janowicz, K., Krisnadhi, A., Presutti, V. (eds.) Ontology Engineering with Ontology Design Patterns - Foundations and Applications, Studies on the Semantic Web, vol. 25, pp. 23–50. IOS Press (2016). https://doi.org/10.3233/978-1-61499-676-7-23
5. Cloud for preservation. https://blog.dshr.org/2019/02/cloud-for-preservation.html
6. Diefenbach, D., Wilde, M.D., Alipio, S.: Wikibase as an infrastructure for knowledge graphs: the EU knowledge graph. In: Hotho, A., et al. (eds.) ISWC 2021. LNCS, vol. 12922, pp. 631–647. Springer, Cham (2021). https://doi.org/10.1007/978-3-030-88361-4_37
7. Eells, A., Shimizu, C., Zhou, L., Hitzler, P., Estrecha, S.G., Rehberger, D.: Aligning patterns to the Wikibase model. In: Hammar, K., Shimizu, C., McGinty, H.K., Asprino, L., Carriero, V.A. (eds.) WOP 2021, Workshop on Ontology Design and Patterns 2021. Proceedings of the 12th Workshop on Ontology Design and Patterns (WOP 2021) co-located with the 20th International Semantic Web Conference (ISWC 2021). Online, October 24, 2021. CEUR Workshop Proceedings, vol. Vol-3011. CEUR.org (2021)
8. Computer science professor, postdoc launch online database on history of slavery. https://cacm.acm.org/news/249167-computer-science-professor-postdoc-launch-online-database-on-history-of-slavery/fulltext?mobile=false
9. A massive new effort to name millions sold into bondage during the transatlantic slave trade. https://www.washingtonpost.com/history/2020/12/01/slavery-database-family-genealogy/
10. Gayo, J.E.L.: WShEx: a language to describe and validate Wikibase entities. CoRR abs/2208.02697 (2022). https://doi.org/10.48550/arXiv.2208.02697
11. Knublauch, H., Kontokostas, D. (eds.): Shapes Constraint Language (SHACL). W3C Recommendation 20 July 2017 (2017). https://www.w3.org/TR/shacl/
12. Shimizu, C., et al.: Ontology design facilitating Wikibase integration - and a worked example for historical data. CoRR abs/2205.14032 (2022). https://doi.org/10.48550/arXiv.2205.14032

13. Shimizu, C., Hammar, K., Hitzler, P.: Modular ontology modeling. Semantic Web **14**(3), 459–489 (2023). https://doi.org/10.3233/SW-222886

14. Shimizu, C., et al.: The enslaved ontology: peoples of the historic slave trade. J. Web Semant. **63**, 100567 (2020). https://doi.org/10.1016/j.websem.2020.100567

15. Wilkinson, M.D., Dumontier, M., et al.: The FAIR guiding principles for scientific data management and stewardship. Sci. Data **3** (2016). https://doi.org/10.1038/sdata.2016.18

16. Zhou, L., et al.: The Enslaved dataset: A real-world complex ontology alignment benchmark using Wikibase. In: d'Aquin, M., Dietze, S., Hauff, C., Curry, E., Cudré-Mauroux, P. (eds.) CIKM 2020: The 29th ACM International Conference on Information and Knowledge Management, Virtual Event, Ireland, October 19–23, 2020, pp. 3197–3204. ACM (2020). https://doi.org/10.1145/3340531.3412768

The World Literature Knowledge Graph

Marco Antonio Stranisci[1](✉)[ID], Eleonora Bernasconi[2][ID], Viviana Patti[1][ID],
Stefano Ferilli[2][ID], Miguel Ceriani[2,3][ID], and Rossana Damiano[1][ID]

[1] University of Turin, Corso Svizzera 185, Turin, Italy
{marcoantonio.stranisci,viviana.patti,rossana.damiano}@unito.it
[2] University of Bari Aldo Moro, Via Orabona 4, Bari, Italy
{eleonora.bernasconi,stefano.ferilli,miguel.ceriani}@uniba.it
[3] ISTC-CNR, Via S. Martino della Battaglia 44, Roma, Italy

Abstract. Digital media have enabled the access to unprecedented literary knowledge. Authors, readers, and scholars are now able to discover and share an increasing amount of information about books and their authors. However, these sources of knowledge are fragmented and do not adequately represent non-Western writers and their works. In this paper we present The World Literature Knowledge Graph (WL-KG), a semantic resource containing 194,346 writers and 971,210 works, specifically designed for exploring facts about literary works and authors from different parts of the world. The knowledge graph integrates information about the reception of literary works gathered from 3 different communities of readers, aligned according to a single semantic model. The resource is accessible through an online visualization platform, which can be found at the following URL: https://literaturegraph.di.unito.it. This platform has been rigorously tested and validated by 3 distinct categories of experts who have found it to be highly beneficial for their respective work domains. These categories include teachers, researchers in the humanities, and professionals in the publishing industry. The feedback received from these experts confirms that they can effectively utilize the platform to enhance their work processes and to achieve valuable outcomes.

Keywords: Knowledge Graph · World Literature · Information Visualization

1 Introduction

The impact of digital media on the literary ecosystem has led to a transformation of reading [23] and researching [24] practices. Digital media represent an unprecedented opportunity for studying the World Literature [10]. Digital platforms are not only open windows on different parts of the world, but also privileged viewpoints on how communities of readers receive and share literary works [34].

M. A. Stranisci and E. Bernasconi—Contributed equally to this work.

The opportunities emerging from this transformation are, however, limited by a series of issues. The knowledge stored in these archives is vast, but fragmented: only a minimal part of writers and works is mapped from one source to another and many archives do not rely on a semantic model. This hinders the study of the writers and their reception by different groups of readers. Furthermore, it has been proved that some of these resources are characterized by the underrepresentation of non-Western people. It is the case of Wikidata [1] and Wikipedia [13] that are both affected by an ethnic and gender bias. In a recent work [33] the analysis of 48, 789 biographies from Wikipedia extends the findings from previous work indicating that representational biases are present in an allegedly objective source such as Wikipedia along intersectional axes [9], namely ethnicity and gender.

The World Literature Knowledge Graph (WL-KG) is a knowledge base developed for tackling these issues. The resource includes 194, 346 writers and their works gathered from three sources of knowledge: Wikidata, Open Library, and Goodreads. Such a collection relies on a common ontology network [35] specifically developed with the aim of emphasizing the ethnic origin of writers and the readers' response about them and their works.

The WL-KG is intended to support two main types of tasks: (i) the analysis of the underrepresentation of non-Western writers; (ii) the reception of works by different communities of readers. These tasks, in turn, can support the implementation of applications like recommender systems [28], and discovery tools [27], which may take advantage from the more balanced representation of literary world provided by the knowledge base. The WL-KG is also intended as a tool for all professionals that work in the literary field (e.g., researchers in the humanities and publishers) and operate in multicultural contexts (e.g., teachers, educators, activists). In order to make the resource accessible to these target, it is hosted on a visualization platform [4] that allows for a graph-based exploration of the KG. Both the platform and the WL-KG were tested by 3 categories of experts who evaluated them along three dimensions: completeness, accuracy, and usability. Results showed that our resource may be considered as an alternative to traditional literary search tools, especially for the discovery of new writers.

This paper is structured as follows. In Sect. 2 related work and theoretical background are presented. Section 3 describes the semantic model on which the WL-KG relies. Section 4 describes the creation of the resource, while Sect. 5 illustrates its implementation in a visualization platform. Section 6 reports on the evaluation of the resource.

2   Background and Related Work

In this section we first briefly describe the World Literature theoretical framework. Then, we review the related work in two fields: semantic resources designed for literary studies and Linked Data visualization platforms.

2.1   Theoretical Framework

World Literature is a recent approach to literary studies that emphasizes the idea of works as windows on different parts of the world [10]. In such a perspective, national and chronological boundaries must be overcome and a crucial step of the analysis is how works transcend their local contexts to be globally received [2,19]. Such a framework gained prominence in last years thanks to the availability of an unprecedented knowledge about writers and their works enabled by social media: this paved the way for the development of distant reading approaches [22] as well as digital humanities studies of digital platforms [18]. The centrality of reception and the emphasis on a non-Western-centric approach are two features from this theory that were adopted for modeling the WL-KG. In fact, our resource can be used not only for discovering writers and works from the world, but also to analyze how communities of readers increase or decrease their underrepresentation, and to devise ways to contrast it.

2.2   Semantic Technologies for Literary Studies

Several digital resources that provide information about literary works and writers are available online. Wikidata [40] is a general-purpose KG which includes knowledge about writers and their works. Other archives are domain-specific: Goodreads is a social cataloging website owned by Amazon, where readers share their impressions about books. Open Library is a project of the Internet Archive[1] where users can borrow books. Among these three archives, only Wikidata relies on the Linked Open Data paradigm. Open Library exposes its data through APIs, while Goodreads dismissed its APIs in 2020. This leads to issues in data gathering and mapping, since there is no unified model to align these resources.

Some digital archives are monographic and curated by teams of experts. It is the case of The European Literary Text Collection[2] [30], a multi-lingual dataset of novels written from 1848 to 1920; DraCor[3] [14], a collection of plays corpora in multiple languages; MiMoText[4], a parallel corpus of French and German novels published from 1750 to 1799.

Other resources are more oriented to explore the intersection between people and society. The Japanese Visual Media Graph[5] [25] gathers data about Japanese visual media (including manga and visual novels) from communities of fans. The Orlando Textbase[6] [31] is a KG developed to explore feminist literature. WeChangeEd[7] [38] is a KG of 1,800 female editors born between 1710 and 1920 aligned with Wikidata.

---

[1] https://archive.org.
[2] https://www.distant-reading.net/eltec.
[3] https://dracor.org.
[4] https://mimotext.github.io.
[5] https://jvmg.iuk.hdm-stuttgart.de.
[6] https://www.artsrn.ualberta.ca/orlando.
[7] https://www.wechanged.ugent.be.

The WL-KG is the first resource designed to study the intersection between literary production and ethnic information about writers. There are research projects that analyze the world of literature according to Wikipedia [18], but this is the first attempt to release a resource which could be at the same time a platform to foster digital humanities and literary studies and a benchmark dataset for analyzing the knowledge gaps that affect an authoritative source like Wikidata in the literary domain.

2.3   Visualization Platforms

Many works deal with interfaces for visualising Linked Data [8, 11, 16, 17, 21, 26, 37, 39], but only some focus on exploring and disseminating domains related to digital humanities, primarily digital libraries [3, 12]. The interaction paradigm and the information reduction strategies are the two main characteristics of an interface for visualising Linked Data.

ARCA [4] is a modular system that deals with knowledge extraction from a digital library, visualisation, and collaborative validation of automatically extracted associations between concepts and books [5]. ARCA uses two different interaction paradigms: the node-link paradigm for visualising resources extracted and linked to the DBpedia knowledge base[8], and the tabular paradigm for the visualisation of additional metadata related to books. As an information reduction strategy, ARCA allows for incremental visualisation of resources.

On the other hand, Yewno Discover [6] allows node-link visualisation of concepts contained in a digital library. Unlike ARCA, Yewno has a static and non-incremental visualisation of resources but uses ranking algorithms to filter the displayed content.

Another tool is ResearchSpace [12], an open-source platform that facilitates working with digital cultural heritage data in a Linked Data environment, enabling improved discoverability and reuse of data. The platform includes a node-link interaction paradigm, which employs incremental visualization for knowledge exploration. Additionally, it allows for collaborative annotation of texts or images.

Thanks to the flexibility and modularity of the ARCA system, we have chosen to build upon it by creating an extension called SKATEBOARD (Semantic Knowledge Advanced Tool for Extraction Browsing Organization Annotation Retrieval and Discovery), as described in Sect. 5. This extension has been customized and updated to meet the specific needs of users interacting with the World Literature Knowledge Graph.

3   The Semantic Model

In this section the semantic model adopted for the WL-KG is described. After a general introduction of the model and the authoritative ontologies to which it is

---

[8] https://dbpedia.org.

aligned, we focus on two aspects that we modeled through our ontology network: the interaction between writers and their ethnic origin and the representation of the publishing history of the works.

3.1 The UR-Ontology Network

The ontology network serves two main functions: modeling ethnic-based under-representation of writers; mapping different digital libraries under a unique data model. Data in the WL-KG are modeled according to the Under-Represented Ontology Network (UR-O) composed of two modules: a revised version of the Under-Represented Writers Ontology (URW-O)[9] [35] and a module for the encoding of works: the Ontology of Under-Represented Books (URB-O)[10].

The ontology network is mapped onto three authoritative ontologies: the Functional Requirements for Bibliographic Records (FRBR) [36], the PROV Ontology (PROV-O) [20], and the Descriptive Ontology for Linguistic and Cognitive Engineering (DOLCE) [15]. FRBR is a standard for modeling the relationship between a work (FRBR:WORK), its expressions (FRBR:EXPRESSION), and manifestations (FRBR:MANIFESTATION). From PROV-O the relationships of attribution, association, and derivation are inherited, in order to make explicit the sources from which data were gathered (**prov:wasDerivedFrom**), the people and organizations involved in specific editions of given works (**prov:wasAssociatedWith**) and their roles (e.g., publisher, translator), and the attribution of a work to its creator (**prov:wasAttributedTo**). DOLCE has been used as a reference model for encoding biographical and publishing events, which are represented as time-bounded perdurants in which entities play specific roles. This allows representing publications as events where sets of entities participate (**dul:hasParticipant**) and life events (e.g., Birth, Migration) as situations which are setting for (**dul:isSettingFor**) agents and their roles.

3.2 Modeling Underrepresentation

For modeling ethnic-based underrepresentation of writers we relied on two criteria derived from post-colonial studies - Gayatri Spivak's work in particular [32]. To be potentially under-represented an author must either (i) be born in a non-Western former colony country or (ii) belong to an ethnic minority in a Western country. Using the country of birth as a criterion is prone to false positives though, since many writers with Western origin were born in former colonies (e.g., George Orwell, Rudyard Kipling). In order to mitigate such issue we chose to adopt the term 'Transnational', which is broader than 'Under-Represented' since it refers to people who "operated outside their own nation's boundaries, or negotiated with them" [7]. Furthermore, we classified as 'Transnational' only people born in former colonies from Latin America and Caribbeans since 1808, and in former African and Asian colonies since 1917, to

---

[9] https://purl.archive.org/urwriters/lode.
[10] https://purl.archive.org/urbooks/lode.

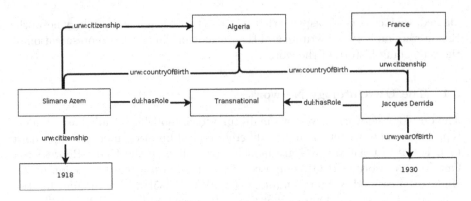

Fig. 1. An example of how the concept of 'Transnational' writer is encoded in our semantic model.

reduce the number of people of Western origin selected by this condition. The first date marks the beginning of the Spanish American wars of independence; the second was chosen as a symbolic beginning of the decolonization process in Africa and Asia. Finally, we coupled the condition of being 'Transnational' with the citizenship of an author in order to reveal potentially false under-represented writers which may be still present in the knowledge base. As it can be observed in Fig. 1, Jacques Derrida and Slimane Azem are both classified (**dul:hasRole**) as 'Transnational' in the KG, since they were born in Algeria, a former African colony, in 1918 and 1930. The specification of their citizenship (**urw:citizenship**) provides additional information about Jacques Derrida, who was not an Algerian citizen despite Algeria is his country of birth. This allows users to infer his European origins.

3.3   Modeling Works Publishing History

Before gathering data from Wikidata, Open Library, and Goodreads we designed a common data model for aligning literary information that the platform represents in heterogeneous shapes. Following the FRBR ontology, we defined each work in the platform as an instance of type FRBR:EXPRESSION, which is described as the "intellectual or artistic realization of a work in the form of alpha-numeric, musical, or choreographic notation". We then defined the concept of URB:EDITION as a subclass of FRBR:MANIFESTATION, namely "the physical embodiment of an expression of a work". These two concepts are linked through the property **frbr:embodiment**. Such semantic relationship is wrapped in a URB:PUBLICATION pattern, which is a subclass of a DUL:EVENT. An event in DOLCE can be used as a reification to provide richer descriptions of a property. In our case this type of pattern is adopted for two reasons: (i) expressing a large number of facts about an edition (place, date, language of publishing and publisher) in a compact way; (ii) encoding roles of people who contributed to a publication without being the author of a work. A final feature of the semantic model is the reception of works from communities of readers. Depending on the source of knowledge from which a work is derived, it may have an average rating (**urb:rated**), a number of ratings (**urb:numberOfRatings**), or a number of readers (**urb:numberOfReaders**). Figure 2 shows an example of our representation of works. 'Harry Potter e il Prigioniero di Azkaban', namely the Italian version (FRBR:EXPRESSION) of the 3rd Harry Potter book, **prov:wasAttributedTo** to J. K. Rowling, has an average rating and a number of ratings from the Goodreads community, and it has as **frbr:embodiment** the '1999 edition'. The latter in turn participates (**dul:isParticipantIn**) to a URB:PUBLICATION, a blank node entity that can be used for expressing several information: country of publication, year of publication, publisher, and translator. The translator is linked to the publication through the property **prov:wasAssociatedWith** and **dul:hasRole** 'translator'. Such representation supports a thorough exploration of the intersections between writers' biographies and their publishing history as well as a more accurate analysis of their relationships with other authors and people working in the publishing industry. It is however a verbose encoding that may affect the usage of this resource. In order to avoid this issue, we defined a set of property chains that directly link works to bibliographical information. Examples of these properties are shown in red in Fig. 2.

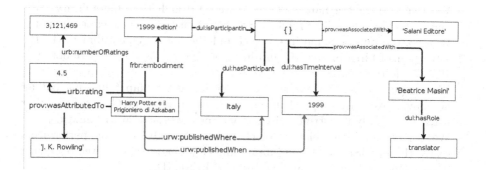

Fig. 2. An example of publication.

4 Creation of the WL-KG

In this section, we describe the process involved in creating our World Literature Knowledge Graph (WL-KG), which can be queried online through the SPARQL endpoint available at https://kgccc.di.unito.it/sparql/wl-kg. We first describe our strategy for mapping knowledge from Wikidata onto Open Library and Goodreads. We then introduce our strategy for evaluating the mapping. Finally, we provide some statistics about the number of literary facts collected from each platform and about the interaction of communities of readers with works.

4.1 Mapping Between Platforms

The data collection process started from Wikidata. From this knowledge base we gathered all the 194, 346 entities of type Person (wd:Q5) with occupation (wdt:P106) writer (wd:Q36180), novelist (wd:Q6625963), or poet (wd:Q49757) born after 1808 and having information about their place of birth. For each author, we collected the ethnic group, gender, date and place of death, Wikipedia page, and all the works associated with them. We converted all geographical information gathered from Wikidata to the "ISO 3166-1 alpha 3" code[11] (e.g., IND, NGA), which is internationally recognized as a standard for referencing modern countries.

To enrich the knowledge base we first conducted a quantitative analysis of their external identifiers in Wikidata pages on writers. We focused on three of them: writers' Virtual International Authority File Name (VIAF) IDs, Open Library IDs and Goodreads IDs. A fourth platform, Library Things, was not included in the data collection process given the low number of links from Wikidata and the impossibility of automatically obtaining authors' IDs from that website. In Table 1 it is possible to observe that the 84% of writers has a VIAF ID, the 18.5% an Open Library ID, and the 4.5% a Goodreads ID. In order to increase the percentage of writers mapped to VIAF and Open Library identifiers, we adopted three heuristics:

– We retrieved all the names of the writers through the OpenLibrary APIs and kept only the entities fulfilling two conditions: (a) an exact string match between the author name in our KG and the one in OpenLibrary; (b) the same year of birth in our KG and in OpenLibrary. As a result, we obtained 19, 737 additional ids.
– We scraped all writers' names from Goodreads sitemap[12] filtering out all homonyms. We then mapped all the names in our KG onto Goodreads author list, keeping only the string matches. We thus obtained 26, 019 new ids.
– We searched all ISBNs related to each authors through VIAF and performed a search through ISBN on Open Library and Goodreads, that allowed retrieving 22, 661 Open Library IDs and 44, 142 Goodreads IDs.

4.2 Quality Assessment of the Mapping

After the mapping, we performed a quality assessment of a sample of links between Wikidata and Goodreads, and between Wikidata and Open Library for removing incorrect links before gathering works. Our evaluation strategy is composed of three steps. We computed the Gestalt pattern similarity [29] between the names of the same writer in different platforms. For instance, Esther Salaman[13] is linked to her Goodreads pagewhere she is referred as 'Esther Polianowsky Salaman'. The two strings have a Gestalt pattern score [29] of 0.7. Then, we

---

[11] https://www.iso.org/iso-3166-country-codes.html.
[12] https://www.goodreads.com/siteindex.author.xml.
[13] http://www.wikidata.org/entity/Q4405658.

manually checked random samples of 100 name pairs with 7 degrees of similarity: $x < 0.1$, $0.1 \geq x < 0.2$, $0.2 \geq x < 0.3$, $0.3 \geq x < 0.4$, $0.4 \geq x < 0.5$, $0.5 \geq x < 0.6$, $0.6 \geq x < 0.7$. As it can be observed in Fig. 3, the percentage of correct links is directly proportional to the similarity between the name by which the writer is referred to in different platforms. In particular, the accuracy dramatically increases with a similarity between 0.5 and 0.6 (77% of correct links) reaching a 89% of accuracy with a similarity between 0.6 and 0.7.

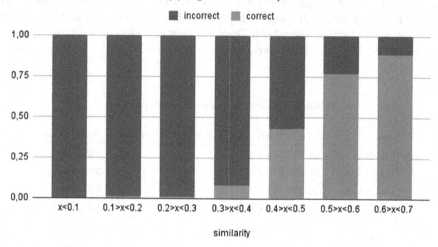

Fig. 3. Results of the evaluation of writers mappings between Wikidata, Goodreads, and Open Library.

Finally, we set a similarity threshold for filtering out potentially incorrect links. In order to privilege precision over recall, we set the threshold at 0.7. As a final result, we obtained $71,706$ (36.8%) writers with an Open Library ID and $79,158$ (40.7%) with a Goodreads ID (Table 1). The percentage of writers linked to at least one of the two platforms is 54%.

4.3   Data Collection and Statistics

After the augmentation of external identifiers of authors, we collected all their works in these platforms. OpenLibrary APIs allow retrieving all works, and for each work it is possible to obtain all editions. Results include a set of useful publishing information, readers count, ratings, and number of ratings. Goodreads does not provide APIs, but allows for web scraping. Hence, we first collected the list of all works from writers pages, their ratings and number of ratings, then we obtained publishing information through Google Books APIs.

In order to emphasize the role of readers communities, we only kept works that had received at least one reception or that were marked as read by at least

Table 1. Number of authors with an external identifier

Identifier	Before Mapping	After Mapping
VIAF	$163,353$ (84.0%)	
Open Library	$36,097$ (18.5%)	$71,706$ (36.8%)
Goodreads	$8,997$ (4.6%)	$79,158$ (40.7%)

one user. Table 2 shows the number of works collected from each platform and the number of writers associated with at least one work from them. As it can be observed, Goodreads includes a higher number of works and writers with at least one work. Furthermore, both Open Library and Goodreads show a higher percentage of 'Transnational' writers than Wikidata: 12.6% and 11% against 8.6%.

Table 2. Number of works for each platform

Source	N. of writers with $\geq$ 1 works (% transn.)	N. of works
Wikidata	$22,515$ (8.6%)	$117,798$
Open Library	$24,370$ (12.4%)	$226,108$
Goodreads	$60,201$ (11.0%)	$627,214$
Total	$71,443$ (10.6%)	$971,120$

The analysis of readers communities may also be observed through the lens of the number of interactions between readers and works. While Wikidata does not include users evaluation of literary works, it is possible to obtain this information from Goodreads and Open Library. Both expose the number of ratings and the average rating, while the latter also exposes the number of readers. Table 3 shows the number of interactions between readers and literary works in the two platforms. As it can be observed, absolute numbers are incomparable: there are 112.708 ratings in Open Library against 1.7 billions in Goodreads. The percentage of ratings about Transnational works is higher on Open Library (6%) than in Goodreads (4.9%), while both platforms show a slightly higher average rating of Transnational writers.

Summarizing, aligning literary facts from different platforms in a unique semantic resource allows for a richer representation of World Literature, with a more balanced knowledge about Transnational writers (+2% of them are associated with at least one work). Furthermore, such data collections shows the impact of communities of readers on the diffusion of writers and their works.

Table 3. Number of readers interactions in Goodreads and Open Library. Interactions about Transnational writers are reported in parenthesis.

Source	Average rating	N. of works	N. of readers
Open Library	3.91 (3.99)	112,708 (6.0%)	1.2M (8.5%)
Goodreads	3.86 (3.77)	1.7B (4.9%)	–

5   Visualization Platform

The World Literature Knowledge Graph is built to support advanced queries and is seamlessly integrated with SKATEBOARD, the Semantic Knowledge Advanced Tool for Extraction Browsing Organization Annotation Retrieval and Discovery, providing users with an intelligent and intuitive way to explore the vast world of literature. With the World Literature Knowledge Graph and SKATEBOARD interface, our goal is to enable users to uncover deep insights and connections within literary works and enhance their understanding of the literary world. The SKATEBOARD platform presented in this research builds upon the work of Bernasconi et al. [4] and represents an extension and updated version of their work to fit our specific context of use. The interface features two main views: "Author" and "Work". The navigation flow that starts with an initial search for a topic of interest. Once a relevant topic is found, the user can drag the resource onto the central board and explore its relationships with other objects and predicates, creating a visual representation of the connections. This feature is illustrated in Fig. 4.

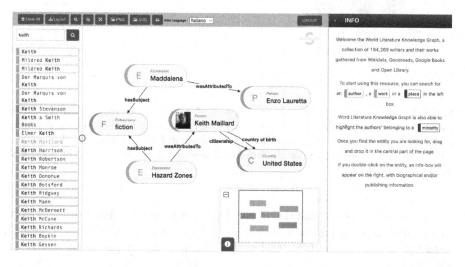

Fig. 4. A snapshot of the visualization platform. On the left, the search box; in the middle, the whiteboard where entities can be dragged; on the right, info pane about the selected entity.

By clicking on resources of type "Person" (as visible in Fig. 5), the user can access information about an author, including both direct relationships such as published works and indirect relationships such as all the topics covered in their works, or a map of all the locations where their works were published. Clicking on resources of type "Expression" (as visible in Fig. 6) displays information specific to a particular work, such as editions, languages, and readers ratings.

Literary searches may also start from different type of entities in the Knowledge Graph. It is possible to retrieve all writers by their country of birth or by their citizenship, as well as perform searches based on specific minorities (eg.: African Americans). The platform also allows navigations based on subjects: users can browse all works linked to a specific URB:FOLKSONOMY. The graph-based navigation encourages serendipitous discovery, allowing users to stumble upon unexpected connections and relationships.

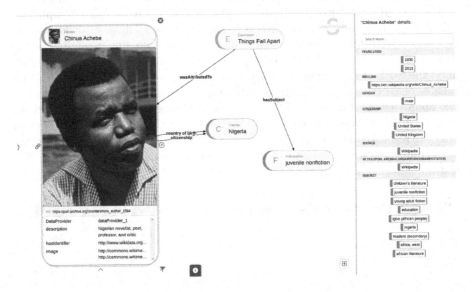

Fig. 5. Person view: on the left, the central area of the interface, where selected entities can be dragged for visualising their provenance and associated media and their relations with other entities according to the node-link paradigm (here, Chinua Achebe); on the right, the Info pane displaying the information about the entity (e.g., biographical dates, citizenship).

In summary, the visualization platform presented in this research offers an updated and customizable interface for exploring and visualizing relationships between topics, authors, and works, with potential applications in various research fields.

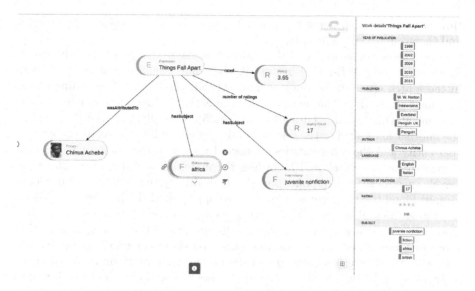

Fig. 6. Expression view: on the left, the central area of the interface where a work (top left, "Things Fall Apart") is connected with its author (Chinua Achebe, see Fig. 5). On the right, the Info pane displaying the information about the work in tabular form (an Expression in FRBR terms), such as publisher, language, rating, etc.

6   Resource Evaluation

The current form of the WL-KG and its visualization platform are the result of a two-year interactive process of design and development carried out in constant interaction with domain experts. The contribution of domain experts to the process has been two-fold: on one side, they helped in defining the geopolitical and temporal boundaries of the resource, suggesting post-colonial studies as the conceptual reference framework for the study of underrepresentation; on the other side, they suggested that a graph-based visualization would be better suited to encourage exploration – and support their professional tasks – than the archival-based visual metaphors employed in the first prototype, for its capability to encourage the discovery of new authors through the connections displayed in the graphical interface.

For the evaluation of the WL-KG we organized a series of structured interviews with a group of potential targets of our resource, in line with the paradigm of user-centered design [41]: 4 teachers, 6 researchers in the humanities, and 3 professionals in the publishing industry. Each interview was articulated in two parts: the first part, targeted on the search of Transnational writers and works, was focused on the use of the platform; the second focused on the potential uses of the resource in the users' field of work and research.

User Experience. After asking the users to search for at least one Transnational author and work of their choice, the user experience was investigated along three dimensions: the usability of the platform, the completeness of the results, and the accuracy of the results.

Concerning the usability of the platform, most users experienced difficulties in navigating the WL-KG. First of all, they didn't realise that every element in the search area can be dragged into central whiteboard – according to the incremental paradigm that controls the interaction between the search area and the central whiteboard (as described in Sect. 5). Secondly, they failed to explore the information linked to the selected entity by expanding the relations between that entity and the other entities connected with it in the graph, which can be navigated in the whiteboard according the node-link paradigm (Sect. 5). Conversely, a minority of respondents who had already experience of Knowledge Graphs found the platform easy to use and appreciated the possibility of selecting the entities of interest by dragging them into the whiteboard, a function that they saw as a way to overcome the limitations of the standard navigation tools for graph-based representations. Based on these observations, we hypothesize that the difficulties in the use of the visualization platform reported in the interviews can be mainly attributed to the users' lack of experience with graph-based resources. For these users, the drag and drop selection of entities and the link-based navigation were not intuitive and can be improved by providing more guidance in the exploration (e.g., through tooltips, demo-mode navigation, etc.). This is in line with the comment made by some respondents who suggested to initialize the platform with an already loaded example. Concerning the entry of the search parameters, some users expressed their difficulty in finding a suitable author or work, motivating it with their limited knowledge of the domain. To bypass this difficulty, a user suggested to create a list of writers' names, indexed by country of birth, in a separated section of the site. We think that this suggestion is valuable, although it partly overlaps with the possibility of exploring the graph by starting from different types of entities (e.g., subjects, countries, topics), which is already available in the current version of the platform.

Concerning the completeness of the resource, a criticism derived from a misconception about its objectives shared by most respondents, who compared it with standard online archives, such as Wikipedia: the latter, being targeted at end users, include richer information about the entities in textual form, but are not suited for the development of applications that rely on the graph-based representations. This issue can be addressed by revising the description of the resource with a clearer definition of its intended usages. A more challenging request, then, emerged from the scholars in post-colonialism, who complained about some missing associations between works and subjects. It is the case of Andrea Levy's work 'The Long Song': although this book is about 'slavery', it is not linked to this subject in the KG, an issue derived from the lack of attribution of this subject within the digital sources from which data were gathered.

As for completeness, almost all respondents found the resource accurate, with a few errors that we could track from sources. For instance, 'Candide oder der Optimismus', namely the German translation of Voltaire's 'Candide', was attributed to Stephan Hermlin, its translator, due to an error propagated from Goodreads. To address this issues, a functionality for signaling missing and wrong information will be added in a future version of the platform.

Use Cases. The discussion of use cases was structured in two main parts: the comparison of the resource with the existing known archives and the collection of feedback about use cases and missing functionalities. Participants tended to rate the resource as useful for the discovery of new writers, but not useful for exploring new works. Such feedback reflects our data collection strategy, that was limited to the existing entities of the type writer on Wikidata and to the works that had received at least one reaction on the platforms where they are archived, aiming at relevance rather than completeness for what concerns works.

Interviews also showed that almost all respondents use general purpose archives like Google, Wikipedia, and Goodreads for the literary searches, showing a gap in the usage of knowledge bases designed for specific domains of application. The discovery of new literary facts has been pointed out as the major use case for all respondents. Interestingly, from the structured interviews with teachers, it emerged that the students themselves may be potential users of the platforms, since they could take advantage of subject-based search for supporting essay writing. Finally, it emerged the need of exposing in the knowledge base all the places where authors lived during their lives, in order to discover deeper connections between them.

7   Conclusion and Future Work

In this paper we presented the WL-KG, a knowledge base of writers and works designed for the discovery of literary facts from different parts of the world and exploring the underrepresentation of non-Western writers. The resource includes 194, 346 writers and 971, 120 works collected from Wikidata, Goodreads, and Open Library. The integration of knowledge from different sources had an impact on reducing the underrepresentation of Transnational writers, about whom there is more available information in Goodreads and Open Library than in Wikidata. Our resource also allows exploring how works are received by different communities of readers.

The WL-KG is publicly available through a graph-based visualization platform that simplify its usage by non-expert users. The resource and the visualization platform were evaluated by a group of professionals whose work may be supported by the KG. Their feedback shows that the platform may be useful especially to discover new writers from multiple kinds of entities: works, subjects, countries, minority groups. Respondents also highlighted the novelty of the platform compared to existing archives: the graph-based browsing experience, designed according the node-link paradigm, has been perceived as a valuable and alternative tool for exploring literary facts, even if its usability is not immediately intuitive, since graph-based resources are not widespread.

Future work will be devoted to improve the WL-KG with feedback emerged during the evaluation: we plan to increase the knowledge base with knowledge from new communities of readers and thematic platforms; we also plan to release a new version of the visualization platform focused on improving its user experience for non-expert users. To do so, the platform will be adopted as a didactic tool in undergraduate and graduate courses that tackle the postcolonial aspects in World Literature. Finally, we plan to test a recommender system based on our knowledge graph, in order to test its impact in providing fairer recommendations.

Acknowledgements. This work was partially supported by the PNRR projects "CHANGES: Cultural Heritage Active Innovation for Next-Gen Sustainable Society", CUP H53C22000860006, and "Fostering Open Science in Social Science Research (FOSSR)", CUP B83C22003950001.

References

1. Adams, J., Brückner, H., Naslund, C.: Who counts as a notable sociologist on Wikipedia? Gender, race, and the "professor test." Socius **5**, 2378023118823946 (2019)
2. Benwell, B., Procter, J., Robinson, G.: Postcolonial Audiences: Readers, Viewers and Reception. Routledge, New York (2012)
3. Bernasconi, E., Ceriani, M., Mecella, M.: Linked data interfaces: a survey. In: Falcon, A., Ferilli, S., Bardi, A., Marchesin, S., Redavid, D. (eds.) Proceedings of the XIX Italian Research Conference on Digital Libraries - Information and Research Science connecting to Digital and Library Science (IRCDL2023). vol. 3365, p. 16. Central Europe (CEUR) Workshop Proceedings, Bari, Italy (2023)
4. Bernasconi, E., Ceriani, M., Mecella, M., Catarci, T.: Design, realization, and user evaluation of the ARCA system for exploring a digital library. Int. J. Digit. Libr. **24**(1), 1–22 (2023)
5. Bernasconi, E., Ceriani, M., Mecella, M., Morvillo, A.: Automatic knowledge extraction from a digital library and collaborative validation. In: Silvello, G., et al. Linking Theory and Practice of Digital Libraries. TPDL 2022. LNCS, vol. 13541. Springer, Cham (2022). https://doi.org/10.1007/978-3-031-16802-4_49
6. Bolina, M.: Yewno Discover. Nord. J. Inf. Literacy High. Educ. **11**(1) (2019)
7. Boter, B., Rensen, M., Scott-Smith, G.: Unhinging the National Framework: Perspectives on Transnational Life Writing. Sidestone Press (2020)
8. Chawuthai, R., Takeda, H.: RDF graph visualization by interpreting linked data as knowledge. In: Qi, G., Kozaki, K., Pan, J.Z., Yu, S. (eds.) JIST 2015. LNCS, vol. 9544, pp. 23–39. Springer, Cham (2016). https://doi.org/10.1007/978-3-319-31676-5_2
9. Crenshaw, K.W.: On intersectionality: Essential writings. The New Press (2017)
10. Damrosch, D.: What is world literature?, vol. 5. Princeton University Press (2003)
11. Desimoni, F., Po, L.: Empirical evaluation of linked data visualization tools. Futur. Gener. Comput. Syst. **112**, 258–282 (2020). https://doi.org/10.1016/j.future.2020.05.038
12. Fenlon, K., Kariuki, B., Welberry, A.: Researchspace: A platform for digital cultural heritage data management and linked data publication. J. Digital Humanit. **6**(1) (2017)
13. Field, A., Park, C.Y., Lin, K.Z., Tsvetkov, Y.: Controlled analyses of social biases in Wikipedia bios. In: Proceedings of the ACM Web Conference 2022, pp. 2624–2635 (2022)

14. Fischer, F., et al.: Programmable corpora: introducing DraCor, an infrastructure for the research on European drama. Digit. Humanit. **2019**, 5 (2019)
15. Gangemi, A., Guarino, N., Masolo, C., Oltramari, A., Schneider, L.: Sweetening ontologies with DOLCE. In: Gómez-Pérez, A., Benjamins, V.R. (eds.) EKAW 2002. LNCS (LNAI), vol. 2473, pp. 166–181. Springer, Heidelberg (2002). https://doi.org/10.1007/3-540-45810-7_18
16. Haag, F., Lohmann, S., Siek, S., Ertl, T.: QueryVOWL: a visual query notation for linked data. In: Gandon, F., Guéret, C., Villata, S., Breslin, J., Faron-Zucker, C., Zimmermann, A. (eds.) ESWC 2015. LNCS, vol. 9341, pp. 387–402. Springer, Cham (2015). https://doi.org/10.1007/978-3-319-25639-9_51
17. Heim, P., Lohmann, S., Stegemann, T.: Interactive relationship discovery via the semantic web. In: Aroyo, L., et al. (eds.) ESWC 2010. LNCS, vol. 6088, pp. 303–317. Springer, Heidelberg (2010). https://doi.org/10.1007/978-3-642-13486-9_21
18. Hube, C., Fischer, F., Jäschke, R., Lauer, G., Thomsen, M.R.: World literature according to wikipedia: Introduction to a DBpedia-based framework. arXiv preprint arXiv:1701.00991 (2017)
19. Jauss, H.R., Benzinger, E.: Literary history as a challenge to literary theory. N. Literary Hist. **2**(1), 7–37 (1970)
20. Lebo, T., et al.: PROV-O: The PROV ontology. W3C Recommendation, World Wide Web Consortium, United States (2013)
21. Lohmann, S., Link, V., Marbach, E., Negru, S.: WebVOWL: web-based visualization of ontologies. In: Lambrix, P., et al. (eds.) EKAW 2014. LNCS (LNAI), vol. 8982, pp. 154–158. Springer, Cham (2015). https://doi.org/10.1007/978-3-319-17966-7_21
22. Moretti, F.: Conjectures on world literature. N. Left Rev. **1**, 54 (2000)
23. Nakamura, L.: "Words with friends": socially networked reading on Goodreads. PMLA **128**(1), 238–243 (2013)
24. O'Donnell, D.P., Walter, K.L., Gil, A., Fraistat, N.: Only connect: the globalization of the digital humanities. In: A New Companion to Digital Humanities, pp. 493–510 (2015)
25. Pfeffer, M., Roth, M.: Japanese visual media graph: providing researchers with data from enthusiast communities. In: International Conference on Dublin Core and Metadata Applications, pp. 136–141 (2019)
26. Po, L., Bikakis, A., Desimoni, F., Papastefanatos, G.: Linked Data Visualization: Techniques, Tools, and Big Data, vol. 10. Morgan & Claypool Publishers (2020)
27. Polley, S., Ghosh, S., Thiel, M., Kotzyba, M., Nürnberger, A.: SIMFIC: an explainable book search companion. In: 2020 IEEE International Conference on Human-Machine Systems (ICHMS), pp. 1–6. IEEE (2020)
28. Rajpurkar, S., Bhatt, D., Malhotra, P., Rajpurkar, M., Bhatt, M.: Book recommendation system. Int. J. Innovative Res. Sci. Technol. **1**(11), 314–316 (2015)
29. Ratcliff, J.W., Metzener, D., et al.: Pattern matching: the gestalt approach. Dr. Dobb's J. **13**(7), 46 (1988)
30. Schöch, C., et al.: Distant reading for European literary history. a cost action. Proceedings of DH2018 (2018)
31. Simpson, J., Brown, S.: From XML to RDF in the Orlando project. In: 2013 International Conference on Culture and Computing, pp. 194–195. IEEE (2013)
32. Spivak, G.C.: Can the subaltern speak? Die Philosophin **14**(27), 42–58 (2003)
33. Stranisci, M.A., Damiano, R., Mensa, E., Patti, V., Radicioni, D., Caselli, T.: WikiBio: a semantic resource for the intersectional analysis of biographical events. In:

Proceedings of the 61st Annual Meeting of the Association for Computational Linguistics (Volume 1: Long Papers), pp. 12370–12384. Association for Computational Linguistics, Toronto, Canada (2023). https://aclanthology.org/2023.acl-long.691

34. Stranisci, M.A., Patti, V., Damiano, R.: User-generated world literatures: a comparison between two social networks of readers. In: Proceedings of IRCDL 2023. vol. 3365, pp. 38–46 (2023)

35. Stranisci, M.A., Patti, V., Damiano, R., et al.: Representing the under-represented: a dataset of post-colonial, and migrant writers. In: Proceedings of the 3rd Conference on Language, Data and Knowledge (LDK 2021), Open Access Series in Informatics, vol. 93, pp. 1–14 (2021)

36. Tillett, B.B.: FRBR and cataloging for the future. Cataloging Classif. Q. **39**(3–4), 197–205 (2005)

37. Troullinou, G., Kondylakis, H., Daskalaki, E., Plexousakis, D.: RDF digest: efficient summarization of RDF/S KBs. In: Gandon, F., Sabou, M., Sack, H., d'Amato, C., Cudré-Mauroux, P., Zimmermann, A. (eds.) ESWC 2015. LNCS, vol. 9088, pp. 119–134. Springer, Cham (2015). https://doi.org/10.1007/978-3-319-18818-8_8

38. Van Remoortel, M., Birkholz, J.M., Alesina, M., Bezari, C., D'Eer, C., Forestier, E.: Women editors in Europe. J. Eur. Periodical Stud. **6**(1), 1–6 (2021)

39. Viola, F., Roffia, L., Antoniazzi, F., D'Elia, A., Aguzzi, C., Salmon Cinotti, T.: Interactive 3D exploration of RDF graphs through semantic planes. Future Internet **10**(8), 81 (2018)

40. Vrandečić, D., Krötzsch, M.: Wikidata: a free collaborative knowledgebase. Commun. ACM **57**(10), 78–85 (2014)

41. Wood, L.E.: Semi-structured interviewing for user-centered design. Interactions **4**(2), 48–61 (1997)

Literal-Aware Knowledge Graph Embedding for Welding Quality Monitoring: A Bosch Case

Zhipeng Tan[1,2(✉)], Baifan Zhou[3,4(✉)], Zhuoxun Zheng[1,3], Ognjen Savkovic[5],
Ziqi Huang[2], Irlan-Grangel Gonzalez[1], Ahmet Soylu[4],
and Evgeny Kharlamov[1,3(✉)]

[1] Bosch Center for AI, Renningen, Germany
[2] RWTH Aachen University, Aachen, Germany
`zhipeng.tan@rwth-aachen.com`
[3] Department of Informatics, University of Oslo, Oslo, Norway
`evgeny.kharlamov@de.bosch.com`
[4] Department of Computer Science, Oslo Metropolitan University, Oslo, Norway
`baifanz@ifi.uio.no`
[5] Department of Computer Science, Free University of Bozen-Bolzano, Bolzano, Italy

Abstract. Recently there has been a series of studies in knowledge graph embedding (KGE), which attempts to learn the embeddings of the entities and relations as numerical vectors and mathematical mappings via machine learning (ML). However, there has been limited research that applies KGE for industrial problems in manufacturing. This paper investigates whether and to what extent KGE can be used for an important problem: quality monitoring for welding in manufacturing industry, which is an impactful process accounting for production of millions of cars annually. The work is in line with Bosch research of data-driven solutions that intends to replace the traditional way of destroying cars, which is extremely costly and produces waste. The paper tackles two very challenging questions simultaneously: how large the welding spot diameter is; and to which car body the welded spot belongs to. The problem setting is difficult for traditional ML because there exist a high number of car bodies that should be assigned as class labels. We formulate the problem as link prediction, and experimented popular KGE methods on real industry data, with consideration of literals. Our results reveal both limitations and promising aspects of adapted KGE methods.

Keywords: knowledge graph embedding · welding quality monitoring · literal embedding · knowledge graph construction · open dataset

Code and data are available under https://github.com/boschresearch/KGE-Welding.

© The Author(s), under exclusive license to Springer Nature Switzerland AG 2023
T. R. Payne et al. (Eds.): ISWC 2023, LNCS 14266, pp. 453–471, 2023.
https://doi.org/10.1007/978-3-031-47243-5_25

1   Introduction

Background and Challenge. In automotive industry, automated welding is essential for manufacturing high-quality car bodies, accounting for over millions of car production annually. Welding is a data-intensive process. Considering the production lines in Fig. 1 with 10–20 welding machines in each line, each welding machine produces one spot in several second or minutes, and a car body can have up to 6000 spots [1]. For each spot, several hundreds of features are generated, including welding status, quality indicators, and sensor measurements, where the sensors measure important physical properties every millisecond, such as current, resistance, power.

This large amount of data increases the demand of data-driven solutions [2,3], which aims to reduce and eventually replace conventional destructive methods. In the case of the latter, only a small sample of welded car bodies can be measured, because the sample needs to be destroyed, making the methods to be extremely expensive and also producing waste. Two core questions need to be answer here as shown in Fig. 1. Q1 is important because the spot diameter is the key quality indicator for judging welding quality. It must be above a certain threshold, because a too small diameter means insufficient connection and can cause severe consequences (e.g., car user safety). The diameter should also not be too large, because this means energy inefficiency and can cause quality deficiency of the surrounding spots (by e.g. short-circuit effect). Q2 is important because it is essential to know the percentage of good spots for each car body, and this percentage must be higher than certain thresholds according to quality standards. Bosch is doing research to develop data-driven solutions [4] and semantic technologies [5–7] for answering the two questions, whereby both classic machine learning (ML) [1] and the recent methods of knowledge graph embedding (KGE) are under consideration.

Knowledge Graph Embedding. There has been a series of research on KGE methods recently [8–10]. In essence, KGE attempts to represents nodes and edges in KGs as vectors/matrices or mathematical mappings. Mainstream works include translational models [11], bilinear models [12], graph neural networks [13], etc. They have studied KGE for downstream tasks such as link prediction [14], entity classification [15], and entity alignment [16]. KGE for industrial applications is a relatively new trend. We observe that there has been limited investigation done especially in the area of KGE for manufacturing industries (to our best knowledge). One recent work applied KGE on ecotoxicological effect prediction [17], where the KGE models are applied to enhance the MLP model for predicting the effects of chemical compounds on specific species. Other works applied KGE in text processing [18], where the user names and name abbreviations are mapped to the same author based on their publications. Inspired by these works, we consider it an interesting and important research question to study whether and to what extent KGE can be applied for manufacturing industry.

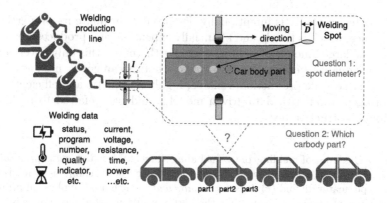

Fig. 1. Two core questions in welding quality monitoring: *Question 1* (Q1), how large is the spot diameter? *Question 2* (Q2), which car body part does this spot diameter belongs to?

Our Approach. To this end, we investigate KGE for answering the two questions in the automotive industry with Bosch data, and compare with a representative classic ML method. In this work, (1) we first give a detailed introduction of the welding quality monitoring use case and welding data (Sect. 2); (2) after that, we formulate regression and classification problems as link prediction problems (Sect. 4); (3) and construct KGs from tabular data, during which we pay special attention to handling literals, and discretise the literals in intervals and create entities on them; (4) we compare mainstream KGE methods such as TransE, RotatE, AttH with multilayer perceptron (MLP) (Sect. 5). In addition, we conduct an ablation study to investigate whether the literals are important. Furthermore, we compare a variant KGE method proposed in a recent application paper [17] to see if this method is applicable; (5) we introduce adapted performance metrics to increase the applicability of KGE to our industrial problems and give recommendations for further adoption in these settings (Sect. 6).

2   Use Case

Welding Process. We refer to automated welding as a family of manufacturing processes where multiple metal parts are melted and then connected together. An example process and production line is illustrate in Fig. 1, during which, the welding robots control welding electrodes move along the car body parts. A high current (several kilo Ampere) passes through the electrodes and car bodies, generates heat on the metal, melting the metal to produce welding nuggets for connecting the car bodies. Welding is heavily applied in automotive industry, accounting for over millions of carbody production annually, where which carbody has upto 6000 spots. Monitoring welding quality has been a key problem for industrial manufacturing, due to the requirement of accuracy and efficiency at the same time. *Traditional quality monitoring* applies destructive testing, where the test carbody is intentionally destroyed to evaluate its properties and performance, which is timely and financially expensive, and produces waste, considering the large amount of welding spot. Furthermore, this only covers part of the welding quality, because the destroyed car bodies can not be used as product. Thus, for large scale production, reliable, highly automatic and efficient quality monitoring method with data-driven model would be preferred to replace the traditional destructive testing.

Table 1. Example of welding data, including three tables: (a) *main protocol* with ids, status, etc.; (b) *welding meta setting* with the carbody component information such as type, material; and (c) *sensor measurements*, which are the physical properties measured per milliseconds. Note that the carbody information does not exist in the welding table data.

ⓐ main protocol

spot_id	machine_id	program_id	program_no	monitor_state	capwearcount
Spot127	machine10	22690	4	0	36
Spot16	machine1	22286	6	0	44
Spot13	machine2	20698	7	0	119
Spot22	Machine5	26680	10	0	122
Spot21	Machine5	20360	9	1	55

ⓑ welding meta setting

program_id	component1_type	comp1_material	comp1_thickness	component2_type
22690	Type1	Aluminium	1	Type3
22286	Type2	Steel	0.2	Type4
20698	Type3	Steel	0.2	Type5
26680	Type4	Aluminium	0.1	Type6

ⓒ sensor measurements

time	Current	Voltage	Resistance
1	0.88	0.8	0.43
2	0.88	0.34	0.5
3	0.9	0.64	0.03
4	0.43	0.08	0.98
5	0.09	0.05	0.16
6	0.39	0.23	0.21
7	0.81	0.91	0.33
8	0.6	0.17	1
9	0.56	0.94	0.49
10	0.44	0.83	0.71
11	0.09	0.18	0.8
12	0.99	0.23	0.27
13	0.4	0.99	0.52
14	0.81	0.14	0.45

Welding Data. Welding data include various information gathered from the welding process (Fig. 1). We exemplify welding data with the three tables in Table 1. Welding machines are installed with different sensors which can detect the parameter values of all the machines, these data will be collected and stored in various sources, including the welding protocol, the welding setting database and the sensor measurements. Table 1 shows an example of the recorded welding data with selected columns. The welding protocol involves all the parameters used for the machines when conducting the welding process, such as the welding machines, the welding program, the welding state etc. This welding setting database (metadata) contain information about the materials being welded, such as the type, materials and thickness of welded sheets. The sensor measurements contain all the numeric literals that are measured during the welding process over different time span, including the current, the voltage, PWM and the resistance. The welding data we are utilising are the combination of data from welding protocol, welding setting database, and the sensor measurements. The details of the columns of Table 1 are given as follows:

- *Welding Machine* records the machines that perform the welding operations.
- *Welding Program* is the program installed in the welding machine used for different welding operation. Literals are the data measured by sensors in the welding process, including current, voltage, resistance, power, and other important sensor measurements.
- *Component Type* is the components of the welding spot. A welding spot will connect a few sheets (components), where each sheet has an impact on the resulting welding spot diameter. The three different components are also closely related to the carbody.

Welding data is important for ensuring that the welding process is performed correctly and that the resulting weld is strong and durable. In our work, welding data will be used for quality control and quality monitoring purposes, such as monitoring the location of the welding spots and the diameters.

Data Anonymisation. Data anonymisation and data simulation are important approaches to keep the privacy of the data. Because Bosch has strict regulations that protects the company privacy, and the production data contain numeric values subject potential leak of confidential information, the production data are not directly disclosed in the open data set for KGE. We anonymise the production data from a factory in Germany and simulate part of the data based on domain knowledge, so that the data capture the statistics of the real data but do not disclose any potentially confidential information. We conducted the anonymisation and the discretisation on the numeric values, which follows the idea of literal embedding of previous works [19,20]. We provide the anonymised dataset in the open source Github repository, aiming at improving the reproducibility of the work, and potential reuse for investigation of KG embedding.

3 Preliminaries

Knowledge Graph (KG) represented as $G = (\mathcal{E}, \mathcal{R}, \mathcal{L})$ is a graph-structured data model, where $\mathcal{E}$ is a set of entities, $\mathcal{L}$ is a set of literals included in the knowledge graph, and $\mathcal{R}$ is a set of binary relations, which can be further divided into two groups $\mathcal{R} = \{\mathcal{P}_o, \mathcal{P}_d\}$, where $\mathcal{P}_o$ denotes the relations between entities ($\mathcal{P}_o \subseteq \mathcal{E} \times \mathcal{E}$, known as object properties), while $\mathcal{P}_d$ denotes the relations between entities and literals ($\mathcal{P}_d \subseteq \mathcal{E} \times \mathcal{L}$, known as datatype properties).

Knowledge Graph Embedding (KGE) in a common setting [21], seeks to find a function (also model) that represents entities ($e \in \mathcal{E}$) as vectors ($v_e \in \mathcal{U}^e$) and relations ($r \in \mathcal{R}$) as mathematical mappings ($r_r \in \mathcal{U}^r$), with a given set of triples $(h, r, t) \in \mathcal{T} \subseteq \mathcal{E} \times \mathcal{R} \times \mathcal{E}$, where the $\mathcal{U}^e$ and $\mathcal{U}^r$ are some choices of embedding spaces for entities and relations, respectively. Commonly a KGE model is trained with ML by solving the problem of link prediction: $(h, r, ?)$, namely given the *query* of the head entity $h \in \mathcal{E}$ and the relation $r \in \mathcal{R}$, to find the most probable tail entity t (for simplicity, we denote the query in both two directions as $(h, r, ?)$). Thus, a KGE model needs to find a scoring function

$s : \mathcal{E} \times \mathcal{R} \times \mathcal{E} \rightarrow \mathbb{R}$, which measures the plausibility of a triple (h, r, t). In literal-aware KGE, the triples are in the form of $(h, r, t) \in \mathcal{T} \subseteq \mathcal{E} \times \mathcal{R} \times \{\mathcal{E}, \mathcal{L}\}$, and the relations have two groups ($r \in \mathcal{R} = \{\mathcal{P}_o, \mathcal{P}_d\}$). Both the literals and the relations need to be handled properly. We list some popular KGE models below.

TransE [11] represents entities as vectors and relations as translation operations between these vectors. Specifically, given a query $(h, r, ?)$ in a KG, TransE predicts the tail entity as $f(h, t) = v_h + v_r$. TransE then minimizes the Euclidean distance between the predicted and the true entity representation while maximizing the distance between the predicted and the false entity representation: $Dist(v'_t, v_t) \rightarrow 0$ for true tail entity, while $Dist(v'_t, v_e) \rightarrow MAX$ for other entities except the true tail.

DistMult [12] models the interactions between entities and relations as dot products in a low-dimensional space. Specifically, The score function is calculated in the matrix multiplication $g_r(h, t) = v_h^\mathsf{T} \cdot Mr \cdot v_t$, here $^\mathsf{T}$ denotes the transpose, while DistMult maximizes the score for true triples while minimizing the scores for negative triples, where the score

RotatE [22] is similar to TransE, but models the relations as rotation vectors. Specifically, tail entities are predicted from head entities and relations through $f(h, t) = v_h \circ v_r$, where $\circ$ denotes rotation in complex number space. The distance function is defined as cosine distance $Dist(h, t) = cos(v'_t, v_t)$.

AttH [21] models the relations as reflections and rotations in the hyperbolic space as well as weights in the attention mechanism which combines the two hyperbolic transformations. In particular, AttH first calculates the two predicted values for the tail entity by relation-specific hyperbolic reflecting and rotating the head entity. The two predictions are then combined into the final tail prediction through an attention mechanism with a relation-specific attention weight. The model is eventually optimized so that the true tail entity embedding is the closest to the prediction compared to the false ones. In Atth, the mapping of hyperbolic spaces is able to better represent hierarchical relationships, thus Atth achieves good accuracy in relatively low dimensions.

Negative Sampling. Negative sampling is a widely used technique in KGE that aims to improve the performance KGE models [23]. The key idea of negative sampling is to sample negative triples that do not exist in the KG and use them to train the KGE model along with positive triples. By doing so, the model learns to differentiate between positive and negative triples and improves its ability to predict missing relationships in the KG. The learning objective is usually set as maximizing the difference between positive triple scores and negative triple scores, so that the positive triples are assigned higher scores and negative triples are assigned lower scores. In this paper, we also explore the effectiveness of negative sampling in KGE by training with different negative size.

Multi-Layer Perceptron. A Multi-Layer Perceptron (MLP) classifier is a type of artificial neural network that is commonly used for classification tasks. The MLP consists of multiple layers of interconnected nodes or neurons that are organized into an input layer, one or more hidden layers, and an output layer. Each neuron in the network receives input from the neurons in the previous layer, and computes a weighted sum of those inputs using a set of learned weights. The weighted sum is then passed through an activation function, usually the sigmoid function or the ReLU function, to produce an output. The output of the final layer is used to make a classification decision. The weights of the MLP are learned through a process called backpropagation, which involves adjusting the weights to minimize a loss function that measures the difference between the predicted output of the network and the true output. MLP is used in many industrial applications such as abnormality detection, predictive quality maintenance [24].

4   Method

Welding KG Construction. A welding KG is constructed from the table data. We have used welding-related information, such as time of welding processes, welding machines, welding programs, and welding parameters (e.g., voltage, current, resistance). The constructions are conducted on welding spots and the car body and diameters. We transform the values of the welding data table into entities and the relationships between these entities as edges in the KG. Figure 4a shows the construction of literal entities, which are entities generated from numeric values. Based on the mean values, the current and voltages will be discretised by value ranges, such that all the numerics values are turned into entities. Discretised values such as machines and program id can be directly converted into entities. Figure 4b shows the Welding KGs, which are constructed from the data table with the form of the Table 1. And the two main research questions of our work. Question 1 is the classification of the welding spot to the diameter classes. Question 2 is to predict the link between the carbodies and the welding spot, to find the correct carbody of the welding spots.

Problem Formulation. Given the information of the welding spot, including the machine ID, program ID and their literal features such as voltage, current, resistance, welding time, welding power, the two research questions are to predict the carbody of the this welding spot and the diameter of the welding spot. To make KGE applicable to the problem, we reformulate the two questions of the quality monitoring in the use case (Fig. 2): Q1: The Spot diameter prediction was a regression problem based on the welding data to predict the real values for the diameters size. Due to resolution when measuring the spot diameter, we discretise the diameters into different diameter classes and constructed the entities based on the diameter classes. We then predict the link between welding spots and the diameter classes. Considering the fixed differences between the neighbouring diameter classes, we use the mean differences between the diameter classes and calculated rmse based on the differences. Q2: For carbody classification, we conducted similar reformulation. Difference is that the carbodies are already discretised values, so we simply create the entities based on carbodies. Then the question is converted to predict the link between the carbody entities

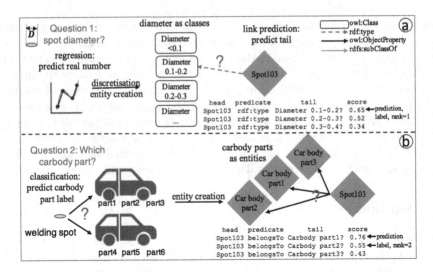

Fig. 2. Formulating regression and classification problems as link prediction problems.

and the welding spots. With both of the reformulated research questions, we can apply KGE models, and their results become comparable to that of the original regression and classification problems.

KG Construction from Tabular Data. The welding data are original in tabular form extracted from relational databases. Since the tabular data are very extensive (over 200 columns) and contain many columns not closely related to the operation (e.g., unused machine settings), we need to construct welding KGs with relevant information describing welding operations. We construct KGs as the following steps: (1) Remove all the empty columns and columns with only unique value, since these columns are not distinguishing information and are thus redundant for the welding knowledge graphs. (2) Choosing the most representative features based on domain knowledge from welding. Those representative features are to be put in the welding KG. (3) Process the literal features to be converted into KGs. Since many KGE approaches do not consider the literals when embedding the entities, we adapted literal-embedding approaches from previous works to convert the literals into entities. [19] (4) Identify the entities and relationships: Look for the unique entries and their attributes in the table as the entities in the KGs. These relationships will be the edges in the KG and connect the entities. For example, one operation with id 1 was conducted on machine id 2, then the entities should be operation1 and machine2, with relationship "conducted_on_machine".

Literal Handling. We did the following steps for literal embeddings inspired by [20]: aggregation, value discretisation, entity creation and linking. In the aggregation step, the sensor measured values are aggregated into the mean values of the three stages and the overall mean values in real numbers. Then in the discretisation step, we discretise the real values into different ranges. And then we create entities based on the discretised ranges. Then we link all the created literal entities with other entities.

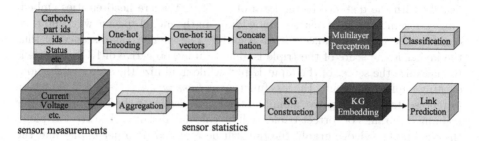

Fig. 3. The workflow of compared methods: the same raw data from relational tables go through different preprocessing (one-hot encoding or KG construction) and modelled by MLP or KGE methods, solving classification or link prediction problems for answering Q1 and Q2.

Multi-Layer Perceptron Classifier. In our work, MLP classifier is used to predict whether there exist connection between welding spot and the carbody or the diameter class, based on the information from welding knowledge graphs related to the welding spot and the carbody. Figure 3a shows the structure of the MLP classifier with embedding layer mapping each entity to a low-dimensional vector. The input of the MLP classifier is all the known parameters that belong to the welding spot, for example the welding machine, weling program, welding current, welding voltage etc. Their one-hot encoding will be fed to the MLP classifier. The output of the MLP classifier is the one-hot encoding of the carbodies or encoding of the diameters.

This model is the most basic model used in the quality monitoring and works as a baseline model for this use-case. Since the traditional manufacturing quality approach is totally different and not predictable, we can not compare directly with traditional method but rather compare all the machine learning approaches.

Knowledge Graph Embedding. As the development of knowledge graph embedding models in the recent years, there are various KGE models focusing on capture the information in the graph structural data. Our KGE models are based on the famous models TransE which treat the entities and relations based on vector translation, DistMult model which treat relation with matrix factorization, AttH which maps the vector into hyperbolic space and calculate the score based on hyperbolic space vector. Those models shows good performance on open dataset and possess good generalization capability. Figure 3b contains the KGE models architecture. The KGE model will embed all the entities and relations into a look-up table with a embedding layer. Afterwards the score or the distance of the input triple will be optimized based on the score functions tailored to different models. The input data of the model are triples in the form of (head, relation, tail) representing the single fact from the welding knowledge graphs. The output of the model is the score based on the distance of the triple, usually with the distance in the form of $d(h + r, t)$ where head entities embeddings are combined with relation embeddings in the model specific way, and then compare the vector distance with tail entity. The smaller the distance is, thus the higher is the score of the triple is. The training objective of KGE models is to maximize the scores of the input triples while minimize the scores of the non-existing triples by building the loss function as $Loss = s(h, r, t) - s(h, r, t*)$ where $t*$ represents all the negative sampling triples. To evaluate the KGE model after training, the ranks of correct triples will be calculated. For each correct triple in the welding knowledge graph, the tail will be replaced by other triples and the rank of correct tail will be calculated with respect to the other false tails.

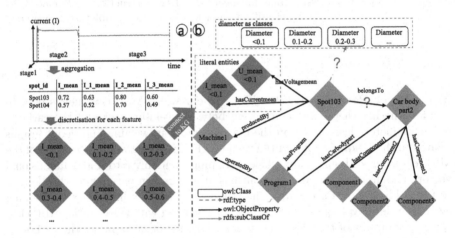

Fig. 4. (a) Procedure of literal embedding (b) Partial illustration of the welding KG

Metrics and Their Meanings in the Use Case. We consider 4 metrics for our questions: Acc(Hits@1), Hits@GroupBy3, *nrmse*, MRR.

Acc(Hits@1) represents the percentage of correct entities that are predicted correctly by assigning them the highest scores. In our case this can be understood as prediction accuracy and we use the Hits@1 to represent the accuracy. It is calculated by the percentage of entities having highest rank in the evaluation. In our use case, the Hits@1 represents the accuracy of the prediction. The range of the Hits@1 is between 0 and 1, where higher score represents the better performance. *Hits@GroupBy3* represents the percentage of correct entities that are predicted correctly when conducting a prediction in the group of 3 welding spots. In the testing, 3 carbody parts are grouped together and the prediction is considered correct if the predicted carbody part is in the same group as the ground truth carbody part. In our use case, the Hits@GroupBy3 is a less strict metrics than Hits@1, but it derives from the industrial scenario where the testing is conducted. It also represents the accuracy of the prediction.

nrmse is the shortcut for normalised-root-mean-square-error, which was used to calculate the accuracy of diameter prediction. The metric is still applicable after we reformulating the problem into the link prediction problem, since the average diameter difference between the different diameter classes are known. It is calculated, as shown in the equation $nrmse = \Sigma_i (D_i - \hat{D}_i)^2 / \bar{D}$, as the square root of the mean value of the squared error.

MRR is a measure of the average rank of the first correct entity or relation among all possible entities or relations. It is computed as the reciprocal of the rank of all the correct tail entities. MRR is more on the research purpose and used to compare the performances of different KGE models.

5   Evaluation

This section compares multilayer perceptron (MLP) with mainstream KGE methods and its KGE-MLP variants to investigate whether and to what extent KGE methods are useful for the two questions of interest in our use case. We also hope to shed light on KGE for industrial applications via discussions on the KGE performance and the KG characteristics.

5.1   Experiment Settings

Baselines. We compare three mainstream KGE methods with the representative classic ML method MLP. The KGE methods include translational models in Eucledian space: TransE, RotatE, and hyperbolic model with attention mechanism: AttH. We select TransE and RotatE because they are representative methods, and are proven to have good generalisability to datasets and applications other than the settings under which they are developed [25]. We select AttH as a representative method for more sophisticated KGE with attention mechanism and non-Euclidean embedding space. We compare all KGE methods with MLP because MLP are widely applied in industrial applications, and have been proven to be universal approximators [26].

In addition, we compare with a special type of KGE method proposed in [17], because this paper is a most close work on KGE for real-world use cases. The KGE method in this work is a combination of MLP and KGE method (thus is referred to as *KGE-MLP*) to binary classification of triples (referred to has prediction triples), MLP is used for learning the probability of the prediction triples as well as the embeddings of the head and tail entities in the prediction triples, and KGE is used for learning all entity and relation embeddings.

Dataset Details. We randomly select welding data in relational tables related to 2000 records of welding operations from a large database with over 260 k welding operations. We consider 2000 records is a balanced number to meaningfully test the method performance, while not spending excessive training time. From over 200 features of the data, we removed certain features, such as constant values, NaN values, and other features according to domain knowledge. The resulting dataset contains 31 meaningful features and 2000 rows, including ids for machines, programs, status, and aggregated values of sensor measurements. Then the data are used for MLP after one-hot encoding, or used for KGE after KG construction, according to the procedures elaborated in Sect. 4. The KG dataset contains 44801 triples, including 3342 entities, 26 relations, among which, 18 machines, 181 programIDs, 613 carbodies, 327 are literal entities.

Data Splitting. We split the table data following the standard 80%/10%10% for train/validation/test, and do the following modifications for the KGE model. To ensure a fair comparison between MLP and no leakage appears, we firstly split the table data into train/validation/test dataset and then conduct the conversion from table data into KGs. The testset only contains triples with entities of *welding spot, carbodypart* and *diameter*. The negative triple samples are generated randomly following the negative sampling of existing KGE approaches.

Table 2. Model performance comparison on answering Question 1 (Q1) and Question 2 (Q2). The best results are marked bold, and second best results marked by underlines. The experiments are repeated 5 times and results are reported as mean ± std. Note that MLP performance is not usable according to domain expert.

		MLP	TransE	RotatE	AttH
Q1	Acc(Hits@1)	0.39 ± 0.01	**0.42** ± 0.02	0.25 ± 0.01	0.31 ± 0.05
	MRR	–	**0.65** ± 0.01	0.49 ± 0.00	0.57 ± 0.04
	$nrmse$	**0.05** ± 0.01	0.06 ± 0.00	0.08 ± 0.01	0.06 ± 0.01
	$time_{train}$	120.6 ± 15.2 s	660.1 ± 30.1 s	1022.9 ± 80.5 s	1829.1 ± 100.1 s
	$time_{test}$	< 0.03 s	< 0.03 s	< 0.03 s	< 0.03 s
Q2	Acc(Hits@1)	0.61 ± 0.01	**0.64** ± 0.01	0.52 ± 0.01	0.53 ± 0.03
	MRR	–	**0.77** ± 0.01	0.69 ± 0.01	0.70 ± 0.01
	Hits@Groupby3	–	**0.85** ± 0.01	0.81 ± 0.01	0.79 ± 0.03
	$time_{train}$	117.1 ± 13.2 s	822.6 s ± 101.7	1722.7 ± 152.7 s	4266.9± 234.5 s
	$time_{test}$	< 0.03 s	< 0.03 s	< 0.03 s	< 0.03 s

KGE Setting. In this setting, negative samples are generated by corrupting existing triplets in the training set. In the case of Q1, the tails in negative samples are the wrong diameter classes. In the case of Q2, the tails in negative samples are the wrong carbody part entities. The embedding size is experimented on a search space of {16, 32, 64, 128, 256} and we choose the best hyper-parameters based on the MRR on the validation set. We chose 128 or 256 as the best trade-off between efficiency and the accuracy.

KGE-MLP Setting. The special variant of KGE-MLP models are tested with TransE [11], DistMult [12] and HolE [27], following [17]. The embedding size is experimented on a search space of {16, 32, 64, 128, 256} and we chose 128 as the best trade-off between efficiency and the accuracy.

5.2   Results and Discussion

Results and Discussion on Question 1. From the results of MLP and KGE on Question 1 (Table 2), we see that TransE performs the best in terms of Hits@1, and MLP performs the best in terms of *nrmse*.

Acc(Hits@1). For Q1, Hits@1 means the percentage of the correctly predicted diameter classes, therefore it represents the accuracy of diameter prediction, making it the most important metric in the use case. In terms of Acc(Hits@1), TransE outperforms all other KGE and outperforms MLP by 6 %. Important to note, for industrial applications, a prediction accuracy of only 0.42 is not sufficient, because industrial applications typically expect high accuracy. In our use case, we consider an accuracy at least over 80% can make the solution usable, and over 90% makes the solution good. However, we should not be too pessimistic, and can relax the evaluation metric by resorting to *nrmse*. The MLP model performs not well on Hits@1 for the diameter class prediction. As only 0.39 for the prediction accuracy, meaning not even half of the diameter is predicted correctly. Among all KGE models, *TransE* achieves the best results and is also better than the MLP model results, with 0.42 accuracy. Other two KGE models RotatE and AttH didn't show improvements compared with the MLP model, but they still manage to predict around 1/4 of the diameter classes correctly.

MRR. For common KGE problems, MRR is also a important performance indicator, and mostly correlates with Hits@1. In the use case, the MRR indicates that TransE is the best KGE model with an MRR of 0.65 and AttH is the second best with 0.57. There exist no MRR for MLP and thus they are not comparable in terms of MRR.

nrmse. Here the *nrmse* is calculated by converting the diameter classes back to real values then using the equation $\Sigma_i(D_i - \hat{D}_i)^2/\bar{D}$. It indicates the average prediction error normalised by the mean value of the prediction target and can be understood as relative percentage error. We see that in terms of *nrmse*, MLP model is the best one, while TransE and AttH are comparable to MLP, and their prediction errors are 5% to 6%. We postulate the reason that diameter prediction was originally a regression problem, and classic ML method such as MLP is well-suited for regression problems.

Considering the industrial adoption, we think the relative percentage error of 5% - 6% are both acceptable for industrial adoptions in our use case and thus both MLP and KGE can be adopted in principle.

Time. In terms of training time, MLP consume much less than all KGE models, while TransE consumes the least time among the KGE models. In terms of test time, all models are comparable. Considering industrial adoption, in the case where training time is critical, MLP has an advantage. In mose cases, models in industrial applications are pre-trained and the test time is more important. In this regards, all models do not have adoption issues in terms of test time.

Results and Discussion on Question 2. From the results of MLP and KGE models on Q2 (Question 2), we can see that TransE also performs the best in terms of Acc(Hits@1), Hits@3Group and MRR (lower part of Table 2).

Acc(Hits@1). This metric means the percentage of the correctly predicted carbody parts. In terms of Acc(Hits@1), TransE is the best model and outperforms MLP model by 5% (relative). We see that for the carbody part problem, which can be regarded as classification problem, TransE is better suited. However, a prediction accuracy of 0.61 means 61% carbody is corrected predicted, which is still not sufficient for industrial application. We also consider relax the prediction and rely on Hits@Groupby3.

MRR. Similar to Question 1, MRR is highly correlated with Hits@1 and TransE is the best KGE model.

Hits@Groupby3. Hits@Groupby3 is a metric we propose that is similar to Hits@3. It is calculated by first splitting the carbody parts into groups where each group has 3 carbody parts then count whether the predicted carbody is within the group. Hits@Groupby3 relaxes the prediction by requiring to predict the correct carbody part group (with 3 carbody parts) instead of one carbody. In industrial practice we can also rely on Hits@Groupby3, because we can consider the carbody part groups as the minimal unit of quality monitoring and evaluate the quality by the groups. With this new metric Hits@Groupby3, we can see all the KGE models have relative good performance, about 0.80. TransE is still the best model with 0.85.

Time. In terms of training time, the models consume time differently, with MLP consuming much less than all KGE models, while TransE consumes the least time among the KGE models. In terms of test time, all models are comparable in the Q2 prediction. Considering industrial adoption, in the case where training time is critical, MLP has an advantage. In the case where the models only conduct inference, the TransE with higher performance si advantageous. In this regards, all models do not have adoption issues in terms of test time.

Comparison with KGE-MLP Models. We observe from Table 3 that all the KGE-MLP variants performs worse than their KGE counterparts in terms of Acc(Hits@1), MRR, and *nrmse*. With 0.34 for accuracy and 0.52 for

Table 3. Comparison with KGE-MLP Models. The KGE-MLP variants are marked with*.

	Metric	TransE	TransE*	DistMult*	HolE*
	Acc(Hits@1)	**0.42**	0.17	<u>0.22</u>	0.21
Q1	MRR	**0.65**	0.45	<u>0.48</u>	<u>0.48</u>
	nrmse	**0.06**	0.11	<u>0.09</u>	0.10
	Hits@1	**0.64**	0.34	0.34	<u>0.37</u>
Q2	MRR	**0.77**	0.48	<u>0.52</u>	0.41
	Hits@GroupBy3	**0.85**	0.45	0.46	<u>0.52</u>

MRR for carbody prediction and 0.22 for accuracy and 0.48 for MRR for diameter prediction, the DistMult based MLP model shows no performance improvement over the baseline MLP model regarding the carbody prediction. Possible reason could be the MLP in this model can not capture the welding information well. The special KGE variants were suitable for the problem of [17], but they seem to be not well-suited for the questions in our case.

This results indicate that the welding KG and KGE based MLP can capture the information of the welding data. However, due to the model design it may not work as well as the KGE models.

Ablation Study on Literals. Table 4 shows the results of the ablation study regarding the literals. We can see that for answering Q1, performance of TransE is even worse than TransE† (without literals), while MLP performs better with

Table 4. Ablation study on literals, models without literals are marked with †

		TransE	MLP	TransE†	MLP†
Q1	Acc(Hits@1)	0.42	0.39	**0.45**	0.36
	nrmse	0.06	0.05	0.04	0.05
	MRR	0.64	–	**0.68**	–
Q2	Hits@1	0.64	0.61	0.53	0.49
	MRR	**0.77**	–	0.70	–
	Hits@GroupBy3	**0.85**	-	0.78	–

literals. We repeated the experiments 5 times and this result is persistent. We postulate the reason is that the *Diameter* class are isolated in the KG, as shown in Fig. 4 that the `rdf:type` is the only link connecting *Diameter* with the rest of the KG. This makes it is difficult to learn the correct links between the *Diameter* and *Spot*. For answering Q2, we see both MLP and TransE models show some performance degradation without literals. This is expected. We can see from Fig. 4 the *Carbodypart* is "well" connected to the rest of the KG via many other links, and thus it does not suffer the same issue as in Q1.

Recommendation for Industrial Adoption. For answering Q1, MLP has slightly better performance than TransE in terms of *nrmse*, which is the most meaningful metric for industrial adoption, but the different of 5% and 6% error is marginal. Considering MLP has less training time and it is easier to understand for domain experts than KGE, it is still preferred than TransE. For answering Q2, TransE has better results than MLP. Although none of the methods are directly applicable considering the prediction accuracy (Hits@1), we can relax the condition by introducing Hits@Groupby3, which requires to group the carbody parts first by 3 and judging the quality for each carbody part group instead of for each carbody. This is a good news for industrial adoption since the carbody classification problem is challenging for classic ML due to the high number of label classes. Overall, we consider the adoptabilty of KGE in industrial applications is promising, although not perfect. The adoptability is increased by the adaptation of problem formulation, handling numerical literals and introducing new metrics.

6   Discussion on General Impact and Related Work

Related Work of KGE. Representative KGE models include translational models in Eucledian space, such as TransE [11], RotatE [22], and model in hyperbolic space with attention mechanism: AttH [21] as the KGE models for quality monitoring.

Related Work of KGE Applications. In the past work, there exist some applications of KGE in real-world applications. Such as the application in natural language processing [18], ecooxicological effect prediction [17], application in biological area [28]. There exist rather less work on KGE in industrial applications. Our work is an attempt to test whether and to what extent KGE can be used in industries, especially traditional industries such as manufacturing, rather than internet industries.

Usability by Stakeholders. Our work is grouped into the Bosch research for data-driven solutions for manufacturing condition monitoring, and under the umbrella of new generation manufacturing monitoring solutions based on neuro-symbolic methods. The project spans over three sub-projects: the resistance spot welding quality monitoring, process optimisation for hot-staking, and plastic data analytics. The project collaborates with several factories in Germany, aiming at smart equipment analytics, process optimisation, etc. Currently the solution is under evaluation environment of both Bosch research and factories, and received positive feedback, where the stakeholders are data scientists, semantic experts, R&D engineers, etc. After the evaluation and prototyping, the solution will be moved to the factories.

General Uptake. We provide our *scripts* of ML and KGE and *anonymised welding KG dataset* in the open GitHub repository. Our scripts of ML and KGE should provide important resource for reproducing the methods and results. Our goal is to facilitate neuro-symbolic research that combines semantic technologies and ML for industrial applications, especially for manufacturing industry. We hope our provided resource can inspire research in the community of neuro-symbolic reasoning, semantic technologies, graph embedding, etc. and advance the state of art in these domains. We observe that the most open-source KG datasets are about common sense domains, and few are about industries such as manufacturing. We thus hope that our dataset can help more researchers to connect their research on KG to industrial cases.

Scalability and Benefits. We have tested our solutions and recorded the consumed resource and time. The results (Table 2) show that the test time which is critical for scalabilty in industry is acceptable. The benefits of this work are quite obvious. Data-driven solutions help to reduce cost and waste and increase quality monitoring covering, by reducing or eventually replacing the conventional destructive methods that destroy samples of welded car bodies. Further benefits are that the work is an attempt of neuro-symbolic reasoning for manufacturing that hopes to inspire more research directions.

Risks and Opportunities. The risks here are that the prediction of both diameters and carbody parts are not perfect. This needs to be documented in the quality monitoring system if the technology is equipped in such a system. Despite this, the risks are comparable to conventional methods and other data-driven solutions, and are manageable by correct understanding of the prediction results and adopting the measures such as safety coefficients. The research provide opportunities for further investigation and improvement of the solutions on other manufacturing condition monitoring questions, datasets, and use cases. This research also provide opportunities for researchers working on industry digitisation and the AI application.

7 Conclusion and Outlook

Conclusion and Outlook. This paper investigats to whether and to what extend KGE can be applied for Bosch welding quality monitoring. We compared KGE methods with MLP on two important questions in manufacturing quality monitoring. To make KGE applicable for our industrial questions, we adapted the KGE methods in these aspects: we formulated classic ML problems of classification and regression to link prediction, proposed strategies for handling literals, including sensor measurements and diamters, and introduced the performance metric *rmse* and Hits@GroupBy3. The KGE are not directly applicable if we only consider the original metrics of KGE such as Hits@1 and MRR, but after relaxing the prediction task by adopting *rmse* and Hits@GroupBy3, the adoptability of KGE is increased and we give recommendations on the adoption.

This paper is under the umbrella of Neuro-Symbolic AI for Industry 4.0 at Bosch [29] that aims at enhancing manufacturing with both symbolic AI (such as semantic technologies [30]) for improving transparency [31], and ML for prediction power [32]. As future work, we plan to investigate larger datasets and improve the KGE performance. We work closely with colleagues from factories and will investigate further the adoptability of the technology.

Acknowledgements. The work was partially supported by EU projects Dome 4.0 (953163), OntoCommons (958371), DataCloud (101016835), Graph Massivizer (101093202) and enRichMyData (101093202) and the SIRIUS Centre (237898) funded by Norwegian Research Council.

References

1. Zhou, B., Pychynski, T., Reischl, M., Kharlamov, E., Mikut, R.: Machine learning with domain knowledge for predictive quality monitoring in resistance spot welding. J. Intell. Manuf. **33**(4), 1139–1163 (2022)

2. Zhou, B., et al.: Scaling data science solutions with semantics and machine learning: Bosch case. arXiv preprint arXiv:2308.01094 (2023)
3. Huang, Z., Fey, M., Liu, C., Beysel, E., Xu, X., Brecher, C.: Hybrid learning-based digital twin for manufacturing process: modeling framework and implementation. Robot. Comput. Integr. Manuf. **82**, 102545 (2023)
4. Zhou, B., Kharlamov, E., Pychynski, T., Svetashova, Y.: Device for and method of automating machine learning. US Patent App. 17/448,487 (2022)
5. Zheng, Z., Zhou, B., Zhou, D., Khan, A.Q., Soylu, A., Kharlamov, E.: Towards a statistic ontology for data analysis in smart manufacturing. In: Proceedings of the ISWC 2022 posters, demos and industry tracks, vol. 3254. CEUR-WS. org (2022)
6. Zhou, D., Zhou, B., Zheng, Z., Tan, Z., Kostylev, E.V., Kharlamov, E.: Towards executable knowledge graph translation. In: ISWC (2022)
7. Rincon-Yanez, D., et al.: Addressing the scalability bottleneck of semantic technologies at bosch. arXiv:2309.10550 (2023)
8. Zheng, D., et al.: DGL-KE: training knowledge graph embeddings at scale. In: Proceedings of the 43rd International ACM SIGIR Conference on Research and Development in Information Retrieval, pp. 739–748 (2020)
9. Ali, M., et al.: PyKEEN 1.0: a python library for training and evaluating knowledge graph embeddings. J. Mach. Learn. Res. **22**(1), 3723–3728 (2021)
10. Li, Z., Liu, H., Zhang, Z., Liu, T., Xiong, N.N.: Learning knowledge graph embedding with heterogeneous relation attention networks. IEEE Trans. Neural Networks Learn. Syst. **33**(8), 3961–3973 (2021)
11. Bordes, A., Usunier, N., Garcia-Durán, A., Weston, J., Yakhnenko, O.: Translating embeddings for modeling multi-relational data, NIPS 2013, pp. 2787–2795. Curran Associates Inc., Red Hook, NY, USA (2013)
12. Yang, B., Yih, S.W.-T., He, X., Gao, J., Deng, L.: Embedding entities and relations for learning and inference in knowledge bases. In: Proceedings of the International Conference on Learning Representations (ICLR) 2015 (2015)
13. Zhang, M., Chen, Y.: Link prediction based on graph neural networks. In: Advances in Neural Information Processing Systems, vol. 31 (2018)
14. Wang, M., Qiu, L., Wang, X.: A survey on knowledge graph embeddings for link prediction. Symmetry **13**(3), 485 (2021)
15. Yan, Q., Fan, J., Li, M., Qu, G., Xiao, Y.: A survey on knowledge graph embedding. In: 2022 7th IEEE International Conference on Data Science in Cyberspace (DSC), pp. 576–583. IEEE (2022)
16. Sun, Z., Hu, W., Zhang, Q., Qu, Y.: Bootstrapping entity alignment with knowledge graph embedding. In: IJCAI, vol. 18 (2018)
17. Myklebust, E.B., Jimenez-Ruiz, E., Chen, J., Wolf, R., Tollefsen, K.E.: Knowledge graph embedding for ecotoxicological effect prediction. In: Ghidini, C., et al. (eds.) ISWC 2019. LNCS, vol. 11779, pp. 490–506. Springer, Cham (2019). https://doi.org/10.1007/978-3-030-30796-7_30
18. Santini, C., Gesese, G.A., Peroni, S., Gangemi, A., Sack, H., Alam, M.: A knowledge graph embeddings based approach for author name disambiguation using literals. Scientometrics **127**(8), 4887–4912 (2022)
19. Kristiadi, A., Khan, M.A., Lukovnikov, D., Lehmann, J., Fischer, A.: Incorporating literals into knowledge graph embeddings. In: Ghidini, C., et al. (eds.) ISWC 2019. LNCS, vol. 11778, pp. 347–363. Springer, Cham (2019). https://doi.org/10.1007/978-3-030-30793-6_20
20. Wang, J., Ilievski, F., Szekely, P.A., Yao, K.-T.: Augmenting knowledge graphs for better link prediction. In: International Joint Conference on Artificial Intelligence (2022)

21. Chami, I., Wolf, A., Juan, D.-C., Sala, F., Ravi, S., Ré, C.: Low-dimensional hyperbolic knowledge graph embeddings. In: Proceedings of the 58th Annual Meeting of the Association for Computational Linguistics, pp. 6901–6914 (2020)

22. Sun, Z., Deng, Z.-H., Nie, J.-Y., Tang, J.: Rotate: knowledge graph embedding by relational rotation in complex space. In: International Conference on Learning Representations (2018)

23. Kamigaito, H., Hayashi, K.: Comprehensive analysis of negative sampling in knowledge graph representation learning. In: International Conference on Machine Learning, pp. 10661–10675. PMLR (2022)

24. Raman MR, G., Somu, N., Mathur, A.: A multilayer perceptron model for anomaly detection in water treatment plants. Int. J. Crit. Infrastruct. Prot. **31**, 100393 (2020)

25. Lin, Y., Liu, Z., Sun, M., Liu, Y., Zhu, X.: Learning entity and relation embeddings for knowledge graph completion. In: Proceedings of the AAAI conference on artificial intelligence, vol. 29 (2015)

26. Pinkus, A.: Approximation theory of the MLP model in neural networks. Acta Numer. **8**, 143–195 (1999)

27. Nickel, M., Rosasco, L., Poggio, T.: Holographic embeddings of knowledge graphs. In: Proceedings of the Thirtieth AAAI Conference on Artificial Intelligence, AAAI 2016, pp. 1955–1961. AAAI Press (2016)

28. Mohamed, S.K., Nounu, A., Nováček, V.: Biological applications of knowledge graph embedding models. Brief. Bioinform. **22**(2), 1679–1693 (2021)

29. B. Zhou, et al.: Neuro-symbolic AI at bosch: data foundation, insights, and deployment. In: Proceedings of the ISWC 2022 Posters, Demos and Industry Tracks, vol. 3254 of CEUR Workshop Proceedings (2022)

30. Yahya, M., Zhou, B., Breslin, J.G., Ali, M.I., Kharlamov, E.: Semantic modeling, development and evaluation for the resistance spot welding industry. IEEE Access (2023)

31. Zheng, Z., Zhou, B., Zhou, D., Soylu, A., Kharlamov, E.: Executable knowledge graph for transparent machine learning in welding monitoring at bosch. In: Proceedings of the 31st ACM International Conference on Information & Knowledge Management, pp. 5102–5103 (2022)

32. Klironomos, A., et al.: ExeKGLib: knowledge graphs-empowered machine learning analytics. In: ESWC (Demos) (2023)

Author Index

T. R. Payne et al. (Eds.): ISWC 2023, LNCS 14266, pp. 473–476, 2023.
https://doi.org/10.1007/978-3-031-47243-5